BODY EXPERIENCE IN
FANTASY AND BEHAVIOR

CENTURY PSYCHOLOGY SERIES

Kenneth MacCorquodale, Gardner Lindzey,
and Kenneth E. Clark
Editors

BODY EXPERIENCE IN FANTASY AND BEHAVIOR

Seymour Fisher

State University of New York
College of Medicine (Syracuse)

APPLETON–CENTURY–CROFTS

EDUCATIONAL DIVISION

New York   MEREDITH   CORPORATION

ACKNOWLEDGMENTS

Special acknowledgments to the *Journal of Projective Techniques and Personality Assessment* for permission to present quotations from the following publication: Fisher, S. and Renik, O. Induction of body image boundary changes. 1966, *30*, pp. 329–334 (reprinted on pp. 180–184).

Special acknowledgments also to the American Psychological Association for permission to reproduce portions of the following publications:

Fisher, S. and Fisher, Rhoda L. Body image boundaries and patterns of body perception. *Journal of Abnormal and Social Psychology*, 1964, *68*, pp. 255–262 (reprinted on pp. 169–177).

Fisher, S. Body sensation and perception of projective stimuli. *Journal of Consulting Psychology*, 1965, *29*, pp. 135–138 (reprinted on pp. 190–194).

Fisher, S. Sex differences in body perception. *Psychological Monographs*, 1964, *78* (No. 14), pp. 2–5, 6–9, 14, 16–20 (reprinted on pp. 528–543).

Fisher, S. Body attention patterns and personality defenses. *Psychological Monographs*, 1966, *80* (No. 9), pp. 2–5, 7–11, 12–14, 18–20, 22–26 (reprinted on pp. 337–346, 360–363, 373–382, 394–396, 409–414, 417–419, 512–513).

Fisher, S. The body boundary and perceptual vividness. *Journal of Abnormal Psychology*, 1968, *73*, pp. 392–396 (reprinted on pp. 234–239).

*To Rhoda, Jerid
and Eve*

Preface

Much intervenes between the stimulus and the response it finally elicits. As our knowledge has grown we have discerned, all too well, how intricate are the values and expectations that guide behavior. These modifying variables derive from what the individual has learned in the course of interacting with significant figures and objects. They are labeled and referred to with terms like "ego structure," "self concept," "authoritarian–non-authoritarian," "rigid–non-rigid," and so forth. They denote that organized experiences acquire structure and become vectors which exert long-term directive effects.

This book is devoted to those organized experiences associated with the perception and assignment of meaning to one's own body. It will be shown that they too take on structure and have long-term directive effects. The attitudes a person adopts toward this body can modulate his responses in the same way as other significant attitudes do. A central theme which will be underscored in the pages that follow is that a person's experiences with his body, as a psychological object, intrude widely into his life. His body is a perceptual object from which he cannot escape. Being an inevitable accompaniment of his awareness, it has great influence upon him.

There are many aspects of the individual's body which acquire psychological significance. He adopts attitudes about its size, strength, attractiveness, sexual potency, cleanliness, agility, plasticity, masculinity-femininity, vulnerability to external intrusion, and proper level of arousal—just to name a few. Such attitudes impinge upon his decisions pervasively. Whether it is his need to decide the kind of clothing he ought to buy or to evaluate if the world is a safe enough place for him to pursue goals and aspirations, his feelings about his body will participate in the decision process.

There are numerous potential approaches to understanding how he learns to integrate his feelings about his body and how he relates them with what he perceives going on "out there" in his environs. The domain of knowledge involved is huge and has been only peripherally glimpsed. It will require years of application by investigators to undertake the necessary explorations. The work presented in this book centers about a series of parameters which, at this stage, seem to be of importance in the organization of the experienced body (body image, body concept). It is concerned with understanding how the individual distinguishes his body from the rest of the world; how he distributes his attention to the various regions of his body; and how he regulates his own stimulation of his body. Particular effort is directed to understanding how characteristic modes of perceiving and appraising one's body are related to personality and also how they influence selective cognition and fantasy construction. Variations in body perception are appraised with reference to sex differences, personality disorganization, body disablement, and developmental factors. Empirical data will be presented which are viewed against the background of the existing body image literature and utilized for fashioning new theories and models.

The experiments which were undertaken presumed that it was possible to obtain meaningful and quantifiable information about the subjective aspects of body experience. It was found that the essentially private domain of body perception can be effectively tapped if the complexity of the reporting process is reduced to a comfortable level and if the reporting individual is given no cues which might lead him to think that he knows the proper, socially desirable thing to say. Naive self observation can be accurate, reproducible, and predictive of significant behavioral phenomena.

Certain of the conclusions to be presented will sound old-fashioned because they represent a turning away from the "central" view of emotions and thinking which dominates psychological theory today. The findings made it necessary to revive old peripheralist concepts, such as typified by the James-Lange theory of emotion. Formulations will be offered which underscore motor aspects of thinking and fantasy. Body experience will be depicted as fundamental to a control system which helps the individual to store affective information, decide what is personally significant, and maintain constancies in his behavior.

Other researchers are also increasingly turning to the analysis of the body as a psychological phenomenon. Studies concerned with the body concept have in recent years continued to accelerate. This has been stimulated by work in diverse areas. Problems related to ego development, personality, adjustment to body disability, and many others have begun to be approached in body image terms.

A man's body is, after all, synonymous with his existence. It should come as no surprise that his perception of its attributes colors his experience of life.

S. F.

Syracuse, New York
July, 1968

ACKNOWLEDGMENTS

This book evolved from work which was initiated at the Baylor College of Medicine and continued at the State University of New York Medical School (Syracuse, N.Y.). The studies to be described were consistently supported by grants from the National Institutes of Health and were immeasurably facilitated by them.

The real beginnings of these studies go back to the joint work, concerned with the body boundary, which my friend and colleague, Sidney Cleveland, and I undertook and later described in a monograph (*Body Image and Personality*). Through the years we have continued to exchange thoughts and ideas about our favorite topic—body perception and experience. I wish to thank him for having read large segments of the present book and having offered numerous cogent suggestions about the organization and interpretation of material.

I also received particularly valuable comments and criticisms from Edward Murray who read a considerable portion of the manuscript. He helped me to grasp and explain a number of theoretical issues which had not been sufficiently clarified

My wife gave me much assistance and also information derived from her own research relating to body perception. She was frequently called upon, over the years, to give opinions, advice and reactions as the book took shape.

I would like to thank Donald Meyer, Howard Friedman, and Marc Hollender for variously providing suggestions, consultation, and necessary chunks of knowledge which expedited the research and writing process.

Let me acknowledge the invaluable assistance of Robert Curtiss whose technical skills and knowledge of electronics facilitated almost every experiment undertaken.

I am, indeed, indebted to Mary McCargar for her outstanding efforts in typing and organizing the manuscript. She maintained a steady grip on what seemed to be an endless profusion of pages.

Contents

SIGNIFICANT DEVELOPMENTS IN THE STUDY AND UNDERSTANDING OF BODY PERCEPTION

1

Introduction

This part will present a review of studies dealing with perception of one's own body. Various terms will be used in a shorthand way to refer to the fact that each individual develops techniques for integrating the feelings and experiences emanating from that unique bit of space he calls his body. Such terms as "body image", "body concept", and "body scheme" will be employed. Some have maintained that they are so vague and imprecise that their use only leads to confusion. It has also been argued that they imply the existence of mentalistic phenomena like "images". One cannot deny their imprecision, grossness, and aura of subjectivity. But, at the same time, they do represent convenient ways of labeling events involved in experiencing and organizing one's body as a perceptual object. Also, they have been widely circulated in the literature and represent a convenient currency of exchange. In any case, there is no harm in using them if one clearly states that they are merely ways of referring to a large amorphous category and are not intended to have mentalistic connotations. They simply denote a special category of perceptual behavior.

The truth is that no one or two or several words or phrases will ever capture the complexity of the events associated with body experience. In the presentation to follow, more precise terms have been substituted whenever the state of knowledge has so permitted.

The objective of this chapter is to review what has been observed and thought about body perception and body experience in the last ten years.

A general historical survey of the work done previous to this time may be found in an earlier publication (Fisher and Cleveland, 1968). The material in that survey encompassed a period beginning with the earliest exploratory observations and extended through the year 1957. It described the origins of body image concepts in the experiences of neurologists and psychiatrists who were confronted with the need to explain the strange distortions in body perception which they encountered in their patients. The gradual evolution was traced of body image studies which began as vague anecdotal observations and which now employ a growing range of complex measuring techniques. Detailed descriptions of these new techniques were provided. It was emphasized too that body image formulations are not only being applied to pathological phenomena, but also increasingly to normal behavior.

The present review, which embraces several hundred publications, is intended to fill in developments since 1957 and to touch on earlier work which was previously either overlooked or which seems, with hindsight, not to have been assigned sufficient importance. It is hoped that such a review will provide the reader with a broad perspective which will enable him to approach more meaningfully the new findings from the author's research which constitute a large part of this book.

The material to be presented has been broadly separated into that relating to normal persons and that involving gross forms of pathology (e.g., schizophrenia and brain damage). Within each of these broad categories there has been a further differentiation of topics based both on certain theoretical considerations and the frequency of various types of studies.

In most instances, considerable detail of the work under consideration has been presented. This is to provide the reader with sufficient information to arrive at independent judgments. At the same time, whenever the evidence appraised justifies it, attempts will be made to extract generalizations and formulations and to offer critical comments.

2
Body Perception
and Normal Behavior

The first section of the opening review which deals with body perception and normal behavior will encompass phenomena involving normal persons who have not suffered significant deficits in their usual structure or function. It will be followed by a second section describing body perception variables characteristic of normal persons who have experienced various kinds of serious body insults.

SELF CONFRONTATION AND PERCEPTION

It has long been known that a person is stirred to special response when he views his own image. Even the very young react with special excitement and gestures when seeing themselves in the mirror (Gullaime, 1925; Boulanger-Balleyguier, 1964; Zazzo, 1948); and by the age of one there seems to be explicit self recognition (Dixon, 1957). Investigators concerned with body image problems have sought increasingly to approach them via measurement of feelings and attitudes toward one's mirror image and other self representations. Subjects have been studied as they are confronted with self representations which vary in degree of distortion, amount of disguise, and ego involvement elicited. A review of pertinent studies follows:

Schneiderman (1956) conducted an elaborate project which dealt with the ability to detect distortions in one's mirror image. Some of the hypotheses underlying his investigation were as follows: recognition of the true proportions of one's face is subject to large error; errors in estimating the proportions of one's face are greater than those involved in judging the proportions of another person's face or of inanimate objects; and individual differences in magnitude of error in self estimations are correlated with amount of human content (H) and human movement responses (M) in Rorschach percepts, on the assumption that these Rorschach indices denote an interest in people and therefore indirectly in the self as a social stimulus. Twenty-one male and 21 female college students served as subjects. A rather ingenious mirror was used to measure ability to detect distortions in one's own image and the images of other persons and things. It consisted of a slightly flexible sheet of Plexi-glass which could be curved in controlled amounts so as to produce 13 different distortion settings. A number of judgmental series were obtained. One involved the individual looking in the mirror at his own image (head and shoulders) which was distorted in varying amounts and in each instance answering the question, "Is this a perfectly true image of yourself or not?" A second series required the subject to make similar judgments about the mirrored face of another person (female) whom he had viewed in an undistorted state just prior to the beginning of the experiment. A third sequence of analogous judgments was made with regard to a number of mirrored objects (e.g., telephone, lamp shade).

The data showed that there was considerable error in recognizing the true proportions of one's own face; but that such error was strikingly minimized if the first image in the judgmental series to which a subject reacted was an undistorted rather than distorted version of himself. There was a significant but low correlation between errors in judging the self on two occasions a week apart. The men proved to be less accurate in judging their own faces than in evaluating the face of another person. The women did not show such a trend. Schneiderman was not in a position to explain this sex difference because the face of the "other person" was a female and so constituted a stimulus with unlike meanings to the male and female subjects. The prediction that self-judgments would be more difficult than those having to do with the proportions of external objects was generally borne out. When the self-evaluation errors of the men were analyzed, it was noted that they were in the direction of representing the self as wider and huskier looking than in reality. However, the women's errors went in the direction of portraying the self as unusually long and "slender-looking". These differences in emphasis between the men and women are certainly congruent with the sex differences in body size preference reported by Jourard and Secord (1955) (viz., men prefer larger body proportions than women do). No relationships were observed between any of the mirror judgment scores and the Rorschach indices pertaining to human content and movement.

Traub and Orbach (1964) and Orbach, Traub, and Olson (1966) described a mirror which could be used to distort one's mirror image in a calibrated fashion. The mirror consists of a sheet of aluminum plated Plexi-glass. Various degrees of concave or convex bending of its parts can be introduced by means of motors. Subjects are typically presented with a given pattern of distortion of their image and asked to use the motor controls to correct the distortion. Except for some data concerning the ability of schizophrenics to make such corrections (to be described later), no systematic hypotheses have been evaluated with the technique. Exploratory work did indicate that normal subjects were not particularly precise in identifying that self image which was least distorted. There was a range of distorted images which were regarded as acceptable self representations. Some subjects complained that they could not remember precisely what they looked like. These observations concur with a similar vagueness concerning one's mirror image reported by Schneiderman (1956). The existence of such vagueness is paradoxical in view of the average individual's infinite number of experiences with his own image. The phenomenon obviously ought to be investigated more thoroughly. Preliminary data from the Orbach, et al. mirror indicated that judgments related to head and shoulders were most accurate and those pertaining to feet and legs least so. Surprisingly, the intercorrelations among scores indicating ability to correct distortions for different body areas were quite moderate. It was noted that one problem in using the mirror technique as a body image measure is the fact that the subject had to express his judgments by means of mechanical controls which constitute a formidable cognitive task. Difficulty in mastering such a cognitive task may in some instances prevent direct and valid expression of judgments concerning one's body.

McPherson, Poppelstone, and Evans (1966) ascertained that independent observers could attain respectable agreement about the behavior of children when confronted with their mirror image. In this first exploratory study they found that six-year-olds who have unusual difficulty in judging the appropriate spatial positions for objects in a series of pictures were characterized by a large number of mouth movements while looking in the mirror. For five-year-olds such a relationship was absent. The authors did not have a ready explanation for their findings. However, the technique employed deserves consideration and further use. Apparently, it is possible for observers to agree upon and quantify a range of mirror behavior. It might be profitable to take time samples of mirror behavior and determine which body parts (e.g., mouth, eyes, legs) are most frequently moved under the stimulus of self perception. There may be significant individual differences related to patterns of body image organization.

Deno (1953) also attacked a problem that concerned the question of self recognition. Individual rear-view photographs were taken of 40 nude male subjects varying in age from 14–16. The subjects were all members of a school group and were well acquainted with each other. The 40 photographs were shown to each individual with the heads masked and he was asked not only to identify them but also to rate them for goodness of physique. One of the pictures was, of course, of himself. A second presentation of the photographs was then made with the heads unmasked. Efforts were also made to measure the social standing or popularity of each subject in the group by means of a sociometric technique. It turned out that only 30 percent of the boys could correctly identify themselves if the heads of the photographs were covered. When the heads were uncovered, correct self identification rose to 37.5 percent. Those who were able to identify themselves correctly were not only better in their ability to identify others but they in turn were easier to identify by others. There was no relation between ability to detect one's own photograph and one's popularity in the group. But there was a positive correlation between popularity and the rate at which one was correctly identified by all other group members. Finally, it is noteworthy that there was a trend for those who were most easily identified by themselves and others to have been rated as especially good or poor in physique. This raised the possibility that their higher rate of identification was due to physical characteristics which made them conspicuous. Perhaps one of the most important findings in this study was the fact that only a third of the subjects could correctly designate their own photographs. This is of special import because it corroborates Wolff's (1943) earlier discovery that it is difficult for an individual to recognize representations of aspects of his own body (e.g., hands, facial profile).

Arnhoff and Damianopoulos (1962) photographed 21 male adults (clad only in jockey shorts) who had no distinguishing scars or moles. The complete head was inked out in all pictures to eliminate it as an identifying feature. Each subject was shown his own photograph in the context of six others chosen to resemble his to varying degrees; and asked if he saw his picture among the seven presented. Identification was 100 percent correct. This finding is quite different from that reported above by Deno (1953). However, since Deno used back rather than front views of the subject's body and also since her sample involved adolescents rather than adults, one must look to these two differences, or their interaction, to explain the divergence. The back view of one's body, which is obviously less often seen by the average individual, may be much harder to identify than the front view. In addition, the ability to identify one's body may be considerably superior in the adult as compared to the adolescent. Perhaps the adolescent has unusual difficulty because of the radical body changes he is experiencing which leave him with a vaguely delineated body concept.

Werner Wolff (1943) amassed a considerable amount of provocative information about how people react to representations of themselves when they are not aware that they are self referring. Typically, in the course of his work Wolff would obtain pictures of an individual (e.g., hands, profile) without his knowledge; and later when they were shown to that individual in the context of similar photographs of other persons he would be unaware that they were pictures of himself. Wolff established that in their unknowing (unconscious) responses to such self representations people not only manifested an unusual degree of affect but also revealed the content of important attitudes about themselves. The potentialities of such a procedure for tapping body image attitudes are obvious.

Numerous studies have attempted to check the validity of Wolff's observations. Huntley (1940), Epstein (1955), Fisher and Mirin (1966), and Sugerman (in Ittelson and Kutash, 1961) were able to show, in agreement with Wolff, that persons do have difficulty in identifying self representations obtained without their knowledge and also that they respond in a selectively enhanced fashion to them. The findings from these studies also indicated that the enhanced response is typically in the direction of being unusually favorable to one's self representation. This differs from Wolff's report that the enhancement was likely to be either unusually favorable or unfavorable.

A particularly exacting test of Wolff's original findings was carried out by Beloff and Beloff (1961). Their experimental design made use of a stereoscope which could, without the subject's knowledge, present different stimuli to each eye. Twenty-three men and 29 women were studied. During a control phase of the procedure the subject was asked to describe and then rate the "attractiveness" of a series of faces which actually consisted of the fused images of different photographs of strangers presented in the stereoscope to his right and left eyes. The experimental phase revolved about presenting the subject's own photograph to one eye and that of a stranger to the other eye. About one-third of the subjects spontaneously recognized themselves during this experimental presentation. However, in the group where self recognition did not occur it was found that significantly more positive ratings of attractiveness were made for the composite involving the self than for the control composites in which the self was not included. These results certainly substantiated Wolff's work.

A related kind of study was done by van der Werff (1967) who used an ingenious technique which was based on eliciting responses to pictures of eyes. Photograph fusions were constructed which combined both eyes of two persons into one pair by means of double printing. Subjects (N = 50) were presented with eye fusions which combined their own eyes with those of another and eye fusions which involved that of control persons and another. They were asked to make judgments of the eye pictures with reference to 23 personality traits. In the 38 cases where self recognition did not occur, subjects described their own pictures in less neutral and more positive terms than they did non-self pictures. These data were once again in agreement with Wolff.

Efforts have been made to trace how personal attitudes and traits might influence the individual's unknowing response to his self representation.

Rogers and Walsh (1959) predicted that defensive people would show greater dislike of self in their unconscious evaluations than would the nondefensive. The K scale of the Minnesota Multiphasic Personality Inventory was used as an index of defensiveness. Evaluation of self was determined by asking subjects (55 women) to look at line drawings of two female faces and to rate the relative attractiveness of each as their expressions apparently changed. Expressions were changed by projecting on to the line drawings at subliminal speeds pictures of female faces. Among the faces projected was the subject's own. None of the subjects seemed aware that she had been shown her own face. Analysis of the attractiveness ratings revealed that the defensive women judged themselves as significantly less attractive than did the non-defensive women. Incidentally, it was earlier established that judges could not detect any real differences in attractiveness among those high and low in defensiveness. Generally, Rogers and Walsh interpreted their data to mean that their high defensive subjects had strong self depreciatory feelings which were denied conscious expression in order to maintain self-esteem—but which were revealed in the self evaluation situation.

With these results as a background, Rogers and Coleman (1959) considered the relationship of an individual's difficulty in expressing aggression to his unconscious evaluation of his own aggressiveness. It was hypothesized that those persons who had greatest difficulty in voicing hostility would unknowingly rate themselves as highest in aggressiveness. Presumably the accumulated unacceptable hostility which inhibited their free response would make them feel that they had unusual hostile qualities. Ability to express aggression was measured by means of the Rosenzweig Picture-Frustration Study which involves the subject writing the verbal responses that frustrated persons in various cartoon situations might make. One scoring category for such responses is called "impunitive" and includes all instances in which hostility depicted in the cartoon situations is completely denied. It is this impunitive score which was used as an indicator of difficulty in expressing aggression. The methodology for determining how the subject would unconsciously evaluate his own aggressiveness was very similar to that described in the Rogers and Walsh (1959) study just cited above. Subjects (30 women) looked at two line drawings of women's faces and were told to rate which of the two looked more aggressive during a series of trials in which pictures of self and others were subliminally projected upon them. Significant trends turned up for subjects who had difficulty in expressing aggression to judge their own pictures as more aggressive than did those who were not characterized by such difficulty.

The impact of anxiety upon self perception was approached in a novel fashion by Schumacher, Wright, and Wiesen (1968). This study tested the hypothesis that one effect of anxiety is to cause a breakdown in discrimination between self and environment. While it did not involve reactions to self representations unknowingly perceived in the usual Wolff type of context, it did elicit reactions to a self representation in a special unstructured setting. The authors actually examined a very complex hypothesis. They expected that anxiety would result in selective response to one's own picture because it disrupts subject-object relations and renders the self "an objective source of threat or fear". Further, they anticipated in terms of Blum's (1954) findings that perceptual defense strategies differ at low versus high awareness of threatening stimuli, that anxiety would have contrasting effects upon perception of one's own picture presented at fast versus slow tachistoscopic speeds. Forty female college students were studied. Each subject was shown a picture of herself, one of another college student, and a third of a famous movie actress. She was told that the pictures would appear repeatedly in a tachistoscope and she was to identify each as it was presented. There was a series of trials at a fast speed and another at a slow speed. One group responded under neutral conditions and another in an "anxiety" condition induced by apparently attaching the subject to a "device" that would reveal things about her personality. The results indicated that the "anxious", as compared to the control subjects, overestimated the frequency of appearance of their own pictures at the high tachistoscopic speed and underestimated it at the low speed. This had been predicted; the findings were explained in terms of the self photograph acting as a "negative reinforcer" for the anxious subjects and as a "positive reinforcer" for the controls. Thus, at the slow speed where identification of self was most possible the controls were more often positively reinforced by identification and therefore encouraged to overestimate the occurrence of their own pictures; while the anxious subjects received augmented negative reinforcement which resulted in underestimation. At the faster speed, the opposite would presumably be true. Failure to attain recognition of a self photograph would act as a negative reinforcer for the controls and result in underestimation, but induce positive reinforcement for the anxious subjects (who wanted to avoid seeing their own pictures because of the associated anxiety). Insofar as these findings indicate that slow versus fast presentation of one's picture elicits different types of responses, they are congruent with the Wolff viewpoint. That is, if one thinks of the high speed presentation as analogous, in some ways, to the unconscious confrontation with self and the slow speed as a condition permitting fully aware perception of self, then the difference in response patterns partially bears out Wolff's view that the level of awareness at which a self representation is perceived influences its apparent attributes. The finding that anxiety level interacts with this level of awareness factor adds to our perspective concerning the complexity of the conditions governing self perception.

One study by Korner, Allison, Donoviel, and Boswell (1963) reported negative results in its attempt to find a link between a subject's conscious ratings of self (Bell's Index of Adjustment and Values) and his degree of liking of his own pictured silhouette. The picture of each subject's silhouette had been secured without his knowledge and he rated it in the context of a number of other silhouettes—without, of course, being aware that it was his own.

Fisher and Mirin (1966) proposed that the more insecure an individual feels about how others view him the greater his defensive need in the Wolff type self-evaluation situation to rate himself in favorable terms. Twenty-three men were asked to respond to four pictures presented tachistoscopically at increasingly slower speeds. One of the pictures (figure posing in front of a camera) was intended to tap narcissistic attitudes related to one's feelings of worth and regard. The other three pictures concerned various hostile themes.

Unconscious self evaluations were obtained by asking subjects to rate the friendliness and intelligence of a series of tachistoscopically presented pictures of shadow profiles and full faces of self and others. Self recognition was rare. A significant positive correlation was found between the favorableness of the subjects' ratings of their profiles and their degree of difficulty in perceiving the picture with the tachistoscopically presented narcissistic theme. This supported the initial hypothesis. But the correlation between ratings of one's full face picture and the narcissism tachistoscope values was not significant. In explaining this negative finding, it was speculated that because the full face pictures provided more self-recognizable cues than the profiles and therefore came closer to being consciously identified they might have been less able to evoke acceptably a self enhancing defensive strategy. This idea that defensive responses are optimally elicited when the subject has the fewest cues that he might be responding to his own self representation was first expressed by Wolff (1943) and also Huntley (1940). However, it must be cautioned that it is quite speculative. One investigator (Epstein, 1955) could find no relationship between extremeness of judgments of self representations and their degree of disguise. Other investigators (Rothstein and Epstein, 1963) found a rather complex model necessary to represent the relationship. They analyzed responses of subjects (N = 20) to their voices presented under six different conditions and degrees of disguise. The findings indicated (p. 484): ". . . increasing disguise results in less extreme reactions to self, both of a favorable and unfavorable nature . . . self judgments were significantly more favorable than judgments by and of others at the level of moderate disguise." The following quote is also pertinent (p. 484): "The curvilinear relationship between disguise and personality revealingness is not surprising, for while disguise may reduce defensiveness, it provides fewer cues which can stimulate reactions at any level, i.e., with sufficient disguise, the stimulus becomes meaningless."

Another matter to consider at this point is that while Fisher and Mirin, in the study just cited above, anticipated that an individual's anxiety about how he appears to others would be balanced defensively by a positive "self admiring" evaluation of self when he was provided with an opportunity to do so "innocently" and "unknowingly", the Rogers and Coleman and Rogers and Walsh studies proceeded from the contrary assumption that unacceptable feelings would be revealed in the self-evaluation situation. The first view portrays the unconscious self judgment as an opportunity to say something defensively nice about oneself; whereas the second view regards it as a context in which repressed feelings are unwittingly revealed. Actually, both kinds of responses have been observed; but most investigators report the positive, self praising one as having highest frequency. Because diverse methodologies have been used it is difficult to deduce from the existing literature what factors are likely to maximize the defensive versus the self revealing mode of response. Exploration of this problem should have priority if it is to become possible to make consistent interpretations of experiments using the self-evaluation methodology.

However, to elaborate further on the issue it should be mentioned that there is another study which has demonstrated experimentally that it is possible for unconscious self ratings to become a direct vehicle for expressing underlying affects or attitudes that might otherwise be concealed.

Sugerman (in Ittelson and Kutash, 1961) appraised the impact of success–failure conditions upon self evaluation. Sixty normal subjects hospitalized largely for surgical treatment were studied.[1] One part of the sample performed a series of tasks (figure drawing, reproduction of Bender designs, writing, make a design, coloring a picture, make a clay man) under "success" conditions. A feeling of success was created by intermittently asking questions of the subject and rewarding him with cigarettes—to indicate that he had done well. Another subsample completed the tasks under "failure" conditions, which involved not receiving cigarette rewards. A third part of the sample performed the tasks under "neutral" conditions. Various of the subject's self products (e.g., figure drawing, handwriting) derived from the tasks were shown later to him along with the productions of six others. He was asked in each instance to rank the products in the order in which they were "most pleasing" to him. If he did not spontaneously recognize his own production, the time was ascertained that he required to do so when a series of cues as to its possible presence were given. The judgments of self products associated with failure were more negative than those of products linked with the success or neutral conditions. It also took significantly longer to recognize the failure self products than those from the other two conditions. Subjects in the success sample did not differ from the neutral subjects in their ratings of self products or the time required to recognize them as one's own.

The results indicated that the negative affect created during the failure condition was transmitted in direct form to the self evaluations. Presumably, failure made subjects feel relatively negative toward themselves; and their productions carried this associated feeling. When they rated these productions they expressed their negative self perceptions in their judgments. One could not ask for a clearer demonstration that it is possible for an unconscious self rating to reveal underlying feelings.

The individual's perception of his own voice at conscious and unconscious levels has been the subject of a series of particularly intensive and careful investigations by Holzman and his colleagues (Holzman, 1964; Holzman and Rousey, 1966; Holzman, Rousey, and Snyder, 1966). They began their studies by simply observing how the average person reacts when he listens to a recording of his voice—with full knowledge that it is his own. They found that typically the initial reaction is one of displeasure, negativity,

---

[1] A schizophrenic sample was also studied, but results pertinent to this group will be cited later.

and autonomic arousal. One unique experiment that was carried out with reference to this response pattern involved bilingual subjects (N = 12) listening to recordings of their voice speaking in their original native language and another learned later in life (Holzman, Berger, and Rousey, 1967). The native language was Spanish and the later learned one English. Subjects listened to recordings of their voice, once in Spanish and once in English, and were encouraged to express their reactions. These reactions were tape recorded and raters later evaluated the content for a number of variables (e.g., affectivity, anxiety). The results conformed to the expectation that more affect and disturbance would be displayed by the subject in response to his voice speaking in Spanish than in English. The original hypothesis predicting these results had been derived in terms of the following formulation. When one learns one's native language one learns not only vocabulary and grammar but also a complex "paralanguage" that expresses unconscious intentions and attitudes, some of which are ego alien and unacceptable.

However, learning a foreign language, particularly late in life, is more of an intellectual process and less likely to be accompanied by an expressive paralanguage. Holzman, et al. therefore state that when an individual listens to his voice speaking in his native language he is more likely to be confronted with disturbing paralanguage information about himself than when listening to his voice in the non-native language. The idea that the individual's voice contains information which he finds unpleasant and wants to avoid has been the paradigm which these investigators have used to interpret a variety of behavior patterns evoked by one's own voice.

Holzman, Rousey, and Snyder (1966) have provided significant information, in terms of physiological measures, concerning subjects' reactions to their voices when they are recognized and not recognized. They designed a study in which one group unknowingly listened to their own voices, which had been recorded 15 minutes earlier, and which was presented in the context of 19 unfamiliar voices all communicating the same message. Responses to these stimuli were measured with GSR, muscle action potential, finger vaso-constriction, and pulse amplitude. A second group participated in the same design, except that their voices had been recorded three months prior to the experiment. The findings indicated that when subjects heard their own voices shortly after they were recorded and knew they were their own they evidenced more physiological reactivity than when they heard the voices of others. They showed a similar (but non-significant) tendency to react more to their non-recognized voices than to voices of others. When subjects heard their voices which had been recorded three months earlier, only those who recognized their own manifested significantly elevated reactivity. But in another analysis, it was established that of 24 subjects whose physiological data indicated they had responded in a differentiated fashion to their own voice as compared to voices of others, 13 had not identified their voices. That is, despite verbal non-recognition, a selective physiological reaction was elicited.

Apparently, in congruence with Wolff's views, the unrecognized voice did "register" at some level in the individuals concerned.

An intriguing question was raised by Holzman, et al. in discussing their results. They asked whether recognition of one's voice produced increased physiological activation or whether the somatic activation comes first and somehow aids in the identification process. In possible support of the second alternative they pointed out that Reiser and Block (1965) had found that if subjects making judgments about very weak stimuli to which they had been aversively conditioned are forced to delay verbal response until a peak GSR reaction has occurred, their decisions increase in accuracy. That is, if the somatic event presumably associated with the GSR response is allowed to occur first, the judgmental process is facilitated. Much more will be said in later chapters concerning the role of such somatic body experiences in cognitive processes.

An experiment has even been performed (Castaldo and Holzman, 1967) to examine the impact of hearing one's voice upon the content of one's dreams. Ten males were studied. Three months prior to the experiment each subject's voice had been recorded as he read a specific list of words. Later, he slept in a laboratory for a number of nights where it was possible to monitor rapid eye movements and elicit dreams shortly after they occurred. During one night the subject was exposed, while sleeping, to the sound of his own voice and on another night to the sound of another voice. A series of dreams were collected on each occasion; and so it was possible to compare the content of those occurring after exposure to one's own voice and those following the voice of another. The dreams were analyzed blindly. The exploratory results suggested that those associated with one's voice are particularly likely to contain a principal figure who is active, assertive, and independent. Hearing another person's voice seems, on the contrary, to stimulate dreams in which the principal figure is passive. Two chief possible explanations for the results were offered. Perhaps hearing one's own voice produces greater physiological arousal than a stranger's voice and this, because of the motor inhibition associated with sleep, is translated into a more active central figure. Or, as suggested by Luria's (1961) experiments which indicate that a child's vocal activity is necessary to him in gaining control over his voluntary action, one's voice is equated with control and competence and therefore hearing it arouses dream themes related to activity and independence. Obversely, the voice of another could set off associations about others telling one what to do and therefore arouse passive themes.[2]

---

[2] Witkin and his associates (Witkin and Lewis, 1967) have also been studying the impact of certain body experiences (e.g., related to induction of hypnosis and watching a movie about childbirth) upon dream content.

It may be recalled that Freud (1900) minimized the importance of immediate body experience upon dream content; but there are accumulating findings which challenge his view.

Comment

There is plenty of evidence that when an individual is confronted with his body or some representation of it as a perceptual object he gets stirred up in fairly unique ways. He is surprised, puzzled, autonomically activated, and motivated to take various kinds of defensive strategies. It is even a bit astonishing to learn that he does not have a precise patent against which to compare his mirror image and may have difficulty in deciding precisely how he looks.

Multiple studies have convincingly validated Werner Wolff's original discovery that one may not recognize pictures or representations of oneself and furthermore that such representations may evoke selectively defensive responses, despite lack of conscious awareness that they are self referring. These studies have variously used methodologies involving stereoscopic presentation of fused faces, photographs of fused eyes, projection of pictures at subliminal levels, tachistoscopic presentation of shadow profiles and full-face pictures, disguised voice and handwriting samples, and even input of one's own voice during sleep. While most observations indicate that self representations evoke positive self laudatory responses, negative ones also occur. Indeed, the unconsciously perceived self representation can apparently function not only to provide an opportunity for defensive self enhancement but also to provoke self revelation of repressed attitudes and affects. Much remains to be learned about how the amount of camouflage of the self representation influences response to it. Wolff thought that with greater disguise a more extreme response would be evoked. Epstein found no relationship between amount of disguise and mode of reaction. But Rothstein and Epstein discerned a curvilinear relation between degree of disguise of the self representation and the degree to which subjects register extreme responses toward it. The facts are obviously complicated and one wonders whether eventually an even more complex model than that proposed by Rothstein and Epstein will turn out to be applicable.

Exciting possibilities exist for innovation in the use of the self image and self representation to elicit body image variables. From the simple variations of spontaneous body movements before the mirror to the complex defensiveness evoked by a camouflaged self representing image there is a continuum of possible useful methodologies. Such methodologies would be particularly attractive because they would involve behaviors with obvious self significance. They would not require elaborate rationalization to be placed in such a perspective. What are some possible ways in which certain of the techniques described could be adapted directly to body image issues? Consider the following two illustrations. Schneiderman's work, cited above, already indicates a possible use of adjustable mirrors to determine preferred size for various body parts. That is, a subject could be presented with a mirror image in which his body was magnified or reduced in size and asked to adjust the image so that a particular part of his body (e.g., shoulders or arms) looked normal. Similar adjustments could be obtained for a variety of other body parts. One may speculate that tendencies would be found for some parts to be adjusted larger and others smaller than actuality. In this way, one could possibly measure the pattern of augmentation and shrinkage of body parts characterizing an individual's body image. Another interesting possibility would be to determine if different kinds of information emerge as a function of the individual reacting to self representations of different areas of his body. For example, if an individual unknowingly responds to a picture of his hands (which Wolff showed could quite feasibly be arranged), will he express different affects or attitudes than if he unknowingly responds to his head depicted in a shadow profile? As will be seen in later chapters, there are, indeed, variations in the values ascribed to the major sectors of one's body which would be interesting to assay with the Wolff type methodology.

New avenues need to be explored to increase the yield of information from the self confrontation methodology. We need to know more about the range of feelings and fantasies evoked when people see themselves in a mirror. Holzman's (1964) study of response to one's voice indicates that special defensive strategies are immediately triggered as one detects the presence of self in some shape or form. We need to know if localized physiological responses occur as the individual focuses his attention upon circumscribed parts of his image. We need systematic procedures for coding his motor and expressive behavior in reaction to self perception. Where does he touch himself? Which body parts does he move the most and least? Since it is known that in the course of unconscious self confrontation there may be special arousal (e.g., physiologically), can one also detect specifically excited patterns of kinesic behavior, such as increase in self directed motor behavior as indicated by increased self touching? There is, indeed, much about self confrontation behavior that remains to be explored.

RELATION TO OBJECTS IN SPACE

To be aware of the position of one's body in space and to localize it as an object in relation to surrounding objects has been considered a fundamental aspect of body image organization (Schilder, 1935; Head, 1926). Werner and Wapner (1949) and Witkin and his associates (1954, 1962) have taken the lead in exploring the spatial aspects of body perception. A stream of productive work has characterized both groups through the years. This work is well known and too voluminous to be presented in detail in the present review. However, it will be helpful to mention some of the highlights which are particularly pertinent to body image phenomena.

Sensori-tonic Work

The sensori-tonic group at Clark University under the leadership of Werner and Wapner has relied on two prime methods for studying the individual's perception of his body in its spatial context. One has involved the subject adjusting a luminous rod to the vertical while his body is tilted to various degrees in a darkened room where he has minimal environmental cues for defining his spatial position. A second has made use of a similar setting, except that the subject is asked to adjust a luminous rod so that it is aligned with his degree of body tilt in a given direction. Detailed studies have been completed to evaluate the effects of various conditions (e.g., starting point of rod, degree of body tilt, sequence of trials) upon these two judgmental situations. But aside from these details, the major findings that have emerged are as follows:

1. Normal subjects who have been tilted tend to perceive the vertical as shifted away from the direction of their tilt.

2. Normal subjects, in directly evaluating their tilt in space, tend to overestimate it in the direction of tilt.

These results have been interpreted within the sensori-tonic theory of maturation and differentiation. That is, the mature adult presumably differentiates himself clearly from the surrounding space; and this is reflected in the polarity of his judgments about other objects versus his own body. Thus, when he is tilted, he emphatically expresses his differentiation by seeing other objects as tilted away from his body. However, when asked to judge his body position directly, he is "pulled" by the opposite side of the polarity and overstates its amount of tilt. As will be later described, this formulation has been applied to "less mature" persons (e.g., children, schizophrenics); and it has been shown, according to theoretical expectation, that their spatial judgments do not manifest the same emphatic differentiation of self and object. A fundamental proposition that emerged from the sensori-tonic experiments is that maturity carries with it a mode of organization in which one's body as a perceptual object is clearly separated from non-self objects. Incidentally, this reaffirmed what has been speculatively asserted by many psychoanalytic theorists (e.g., Freud, 1927; Fenichel, 1945; Federn, 1952).

Another noteworthy discovery of the sensori-tonic group is that it is possible to modify the experience of separation of self from objects by adopting "polarized" versus "depolarized" attitudes toward them. An individual can, with the proper instructions, be induced to take a "depolarized" attitude in which he focuses on the potentiality for interaction and "linkage" between self and object. A "polarized" attitude is, on the contrary, encouraged by emphasizing the separateness and independence of self from a given object. It has been shown by Glick (1964) and Porzemsky and Wapner

(1965) that the apparent positions of objects in space, and particularly with reference to one's own body, may be varied as a function of taking polarized versus depolarized attitudes toward them. For example, under depolarized conditions objects appear to be relatively closer to self than when regarded from a polarized perspective. In this vein, one of the major contributions of sensori-tonic endeavors has been to show that many perceptual-cognitive phenomena may be modified by varying the observer's experience of his body. Such variables as degree of body tilt, distribution of right-left body tonus, prone versus upright position, and patterning of tension in one's eyes have been demonstrated to affect varied phenomena like light touch threshold, apparent direction of autokinetic movement, and the apparent position of the "straight-ahead". In fact, as one surveys such accumulated findings, one realizes how seriously most psychological theories underestimate the influence of the body as a perceptual anchor upon how the world is interpreted. Much more will be said about this issue in later chapters.

Witkin's Formulations

The energetic searches of Witkin and his colleagues have underscored the interrelationships between the individual's ability to maintain realistic perception of his position in space and various cognitive and personality variables. Typically, this group creates situations in which the subject has minimal cues, aside from those emanating from his own body, to localize either himself or other objects spatially. He is asked to determine the vertical for himself or an object such as a luminous rod in the presence of distractions like being tilted or visual stimuli introduced to provide misleading spatial information. The ability to make accurate spatial judgments under such distracting circumstances is considered to reflect one's capability of utilizing orienting cues which are provided by kinesthetic experience; and at a more general level it is interpreted as a capacity for separating out what is significant from the context in which it is embedded. Empirically, this is reflected in a significant positive correlation between facility in making accurate spatial judgments and adequacy of performance on embedded figure problems. It has been established that accuracy in defining spatial positions accurately (presumably with respect to one's body) is a stable attribute of the individual—even over a period of years. Furthermore, one's spatial accuracy is positively correlated with how mature and differentiated a figure one sketches when asked to draw a human figure.

Those who are particularly proficient in dealing with the Witkin spatial tasks (referred to as "field independent") have been shown to manifest a variety of traits like independence, low suggestibility, special tolerance for stress, and so forth. In addition, they seem to have had experiences with parents who respected integrity of self. The poor performer ("field dependent") is described as being at the opposite end of the continuum for the various attributes and dimensions enumerated.

A prominent and well validated aspect of this work is the fact that males seem to be more "field independent" than women. Witkin has suggested that it may partially be a function of the woman's difficulty in regarding her body as adequate (because it lacks culturally valued male features) and being able to experience it as a stable orienting reference in the total perceptual field. Much discussion has been stimulated by these observations concerning possible differences between the way males and females perceive and evaluate their bodies. Views have ranged from the assumption that males have a much more stable and well integrated body image than women—to just the opposite position (e.g., Fisher, 1964E).

It is a problem to evaluate what Witkin's findings signify for body image theory because facility in dealing with his spatial judgment tasks has turned out to be positively correlated with ability to perform a variety of cognitive tasks (e.g., embedded figures, Block Designs). He sees ability to perform the spatial tasks as part of a general ability to separate an item from its context. Where does body experience or body concept enter into this general cognitive-like level of response? Perhaps the best way to cut through the potential confusion is to say that Witkin regards a clear sense of one's body, a definite concept that one's body is a separate entity, as a necessary condition for being able to differentiate an object from the context in which it is embedded. The confusion, if there really is any, relates to the fact that learning to differentiate one's body as an entity is portrayed by Witkin as parallel, and yet interacting with, learning to differentiate non-self objects. The two processes are overlapping; and ultimately there is obscurity about cause and effect. Inter-relations between cognition and body experience are similarly explicit in the sensori-tonic experiments. Findings by the present writer, to be cited at a later point, point in the same direction.

BODY CONCEPT AND SELF CONCEPT

As Wylie (1961) remarked, there has been confusion about the relation of self concept and body image variables. Part of the confusion has probably resulted from a reluctance to come to terms with the fact that the two classes of variables are inextricably interdependent. The body concept is a perception of one's body against the whole context of self feeling and developmental experiences which also shape the self concept. This does not mean that body concept and self concept do not broadly have different referents; and certainly they lead to different perspectives toward many phenomena.

Empirical work concerned with the correlation between body concept and self concept has been sparse. In addition, as will be seen, the work that has

been done largely involves measures which are vulnerable to social desirability effects. The typical self concept scale is known to be heavily influenced
by social desirability. Pantleo (1966) has also shown this to be true of verbal
body concept measures like the Secord-Jourard (1953) Body Cathexis type
scale, which measures degree of satisfaction with various body areas, and has
been most frequently reported in studies comparing self concept and body
concept measures. Therefore, many of the fairly high positive correlations
reported between self and body concept indices may reflect their shared social
desirability variance. A brief overview of studies pertinent to this general
matter follows.

Jourard and Secord (1954) originally reported that Body Cathexis (degree
of feeling of satisfaction or dissatisfaction with the various parts or processes of
the body) was significantly related to feelings about the self. They had used a
Body Cathexis scale and a Self Cathexis scale composed respectively of 46 and
55 items which the subject rated on a five-point basis ranging from strong
positive to strong negative feelings. Some of the items in their Body Cathexis
scale were "legs", "health", and "teeth"; while self concept items were
represented by such examples as "will power", "taste in clothes", and
"popularity". Johnson (1956) substantiated the correlation between Body
Cathexis and Self Cathexis which they had reported; and Gunderson and
Johnson (1965) further verified it. Incidentally, Secord and Jourard had also
utilized an Homonym test in their study which required the subject to respond
with associations to a series of words having common body or non-body
meanings. Words like "colon" and "graft" are examples. Body responses to
these words might be: colon–intestine, graft–skin; whereas non-bodily
responses might be colon–comma, graft–politics. It was presumed that a
high number of body associations was correlated with high concern with
one's body. Secord and Jourard described a significant positive relationship between Homonym scores and an index of body anxiety derived
from items in the Body Cathexis scale. In addition, they indicated that
psychological insecurity (as measured by the Maslow Security–Insecurity
Inventory) was positively linked with anxious or negative concern on the
Body Cathexis and Self Cathexis measures. Weinberg (1960) in 1960
attempted to cross-validate the results which have just been summarized.
He administered the Homonym, Body Cathexis, and Self Cathexis scales
and also Maslow's Security–Insecurity Inventory to 212 college students, of
whom 108 were male and 104 female. In general, his results supported the
previous observations. The Body Cathexis and Self Cathexis scores once
again proved to be significantly positively interrelated. They were also again
correlated with the Maslow insecurity test. The original finding was not
reaffirmed that negative feelings about the body (as indicated by the Body
Cathexis score) are correlated with body concern in the Homonym test. An
unexpected result that emerged was the fact that in the male group (but not
in the female group) high insecurity on the Maslow test was accompanied by

high body concern on the Homonym test. An interesting sidelight in the data was that women evidenced significantly higher body concern on the Homonym test than men, which was in keeping with a similar report by Secord (1953).

Rosen and Ross (1968) raised the question whether the relationship between the Secord-Jourard Body Cathexis measure and self concept might not turn out to be even more positive than generally reported, if one took into account the relative importance to the individual of the various body parts he rated. The lumping together of ratings of parts that are high and those that are low in their significance to the individual could attenuate the meaning of the derived total score. Eighty-two college students were studied to evaluate this matter. They rated their satisfaction with a variety of their body parts and also indicated how important they considered each to be. Self concept was measured by means of self ratings in relation to bi-polar dimensions defined by 17 adjectives. The findings indicated that the self concept scores were much more positively correlated with the Body Cathexis scores derived from ratings of body parts seen as having high importance than with Cathexis scores based on body parts having low importance.

Zion (1965) considered the relationship between a self concept measure (Bell's Index of Adjustment and Values) and an elaborate scale for evaluating attitudes toward one's body. The following self concept scores were used: self description, self acceptance, ideal self, and self description—ideal discrepancy. The body attitude measure involved five different dimensions: physical attractiveness, feelings about body movement, grooming, body expressiveness, and masculinity-femininity. In a population of 200 college women a strong trend was observed for self concept and body concept ratings to be positively correlated. There was a clear parallel between the way the subject appraised herself as a person and the way she evaluated her body.

The only study which has not discerned a positive relation between Body Cathexis and self concept was carried out by White and Gaier (1965). They obtained from 104 male members of Alcoholics Anonymous responses to the Secord and Jourard Body Cathexis and Self Cathexis scales. The subjects were also asked to estimate how long they had maintained sobriety. It was established that during the first 12 months of sobriety there was a gradual increasing satisfaction with one's body, as defined by the general Body Cathexis score. But this satisfaction tended to decline at 36 months or beyond. An opposite pattern appeared for the self concept ratings. Subjects indicated high self evaluation at the beginning of sobriety and then increasingly more negative self feelings from that point until about 12 months, when self evaluations stabilized. It was of particular interest that the pattern over time for the self concept ratings tended to be the opposite of the Body Cathexis ratings. White and Gaier suggest this reflects the fact that improvement in control of drinking is particularly evident in body appearance, which other AA members frequently observe and evaluate. But the alcoholic's initial self concept is artificially high because of the "residual effects of alcohol"; and as sobriety is maintained he takes a more realistic attitude toward himself.

A clear demonstration of the fact that an individual's feelings toward self and his body overlap awaits the development of measures for both of these parameters which are minimally influenced by social desirability effects. Perhaps such a demonstration would be possible if some of the Wolff (1943) self confrontation techniques referred to above were adapted to measure both feelings about self and evaluative attitudes toward a number of different body areas.

PERCEPTION OF BODY SIZE IN ADULTS

General Literature

One of the fastest moving developments in body image research has been a series of studies emanating from diverse sources which focuses on the dimension of perceived body size. The individual's perception of the size of his body has been diversely related to his actual body size, personality traits, sex, level of ego integration, and so forth. Retrospectively, one can see suggestions in earlier work that the concept of size might provide an important context within which to interpret body image phenomena. Schilder (1935) and Federn (1952) referred to the significant body size changes experienced during the ordinary course of a day as one does such things as wake up, ride in an elevator, become fatigued, and go to sleep. Some of the most classical observations concerning how the amputee adjusts to his loss concerned his inevitable experience of a phantom limb which gradually shrinks and retracts and finally disappears. Savage (1955) described dramatic sensations of shift in body size under the influence of LSD; and Gill and Brenman (1959) reported similar alterations during hypnotic states. Katcher and Levin (1955) found evidence that body size experiences are important in the process of development and attaining identity.

Nash (1951) was actually one of the first to undertake systematic study in which the individual's perception of his own body size, as a body image problem, was of central importance. He was impressed with the fact that there is a "primitive evaluation of size which is related to power or powerlessness in others or in oneself"; and he felt that it was an important aspect of how one viewed one's body. His study had two objectives: (1) to determine whether there are attitudinal correlates of the sizes ascribed to body areas; (2) to ascertain whether there are changes in perception of body size associated with the radical physical transformations of puberty. The experimental population consisted of prepubescent and postpubescent boys. The procedure used to measure subjects' body size concepts is described by the following quote (p. 24):

> The subject is told that the height of an X mark . . . (as shown on a sheet of paper) represents his stature. He is asked to place an X mark at the height above the baseline . . . where he could expect his eyes to be, compared to the standard representing his stature. Provision is also made for recording his shoulder height, belly-button height, height at which legs join, and knee height. . . .
>
> Likewise the subject is told that the height of a second given X mark above the baseline represents the stature of the average boy of his age. With this standard he is asked to compare (in the same manner as previously) his own stature, those of the tallest and shortest boys of his age, those of the average man and woman and of the average girl of his age, as well as the stature of a two-year-old, and the height at which the legs of a two-year-old join.

The discrepancies between subjects' estimates of their own body dimensions and the actual measurements of these dimensions were computed. Similar discrepancies were determined between subjects' estimates of the sizes of other persons in various age and sex groups and the size norms available for such groups. A vaguely defined test of "ego expansion" was also included in the study. It required the subject to do such things as depict the size of his personality by drawing a circle representation of it on a sheet of paper and draw a circle equal to the size of a quarter. Scoring of responses was based on their size or expansiveness. There were significant findings for both the prepubescent and postpubescent groups.

The relative heights of one's body landmarks tended to be underestimated; and the pattern of underestimation was congruent with the body proportions characteristic of a young child. There was a relative exaggeration of the size of the head. Nash remarked with regard to this matter (p. 98), "It is possible that the highly differentiated nature of the head, which places it virtually at the center of one's spatial world, results in feelings of the expansion of the head at the expense of the distant organs on the 'periphery'." Those whose stature differed markedly from the average of their peers distorted the stature of others in the opposite direction.

In the prepubescent group only it was noted that overestimation of the size of the upper body areas was correlated with overestimating the size of certain non-human objects. Also, it was observed in this group that there was a high degree of error in estimating stature that possibly reflected the uncertain status of being a prepubescent who stands uncertainly in between childhood and manhood. No consistent relationships appeared in either of the groups between body size estimates and the test of "ego expansiveness" that was employed. Nash's exploratory venture turned up a few interesting leads. However, years elapsed before further systematic investigations of body image size perception were undertaken.

When one next encounters the size variable in the body image literature it is within the context of work carried out by Jourard and Secord which dealt with the individual's subjective feelings about various parts of his body. As earlier described, they developed a technique which tapped how positively or negatively persons felt toward their bodies. This technique, which they refer to as the Body Cathexis scale, requires subjects to rate approximately 40 different areas (e.g., hair, hands, ears, sex organs) of their own bodies on a five point scale ranging from "strong positive feelings" to "strong negative feelings". In one study (1954) they had 62 college males fill out the Body Cathexis scale and then measurements were taken of their height, weight, width of shoulders, circumference of chest when relaxed and expanded, and circumference of biceps when relaxed and expanded. Correlations were computed between these measurements and five pertinent Body Cathexis ratings: height, weight, shoulder width, chest, and muscular strength. There were low but significant correlations which indicated that "large size of the relevant body parts is associated with positive cathexis, while the reverse is true for small size." In this masculine group positive attitudes toward one's body were associated with bigness.

Magnussen (1958) successfully replicated this finding in another male sample. He also found that body satisfaction was positively correlated with weight.

Quite relatedly, Gunderson (1956) obtained from 670 Navy enlisted men self ratings of various body areas on a modified version of the Secord and Jourard Body Cathexis scale. Information was available concerning the actual heights and weights of these men. It was shown that amount of dissatisfaction with either height or weight tended to increase with its degree of deviation from the most preferred ("ideal") value in the group. Those who were either too short or too tall and those who were too light or heavy were most dissatisfied. The curvilinear relationship between height and satisfaction with height differed from that originally reported by Jourard and Secord (1954) which was linear.

In a study by Jourard and Secord (1955) involving 60 female college students a somewhat different pattern than that encountered in men characterized the relationship between Body Cathexis ratings assigned to body areas and their size attributes. Body Cathexis ratings of 12 body parts (e.g., height, weight, bust, waist, hips) were obtained. Direct measures of these areas were also secured. Correlations indicated that in this female group positive feelings toward body parts were linked with smallness in size of such parts. The only exception was the bust where large size was generally desired. Another pertinent aspect of this study had to do with the relationship of Body Cathexis scores to the discrepancies between subjects' estimates of the ideal sizes for given body parts and the actual sizes they ascribed to these parts. There were significant indications that the greater the discrepancy between estimated ideal and estimated size for certain body dimensions (height, weight, waist, hips) the more negative was the cathexis rating assigned.

Calden, Lundy, and Schlafer (1959) observed sex differences in attitudes toward body size which are supportive of those reported by Jourard and Secord. They had 196 female and 110 male college students fill out a questionnaire which asked for estimates of the sizes of various body features and also statements of extent of satisfaction or dissatisfaction with these features. Such questions as the following were included:

> What is your own weight?
> What is your own height?
> Are you satisfied with your own weight?
> What would you like to weigh ideally?
> For the following parts of your body (shoulders, hips, waist) indicate how you would like them to be (bigger, smaller, okay as is).

In addition, each subject rated the attractiveness of seven male figures ranging over a continuum which included endomorphs, mesomorphs, and ectomorphs. The results demonstrated that males prefer largeness of bodily proportions, i.e., broader shoulders, thicker arms, bigger chest, and more prominent chin. Females, on the other hand, wished to be smaller in all dimensions except for bust. An interesting sidelight was the fact that the body parts which men most wanted to see changed in themselves were from the waist up; whereas the women wanted change in body parts from the waist down.[3] In reacting to the pictures of men with different body types the subjects of both sexes perceived the extremely stout person as being least attractive in build. But, in general, the women were significantly more negative in their evaluations of figures with large body proportions (viz., extreme endomorphs and mesomorphs) than were the men. Since women in contrast to men reject bigness in themselves, the hypothesis was offered that their negative reactions to bigness of the figures in the pictures represented a projection mechanism. This projection hypothesis presumes that the qualities which are judged undesirable in one's own body are the same qualities that are considered undesirable in others.[4] Parenthetically, it should be noted that significantly more women than men indicated in their questionnaire responses that they were satisfied with their height, whereas the obverse was true for responses relating to one's facial attractiveness.

The preference of women for small body proportions was evident again

[3] This finding bears an interesting analogy to the Wittreich and Grace (1955) and Fisher (1964E) findings (which will be described later) that females have more difficulty than men in experiencing aniseikonically induced perceptual alterations of their legs than do men.

[4] It is apropos to note that evaluations concerning whether others are fat or thin or tall or short are significantly influenced by the weight and height attributes of those making the judgments (e.g., Fillenbaum, 1961; Hinckley and Rethlingshafer, 1951). The influence of personal needs upon reactions to the physical attributes of others is illustrated by the work of Scodel (1957). He has shown that ratings by men of the attractiveness of women with different sized breasts is significantly a function of how dependently oriented the male rater is. The greater a male's dependency the more he finds small breasted women attractive.

in the findings of Singer and Lamb (1966). Ninety-three female college students responded to a series of questions. There were inquiries concerning their actual and preferred physical size (e.g., with reference to height, bust, hips, ankles); and measures were taken of the corresponding dimensions. Forty-nine of the subjects estimated their own body attributes without knowing measurements would be taken later; whereas 44 were informed in advance that this would occur. It was found that there were significant trends for all subjects' ideal preferences as to waist and hip size and also weight to be smaller than their self estimates. But short girls wanted to be taller and tall girls wanted to be shorter. Almost all wanted larger bust sizes. Interestingly, those who knew their actual measures would be taken were significantly more accurate in estimating their size attributes than were those who did not know. It was also noted that subjects who were first-born children distorted their estimates more in the "unaware" condition and less in the "aware" condition than subjects who were later-born children. The authors speculated that this might reflect relatively greater body anxiety on the part of the first born. This speculation has been affirmed by Nisbett's (1968) report that first born are less likely to participate in dangerous sports than later born. Similarly, Helmreich (1966) observed that first borns express more fear than later borns in a situation with life threatening implications.

Arkoff and Weaver (1966) applied the Jourard and Secord Cathexis scale to students at the University of Hawaii [87 Japanese-Americans (35 male and 52 female) and 53 Caucasian-Americans (29 male, 24 female)]. The subjects also estimated the sizes of various areas of their bodies (e.g., height, biceps, waist, hips) and indicated ideal preferred sizes for them. Actual measures of the body dimensions were subsequently taken. The data indicated once again that males generally wished to be larger and females to be smaller. But the Japanese men exceeded the Caucasian men in the degree to which they wanted to be taller and have larger biceps. Contrary to most past reports, females in both groups wanted to be taller, but this was particularly true of the Japanese females. It was observed that the Japanese females expressed significantly greater overall body dissatisfaction than males of the same ethnic background and also more than the female Caucasians. The Japanese males and the Caucasian males and females did not differ from each other in this respect. The body dissatisfaction expressed by the Japanese women was speculatively attributed by Arkoff and Weaver to the fact that this group is unusually self abasing and self critical. When the accuracy of estimation of body size was considered by comparing estimates with actual body measures, the Japanese and American females were found not to differ. Similarly, the two male groups differed for only one dimension. The Japanese males were more accurate [5] in estimating their height. Paradoxically, this was true despite the fact they were more dissatisfied with their height.

[5] But in another instance, Arnoult and Duke (1961) concluded that native Japanese college students make larger errors in estimating their height than do American students.

The question whether there are truly fundamental differences in the way males and females experience the size aspects of their bodies has stimulated a good deal of work. Boraks (1962) conducted one of the most elaborate inquiries in this area. But he sought to look simultaneously at several other aspects of sex differences in body image. His subjects were 24 male and 24 female college students. The various body image dimensions he sampled were as follows:

1. Perception of body size was determined by asking subjects to draw lines (while blindfolded) which equaled the lengths of seven specific body parts (e.g., arm, head, leg, shoulders). The actual dimensions of the body parts in question were subsequently measured.

2. Semantic Differential ratings (Osgood, Suci, and Tannenbaum, 1957) were obtained from each subject of seven areas of his body (e.g., hand, shoulders, leg, head), the general concept "My Body", and also "Myself" and "My Mood Today".

3. Subjects were asked to sketch a picture of a person and also a picture of themselves. The pictures were evaluated in terms of their size and rated for variables like attractiveness, strength, and activity.

4. A multiple choice version of the Secord (1953) Homonym test for measuring body awareness was administered. This test measures body awareness in terms of the number of body associations given to words that have both body and non-body meaning (e.g., colon, stitch). Not only were number of body associations ascertained but also the number of such associations subsequently recalled in a memory test.

The findings indicated that the sexes did not differ in the degree to which they over- or under-estimated the sizes of their body parts. But men were noted to be more variable in their body part estimation. Males further proved to be more variable than women in their ratings of their bodies. These last results did not agree with those of Secord and Jourard (1953) and Jourard and Remy (1957) who reported that females were more variable than males in Body Cathexis ratings. Females were observed by Boraks to rate their bodies as less potent (e.g., strong) than did the men. No consistent relationships were found between Body Cathexis scores and size estimates for the corresponding body areas. Few findings of significance emerged for the figure drawing and the self drawing measures. The Secord Homonym data revealed no meaningful sex differences.

Based upon a complicated and somewhat *ad hoc* mode of analysis, it was concluded that the male has a more global or unitary body image than the female. However, the male was described as being more differentiated at specific levels of the body image (e.g., with reference to body fantasy as portrayed in figure and self drawings). This formulation is highly interpretative and should be regarded with caution. Indeed, one can easily conclude from a survey of the findings that there were few solid differences revealed between the sexes in their body perceptions and evaluations. This was especially true with reference to over- or under-estimation of the sizes of various sectors of one's body.

Shontz (1963C) studied 22 male and 22 female college students to determine, among other things, whether there were sex differences in body size estimation. Subjects estimated the sizes of ten different parts of their bodies (e.g., hand, hips, trunk, arm) and the sizes of three different wooden sticks. At a later point measures were taken of the pertinent body areas of the subjects. Attitudes toward various body sectors were evaluated with 40 items similar to those in the Secord-Jourard Body Cathexis scale. Women were found to over-estimate body part sizes; whereas the judgments of the men were more accurate. No sex differences occurred in judging the sizes of the non-body objects. No differences were detected in over-all level of body acceptance; but women showed greater variability (differentiation) in their evaluations of the acceptability of a range of body areas. Shontz felt that his data indicated that, "Important sex differences seem to exist in body cognition. Men show greater veridicality of response at the level of sensorily-mediated perception of the body. Women demonstrate a greater degree of differentiation among body parts and functions" (p. 665).

"It might be supposed that men's orientations toward the body tend to be more global, while women tend to judge somatic characteristics more on a part-by-part basis" (p. 671). In some ways this conclusion is congruent with those of Boraks.[6]

Fuhrer and Cowan (1967) compared 20 male and 20 female college students in their estimates of the sizes of six body parts (e.g., shoulder to elbow, shoulder width, hip width, head width) and also two non-body objects (viz., 12 inch ruler, dollar bill). Judgments were made under lighted and dark conditions. Also, two sites (shoulder to elbow and wrist to middle finger) were estimated under non-movement and active movement conditions. Active movement was achieved by asking subjects to move each joint bounding the given body part vigorously. The actual dimensions of the pertinent body areas were measured. No gross sex differences in degree of error in making body size judgments could be demonstrated. One particularly interesting finding was that while females tended to underestimate body size more than males under non-movement conditions, the difference disappeared under conditions of movement. Fuhrer and Cowan interpreted this as congruent with the Witkin, et al. (1954) conclusion that women customarily use more visual and fewer body cues than men in making spatial judgments. Thus, when the women were forced by the experimental condition to use proprioceptive information their difference with men in this respect was reduced; and so their judgments of body size approached those of the men. Incidentally, it is not surprising to learn further that size estimates under normal illumination prove to be more veridical than under darkness conditions.

[6] Boraks' dissertation was completed under Shontz's direction.

Kurtz (1966) addressed himself directly to the question whether the size and "build" attributes of an individual's body influence his satisfaction with it and whether the direction of the relationship varies with sex. It was hypothesized that men of large size or mesomorphic build would evaluate their bodies more positively than would men of small size or leptomorphic (thin and narrow) or eurymorphic (wide and squat) body build. For women more complex hypotheses were formulated. It was anticipated that the larger a woman's body size the more negatively she would evaluate her body, but the more potent (powerful) she would perceive it to be. Also, the more mesomorphic (as compared to leptomorphic or eurymorphic) a woman's body the more she would feel positively toward it. At a more general level, it was predicted that women would have a more clearly differentiated idea of what they like and dislike about their bodies than would men.

Eighty-nine male and 80 female college students served as subjects. Each was asked to rate on a series of Semantic Differential scales (e.g., good-bad, ugly-beautiful) 30 different aspects of his body (e.g., size of my hands, my weight, my height). Data were also obtained about weight, height, and body build.

A borderline trend was noted for large men to like their bodies better than small men; and mesomorphic men proved to like their bodies significantly more than non-mesomorphs. Large mesomorphs rated their bodies more positively than did any other group. With reference to women, the hypothesis was not supported that those who were large would dislike their bodies more than those who were medium or small. The hypothesis was also unsupported that mesomorphic women would like their bodies more than non-mesomorphs; but the former did rate their bodies as more potent than the latter.

In terms of the self ratings, women had a clearer, more differentiated concept of what they like and dislike about their bodies than men. This is in agreement with the previous reports of Jourard and Remy (1957), Secord and Jourard (1953), and Shontz (1963C); but not in accord with Boraks' (1962) findings. Kurtz attributed the greater differentiation of the women's body judgments to the fact that "it is part of the female's role prescription to focus attention upon the details of their bodies whereas men are expected to be more subdued in the interest they take in the appearance of their bodies" (p. 113). It is of interest too that the women were more positive toward their bodies than the men; but men did see their bodies as more potent and active.

Certain generalities emerge from the studies cited. Men tend to prefer large body size. Women prefer small body size; but there have been notable exceptions. For example, women do prefer large breasts and in some instances they wish to be taller. No consistent sex differences have been observed in accuracy of body size estimation or in tendencies to over- or under-estimate the sizes of one's body parts. There are no consistent correlations between the absolute sizes individuals ascribe to specific body areas and their degree of dissatisfaction with them; nor are there significant correlations between degree of error in judging the sizes of specific body areas and dissatisfaction with them. Men who actually possess large body size or who are mesomorphic seem to regard their bodies more positively than do small men or non-mesomorphs. Simple equations of this sort do not seem to apply to women. Finally, it may be said that women are inclined to give more differentiated judgments about their satisfaction with various sectors of the body than do men.

Mention should be made of a paper by Prelinger (1959) which bears somewhat indirectly upon body size experience. Its title is "Extension and Structure of The Self"; and one of its important objectives was to determine if persons differ in the bigness or extent they ascribe to the self structure. Prelinger pictures the self as constituting a spatial "region which can vary in its degree of extension depending upon what is included within its boundaries." His way of conceptualizing the self reminds one of models that have been proposed to represent the body image. In order to arrive at a measure of the extent of the "self" as compared to the "non-self region", he had subjects classify 160 different items as being or not being part of the self. There were eight groups of items: psychological or intra-organismic processes (e.g., the conscience, itching of the foot); body parts; objects within the close physical environment (e.g., dirt on hands, furniture in the room); distant physical environment; personal identifying characteristics (e.g., age, occupation); possessions; other people; and abstract ideas (e.g., law, the morals of our society). In a group of 60 normal men the number of items included as part of the self region varied extremely from 25 to 129. Separate scores for each of the eight clusters of items proved to be highly intercorrelated. It is interesting that the group of items consisting entirely of body parts correlated as high as .60 with other categories of items. But as might be expected, body parts were considered to be parts of the self with greater frequency than other concepts or objects. It was also found that items most likely to be included in the self region are those which refer to things under our control or which can influence us. At another level, it was noted that the likelihood of objects in the external world being classified within the self was negatively correlated with their physical distance from the body.

Sensori-tonic Contributions

Some of the most sustained and theory-derived work dealing with body image size variables has emerged in the last several years from the sensori-tonic group at Clark University. Just as they have in the past been interested in examining the manifold variables which affect perception of external objects, they are similarly concerned with investigating the factors which influence perception of one's own body. A dimension which they have focused upon concerns the size attributed to various body parts. Some of their earlier experiments dealt particularly with perception of head size. Werner, Wapner, and Comalli reported in 1957 a study involving 24 subjects which concerned the effect of an imposed boundary upon perceived head size. Each subject was asked, with his eyes closed, to estimate his own head size by pointing. He indicated, with his index fingers, a horizontal distance on a metal rod which he considered to be equal to the width of his head. There was an experimental condition during which the experimenter lightly touched the subject's temples as he made his judgments and there was a control condition when no attempt was made to influence judgments by imposing the boundary experience of touch. At the conclusion of the procedure measures were taken of the subjects' actual head widths. The results indicated that under both conditions there was an overestimation of head size, but that the overestimation was significantly less when a touch boundary was imposed. It was concluded that (p. 71), "Touching the temples serves to delineate or articulate the borders of the head; and in that manner makes for a reduction in perceived size." The authors called attention to the fact that others had observed a similar phenomenon with regard to perception of external objects, viz., that with an increase in degree of segregation of a figure against its ground there is a reduction in apparent size.

Continuing this train of exploration, Wapner, Werner, and Comalli reported a study in 1958 which concerned the effects of various types of boundary enhancing stimuli on the perception of the size of specific areas of the face. Three separate experiments were performed. In all of the experiments it was the subject's task to estimate, with his eyes closed, the distance from his nose to his cheekbone by pointing to a meter stick in the frontoparallel plane either with his right or left index finger where he felt his cheekbone was projected. The meter stick was 18 cm. from the subject who was seated with his nose touching a rod-like projection that was mounted perpendicularly to the meter scale and in his median sagittal plane. Under one condition the boundary on one side of the face was enhanced by touching the cheek and it was predicted that the touched side would be perceived as smaller than the side that was not enhanced in this fashion. A second condition concerned a similar comparison but the enhancing condition consisted of the application of a cold stimulus (dry ice); and the third condition involved the boundary enhancing effect of a heat stimulus (held a meter from the face). In all three instances the side of the face whose boundary had been emphasized was judged to be significantly smaller than the nonstimulated side. The heat stimulus was the least effective of the three types of stimulation used. These results were clearly supportive of the first study reported by Wapner, Werner, and Comalli (1958) in which touch decreased the perceived width of the total head.

Analogous data have been obtained with reference to perceived arm length by Humphries (1959). She had subjects adjust a luminous marker to indicate a point which they considered to coincide with the location of the tips of the fingers of the outstretched hand. This was done in one series of trials with the tips of the fingers touched and in another series with the fingers untouched. The results indicated that touch or articulation reduced the apparent length of the outstretched arm. It is noteworthy that there was a significant trend for men to overestimate and women to underestimate their arm length. There was also a significant tendency for the arm to be perceived as shorter when outstretched sideways than when in the forward position. This last finding bears some analogy to Davidon's (1960) observation that perception of touched distances on the arms differ when they are outstretched sideways as contrasted to a forward position.[7]

Another variable having to do with perceived arm length which the Clark group has considered is the effect of the openness of the visual context in which the perception occurs (Wapner, McFarland, and Werner, 1963). It was predicted that arm length would be experienced as relatively longer in an open, extended spatial situation than in one in which the spatial vista was blocked or cut off. This hypothesis was tested by having subjects judge arm length under three different conditions: one hand almost touching a wall and the other with an open space before it; both hands almost touching a wall; both hands with extended space in front of them. The findings sustained the hypothesis. When an arm is stretched out toward a barrier it is regarded as shorter than the arm stretched out toward an open space. Apropos of this indication that the spatial framework influences the experience of body size, an experiment carried out by Schnall (as cited by Wapner, 1960) in the Clark laboratory is noteworthy. He was concerned with the effects on body image of being in a very small space for an extended period. Subjects remained in a "Lilliputian" room (with lowered ceiling and miniature furniture) for half an hour. Their evaluation of their arm length was taken upon first entering the room and upon completion of the half hour. In general, the room induced a sense of increased body size. The perceived arm length was larger than usual after first entering the room and still larger after a longer period of exposure to the Lilliputian effect. Observations at Clark (cited by Wapner, 1960) also suggest that special attitudes about the immediate functional significance of a body part may influence its apparent length. Thus, arm length has been judged under conditions when the arm is simply extended versus conditions in which there have been instructions to point at something. Significant evidence emerged that with a set to point the arm is experienced as longer than when it is extended without purpose in space. Quite relatedly, the question was pursued by McFarland, Wapner, and

[7] It is pertinent to note at this point the great sensitivity of body size estimation to measurement procedure, instructions, subject set, and many other variables. Sequence effects have been demonstrated by Boraks (1962); anchor effects by Dillon (1962A); illumination effects by Fuhrer and Cowan (1967); special effects related to the body unit used by Barton and Wapner (1965) and also Shontz (1967); etc. This introduces considerable difficulty in comparing studies which have used different experimental conditions and procedures.

Werner (1960) whether the phenomenal length of the arm may be increased by the use of a tool. There were four principal experimental conditions: pointing at a target with hand and not touching it; pointing at target with hand and touching it; pointing at target with rod but not touching it; and pointing at target with a rod and touching it. It was found that with touch and no touch conditions pooled there was a significant trend for the arm to be perceived longer when pointing with a rod than when pointing without a rod. For the touch condition alone a significant difference in this same direction occurred; but the difference failed to appear in the no touch setting. Further-more, the data indicated a significant tendency for the arm to be perceived as shorter when contact was made either directly or indirectly with an object than when such contact was not made. In still another of such preliminary investigations (cited by Wapner, 1960) the question was approached as to whether perceived arm length would vary as a function of the positive or negative value of the object toward which the arm was extended. The results indicated (p. 7) "that when the S reaches for a negative object, i.e., some-thing that is distasteful to him, arm length appears shorter than with a positively toned object, i.e., something he desires."

An important concept in the body of theory underlying the research of the sensori-tonic group at Clark is that degree of differentiation between the self and the world is inversely proportional to level of maturity. Illustratively, children and schizophrenics would be considered to have less clearly differentiated boundaries between themselves and outer objects than would normal adults. This viewpoint has stimulated a number of studies relevant to perceived body size. It has been reasoned that since there is evidence that enhancing the boundary of a body area decreases its apparent size, one would expect that persons with vague boundaries would perceive their bodies as larger than those whose boundaries are well articulated. Liebert, Werner, and Wapner (1958) reported a project which tested this formulation in terms of the primitivizing effects of LSD-25 (lysergic acid diethylamide) upon normal subjects. They predicted that LSD would produce regression which would in turn reduce the definiteness of body image boundaries and therefore increase perceived body size. In order to check out this presumption they conducted three experiments. The first dealt with the effects of LSD on perceived head size in both normal and schizophrenic subjects. Estimated head size was obtained by means of a device which consisted of an adjustable frame which could be made narrower or wider, or taller or shorter, thus exposing a greater or smaller area of a white background. The subject in-structed the experimenter how large an expanse of the white background to expose in order to represent an area just large enough for him to squeeze his head through. Estimates were obtained in a control situation and also while under the influence of LSD. LSD produced a significant increase of estimated head size from the control to the LSD condition in both the normal and schizophrenic groups. As part of this same experiment, the subjects had also estimated the sizes of a number of external objects (viz., dollar bill, 10 × 10 square, pack of cigarettes, a $20 bill). Contrary to the pattern of change characterizing estimates of one's own head size, there were no significant increases from control to LSD in the estimated sizes of the objects. In a second part of this experiment the effects of LSD on perception of arm length were examined. The subject was asked to indicate in a darkroom how far from him a luminescent marker should be placed so that it would correspond to where his finger tips would be if his arm were fully extended straight out in front of him. There were four trials. The marker was started for two trials at the body and for two it was started 200 cm. away from the body. In the normal group the mean judged arm length was greater under LSD than without LSD. The same trend was apparent in the schizophrenic group, but it was not significant. When the schizophrenic judgments were separated according to the two starting positions (at the body and away from the body), there was a significant increase during the LSD condition in judged arm size for the series with the starting position away from the body. However, when the starting position was close to the body such an increase did not manifest itself. The third phase of this undertaking had to do with the effects of LSD on the size of drawing of a human figure. It was requested that each subject "draw a picture of a person"; and after he had completed the first picture he was asked to draw a person of the sex opposite that of the first drawing. This was done, of course, under control conditions and also under the influence of LSD. Measurements were taken in each drawing of total length, length of head, width of shoulders, and width of head (ear to ear). In the normal group all of the measures from the pairs of drawings increased during the LSD condition, but none of the increases attained statistical significance. The results in the schizophrenic population were in the same direction and a majority of the differences were significant. The outcome of the three experiments cited above led Liebert, Werner, and Wapner to conclude (p. 583), "The findings support the hypothesis that under the influence of LSD there is an increase in the perceptual size of one's own body, with little or no change in size of external objects." They underscored the fact that perception of one's own body seems to be much more influenced by an agent like LSD than is perception of external objects. It was their speculation that this mirrors the fact that one is able to assign more definite boundaries to external perceptual objects than to the body as a perceptual phenomenon. They cited a study by Rosenblatt which also revealed differences in the perception of that which has body as compared to object reference. Rosenblatt found that manic and depressed patients did manifest differences in size perception (reflecting organismic states of elation vs. depression) in the way they depicted the human figure but did not manifest such differences in representations of geometric forms. Incidentally, Lewisohn (1964) has also shown that the drawings of a human figure by depressed patients are significantly shorter than those drawn by non-depressed patients.

A further pertinent study by Wapner and Krus (1959) concerned the effects of LSD on the individual's estimate of his total height. Normal subjects were asked to stand in a darkroom and to indicate how a line ten feet distant should be adjusted so that it was just high enough to "walk under". The starting position of the line was the individual's own objective height. Judgments were made under control conditions and under the influence of LSD. There was a mean increase in apparent height during the LSD condition, but it did not attain statistical significance. It was also noted that in the control situation there was a tendency to underestimate one's true height, whereas during the LSD condition one's height was overestimated.

Silverstein and Klee (1958), while focusing on the ability of raters to distinguish figure drawings made under normal as contrasted to LSD conditions, uncovered some results which have to do with body size perception. They evaluated 18 normal men who were instructed first to draw a human figure; then one of the opposite sex; and finally a "picture of themselves". It was not possible to separate the LSD from the non-LSD figure drawings on the basis of size differences. However, the self drawings did increase significantly in size from the control to LSD context. The fact that the figure drawings failed to manifest an appreciable size shift is congruent with the findings of Liebert, Werner and Wapner (1958) involving normal subjects which were cited above. An interesting question arises as to why the sizes of the self drawings change in contrast to those of the figure drawings which do not. One might speculate that the self drawing taps a deeper level of body image involvement than does the usual figure drawing. However, this possibility is not supported by Silverstein and Klee's observations that other figure drawing characteristics besides those related to size (viz., attention to detail, distortions, and line quality) did change perceptibly from control to LSD conditions. The LSD drawings were less detailed, more distorted, and more disturbed in line quality.

Kolb (1959) described an exploratory investigation which has potentially important implications because it suggests that the increase in perceived body size associated with the ingestion of LSD may apply not only to an individual's real body but also to phantom representations of himself. In the course of this exploratory work an amputee with a painful arm phantom was observed under three different LSD dosages. The smallest dose produced no change in the phantom experience. The next larger dose made the phantom more perceptible; and the largest dose enlarged the size of the phantom. If this enlargement phenomenon were firmly substantiated, it would indicate that the primitivizing and consequent boundary blurring effects of LSD result in a perceived increase in the size not only of one's real body parts but also of parts that exist only in one's fantasies. This would dramatize the fantasy aspects of the body image.

The presumed effect of primitivization in making the boundary more hazy and thereby increasing perceived body size has been tested in a number of studies of schizophrenic patients. Presumably the average schizophrenic individual should, because of his regression in level of ego functioning, be left with poorly articulated boundaries and therefore perceive his body as larger than the average non-schizophrenic person. Many projects have been carried out to test this proposition. Some are supportive (e.g., Wapner, 1961A, B; Cleveland, 1960; Cleveland, et al., 1962). Others are not (e.g., Cappon and Banks, 1965; Fisher, 1966B). A detailed analysis of these projects involving schizophrenic patients will be presented in the literature review section dealing with psychopathological phenomena.

With minor exceptions, the studies cited above concerning body size perception in relation to boundary articulation which have involved normal subjects or utilized the effects of LSD have shown that conditions which foster boundary definition reduce experienced size and those which impede boundary maintenance have the opposite effect. However, Epstein (1965) in a major study designed to test several aspects of the boundary hypothesis as applied to body-part size perception reported that he could find no support for it. His initial view was that the boundary formulation regarding size experience was too "structural" and not sufficiently concerned with how motives and values affect the experience of stimuli applied to one's body. For example, while the sensori-tonic position would regard almost any stimulus applied to the body periphery as likely to have boundary reinforcing effects, he suggested that one needs to know how pleasantly or unpleasantly, expansively or constrictedly it is experienced to predict its effect. His experimental procedures secured body size estimates under neutral conditions and also under conditions designed to alter the boundary; and a determination could be made of the impact of the alterations upon apparent body size. In one study he was specifically interested in the effects of electrical vibration of the hand (presumably producing boundary stimulation) upon estimates of its size. Thirty-six subjects (college students) had their right and left hands each vibrated for two minutes. Measurement of the apparent size of the hand was made before and after vibration. The 36 subjects were divided into groups of 12. One received instructions which portrayed the vibration to be received as positive in its effects; a second was told the vibration was possibly injurious; and a third was given neutral instructions. A special control group received no vibration; and merely had a rest period equal to the usual vibration period. Epstein expected that vibration under positive conditions would result in a sense of increased body size and the negative vibration would have the opposite result. In general, the experimental findings indicated that none of the vibration conditions significantly affected size perception. In a supplementary experiment involving 13 subjects, size estimates were obtained from them before and after hand vibration; and questions were asked to determine whether they experienced the vibration as pleasant or unpleasant. A significant trend appeared for those who felt the vibration to be pleasant to show increased size estimates and for a slight decrease to occur in those who described the vibration as unpleasant. This finding was considered by Epstein to go along with his view that the sensori-tonic concept of the boundary is too simple. He indicated that the differential effect upon size estimation produced by the stimulus to the boundary when it was experienced positively versus negatively could not be predicted from the sensori-tonic model.

In a second series of experiments he asked whether there are differential effects on apparent head size when the stimuli applied to the boundary are experienced as directed "toward" as compared to "away" from self. He also asked whether pleasant versus unpleasant stimuli applied to the periphery of the head would have contrasting effects on apparent head size. Twenty-four college students were studied who estimated head size in a neutral context and also seven conditions designed to make them feel that their heads were being exposed to a number of different conditions. The seven conditions involved blocks, sticks, arrows, pleasurable pictures, and threatening pictures which were in each instance placed so as to surround the subject's head. The data analysis revealed no effects upon head size estimation from any of the stimuli which were directed toward the head. Neither the sensori-tonic nor Epstein formulations adequately explained the results. This study constitutes the first important challenge to the sensori-tonic concept of the body boundary as it relates to body size perception. It remains to be seen how serious the challenge actually is.

BODY SIZE JUDGMENTS IN CHILDREN

There have been appraisals of children devoted largely to developmental differences in body size experience. Wapner (1960) described a project based on the assumption that children would overestimate head size to a greater degree than adults because they possess less definite boundaries between themselves and the world. A subject group consisting of 463 persons (248 male and 215 female) varying in age from four through 25 was studied. Estimates of head size were secured by asking the subject, with eyes closed, to indicate by pointing with index fingers where the cheekbones of his face would be projected on a meter stick horizontally mounted 18 cm. from his nose. These estimates were compared with actual measures of head size. A marked overestimation of head size at all ages was apparent. However, the overestimation is greatest in younger children, with a sharp decrease at age nine. The difference between the degree of overestimation by the subjects below age nine and those in the older age groups was, of course, confirmatory of the initial hypothesis. As another phase of the study it was established that when the head boundaries were enhanced by touching the temples, all age groups perceived a decrease in head size to a rather uniform degree. Wapner pursued his ontogenetic hypotheses by determining the pattern of head size evaluation in retarded children. It turned out that in a retarded group of 13- and 14-year-olds the degree of overestimation of head size was comparable to that found at the four-year-old level.

One should note, apropos of the matter of size estimation in the retarded, a study by Shontz (1963A). He appraised size judgment of body (e.g., head, trunk, waist) and non-body objects (e.g., 12 inches) in 20 college students and 20 mentally retarded subjects. He discovered that the retarded under-estimated the size of their body parts more than the college students. Their judgments were also less accurate. But there were no differences between the groups in accuracy or directionality of judgments pertaining to non-body objects. Further, a high correlation was found between tendencies to over- or underestimate sizes of body and non-body objects in the retarded but not in the college group. It was concluded from the results that the retarded do not know how to make appropriate distinctions between body and non-body space. The author states: ". . . the data imply that a different kind of spatial organization is required for dealing effectively with pure body stimuli than for dealing with non-body objects;[8] the college students were evidently considerably more able to make the cognitive shift than the mentally retarded subjects" (p. 372).

Gellert and Stern (1964) concerned themselves with some of the basic cognitive parameters which contribute to a child's reporting of his own size attributes. They studied a large population (152 boys, 107 girls) ranging in age from five to 12 years. The subjects were asked to estimate their height by using a pointer to designate a spot which they considered to be level with "where the top of your head would be". A portion of the sample was also asked to estimate in a similar manner the height of a yardstick. The actual stature of each subject was subsequently determined. It was found that accuracy of self estimated height increased chronologically until about ten years when it levelled off. Tendencies to make over- or underestimation errors were not associated with being unusually tall or short. Boys tended to be more accurate than girls in their self estimates and their judgments of the height of the yardstick. Errors in self estimate by boys tended in the direction of underestimation and that for girls in the direction of overestimation. A significant, but quite small, positive correlation was discerned between self and yardstick estimates. Gellert and Stern considered the smallness of the correlation to indicate that the factors involved in judgment of self height

[8] Shontz (1967) has shown in other studies that body size judgments differ in variability and degree of overestimation from non-body size estimates. He and his co-workers have also taken the lead in trying to establish whether there are consistent trends for persons to under- or overestimate the sizes of particular body parts. His most recent conclusion (Shontz, 1967) was that body parts in the region of the lower extremities are underestimated while those in the head region are overestimated. Further, hand length tends consistently to be under-estimated.

were only minimally accounted for in terms of the ability to make height judgments in general. Interestingly, yardstick judgments were positively related to IQ but self judgments were not.

In another phase of this study the subjects were shown a number of pictures, four containing human figures, one a series of keys, and another a series of blocks. The humans were drawn so that in each series one body part (viz., head size, leg length, trunk length, arm length) varied from unusually small to large in relation to the rest of the body. Similar variations in distortion were introduced into the key and block picture series. Subjects were asked to pick out in each group of human pictures the one most like themselves. For the key and block their task was to find one that most accurately matched respectively the proportions of a real key and a real block construction. With increasing age, realism improved in all the judgments made. Apropos of Wapner's (1960) reports about the tendency of children to grossly overestimate head size, it is noteworthy that the most marked deviation from true proportions was in overestimating the head. This was especially pronounced in the girls. Boys were more realistic than girls in their body proportion judgments, but not so for the proportions of key or block. The relationship between accuracy in evaluating body proportions and proportions of non-body objects was not significant.

Woods (1966) obtained body size estimates from samples of boys and girls at age levels eight, ten, and 12. The subject indicated his size estimates of various body areas by drawing lines on a scale representation of body dimensions which was presented to him on a sheet of paper. Actual measures of the body areas in question were later secured. Measures of motor skills and concept of body boundaries as defined by the Fisher–Cleveland Barrier score (1968) were also secured. The findings revealed a tendency toward underestimation of one's height. But there was a trend to overestimate horizontal dimensions like shoulder and hip width. Scattered correlations between size estimates and motor skill indices appeared, but they did not fall into a coherent pattern. Some correlations between degree of boundary definiteness and size estimates were found. These were in the direction of indicating that those with more definite boundaries were less likely to overestimate their size dimensions. However, the results were of a borderline character; and it will be shown at a later point that boundary definiteness and body size estimates are not consistently related in adult populations.

The matter of whether children have a realistic concept of their body proportions was one among several issues which concerned Gunvald (1951) in his appraisal of 64 girls (ages nine–11). He provided the girls with a series of cardboard body parts (e.g., head, neck, trunk, arms, legs). Each part was represented by three lengths and three widths. Half of the subjects used the parts to construct four different figures based on four different live children models (representing fat, lean, tall, and short types); and then constructed a representation of self. The other half of the subjects were asked to construct a representation of self; but in one instance they did so by freely building an entire model of self and in a second instance chose each individual part that was most like the same part of self. Little of significance was revealed by the data. However, a clear trend was found for those children who were tall to represent self with tall body parts and for those of a fat body type to depict self with wide body parts. It was concluded from this and other results that girls in the nine–11 age range do have a realistic concept of their body proportions.

Several approaches to determining how children perceive their body size and relative body proportions have been presented as formalized tests. Adams and Caldwell (1963) developed a procedure (Children's Somatic Apperception test) designed to determine how an individual perceives the size attributes of his body; how he would like such attributes to be; and the discrepancy between what is actual and desired. It takes the form of a test which involves ten wooden boy representations of varying size, each with a removable head, arms, and legs. The subject picks one of the ten which he thinks looks most like himself and then one "you would like to be". Finally, from a tray containing ten different sized versions of each body part (e.g., head, trunk) he chooses those he needs to construct the figure he would like to be.

A number of samples were evaluated with this technique: (1) 35 normal boys in the seven–12 age range; (2) 13 "moderately disturbed" boys seven–11; (3) ten boys (ages nine–14) with IQ's in the 45–70 range. The actual dimensions of a number of body areas were measured for each boy. The results obtained were not very revealing. The various groups did not differ in the frequency with which their preferred choice deviated from their judged actual representation. Many subjects in all groups chose the same figure as representative of how they actually look and how they would like to be. But if one inspects all instances where the preferred figure differed from the actual, the degree of difference between actual and preferred was greater in the disturbed than in the normal or retarded. A further analysis of the shifts indicated that in normals they were more often in the direction of the ideal having larger dimensions than was true for the disturbed. This last finding elicited the speculation that normal children may be more realistically aware than the disturbed of future growth processes which will result in increased body size.

A related kind of test (Somatic Apperception test) has been described by Rowe and Caldwell (1963). Male figures representing seven major classes of Sheldon's somatotypes [9] were drawn on an illustration board. The task of the subject is to select one that looks most like himself and subsequently one

---

[9] Variations of this technique have been described by Caldwell and Matoon (1966) and Gottesman and Caldwell (1966) for evaluating respectively feelings about one's skin color and feelings about the masculinity-femininity of one's body.

that looks least like himself. Data derived from the application of this procedure to 58 male Negro adolescent delinquents were presented. The height-weight ratios of the delinquents had been determined and could be compared with the equivalent ratios characteristic of the seven somatotype categories. A significant positive relation was found between the subjects' actual height-weight ratios and those of the figures they chose as being most like themselves. The choices were apparently moderately accurate. Generally, there was a trend to underestimate body size. This finding was interpreted as reflecting either self depreciatory tendencies or the fact that there may be a lag in the adolescent, because of his rapid growth, between his feeling about his size and his actual size.

Although it was not developed in work with children, it is appropriate to mention at this point a test (Body Image Projective test) which is analogous to the Somatic Apperception tests referred to above. Hunt and Weber (1960) devised this test for measuring body image attitudes and it is based on the individual's preferences for body representations varying in size proportions. One section consists of a series of pages, each containing four pictures of anterior views of female figures. Each drawing was made up at random of various parts (viz., arms, shoulders, torso, abdomen, hips-legs, and breasts) from seven original silhouettes which were constructed to depict a range of categories of body size and proportion. These categories were portrayed in terms of seven types of figures: normal height, normal contour; normal tall, normal contour; short, normal contour; tall, thick figure; tall, thin figure; short thick figure; and a short, thin figure. There was also a second series of lateral view drawings devised in a manner analogous to that of the anterior view picture. All of the drawings were of females and so the test was restricted to use with women. In administering the test, instructions are given the subject to choose the one figure from each page which looks most like herself; the one which she would most like to look like; and the one which she would least like to look like. Various scores can then be derived which depict the subject's preferences relative to body size (e.g., thin, long, thick). Also her degree of body insecurity can be evaluated via a number of indices which take into account discrepancies among the categories of judgment "What I am", "What I want", and "What I least want". The test-retest reliabilities of the various scores have proved to be mainly in the .80–.95 range. Exploratory work with the test has indicated that it taps a level of response which is different from that sampled by simply asking subjects to rate the sizes of parts of their bodies. Some evidence has presented itself that the more secure an individual is about his body image the greater the test-retest reliability of his Body Image Projective test responses. Furthermore, Hunt and Weber have attempted to demonstrate that the scores from their test are linked with more general perceptual processes. Thus, they found significant positive correlations between body image security indices and ability to perceive the figures in the Gottschaldt Test.

Pertinent to the question of what body size proportions are preferred are the findings of Staffieri (1967) who measured children's attitudes toward different body types. His sample consisted of 90 male children (ages six–10) who were classified as endomorph, ectomorph, and mesomorph. Each subject was asked to choose adjectives he considered most descriptive of silhouettes representing each of the three major body types. There was a child and an adult version of each silhouette. Also, subjects were presented with five silhouettes representing a range from ectomorph through endomorph and asked which they preferred to look like. The favorableness of adjectives applied to the various body type silhouettes was not related to the subject's own body type. Most children preferred to look like the mesomorph. Ecto-morphic and endomorphic silhouettes were generally disapproved and given low evaluations. Finally, in a selected portion of the sample it was possible to demonstrate reasonable accuracy in the individual's perception of his own body type. Ten-year-olds were more accurate in this respect than seven-year-olds. With reference to this matter of accuracy, the author states (p. 104): "The point at which accuracy of self-perception becomes apparent (probably eight to nine years of age) may also be the beginning of dissatisfaction with one's body, and the degree of dissatisfaction may well be proportional to the extent that one's body differs from the mesomorph image." He emphasized too that the strong approval-disapproval attitudes which seem to apply so differentially to the various body types may well elicit and shape the social behavior of those with particular body types.

A number of studies have aimed at exploring possible personality and maturational correlates of body size estimation in children. They will be presented below.

Shaffer (1964) carried out an extensive project which dealt with per-ception of body height in children. It involved 220 children (112 girls and 108 boys) in grades five–eight. Several hypotheses were proposed:

1. Persons of greater perceived importance are overestimated in height relative to other persons.

2. Children of low intelligence underestimate themselves in height as compared with children of high intelligence.

3. Children who experience failure decrease in perceived self height. The assumption basic to this study was that the judged height of a person (whether of self or others) would be underestimated or overestimated as a function of his perceived importance, success and power. The experimental procedure required the children to estimate the heights of themselves, their mothers, their fathers, the school principal, their teachers, their teachers the previous year, and the experimenter. Their height estimates were obtained by first having them imagine that a vertical line on a sheet of paper was equal in size to a stick which stood in the testing room. Then, they were asked to place a mark on the vertical line which would be equivalent to where the tops of their heads would come if they stood next to the measuring stick.

They similarly designated the heights of other persons on a number of vertical lines. At a later point they repeated all of these judgments while using a larger measuring stick as a reference. In another phase of the procedure they were requested to judge their own heights in relation to the six other figures they had previously rated. The subject once again registered his estimates on a vertical line on a sheet of paper. However, in each instance he was told to imagine that the total length of the line represented not an actual measuring stick but rather the height of a given person (e.g., mother, father). He marked on the line where the top of his head would be relative to the height of that person. Two weeks following the initial testing session one half of the group was retested with identically the same procedure. However, the other half was first asked to take a five minute anagram test which was designed to produce a feeling of failure; and only afterwards were the height judgment tasks readministered.

The various scores representing perceived height proved to have satisfactory test-retest reliability. The children displayed a significant inclination to underestimate their own heights relative to their actual heights and also in relation to the estimated heights of various adult authority figures.[10] No relationship was found between height estimates and intelligence for the girls. However, in the boys' group there was a moderately significant trend for intelligence to be inversely related to the minimizing of self height in relation to that of adult figures. There were no meaningful differences in height estimates among the grade levels represented in the sample; but sex differences were prominent. Thus, girls underestimated themselves more than boys with reference to all adults. They also overestimated the heights of men in relation to women to a greater degree than the boys. A sex difference was further observed in considering the effects of the anagram failure experience upon height evaluations. Failure seemed not to affect such evaluations in the girls, but it did produce perceptible decreases in the boys' self height judgments. Shaffer raised the question whether height might not be a more sensitive area of concern for boys than girls which would result in their expressing feelings about the self via height judgments to a greater degree than girls. In summarizing the results, Shaffer considered that they did support the relationships hypothesized to exist between the importance attributed to figures and their apparent height.

With reference to this last point, it is of parenthetical interest that Dannenmaier and Thumin (1964) showed a significant positive relationship between the degree to which nursing school students (N = 46) overestimated the heights of various persons and the actual positions of such persons in the

---

[10] Apropos of this tendency for children to exaggerate their smallness relative to adults, it is interesting that Wolfenstein (1954) found in an analysis of children's humor that there was considerable preoccupation with themes that had to do with defensively making fun of adult bigness.

authority structure of the nursing school. The higher an individual's authority role the greater was his height overestimated.

Hypotheses dealing with the influence of dependency and achievement feeling in children upon their perception of body size in themselves and others were explored by Beller and Turner (1964). They predicted that the greater a child's dependency the more he would overestimate the size of "dependency objects" (e.g., mother, teacher) and underestimate his own size. They anticipated, in addition, that the greater a child's striving for autonomous achievement the more realistic or accurate he would be in estimating his own and other person's sizes—when the measurement situation is non-ambiguous and stressed the metric properties of the stimulus to be judged. The limiting of this last hypothesis to situations in which the physical attributes of the judged object were emphasized grew out of previous research by the authors which had indicated a correlation between autonomy behavior and sheer accuracy in judging physical objects.

The subjects were six boys and eight girls (age range three–six) attending a "therapeutic nursery". Each was rated by nursery school teachers for dependency in terms of how frequently he sought adult help, contact, and recognition. Ratings of autonomous achievement striving were based on the frequency with which the child tried without assistance to initiate activities and overcome obstacles. Size estimates of self and others were obtained with reference to an impersonal moving bar and also projected pictures with appropriate human representations (e.g., man, woman) which could be varied in size as the child directed.

The results did not support the expectation that the child's estimate of his own size would be correlated with his amount of dependency. A significant trend was detected for overestimation of mother and teacher size to go along with degree of dependency, when only those children above the median in dependency were considered. Support was found for the proposition that the accuracy of a child's size estimates of others in an impersonal context would be positively correlated with his rated autonomy. In general, nothing of real import emerged with respect to the child's perception of his own body size.[11]

Since the drawing of a human figure is often used as means for evaluating body concept [12] several studies of children involving size of the figure

[11] In contrast to these results, Fisher (1964D) was able to show in 52 college males that the degree to which they overestimated their height was positively correlated with their commitment to the idea of the superiority of the male over the female and also their Achievement and Dominance scores derived from the Edwards Personal Preference Schedule. Power aspirations seemed to find expression in the subjects' body size estimates.

[12] The use of figure drawing size to represent an individual's perception of his own body size is a questionable procedure. Size of figure drawings is influenced by many other variables besides the size of the individual producing such drawings. For example, Craddick and Stearn (1963) observed that figure drawing height was reduced in a stress situation; and Zuk (1962) found in children that size of figure drawing was positively correlated with mental age. Even further, Silverstein and Robinson (1961) discovered that the height and volume of children's

portrayed should be mentioned. McHugh (1964) looked at the relationship between figure drawing size and over- and underachievement in school. The data did not demonstrate a meaningful connection between the two variables. Bennett (1964) considered the possibility of a connection between a child's self concept and the size of his figure drawing. A Q sort was used in a sample of 198 sixth grade children to measure lowness versus highness of self concept. Those who were "low" did not differ from the "highs" in the size of their figure drawings. Actual size of the child was also not correlated with figure drawing size.

Fish (1960) undertook a study of children which had as one of its important variables the changes in perceived body height that occur developmentally. The subjects were seven, nine and 11-year-old boys of normal intelligence. Each individual's concept of his total height was obtained by asking him to estimate his height relative to a six foot pole. He was instructed to pretend that he was standing next to the pole and to estimate how high on the pole the top of his head would reach. Then he was to place a mark on the picture of the pole to show how high this point was. His estimate was converted into inches and compared with his actual measured height. A number of other body image measures and procedure for evaluating maturity of outlook were also administered to the children. One of the body image measures was based on the degree of resistance shown by the child to perceiving changes in his mirror image while wearing aniseikonic lenses. It was presumed, in terms of previous work by Wittreich and Radcliffe (1955), that the readiness to accept changes produced in one's body appearance by the lenses was an indicator of body image maturity or adequacy. Wittreich and Radcliffe presented data which suggest that resistance to perceiving change in one's body while wearing aniseikonic lenses is related to bodily anxiety and insecurity. A second body image measure included in the battery of procedures was a multiple choice test which sought to evaluate degree of body image boundary definiteness in terms of the Barrier score which was developed by Fisher and Cleveland (1968). Subjects were shown the Rorschach blots and asked to select from lists of multiple choice alternatives those best descriptive of given blot areas. These alternatives were presumed to vary in the degree to which they tapped barrier attitudes. In addition to the body image measures, several techniques were employed to evaluate the maturity of the child's concepts of adulthood and of time. Concepts of adulthood were sampled by means of two categories of tasks:

1. One involved composing stories and lists of criteria having to do with how "to tell when you're a grown-up".

---

figure drawings lacked any meaningful relationships with their actual or estimated heights and weights. Shontz (1967) found significant differences between the way subjects expressed body size proportions in figure drawings and in size estimates of various parts of their own bodies.

2. A second category was based on the degree to which subjects could, when asked to draw successively a current picture of themselves and then one representing their "grown up" appearance, improve the Goodenough figure drawing maturity score of the second over the first. Maturity of time perspective was evaluated by having each subject mark on a ten-inch line representing his life span the point at which significant adult milestones (e.g., getting married, having a full-time job) would occur in his life. It was considered that maturity of time perspective would evidence itself in the placing of future events at a far distance from the present.

Most of the findings that emerged from the study will be described here and others involving the Barrier score will be taken up at a later point. With regard to the estimation of one's height it was found that average error decreases with increasing age, especially between ages nine and 11. There was no consistency in the direction of error in the nine- and 11-year-olds; but there was strong inclination among seven-year-olds to underestimate their heights. The discrepancy between estimated height and real height proved not to be significantly correlated with any of the other body image or "maturity" variables. The aniseikonic body image index demonstrated that there was a clear developmental increase in ability to accept the existence of change in one's distorted mirror image. Further, there were indications that it was more difficult to perceive alterations in one's mirror image than in external objects. In the seven- and 11-year-old groups there were suggestions of a positive relationship between receptivity to aniseikonic changes in the self and ability to formulate mature definitions of adulthood. That is, degree of maturity in terms of a body image variable was positively correlated with the maturity displayed in ability to conceptualize the adult role. Interestingly enough, the subject's ability to increase the Goodenough score of a second self drawing over a first drawing was also positively linked (in seven- and 11-year-olds) with a mature image of the adult role. Summarizing her general results, Fish stated (p. 115): "The total patterning of the data suggests the tentative generalization: the child whose body scheme is less differentiated or articulated presents relatively less mature criteria for judging adulthood—and he experiences adulthood as psychologically near. The child whose body scheme is relatively more articulated presents relatively more mature criteria for judging adulthood—and he experiences adulthood as psychologically more distant from him."

Epstein (1957) evaluated in a group of 35 adolescent boys (mean age = 16) the relationships of a number of body image variables to the ability to make spatial judgments in an unstructured setting. He hypothesized that the more integrated and stable an individual's body image the greater the likelihood of his making use of body sensations, as against visual cues, in judging the true vertical in a situation in which the normal information required for such judgments is not available. Witkin's space orientation tests were utilized in order to evaluate mode of spatial orientation. The subjects were

asked to determine the true vertical under various conditions in which conflicting visual and kinesthetic cues were present; and degree of error in judgment
was measured. The following body image techniques were employed:

1. The Finger-Apposition test consists of a series of 14 pictures of two
hands in various positions relative to each other. It was the subject's task to
imitate these pictured hands with his own as quickly as possible. Performance
was scored in terms of total time required to perform the entire series of hand
positions. It was conjectured that this technique taps the individual's ability
to manipulate certain aspects of his body image.

2. A second procedure involved the subject estimating his height in a
dark room where he did not have the usual visual cues for anchoring his
judgment. This estimate was made in terms of a luminous line whose length
could be varied. The deviation of the judgments from the individual's actual
height was noted.

3. Estimates of the sizes of five specific body areas (e.g., width of
shoulders, thickness of body) were made by designating distances between
two parallel upright luminous rods. Deviations of the estimates from the true
sizes of the given areas were determined. Control size estimates of non-
bodily objects (viz., 12 and 18 inches) were also obtained.

4. A so-called "motor test of the body image" was used which determines how well the subject can keep a small follower in contact with a
moving target.

5. The figure drawing test was administered and scored in terms of the
Witkin-Machover scheme (Witkin, et al., 1954) which presumably measures
the integration and differentiation of the body image depicted in the drawing.

6. Secord's word association Homonym test was included. It requires
the subject to give associations to a series of words that have both bodily and
non-bodily meanings; and is considered to sample degree of body concern.

7. Also present in the battery was the Secord and Jourard (1954) Body
Cathexis scale.

It was found that the tendency to rely upon visual rather than kinesthetic cues in spatial judgments (field dependent) was positively correlated with
the perception of one's self as short and to a lesser extent with the tendency to
see other areas (e.g., width) of one's body as small. Epstein suggests that the
field dependent person experiences himself as small in relation to the
surrounding field. Field dependent subjects were significantly less successful
on the Finger-Apposition test than those who were field independent. The
figure drawing data indicated that degree of field dependence was positively
linked with the presence of signs of distortion in the drawings. No results of
real importance appeared between field dependence and any of the following
body image tasks: Secord Word Association test, Body Cathexis scale, Two
Hand-Coordination test. Certain significant relationships occurred among the
body image measures themselves. There was a positive correlation between
perceiving one's height as large and perceiving sections of one's body as large.

Also, the more subjects overestimated the thickness and width of their bodies, the less distorted were their figure drawings.[13] Those who expressed much conscious acceptance of their body on the Body Cathexis scale tended to manifest high body concern on the Secord Homonym test.

Epstein was impressed with the lack of inter-relationships among the various body image indices; and concluded that the concept of body image may be a less unitary one than has been supposed by some, especially Schilder (1935).

Harvey Nash (1958) discovered evidence in a sample of children which indirectly reinforced the fact of an interplay between sex role attitudes and perception of body size. He noted that often when people use terms to describe body parts they are implicitly assigning gender to them. He set himself the problem of determining how much agreement there is regarding the masculine vs. feminine classification of various body areas. His subjects comprised 33 boys (20 seventh-graders and 13 ninth-graders). They were presented with a list of body regions in the following order: head, face, eyes, nose, mouth, teeth, chest, abdomen, rear end, arms, hands, fingers, legs, feet, and toes. It was pointed out to them that objects are labeled as masculine or feminine in some languages; and they were asked to designate each of the body regions on the list presented to them as masculine or feminine. Marked differences occurred in the masculinity-femininity ratings of the various body areas. The distribution of the ratings (in rank order) are listed below:

Body region	Rank order (Rank 1 indicates high masculinity)
Chest	1
Arms	2
Abdomen	3
Feet	4
Toes	5
Rear end	6.5
Nose	6.5
Head	8
Mouth	9
Legs	10
Teeth	11.5
Hands	11.5
Fingers	13
Eyes	14
Face	15

[13] Shontz (1967) could find no significant relationships between a modified version of a figure drawing measure of body distortion originally developed by Witkin, et al. (1954) and subjects' estimates of the sizes of various parts of their bodies. He also noted a lack of correlation between body size estimates and scores derived from a number of paper and pencil personality tests.

In the process of interpreting the determinants of such ratings, Nash hit upon the idea that the more gross (i.e., larger) a body area the greater the likelihood it would be viewed as masculine. He did, in fact, find that there was a significantly greater average masculinity value attributed to the aggregation of grosser body parts (head, arms, legs, chest, abdomen, rear end) than to the group of less gross areas (each of which is a sub-division of one of the grosser parts). One cannot help but be impressed with the analogy between these results and those reported by Jourard and Secord (1954, 1955) concerning the preference of men for large, and of women for small, body size in themselves. Apparently, the association between size and gender may extend into a number of dimensions related to body perception.

A brief digression from the topic of body size evaluation is in order at this point in order to describe a study by Coats (1957) somewhat related to that which was undertaken by Nash. Coats made use of a technique originally developed by Korner (cited by Coats) which was intended to determine what symbolic values or meanings the individual ascribes to the major sub-divisions of his body. This technique posed for the subject the task of responding to a series of nine stimulus words, each in the context of a simple sentence, by spontaneously pointing to some part of his own body. Special interest was directed at the question of whether subjects of various age levels would differ from each other in the symbolic properties they attributed to body areas. The age groups that were compared were comprised of men in their 20's, 30's, 40's, and 50's–60's. Each subject was shown the nine stimulus cards, one at a time, and requested "to point to the part of your body that you think of first". The nine stimulus sentences were as follows:

> Brother is Strong
> Sister is Angry
> Father is a Man
> Mother is a Woman
> Food is Good
> Sin is Bad
> Baby is Sick
> A man is Strong
> A person is Sexy

An analysis of the responses indicated that in all of the age groups the word Strong was typically associated with the torso area; the word Angry with the head area; the words Sick and Sexy with the lower part of the body. Several age differences appeared in body designations. The 20-year-old group selected the torso and the 50-year-olds the lower area of the body to represent Woman. None of the other age groups made this differentiation. The 30-year-olds used the torso and the 40- and 50-year-olds the lower parts of the body to symbolize Man. Except for the 40-year group, all of the others chose the head region to symbolize the phrase Food is Good. The 40- and

50-year-olds significantly selected the head to designate the phrase Sin is Bad; whereas the other groups did not focus on any one body region in response to this stimulus. Coats underscored two facts as being of principal importance in his findings. The first was that there seemed to be a high frequency of agreement in ascribing meanings to certain body regions. The second was that the concepts Man and Woman seemed to show the clearest changes in body associations with age. If one compares Coats' results with those obtained by Nash, the only point at which one can readily relate them is the apparent contradiction in the significance attributed to the torso. Torso areas were rated as high in masculinity by Nash's subjects. However, many of Coats' subjects associated torso regions with both the masculine concept Man and the feminine concept Woman.

Conclusions

What has emerged from the mass of observations concerning the individual's perception of his own body size?

1. There does seem to be a consistent trend for that which is large (or mesomorphic) to be labeled as masculine and that which is small to be linked with femininity. But one cannot say that there are consistent sex differences in over- or under-estimating the size of one's body or in the accuracy of such estimation. Incidentally, women seem to rate their degree of satisfaction-dissatisfaction with their various body sectors in a more differentiated way than men do.

2. To generalize about the accuracy of the average individual in judging his own size dimensions is difficult. First of all, the fact that the method of estimation itself strongly influences amount of error and also over- versus under-estimation complicates comparisons across studies. But, generally, one gets the impression that with conditions of good illumination and when the method of estimation is not too indirect, the majority of individuals are quite accurate. This is also true of children by the time they reach the nine–11 age range.

3. In most studies the correlations between estimation of body size and size of non-body objects have been non-significant. Even when significant, they have been low. There do seem to be different factors participating in body as compared to non-body judgments, and they are reflected in differences in variability and degree of over- versus under-estimation. The nature of the differences remains obscure.

4. Few dependable relationships have been demonstrated between size estimation and personality or trait variables. One can only make a few disconnected statements. Failure or the sense of being depreciated apparently results in feelings of smallness. Field dependence is linked in adolescent boys with perception of self as small. Men who are particularly competitive with

women and who are aggressively oriented seem (perhaps defensively) to exaggerate their height.

5. The sensori-tonic theory concerning the function of the boundary in perception of body size has stood up well to a variety of tests. One major failure to support it has been described by Epstein (1957). But otherwise it has successfully predicted the effects upon size judgments of stimuli applied to the body periphery, the nature of response distortions produced by LSD, and certain overestimation trends observed among the immature. In the case of the immature, the evidence is especially strong when one reviews the number of instances in which head size is grossly overestimated by young children. Acknowledgment must be given that the sensori-tonic formulation has not accounted consistently for the size estimation behavior of schizophrenics, who because of their primitivized functioning should presumably have poor boundaries and be inclined to overestimation. This matter will be dealt with at a later point.

6. An individual's perception of his body size is not related to how aware he is of his body, at least as measured in several studies by the Secord Homonym Test.

7. There are findings which indicate a trend for body parts in the vicinity of the lower extremities to be underestimated and those in the region of the head to be overestimated.

The total findings are not impressive. They suggest a few promising leads; but one can see that there is still a long way to go. One major obstacle to progress on this problem has been the paucity of theoretical statements (with the notable exception of sensori-tonic concepts). Another relates to the unbelievably diverse methods of measuring body size perception which have been used. Some of these methods have resulted in consistent overestimation of body size and others when applied to similar populations have led to underestimation! Comparisons across studies have consequently lacked meaning. In ways which are not yet clear, it is apparent that body size estimates can, at times, be strongly influenced by non-body variables, such as the subject's individualistic concept of the judgment units used. His definition of a unit like an inch or his general concept of what looks "big" versus "small" on the measuring rod provided him for his judgment may be quite idiosyncratic. This is a highly important and complicating matter because one is left with the dilemma of not knowing what part of the variance of body size judgments mirrors the subject's actual perception of his body size. We also know from Singer and Lamb's (1966) study that just knowing that one's size judgments will later be checked by actual body measurement is enough to make them significantly more realistic. That is, there may be a special kind of social desirability effect with which one has to reckon. These and other complicating phenomena raise serious questions about whether we will be able in the near future to develop reliable and meaningful ways of determining how the individual experiences the size aspects of his body.

OTHER APPROACHES AND OBSERVATIONS

In the course of probing the amorphous body image domain, investigators keep trying new approaches and tangents. Often such tangents involve one study and no more. Something is tried and dropped—or simply forgotten. It is difficult to review studies of this sort because they are so disparate. However, an attempt will be made to provide an overview of their range and character.

The central concern of several investigations by Mason (1961) was to find out about the background of body sensations accompanying various types of experiences. He was particularly interested in whether "people with different personality constellations react with different internal sensory patterns in feeling-toned situations". There were three phases to his study. In phase one, eight different subjects were repeatedly interviewed regarding their body sensations during various daily activities over a period of several months. Judgments were made as to the quality and body location of such sensations. During phase two an evaluation was made of 36 college students who were exposed to a series of TAT pictures and accompanying recorded stories that dramatized particular emotional effects. The students rated the kinds of experiences evoked by each story in ten different areas of their bodies. Phase three embraced 139 psychiatric patients and 176 non-patients, all army enlisted personnel. Brief film excerpts depicting emotionally arousing action were shown to them and they rated ten different areas of their bodies as to the sensations stimulated in each instance. The Harrower Multiple Choice Ink Blot Test and a Multiple Choice Sentence Completion Test were administered to obtain supplementary information.

The findings indicated that subjects tend to experience most emotional states in terms of body sensations in a relatively limited number of body areas. These focal points were as follows: (a) In the front body plane: head, neck, center chest and diaphragm, center midriff, pubic-genital area, left groin-hip area, right forearm, and right biceps; (b) in the back body plane; (c) center back areas above the upper hip line and between vertical lines through the tips of the shoulder blades. When describing the depth of the body at which they experienced various emotional body sensations, subjects usually referred to the striate muscle layers. Sexually tinged emotions were typically perceived as involving the lower-most front trunk region. Sensations in the lower central back areas were frequently linked with unpleasantness or avoidance. Fear and anger were both generally associated with the chest-abdomen region. There was apparently some tendency for normal subjects who obtained "healthy" scores on the Harrower Multiple Choice test to report more body sensations related to their emotional reactions than subjects with less "healthy" scores.

Individual differences in patterns of body sensation perception were clearly apparent; and the serious possibility presents itself of being able to classify persons by means of such patterns.

D. J. van Lennep (1957) approached the matter of body sensation experiences in terms of responses to his Four Picture Test (FPT) which consists of four unstructured pictures which subjects are asked to integrate into a story. One of the content scores which he derived from the story protocols was called "Body Sensations". It embraces all references to physical sensations; and includes statements about body temperature, fatigue, illness, eating, drinking, and others of a similar nature. When Body Sensation scores were plotted for males and females over the age range 13–40, notable sex differences became evident. In the 13–15 age period the two sexes obtained very similar scores. However, with further increase in age the males manifested a continuous sharp decline in their scores. This contrasted with a moderate rise in scores which characterized the females. It was conjectured by van Lennep that these differences represented the fact that maturing males in our culture are supposed to transcend their bodies and turn their energies toward the world; whereas females are given social approval for continuing and even increasing their investments in their bodies.

Petrovich (1957, 1958, 1959, 1960) too has used reactions to pictures as a means for getting at body experiences. However, he was specifically interested in the individual's attitudes toward having pain inflicted upon him. He constructed a series of 25 pictures which depict situations in which pain is a prominent element. Ten of the situations involve people who are in the process of experiencing some type of pain (e.g., man with a broken leg). Eight deal with pain that is anticipated or about to occur (e.g., man about to receive hypodermic injection). The last eight in the series vary with reference to the origin of the inflicted pain, viz., whether it is self or other inflicted. Subjects rated each pictured pain situation on a seven-point scale relative both as to how much pain was being experienced by the person in the picture and also how long the pain might be expected to last (e.g., seconds, weeks, months). In a population of V.A. medical patients there proved to be significant positive correlations between both of these indices and the Taylor Manifest Anxiety Scale and the Eysenck Medical Questionnaire which was designed to assess neuroticism. Petrovich reported considerable intra-individual consistency in apperceptive evaluations of the projective pain stimuli. He felt that his Pain Apperception Test could provide insight into the manner in which the individual incorporates body pain into his total personality.

A matter that has intrigued some concerns the question where the average individual localizes his "ego" in his body. Is there a primary place or area equated with self? Claparide (1924) thought most people located the ego at a position equivalent to the pineal gland (between the eyes); but he failed to obtain empirical support for his idea. Horowitz (1935) asked 45 men to indicate which body area they most identified with self, and found that a majority chose the head. Later, Himelstein (1964) approached the same issue in a population of 52 male and 37 female college students. He too found the head most frequently linked with self. There was a significant trend for females to localize self in the chest and body area more often than did the males. Males were inclined to localize self in the head. Himelstein speculated this difference might be a function of greater "body narcissism" in the women.

Equation of self with head was considered by Machover (1951) and others (e.g., Baldwin, 1964) to be particularly true of schizophrenics and senile patients. They indicate that in the figure drawings of such persons the body is often fragmented and even missing, but the head is sketched in a relatively clear fashion. This is assumed to reflect a loss of realistic perception of one's body—with only head awareness remaining moderately realistic. Relatedly, Gittleson (1962) speculated that patients with "psychogenic headache" unconsciously "chose" this symptom as a function of the fact that they regarded the head as the most vital part ("containing" the ego) of their corporeal being. He compared the responses of 45 patients with psychogenic headache and a control group of surgical patients (N = 45) to the question "What is the most vital part of your body?" As predicted, the patients with headaches mentioned the head significantly more often than the controls. In the control group, the heart was the organ mentioned with greatest frequency as "vital".

Pezzella (1964) studied 60 boys and 60 girls (ages 5–11) when they were asked "Point to yourself" while standing in front of a mirror. Eighty percent of the responses were to the torso. The head was designated in only about seven percent of the responses. A definite trend was found for boys to point to the head more often than girls did. This supports Himelstein's observation that girls link self with body rather than head to a greater degree than is true of boys.

Weinstein, Sersen, Fisher, and Vetter (1964) asked subjects (1045 men, 986 women) to rank various body areas in terms of the degree to which they would miss them.[14] Considerable consistency was shown, with tongue, leg, eye, and nose most often ranked as likely to be missed. Tooth, large toe, and thumb received the lowest rankings. A similar kind of evaluation of the worth of various body parts was obtained by Gorman and Abt.[15] The results indicated that subjects rated the heart as the most "important" organ in old persons; the sex organs of greatest importance in adults; and in children brain, heart, and digestive organs were assigned equal value.

Finally, in the same context, a study by Bennett (1960) should be mentioned. He concerned himself with the differences in body concept

---

[14] Thorndike (1937) asked subjects how much money they would require in exchange for suffering certain body insults and was impressed with the high prices set by most individuals.

[15] Unpublished paper (Is the Brain the Most Important Organ?).

among normal, blind, and schizophrenic subjects. He used a method which he calls "associative listing". The subject was asked to respond to a sheet of paper with three columns, one headed "Names of Colours", a second "Parts of the Body", and a third "Names of Occupations". He was told to write under each heading a list of ten names. No further instructions were given. Only the list relating to "Parts of the Body" was pertinent to the study. One hundred-and-ten adult sighted normals, 29 totally blind normals, and 83 schizophrenics were evaluated. There was an absence of meaningful differences between the normals and schizophrenics in the frequencies with which they listed various parts of the body. However, the blind subjects tended to list facial areas more often than sighted subjects. The parts mentioned with greatest frequency by the average subject were as follows: arm, leg, head, foot, hand, finger, eye, neck, ear, nose, toe, and chest. Bennett speculates that these particular parts are "integral" to the body concept of most persons. He points out also that the first five in the list are all capable of movement; and he raises the question whether the experience of movement is not of special importance in determining the place of a body part in the body concept.

Looking back at the studies enumerated which have dealt with the localization of the ego and sought to determine which body parts are considered to be most vital or important, it is apparent that the head tends fairly consistently to be given high significance. The heart and legs are also ascribed unusual value. However, while there are consistencies in the findings, it is also clear that large differences can occur as a function of the way questions are asked or ratings obtained.

Jourard (1966) hit upon the novel idea of finding out how "accessible" an individual's body is to others. He asked 168 male and 140 female college students to answer a questionnaire which inquired as to the extent to which they permitted their parents and closest friends of each sex to see and touch 24 different areas of their bodies. They were also to indicate the extent to which they were allowed to see and touch the same areas in these "target persons". As one might expect, greatest tactual interchange was found between close friends of the opposite sex. Males reported being touched less by their parents than did girls. Protestant and Catholic females indicated they were touched on more body areas by their boy friends than did Jewish females. Also, those who rated themselves as average or attractive in appearance indicated they were touched more than those rating themselves as unattractive. Jourard indicated there were especially interesting possibilities for future research with respect to the ethnic and sex differences observed. He speculated that the experience of being touched is basic to developing a sense of "embodiment" and therefore emphasized the importance of continuing the line of research he initiated.

It is known that the periphery and interior of one's body are perceived differently. Spiegel (1959) has referred to an observation by Hartmann concerning the difference in the way the periphery and interior of the body are experienced. Thus, when an individual touches his body periphery he has two sensations, one from his own finger and one from the part touched. This duality of sensation does not occur when he touches another person or thing; and it obviously cannot occur with reference to his body interior. The interior is never perceived within the context of this dual source of sensations. In what way this affects the relative modes of perception of body exterior and interior can only be conjectured. Schilder and Wechsler (1935) and Michel-Hutmacher (1955) have actually questioned groups of children to determine how they picture the relatively unknown body interior. In both studies it was found that there is a tendency for children to think of the interior as being largely a container full of food recently eaten. Nagy (1953) concluded, after interviewing children, that they perceive and interpret internal body events in an extremely over-simplified fashion. More recently, Gellert (1962) undertook a very detailed inquiry into the ideas that children (N = 99) in the four–16 year age range have about the body interior. She affirmed that in younger children ideas of the body interior were similar to those described by Wechsler and Schilder, Michel-Hutmacher, and Nagy. However, by the age of nine–11 quite realistic concepts were expressed; and the interior was accurately perceived as consisting of differentiated organs and systems.

Dramatic proof of the role played by body feelings in long-term behavior has been provided by Kagan and Moss (1962). They were able to trace the impact of certain body attitudes upon later adjustment in a sample of 89 subjects who were followed in the Fels Research Institute longitudinal study. The subjects were observed periodically from birth until adulthood. Early in their development they were rated with regard to fear of bodily harm. This was based on how much they avoided dangerous play; the presence of certain irrational fears (e.g., the dark, animals); and degree to which they were disturbed by injury or illness. Repeated ratings of this kind proved to be moderately stable during a large part of the developmental sequence. Fear of bodily harm seemed to be a consistent attribute of the individual. One of the chief findings that emerged was that (p. 191), "The boys who showed evidence of intense physical harm anxiety during the preschool years were, as adults, anxious about sexuality, uninvolved in traditional masculine activities, and highly concerned with intellectual competence and status goals." In girls, fear of bodily harm (during first ten years) was much less predictive of adult behaviors. However, the following trend was noted (p. 192): ". . . girls who avoided dangerous activities during age ten to 14 were, as adults, dependent on love object and family, aggressive in the face of attack, and unconcerned with intellectual goals or social recognition." In many ways the patterns for males and females were reversed. Kagan and Moss noted that the reversal was, at least partially, a function of the fact that boys who exhibited fear of bodily harm at an early age came from well-educated families; whereas girls with such fear came from poorly educated families.

No relation was found between early ratings of fear of bodily harm and the subjects' own ratings of their fears in this area when they were adults. It was also observed that for boys fear of bodily harm was positively correlated with a protective ("overly nurturant") attitude on the part of mother.

As adults, the subjects were asked to identify a series of pictures exposed tachistoscopically. Among them, were two pertaining to physical harm (person falling, person being attacked by a dog). Analysis of responses of male subjects to the pictures indicated that those who had the most difficulty in seeing them were, during childhood, rated as aggressive with peers and likely to show aggressive outbursts when frustrated. Consistent relationships were not discerned for the female subjects.

This work, which has just been briefly summarized, indicates that amount of body anxiety is a consistent characteristic of an individual. It suggests, too, that behaviors related to sex role, aggression, and intellectual mastery may be significantly influenced by body anxiety. Finally, important differences seem to exist in the way males and females express body anxiety.

More than 40 years ago Flugel (1930) published a speculative analysis of the psychological function of clothing. In his view, clothing was often used to express feelings and wishes [16] and also in identifying and protecting oneself psychologically. Many studies have since shown that clothing is widely recognized as a designator of status and is used to enhance one's apparent value in the eyes of others. Bergler (1953) proposed, "The way a person dresses has an intimate connection with the unconscious perception of herself which she wishes to convey." Empirical evidence exists that the qualities one ascribes to others are influenced by the kinds of clothing they are wearing. For example, Douty (1962) had subjects photographed in different costumes and demonstrated that ratings of their pictures with reference to an assertive-compliant continuum did vary as a function of their mode of dress. A number of other studies have given essentially similar results. Rosencranz (1960) has shown that the clothing worn by figures in TAT pictures affects the stories created about them. Also, individual differences were discerned in the degree to which subjects seem to be aware of, and influenced by, clothing cues in such pictures.

Hall (1898) undertook one of the first questionnaire studies concerning the psychological import of clothing. Based on the responses he obtained from a sample of children, he felt that clothing played a role in the development of the self. The need to secure approval from others seemed to be a necessary factor in the child's enjoyment of clothing. This was especially true in girls. In a follow-up of this study, Flaccus (1906) found that girls felt a greater sense

---

[16] Anatole France once wrote, "If I were allowed to choose from the pile of books which will be published one hundred years after my death, do you know what I would take? I would simply take a fashion magazine so that I could see how women dress one century from my departure. And these rags would tell me more about the humanity of the future than all the philosophers, novelists, prophets, and scholars." (As reported by Rudofsky, 1947, pp. 17–18.)

of power and worth when they were well dressed. Cantril and Allport (1933) discovered that men's general interest in clothing was not related to their values; but women with a high interest in clothes had high aesthetic and economic values. Women with high theoretical or religious values manifested low interest in clothes. Silverman (1945) was able to show that high school girls with good-appearing clothes differed from those with poor-appearing clothes. The poor-appearing subjects expressed more dislike of social interaction and any situations which gave them prominence in the group.

The above studies have been cited largely to indicate that significant relationships have been demonstrated between clothing behavior and a range of other behaviors with psychological connotations.

If indeed, an individual's clothing affects how others see him, it is also likely that it influences his perception of self. There are studies in which subjects report that "dressing up" changes their evaluation of self. The next question is how does one's clothing affect the experience of one's body? Also, is clothing used by the individual to reinforce or deny certain body image attitudes? Only a few experiments have been done in which clothing behavior and body image variables have been correlated. Studies by Compton (1964) to be described at a later point, do suggest that women who are insecure may wear clothes which emphasize certain colors and designs as a way of reinforcing their boundaries and reassuring themselves that a clear line of demarcation exists between their own body and others. Further, Fisher and Osofsky (1967) have done work, to be described in a later chapter, which indicates that there are different body feelings related to wearing and not wearing clothing.

Our pool of knowledge concerning the role of clothes in the development and functioning of the body concept is currently almost non-existent. There is no doubt that much will be learned from even exploratory investigations of the problem.

3
Disturbed Body States
in Normal Persons

This section will concern itself primarily with body perception in normal persons who have experienced serious threats to, or actual deficits in, their body functioning.

When an individual suffers severe crippling or disfigurement, his modes of organizing body experience are put to great strain. If he loses a limb or suddenly cannot move a major part of his body, or finds his appearance grossly altered, disturbing disparities arise in the assumptions he has long accepted about his body. As will be seen, in the case of loss of a limb, this disparity seems typically to produce hallucinatory-like experiences. Hallucinatory response is usually considered in other realms of behavior to indicate severe ego regression. There is much to be learned about the body image in the course of observing the strategies which persons evolve in adjusting to body disablement. What are the first responses to the catastrophe? How long does it usually take to readjust to the new and disturbing body experiences? Is the disturbance in body concept focused in the area of disfigurement or does it spread widely? How does disturbance manifest itself? Does it primarily take the form of alterations in how positively or negatively one feels about various body areas? Does it involve other dimensions like changes in total amount of body awareness; or the relative distribution of attention to major body sectors; or ability to experience size attributes of one's body realistically? For example, does the crippled area seem to shrink in size? Does the individual "shut out" this area and rarely admit it to awareness; or does he find that it fills the whole perceptual field?

It is the fact that crippling requires a revision of the body concept in otherwise normal persons which makes this phenomenon such a potentially important channel for gaining new insights about the organization of the body image. The opportunities for observing radical changes in the system which integrates body experience in normal persons are rare. Most radical changes in this system are associated with gross disorganizing processes like schizophrenia and central nervous system damage whose effects are so complex and pervasive as to make observation of specific body image variables extremely difficult. The normal individual, who as the result of crippling is unexpectedly confronted with a drastic shift in how his body appears to him, represents a unique natural experiment from which one ought to be able to learn a great deal.

PHANTOM EXPERIENCES

The phantom-limb phenomenon has often been cited as one of the prime examples of a normal body image response to body mutilation or loss. This "phantom" phenomenon refers to the fact that after an individual has suffered the loss of a limb he usually reports an illusory feeling of continued presence of the missing member. It is as if the amputated member were still part of the body and a source of sensations. The individual may feel that he can still move it and will unthinkingly undertake sequences of action which assume its reality. In the normal course of events the phantom part becomes smaller and smaller and finally fades away. However, there are instances in which the phantom becomes a source of pain which persists for many years. Much research interest has in the past been devoted to phantom phenomena because they represent a unique example of a highly visible and unrealistic body image distortion which is at the same time a normal mode of adjustment to body loss. A survey of some of the major research findings published up to 1957 in this area has been compiled elsewhere (Fisher and Cleveland, 1968). Kolb (1959) published a later résumé in 1959 which nicely highlights earlier significant findings. He emphasizes that phantoms occur not only following amputation of major body members but also in consequence of the removal of a great variety of smaller parts (e.g., nose, eye, teeth, breast, penis, mandible). Apropos of this point, Szasz (1957) suggested that there might even be phantom equivalents for the removal of internal organs like the stomach. Kolb refers also to the fact that phantoms may arise from denervation of limbs or severance of the spinal cord; and he notes that such phantoms do not shrink away and telescope in the same fashion as those elicited by amputation. He offers some novel comments about the length of time required for the usual phantom to fade away (p. 762):

> The life of the phantom has been variously reported to persist from a period of a few months to as many as twenty or thirty years. While it is common to hear that the usual phantom disappears within two years after amputation, no firm evidence is available on the period of survival. It seems probable that the failure to reorganize the body-image with disappearance of the phantom extends over a much longer period than is usually thought.

In the same vein, he points out that even after a phantom has apparently disappeared it may be revived by experiences that cause the individual to regress. He indicates that it may be revived too by various kinds of sensory stimulation to the stump, e.g., such as that occasioned by the fitting of a prosthesis. In discussing the variables which determine how a person will react to amputation, he cites observations which suggest that (p. 764) "maladaptation is frequent among those individuals in which the integrity of the body image, as it existed prior to illness or trauma, is overevaluated for maintaining self esteem. Limb amputees, in whom the presence of a limb symbolized either masculinity or femininity, generally adapt poorly to limb loss." Complaints of pain in the phantom, which can in some instances become intractable, are conceptualized by him as being symbolic expressions of anxiety and also sado-masochistic identifications. The possible importance of sado-masochistic identifications in this respect was highlighted by his finding that 70 percent of a group of amputees with painful phantoms had lived in close association with an amputee before their own loss had occurred; whereas the percentage reporting a similar association was considerably smaller in several control groups. It would appear as if the individuals who developed painful phantoms had been particularly exposed to an amputee as a possible identification model.

The problem of pain (which includes phantom pain) following amputation has received attention not only as a theoretical issue but also because it plays an important role in the amputee's ability to adjust to wearing a prosthesis. Korin, Weiss, and Fishman (1963) examined pain thresholds in 44 amputees, not only on the stump but also an homologous area on the intact limb. It was found that sensitivity to pain was greater on the stump than the intact homologous area. A similar kind of finding has been reported with respect to sensitivity for other classes of stimuli. Shapiro (1965) studied 32 amputees and compared the sensitivity of the stump and an homologous intact area for a variety of stimuli (e.g., light touch, two-point discrimination, roughness discrimination). The stump area proved to be significantly more sensitive with respect to two-point discrimination and point localization. There was a trend, though not significant, for it to be more sensitive to light touch. Further, size and form discrimination were superior on the stump as contrasted to the homologous area. The fact that the stump acquires a new level of unusual sensitivity had been previously observed (e.g., Haber, 1955). Considerable difficulty arises in arriving at a formulation which will explain this change. Disputes have arisen between "peripheral" versus "central" explanations. Shapiro (1965), after reviewing the pertinent literature, suggests that both peripheral and central factors are involved. He notes that physical and chemical changes do occur in the stump itself which can increase nerve ending sensitivity. Also, at a central level, the sensations from the stump can be regarded as entering (p. 62) "the somesthetic cortex against a reduced background of nervous activity as compared with the undiminished level on the contralateral side. Therefore, a tactile stimulus applied to the stump will be more readily discriminated than an equivalent stimulus to the homologous area of the intact limb."

Jarvis (1967) made an interesting point with regard to phantom pain. He determined in a sample of women with mastectomies that about 30 percent of those with phantoms reported phantom pain. This is considerably higher than the range of one to 13 percent found for such pain in most other kinds of amputations. Jarvis speculated, however, that the difference might be a function of how pain is defined. He included transitory and long continuing pain experiences; whereas most studies have ignored the transitory phenomena. If one includes briefly experienced pain sensations, phantom pain may be quite common whenever there is loss of a body part. Incidentally, Jarvis and others, e.g., Barglow (1964) and Malerstein (1963), have established that phantom type experiences occur with fair frequency in women who suffer body loss related to their breasts or the genital system. Thus, in the Jarvis study 24 percent of 104 patients with mastectomies had phantom breast sensations. Of a range of variables examined (e.g., marital status, size of breasts, attitude toward one's breasts) in an attempt to find "predictors" of the occurrence of the breast phantom, only age turned out to be of real significance. Younger women experienced phantoms more often than older women.

One of the puzzles regarding the phantom which has resisted solution concerns its duration. Why does the phantom begin to "telescope" or grow shorter and then quickly disappear in some amputees; whereas in others it persists in "extended" (non-shortened) form for long periods of time? Systematic studies of this matter have been practically non-existent. A particularly important investigation related to this point was carried out by Weiss and Fishman (1963). Their sample of 239 persons contained above elbow, below elbow, above knee, and below knee unilateral amputees. An interview was arranged with each subject to determine his phantom experiences. One of the prime conclusions derived from the data was that the nature of the phantom is a resultant of the interaction of the central image of the previously existing limb and the new cues provided by sensations from the stump. The more vivid the sensations from the stump itself the more likely the phantom is to develop gaps; "telescope"; and finally disappear. When stump cues are weak the phantom persists. This was illustrated by the fact that diabetics in the sample who, because of their disease have relatively low stump sensitivity, were characterized by persisting "extended" phantoms. It is known too that paraplegic amputees, whose stumps are relatively insensitive because of the effects of spinal damage, retain their extended phantoms.

In a detailed analysis of their data, Weiss and Fishman found, as Kolb has also observed, that contrary to the belief that the phantom invariably shrinks in a few years, numerous amputees in their sample experienced extended phantoms even after many years. A cephalocauded pattern was noted, with intensity and persistence of phantoms tending to decline from the upper to lower regions of the body. Thus, above elbow amputees reported the strongest and below knee amputees the weakest phantom sensations. Individuals whose limb loss had occurred as the result of war rather than civilian injury tended to have more persistently strong phantoms. It was proposed that the unusual tension of the soldier just before and at time of injury might play a role in this phenomenon. However, it is difficult to know how to compare this observation with that of Hirschenfang and Benton (1966) who found that patients who had a traumatic amputation showed shorter phantom duration than patients whose amputation occurred after an extended period of illness.

Siller (1960) explored the reactions of 52 children who had suffered amputations. He used a broad approach which involved interviews and various projective techniques (e.g., Draw-a-Person and Thematic Apperception test). In addition, he conducted interviews with the parents of the children. There were no clear indications that these amputee children were in general more disturbed psychologically than normal children. Some evidence was found that the best adjustment to the amputation was one in which there had evolved active compensatory modes of behavior. An important point that emerged from the data was that children who had suffered amputations as the result of traumatic factors were more disturbed than those whose loss was congenital. Siller remarked apropos of this point (p. 114), "Congenital amputees are less likely to mourn for that which they have never had."

Money (1960) examined the nature of erotic experiences in paraplegics who had lost all sensation from the lower half of the body. Fourteen men and seven women were interviewed as part of the study. It was found that erotic sensations from the affected body areas were completely abolished. However, it was discovered that (p. 74) "it is possible for vivid orgasm imagery to occur in the dreams of paraplegics, despite total lack of somesthetic sensation from, and paralysis of the genito-pelvic area." Money regards such imagery to be a special kind of phantom phenomenon.

Murphy (1957) noted in the course of intensive psychoanalytic interviews with amputees that phantom sensations sometimes reflected attempts to produce movement in the missing member. Kinesthetic experiences in the area adjacent to the amputation were apparently maximized in an effort to defend against the sense of loss. Murphy postulated that painful phantoms would be most likely to occur in men who had laid special stress on athletic activity and its associated highlighting of body existence. He seems to have reasoned that such men would have the greatest defensive need to feel intense sensation as compensation for the lost part. He indicates that in 11 cases with phantom pain that he investigated there did prove to be a previous unusual degree of interest in muscular activity.

Weiss (1958) reviewed some of the paramount features of phantom sensations in amputees and formulated a theory for explaining phantom pain and discomfort which minimizes their neurotic or maladjustive significance. He hypothesized that phantom pain or tingling has a positive functional value to the individual in comforting him with regard to his loss. He proposed that (p. 27), "The painful sensations thus are employed by the amputee to allow him to reason as follows: 'I have pain. Since I have pain in the area where my limb was, I must still have the limb.' "

Szasz (1951) has devoted a good deal of effort to ordering phantom limb phenomena into a frame of reference which includes other categories of unreal perception and imagery. He views the phantom as a means for cushioning sudden body loss by providing an illusory substitute which gradually fades away and thus permits the ego to reexperience "the trauma in small doses". His formulation is, of course, analogous to that presented by Weiss (1958). Paranoia is one of the major classes of unreal perception with which he compares the phantom experience. He hypothesizes that the paranoid has lost or been forced to disclaim something of vital importance and that the person or object he labels as a persecutor is an unconscious substitute for it. He states (p. 158), "The delusion of persecution may also function as a reassurance against object loss: 'If I am persecuted—then I cannot be alone.' " It seems to him that (p. 158) "there is an arresting analogy between the 'noisy claim' of the persecutory delusion and of the phantom pain." That is, paranoia and the phantom may be both regarded as illusory substitutes for serious loss. They both apparently signal the loss and yet simultaneously provide a paradoxical reassurance against it. Szasz would go further and treat any fantasied alteration in the body as falling on a continuum which includes the phantom. He sees a quality akin to the phantom in fantasied additions to the body such as might occur when a woman wishes she had male attributes (e.g., a penis) or when a man desires female characteristics (e.g., as evidenced in transvestite behavior). In general, his theorizing represents a provocative attempt to integrate what might at first appear to be diverse types of events.

Simmel (1959) expressed disagreement with Szasz' formulations and also with those of others who regard the phantom as representing primarily a means of denying body loss. She raises a number of questions which she considers to contradict such a view. She notes that phantoms persist in some amputees for decades despite the fact that these amputees utilize their prosthesis well and appear to lead normal lives. She questions whether they would continue to deny (via the phantom) the amputation while apparently reconciled to it at most other levels of their behavior. She further asks whether the various changes that occur in the concept of the phantom (e.g., telescoping) and which render its image very different from the normal contralateral member would not constitute an inefficient and unsatisfying defense against recognizing the loss of the body part in question. Her third major criticism is derived from her observations (1956) that lepers experience phantom sensations for parts that are lost through amputation but not from parts lost through absorption associated with the disease process. She points out that it is inconsistent with the denial theory that an individual should use the phantom as a defense against loss in one instance but not in the other.

Her own theory is that the phantom is an indication of a stable body scheme that persists beyond the time of amputation. She says (1966, p. 18), "The lost limb continues to be represented in the schema and manifests itself experientially as the phantom." In support of this view she notes that whenever an individual has not had sensory experience with a given body part, its loss or absence is not accompanied by a phantom experience. Illustratively, phantoms do not occur in those with congenitally missing limbs or who lose a malformed extremity which lacked sensation. She points out that the absence of phantom experiences in patients with leprosy who lose parts by gradual absorption over many years supports her view too, because in such instances one can take the view that the slow pace of the body changes permits the body scheme to keep in step with the physical reality—eliminating the persisting unrealistic body concept which presumably arouses phantom sensations. By the way, she specifies that the phantom will occur even in relatively immature persons (e.g., very young children, mental defectives) if they have had sensory experience with the body part before it is lost.

GROSS BODY DISABLEMENT

This section will look at studies which have appraised body image or related processes associated with forms of body damage besides amputation and loss of a body part. A variety of different conditions will be reviewed. Responses to polio, heart disease, spinal damage, retarded sexual development, dwarfism, and cleft palate are among those which will be considered.

Response to Crippling

Several papers have dealt with the effects of paralytic poliomyelitis upon body feelings and attitudes. There are few conditions which produce such radical body incapacitation; and one might consequently expect that it would have quite demonstrable body image implications. Ware, Fisher, and Cleveland (1957) were able to demonstrate in 1957 that the individual's adjustment to poliomyelitis is significantly related to the definiteness or firmness of his body image boundaries. Patients who perceive their body boundaries as well articulated (as defined by the boundary characteristics of their Rorschach images) made better long-term adjustments to their disablement than patients with poorly demarcated boundaries.

Lebovits and Lakin (1957) used several different techniques to evaluate body image changes in persons with paralytic polio. Their subjects consisted of 15 polio patients and a control group of female student nurses. One of their evaluation procedures was based on asking the subject to make a series of size estimates about his body. Illustratively, he was asked such questions as:

> How many inches is it around your ankle?
> How many inches is it from your elbow to your armpit?
> How long is your spinal cord?

It was intended in this way to uncover distortions or overcompensations that might have occurred in experiencing various body areas. A second procedure was concerned with how active or passive the subject perceived his body to be. He had the task of rearranging a series of scrambled sentences which could be interpreted as depicting either an active or a passive mode of response. The degree to which he chose active vs. passive alternatives was noted. Finally, a series of cards were shown to the subject. Each of the cards contained a stimulus word followed by four adjectives ranging from positive to depreciatory in connotation; and the task was to incorporate the stimulus word and one of the four adjectives into a sentence. The first two cards in the series involved neutral stimulus terms and the last four presented body image words. Analysis of the data from the three tasks revealed that there were no differences between the polio patients and the controls so far as the content of any of the types of responses obtained. That is, polio patients did not deviate from the normals in their body size estimates; in their references to active vs. passive body sequences; or in the kinds of adjectives used to refer to body areas. However, there were some significant and apparently meaningful differences between the two groups in their reaction times to certain of the experimental tasks. In the instance of the body size estimate task the polio patients had significantly longer reaction times and therefore presumably greater anxiety than the normals in responding to three of the items: length of spinal cord, length of hand, and distance from navel to chin. It was conjectured that the three body areas involved are particularly critical in a polio patient's life. Thus, he spends most of his time in a supine position where sensations from the spinal area might be magnified. Similarly, it has been observed that he is often particularly disturbed about the loss of function in his hands; and the body region from navel to chin is the locus of the chest shell which maintains his respiration.

Lebovits and Lakin (1957) were inclined to view their results as indicating that polio patients do not suffer a gross revision of the body schema, at least not during the early phase of incapacitation which was characteristic of their sample. They interpreted the reaction time differences between the polio and normal subjects as having limited significance; and stated (p. 521), "The fact that no significant differences were obtained with respect to body part estimates and symbolic body attributes suggests that even in the face of such major incapacitation as is involved in paralytic polio, people do not suddenly and drastically alter general body image schemas." In another instance they indicated (p. 522), "No differences were found in body image per se. Certain body parts tended to arouse greater concern among the polio patients. General body-image-related-anxiety was found to be characteristic of the polio group. This anxiety was inferred to be a result of conflict engendered by the attempt to retain the pre-onset body image as reference point in the face of the realistic impairment experienced by the patients."

Parenthetically, a project by Potter and Fiedler (1958) should be mentioned which dealt with the question whether a group of college students who had been disabled by polio differed from a non-disabled group in the way in which they perceived themselves and others. Each subject described himself, his ideal self, and the most and least preferred co-worker he had ever had on a 24-item, six-point scale containing bipolar items such as "friendly-unfriendly", "cooperative-uncooperative". The disabled and control subjects did not differ in self-satisfaction or in the degree of psychological distance they perceived to exist between themselves and others. However, subjects who had been disabled for a short period were significantly less self-satisfied and felt less personally close to others than subjects who had been disabled over a long time span. Apparently, there was more disturbance present in those who had been relatively recently disabled than in those who had had a longer period to adjust to their handicap.

It may be added that a majority of studies have found that the disabled have lower self-esteem than the non-disabled. Some (e.g., Pomp, 1962) emphasize the relative large disparity between self concept and ideal concept characterizing the disabled.

At a more clinical level of observation, Glud and Blane (1956) reported deep anxiety about the body image in polio patients. They highlight the fantasies of body annihilation which attend the acute phases of the disease. It was noted that a variety of compensatory body image changes occurred in the process of dealing with long term disablement. Thus, less interest seemed to be shown in the non-functioning regions of the body and heightened attention was focused on normal areas. For example, relatively greater attention would be directed to the head and to the excretory regions than to the paralyzed trunk. Indeed, there was even an apparent compensatory extension of the body image to include equipment (e.g., respiratory) necessary for the patient's survival.

Bierman, Silverstein, and Finesinger (1958) followed the course of a six-year-old boy who was hospitalized for acute lower extremity paralytic polio and who subsequently recovered with only mild residuals. During the period of his illness and his convalescnece he was interviewed many times. Various projective tests were administered to him and his reactions to play materials were recorded. It was noted that at a conscious level he had almost nothing to say about his body disability; but he evidenced considerable concern about it in more indirect ways. At one point he drew a picture of a "hot rod racer" and said that it had been in a wreck and was "all beat up". He pointed out that a rear wheel had a "flat tire". In his doll play interviews his body concern seemed to manifest itself in a preoccupation about things being unstable and likely to fall over. He used phrases like "then the refrigerator fell over" and "the whole place is falling down". Similarly, his Rorschach responses focused on such themes as "bones are going to break" and "he got wrecked". His degree of concern about body image and mutilation seemed somewhat out of proportion to the fact that he had only a relatively mild case of polio. One of the methodologically instructive aspects of this study was the contrast between the limited body image disturbance revealed in conscious verbalizations and the considerably greater disturbance that apparently appeared in projective type responses.

Cath, Glud, and Blane (1957) elaborated from a clinical point of view some of the body image variables which influence the polio patient's ability to adjust to his crippling. They concluded that one of the major obstacles to a successful reintegration is the patient's denial of his disability. It is, they indicated, as if he refused to recognize the permanency of his radical loss of function. They suggest that such denial prevents the elimination of what have become the unrealistic pre-morbid aspects of the body image and consequently interferes with the revision necessary to take into account the new state of affairs. They emphasize that such revision is further hindered by the patient's awareness of the threat of death, due to his difficulty in breathing which reactivates regressive anxieties associated with earlier experiences that carried connotations of mutilation and attack upon body integrity. Finally, they observed that one of the constructive steps necessary for successful change is the incorporation into the new body image of compensatory external objects (e.g., wheelchair substituting for lost leg function).

The role of denial in maintaining adjustment to serious body disability is highlighted in a paper by S. H. Fisher (1958). He referred to three patients he had seen in the course of psychotherapy who had serious body damage (e.g., paralysis due to spinal injury). A similarity they shared was the fact that they had all reacted to their body defects with attitudes of denial which radically minimized their seriousness. However, the similarity went further in that each had been suddenly precipitated into a period of serious disturbance by being exposed to a visual experience which dramatized his body disablement and undermined the self-protective denying defense that had prevailed. For example, in one instance a woman had suffered a spinal injury which had left her with spastic paraparesis and a scissors gait that required her to walk with the aid of a cane. For a number of years she lived productively despite her handicap. However, on one occasion a friend took some movies of her walking up a path; and when she later saw the film projected she was shocked at her appearance. The film revealed to her an image of herself that was catastrophically ugly, crippled, and awkward. She then lapsed into a depression and could not go on with her usual life. The other two patients whom Fisher described were apparently similarly precipitated into serious disturbance by suddenly being confronted by their images in full length mirrors. One cannot help but be impressed with the potential significance of these phenomena. It would appear as if body image alterations which the individual has resisted making in the face of actual changes in his body may be accelerated by vivid visual stimuli which confront him with the unreality of his current body image.

Wachs and Zaks (1960) studied a disabled group composed of 30 male veterans with spinal cord injuries. These patients had all suddenly lost lower limb, bladder, bowel, and sexual function; and could logically be regarded as having suffered great trauma to their usual body concepts. The question was posed whether such catastrophic body insult would manifest itself in their drawings of a human figure. Figure drawings were obtained from them and also from a control group of 30 male veteran patients who had serious chronic diseases but who were ambulatory and had not experienced gross body disablement. By and large, it was discovered that the drawings from the experimental and control groups did not differ appreciably. In seeking to explain this lack of differentiation Wachs and Zaks raised the question whether the control subjects, who were after all suffering from serious illnesses, had not experienced almost as serious attacks upon the body image as had the spinal injury patients. Of course, the additional question could be raised whether figure drawings truly mirror the body schema alterations occurring in persons with spinal injuries. This is a significant question if one considers that in 1956 Silverstein and Robinson (1956) reported that the figure drawings of children with polio could not be distinguished from those of normal healthy children.

DRAWING OF HUMAN FIGURE AS A MEASURE OF BODY ATTITUDES

It would be apropos at this point to digress and consider the evidence for and against the proposition that figure drawings can be validly used to measure body image attitudes and feelings. A profitable beginning is a paper by Levi (1961) which sought to determine the effects of body disablement upon the perception of drawings of human figures. Levi indicated (pp. 1–2), "even assuming that a drawing is a projection, before we can attribute a bit of elaborate overemphasis in the drawing to its creator's undue preoccupation with the part in question, we have to insert a middle step and show that his perception—as yet uncomplicated by the act of bodying forth mental images through paper and pencil—has already been shaped by that particular preoccupation". She regarded her study as a first step in dealing with the question whether the body image and a drawn figure stand in an "isomorphic relation". The hypothesis she tested was that subjects with leg disabilities and those with arm disabilities would be unusually sensitive to the legs and arms respectively in drawings of the human figure. There were 12 subjects with traumatic arm disabilities (e.g., amputation, fracture); 12 with traumatic leg disabilities; 13 with low back disabilities of poorly defined etiology; and 35 normal subjects serving as controls. In order to measure perceptual sensitivity to the particular body areas under consideration, reactions were obtained to a series of stick figure human representations. The series consisted of 27 cards, each displaying a pair of stick figures and a single large card on which there was a model stick figure. All figures comprised three sections: an arm unit, a leg unit, and a head-and-spine unit. The three parts of which the model was composed were taken as the standard units of reference. Each of the paired figures on the 27 cards contained only one standard unit, the other two units being variants. The pairing of the figures was such that 18 contained the standard arm unit, 18 the standard leg unit, and 18 the standard head-and-spine unit. It was the subject's task to indicate for each pair of stick figures the one most resembling the model. Scores were tabulated in terms of the total number of times the figures chosen contained the standard arm unit, leg unit, and back unit. As hypothesized, the arm disability group chose figures with the standard arm unit to a significantly greater degree than the control group. The leg disability group was likewise differentiated from the normal controls in terms of standard leg units. However, the back group was not different from the control group in choice of back units. This last finding had been anticipated by Levi because of the vague and poorly defined nature of the complaints in the back group. Altogether, Levi felt that the results supported the view that if a given region of an individual's body is disabled he is particularly sensitive to the perception of this region in representations of the human figure. However, the fact that this did not hold true for the back region suggested that such perceptual sensitizing does not occur unless the body disablement takes a clearcut visible form.

Apfeldorf (1953) probed into the matter of whether the individual projects his "bodily self" to a recognizable degree into his figure drawings. He felt this was an important issue because it touched on the more general question of whether one projects recognizable aspects of one's "bodily self" into any task which involves some creative activity or expression. To implement his investigation he determined whether judges could successfully match subjects' figure drawings with their full-length photographs. Two categories of subjects were studied that were regarded as differing in how much they were invested in their bodies. There was an unselected college student group considered to be typical of those with a normal amount of body interest and a group majoring in physical education which was viewed as having unusually high body investment. On the basis of observations from an earlier exploratory study Apfeldorf decided that it was best to use as representative of an individual only a like-sex drawing portraying the left profile view. The decision to use only left profile, like-sex drawings resulted in only 18 of the 84 drawings originally collected from the unselected subject group and 17 of the 75 from the physical education major group qualifying for inclusion in the experimental design. Three groups of judges attempted to match the drawings and photographs: 40 college students, eight artists, and eight clinical psychologists.

It was found that judges were capable of matching the drawings and corresponding photographs of the unselected student group significantly better than chance. They were much less successful in their matchings for the physical education majors. In evaluating his data, Apfeldorf was impressed by the fact that the drawings of the physical education majors were more difficult to match correctly with their photographs than were those of the unselected subjects. He also observed that drawings which were correctly identified were more often characterized by obvious movement than drawings not correctly identified. This led him to conclude that the greater one's interest in one's body as an object of physical development and the more one is muscularly active, the less the capability for body self projection. He suggested that muscular mobility decreases kinesthetic experiences and that a low level of body activity maximizes such experiences.

These findings which showed that a person's figure drawing and his photograph could be matched were later followed up in another study by Apfeldorf and Smith (1965). A similar design was employed. Judges were asked to match 25 frontal drawings of the female human figure with 25 frontal photographs of the college women who drew them. The judges were 30 male psychology graduate students and 30 women religious graduate students of art. Matchings of drawings and photographs were significantly higher than chance. The data clearly supported the proposition that when the subjects sketched the figures they introduced elements resembling themselves.

An investigation bearing on the question of whether an individual's body experiences find expression in his figure drawings was published by Schmidt and McGowan (1959). Figure drawings were secured from 30 adult persons with visible physical disabilities (e.g., amputation) and 30 adults without disabilities. These drawings were presented to judges with varying theoretical orientations and degrees of training in figure drawing analysis; and the request was made to sort them into "disabled" and "normal" categories. The judges were able to distinguish the disabled from the normal drawings significantly better than chance. Success in differentiating the drawings was not a function of the judge's degree of training in figure drawing analysis. Schmidt and McGowan raised the question whether the past failure of Silverstein and Robinson (1956) to differentiate the drawings of disabled subjects might have been a function of the fact that they studied only children. They suggested that children's drawings might simultaneously reflect so many developmental variables as to obscure the effects that body disablement itself might produce.

Other studies which have found data supportive of the view that the figure drawing reflects body image variables may be briefly enumerated.

Berman and Laffal (1953) reported a significant positive correlation in a sample of VA hospital patients between their body types and the rated body types of their figure drawings.

Kotkov and Goodman (1953) concluded that obese women draw figures that cover an unusually large area of the page.

Lehner and Silver (1948) found a trend for the age ascribed to figures which had been drawn to match those of the drawer.

Craddick (1963) compared the characteristics of subjects' figure drawings with the attributes of their self drawings. Significant similarities in size, among other, were noted.

Gellert (1968) found that children's drawings of self differed only in minor ways from drawings of non-self figures. No differences were observed for detail, symmetry, proportion, placement, and line quality. There was, however, a significant trend to draw the self representation larger than the non-self figure.

Marais and Struempfer (1965) determined a significant positive correlation between indicators of body anxiety in the subject's drawing and amount of anxiety elicited by tachistoscopically exposed pictures depicting body mutilation.

Wysocki and Whitney (1965) showed that the figure drawings of crippled children had significantly more "areas of insult" (i.e., special distortion) than those of normal children. The area of "insult" was often correlated with the locus of body crippling.

Holden (1962) described a study in which handicapped children who had had a presumably therapeutic camp experience showed "improvement" as defined by judges' evaluations of their pre-camp versus post-camp figure drawings.

Kamano (1960) was able to show in a sample of schizophrenic women that there were significant positive correlations between their semantic differential ratings of the concept of My Actual Self and their ratings of their own like-sex figure drawings.

A particularly detailed and careful study was undertaken by Simmons (1966). College students who had produced figure drawings were asked to evaluate themselves by means of Semantic Differential ratings and adjective check lists. They applied the same evaluations to their figure drawings. Significant positive correlations were found between ratings of Actual Self and ratings of the like-sex drawing—but the results were not significant when the opposite sex drawing was involved. Artistic ability proved not to have appreciably affected the findings. Simmons cautioned that although a significant relationship was observed between self ratings and ratings of the like-sex drawing, the overlap was of a low order and raised questions about the validity of most clinical evaluations which presume similarity between an individual and his figure drawing.

The following are studies which have not supported the hypothesis that the figure drawing portrays aspects of the body image of the drawer.

Hunt and Feldman (1960) related Body Cathexis scores to certain figure drawing attributes with presumed self significance. They administered a modified version of the Secord and Jourard scale to 65 students, 39 men and 26 women. Each subject was asked to rate 25 areas of his body twice, first as he perceived them in the present and secondly as he recalled his feelings toward these areas to have been when he was an early adolescent. Further, he was requested to draw an unclothed human figure. Three clinicians rated the same 25 body parts in the figure drawings as were mentioned in the Body Cathexis scale. The ratings simply indicated the presence or absence of disturbance in the representation of each given area. The trend of the results indicated a lack of meaningful congruence between the Body Cathexis ratings and the corresponding evaluations which had been applied to the figure drawings. However, there was one significant positive correlation in the male group between degree of figure drawing disturbance and degree of negative Body Cathexis expressed in the retrospective self ratings.

Silverstein and Robinson (1961) considered how children represent physique in their drawings. Thirty boys and 30 girls were asked to draw a person and then one of the opposite sex. They were also asked to estimate their height and weight. No significant correlations were found between actual height and weight and respective indices of height (total length) and weight (volume of figure) derived from the drawings. The one exception involved significant negative correlations between estimated height and weight and the corresponding figure drawing indices which were derived from the figure of the same sex as the subject. Silverstein and Robinson concluded, in general, that a human figure drawing is not a direct representation of the body image.

It should be recalled at this point too that Silverstein and Robinson (1956) were not able in another study to distinguish the figure drawings of children with polio from those of normal children.

Sims (1951), Corah and Corah (1963), Johnson and Wawrzaszek (1961), and Centers and Centers (1963) found that the figure drawings of physically handicapped children and those of normal children could not be meaningfully distinguished. That is, they could not be differentiated with reference to the presence of specific kinds of body deformities.

The weight of the pertinent evidence that can be extracted from the literature suggests that the like-sex figure drawing produced by an individual does mirror some aspects of his feelings about his body and perhaps more broadly certain attitudes toward himself as a person. Body type, age, physical appearance, and body anxiety do seem, in many cases, to find representation in the individual's drawing. However, the presence of gross body defects is apparently not usually revealed in figure drawings. Perhaps the anxiety linked with body defects triggers compensatory strategies which result in exclusion of the defect from the drawing. The positive trends that do emerge are encouraging; and will hearten those who have, without real empirical support, assumed that figure drawings somehow sample body attitudes.

THE CHILD'S RESPONSE TO DISABLEMENT

A number of studies and observations concerning the responses of children to body damage will be taken up at this point.

Watson and Johnson (1958) discussed a series of clinical cases in which children had suffered gross physical alterations as the result of trauma, surgery, or disease. It was considered that the severity of their reactions to such alterations was often a function of how well their parents were able to accept them in their disfigured states. Rather detailed protocols of interviews with the children indicated that intense rage was usually the reaction to the body loss. This rage sometimes resulted in wishes to inflict the same type of body loss on others. Also grief reactions about the lost body parts were common. Concern would often be verbalized as to whether proper consideration had been given to the disposal of the amputated part. It was striking that some of the very young children (e.g., age three) complained of phantom sensations and pain. This would seem to contradict assertions by others [Riese and Bruck as cited by Simmel (1966)] that phantom sensations do not appear when amputation occurs in children before the age of six. Apropos of this last point, Easson (1961) too has reported the case of a 37-month-old boy who reported phantom sensations after the amputation of an arm.

Schechter (1961) has given his impressionistic observations of children with serious body defects in an orthopedic hospital. He portrays such children as rarely without an undercurrent of depression and usually adopting a pessimistic view toward the future. It was his formulation that the body image disturbance they manifest is often a result of the negative reactions they detect in others to their body disablement. He was impressed with the number of instances in which the body deformity was interpreted as punishment for past misdeeds. It seemed to represent a visible badge of badness. More will be made of this matter in a following section dealing with children's responses to surgery.

The negative attitudes that crippled children feel toward their disablement was indirectly demonstrated in a study by Richardson, et al. (1961) in which crippled children, among other groups, ranked a series of six pictures of children in terms of how much they liked them. The pictures included a child with no physical handicap and others with various types of disfigurements (e.g., walking with a crutch, amputated hand). It was found that the crippled children, like normal children, expressed highest liking for the picture of the non-handicapped child and lower preferences for pictures of the handicapped. That is, the association of the body disablement with a child's picture caused them to feel less positively toward that picture. In this way they revealed an underlying depreciation of the very condition characteristic of themselves.

Many impressionistic papers concerning the effects of body defect upon children may be found in the literature. Green, Schur, and Lipkowitz (1959) provided a psychiatric analysis of the life of a dwarf in which they speculated about the influence of his small stature upon his body image. Alpert (1959) referred to the "damaged self image" which evolved in a child who was born with a cleft palate. Fineman (1959) published preliminary findings concerning the special problems of ego and body image development in children with gross congenital anomalies of the urinary excretory apparatus. Miller, et al. (1959) commented upon the body image factors involved in adjusting to deafness and wearing a hearing aid.

Sabbath, et al. (1961) made observations of seven adolescent girls with ovarian dysgenesis. These girls were characterized by genital infantilism, absence of menstruation, unfeminine shape, and unusually short stature. Interviews with them revealed that beneath their superficial blandness there was much anxiety and concern about being a "freak". It was concluded that they experienced serious distortion of the body image which prevented them from working through an adequate sense of identity. Similar body image distortions have been observed in boys with abnormal breast enlargement (Schonfeld, 1962) and also those unusually obese or short (Schonfeld, 1964).

Lussier (1960) presented data from psychoanalytic treatment sessions with an adolescent boy who had been born with grossly malformed shoulders and arms. It was pointed out that this boy was consistently driven to compensatory behavior to prove that his body defect did not make him inferior to others. However, it was also true that his malformed arms, which had been part of his body from birth, appeared to have become an integral valued part of his body image and he strenuously resisted the idea of amputating them so that artificial arms could be substituted.

Offord and Aponte (1967) obtained Inside-of-the-Body (Tait and Ascher, 1955) and human figure drawings, among others, from a sample of children (N = 20) with congenital heart disease and a control group (N = 20). The heart defect group tended at a borderline level of significance to draw larger hearts and fewer other internal organs than the control group. No difference was found with reference to the drawing of a human figure. It was conjectured that because the Inside-of-the-Body drawing was relatively more differentiating than the figure drawing that the "body image distortion in congenital heart children pertains more to their perception [1] of the inside of the body than to their external view of it" (p. 62).

[1] Cassell and Duboczy (1967) found that subjects with a large number of heart symptoms required significantly longer to identify correctly a tachistoscopically presented picture of a heart than did subjects with a low number of heart symptoms. It is of related interest that defects like paralysis or loss of a limb may affect space perception (e.g., Comalli, 1966).

In contrast to the studies enumerated above in which body defect seems to be associated with distortion in body concept, Poeck and Orgass (1964) could not distinguish a group of largely congenital blind children (N = 30) from normal controls (N = 30) in terms of a special battery of body image measures. The battery included tasks which involved identifying parts of one's body, making right-left discriminations, and differentiating the fingers from each other. Of course, one must keep in mind that blindness is different from any of the classes of body defects discussed above, especially in the fact that blindness prevents the individual from experiencing his body defect as a *visual* phenomenon.

Arnaud (1959) has touched on a problem which is indirectly relevant to the question of reaction to body defect, particularly as it applies to children. She evaluated a group of children who were growing up in families in which one of the parents had a crippling ailment (multiple sclerosis). Aside from the disturbing effect upon the child of being in a family disrupted by the illness of an important member, this situation also exposed him to "omnipresent" stimuli related to body malfunction and damage. It is an important theoretical issue whether exposure to such stimuli would create an unusual degree of body anxiety in a child. Sixty children (26 boys and 34 girls) from families in which one of the parents had multiple sclerosis were compared by means of the Rorschach test with 221 children (131 boys and 90 girls) whose parents had been free of serious chronic illness. Body concern was measured in the Rorschach protocols by tabulating references to anatomy, mutilation, and deformed human figures. The children from the multiple sclerosis families proved to have significantly higher body concern scores than the controls. There were indications too that such intensified body concern was particularly characteristic of the boys in comparison with the girls. This led Arnaud to speculate that boys may have "more intense and lasting anxieties about body integrity and function" than girls. Incidentally, the experimental subjects were also found to exceed the controls in amount of dysphoric feeling, hostility, dependency longings, constraint in interpersonal relations, and a tendency to adopt a facade of "false maturity".

It should be added that mothers with handicapped children have been shown to be influenced by this fact. For example, Howell (1962) found such mothers to have lower self-esteem than mothers of well children. Dow (1965) was able to demonstrate that parents of disabled children are best able to adjust to the whole problem by a general de-emphasis of the importance of physique in the world.

The Arnaud study cited above indicated that children exposed to parents with body damage registered the impact of this damage. What factors determine how the perception of body damage in others will register? What role does an individual's feelings about his own body play in his reactions to perceiving disability? It is well established that the sight of body distortion in others arouses anxiety (Fisher and Cleveland, 1968). Indeed, Noble, Price and Gilder (1954) and Wittreich and Radcliffe (1955) have shown that an amputee viewed through aniseikonic lenses is perceived as less distorted than a normal figure. This phenomenon has been attributed to the fact that the greater an observer's anxiety about a stimulus he views aniseikonically the more he tries to stabilize the perceptual field in which it is embedded by excluding the lens induced distortions.

BODY IMAGE AND ATTITUDES TOWARD THE DISABLED

Several studies have been done which directly appraise the role of body image variables in mode of response to the disabled. Epstein and Shontz (1962) obtained evaluations from 49 college students of their own bodies via the Secord and Jourard Body Cathexis scale. They also assessed their attitudes toward persons with physical disabilities by means of a special test that was constructed for this purpose. The test presented a series of dilemmas involving disabled persons and the subject wrote a short essay about each. Analysis of the data indicated that the more favorable an individual's attitude toward his own body the more favorably he views the disabled. For example, those with high Body Cathexis scores were particularly willing to date persons with physical disabilities. One difficulty in interpreting these results is the fact that responses to both the Body Cathexis measure and the scale for assessing feelings about the disabled were probably significantly influenced by social desirability sets. To some degree the positive correlations obtained were probably a function of the overlapping social desirability variance.

In a related investigation Centers and Centers (1963) were concerned with how parents with malformed children perceived the bodies of these children and also their own. They administered the Secord-Jourard Body Cathexis scale to one of the parents (largely mothers) in 26 families in which there was a child with a congenital upper extremity anomaly or early amputation. The parent was first asked to fill out the scale as it pertained to the child. Then he applied the scale to his own body. The same procedure was used with a control group of families (N = 21) in which there were no malformed children. The results demonstrated, as predicted, that parents of the deformed upper extremity children rated the upper extremity regions of such children less favorably than the parents in the control families did with reference to their children. No differences occurred in ratings of other areas of the children's bodies. Also, the parents of malformed and normal children did not differ in how favorably they rated their own bodies. One particularly interesting finding that emerged was that the parents of the deformed children manifested a significant positive correlation between the way they rated their children's bodies and their own. The analogous correlation for the control parents was not significant. Centers and Centers speculated this difference represented a greater emotional involvement and identification with the child's body in the instance of the parent with the deformed child than was true in the case of the control parent and his child. It was proposed that the special involvement of a parent with the body of his deformed child prevents him from clearly distinguishing it from his own.

In still another pertinent study involving 150 college students Noonan (1966) measured conscious evaluation of one's body by means of the Secord and Jourard Body Cathexis scale and unconscious body concern with the Secord Homonym test (1953). Other measures were also taken (e.g., authoritarianism, ego strength). They were all correlated with degree of favorableness toward the disabled as appraised by two instruments. It was found, as predicted, that the more favorable the subject's conscious attitude toward his body the more favorable was his attitude toward the disabled. However, the Body Cathexis score was discovered to be significantly correlated with a measure of social desirability which had been included. As mentioned above, this calls into question a direct interpretation of cathexis scores as indicators of body attitudes. The data indicated further that the less unconscious concern manifested by an individual about his body in terms of the Homonyms test, the more favorably he viewed the disabled. Field dependence, which Witkin regards as having important body image connotations, also proved to be negatively correlated with liking for the disabled. Incidentally, a similar negative relation appeared with respect to authoritarianism. In a second sample of subjects, Noonan was not able to find support for any of the findings pertaining to the body image measures. Only that pertaining to authoritarianism held up successfully. Apropos of the negative correlation between field dependence and acceptance of disability which appeared in the first sample (but not in a second), it should be indicated that Webb (1963) could not find (in a large sample of men and women) a significant correlation between Embedded Figures Test scores and measures of attitudes toward the disabled. Thus, in two of three instances the results were of a chance order. If field dependence bears on response to the disabled, its influence is rather ephemeral.

Finally, it is pertinent that Jabin (1965) detected (in a population of high school students) low but significant positive correlations between body concern, as measured by the Hypochondriasis scale of the MMPI, and anxious, negative attitudes toward the disabled.

Looking back at the last several studies, one is not impressed with the consistency or magnitude of the relationships found. It has not been easy to show that body image variables predict an individual's perceptions of the disabled.

VISIBLE VERSUS INVISIBLE DEFECTS

An issue remaining to be discussed concerns the differential impact upon an individual of visible versus invisible body defects. Is there greater disturbance if a severe body disability is visible to the public (e.g., amputation) than if it is of a concealed type (e.g., heart disease)? Are the problems of body image reorganization in these two opposing cases of a different order?

The available research gives conflicting answers. Barron (1955) could not detect gross personality differences between those with "visible" and "invisible" disabilities. He used Rorschach and sentence completion techniques to measure personality variables. Smits (1964) examined self ratings, among others, in an adolescent sample of the disabled who varied not only with reference to the rated visibility of their disabilities but also severity. He could find no differences in self concept among those varying in the visibility of disability. A tendency was noted for obviously disabled female subjects to have a more negative self concept than obviously disabled males. A similar result was reported by Meissner, Thoreson, and Butler (1967) when comparing male and female disabled adolescents. Yuen-Chi-Wu (1963) interviewed samples of males with visible and invisible impairments. He found that the "visible" defect subjects (orthopedic) differed from the "invisible" defect subjects (cardiac) insofar as they were more inclined to blame other persons or things (rather than themselves) for their impairment and also were less likely to be interested in learning more about the cause of the impairment. No differences were detected between the groups in adjustment as defined by the Bell Adjustment Inventory. No differences were found with reference to self evaluations. But one of the conclusions drawn from the difference between the groups in direction of blame (outward versus inward) was that the individual with an invisible defect can seek compensation for it only by turning to himself—requiring some change in himself. However, he who has a visible defect is somehow able to seek compensation via outward directed aggression.

Koechel (1964) predicted that the obviously disabled, because of the visibility of their defects, would have more anxiety about interacting with others than would the non-obviously disabled. That is, they would expect more immediate negative reactions to be elicited by their visible defects. This view was tested by comparing the reactions of amputees and persons with cardiac disease to tachistoscopically exposed pictures either containing or not containing people. It was predicted that the amputees would show more defensive responses than the cardiac subjects to the scenes containing people —as compared to those without such content. When defensiveness was defined in terms of either extreme difficulty with, or unusual sensitivity to, the pictures, the hypothesis was significantly supported.

Anticipating a finding to be reported in a later chapter, it may be added that Sieracki (1963) found no differences in definiteness of body boundaries between subjects with visible (orthopedic) and invisible (cardiac) defects.[2]

Obviously, the existing literature is too sparse and scattered in its intent to give any meaningful answers to the question whether visible and invisible body defects have a differential impact upon the body image.

COMMENT

Severe body disablement sometimes produces surprisingly little apparent effect upon the body concept. Whether this is partially a function of the insensitivity of the measuring devices used remains to be seen. But it is probably even more a reflection of the ability of the individual to deny a transformation which is too threatening to acknowledge. There is no doubt that great anxiety is aroused by body disablement. In fact, even the process of interacting with the crippled is disturbing. The members of families containing a crippled child or parent register the impact of what they witness. Their feelings about self and body can be quite negatively influenced. One factor which seems to be involved in how much they are affected is their own degree of body insecurity.

REACTIONS TO SURGERY

The need for surgery is one of the most common situations to arise in which a normal individual suddenly finds his body integrity threatened. An increasing number of publications may be found which deal with the implications of such threat. Most studies have been preliminary and scanning in character. They usually describe the anxieties and irrational defense mechanisms triggered off by the surgery experience. Also, they directly or indirectly recognize that there are few stresses which compare in intensity with that occasioned by potential body disruption. The possibility of attack upon one's own body seems to stir a unique pattern of anxiety.[3] This is a key theme of a book entitled *Psychological Stress* by Janis (1958) which examines surgery experiences in detail. Janis presents an extended account of a female patient

[2] Tangential to this matter, it should be noted that Kimmel (1958) found less body confidence and esteem (as defined by figure drawing criteria) in children with acquired orthopedic defects than in those with congenital defects.

[3] As (1958) and Speisman, Lazarus, Davison, and Mordkoff (1964) have shown that merely witnessing a movie in which the body is cut arouses intense autonomic reactions.

who while undergoing psychoanalytic therapy entered a hospital for surgery. He was able to observe her reactions to the news that she needed surgery and to follow her behavior step by step through surgery and into the recovery period. Despite the fact that her surgery was of a relatively minor character, she responded to it as having catastrophic implications. Janis was impressed by the number of childhood conflicts and attitudes that were stirred up by her anticipation of the surgery. He was prompted to hypothesize (p. 196): "In adult life, exposure to any signs of potential mutilation or annihilation will tend to reactivate the seemingly outgrown patterns of emotional response which had originally been elicited and reinforced during the stress episodes of early childhood." He found that threat of body mutilation particularly sensitized the patient to the existence of hostility in both herself and others; and tended to elicit defense mechanisms designed to minimize aggressive interchange. The imminence of surgery seemed to create great fear about being abandoned and being unable to cope with life and there was an intensified need to be reassured that affection was still available from significant emotional figures. One of the most interesting aspects of Janis' study were the detailed free associations he obtained from the patient concerning her images of body dissolution. Although her operation was to be restricted to her leg, she had fantasies in which she variously pictured herself becoming diseased; being genitally mutilated; having her mouth eaten away by cancer; emitting hideous secretions; having to submit to a dangerous hemorrhoid operation; and so forth. Apparently, many different zones of her body schema, aside from her leg, became targets for her anxiety. Janis has referred to the threat linked with surgery as being unique in the sense that it (p. 411) "requires passive submission to a direct medical assault at the hands of an authority figure who will cut an opening with his knife and remove something from inside the body."

As part of his project, he also undertook to evaluate 30 patients who were in a general hospital for surgery and 149 college students who had experienced surgery at some earlier time. He studied the 30 surgical patients pre- and post-operatively with a series of questions touching on such matters as their thoughts about the operation; their degree of anxiety; and their pain experiences. The college students were asked to fill out a survey questionnaire which inquired at some length about similar matters. The principal finding that emerged from this data was that persons who experience very little or very high anxiety pre-operatively are those most likely to develop emotional disturbance during or after the surgical stress. Those who have a moderate amount of anxiety previous to surgery seem to make the best overall adjustment to the situation.

Gibson (1959) studied a group of children with congenital anomalies who required considerable surgery during the first four months of life. He evaluated them with interviews and projective tests five to eight years after surgery. They proved to be more disturbed than a control group that had not experienced surgery. No relationships could be solidly ascertained between the child's personality and his degree of disturbance during hospitalization. Quite relatedly, Jessner, Blom, and Waldfogel (1952) concluded from their impressionistic survey of 143 children undergoing tonsillectomies that those who drastically denied their anxieties pre-operatively tended to evidence a relatively high degree of disturbance post-operatively. They also called attention to the variety of symbolic and fantasied meanings attributed to the surgery and to the body area to be cut or removed. Very frequently the operation was perceived as retaliatory or punishing in its implications. The parts to be removed (viz., tonsils and adenoids) were described as if they were bad, "poisoned", and a generalized source of evil. Fears were even verbalized by some children that the operation might produce a change in their sex. Apropos of this point, Kaplan (1956) reported that some adult patients awaiting heart surgery "regarded the operation symbolically as an attack upon their sexual organs" (p. 226). Anna Freud (1952) and Falstein, Judas, and Mendelsohn (1957) have highlighted the magical nature of the body fantasies of children who are ill or awaiting surgery. Anna Freud suggested that children were particularly likely to interpret surgical procedures as aggressive attacks which are in the way of retaliation by those with whom they happen to be most in conflict at the time. Incidentally, Vernon, Foley, and Schulman (1967) have shown in a controlled study that the anxiety of a child in a surgical situation may be significantly reduced by the presence of the mother during induction of anesthesia. Vernon, Foley, Sipowicz, and Schulman (1965) concluded after an exhaustive review of pertinent literature that separation from parents is a prime variable in the child's disturbed response to hospitalization. Degree of preparation for the experience also plays an important role.

Titchener and Levine (1960) reported that high manifest pre-operative anxiety in adults is correlated with low post-operative anxiety and with a good post-convalescent adjustment. They state that low pre-operative fear heralds a poor post-convalescent adjustment and a moderate degree of post-operative disturbance. Further, they describe an "intermediate" degree of pre-operative anxiety as indicative of a "worse" post-convalescent adjustment and of a high level of post-operative anxiety. This last point is, of course, contradictory to Janis' findings. Two variables were noted by Titchener and Levine to maximize fear of surgery: (1) knowledge that the operation in question had an unusually high risk of death and suffering; (2) awareness that the incision would be near the genital region rather than in the upper part of the abdomen or the chest. Also, as in other studies, it was discovered that the imminence of surgery arouses many distorted and unreal images about one's body and one's relationships with others.

The peculiarly threatening character of surgery which involves the genital region was highlighted in a clinical investigation by Drellich and Bieber (1958) of 23 women who required hysterectomies as the result of benign or malignant disease. These women were interviewed at some length, both pre- and post-operatively, concerning their expectations of the surgery and also their fantasies regarding the loss of the uterus. Generally, there was a high level of pre-operative anxiety. Much concern was expressed about the fact that there would be a loss of childbearing ability. Even the loss of the menstrual function itself, which is usually considered to be of negative value to women, was viewed with serious regret. Many of the patients ascribed to their menstruation not only a basic feminine significance but also various excretory and rhythmic functions which they fantasied necessary for their well-being. Many unreal ideas were noted in which the removal of the uterus was equated with having one's womanliness and strength destroyed. One woman said (p. 328), "I know this operation definitely affects your strength. It may sound silly but I believe your strength comes from your womanly organs." A number of the patients acted out this view for months following the operation in a continued unfounded insistence that they were "raw" and "weak" inside and therefore unable to engage in sexual activities or to sustain their usual responsibilities. As in other studies, there was evidence that some individuals perceived the surgery as punishment for past activities about which they felt guilty. The fact that the genital region was involved seemed to make it particularly easy to regard it as punishment for sexual transgressions. The authors concluded that women may experience "castration anxiety" about the loss of body organs linked with femininity in a manner quite analogous to that which a man is presumed to experience when his sexual organs are threatened.

The degree to which castration anxiety is aroused by surgery has been considered in two controlled studies by Lane (1966) and Schneider (1960).

Lane (1966) was sufficiently encouraged by the observations of Wadeson (1966), which indicated that the dreams of a patient before and after surgery did reflect intensified anxiety, to attempt the systematic measurement of several parameters in the dreams of a sample of surgical patients (N = 5). There were also control subjects (N = 2) not undergoing surgery. The dreams of the subjects were collected on four separate days before they underwent surgery and during a subsequent three-day post-operative period. Recording of dreams took place in a dream laboratory where rapid eye movements were used to ascertain the occurrence of dreaming. Thirteen different aspects of the content of the dreams were measured by means of ratings. Such dimensions as the following were evaluated: anxiety, primitivity, body imagery, castration. It was found that the castration category (involving injury to a part of one's body) was one of those most affected by the surgery. Surgery patients manifested more castration themes before and after surgery than did the test-retest dream protocols of the non-surgical controls. There was a significant drop in castration themes from pre- to post-surgery. Of special interest is the fact that male patients' dreams contained much more castration material than did those of the females. A category of dream content referred to as "body imagery" was also utilized which reflected the general degree of health [4] and well-being of the human and animal characters and also the physical integrity of inanimate objects. This category was significantly higher in the surgical than control patients; but it did not decline from the pre- to post-surgical period. In speculating about the failure of the body image themes to decrease from pre- to post-surgery, whereas castration themes did decline, Lane indicated that it might be due to the fact that the threat of acute body damage would have partially faded post-operatively—but there would still be much general preoccupation with one's body. A general conclusion derived from the study was that the roles surgical patients "assigned" to principal figures in their dreams mirrored the strategies that they actually adopted in the hospital situation to cope with their anxieties. [5]

Schneider (1960) used TAT, story completion, figure drawing, and dream report techniques to investigate the nature of the anxieties and fantasies experienced by children (N = 96) awaiting surgery. A control group (N = 50) of children not awaiting surgery was also studied. Apropos of the dream results just described above, it may be first noted that the dreams of the children in the surgical sample were characterized by more themes of getting "hurt" than were those of the controls. Further, in congruence with the Lane study, boys revealed more fearful content in their dreams than girls. Indeed, the possible existence of sex differences was one of the central concerns of the analysis of the various test responses obtained. Boys awaiting surgery and their controls did not differ in the number of castration themes they produced (in projective images). Instead, it was found that both groups were generally higher in this respect than the control girls. The girls in the surgical sample evidenced as much castration anxiety as the boys, but it was significantly higher than that of the control girls. Schneider interpreted the pattern of findings to mean that boys tend generally (even when not hospitalized) to be characterized by a high level of castration anxiety and that the surgical threat did not produce a sufficient increment to be detected by the instruments used. However, girls were viewed as normally operating at a relatively low level of castration anxiety; and it was only under the impact of the surgical threat that a high level was elicited. [6] It should be mentioned that

[4] Gleser, et al. (1961) have shown that even the spontaneous speech productions of normal subjects differ considerably in the number of references to themes involving body destruction and illness. Ames (1966) has similarly observed large individual differences in number of references to death and body destruction in the spontaneous stories of children.

[5] Lerner (1966, 1967) has proposed the interesting hypothesis that (p. 90) "a function of dreaming is to strengthen body image by reintegrating the body into those fantasies which the dreamer cannot allow himself to act out physically in his waking life". It is assumed that kinesthetic fantasy is necessary to maintain the integrity of the body image; and dreaming provides one important opportunity for such fantasy.

[6] However, the Vernon, et al. (1965) detailed review of children's responses to hospitalization did not discern consistent sex differences in degree of overt disturbance.

the projective responses of the surgical sample contained an unusual number of themes of guilt. This goes along well with previous reports cited that illness often reactivates guilt and is unconsciously perceived as a punishment for wrongdoing. One may add that Richter (1943) and Gellert (1961), who have used techniques ranging from the interview to projective tests, have consistently observed feelings of guilt and self blame in sick children. For example, Gellert asked a sample of such children about how a child pictured in bed might have become ill; and two-thirds perceived the illness as related to misdeeds or bad behavior on the part of the child. Similarly, Cruickshank (1951) found that the responses of adolescents with body disabilities to a sentence completion test contained an unusual number of guilt themes.

There have been limited attempts to apply more quantitative test techniques either to predict response to surgery or to record its effects. Price, Thaler, and Mason (1957) found that the adrenal hormone levels of patients on the day before they were to undergo surgery were positively correlated with degree of overt disturbance and also with indices of anxiety derived from Rorschach protocols. It is interesting that a Rorschach index based on the amount of reference to the body did not correlate with steroid levels.

Lasky and Berger (1959) administered the Blacky Pictures (which tap 11 psychoanalytically defined variables in terms of responses to cartoon situations) to 30 male urological patients. The test was given soon after admission to the hospital and usually six days following surgery. Seven scores changed significantly from test to retest. The three scores (Masturbation Guilt, Castration Anxiety, and Narcissistic Love-Object) which manifested the greatest change were considered (p. 58) "the dimensions that one would expect to be affected most by surgery performed on the genitalia".

Meyer, Brown, and Levine (1955) analyzed the changes that occurred in the drawings of a house, a tree, and of a person of both sexes (H-T-P test) under the impact of surgery. The H-T-P tests were obtained before and after surgery from 22 patients, most of whom underwent rather radical mutilating procedures. Almost all patients evidenced gross changes in their drawings and these were interpreted as resulting from the surgery experience. However, the changes were not of a consistent type and were detectable mainly, via qualitative clinical analysis. It was considered that the (p. 454) "preoperative drawings were usually characterized by multiple indications of psychologic regression . . .". In describing the post-operative drawings, it was said (p. 454), "where the operations resulted in obvious mutilation the post-operative drawing appeared to reflect psychic reactions to it. Here again direct representation of body change was unusual. Allusion to the physical alteration tended to be expressed either symbolically or through multiple psychic defenses and through changes in mood." Very similar findings emerged in a further study by Meyer, Blacher, and Brown (1961) of 29 patients undergoing mitral surgery. Their investigative techniques included interviews, H-T-P drawings, and a drawing of the inside of the body.

Herring (1956) explored the power of a variety of physiological and psychological measures to predict the clinical and physiological responses of 25 surgery patients to the stress of anesthesia. Only a limited few of the measures proved to be of value in this respect. Paradoxically, one of the indices which was positively correlated with a stable response was the number of Rorschach percepts in which things were described as "deformed". No obvious explanation presented itself as to why such a relationship should exist.

Both Giller (1960) and Weiss (1965) obtained evidence that the Barron Ego Strength Scale (1953) predicts important aspects of behavioral response to surgery. The Barron scale is based on items from the MMPI and is defined as a measure of personality adaptability and resourcefulness. In the Giller study the MMPI K scale, an Attitude Toward Surgery Scale, and a Self Report of Fear of Surgery rating were used in addition to the Ego Strength Scale to predict reaction to surgery. Criteria for evaluating such reaction were based on amount of pain-reducing medication required by the patient, nurses' ratings of recovery, global ratings of recovery based on material in the patient's chart, and number of days spent in hospital post-operatively. The subjects were 50 male surgical patients. Most of the predictive variance in the battery of personality and attitudinal measures came from the Ego Strength scale. As for the Weiss study (1965), it involved open heart and general major surgery patients (N = 30). Besides the Barron Ego Strength scale, the following measures were employed to predict response to surgery: MMPI, Cornell Medical Index, Taylor Manifest Anxiety Scale. Recovery behavior was evaluated largely on the basis of interview observations. Significant prediction of adequacy of recovery behavior was largely due to the contribution of the Ego Strength scores. Conventional indices of anxiety, as measured by the Taylor scale, were not at all predictive. Indeed, Weiss pointed out that his results did not support Janis' (1958) formulation, cited above, of a curvilinear relationship between "anticipatory fear" and post-operative emotional disturbance. Giller (1960) noted, in the same vein, that his results which pertained to the relationship between a measure of pre-operative anxiety and post-operative behavior did not support Janis' curvilinear model. In view of the negative results from these two sources, one should take a cautious position concerning the generality of Janis' original findings.

Comments

Numerous studies have confirmed what is well known to most people, viz., that it is disturbing and threatening to submit to surgery. This is especially true in the case of children in which the surgical experience involves separation from parents at a time of major stress. It is intriguing to learn the range of meanings consciously and unconsciously attributed to the surgical experience. Themes of castration, body transformation, sexual distortion, and guilt have been noted by various observers. It is particularly surprising how often the need for surgery (and illness in general) seems to be interpreted as punishment for past transgressions. Is this due to the link between spanking and punishment which early sets up a primitive equation such that anything painful which happens to one's body is the result of wrongdoing? The threat of surgery may result in regression to early body image attitudes of this sort.

The Janis formulation which seemed to offer a neat statement concerning the relationship between amount of pre-surgical anxiety and actual response to surgery now stands in doubt. Several studies have not supported the curvilinear model which Janis proposed. The most consistent predictor of post-surgical behavior has turned out to be the Barron Ego Strength scale. This scale has in the past also shown some efficacy in predicting response to psychiatric treatment and hospitalization. Perhaps this is not mere coincidence. It may be that the threat of surgery typically induces transient disturbance approaching that found in the so-called psychiatric patient. The kind of ability required to adapt to the regressive effects produced by anticipating surgery may be in some ways analogous to that needed to recover from the disorganized states found in neurotics and schizophrenics.

The existing data on sex differences in response to surgery certainly invite further study. While Vernon, et al. (1965) concluded from a literature survey that girls and boys do not consistently [7] differ in their overt response to hospitalization experiences, both Schneider (1960) and Lane (1966) found evidence that the pre-operative dreams of boys are characterized by more disturbance (especially with reference to castration and "getting hurt" themes) than are those of girls.[8] It may be recalled too that Arnaud (1959) found that boys were more disturbed by exposure to body damage in a family member than were girls. Whether such sex differences are real is of fundamental significance because it touches on the whole matter of whether men and women are differentially sensitive to body threat. As will be shown at a later point, there is accumulating evidence that, contrary to the usual stereotype, the female may be less disturbed with reference to body threat than the male.

[7] They actually stated that boys seem more upset by hospitalization than girls at very early ages (one–four); but this is reversed at older age levels. They suggest that very early the boy may be more dependent on mother than the girl and therefore would be more upset by the separation related to hospitalization. However, as boys grow older and encounter demands that they behave in a brave and manly fashion, they may exhibit progressively smaller degrees of upset. Such "manly" behavior is not required of the girl.

[8] One may add that Cohen (1963) concluded that women were less defensive than men in responding to a stressful film which depicted a person with gross body deformities.

PLASTIC SURGERY

A discussion of the body image implications of surgery would not be complete without also considering the phenomenon of elective plastic surgery. It has become common for individuals to call upon surgeons to change their appearance by reshaping parts of their bodies (e.g., nose, breasts, eyelids, chin). The usual fear of surgery is apparently more than counterbalanced by the wish to eliminate some ugly or depreciated body feature. One can find numerous studies which have examined the personalities and motivations of those who seek plastic alterations (e.g., Macgregor, et al., 1953; Meyer, et al., 1960). These studies have relied almost entirely on interview material, with a few also including the analysis of psychological tests. Several will now be discussed which have particular body image implications. Macgregor, et al. (1953) collected data on 74 patients with mild to grossly deviant facial defects who were candidates for plastic surgery. Interviews, Rorschach, Draw-A-Person, Thematic Apperception, and various other tests were used to get at their reactions to their deformities and to their altered features following surgery. The results did not permit any simple generalizations about their modes of response to such body defects and body alterations. Little relationship was found between the severity of a defect and the manner in which it was handled. Some individuals with minor deformities had much greater difficulty in accepting themselves than did others with very gross deformities. Interestingly, it was observed that complaints about minor facial defects seemed often to be a cover for deeper personality difficulties. It was as if the facial defect symbolized to the individual some basic problem or frustration in his life. There was a strong tendency to reject the reality of disfigurement and to treat it as "an object in the outside world" alien to one's own body. Such rejection was especially prominent in patients who acquired their disfigurements later in life and who presumably were faced with a more radical kind of "readjustment of the body image." Wide variations occurred in reaction to post-operative changes in appearance. Some patients derived marked satisfaction from very minor improvement and others were dissatisfied with what objective observers considered to be great improvement. Likewise, some patients integrated the post-operative change within a few weeks and others required several months to do so. It was indicated that (p. 199) "a clear concept of the body image seemed . . . to predispose to post-operative satisfaction." This led to the conclusion (p. 206): "More extensive study of the body image, as it is related to facial deformity, may show its evaluation to be the single, reliable tool in determining the advisability of a corrective operation. . . ."

In a later study involving 89 patients requesting cosmetic rhinoplasty, Macgregor (1967) concluded from interview data that cultural role factors contribute greatly to an individual's decision to revise his nose. He observed that half of his sample consisted of persons who felt their noses looked "too Jewish" or too much like that of some depreciated minority group. The decision to seek rhinoplasty seemed to be an attempt to escape from an ethnic identification that was disadvantageous in the current American scene. A second half of the sample was comprised of those who felt their noses provided a target upon which others could project negative evaluations. They wanted (p. 134) "to escape the psychic assaults that result from the dichotomy between 'what I look like' and 'what I am'." Macgregor generalized (p. 135), "Regardless of what deeper psychological forces may be operating in the desire to alter one's nose, the wish to do so must also be seen as having its roots in the social and cultural pressures to conform."

Meyer, Jacobson, Edgerton, and Canter (1960), who are part of a group at Johns Hopkins that intensively explored the psychological aspects of plastic surgery, reported a review of 30 female patients who had been seen for elective plastic surgery of the nose. Interviews and psychological tests (e.g., Guilford-Zimmerman Temperament Survey, Draw-A-Face, Draw-A-Person) were employed in order to determine the motivations for rhinoplasty and also to examine what impact it makes upon the individual post-operatively. Various motivations for altering the nose were described. In some instances it seemed to represent the wish to become more attractive as a step toward increased friendship and courtship opportunities. Often there was a sense of being alien or different which was condensed into self-consciousness about the nose being "different." The general wish to shift from a passive restricted way of life to one more active and assertive was also prominent. There seemed to be an urge to create a new identity which would be symbolized in a new physical appearance. Taking a very speculative position, it was suggested that the typical woman presenting herself for rhinoplasty had had special difficulty in identifying with the mother figure. Instead, she had tended to model herself after father. But this use of a masculine model became a serious obstacle to assuming a normal feminine role with the coming of adolescence. The nose, in such individuals, could presumably be regarded as symbolic of the identification with father; and the wish to alter the nose might be interpreted as an attempt to eliminate that which is masculine in the self as a step toward becoming more feminine. When changes in physiognomy were actually produced surgically, surprising emotional responses often followed (e.g., great anxiety, crying, panic, exhibitionism). It was noted (p. 198) that "the initial effect of (plastic) surgery is a symbolic change in the body image with the liberation of affects previously bound." It is an interesting sidelight that at times there was considerable anxiety which reflected concern that one was no longer recognizable as one's former self and that one had lost all of the positive aspects of the old identity.

The frequent choice of the nose for plastic alteration has raised the question whether it occupies an unusually important role in the body scheme. Meerlo (1956) has pointed out that it is the "central and the most representative part of the face" which is in turn one of the most visible and expressive aspects of the individual's total self. Similarly, Hollender (1956) has speculated that (p. 375), "The nose with its external configuration, openings, cavities and contents (mucus and debris, vibrissae, etc.)" is an unusually good target upon which to project and discharge feelings. He cited clinical instances in which the nose seemed variously to be equated with the phallus, the female sex organ, the anus, and the mouth.[9]

Jacobson, et al. (1960) have come to the conclusion that men seeking elective plastic surgery are typically more maladjusted than women who do so. In fact, they found a large proportion of the 18 men they evaluated "to have serious emotional illness." For example, seven were diagnosed as psychotic. Interviews and a battery of psychological tests (e.g., Guilford-Zimmerman Temperament Survey, MMPI, Draw-A-Person) constituted the primary sources of data for the study. An attempt was made to formulate the pattern of attitudes underlying the typical male patient's wish for body alteration. This formulation can be best conveyed by the following quotation (pp. 369–370): "In the male patient, the sense of deformity is frequently linked with a conscious wish to dissociate himself from the father's undesirable traits or weaknesses. At the more unconscious level, the male cosmetic patient's motivation involves a wish to dissociate himself from a primitive destruction rage, primarily directed at the mother, from which he has not been rescued or helped by his father. The cosmetic concern contains the joint message of his failure to master intense ambivalence in relation to his mother and failure on the part of the father to help the patient out of this situation. . . . The symbolic representation of these problems in a sense of facial deformity provides a symptomatic solution or alternative to more direct dealing with conflicted feelings." In general, material from the male patients underscored the frequency with which a sense of body deformity may be a body image representation of role conflict. The authors of the study labeled this "the sequestering of a psychologic problem into an anatomical representation."

In another study by the Johns Hopkins group (Webb, Slaughter, Meyer, and Edgerton, 1965) attention was focused on the patient who comes for plastic "face-lift" surgery to remove evidences of aging from the face. Interviews and some psychological testing were done with a sample of 72 patients. The typical patient turned out to be a 48-year-old, married, Protestant female, high school graduate from the upper-middle class, with a comfortable income. She was also described as activity (accomplishing) oriented, socially

---

[9] The fact that certain areas of the body lend themselves particularly well to symbolic roles is highlighted in a paper by Hart (1950) which considers in detail the multiple significances that have been ascribed to the eyes and also in papers by Bell (1961, 1965) concerning the scrotal sac and testicles.

poised, and distant in her relations with others. The younger the age at which "face lifting" was requested the more evidence there was of unsatisfactory childhood relationships. A majority of the patients seemed to have a more positive attitude toward self post-operatively. As was true for rhinoplasty, men seeking the "face lift" procedure seemed much more psychiatrically disturbed than women who were candidates.

Some of the formulations presented in the plastic surgery studies have been extremely speculative and gone considerably beyond the facts. However, one also finds a number of interesting and provocative formulations. They stimulate questions whose solution might contribute to an understanding of body image phenomena. Illustratively, one wonders what types of body image patterns are most likely to result in the extreme negative body feeling that will spur an individual to seek surgical alteration in his appearance when it realistically does not require change? What factors determine the body area which will become symbolic of the wish for body change? Does actual surgical re-shaping of a body sector which is a prime focus of negative feeling result in any significant changes in the general characteristics of the body image? Are there equivalents to phantom experiences from a body region which has been surgically revised for cosmetic reasons?

Comment

As one surveys the multiplicity of accumulated observations concerning response to surgery and body crippling, there is no doubt that they provide a somewhat unique opportunity for examining body image systems in the process of alteration. Such alterations cannot be produced in the laboratory. Responses to gross body distortion seem to vary greatly. What are some of the principal shifts in the body image that have been described as occurring in the sick and disabled?

One finds, after surveying the literature, that only a small beginning has been made in detecting and classifying such shifts. Those which have been noted will be briefly enumerated below.

1. One pattern of change seems to be directed at shutting out and denying the existence of one's body. If an individual can turn away from his body, minimize its presence in his perceptual field, he can continue to exist in a world in which the catastrophic crippling of his body has not occurred. This mode of adjustment has been fairly well documented in polio patients. It is also typified in a diluted way by the behavior of parents with handicapped children who strongly de-emphasize the importance of the body and physique in man's affairs.

2. Another form of defensive response attempts illusory restitution of the lost body part. Probably, when an individual experiences a phantom limb,

which occupies the space of the lost limb, some such restitutive process is at least partially involved. If, indeed, this does turn out to be one of the adaptive purposes of the phantom, it would represent the most frequent method of restoring body image equilibrium when there is actual loss of a body part. This would be true by virtue of the fact that phantom experiences are almost invariable consequences of body part loss. As more and more detailed observations are made, it is beginning to appear that phantom experiences are not restricted, as previously believed, to projecting body areas—but may also involve internal organs and relatively small non-projecting regions.

3. A third adjustive process that has been observed revolves about focusing attention on a healthy part of one's body as a way of denying or shutting out damage to some other part. The use of this strategy has been detailed with reference to polio patients who become preoccupied with their heads or their genito-urinary systems and seem to pay no attention to their paralyzed body members.

4. Finally, may be mentioned what is ultimately the most common and normal resolution. The average individual confronted with catastrophic body change goes through a period of crisis in which he may resort to highly unrealistic defenses; but gradually he begins to accept his altered body and the area of disfigurement is reduced to manageable significance. This seems to occur rather quickly in most persons. A number of observers have been impressed with how realistic the crippled individual becomes about his body (e.g., Richardson, Hastorf, and Dornbusch, 1964). The drive for such mastery may account for the fact that many studies employing quantitative techniques have not been able to demonstrate gross differences between the disabled and normal controls with reference to body image parameters. It has not been possible to show consistently that such groups differ in accuracy of body size estimates, degree of body awareness, definiteness of body boundaries (e.g., Fisher and Cleveland, 1968), or even total body anxiety. One cannot but be surprised by the capacity of the average person to assimilate gross body distortion and to come to terms with it. This ultimate mastery is all the more impressive when one recalls the intense disturbance that the mere sight of body distortion in others seems to arouse in oneself.

Several sources of data tentatively suggest that one of the first effects of serious body threat is to activate childhood fantasies concerned with castration, dissolution, and destructive incorporation. In the same spirit of childhood, the threat is perceived in the context of moralistic images relating to evil and wickedness. There is apparently a tendency to assume at some level that catastrophic threats to one's body can only mean that one has been wicked and deserves punishment. Perhaps this reflects an early equation between receiving body punishment (spanking) and wrongdoing. This is a potentially profitable area for intensive investigation. To what extent is there an intensification of moralistic standards during the acute phases of body loss? Does the strictness of one's moralistic values play a role in one's ability to resolve the implications of body impairment realistically? To continue to experience an impaired area of one's body as a form of punishment or a badge of badness would, in all probability, interfere with its integration into the body concept.

The question of sex differences has reappeared again and again in the literature reviewed. With minor exceptions, the evidence seems to favor the view that the female is less disturbed by threat to her body than the male. Whether this is generally true remains to be seen. Would it, for example, apply to facial disfigurement? One would guess that facial attractiveness is more important to the female than the male in making an adequate social adjustment. It is also possible that males and females vary differentially in their sensitivity to body threat at various developmental points. The boy who is trying to establish a sexual identity at the time of adolescence may be much more concerned about body threats (with their apparent potentiality for harming vulnerable body projections) than the adolescent female who may be more preoccupied with the significance of inner and better protected reproductive body regions. If there is a time when the female does become particularly concerned about the importance of a projecting organ (e.g., her breasts), this could initiate in her a phase of special sensitivity to body threat.

Considerably more material relating to sex differences in body image organization will be presented in a later chapter.

4
Pathological Phenomena

This section will be devoted to a review of material which bears on the deviant states which occur in persons with brain pathology and in those with various types of serious psychiatric disturbance.

BRAIN DYSFUNCTION

Introduction

It was the unusual body experiences reported by patients with brain damage which played an important role in first attracting attention to the consequences of disorganizing the body scheme.

Even relatively mild forms of disturbance of brain function such as are linked with migraine can produce alterations in the body scheme. Lippman (1952) has recorded in rich detail the introspections of patients concerning their body sensations during the course of migraine attacks. Some of these introspections should be quoted because of their unique richness of detail:

... I experienced the sensation that my head had grown to tremendous proportions and was so light that it floated up to the ceiling, although I was sure it was still attached to my neck. I used to try to hold it down with my hands [pp. 348–349].

Today my body is as if someone had drawn a vertical line separating the two halves. The right half seems to be twice the size of the left half. I wonder how I am going to get my hat on when one side of my head is so much bigger than the other [p. 350].

Similar unusual body experiences in epileptics have been described by Arseni, Botez, and Maretsis (1966).

Gross brain pathology, particularly if it involves the parietal lobes may produce widespread, vivid body image distortions. These distortions are often quite bizarre. A general description of their range and character has already been provided elsewhere (Critchley, 1953).

Anosognosia

One of the most extreme forms of body scheme distortion arising from brain damage involves the literal denial of the existence of one's body. Considerable investigative attention has been devoted to this type of body denial; for an individual's renunciation of a sector of his own body is indeed a dramatic occurrence. Typically, the target for such renunciation is a limb or region that has been disabled in some way (e.g., paralyzed arm, blinded eyes). The term anosognosia is used descriptively to refer to this phenomenon.

Nathanson, Bergman, and Gordon (1952) found an incidence of 28 percent of anosognosia in 100 consecutive cases of hemiplegia studied. Weinstein and Kahn (1955) have written a book, *Denial of Illness*, which considers in detail various kinds of anosognosia and the manner in which they are integrated into the general behavior pattern of the individual. They point out that the denial of a disabled body region may take different forms, e.g., complete refusal to recognize the disability; attributing its ownership to someone else; paying no attention to it. They indicate too that the rejection of a body disability may at times be an aspect of a more inclusive shutting out of traumatic experiences. That is, it may be part of a general defensive refusal to recognize anything with an unpleasant impact, whether it be an unhappy marriage, a body defect, or the death of an important figure. Parenthetically, it should be remarked that Guthrie and Grossman (1952) observed a similar generalized denial of defect in patients with anosognosia they had evaluated. Indeed they found that if they bound the right hand of such a patient whose left hand was already disabled as the result of a hemiplegia he not only denied the disability of his left hand but also his inability to move his right hand. One of the most significant observations made by Weinstein and Kahn in the course of their study was that patients who denied body disability following brain damage had been characterized by certain special body attitudes previous to the onset of gross breakdown. The following quotation defines this matter (p. 73):

The outstanding characteristic of patients in this group concerned their attitudes toward illness and the mode in which they had been expressed. All had previously shown a marked trend to deny the existence of illness. They appeared to have regarded ill health as an imperfection or weakness or disgrace. Illness seemed to have meant a loss of esteem and adequacy.

It appeared as if the brain damage had provided a context in which long-standing body attitudes found expression in a grossly caricatured fashion. Weinstein and Kahn (1955) dispute the usual description of anosognosia in the literature as representing a breakdown in the body scheme. They direct their disagreement especially to those who would define "body scheme" as a three-dimensional image of the body represented in the parietal region. Thus, they note that in a group of patients with similarly situated parietal lesions some will manifest anosognosia and some will not. If the body scheme were, indeed, a specific configuration in the parietal region, similar lesions would be expected in general to produce the same effects. It was concluded that anosognosia can be linked to disturbance of the body scheme only if one defines the "scheme" as having no specific brain localization and as embracing not only the physical appearance of the body but also other spatial, temporal, and interpersonal dimensions of the self.

Weinstein and Kahn also called attention in their book to the phenomenon of reduplication of body parts which appears in persons with anosognosia. This involves the delusion that one has more than the usual number of a given body part (e.g., two heads or three hands). Typically, the reduplicated part is one that has been incapacitated. Since the early 1900's examples of the reduplication delusion have been cited in the literature. It is stated by Weinstein and Kahn that reduplication always expresses itself in a number of spheres of behavior and not merely in body terms. It may, for example, take the form of a belief in the existence of two or more places of the same name (place reduplication) or of confabulations that a current incident has already been experienced at some earlier time (time reduplication). From this viewpoint body part reduplication is simply one form of a generalized reduplicative pattern. In another context Weinstein and Kahn (1959) reported that special characteristics and meanings were at times ascribed to reduplicated parts which indicated that they might be serving some symbolic reparative function in the individual's economy. Apropos of this point, they stated (p. 972): "As in the other forms of reduplication, the phantom member may symbolize an interpersonal relationship. A nurse with a hemiplegia said that the 'extra' arm belonged to her friend, also a nurse. She described the arm as 'heavier, thicker, and darker'. The friend was a large, physically powerful woman who had literally taken care of the patient for many years."

Ostow (1958) has, from a psychoanalytic viewpoint, underscored the symbolically restitutive role of the reduplicated member. He theorized that it represents a mechanism for "regenerating" that which has been lost.

It has become common to regard anosognosia and its associated phenomena not as specific patterns of behavior which are a direct function of brain lesions, but rather as general adjustment strategies triggered off by the catastrophic losses in function which accompany brain dysfunction. That is, the emphasis has been put upon the symptom as a mode of response of a disabled person to social and personal demands. A study by Jaffe and Slote

(1958) reinforces this perspective. They attempted to demonstrate the "interpersonal, defensive quality of anosognosia". Apparently, one of the factors which stimulated their undertaking was the notation in Weinstein and Kahn's book (1955) that a patient who denied the existence of a paralysis while communicating with doctors would admit it when talking with her mother. The specific design of their work was intended to evaluate the degree to which a patient's denial of the severity of his illness would be influenced by the interpersonal role of the person with whom he was communicating. Ten patients were evaluated, most of whom had some type of brain pathology. Each was interviewed by two different physicians. One physician systematically phrased his questions in a manner which would encourage a minimizing and denial of symptoms; and the other attempted to elicit a grave exaggerated description. Analysis of patient responses to these two conditions indicated that there was a significant difference which was in the direction encouraged by the interviewer. That is, degree of denial of body incapacitation was altered by the examiner's attitude.

Ullman, et al. (1960) considered the interplay of structural and motivational variables in anosognosia. During one phase of the project they interviewed patients who had had strokes and who manifested denial of the hemiplegia. An attempt was made by questioning both the patients and their relatives to determine what events might have contributed to the denial syndrome. It was observed that anosognosia always occurred in a context of diffuse brain dysfunction which seemed to produce a concrete attitude toward body sensations (particularly those from the disabled body sector), such that they were interpreted without reference to a social context. Thus, if an impaired limb because of its decreased sensitivity felt different or detached it would be literally perceived as not constituting a part of the self, especially if there were predisposing personality needs for such denial.

A second phase of this project explored the possibility that many patients who do not develop overt anosognosia actually have transitory anosognosic-like experiences which they are able to correct and master. Thirty-four patients were studied who had had strokes but who did not manifest any apparent denial of their impaired body members. They were asked to respond to a questionnaire which was designed to evaluate their body experiences following the onset of hemiplegia. The questionnaire contained such questions as the following:

At the time you became ill, tell me in detail the very first thing you noticed about your right/left arm/leg.

Did your arm/leg ever feel as if it were dead?

Did your arm/leg ever feel as if it were not part of your body?

Fifteen of the 34 patients reported transitory reactions similar to those characteristic of patients with anosognosia. For example, they made such remarks as:

"It felt like I don't have a right side at all."

"At first it felt as if it wasn't my arm—as if it was out in the air."

"I didn't even know I had it. I would go to sleep at night and I couldn't find it."

It is suggested by such data that the anosognosic reaction may represent the extreme form of a species of fantasies about disabled body sectors occurring normally in persons with brain dysfunction.

Studies of Hemiplegia

Although anosognosia has absorbed the major interest of those studying body image alterations produced by brain pathology, there has also been work dealing with other types of alterations. Shontz (1956) examined several varieties of body-concept disturbances in patients with hemiplegia. His subjects included 16 persons with cerebral lesions in the dominant hemisphere; 16 with lesions in the non-dominant hemisphere; 16 with a chronic physical illness other than hemiplegia; and 16 normal subjects without illness. Two techniques were employed to get at body concept disturbance. One was termed the Hemiplegia Research Instrument and was derived from a section of the Eisenson Examination for Aphasia. It involved asking the subject to point to six different parts [1] of his body (eye, foot, ear, shoulder, leg, elbow) and also to differentiate the right and left locations of four body areas. Signs of body concept disturbance were scored if the subject pointed only to parts of one side of the body; if he designated his elbow in a unilateral rather than bilateral manner (e.g., tried to point to right elbow with right hand); or if he misidentified body parts or their right-left locations. The second technique for evaluation of body concept was the Draw-A-Person test. Disturbance was scored if certain major areas of the figure were omitted (head, trunk, arm, legs) or if the drawing was so primitive as to be grossly unrecognizable. The hemiplegia group with dominant hemisphere lesions evidenced significantly more body concept deviation in the body parts identification task than did any of the other three groups. But there were no real differences among the other groups in this respect. The Draw-A-Person test did not reveal any significant body concept differentiations between the hemiplegic and the control subjects. Incidentally, Prater (1950) in an earlier study also failed to find figure drawing differences between hemiplegics and non-hemiplegics. But overall, Shontz interpreted his results to mean that in hemiplegics with dominant hemisphere lesions there is a "body-concept aphasia" which has a negative effect upon cognitive functions related to "body senses".

[1] Weinstein (1964) used a similar procedure for evaluating body image function in 75 cases with various traumatic brain wounds; and found the brain damage had caused considerable disturbance in the body scheme. Also those who were severely aphasic showed more deficit than those with limited aphasia in naming parts of the body but not in naming inanimate objects.

Fink and Shontz (1960) devised an original method for appraising body image disturbance in a group of 12 right and 12 left hemiplegics and in a non-hemiplegic group of 16 patients with chronic disabling symptoms (e.g., hip fracture, arthritis, amputation). They also included a control group of 24 physically healthy individuals. Their interest was in determining how well the individual could represent in an external spatial framework certain spatial experiences which occurred on the surface of his own body. Thus, each subject was asked to adjust the distance between two visually perceived points so as to equal the distance between two points simultaneously touched on his body by means of calipers. Stimulus sizes of eight, 12, and 18 inches were used among 18 different body regions. A control task was introduced which presented the subject with *visual* caliper settings which he then reproduced in the same fashion as he had the distances on his own body. On this control task no differences were found among the various experimental groups. However, there were significant differences with respect to the measure based on translation of body experience. The physically healthy group was characterized by the smallest and the hemiplegics by the largest degree of error. The non-hemiplegic patients fell in between these two groups. There were also significant differences among the groups relative to the degree of over vs. underestimation of the body stimuli. It was found that the physically healthy group overestimated the stimulus; while the other two groups tended to underestimate it—with the hemiplegic group being most extreme in such underestimation. This suggested that a progressive constriction or shrinking of the body image accompanied increasing disablement. The results were considered to demonstrate that chronic disease results in body image disturbance even when there is no obvious cerebral damage present. However, the fact that the hemiplegic group displayed greater error and constriction than the non-hemiplegic chronically ill group in interpreting the body stimuli, suggested that brain dysfunction may result in a significant increment of body image disturbance beyond that due to peripheral body disablement itself. Fink and Shontz summarized their conclusions as follows (p. 240): "The body-image phenomenon may, therefore, be expected to be altered by either central or peripheral changes in the overall system. Disturbance in the body-image may result from either direct damage to the central mechanism or damage to any of the peripheral sources of information. Conceivably, this latter type of damage results in a weakening, or eventual loss, of central associative connections; and this weakening becomes manifested in a reduction in stability of judgment about distances between body parts."

Birch, Proctor, and Bortner (1961A, B) approached the question of body scheme distortion in hemiplegics via their ability to locate points touched on their body surface. The sample studied consisted of 31 patients with cerebral vascular accidents (15 right hemiplegics, 16 left hemiplegics) and 14 controls consisting of three normal subjects and 11 patients with peripheral motor dysfunctions (e.g., arthritics). A series of touch stimuli were applied to various places on the lower limbs. Some were applied while the subject was blind-folded and some while he was not. In the non-blindfold condition an opaque screen prevented him from seeing where the stimulus had been applied, but he could look at the limb while later making his decision about the point of application. The data which were obtained indicated that the hemiplegics were in general significantly less accurate in their localizations than the con-trols under both blindfold and non-blindfold conditions. The difference was highly significant when the disabled limb was touched and at a borderline level when the non-affected limb was involved. The authors interpreted the localization difficulties of the hemiplegics as indicative of a change (decline) in the body scheme.

A sensori-tonic approach to body perception in the hemiplegic is exemplified in the work of Barton (1964). He compared 12 right hemiplegic brain-injured male patients and 12 non-hemiplegic brain-injured male patients. A variety of tests were administered. Several were concerned with estimation of body size, judgment of the position of one's body in space, ability to discriminate and recognize body areas, and the effects of body tilt upon the position of the apparent vertical. There were also a number of perceptual tests. It had been anticipated by Barton that the hemiplegic group would be more regressed than the non-hemiplegic brain-injured sample because of the saliency of body associated with the paralysis and also the aphasia linked with right hemiplegia. Several lines of evidence did, indeed, indicate that the hemiplegics experienced their bodies in a more primitivized manner than the non-hemiplegic patients. Their perception of the median plane, of the position of the vertical during body tilt, and of their own body position during tilt conformed to patterns observed in previous sensori-tonic research to be characteristic of the young and the regressed (e.g., schizophrenics). With reference to the findings involving perception of the median plane and the vertical, Birch, et al. (1960A, B) found similar regressed response patterns in hemiplegics. The prediction had been made that paralyzed parts of the body would be experienced as relatively larger than corresponding non-paralyzed parts because the boundary of the former would presumably be less definite than the boundary of the latter. It will be recalled that sensori-tonic theory concerning the relationship between boundary definiteness and size perception was reviewed in an earlier portion of this chapter. As predicted, Barton was able to show a significant trend for the hemiplegic to judge his paralyzed arm as longer than the non-paralyzed one. However, chance results were obtained with reference to a comparison of size estimates of the shoulder on the paralyzed side with the estimates of shoulder size on the other side. It was concluded that the basic trends in the data supported the proposition that the hemiplegics perceived and utilized body cues in a more primitive fashion than the non-hemiplegics.

Brain Damage and Drawings

During the course of a psychotherapy relationship Sarvis (1960) intensively followed for several years the development of a six-year-old boy with temporal lobe damage. She found that body image themes were extremely prominent in his stream of thought and fantasy. The dysfunction associated with his brain damage seemed to signal to him the momentary possibility of complete body destruction. His drawings and play constructions suggested that it was a struggle for him to establish firm body image boundaries between himself and the outer world. He pictured his body as a series of rooms with a control box in the head region that represented his brain pathology. He visualized his disease (which he personified as Mr. Cephalitis) as lurking within his body; and he concerned himself with how to keep it confined and contained ("in jail"). As he grew older and compensated for some of the deficits, his drawings and productions manifested a significant decline in signs of body image disturbance.

Robert Cohn devoted an entire book (1960) to an evaluation of what he calls "person symbol" alterations in patients with various types of brain damage and brain dysfunction. He considers that the drawing of a human figure may be used to sample the patient's concept or mode of representation of a person. He assumes that an individual's drawing may be a blend of both his general concept of a person and his more specific image of his own body. His clinically oriented study involved an analysis of figure drawing distortions in a wide range of neurological patients (e.g., with brain lesions, convulsive disorders, alcoholic encephalopathy) who had been carefully examined with standard neurological tests, EEG, and language tests. In numerous instances he found correlations between brain dysfunction and figure drawing distortions. Some of his observations with regard to asymmetries in the drawings were particularly interesting. He indicated that a disabled body part (e.g., arm) was usually represented in the figure drawing by omission or perserverative delineation on the corresponding side. In instances of hemianopsia resulting from brain lesions, the asymmetry of depiction was in the disturbed field of vision and therefore usually projected on the side opposite to that of the patient's peripheral symptom. There were clear tendencies for figure drawing representations to deteriorate in quality during the early phases of grave brain injury but also to manifest increased integration when clinical improvement occurred. However, it was cautioned by Cohn that the figure drawing not infrequently fails to be directly representational of the body difficulties resulting from brain damage.

Actually, the few reported empirical attempts to use the figure drawing for detecting the effects of brain damage have given mixed results. Weinstein, Johnson, and Guerra (1963) asked judges to differentiate the pre-temporal lobe surgery drawings of 12 epileptics from those of 12 schizophrenics and also the post-temporal lobe surgery drawings of the 12 epileptics from those of the schizophrenic sample. There was only chance success in making such distinctions. Riklan, Zahn, and Diller (1962) appraised the pre- and post-surgery (chemosurgery of basal ganglia) drawings of 47 Parkinsonian patients. Two test-retest control groups (N = 11, N = 7) of Parkinsonian patients who did not undergo surgery were also included. The results indicated a long-term trend for the drawings of those who had had surgery to decline in terms of how well they conveyed human qualities. It was considered that the damage done to the basal ganglia had produced a decline in body image integration. Alexander (1963) found few differences between the figure drawings of children with central nervous system damage (some form of encephalopathy) and those of normal children or children with behavior disorders (apparently with no organic basis).

NEUROSIS AND PSYCHOSIS

Introduction

The reports of neurotic and psychotic patients have constituted one of the richest sources of material about body image phenomena.[2] This has been due partially to the dramatic alterations in body feeling that often accompany personality disorganization. It is also a function of the fact that disturbed individuals who are in psychotherapeutic treatment are often motivated to describe body experiences which would normally be considered private and therefore remain unverbalized. There are a myriad of unusual body image distortions that have been described as occurring in the course of neurotic or psychotic disturbance. These range from depersonalization and unrealistic body size valuations to denial of one's body parts and experiencing sensations of body deterioration. Breuer and Freud (1936) were among the first to devote systematic attention to the symbolic values which may be ascribed to various body areas and to point out that these values may become vehicles for expressing psychopathology. For example, in their work with conversion hysterics they arrived at the formulation that a body part rendered non-functional by a conversion symptom is typically one to which unconscious sexual significance had been assigned and the incapacitation of the part represents an attempt to block the expression of sexual wishes. Since this early work the psychoanalytic group has continued to be in the forefront of those interested in the interrelationships of body image and personality pathology.

---

[2] Brown (1959) has also reviewed a number of significant body image phenomena related to neurosis and psychosis which will be described in this section.

A long line of successors from Freud to the present have directed attention to such interrelationships (e.g., Jung, Abraham, Ferenczi, Schilder,
Fenichel, Reich, Hoffer, and Federn). Many of their contributions in this
area have already been discussed in a previous publication (Fisher and
Cleveland, 1968). One may broadly conceptualize the body image questions
which they raised that are pertinent to matters of psychopathology as being
of the following order:

1. Are body image variables important in the process of ego formation;
and, if so, what kinds of body image deficiencies are most likely to produce
ego instability?

2. What conditions affect the developing individual's ability to establish
firm or differentiating body image boundaries and how significant is such
differentiation for later maturity?

3. How do body image attitudes affect the translation of repressed
affects and fantasies into body sensations and body dysfunctions?

4. What body image factors may produce disturbance in the individual's
ability to adopt a consistent sex role and to be sexually expressive?

5. Under conditions of severe regression how do body image distortions
influence misinterpretations of the outside world?

As one peruses pertinent psychoanalytic publications of recent years, it is
apparent that they continue to be concerned with the same fundamental
questions. A survey of such publications will now be presented.

Felix Deutsch has, in the original Freudian tradition, maintained a long-
standing interest in conversion hysteria. In the course of psychoanalytic
therapy with conversion patients he has sought to determine how they assign
symbolic meanings to their bodies and how this symbolization process affects
the channeling of body excitation (1952). He has also carefully reviewed
Freud's original work in this area; and notes that Freud regarded conversion
as a "regression of libido" to a body part which results in that part becoming
unusually erogenized. He refers to Freud's view that the erogenized parts
(p. 36) "take on the functions of genitals, a fact which leads to disturbances in
their function". His own observations led him to conclude that a conversion
symptom is only an extreme manifestation of a continual process which
occurs in every person of assigning values and significances to the various
sectors of one's body. A rather elaborate theory has been developed by him as
to how the individual attaches symbolic meanings to his body. He suggests
that a newborn child recognizes the existence of only his own body. Everything he perceives seems to be a part of him. However, he soon discovers that
what he considers to be part of himself (e.g., mother) can be lost for varying
periods of time. What he thought was part of his own body disappears and he
is left with a sense of body loss. This, indicates Deutsch, results in persistent
wishes to restore the body's losses by regaining body possession of important
outside objects. Such objects are linked with various body regions in terms of
memories of the roles they played in arousing or placating sensations in those

regions. He designates this mode of linkage as "symbolization".[3] He states further that conversion occurs when at some point the individual suffers an object loss which is so serious that he has to "retroject" in fantasy important substitute objects ("lost" early in life from his body). Presumably, in the course of such "retrojection" body sensations and body events originally associated with the retrojected object may be aroused and result in the pathological physiological disturbances which are labeled as conversion symptoms. Deutsch states that the conversion (p. 77) "symptom is the protective device against an impending loss of the object which has been retrieved through retrojection and which rests symbolized in the body, where it maintains the body's unity."

Szasz (1961) views the hysterical symptom as an "iconic sign", a mode of communication between a sufferer and another person. He hypothesizes that the individual is particularly likely to use his body as a means for communicating things which cannot be transmitted via ordinary channels. He refers to the "body language" as a "protolanguage". The body language characteristic of the conversion hysteric is thought to focus upon such messages as:

"Feel sorry for me."

"Take care of me."

"I am suffering and so you should do something for me."

Szasz pictures many varieties of body complaints, sensations and pains as primarily serving communication functions.

Phyllis Greenacre devoted a good deal of attention to body image variables underlying behavioral disturbance. She speculated on the basis of her clinical work (1955, 1958A, B) that early body experiences, body rhythms, and modes of body exploration are basic to the individual's sense of identity. She proposes that an individual's images of his face and genitals are particularly fundamental to his body scheme and that distortions in these images enhance vulnerability to later disturbance. In one study (1958A) she illustrated this point by citing the difficulties encountered by a girl with a genital defect (absence of vaginal opening) in establishing a meaningful body image and identity. So disturbed was this outwardly attractive girl about her image that she developed a severe phobia of mirrors. Greenacre (1958B) proposes too that a person's patterns of thinking and verbal expression may be influenced by body image models. For example, she suggests that he may impose the same degree of inhibition upon his thinking as he associates with the functioning of his body sphincters.

In this vein, a paper by Keiser (1958) should be cited which attributes difficulties in learning and abstract reasoning to body image distortions. He reports that in several patients who had outstanding problems in learning and

---

[3] A similar theory concerning the function of the body image and its role in symptomatology has been proposed by Fliess (1961).

abstracting there was an unusual lack of knowledge about, and even denial of, body openings, particularly the vagina and anus. The patients' needs to ignore the existence of their orifices seemed to be due to anxiety about being invaded, penetrated, and disrupted. Keiser indicates that their denial was facilitated by the fact that such body orifices are not easily available for direct visible inspection. He points out that acceptance of the existence of certain body orifices which are not readily visually apparent requires acceptance of certain presumptive data acquired by description and by deduction. It is his theory that when an individual fears to integrate the concept of body orifices into his body scheme this results in a disturbed and fragmented body image. Furthermore, he states (p. 630), "This failure to accept bodily parts that can be known only by deduction was a prototype for the disturbance in aspects of thinking that required the formulation of logical conclusions and the use of abstract thinking." Pertinent to this matter, is the fact that Reiff (1963) empirically evaluated the hypothesis that ability to abstract is related to the state of the body image. She studied 31 male subjects who had been charged with crimes and who had been referred for psychiatric evaluation. Their degree of body image disturbance was measured by rating various aspects of human figure drawings they had produced. The Similarities and Block Design subscales of the Wechsler Adult Intelligence scale were used to evaluate verbal and visual-perceptive abstraction ability. Although there were a few promising trends in the predicted direction, no consistent relationship could be established between an overall measure of body image disturbance and the indexes of ability to abstract. It is true that one specific sub-measure of the body image score which was concerned with the degree of realism of the size and proportions of the figure drawings did correlate significantly in the expected direction with ability to abstract verbally. As an additional phase of the study, the Holt (1956) measure of ability to regulate and control primary process fantasy was obtained from Rorschach responses which had been elicited from the subjects. When this measure was correlated with the figure drawing index of body image integration, it was shown that the greater the individual's ability to deal effectively with primary process fantasy the less disturbed was his body image. The overall results are actually difficult to interpret; and clarification of the question whether disturbance in the body image and ability to abstract are related awaits further investigation.

Fetishism and Transvestism

Greenacre (1953) has applied body image concepts to an analysis of fetishism. Her definition of fetishism is as follows (p. 79): "the obligatory use of some non-genital object as part of the sex act without which gratification cannot be obtained". She notes that it very rarely occurs in women. She states that the fetish may be some other body part or an article of clothing or, in fact, any object. In illustration, she cites the following as frequently chosen objects: foot, shoe, corset, and rubber or leather goods with ties and lacings. The fetishist requires the presence of such objects in order to achieve sexual excitement. Greenacre indicates that Freud viewed fetishism as a defense against "castration anxiety" and that he regarded the fetish as a way of symbolically endowing the woman (mother) with a phallus and thus denying the castration threat implicit in observing that she lacks a penis. Greenacre's own clinical analysis of patients with fetishistic symptoms led her to conclude that they are unusually anxious about sustaining body damage. She sees their symptoms primarily as manifestations of body image disturbance. As she reconstructs it, the early existence (18 months) of the fetishist is typically marked by gross disrupting fluctuations in body image due to such variables as erratic handling by the mother and repeated sudden shifts in body sensation arising from severe illness or massive over or understimulation of the body. She adds that such disturbing body image experiences are often reinforced later (two–four years of age) by witnessing unusual events which vividly dramatize body injury or mutilation (e.g., an operation, mutilating death, abortion). She indicates that the intense body insecurity which ensues from such conditions is even further increased by the fact that the fetishist (almost invariably male) is usually characterized by a childhood in which there is very close contact with a primary woman figure whose body is taken as an identification model and therefore instigates confused bisexual fantasies. The fetish is theorized to represent a means for stabilizing the body image in the face of stresses related to functioning as a phallic male. Apropos of this point, Greenacre says (p. 96): "The support is attained through the use of the fetish; which is tangible, visible, generally inanimate, unchanging in size, also not readily destroyed. It offsets the identification with the partner, and 'pegs' the genital functioning by furnishing this external and material symbol of the phallus to be reintrojected and reaffirm the genital integrity of the fetishist." In a later paper (1955) she referred to the fetish as a (p. 188) "safeguard against the anxiety due to feelings of change of body size, resulting primarily from body-phallus problems and to dissolution anxieties which may have further become attached to fear of the orgasm."

To digress for a moment, it is noteworthy that some observers have regarded the behavior of the male transvestite who wears woman's clothing as analogous to that of the fetishist. Friedemann (1966) described transvestism as closer to fetishism than any other sexual perversion; and Benjamin (1954) regarded it as a special form of fetishism. Friedemann (1966) states (p. 277), "the transvestite treats female garments and underwear as a fetish, with the difference that this fetish becomes a part of himself, that he feels in the fetish as if in a cocoon". Friedemann and others (e.g., Greenson, 1966; Lewis, 1963; and Yazmajian, 1966) conceive of the typical transvestite as one who has not been able to establish a clear body concept separate from that of mother's and who struggles with feelings of body disintegration. The donning of woman's clothing is interpreted as a way of simultaneously being self and mother. Only in this way can a tolerable body concept be maintained. This formulation differs from the more conventional psychoanalytic theory regarding transvestism. As suggested by Freud and others (e.g., Fenichel, 1945; Peabody, Rowe, and Wall, 1953), the transvestite is paradoxically reassuring himself that the female does not lack a penis. That is, by dressing up as a woman he acts out the reassuring fantasy that all women, like himself, possess a penis; and therefore he has no need to fear the genital mutilation which he assumes has caused the loss of the penis in women.[4]

Several of the speculations just cited regarding the disturbed body image of the transvestite have been explored empirically, at least initially, by Goldfarb (1963). He studied 60 male transvestites, 26 normal males, and 29 normal females who were equated for age, education, and occupational level. They were asked to rate their bodies (e.g., My Body), aspects of self (e.g., The Kind of Person I am), their parents and some neutral concepts on Osgood (Osgood, et al., 1957) semantic differential continua. They also responded to Thematic Apperception test pictures, scales from the Guilford-Zimmerman Temperament Survey, and a personal history questionnaire. It was found that the transvestite's body concept, as measured by the self ratings, differed significantly from that of the male's and also the female's. The normal males particularly perceived their own bodies as more rugged than did the transvestites; but the normal females experienced their bodies as softer and less rugged than the transvestites. The transvestite also showed a larger discrepancy than the normal male in the way he rated his self concept as compared to his body. Goldfarb noted further (pp. 125–126), "When the identification pattern of the transvestites was evaluated, the evidence indicated that in terms of the body-image, the transvestites did not identify with either parent as closely as normal males. . . . It appears that the transvestites were less able than normal males to incorporate major aspects of either parent into their identity; but of the aspects which have been accumulated, the body-image of mother appears to predominate." It is of interest that actual homosexual relationships were not found to characterize the transvestites to a prominent degree. Goldfarb interpreted his total findings as indicating that the transvestite does have unusual anxiety about his body and that his "dressing up" represents a way of denying this anxiety and stabilizing his body image.

Returning to the matter of fetish behavior, it was reported by Buxbaum (1960) that she had worked with two children who treated their own hair as a kind of fetish and who had had traumatic body image experiences similar

---

[4] Devereux (1958) asserted that the problem of male anxiety about the absence of the penis in the woman occurs in many cultures. He illustrated the point by descriptions of techniques used in some African cultures to give the female genitalia a more masculine appearance.

to those considered by Greenacre to be typical of fetishists. They pulled their hair out and used it to tickle themselves and even swallowed it. Buxbaum considered the hair pulling to represent not only a form of aggression by the patient against the self but also an indirect way of relieving loneliness by stimulation which reminds himself that he exists by making himself feel. Similar modified versions of fetish behavior have been described by Green-acre (1953). She provided clinical material concerning several patients with disturbed body concepts who sought to control their disturbance by such devices as the ritualistic use of drugs and medicinal substances and the wearing of "lucky stones" or amulets. These patients were considered to have had early experiences marked by the same types of body image trauma which presumably typify the overt fetishist. However, their modes of body reassur-ance took less flamboyant and only quasi-fetish forms. These observations and those of Buxbaum suggest that the need for bolstering one's body image may result in compensatory forms of behavior which range in severity from overt fetishism to moderate quasi-fetish behavior and even to fetish-like habits which are accepted as normal. Winnicott (1953) and Wulff (1946) have both in their own fashion pointed out that most children pass through a phase (beginning somewhere between four to 12 months of age) in which they attach extreme importance to an object (e.g., blanket, doll, teddy bear) they carry about and have particular need of at times of anxiety, or when going to sleep. Wulf regards the child's dependence on such an object as an early example of fetish-like behavior. But Winnicott sees it as a more normal phenomenon which is part of the process of learning to distinguish "me" from "not-me". He labels the object to which the child is attached as a "transitional object". He feels that it represents to the child a part of himself and yet also a posses-sion to which he gradually attributes "not-me" qualities as he learns what is self and not self. It presumably provides an intermediate experience which cushions the growing obligation to set clear boundaries between what is inner and outer.

A number of writers have commented on the frequency with which fetish behavior is apparently encouraged by a mother who overwhelms her child and allows him no identity of his own (e.g., Sperling, 1963; Parkin, 1963; Meyer, 1964). She seems to allow him no sense of having a body that is delimited from hers. The fetish provides a partial means for retaining an identity with mother and yet gaining some distance from her. Sperling (1963) studied a child who manifested fetish-like behavior and concluded that the mother encouraged it in several ways. She described the mother as resisting separation or differentiation from her child and encouraging attachment to a fetish object which she actually supplied for him. In giving him the fetish object, the mother was depicted as unconsciously hoping to conceal her wish that he remain dependent upon her, but at the same time urging him into a dependent relation with an object. Sperling added (p. 381), "The fetish has the double function of making it possible for mother and child to separate in reality by magically undoing this separation. Thus the fetish enables both mother and child to maintain a facade of normality. Gratifications not obtainable from the mother are gained from the fetish."

Hypochondriasis

For centuries there has been curiosity about a category of distorted body experience which has been labeled "hypochondriasis". This term refers to an unreasonable feeling that one is sick. It may involve perception of a completely healthy body area as impaired or it may represent the exaggeration of minor impairment so as to make it appear to be of major proportions. Kenyon (1965) and Ladee (1966) have provided extensive reviews of the evolution of the concept. It is apparent from these reviews that hypochondriasis occurs widely in the world; may involve any area of the body; does not restrict itself to any particular psychiatric diagnostic category; and has not been empirically demonstrated to be associated with a particular personality pattern.

Many theoretical statements have been issued concerning the etiology and significance of hypochondriasis. It was a stimulating but puzzling topic to Freud (1914). He emphasized the role of withdrawal of libido from objects and its concentration on organs of one's own body. This presumably led to an unconscious genitalization of such organs and they could provide symbolic and indirect forms of gratification for various fantasies. Freud (and Ferenczi) considered the "hypercathected" organ to be particularly a means of symbolically expressing and denying anal erotic wishes. However, in general, he was dissatisfied with his formulations concerning the nature of hypochondriasis.

Grayden (1958) has summarized well a number of current positions regarding hypochondriasis. He points out that the orthodox psychoanalytic position stresses three variables as having etiological importance: libidinal frustration, narcissistic withdrawal, and guilt feelings. That is, presumably when satisfaction cannot, for some reason, be gained from the usual libidinal objects in the environment, the individual reinvests the libido in himself. This results in a hyper-narcissistic state in which the prominence and importance of one's own body is intensified. At the same time, since the impulses withdrawn from external objects are to some degree of a hostile and sadistic character, they represent, when turned back upon self, a form of self attack. They cause pain and suffering, but also may serve an important guilt relieving function. Hypochondriasis is, from this viewpoint, a state of magnified narcissism which is a reaction to frustration and also a form of self attack which assuages guilt. Alexander (1948) stated a similar view as follows concerning persons with hypochondriacal symptoms (pp. 232–233):

When frustrated in their demands for admiration by others, they themselves give their bodies all the attention they previously received. . . . Frustration also mobilizes competitive hostile impulses which have been dormant as long as they received love and attention. . . . These hostile impulses revive earlier competitive conflicts of family life, oedipal guilt, and sibling rivalry. This guilt creates a need for suffering. The hypochondriacal symptom satisfies both needs; the patient gives love and attention to her own body and at the same time relieves her guilt by suffering.

Related analytic positions have been expressed by Masserman (1946), Fenichel (1945) and many others. It should be added that the hypochondriacal anxiety experienced with reference to given organs has often been interpreted by analysts as representing castration anxiety (Fenichel, 1945; Deutsch and Murphy, 1955). One should note too that Horney (1945) placed special importance upon the self punishing aspects of the hypochondriacal experience.

Cameron (1947) sketched a view somewhat different from the usual psychoanalytic formulation. He portrayed hypochondriasis primarily as a means for displacing inadequacy from oneself to one's body. It presumably provides a means for avoiding responsibility and denying failure. Cameron also suggested that it could be utilized to control others—to manipulate them into acceding to one's expectations and demands. Further, he cites instances in which it may serve paradoxically as a way for an individual to integrate and focus his energies. Body preoccupation can become a distorted vehicle for channeled self expression.

Schilder's (1935) thoughts concerning hypochondriasis are of interest. He agrees with the Freudian formulation which ascribes it to an increase of narcissistic libido focused on an organ. He was especially impressed with the idea that the affected organ is unconsciously genitalized and representative of a strongly denied wish. But at the same time that its genitalization provides indirect self gratification, it is also a source of anxiety because it represents that which is forbidden. Schilder says, in this respect, that (p. 142) "Hypochondria is a fight against narcissistic libido; the individual defends himself against the libidinous overtension of the hypochondriac organ; he tries to isolate the diseased organ, to treat it like a foreign body in the body-image." As was true of Freud, Schilder stressed that once libido and attention had been focused upon a body area, physiological changes (e.g., vasomotor) are incited in it which in turn attract more of the individual's attention.

Ladee (1966) has written an entire book which minutely scrutinizes the literature dealing with hypochondriasis. One cannot but be impressed with the amount of thought and observation which has been devoted to this phenomenon. Ladee describes a large array of past speculations about the role of the body image in hypochondriacal behavior. One finds that such speculations have been generally vague and rarely presented in an empirically testable form. Illustratively, there are assertions that the hypochondriacal individual is using his body to express conflicts; to mobilize interest and help from others; to symbolize his sense of vulnerability in a threatening world; to experience life only through his body.

Controlled attempts to investigate the variables underlying hypochondriasis have been few. This is true despite the fact that the Minnesota Multiphasic Test (MMPI), which is one of the most widely used "paper-and-pencil" tests, contains an Hypochondriasis scale. This scale was developed by assembling items which would differentiate psychiatric patients with predominant hypochondriacal complaints from normals and neurotics without serious hypochondriacal complaints. A variety of correlates of the Hypochondriasis score have been reported; and they may be found summarized in a paper by Kenyon (1964). These correlates have neither been consistent nor particularly revealing. One does not detect sensible continuity in the disparate results published.

There are, nevertheless, several studies which should be particularly mentioned because they represent unusually direct and carefully designed approaches to the significance of the Hypochondriasis scale. One was carried out by Sweetland (1948). He demonstrated that when hypnosis is used to create an hypochondriacal state it resulted in an MMPI Hypochondriasis score similar to that found in patients with hypochondriacal symptoms. Endicott and Endicott (1963) were able to establish that the MMPI Hypochondriasis score successfully correlated in a psychiatric population with degree of somatic concern, as defined by interview ratings. Indices of somatic concern derived from the Rorschach and TAT which were used also correlated with the somatic concern ratings. Disappointing results were obtained by Poppelstone [5] and Van Every (1963) when they contrasted the MMPI Hypochondriasis scores of a group of prisoners with marked hypochondriacal symptoms and a group with very positive attitudes toward their bodies. No MMPI differences between the groups could be detected. The Rorschach protocols of the hypochondriacal prisoners contained significantly more references to internal anatomy and organic deterioration than did those of the other prisoner sample. Finally, negative results were obtained by Greenfield and Roessler (1958) who found that subjects with high Hypochondriasis scores did not visit a physician any more often than those with low scores.

There is a study by Grayden (1958) which is outstanding in that it proposed, on the basis of a literature survey, a complex hypothesis concerning the trait and attitudinal correlates of an hypochondriacal orientation and sought to test it empirically. This study focused on Alexander's (1948) theory that neurotic hypochondriasis grows out of a dynamic constellation in which

[5] Poppelstone (1963) has formulated the concept of the "exoskeletal defense" which involves "armoring" oneself by strengthening the body, emphasizing the sexuality of the body and equipping the body with signs of invulnerability (e.g., amulets, tattoos). He has work in process which seeks to measure the degree of "exoskeletal defense" in various kinds of groups.

an individual feels rejected by others; turns compensatorily to bestow upon his own body the outside interest he has lost; and at the same time is disturbed by newly mobilized, angry, competitive impulses which create a need to suffer. The individual is presumed to find in the hypochondriacal symptom a means for focusing attention upon his body and also suffering and relieving guilt. Grayden reasoned that if this formulation were correct, there should be a significant positive association between hypochondriasis and feelings of being unloved, narcissism, and guilt feelings. The subjects for the experiment consisted of 15 neurotics with hypochondriacal complaints (and also elevated MMPI Hypochondriasis scores), six neurotics without such complaints, and nine normal subjects. All groups were equated for sex, age, socio-economic status, and intelligence. One of the techniques for measuring the trait and attitudinal variables (viz., feeling unloved, narcissism, guilt) was semi-projective. It involved sorting (Q sort) a series of 60 statements in terms of how applicable they appeared to be to a woman depicted in a Thematic Apperception picture (8GF). The statements concerned qualities pertinent to the trait-attitudinal parameters; and it was assumed that the manner in which they were ascribed to the TAT figure represented a projection of self attributes. In addition, several cartoons (viz., Sibling Rivalry, Narcissistic Love Object, Guilt Feelings) from the Blacky Pictures series (Blum, 1949) were used to elicit stories and other responses which could be scored in relation to the three prime trait-attitudinal parameters mentioned above.

The data collected indicated that, as defined by the Q-sort task, the hypochondriacal subjects had significantly higher feelings of not being loved and guilt than the non-hypochondriacal subjects. Narcissism differences were negligible. As for the Blacky test results, they indicated a significant association between hypochondriasis and selective concern about Narcissism and Guilt Feelings. While the findings for the sorting procedure and the Blacky test were not completely congruent, it was considered that they collectively gave good support to Alexander's theory concerning the etiology of hypochondriasis. Since Alexander's theory is a variant of one commonly accepted in psychoanalytic circles, the findings encourage further application of a psychoanalytic framework to understanding the hypochondriacal symptom. It would be profitable to cross-validate and extend Grayden's results; and this should be given priority by those who become involved with this area of work.

Body Anxiety and Gross Body Image Distortion

The vicissitudes of vague or inadequate body image integration have been taken up from numerous perspectives in the psychoanalytic literature. Spiegel (1959) has suggested that one's identity or self rests upon organized body perceptions which provide a framework for interpreting events. He theorizes that unless this organization process has been adequate the individual's sense of identity is easily vulnerable to stress. He clarifies this view by describing patients whose vague body concepts were accompanied by such symptoms as fear of being incorporated by others, anxiety about loss of body substance, and sensations of depersonalization. One point he particularly underscores is the degree to which a weak body image is strained by experiences that alternately make a body region part of the self and not part of the self. He notes, for example, that during masturbation the individual is exposed to such experiences insofar as he simultaneously treats his genitals as part of himself and also as an object from which satisfaction is channeled toward the self. Brodsky (1959) describes several patients in whom unusual fears concerning death seemed to be linked with previous events which had emphasized the fragility, passivity, and vulnerability of their bodies. In these cases the sense of body fragility was traced particularly to parental overconcern about anal functions which was used to control and infantilize. Annie Reich (1950) discussed a female patient who had marked feelings of body deformity and "castration" which she expressed by exhibiting herself in various ridiculed roles. What was of special import was that the patient had learned how to "sublimate" her sense of being ridiculous into skilful grotesque-comic acting which could actually be used to attack and satirize those toward whom she was hostile. Reich hypothesizes that grotesque-comic acting is, in general, a means of representing by deformation of one's own body what one would like to happen to one's adversaries.

Elkisch and Mahler (1959) present details of the psychoanalytic treatment of a seven-year-old psychotic child who regarded his own body as possessing machine-like attributes and who also reacted to various mechanical devices (e.g., telephone) as if they were sources of animistic influence over him. They indicate that he seemed to be flooded by "aggression-saturated" sensations which dominated his body image and which he defensively denied by projecting them outward upon the mechanical objects. In this way, overpowering unacceptable impulses could be (p. 223) "experienced as if the body were powered by more or less demoniacal, ego-alien mechanical forces . . .". The point was made that this process is analogous to that described by Tausk (1933) in a paper which postulated that the "influencing machine" which appears in schizophrenic delusions is a disguised and projected representation of unacceptable parts of the individual's own body. Linn (1958) described a female schizophrenic who felt that she was being influenced and controlled by a machine similar to the Tausk "influencing machine". He agreed with Tausk in considering the "machine" to be a symbolic representation of an unacceptable part of the patient's own body. Sachs (1957) published a case report of a seriously disturbed young boy (age five) with sensations of body destruction who also was strongly identified with machines and used them as projection targets. Relatedly, Niederland (1959) analyzed many of the bizarre delusions of body change which were described

by Schreber in his autobiographical account (Freud, 1911) of his schizophrenic breakdown. He has documented their similarity to strange body
image traumas imposed upon Schreber by his father who demanded that he
submit to a training program which involved wearing highly restrictive
mechanical appliances and engaging in taxing calisthenic exercises. Fox
(1957) provided an extended account of a patient who used photography as
a means of bolstering his body image. Unconsciously, the patient appeared to
view his camera as being part of his body. It was presumed that he used his
camera as an indirect way of looking at what was forbidden and also as a
substitute representation of areas of his body (e.g., penis) which he guiltily felt
should be denied and minimized.

Peto (1959) pictured a striking form of body image regression in certain
seriously disorganized types of patients involved in psychoanalytic therapy.
During the course of an analytic session a typical patient of this sort would
suddenly lose awareness of his body boundaries and begin to hallucinate that
he was fusing into an amorphous mass with the therapist. The fusion might
be phrased in terms of being absorbed via anal and genital body orifices; or
by intermingling of substance through the skin; or by mutually devouring
each other. The bizarre nature of these boundary dissolution experiences can
best be conveyed by illustrative quotations:

> Then she [patient] hallucinated the following: a gradual shrinking of her body,
> turning into a baby and being cuddled and held with infinite care by the analyst. In
> the hallucination the analyst's whole body softened up, gradually lost shape and
> became jelly-like or even liquid. Then the patient's minute body, which had softened
> up to the same extent, penetrated the analyst's body or merged with it. (p. 3.)
> . . . she [patient] began to feel a gradual enlargement of her limbs and her vulva.
> They were hers, yet they were not. . . . They continued growing and engulfed the
> analyst and the whole room. (p. 3.)

Peto indicates that the patients who manifested such body image regression
had displayed long standing disturbances in body schema organization. He
assumes that the regression permitted the reappearance of an early archaic
body image reflecting certain of the body experiences of the young infant.
Furthermore, he postulates that this archaic image represents a stage in
development in which thinking and perceiving are not translated into
symbols but rather into body image sensations and changes. He notes that
psychosis may produce a lasting regression to this level "where mental
functioning corresponds to cathectic changes in the body image" (p. 8).

Blumstein (1959) delineated a type of patient he has seen in analytic
therapy who unconsciously sees his body as worthless and insubstantial and
who apparently prepares in various ways to offer it as a sacrifice ("to be
devoured") to authority figures in order to placate them and win their favor.
This sort of patient is described as having very vague boundaries and as
recurrently experiencing gross shifts in patterns of body sensation (e.g.,

feelings of contracting and becoming small or of "evaporating" and being "consumed").

Rodrigue (1955) provided a detailed clinical account of a woman with blurred body image boundaries who perceived menstruation as signaling destruction of her body integrity and invasion by foreign objects.[6]

Depersonalization

Depersonalization has been a phenomenon of major interest to psychoanalytic observers. Dugas (as cited by Saperstein, 1949) was the first to use the term "depersonalization" and meant it to refer to a feeling of loss of ego. More and more it has come to refer to a state in which the individual regards himself, and particularly his body, as a foreign object. He is estranged from his own body and does not experience it as belonging to self. There are associated feelings of being without will and being like a machine. It is agreed that depersonalization may vary from a fleeting experience to a chronic one. Some have recognized that it occurs not only in the severely disturbed but also the normal. Saperstein (1949) underscores that when it is found in psychiatric patients it cuts across diagnostic categories and cannot be attributed to any one dynamic problem or conflict.

Jacobson (1959) has been particularly energetic in reviewing and appraising psychoanalytic formulations concerned with depersonalization. In her review of this phenomenon she notes:

Nunberg (1955) viewed it as a response to loss of love and as growing out of a "sudden transposition of the libido from the object to the ego".

Schilder (1935) stated that it occurs when the individual feels he cannot invest libido either in the outside world or his own body.

Oberndorf (1935) portrayed it as a defense mechanism for hiding something unacceptable from the ego and also as a way of "playing dead" like some animals do in the face of danger.

Blank (1956) described it as a defense against very intense feelings of deprivation, rage, and anxiety.

Fenichel (1945) referred to it as a means for repressing over-charged feelings, particularly as they find expression in body sensations.

Jacobson too notes that depersonalization may occur in both schizophrenics and neurotics and also transiently in normal persons. Based upon her observations of neurotic patients in treatment and also of political prisoners in Nazi Germany she has formulated her own theory of the mechanism basic to depersonalization. She proposes that it typically involves

---

[6] Weiss (1964), Ruddick (1961), and others have suggested that the fears characterizing the patient with agoraphobia (fear of open spaces) may partially express a sense of vulnerability related to the loss of boundaries.

an attempt to solve a "narcissistic conflict" or to mediate very opposing identifications. She indicates that when the individual is faced with having to identify with a degraded role which stands in contradiction to a more idealized "good" role he may respond by denying part or all of his body which is symbolic of the degraded role. This denial of self presumably manifests itself in feelings of depersonalization. To illustrate her point, Jacobson describes how political prisoners in Nazi Germany, who had been substantial citizens prior to their imprisonment but who were treated as criminals by their captors, would frequently react with depersonalization symptoms in their attempts to deny the criminal role assigned to them. Thus, she notes that they would awaken at night feeling that their face or limbs did not belong to them. One particularly interesting conjecture that she offers is that depersonalization in chronic schizophrenics represents a restitutive attempt to deny and disown the more regressed aspects of the self.

Stamm (1962) pointed out certain parallels to depersonalization in experiences associated with falling asleep and hypnagogic states. He speculated that it was most likely to occur in passive, oral-dependent persons when they encounter stresses which encourage giving up one's identity and attaching oneself to mother representations.

Sarlin (1962) conjectured that depersonalization was encouraged by an individual internalizing extreme conflicts between his parents which then prevent him from forming a unified identity of his own. That is, when the individual is pulled in opposite directions by the demands of his parents, he cannot synthesize a meaningful self representation and therefore he becomes vulnerable to experiencing himself and his body as weak, hazy, and even foreign in quality. This formulation obviously resembles that of Jacobson's concerning the role of opposing identifications in depersonalization.

It should be indicated that some observers have found depersonalization to be more common in women than in men (Ackner, 1954; Mayer-Gross, 1935).

Azima and Cramer-Azima (1956) reported in the course of a study of psychiatric patients subjected to sensory isolation that depersonalization was one of the common body image distortions elicited by this procedure. The nature of this depersonalization may be illustrated by quoting from the spontaneous verbalizations of one patient (p. 63):

> I feel I am not here. I am scared. I want to grab somebody and hold on. I am in another world . . . I don't feel real, as if I had two spirits. My hands are crossed but I don't feel them. I don't feel part of the world. I find myself in a different world. . . .

It was considered by Azima and Cramer-Azima that depersonalization of this sort and other serious body image alterations occurred mainly in patients who strongly repressed and introverted their aggressive feelings.

There are accounts in the literature dealing with depersonalization which suggest that fetish-like ("transitional") objects may play an unusually important role in the backgrounds of patients with depersonalization symptoms. Searl (1932) stated that several such patients whom he had treated had identified strongly with specific inanimate objects not only as substitutes for losses which they incurred but also as a way of denying more animate and potentially uncontrollable aspects of the self. Apparently, inanimate objects (e.g., clothes, pieces of furniture) would become unusually equated with the self and be used (symbolically and in fantasy) to reassure and anchor certain aspects of one's identity. Oberndorf (1935) provided some confirmation for Searl's view by presenting a case of a woman with marked feelings of depersonalization who had bolstered herself from an early age by sleeping with, and clinging to, a little pillow which she called her "pilpil". This pillow seemed to be of special comfort to her when she felt estranged and unsure of her boundaries. Bird (1958) has speculated that depersonalization is a "state where there is uncertainty as to what is object and what is self . . . a return to the time in earliest infancy when there is no differentiation between objects and self" (p. 473). Peto (1956) also points out the breakdown in body image boundaries in the course of depersonalization. With this in mind one can see some analogies between the individual with depersonalization problems, the fetishistic type of patient described by Greenacre (1953), the transvestite portrayed by Friedemann (1966), and the child [7] depicted by Winnikott (1953) who uses "transitional objects" (e.g., teddy bear) to learn the difference between "me" and "not me". In all these instances there is involved the bolstering of a vague and poorly defined body image by the use of inanimate objects which symbolize the replacement of a lost part of the self, but which at the same time because of their inanimate qualities highlight the confusion in the individual between self and non-self, animate and non-animate.

Evidence has accumulated that depersonalization is a common occurrence in normal persons. In fact, the question has arisen whether its incidence is any greater in psychiatric than normal populations. Roberts (1960) examined by means of questionnaire the occurrence of depersonalization in a population of 33 females and 24 males who were college students. Almost half of the sample admitted to depersonalization experiences. No sex differences were found. Dixon (1963) administered a questionnaire concerned with depersonalization experiences, among others, to one sample of 69 male and 58 female college students and to another sample of 19 men and 22 women. He found in the first sample that depersonalization had occurred in half of the subjects. There were no sex differences in this respect. Introversion-extraversion was not meaningfully related to reported amount of previous depersonalization. These findings were successfully replicated in the second sample. Sedman (1966) surveyed a population of 50 normal subjects (26 male, 24 female) for frequency of depersonalization. Thirty-five reported

---

[7] Salfield (1958) has reported children as young as nine who manifested depersonalization feelings.

previous feelings of depersonalization—usually under conditions associated with alteration of consciousness (e.g., after drinking alcohol or being unusually fatigued). No sex differences were detected. Depersonalization frequency was not correlated with measures tapping a dimension similar to extraversion-introversion. This last negative finding and a similar one by Dixon (1963) referred to above do not agree with a report by Reed and Sedman (1964) who did observe a significant correlation in normal subjects between introversion and the tendency to experience depersonalization during sensory deprivation.

Cappon and Banks (1965) could not find anything distorted about the body image of the psychiatric patient who has prominent symptoms of depersonalization. Twenty such patients were compared with non-patient controls. Measures of body size perception (e.g., length, width, and thickness of body) and body orientation (e.g., identifying one's midline) were obtained under the following conditions: rest, caloric labyrinthine stimulation, rotation, sensory deprivation, and sleep deprivation. The special conditions were introduced because they have been reported to intensify depersonalization states. The number of significant differences between the patients and controls for the various measures over the range of conditions did not exceed chance. Whether the results reflect the insensitivity of the experimental procedures or the absence of serious disturbance in the body image organization of those experiencing depersonalization remains to be seen.

It is a matter of related interest that Fisher has shown in one study (1964C) that normal subjects (close relatives of hospitalized schizophrenics) do not differ from hospitalized neurotics or schizophrenics in the frequency of reported depersonalization. This study involved the comparison of 61 normals with 62 neurotics and 56 schizophrenics. Depersonalization was measured by asking subjects to indicate which of a wide range of possible depersonalized body experiences (e.g., "My body feels dead", "My body feels strange") they were currently aware. In a second study Fisher (1966B) found, using the same methodology, that hospitalized neurotics (N = 40) did not differ with references to depersonalization from hospitalized schizophrenics (N = 91). The two studies were somewhat unique in that subjects were asked to indicate body experiences occurring at the time they were replying to the questionnaire—rather than giving retrospective reports, as has been true of previous investigations. The results indicated that persons with varying degrees of psychopathology could not be distinguished with reference to feelings of depersonalization.

Of course, the question still remains whether the depersonalization experiences of normals and neurotics are not less intense and long persisting than those occurring in schizophrenics. This is a matter for further investigation. But there is a possibility that depersonalization, even of some chronicity, is common among normal and neurotic persons as they respond to the usual range of life stresses and crises.

Formulations Concerning Schizophrenic Distortions

Szasz (1957) discussed the occurrence of certain patterns of bodily feeling in schizophrenia (e.g., hypochondriasis, somatic delusions, being "dead"). He theorizes that these feelings reflect the schizophrenic's need to take his own body as an object of relationship to replace the objects he has lost in the external world. He outlines a progression of attitudes that an individual may adopt toward his body as he regresses from a pre-psychotic to an advanced stage of schizophrenia. The progression may be described as follows:

1. In the pre-psychotic state personal investments are primarily in outside objects of personal significance.

2. Disappointment with, or loss of, outside objects results in withdrawal from such objects; and one's own body becomes a substitute object to which to relate. This is accompanied by a transfer of feelings and fantasies to one's body which were previously invested in outside persons and things.

3. The body becomes "the only remaining foothold for the ego's survival" (p. 136) and therefore the individual becomes fearful that he may lose this object too, just as he has lost most outside objects. He develops intense body concern and focuses upon hypochondriacal (and delusional) body sensations which serve to reassure him that he still possesses his body and also to warn him of the potential danger of losing it. That is, the body becomes a "noisy" perceptual phenomenon as part of a process of accentuating its importance.

4. Regression may proceed further and even the individual's own body is given up as an object of investment. Therefore, sensations of "deadness" and also anesthesias become prominent which symbolically dramatize the sense of body loss.

5. In an even more regressed state there may be attempts via self mutilation to remove body parts which do not fit in with the revised "deadened" and curtailed body image.[8]

Stuntz (1959) presented a case of a schizophrenic male whom he considers to illustrate the various stages of body image change delineated by Szasz. In this instance the patient went through cycles in his relationships to

---

[8] A related concept with regard to the revision of the body image was presented by Flescher (1948). He put forth the idea that areas of the body may be unconsciously eliminated from the body image in order to avoid anticipated punishment for the aggressive fantasies associated with such parts. He refers to "mutilation" of the body scheme with the intent of severing body parts whose presence is experienced as a severe threat to the entire organism. In some of his clinical accounts of neurotic and schizophrenic patients he illustrates how they attempted at times to act out in reality body image revisions which they made in fantasy. Thus he describes a psychotic patient who attempted to bite off his own tongue which he had labeled as a "devil's tongue".

others and to his own body (as defined by growing and shaving a beard) which appeared congruent with Szasz's scheme. Cowden and Brown (1956) described a schizophrenic man who became less grossly psychotic when various methods were used to get him to focus his anxieties and feelings upon a body symptom (viz., back pain) rather than upon his delusional fantasies. One might interpret this phenomenon as exemplifying Szasz's view that investment in one's body may have substitute and reassurance value.

There is no end to the observations and discussion concerning the role of the body image in schizophrenia. Arguments have been offered which would make body image disturbance basic to schizophrenic regression (e.g., Herner, 1965; Des Lauriers, 1962; Woodbury, 1966; Schilder, 1935). Bruch (1962) insists that a defect in learning to interpret sensations from one's body is a (p. 24) "prerequisite for later schizophrenic development". Multifarious lists of body image distortions experienced by schizophrenic patients have been compiled (e.g., Schilder, 1935; Fenichel, 1945; Fisher and Cleveland, 1968). There is also a growing literature concerning the effects of tranquilizing medications on body feelings in schizophrenics and other psychiatric patients (e.g., Klein and Fink, 1962). One should refer, in addition, to increasing interest in the body image distortions produced in normals who have been made to experience psychotic-like states by ingesting drugs like LSD (e.g., Linton and Langs, 1964; Kuramochi and Takahashi, 1964).

The gross breakdown in body image boundaries that apparently occurs in severely disorganized persons has been a special topic of interest for both psychoanalytic and non-psychoanalytic observers.

Descriptions of such boundary disturbance have been particularly well presented by Rose (1966). He conceives of many symptom patterns as maneuvers designed to obtain indirect bolstering of poorly defined boundaries. He traces boundary difficulties to relationships with parents who were too intrusive, "close", and in need of symbiotic interchange. Incidentally, the role of the intrusive and destructive parent in producing body image pathology has been heavily emphasized by Fliess (1961). Rose mentions that in autistic children symptoms like head knocking and self biting may be paradoxical ways of producing input into otherwise hazy boundary regions of the body. Apropos of this point, Green (1967) reported after studying self mutilation in 70 schizophrenic children that head banging was often a precursor to such mutilation and that it may have originally served to provide increased sensory input and greater ego boundary delineation. Woodbury (1966) too has given a good deal of thought to boundary alteration and other body image distortions in psychiatric patients. He refers to some who apparently perceive themselves as hollow containers with defensive circumscribing walls or boundaries. Feelings of being vulnerable, empty, not real, and small seemed to be traceable to defects in boundary maintenance. Woodbury mentions a study he carried out in which psychotic and depersonalized states leading to self laceration and destructiveness were quickly terminated by applying cold-wet-sheet packs; and proposes that the effectiveness of the procedure was due to the fact that (p. 287) "the body-ego boundaries are re-established through the sensory stimulation of the pack in the presence of another person from whom the patient is clearly and definitely differentiated". Such therapeutic use of boundary delineation and related body image techniques has been explored and recommended by a number of individuals.

Des Lauriers (1962) stated that making the schizophrenic aware of his body, particularly his boundaries, is one of the prime methods for restoring his individuality and reality testing. Freytag (1961) has proposed a treatment method for schizophrenics and other types of psychiatric patients based on using hypnosis to induce them to hallucinate their "unconscious body image" and then capitalizing on the insights about self so obtained to eliminate pathological adjustment modes. May, Wexler, Salkin, and Schoop (1963), Goertzel, May, Salkin, and Schoop (1965), Paige, McNamara, and Fisch (1964) and Christrup (1958) have described novel approaches to treating schizophrenics which are based on making them body aware and teaching them to relearn the patterns of body sensations that go along with various postures, sets, and emotional states. In the last four instances cited, empirical evaluations (e.g., psychiatric ratings) of initial results with rather regressed patients appear to be promising. More controlled studies will need to be done before a valid judgment can be formed concerning the therapeutic effectiveness of such body image approaches.

Brown (1960) presented some unusually direct and cogent clinical material concerning 24 schizophrenic children which bears on boundary phenomena. She reports that it is not unusual for a schizophrenic child to treat part of his body as if it were something "out there", not part of himself. He might pick up one of his hands with the other and examine it with a puzzled air, as if he had never seen it before. Brown describes a variety of other strategies which schizophrenic children seem to use to bolster their body identity and to banish sensations of body insubstantiality. She refers to their great interest in looking at themselves in the mirror; their frequent outlining of parts of their bodies (e.g., hand) by tracing around them with crayon on paper; and their close compensatory attachment to dolls and figures to which they gave their own names. From her viewpoint a defective body image is one of the paramount characteristics of schizophrenic children. The mention she makes of their looking into the mirror to reassure themselves of the constancy of their self image is analogous to Elkisch's (1957) reports of the mirror behavior [9] of several adult schizophrenic patients she had in treatment. She describes instances in which they would gaze at themselves in the mirror for protracted periods without awareness of anything

---

[9] Previous descriptions of the unusual mirror behavior of schizophrenics may be found in the literature (e.g., Rosenzweig and Shakow, 1937).

else occurring in their vicinity. It was her interpretation that they sought to retrieve by means of their mirrored images some part of the self or ego or boundary which they experienced as lost. Analogously, Friedemann (1966) has suggested that the intense interest of the transvestite in studying his mirror image while wearing woman's clothing may serve as reassurance against feelings of body dissolution. It is somewhat paradoxical, as Elkisch points out, that in folklore and myth to look at one's mirrored image was considered to be a dangerous thing which could result in loss (as contrasted to the hope of regaining) of some vital part of the self.

Lukianowicz (1958) has reviewed the literature dealing with autoscopy which he defines as a "complex psychosensorial hallucinatory perception of one's own body image projected into the external visual space" (p. 199). This phenomenon bears some relation to the mirror behavior of the schizophrenic in that it usually involves the individual hallucinating a duplicated version of himself in the space in front of him. It occurs rarely and may be linked with a range of disorganized states (e.g., brain damage, migraine, schizophrenia). The etiology remains vague, but the question arises whether it may not function at least partially to provide the same reassurance concerning body substantiality that the schizophrenic apparently seeks in prolonged examination of himself in the mirror. Lukianowicz (1967) has also compiled an unusually thorough inventory of all of the categories of body image distortion which have been observed in many different types of psychiatric patients.

Cappon (1959) elicited descriptions of dreams and other types of imagery from a large number of schizophrenics and also groups of less disturbed subjects, both in their usual state and after nitrous oxide and carbon dioxide inhalation which produced light anesthesia. He roughly rated the imagery with regard to how appropriate and realistic it was relative to that which it was apparently supposed to represent. He found, among other things, that the schizophrenics represented the human body with greater distortion than did any of the other groups. For example, the schizophrenic tended to depict himself via such dysplastic and deviant forms as "gargoyle" and "werewolf". Schafer (1960) similarly finds, on the basis of his experience with the Rorschach test, that schizophrenics are characterized by body image "fragmentation". He indicates that the body percepts in their Rorschach protocols (p. 281) "split, inflate, get crushed or crippled, die, or get lost in each other or in undefined and topsy-turvy space." His paper contains an extremely detailed analysis of the Rorschach record of a patient which is intended to illustrate the profusion of body breakdown concepts typifying the schizophrenic.

Zucker (1962) evaluated the "ego boundary" and body image characteristics of 60 paranoid schizophrenics. Half of the patients were sufficiently disturbed to require hospitalization and half were able to maintain themselves by therapy on an ambulatory basis. The Rorschach, Mosaic, and Figure-Drawing tests were used as evaluation techniques. Many of the measures derived from the tests were concerned primarily with how appropriately the patient was able to differentiate and segregate unlike ideas and concepts. However, some of the measures focused upon body image distortion and inability to establish body boundaries. It was found that the ambulatory schizophrenics manifested significantly less body image disturbance than the hospitalized group. One of the Rorschach scoring categories devised by Zucker, which she labels "fluid contours" and which involves percepts like "jellyfish" and "shapeless mass", bears a certain resemblance to a type of response considered by Schafer (1960) and Fisher and Cleveland (1968) to refer to disruption of body image boundaries. This category occurred with greater frequency in the hospitalized than in the ambulatory group.

Jortner (1966) was concerned with body image boundaries, among other variables, in a study of 25 schizophrenics and 24 non-schizophrenics (most of whom were alcoholics or neurotics). Ink blot responses were obtained from these patients. One of the scores derived from the responses was labeled "Inside and Outside" and referred to images in which the inside and outside of a person were seen simultaneously. This was taken as an index of the extent that the patient's body-image boundaries were disrupted. The Inside-Outside score [10] was found to be significantly higher in the schizophrenic than non-schizophrenic sample. It was positively correlated with ratings and other measures derived from the ink blot responses indicating unusual suspiciousness and difficulty in maintaining boundaries between cognitive categories and different levels of abstraction. One of the major conclusions derived by Jortner was that schizophrenia seems to involve a breakdown in the body boundary.

The matter of body boundary fluidity in schizophrenia was evaluated by Victor (1964), whose work was guided by Federn's (1952) concept of ego boundaries. He predicted that the more fluid an individual's body image boundaries the greater the number of errors he would make in identifying whether stimuli were real and external to himself and also whether they were internal and imaginary. A sample of 62 male hospitalized psychiatric patients (many of whom were schizophrenic) and another of 19 normal male hospital employees were studied. Boundary fluidity was measured in terms of judges' ratings of a number of aspects of human figures sketched by the subjects. Such variables as the following were considered to be pertinent to boundary fluidity: discontinuity in the outline (e.g., dotted, vague), transparency of clothing or skin, confusion of clothing and skin. In order to appraise the subject's ability to distinguish what is real from unreal he was asked to identify a variety of objects solely by touch and to indicate whether he felt each judgment was "real" or "imaginary". Also, he was asked to describe a

---

[10] As will be seen, Jortner's score is similar to the Fisher-Cleveland Penetration score which will be discussed in the next chapter. Material to be presented will make it clear that the boundary of the schizophrenic need not be vague and fluid. It can under certain circumstances be quite definite and firm.

special series of forms depicted in ink blots and to state whether each form was "actually pictured" or "from his imagination". It was found that boundary fluidity was positively correlated with the tendency to judge as possibly unreal those perceptions which were actually accurate. But boundary fluidity had a chance correlation with actually misperceiving the true identity of an object or percept and assuming that the misperception was correct. No differences of significance were detected in boundary fluidity between patients and normal subjects. With respect to this finding, Victor (1964) makes the interesting point that Federn's theory of ego and boundary change during psychosis does not demand that the schizophrenic boundary be unusually fluid. Federn conceptualized the boundary as becoming very fluid during the early stages of severe regression, but in the later stages it could, while encompassing a much smaller part of the self than is true in the normal state, take on very firm and rigid properties.

Lerner (1960) reported that certain scores derived from figure drawings predicted relative degree of recovery of 75 schizophrenic women treated with psychoanalytically oriented psychotherapy. One of the figure drawing scores which successfully predicted in this fashion was the quality and consistency of the bounding lines comprising each drawing. Lerner regards this line quality as an important indicator of the state of the patient's body image boundaries. Poor boundaries were presumably indicated by incomplete, vague, dotted, and only lightly indicated lines. However, it should be pointed out that the equation of the line quality of the drawing with the state of the individual's boundary which is made in this study and others referred to above is without empirical support. No direct evidence has ever been mustered for this view. Indeed, in view of Nichols and Strumpfer's (1962) findings that many figure drawing scores are a function of drawing ability, one must be skeptical about unvalidated claims concerning the specific meaning of given figure drawing indices.

Kaufman and Heims (1958) have pointed out that preadolescent and adolescent delinquents produce Rorschach percepts which dramatize sensations of body damage. They refer to delinquents as registering the loss of early primary figures (e.g., mother) in a sense of body mutilation which takes the form of an image of the body with either the interior hollowed out or a portion ripped from the periphery. They hypothesize that heightened motility and aggression increase interaction with the environment and thus help to define body image boundaries; and they consider this to be an important motivation for aggressive delinquent behavior. Incidentally, they suggest that there are substantial similarities between the distorted body fantasies of the delinquent and those exhibited by psychotically depressed patients. Zuk (1960) has published an account of mental defectives who injure or attack themselves when angry. He conjectures that in such cases there has been regression to the point where the individual does not differentiate his own body from other objects in his vicinity. He suggests (p. 59), "The body is no longer perceived as an extension of the self but as an *object* in the environment". In these patients the boundaries that ordinarily define identity seem to be absent.

An unusual theme which bears tangential relationship to the matter of body boundaries and psychopathology is dealt with in a paper by Benedek (1960) concerning sexual and reproductive behavior. The theme in question concerns the impact upon the pregnant mother of the foetus inside her body. Benedek states that if certain negative and ambivalent meanings are ascribed to the foetus this may lead to disturbance in incorporating the foetus into the existing body image and therefore result in serious disturbance or even psychosis. She describes a wide range of representational roles which the foetus may fill. In some instances it appears to represent parts that are experienced as missing (e.g., wished for penis) or it may be perceived as symbolizing envied attributes of the mother. It may also be identified with such negative objects as the "bad, aggressive devouring self", "feces" or some hated or feared person. A normal image of the foetus is presumably one in which it is positively identified with the pregnant woman's own body and self.

Body Size Perception in Schizophrenia

Considerable research interest has been invested in the question whether there are characteristic size distortions in the body concept of the schizophrenic individual. Early studies gave promise of demonstrating a fundamental difference between schizophrenics and non-schizophrenics in the perception of the size attributes of their bodies. But, as will be seen, the accumulation of new information has raised questions about the existence of such a difference. A review of developments concerning this issue follows.

Weckowicz and Sommer (1960) were among the first to look at body size perception in schizophrenics. Their interest evolved as they explored a number of aspects of how schizophrenic patients regard their bodies. In an initial phase, they examined the reactions of a variety of subjects (34 schizophrenics, 18 non-schizophrenic patients, 29 normal persons) as they were asked to view themselves in a three-paneled mirror. Each subject was asked:

1. What do you see?
2. What else do you see?
3. How many people do you see?
4. Do all these people look alike?
5. Which is the real you? (Point to it.)

He was later requested to describe the person in the mirror as if he were looking at a photograph of someone else. All responses were recorded verbatim. It was found that the schizophrenics differed significantly from the control subjects only in the degree to which they used the words "my", "myself", and "me". To extend the implications of this result another study was conducted in which the experimenter pointed to several different parts of the subject's body (viz., hand, ear, foot, shirt, nose, ankle) and asked "What is this?" As predicted, the schizophrenics used the word "my" to precede their answer less often than did the controls. They tended to respond with "a hand" or "the hand"; whereas the normals would reply with "my hand". These findings were tentatively interpreted to mean that schizophrenics have a more limited self concept and are less ego involved with their bodies than normals.

Weckowicz and Sommer proceeded in a further phase of their exploratory work to have subjects (24 schizophrenics, 30 normals, 11 non-schizophrenic patients) stand in front of a mirror while the upper half of the mirror image was covered with white paper. They were then asked to draw in the missing parts, including the head and left arm. The principal significant result indicated that the schizophrenics drew smaller hands than the controls. It was on the basis of this fact that Weckowicz and Sommer organized an elaborate study which compared schizophrenics and non-schizophrenics with respect to how they perceive the size of their extremities. The subjects (20 schizophrenics, 20 normals, and 20 non-schizophrenic psychiatric patients) were shown a series of 15 photographs of a hand varying in size and a similar series of pictures of a foot. They were to indicate whether each picture was larger, smaller, or the same size as equivalent members of their own bodies. Also, each subject stood in front of a semicircular rod on which were hung 12 brown men's socks varying in size; and he judged which one would best fit him. The judgments with regard to the photographs and the socks were subsequently compared with the actual sizes of the subject's hands and feet. It was found that in terms of the judged sizes of the photographs that the schizophrenics regarded their hands and feet to be significantly smaller than did the non-schizophrenic controls. However, there were no significant differences between the groups with regard to the sock chosen as being one's best fit. Weckowicz and Sommer considered their results to indicate that the schizophrenic perceives the distal parts of his body as relatively small. They offered two possible explanations for this finding.

One is derived from the theories of Schilder and Federn to the effect that schizophrenics are characterized by a narrowing of the self boundary which results in their investing less value and cathexis in the distal parts of the body. The minimizing of the size of the hands and feet could be considered to reflect the lessened investment in the periphery. But a second possible explanation, which Weckowicz and Sommer favor, is that the small size attributed to the distal parts by the schizophrenic is a function of breakdown in size constancy and distortion in space perception. They note that the schizophrenic has lost some of his ability to correct size perceptions in relation to the distance of the perceived object from himself and therefore a distal body part would be seen as smaller than body parts nearer to the eyes. They speculate that the perception of the body space and the space surrounding it are subject to the same controlling principles.

Cleveland (1960B) utilized a eries of pictures of body parts varying in size (adapted from the Weckowicz and Sommer procedure) to determine how schizophrenics experience the sizes of various areas of their body. There were photographs of a hand, foot, stomach, heart, and a baseball. Thirty male schizophrenics and 30 hospitalized non-psychiatric patients were used as subjects. The instructions to each were to indicate whether each picture was larger, smaller, or the same size as his own corresponding body part. The resulting judgments were compared (except for heart and stomach) with the actual dimensions of the parts in question. There was a significant trend for the schizophrenics to exceed the controls in size judgments for all four body parts and also to overestimate the true size of their own hands and feet. No differences appeared between the groups with respect to judgments of the baseball. Cleveland viewed his findings as indicating that schizophrenics have suffered a loss in boundary definiteness which results in an increase in perceived body size. He pointed out that his results were comparable to those obtained by Liebert, et al. (1958) which indicated that when LSD was used to disrupt body image boundaries in normals and schizophrenics it resulted in an increase in the size they attributed to their own bodies but not to non-self external objects. Of course, his findings contradicted those of Weckowicz and Sommer (1960).

Cleveland, et al. (1962) undertook a comprehensive follow-up of the results obtained by Cleveland. Three samples of schizophrenic patients (N = 100) and two non-psychotic psychiatric control groups (N = 50) were studied. Judgments of the size of hand, foot, head, heart, stomach, and a baseball were obtained with the same picture representations of body parts used by Cleveland. Judgments of body size were also secured by having subjects indicate proper distances between luminous markers which would be equivalent to given body dimensions. Height estimates were secured in this fashion too. The findings demonstrated, in congruence with the earlier Cleveland work, that while the schizophrenics did not overestimate the size of a non-body object like a baseball to a greater degree than the controls, they did show greater overestimation for most of the body dimensions. These results were interpreted within the sensori-tonic body boundary model. That is, the diffusion of the boundary in schizophrenics presumably resulted in their feeling relatively "spread out" and therefore large.

Additional evidence concerning this issue accrued when Reitman (1962) obtained a number of body size estimates from 20 schizophrenic patients and 20 non-schizophrenic psychiatric patients. These estimates involved height, hand, stomach, and head. Two non-body judgments (viz., size of baseball and 12 inches) were also secured. Size estimates were measured with both the luminous marker and photograph (of body parts) techniques described with reference to the Cleveland studies (1960). For *all* body parts the schizophrenics exceeded the controls in their degree of size overestimation. It is true that they also overestimated more for the non-body 12 inch distance; but such overestimation was not evident for the baseball.[11] It would be fair to say that the results did indicate trends for overestimation of the size of one's body parts in schizophrenics.

Burton and Adkins (1961) have also examined the question of body size perception in schizophrenia. Their study embraced a group of female schizophrenics and a group of normal women who did not differ significantly in dress size, shoe size, height, or weight. Each subject was shown a schematic drawing of each of 30 different body parts (e.g., arm, foot, tongue, stomach, bladder). She was asked in each instance to indicate which of 21 wire frames (ranging in size from 1/4 inch squared to 18 inches squared) would be the "best fit" for the body part in question. The idea was conveyed that the frame chosen should "best approximate" the size of the given body part. An analysis of the judgments indicated a significant trend for the schizophrenics to perceive their body parts as larger than the normals. This result supported Cleveland's work and the overestimation hypothesis. It is the fourth to be cited which was supportive in this fashion.

However, when Dillon (1962A) compared body size estimation in 21 schizophrenic patients and 20 non-patient controls, he could not detect significant differences. Estimates of height, width, and depth of body were obtained. This was done by having each subject instruct the experimenter to move one beam closer or further away from another so as to make the intervening space match the size of each given body part.

Another study, previously described, which was carried out by Cappon and Banks (1965) and which involved patients with marked depersonalization symptoms, could not find differences in body size estimation between such patients and normal controls. A problem arises in evaluating the pertinence of this study because it is not clear what percent of the depersonalized sample had been formally diagnosed as schizophrenic. One cannot decide how far the results are applicable to schizophrenic behavior.

Fisher and Seidner (1963) observed, while measuring subjective body size feelings in 30 schizophrenics, 25 neurotics, and 25 normals, that schizophrenics did not *feel* that any sectors of their bodies were unusually large. A Body Distortion Questionnaire was used for the first time which inquired of the subject whether he was experiencing any of a variety of unusual body sensations or distortions. Among the items were several concerning sensations of increased body size (e.g., "My hands feel unusually large") and also several related to sensations of decreased body size (e.g., "My hands feel unusually small"). No differences turned up among the groups with respect

---

[11] There were no differences in the sizes of figure drawings produced by the schizophrenic and non-schizophrenic samples. Nickols (1962) similarly reported no size differences in the figure drawings of schizophrenics and normal controls.

to feeling large, but the schizophrenics indicated significantly more sensations of decreased body size than the neurotics and the normals. This observation was puzzling in view of the several studies which had shown that schizophrenics overestimate their body size. However, the idea presented itself that the schizophrenic might actually feel small, but that this feeling could lead him to make compensatorily large body size judgments, especially in the relatively unstructured situation (e.g., lights dim) in which size judgments are typically made. That is, because feeling small has negative, undesirable significance, there might be a need for defensive denial which would take the form of overestimating one's size.

Fisher (1964C) sought to replicate the findings concerning the subjective sense of body smallness in schizophrenics. A longer and more carefully fashioned version of the Body Distortion Questionnaire was administered to both males (21 schizophrenics, 21 neurotics, 20 normals) and females (25 schizophrenics, 40 neurotics, 21 normals). Unusual care was taken to make the normal and psychiatric samples comparable. Subjects responded Yes, No, or Undecided to 82 statements dealing with body image distortions in eight basic categories. One category (14 items) dealt with perception of one's body as small. Other categories included were as follows: loss of boundaries, feelings of being dirty, blocked body openings, unusual skin sensations, depersonalization, and sensations of increased body size.

The groups did not differ with reference to feelings of being unusually large; but the neurotics and schizophrenics of both sexes reported significantly more sensations of body smallness than the normals. The neurotics and schizophrenics did not differ. These findings were somewhat supportive of the previous Fisher and Seidner (1963) results. However, while the feeling of bodily smallness differentiated the psychiatric samples from the normals, they did not distinguish the schizophrenics from the neurotics. The feelings of smallness reported by the schizophrenics were also present in non-psychotic psychiatric patients. The fact that sensations of smallness rather than largeness once again characterized the schizophrenic patients reinforced the Fisher and Seidner speculation that the overestimation of body size said by Cleveland and others to typify schizophrenics might be a compensatory form of behavior. That is, because they feel small, they might be wishfully motivated to find ways of magnifying their size.

A direct test of this hypothesis was designed by Fisher (1966B). He studied 91 schizophrenics (45 male, 46 female) and 40 neurotics (20 male, 20 female). The Body Distortion Questionnaire was used to measure the degree to which there were sensations of body smallness. Each subject was also asked to estimate his height, the sizes of various parts of his body (e.g., shoulders, mouth, stomach), and 12 inches. All of the estimates, except those for height, were made (with eyes closed) by setting distances between two tabs that moved on a measuring rod. Results obtained for the male schizophrenics tended to support the hypothesis in a borderline fashion. The greater the individual's feeling of body smallness the more he overestimated his shoulder size (p .10) and the larger were his estimates of his stomach size (p .10). Chance results appeared for the height and mouth estimates. There was also a borderline positive correlation (p .10) between how small the subject felt and his degree of overestimation of a 12 inch distance. A very significant positive correlation was noted (p < .001) between sense of smallness and the magnitude of the pooled shoulder, stomach, mouth, and 12 inch estimates. Significance was maintained even when the 12 inch estimate was not included among the pooled values.

However, in the female schizophrenic group there were only chance correlations between sense of smallness and the various size estimates.

The general results did not provide much formal affirmation of the hypothesis. But the positive trends in the male schizophrenic sample invite further consideration.

It should be additionally reported that when the body size estimates of the two schizophrenic groups were compared with those of their respective neurotic controls, the differences were of a chance order. The schizophrenics did not overestimate their body size to a greater extent than the neurotics. These findings obviously do not correspond with a number of previous reports cited above.

Incidentally, data based on subjects' responses to the Body Distortion Questionnaire once more indicated that the schizophrenics and neurotics were characterized by significantly more sensations of body smallness than a matched normal control group which had been included particularly to enable a comparison with reference to this variable. The neurotics and schizophrenics did not differ.

In interpreting his findings with reference to the existing literature pertinent to body size estimation in schizophrenics, Fisher arrived at the following conclusion:

> As one surveys the trends of the results accumulating for body size estimation in relationship to psychopathology, it is becoming apparent that the phenomena involved are volatile. One has to presume that the inconsistencies in the literature reflect differences in sampling, measurement techniques, experimenter orientation, and so forth. If there are variables linked to the schizophrenic state which do stimulate overestimation of one's body size, they are obviously not of great force and can be easily nullified by slight variations in experimental conditions. (p. 98.)

This last statement is probably too negative. One must remember that Wapner, et al., Cleveland, et al., Burton and Adkins, and Reitman have produced a series of findings which point to an expression of exaggerated body size in schizophrenics. Such findings cannot be easily dismissed; and they deserve additional consideration and investigation. Perhaps it will be possible to demonstrate that the inconsistencies in the literature are due to procedural matters which can be ultimately controlled. It is noteworthy, for example, that most of the positive results have been obtained with procedures that involve judgments about pictures or representations of body parts. Most negative findings have emerged from studies in which size judgments were reported in terms of abstract or impersonal measuring rods (e.g., distance between two beams). It may require a personalized representation of a body part to evoke the schizophrenic's perception of his body as large. Of course, even if overestimation of self size can be shown to be consistently true of schizophrenic patients, this will have to be squared with Fisher's consistent observations that schizophrenics *feel* as if their body parts have shrunk in size. One would need to decide whether the overt size judgments were compensatory for the sense of smallness. One could also conceivably, but perhaps less convincingly, entertain the obverse possibility that the sense of being strangely big, "spread out", and without limits is so frightening that it produces a defensive need to try to "shrink up" or contract which is reflected in subjective feelings of smallness. These are questions and issues which a fairly limited number of well designed studies could probably resolve adequately.

Spatial Aspects of the Body Image in Schizophrenia

There have been assertions that the schizophrenic individual has unusual and distorted perceptions concerning the position of his body in space. Several approaches to this matter may be found in the literature.

Wapner and his associates have devoted much attention to investigating the schizophrenic's perception of the relation of his body to the surrounding space. Their work derived from the basic sensori-tonic formulation that the greater a person's maturity the more clearly will he differentiate self from outside space. Such differentiation is illustrated by the fact that when a normal adult in a darkened room is tilted and asked to adjust a luminous bar so that it appears to be vertical, he tends to set the bar in a direction opposite to his body tilt. There is, says Wapner (in Wapner and Werner, 1965) a normal polarity or differentiation between self and object which, in this case, results in a "compensatory" shift of the apparent position of the bar. It is perceived as "emphatically" separated from the position of one's own body. However, sensori-tonic theory asserts that if an individual is immature or regressed, as would be true of the young child or the schizophrenic, the differentiation between self and object is minimized. Consequently, it would be expected that when the body of a schizophrenic patient is tilted and he is asked to adjust a luminous rod to the vertical he would not display the tendency to set it opposite to his direction of tilt—since the sense of separation between self and surrounding space would be blurred. In several studies this predicted result has been obtained (Wapner, 1961 A, B). Schizophrenics shift the apparent vertical away from their tilted body position to a significantly smaller degree than do normal subjects.

In other experiments Wapner and his associates have found that when normal subjects who have been tilted are asked not only to adjust one luminous rod to the vertical but also another to represent their own degree of body tilt, the adjustment of the first rod is opposite to body tilt and that for the second tends to overestimate the amount of body tilt. That is, the separation or differentiation in the position of the non-self rod and the position of one's own body is even more clearly exaggerated. But, as would be expected from sensori-tonic theory, when schizophrenics are asked to make the same kinds of judgments, the difference in the position they assign to the rod adjusted to the vertical and the rod presumably aligned with their own body tilt is significantly smaller than that found in normal adult samples.

The sensori-tonic work has been ingenious and productive. It has provided the only consistent demonstration that the schizophrenic differs from the normal individual in the way he experiences his body with reference to the space "out there". An underlying assumption in this work is that the schizophrenic's boundaries are hazy and provide poor differentiation between self and other objects. Such a view is certainly consonant with many clinical reports concerning the breakdown of boundaries in schizophrenia. However, it should also be mentioned that a number of previous attempts to show empirically by means of a variety of methods that schizophrenics have vague boundaries have not succeeded. The present author's difficulties in this respect are described in a later chapter.

A research group directed by Witkin (1954) has also looked closely at the ability of schizophrenics and other psychiatric groups to make spatial judgments based on using one's body as a frame of reference. Their methodology, as earlier described, has typically involved adjusting either a rod or one's body to the vertical in the presence of stimuli (e.g., tilt, visual cues) which are distracting. For example, a subject tilted in a chair will be asked to adjust a luminous rod to the vertical in a darkened room. Findings from a number of studies have indicated that schizophrenics do not consistently differ from normals in their ability to make such spatial judgments accurately. Apparently, they are able to utilize orienting body cues as adequately as normal individuals. However, there is evidence that paranoid schizophrenics are superior to other schizophrenic subcategories in this respect. Further, Witkin (1965) indicates that schizophrenics with hallucinatory symptoms are less capable in making spatial judgments than are non-hallucinating schizophrenics.

It is of interest that the Witkin methodology which is based upon accuracy of spatial judgments does not distinguish the schizophrenic; whereas the Wapner methodology, which is distinguishing in this respect, evaluates the patterning or directionality of the way the individual localizes the spatial position of self versus non-self objects. This reminds one that few of the body image measurement techniques which have been devised which are based on accuracy of perceiving one's body have proven to be productive. This applies to measures of accuracy in estimating one's body dimensions; ability to correct errors introduced in one's mirror image; and degree of realism in self drawing representations.

There are a number of other less programmatic approaches pertinent to the schizophrenic's perception of his position in space which should be mentioned.

Hozier (1959) studied a group of 25 schizophrenic women and a normal control group of 25 women to ascertain whether they would manifest differences in body image integration and also in reality of perception of the body's spatial position that one might anticipate on the basis of Des Lauriers' (1962) concepts of the role of the body image in schizophrenia. Three types of tasks were used to investigate the problem.

1. The first involved the subject's ability to make realistic spatial placements of human figures. He was successively presented with two different pictured scenes taken from the Make-Picture-Story test (MAPS); and he was asked to place male and female cut-out figures of various sizes in the pictured scenes where he felt they would be most appropriate. His placements could then be compared with the pooled evaluations of normal judges concerning the possible range of appropriate spatial placements for each figure.

2. A second task required the subject to reproduce a model doll figure from an array of 30 different doll parts (e.g., legs, arms, head, feet) varying in size. The parts of the figures could be assembled by means of snaps. Omissions and deviations in placement and size were scored as errors.

3. The third task was the drawing of a "whole person". This drawing was scored in terms of a modified version of the Goodenough system which had proved successful in differentiating schizophrenics and college students.

The results indicated that the schizophrenic subjects were more inappropriate than the normals in their placements of human figures in a spatial context. The schizophrenics also made more errors and misinterpretations in their doll constructions. Similarly, the schizophrenics evidenced a greater degree of distortion and omission of body parts in their figure drawings. Hozier interprets such findings as indicating that schizophrenics have difficulty in the perception of the body in relation to space. She describes them as suffering a "diminution of narcissistic cathexis of the body" which results in a breakdown in the bodily self and further in a disturbance in space perception. The dependence of realistic space perception upon an adequate body image is stressed.

Considerable importance has been assigned by Horowitz (1965, 1966) to a spatial aspect of the body image which he calls the "body buffer zone". This refers to the idea that each individual conceives of a certain area of space contiguous to his body as particularly his own. He may have varied feelings and attitudes about the size, shape, and vulnerability to penetration of this space. Horowitz sought to explore the influence of the body buffer zone upon how one relates to others. He noted clinically that schizophrenics may require an unusually large intervening space between themselves and others—but also may relate as if intervening space were non-existent. He observed too that when recovery occurred those with unusually large "buffer zones" showed shrinkage and those who had lost "buffer zones" began to re-establish them.

Several empirical studies of "buffer zone" phenomena were carried out by Horowitz, Duff, and Stratton (1964). They attempted to measure the size of each individual's "buffer zone" in terms of how closely he would approach various objects and persons in unstructured situations. The greater the distance maintained the greater was the size of the zone presumed to be. Another method used to evaluate the "buffer zone" was to ask subjects to draw a line around a representation of a person which would depict "the distance they preferred people to stay from them in ordinary situations". Quite consistently, in several samples, schizophrenic patients were observed to maintain greater distance between themselves and others. The importance of the "buffer zone" in the schizophrenic's style of interaction was underscored. Horowitz argues, as would Schilder (1935), that the space adjacent to one's body should be regarded as an integral part of one's body image.

Zierer (1950) devised a "body-space" test with the intent of differentiating normals and neurotics from psychotics. The patient is asked to draw with crayons five different scenes which he largely creates from imagination (e.g., a landscape consisting of ground, sky, and a tree; a steep hill with a house and tree on its slope). It is apparently assumed by Zierer that the spatial arrangements used by an individual in such drawings are a direct manifestation of the way in which he relates his body to his surrounding space. Psychosis is considered by him to express itself in a regressive way of depicting the body-space interaction. He indicates on the basis of clinical use of the test that psychotics typically use such primitive modes of picturing spatial positions of objects as simply assigning them to different horizontal levels; or by stratifying them one behind the other (as if those in front were transparent); or by arranging them arbitrarily about some imagined position or viewpoint of the self in the panorama.

Abstracting from the results reviewed, it seems probable that the schizophrenic individual does somehow experience his position in space differently from the normal person. The Wapner data imply that one important aspect of this difference concerns the ability to make a clear distinction between the space equated with self and the space occupied by non-self objects. While the Witkin research could not establish a difference in terms of the ability to make accurate spatial evaluations, it is true that Hozier's more indirect measures did show such difference. But it remains to be seen whether Hozier's measures based on responses to miniature stage-like tasks tap spatial perceptions in the same sense that the more direct and realistic tasks employed by Witkin do.

Self Perception and Body Identification in Schizophrenia

Clinical reports have suggested that schizophrenics may have unusual difficulty in dealing with their bodies as perceptual objects. At times they seem to be too aware of body events and at other times not sufficiently aware of them. Goldfarb (1963) has provided instances at both extremes in which schizophrenic children either behave as if body sensations do not exist (e.g., ignoring pain) or become so preoccupied with a body experience that all else in the world is ignored. Such phenomena have led to investigations to determine whether schizophrenics can be distinguished from normals in terms of the immediate aspects (e.g., evaluative, affective) of their responses to perceiving their bodies or representations of them. Somewhat unsystematically, a number of questions pertinent to this area have been considered.

Traub, Olson, Orbach, and Cardone (1967) made use of a mirror, which could be systematically distorted by the examiner and then readjusted by the subject to look like his normal image, to ascertain if schizophrenic patients (N = 20) could be distinguished from normals (ten psychiatric aides) in their ability to make accurate perceptual judgments regarding their bodies. The subjects made judgments not only about distorted versions of their own mirror image but also a control stimulus without body significance. While the schizophrenics made more errors than the controls in their body judgments, they also exceeded them in errors relative to the non-body stimulus. It was concluded that when schizophrenics misperceive their bodies it is because their perception of things in general is impaired.

Arnhoff and Damianopoulos (1964) obtained photographs of 34 male schizophrenic patients in which all facial and clothing identifying cues were absent. Each patient was asked to look at a series of seven pictures, one of which was his own. The other six had been chosen to match his somatotype as closely as possible. He was asked to indicate if his picture was one of those shown to him. Only nine correct self identifications occurred. This was significantly inferior to the accuracy obtained when 21 normal college students had been asked (Arnhoff and Damianopoulos, 1962) under similar conditions to identify photographs of their bodies. Because of gross differences in education and intelligence between the schizophrenics and controls the authors urged caution when interpreting the results. However, they were inclined to the view that schizophrenics are characterized by defects in body perception.

Harris (1967) secured figure drawings (figure of same sex and another of opposite sex) from 20 schizophrenic patients and ten non-schizophrenic, psychiatric controls. Each subject was subsequently asked to identify a series of tachistoscopically presented pictures (e.g., geometric figure, a photograph of the examiner, the word "you") which included his same sex and opposite sex drawings and also a control drawing by another patient. The schizophrenics were observed to have more difficulty in correctly identifying the opposite sex drawing than the same sex drawing. Among the controls the obverse was true. Harris proposed, on this basis, that the schizophrenics "have substituted an image of another for their own image, and they treat it as if it were their own". That is, the opposite sex drawing was, quite speculatively, interpreted as a representation of an important "other" in the patient's life who had been incorporated into the body image. The patient's relatively greater difficulty in seeing the "other" than the self representation was regarded as being due to a greater investment in the "other" than the self. But in the controls the greater investment in the self than the "other" presumably resulted in more difficulty in perceiving the self than the "other" representation. Harris speculated that the fusion of an image of an important other with one's own image, which he regards as occurring in schizophrenia, does not provide a "suitable organizational framework for the interpretation of inner sensations, and thus a sense of body estrangement develops" (p. 683). This is an interesting, if somewhat metamorphic, idea that needs to be more clearly formulated and cross-validated. From an operational view, one of the big uncertainties is whether an individual's drawing of a figure of the opposite sex necessarily reflects his concept of an "important other".

Epstein (1955) compared schizophrenics and normals in their ability to identify self representations under various conditions. It will be recalled that Wolff (1943) discovered that when persons were asked to react to shadow pictures of their profile, samples of their own voice, and other self referring stimuli in a context where they did not expect to encounter them, they rarely recognized themselves. But they did evidence selectively enhanced affect toward the self representations. Epstein arranged for schizophrenic subjects (N = 30) and matched medical patients (N = 30) to rate how much they liked a series of self representations (e.g., their voice played backwards, their drawing of a man, their handwriting upside down) which were, unknown to them, presented along with samples from other patients. It was found that the schizophrenics rated their own self representations relatively more favorably than did the normal controls. This was interpreted to mean that the schizophrenics had a greater defensive need to enhance themselves and unconsciously used the opportunity provided by the experimental situation to do so. Interestingly, the normals and schizophrenics did not differ when asked to make *conscious* rather than unconscious ratings of several aspects of self (e.g., voice, handwriting).

A comparison of normal and schizophrenics in their responses to self representations is found also in the work of Sugarman (in Ittelson and

Kutash, 1961) which was mentioned earlier in this chapter. He set up an experiment which included 60 schizophrenic males and 60 males hospitalized largely for surgical treatment. He obtained a number of self representations from each subject (e.g., figure drawing, reproduction of Bender designs, handwriting). The various products were secured from sample subgroups during three different conditions: failure, success, neutral. Subjects later rated their own products when they were presented along with those from other patients. Initial recognition of one's own product was rare during the rating process. Subsequent to rating, it was determined how long it would take the subject to recognize his own product when cues were given that it was present among those he was viewing. For products created under neutral conditions, the schizophrenics and normals did not differ in the extremeness of their ratings or the length of time it required to recognize them as one's own. While both schizophrenics and normals rated products created under failure conditions in a relatively negative fashion and required a long time to recognize them, there was no difference between the two groups in these respects. But for products created under success conditions, schizophrenics took longer to recognize them than did the normals. There was no difference between the groups in extremeness of ratings of self products. Furthermore, within the schizophrenic group no difference was found between the extremeness of ratings assigned to products which were recognized while rated and those which were unrecognized. This last cited result for the schizophrenics, as contrasted to that for the normals, is not congruent with Wolff's or Epstein's results (although in the normal sample unrecognized self products were rated more extremely than the recognized). Whether this discrepancy was a function of differences in methodology remains to be seen.

A potentially significant lead concerning the dynamics underlying unconscious self evaluation was provided by the fact that schizophrenics took longer than normals to recognize self products created under success conditions. One might have viewed this as a defensive response on the schizophrenic's part designed to protect a source of special self enhancing experience which could be lost if its true identity entered into conscious awareness. However, this hypothesis is doubtful in view of the fact that the schizophrenics did not rate their self products produced under success conditions any more favorably than they did those produced during failure. That is, the success condition did not seem, in terms of the self ratings, to have been any more self enhancing than the failure condition.

Ray, Dickinson, and Morehead (1966) recorded GSR responses from one sample of schizophrenic women (N = 36) while they were watching silent, colored motion pictures of self. GSR was also recorded while they observed a motion picture of another patient. Significantly greater GSR response to the self as compared to the "other" pictures was found. A second sample comprised of eight normal and seven schizophrenic women was likewise studied. One modification in the procedure involved subjects viewing a self picture, another of a friend, a third of an unknown normal woman, and a fourth of an unknown schizophrenic woman. GSR response to the self pictures was greater than that to any of the control pictures. It was noted that even when schizophrenic subjects denied recognizing their own pictures, their degree of GSR response indicated the presence of special affective reactions.

Comparisons of the responses of hospitalized psychiatric patients ($N = 9$ males) to pictures of self versus pictures of others were made by Thomas and Stasiak (1964). A control group of ten normal subjects was included. Responses to pictures of males, females, and self were determined by photographing the distribution of the subject's eye movements as he examined each picture. It was possible, in this fashion, to measure how long he looked at the various parts of a picture. A trend was detected for the psychiatric patients (as compared to the controls) to scan their own pictures a relatively shorter or longer time than they did the non-self pictures. Also, while the normals, in examining their own pictures, focused largely on the face, the patients avoided the face and concentrated on the body. This last finding is exceedingly interesting. Thomas and Stasiak conjecture that it may somehow reflect a tendency on the part of the psychiatric patients to avoid the rich information conveyed by the face and that it may, in fact, be part of a general avoidance of information intake. There is no way of knowing at this point how valid this idea may be. But one cannot help but be impressed with the potentiality of the methodology employed. Here is a technique which permits fairly precise measurement of how an individual distributes his attention to the various sectors of his body. Perhaps it could even be modified to trace how an individual allocates his interest to a full-sized mirror image of himself. The importance of such body attention patterns will be taken up in a number of later chapters.

Confrontation with pictures of self is the basis of a treatment technique which has been under investigation by Cornelison (Cornelison and Arsenian, 1960) and others in a group at Jefferson Medical College (Cornelison and Bahnson, 1966). Typically, motion pictures are taken of patients during periods of disturbance or in special interview situations and they are later shown these pictures—with the assumption that a vivid visual confrontation with their own behavior will lead to insights and corrective responses. While dramatic responses to such self confrontation occur in various kinds of psychiatric patients, it has been difficult to establish general or persisting therapeutic effects. Some encouragement has been provided by results obtained by Moore, Chernell, and West (1965) and Boyd and Sisney (1967) which indicate greater improvement in psychiatric patients exposed to self confrontation stimuli than in controls without a self confrontation experience.

Frenkel (1964) has urged the importance of self confrontation in treatment of schizophrenics. He introduces a mirror into interview and therapy sessions and encourages the patient to associate to his perception of his mirror image. He reports that unusually rich and significant material is elicited in this fashion.

It is impossible at this point to integrate the several studies cited above which bear on the responses of schizophrenics to representations of themselves. Methodologies have been confusingly diverse. One can only say that there has been a trend for schizophrenics to react differently than various control subjects to self image stimuli. The significance of such differences remains in doubt in view of the Traub, et al. (1967) observation that what appeared to be a difference between schizophrenics and normals in the accuracy of perception of their mirror image was actually a special case of a more generalized perceptual difficulty. Of course, one can reverse one's perspective and consider that generalized perceptual difficulty results when serious distortions arise in the perception of one's own body. Perhaps distortion in body experience precedes distortion in what is "out there".

Miscellaneous Body Image Studies of Psychiatric Samples

Scattered approaches, not easily classified under previously cited categories, have been explored in the process of trying to understand the role of the body image in psychiatric symptomatology. Considerable ingenuity characterizes some of these efforts, which will be outlined below.

Bender and Nathanson (1950), Bender, Shapiro, and Teuber (1949) and others, working principally in a neurological context, have highlighted the potential value of the double simultaneous stimulation technique (DSS) for detecting body image pathology. This technique involves the subject reporting (with eyes closed) what he perceives when he is touched simultaneously on two different parts of the body. There is a tendency under such circumstances for certain parts of the body to have dominance over others. That is, the stimulus to the dominant part is perceived whereas that to the less dominant part is not perceived. Patients with brain dysfunction and also very young children manifest this response pattern most clearly. Normal individuals quickly learn to correct their errors and to detect both of the points simultaneously stimulated. Typically, the face and genitals have proven to be dominant over other body areas; and the hand has been lowest in the hierarchy. There has been considerable speculation as to why the face should be so high and the hand so low in the dominance series. Bender proposed an explanation in terms of a psychoanalytic model which depicts the ego as having a center and a periphery—with the face representing the center and the hand the periphery. He states that in visualizing the self the face comes most clearly to mind and, as such, represents the inner or center portion of the ego. But the hand may be viewed as the part which makes contact with the outside world and therefore is on the periphery. The difference in dominance between the face and hands would therefore reflect the contrast in their ego significance. Linn (1955) has proposed another psychoanalytic theory which visualizes the face and hand as originally fused in perception by their common function of relieving oral tension, but then becoming sharply differentiated from each other as the individual matures. Supposedly, as the child learns to separate himself from mother he begins to use his hand as a substitute for her to relieve oral tensions. The hand becomes more of a helper and therefore it is subordinated in stimulus value because it might distract from the appreciation of that which is providing relief for tensions. Thus, indicates Linn, the hand assumes low sensation dominance; and this is evident in the course of DDS.

Morris and Young (1967) undertook to apply Linn's theory in an objective study. They reasoned that the greater the oral orientation (in the psychoanalytic sense) of an individual the more likely he would be fixated at an early stage in which the face and hand were still fused in their oral significance. Furthermore, since the "oral character would be expected to have extinguished the sensations from his hands more often in the past because he would have used them more often to satisfy his oral needs", he "would be expected to have developed hands less sensitive to double simultaneous stimulation" (p. 14). This line of reasoning resulted in the prediction that there would be a positive relationship between degree of orality and occurrence of errors on DSS of face and hand. Two experimental groups were chosen to represent an extreme of oral fixation: 20 alcoholics and 20 patients with peptic ulcers. The control groups were comprised of 40 non-hospitalized normals and a mixed sample of patients with either rheumatoid arthritis or neurodermatitis. DSS measures were obtained in each group. In addition, the Rorschach was administered to the normals and each response was scored with reference to its degree of oral reference. It was found that the alcoholic group was not significantly different from any of the other groups in DSS errors, but the ulcer patients did manifest more such errors than the normals. Further, the combined alcoholic and ulcer groups obtained significantly higher error scores than the combined normal and patient groups. No relationship appeared between DSS error frequency and the Rorschach index of orality in the normal group. Morris concluded that her results were partially supportive of the hypothesis that degree of orality influences the manner in which the individual has learned to differentiate his head and hand.

With regard to the DSS method, it should be noted that past studies have not detected any consistent differences between schizophrenic and normal adults. However, Pollack and Goldfarb (1957) report that young institutionalized schizophrenic children do make more DSS errors than institutionalized non-schizophrenic children and also normal children. They raise the question whether schizophrenic children do not suffer from a degree of integrative impairment equivalent to that found in individuals with brain dysfunction.

Felix and Arieli (1966) compared a number of normal and pathological groups with regard to their ability to put together a model of a hand and also a human figure which were presented in disassembled form and which were taken from the Object Assembly subtest of the Wechsler Adult Intelligence Scale. They assumed that ability to assemble the parts of the hand and figure accurately provided information about the adequacy of the subject's hand concept and his body image in general. The groups studied consisted of normal children, normal adults, children with cerebral palsy, post-polio patients, children with severe behavior disorders, childhood schizophrenics, children with suspected organic disorders, chronic and acute schizophrenic adults, and adults with cerebral lesions. The primary findings were that the chronic adult schizophrenics, childhood schizophrenics, and children with cerebral palsy manifested the greatest difficulty in correctly reconstructing the hand and the human figure. This was interpreted as indicating unusual disturbance of the body image in such groups.

Blatt, Allison, and Baker (1965) used the same hand and human figure from the Object Assembly subtest to determine if they would distinguish a group of children (N = 7) who had come to a child guidance clinic with symptoms of unusual body concern from a group (N = 6) with minimal body anxiety. Those with high body concern performed significantly poorer on the assembly tasks, but not on other Wechsler subtests. In a second phase of this study, the Rorschach protocols of 20 adult psychiatric patients whose Object Assembly scores were low in relation to their own Wechsler subtest scores were compared with the protocols of 20 patients with relatively superior Object Assembly performance. As expected, the poor performers displayed more body concern and anxiety in their Rorschach responses than did the good performers. Body anxiety was evaluated in terms of the presence of Rorschach responses referring to such themes as anatomy, death, and distorted body parts. Blatt, Allison, and Baker considered their results to affirm that cognitive processes involving material with body connotations are vulnerable to disruption by body anxiety. However, one must regard these results cautiously because Rockwell (1967) in a later study involving 30 boys with unusual body concern and 15 without such concern could find no Object Assembly score differences between the two groups.

McClelland and Watt (1968) have made use of attitudes toward "masculine" versus "feminine" parts of one's body as a means of differentiating schizophrenic and normal persons. They assumed that sex role alienation was particularly characteristic of schizophrenics. They studied male (N = 23) and female (N = 22) schizophrenics and male (N = 20) and female (41) normal controls. Among other tasks, they asked that each subject indicate whether he was satisfied or dissatisfied with 20 different body parts. Eight had been earlier judged by experts to be relatively feminine (e.g., lips, face, skin, legs). Eight had been judged to be relatively masculine (e.g., ears, elbow, fingers, back), and four were designated as neutral (e.g., knees, profile). Incidentally, these judgments of masculinity-femininity were similar to those obtained by Nash (1958) from adolescent boys—although the two studies arrived at opposite conclusions concerning the relative masculinity-femininity of legs and fingers. McClelland and Watt discovered in their data that female schizophrenics were less dissatisfied *in general* with their bodies than male schizophrenics. This was especially true in terms of the body parts the experts had judged to be feminine, but not significantly so for the parts judged to be masculine. In the normal samples, the males generally showed less body dissatisfaction than the females. Also, the females were more dissatisfied with female body parts and males more dissatisfied with male body parts. This was the opposite of the patterns characterizing the schizophrenics. It was concluded that (p. 235) "schizophrenic males have replaced the normal male concern for masculine body parts with a greater concern for their appearance, like normal females. Schizophrenic females simply show less concern for all parts of their bodies whether masculine or feminine. . . . It seems plausible to conclude that some part of the schizophrenic woman's unconscious self-image is insensitive and more masculine, whereas some part of the schizophrenic man's self-image is sensitive and more feminine."

5
Trends and Generalities

What generalities and formulations can be extracted from the array of information that has just been presented?

To begin with, it is evident that body image variables have been seriously implicated in an amazing variety of behavioral phenomena. Investigators have been willing to invest time and energy in considering the role of body attitudes in psychopathology, body disablement, motivation for plastic surgery, self concept, organization of spatial perception, response to central nervous system damage, trait patterns, response to drugs, ability to tolerate stress, social interaction, and so forth. It is difficult to think of an area of behavior which has not been at least scanned within the context of the possible influence of the body image.

However, one must admit that a disconcerting range of ideas exists as to the nature of the "body image" and which of its aspects are worthy of study. For some, the "body image" is largely what an individual is willing to tell us when we ask him how he feels about the parts of his body. This view is illustrated by many of the Jourard-Secord (1954, 1955) studies. For others, the "body image" is a more cryptic phenomenon whose measurement requires devious strategies. It can only be indirectly tapped as it appears in a figure drawing or responses to an unknowing confrontation with a representation of self. However, one gets the impression that these differences are only, in part, a function of unlike concepts as to the nature of the body image. They may largely reflect disagreements on the current psychological scene concerning the relative efficacy of direct (e.g., questionnaire) versus indirect (e.g., projective) methods for obtaining useful information. Therefore, it might be sensible to side-step this issue for the moment; and simply consider what body image dimensions have emerged which seem to offer promise. There may be value in taking stock of the various body image parameters which have been conceptualized and, in most instances, also measured. Once such parameters have been identified, their investigation becomes fair game for any methodology which will lead to sensible findings.

Let us systematically list and discuss what seem to be the prime dimensions of body perception which explicitly or implicitly recur in the literature.

1. A popular dimension, in terms of the frequency with which it has been studied, concerns how positively or negatively the individual regards his body. Such body evaluations typically involve stating how satisfied one is with the appearance of a number of different areas of one's body. They relate to the basic question whether the individual likes or dislikes his body. Subjects' ratings of degree of body satisfaction have shown fairly consistent positive correlations with self concept ratings. They have also proven to be positively correlated with variables like self reported degree of ego strength, sympathetic attitudes toward the disabled, and absence of anxious concern about one's body, as defined by the Secord Homonym test (1953). However, there are studies which indicate further that they are positively and significantly linked with social desirability. This means that when they do corrclate with other measures (e.g., self reported ego strength) one must determine how much this is a function of shared social desirability sets.

Few would question that whether a person is satisfied with the attractiveness of his body represents an important facet of how he experiences it. But is this variable best measured by self report techniques which are influenced by social desirability? Might it be possible to adapt unconscious self confrontation procedures to obtain self evaluations less influenced by the intent to make a good impression? Or might the Osgood scales (Osgood, et al., 1957), which obtain evaluations in a moderately devious fashion, provide ratings less consciously manipulated?

2. Perception of one's body size is another important dimension. More empirical studies have been devoted to it than any other body image variable. The accumulated data indicate that when an individual judges the size of a part of his body he is influenced by factors aside from the real magnitude of the part. He seems to be affected not only by the situational context of his body (e.g., the spatial extent of his environs) but also by emotional attitudes toward himself and his body. Illustratively, his perception of his bodily size may reflect his level of self-esteem; or his degree of field independence; or his need to prove his superiority to women. It is equally important that impressionistic and clinical studies have reported that sensations of change in body size often accompany special behavioral events. Florid experiences of body size change have been described in relation to schizophrenic regression, migraine attacks, transference attitudes during psychoanalytic therapy, and brain damage. Gross shifts in the individual's adjustment level seem to be

translated into alterations in perceived body size. Also, shifts in how he feels about himself are similarly channeled.

It is an unsettled matter whether the empirical evidence justifies the statement that schizophrenic disorganization results in a sense of increased body size, although it is fair to say that the weight of the evidence does currently favor this view. In any case, where such evidence has been assumed to be sufficient it has typically been interpreted within a boundary model derived either from psychoanalytic or sensori-tonic theory. Presumably, the schizophrenic perceives himself as large because disorganizing processes have disrupted his boundaries and left him with sensations of being without limits and "spread out"—therefore unusually large. However, this interpretation may be questioned on the basis of Fisher's (1966B) work which indicates that schizophrenics actually have subjective feelings of shrinking and becoming small. Fisher suggests that the overestimation of body size encountered in schizophrenics may be compensatory for the subjective sense of smallness. This entire matter requires clarification.

Another issue to consider is that body size estimation may not be a unitary variable. Correlations between degree of over- or underestimation of the sizes of different body areas have been moderate and in some cases only of a chance order. The factors that determine size estimation of one's head may possibly be quite different from those basic to estimation of hip size. Or height estimation may relate to vectors of quite a different order than those affecting the horizontal body dimensions. There are already reports in the literature which indicate that perception of the size of upper versus lower body regions calls forth different degrees of over- and underestimation.

Finally, we need to get closure concerning the most appropriate ways to measure an individual's perception of his body size. How can we minimize the interfering influence of his own idiosyncratic concept of units like an "inch" and obtain estimates that truly reflect his body size experiences? The work of Fisher (1966B) implies that in addition to eliciting overt judgments of body size from him we ought to ask how he subjectively feels about his size. He may be able to make accurate estimates of his body size and yet simultaneously have sensations of being unusually small or that some body part is shrinking. But returning to the matter of actual body size estimates, one gets the impression that some of the most consistent and meaningful judgments have been obtained with techniques which are ego involving—which require evaluations of lifelike body representations (e.g., the pictures of body parts used by Cleveland, 1960B) rather than impersonal measuring rods.

3. Here and there in the literature one finds indications that people differ in how aware they are of their bodies as compared to the total perceptual field. That is, some have high awareness of the body and others are minimally aware of it. In the case of the hypochondriacal individual, who is completely wrapped up in his body, the fact that extremes of body awareness can occur is obvious. But evidence for variation in body awareness comes

from other sources too. For example, it has been noted that subjects differ a good deal in the frequency with which they use words referring to the body when they produce TAT stories. Differences in mirror behavior have been observed which suggest a range of interest in looking at one's image. There is variation in the number of body associations given to the stimulus words in the Secord Homonym test. This procedure, it will be recalled, was devised to measure how concerned the individual is about his body by determining how often he gives body versus non-body associations to homonyms (e.g., colon, graft) which have both body and non-body meaning.[1] One can further point to the individuality in body awareness by referring to differences in number of anatomy and body responses found in Rorschach images and spontaneous word samples. It is also pertinent that in some disorganized states (e.g., schizophrenia, brain damage) marked tendencies may appear to be either totally focused upon one's body or to ignore it (even to the extreme of denying its existence).

The literature suggests a good likelihood that a dimension of body awareness exists and that it may have significance as a long-term attribute of the individual. Research by the present writer which has reaffirmed this possibility will be described at a later point. In this work degree of body awareness has proven to be a viable variable for study. For example, it has shown itself to be meaningfully related to a number of personality and defense strategy parameters.

Another point to consider with reference to body awareness is how a person distributes or channels his attention to the major sectors of his body. Does one individual focus primarily on his head and rarely upon the lower sectors of his body; whereas another shows the obverse pattern? At another level, this question might be translated into the inquiry whether unlike values or degrees of importance are ascribed to body parts. What indications are there in the past literature that such questions are sensible and would provide a profitable approach to analyzing the organization of the body image? Is there any evidence from previous work that differential attention or value is assigned to body regions? Suggestions that such is the case come from several sources. To begin with, one finds, in psychiatric patients, abundant examples in which a specific body area selectively becomes the focus for hypochondriacal concern or delusional ideas or "strange" sensations. The behavior of certain patients who ask for plastic surgery certainly implies special awareness of, and feeling about, a given body part. A circumscribed region is obviously assigned heightened significance. Other kinds of pertinent observations have been made in normal samples. Thus, there are

---

[1] Parenthetically, let it be said that aside from the appealing "face validity" of this technique its actual validity has not been directly demonstrated. Indeed, its efficacy in predicting behaviors (e.g., sympathy for the handicapped, rate of adjustment to disability, psychopathology) has not been impressive.

reports that subjects vary in the valuations they place upon body areas when asked to judge their worth and importance. Individuals also differ with respect to which body areas they experience as most and least altered when viewing them through aniseikonic lenses. Subjects display their own idiosyncratic reactions when evaluating the masculinity-femininity of specific body areas; and similar individuality has been observed in deciding which body areas remind one of certain emotional themes. It was evidence of this nature, among other cues, which encouraged the present writer to undertake a program of studies concerned with the distribution of body attention, which is outlined in later chapters. As will be seen, individuals do consistently focus a good deal of attention upon certain body sectors and minimal amounts upon others; and these patterns make sense psychologically.

4. The concept of the body boundary derives from the formulation that individuals differ in the way they experience the demarcation between their bodies and the outer world. Some presumably perceive themselves as possessed of a well differentiated boundary which clearly indicates the borders of the body. Others feel only a hazy line of demarcation and do not have a sharp awareness of the separation between self and non-self. The body boundary has appeared as a prominent explanatory idea in the research of Wapner and Werner (1965) and Witkin, et al. (1954, 1962). Likewise, Fisher and Cleveland (1968), whose work will be reviewed in the next chapter, have emphasized the importance of boundary phenomena.

The boundary model has been pressed into service to explain early formation of identity, variations in perception of body size, disturbance in delinquents, disorganization in schizophrenics, and many other phenomena. Fisher and Cleveland have shown that boundary definiteness is related to a spectrum of personality variables. One cannot but be impressed that most of the major programs of research dealing with body image and body perception have found it necessary to propose the existence of a body boundary which influences behavior in manifold ways. The methods used to measure the attributes of the boundary have certainly been diverse. The sensori-tonic group deduces boundary characteristics from the degree to which an individual's spatial judgments indicate separation between self and object. Witkin also makes boundary determinations from spatial judgments; and more recently has relied on figure drawing productions for this purpose. Fisher and Cleveland assay boundary definiteness from the qualities ascribed to imaginative images (e.g., how protected or covered they are) evoked by ink blot stimuli. Unfortunately, systematic attempts have not yet been made to ascertain how the three different methods for measuring boundary definiteness are intercorrelated. Each group seems to be too preoccupied with its own problems and methodology to take the necessary time for such studies.

5. While sensori-tonic and other investigators use spatial judgments (of self and non-self objects) to make deductions about the body boundary, it is also true that ability to judge the position of one's body in space is an

important dimension in its own right. Head (1920) considered that one of the prime functions of the body scheme is to provide a realistic context for maintaining posture and spatial orientation. Witkin's findings (1954, 1962) certainly indicate that some people have excellent facility in accurately monitoring body position, even under very difficult circumstances; whereas others are easily confused by being put into slightly unusual body positions. We know, too, from Witkin's data that these differences are linked with a string of personality traits and stylistic variables. A great deal of effort has already gone into understanding "position in space" responses. Large masses of pertinent empirical data have accumulated concerning them. As these data expand our understanding, it has become apparent that the spatial dimension is probably part of a broader category related to one's ability to separate what is significant from its context. Even traditional cognitive measures underlying the IQ have turned out to be correlated with ability to orient one's body in space. While this is confusing and raises questions about the independent existence of body image variables, it does, at the same time, begin to provide bridges between spheres of perception and cognition which have ordinarily not been juxtaposed. One would hope that the ultimate attainment with reference to most body image dimensions would be, in similar fashion, to demonstrate their relationships to broader levels of response and function.

6. There seems to be a need among those studying the body image to assume that a continuum exists defining how anxious one is about one's body. Some people are apparently chronically afraid of body damage; and others are quite unconcerned about the possibility. The existence of such a dimension has long been proposed by Freud and other psychoanalysts in their formulations dealing with "castration anxiety". Fear of body damage is dramatically highlighted in the behavior of the severe hypochondriac; and is easily apparent in the patient awaiting surgery. But its existence has also been detected in varying amounts in other contexts: e.g., research indicating differential aniseikonic lens response to mutilated and non-mutilated human figures; work concerning reactions to tachistoscopically exposed pictures of persons with body mutilations; findings indicating the apparent interfering effects of body anxiety upon ability to put together representations of the body (e.g., human hand from the WISC Object Assembly); and the prominence of body damage themes in dreams, children's stories, and spontaneous speech productions.

It is not at all obvious how body anxiety is related to other kinds of anxiety. Little or no information is available concerning the correlations between indices of body anxiety and measures like the Taylor Manifest Anxiety scale. One might expect moderately high positive relationships between them; and yet they are probably far from synonomous. A mature adult can fear all kinds of things in the world without seriously anticipating that they will damage his body. It is tempting to speculate that the child's earliest sense of identity revolves about coherent and cyclic body experiences and that consequently some of his first fears are associated with a body context. That is, threat to self might for the child be primarily experienced as a threat to body (e.g., a potential interruption of a pleasant body state). It may be this early prototype of fear which is particularly reactivated by threat of surgery, body crippling, and schizophrenic regressive processes. In such instances fear and body fear may become more and more synonomous. Instead of seeing differentiated kinds of threats in the environment, the individual may rephrase them all into literal body destructive terms. Interesting investigations remain to be done in which the ratio of body anxiety to other types of anxiety is measured in a range of fear arousing situations and also in persons with differing amounts of ego strength. We also need to know a good deal more about this ratio over the developmental sequence from childhood to adolescence to adulthood to advanced aging.

7. One would expect that feelings pertaining to masculinity-femininity would participate influentially in the body image. In most cultures it appears to be important that an individual be able to experience his body as possessing a quantity of masculinity or femininity appropriate to his defined sex role. Perhaps it is even important that there be a patterned distribution of attributed masculinity or femininity, such that some sectors (e.g., the genitals) are perceived as highly "charged" with it and others (e.g., heart, brain) much less so. However, we actually know little about such matters despite the existence of a large literature concerned with sexual identity. One of the problems in doing adequate research in this area is that it is very difficult to obtain criterion information about feelings pertaining to masculinity-femininity without arousing powerful defensive responses. With rare exceptions, the male wants to tell you he feels masculine and the female that she feels feminine. Social desirability effects are pervasive and have rendered most masculinity-femininity scales ineffective. Of course, we do have the obvious distinction between male and female as one criterion of masculinity-femininity. But finer criteria distinctions based on measuring masculinity or femininity within each sex are relatively lacking.

Research concerned with masculinity-femininity from a body image perspective has dealt primarily with the following: degree of portrayal of sex characteristics in figure drawings; how global or differentiated men, as compared to women, are in rating their satisfaction with a number of areas of their bodies; differences between men and women in preferred body size and also modes of estimation of body size; sex differences in perception of one's body while wearing aniseikonic lenses; amount of body awareness and also body anxiety in men versus women. As earlier stated, the results from these multiple procedures have been rather fragmentary. There are leads here and there. However, we currently lack an understanding of the simple facts of masculine versus feminine body experience. Is it largely a difference in feelings about the genitals and the reproductive system? Does it revolve about feelings of strength and aggressive muscular prowess as opposed to sensations of body softness? Are there differences in gross body awareness? Are there differences in the way attention is distributed to the major body regions?

Many theorized differences between the masculine and feminine body image which are referred to, particularly in psychoanalytic papers, have been difficult to demonstrate objectively. Even the gross differences in body configuration, genitals, and social roles obtaining between the sexes have not easily translated into corresponding differences in most of the usual body image measures. However, some of the results obtained offer leads that may be worth thinking about. For example, it has been shown that men seek to dramatize the bigness and women the smallness of their bodies; and these findings have stood up well to cross-validation. It has been shown, in a related vein, that males are more likely than women to convert feelings of failure into sensations of diminished height. Such results imply that there may be a fundamental sex differentiation in the size scale which is applied to the perception of one's body. Women tend to shrink and men to augment the extent of most of their body proportions. Another interesting sex difference which has been reported concerns the upper versus lower regions of the body. Girls are apparently more anxious than boys about perceiving distortions in the legs. Also, it has been reported that women are more dissatisfied than men with the lower areas of their bodies. Perhaps the sexes have different degrees of difficulty or anxiety in organizing upper versus lower body sectors. As will be shown at a later point, this is a possibility of considerable potential significance which may relate to differential cultural rules about motility in the two sexes. Another lead regarding sex differentiation should be mentioned. Data have been obtained which indicate that there may be a contrast in total body consciousness or concern. For example, after the age of 13 males clearly manifest less focus upon the body than do girls in their story compositions. Analogously, female college students have been found to be higher in body concern on the Secord Homonym test than male students. Any of the observations just cited would be reasonable starting places from which to explore further the nature of the body experiences that go along with being a man or a woman.

It is possible to conceive of other dimensions, aside from those listed above, which might eventually turn out to be important in understanding body experience. A few that come to mind will be further mentioned:

Rigidity versus fluidity of body image: studies have been done which indicate that persons differ in how easily they are able to see their usual mirror image as changed when viewing themselves through aniseikonic lenses. Some cannot perceive themselves as changed at all and others do so immediately. Also, experiments involving the impact of conditions like sensory isolation, LSD, and sleep deprivation demonstrate a range of susceptibility to experiencing one's body as altered.

Character of sustaining sensations: the kinds of body sensations that provide a sustaining framework for experiencing one's body with some constancy may differ from person to person. Kinesthetic sensations may be paramount to one; whereas another may find visceral sensations the "core" about which a sense of "my body" is constructed. There is little in the literature concerning this issue except the work of Fisher and Cleveland (1968) which has shown that exterior versus interior body sensations may have unlike experiential impact upon persons, with consequent differences in their ability to maintain boundaries.

Strategies for maintaining existing body image organization: once an individual is satisfied with the way his body "feels" he may develop techniques for insuring constancy in this experiential pattern. There may be interesting individual strategies directed to this end. For example, one person might rely upon wearing clothing of a particular tightness or visibility to create a specific body "feel". Other strategies for insuring body constancy might depend upon a certain rate of self touching, or a regular sequence of intimate contacts with a spouse's body, or eating large quantities of food. It should be possible to classify such strategies and define those which are of special adjustive value for each individual.

Cleanliness: much emphasis is placed in Western culture on keeping one's body clean. This is apparent in the amount of time spent in the socialization process teaching the child how to groom and clean his body. It is also apparent in the considerable effort, money, and time the average adult expends on attaining proper clean, "good smelling" standards. Of course, there are marked individual differences in the importance attached to body cleanliness; and there are probably also differences between men and women in this respect. Certainly age related variations occur. Psychoanalytic observers have been inclined to link attitudes about body cleanliness with the severity or conflict originally associated with the individual's toilet training. The "anal character" in the Freudian typology responds to his conflicts about anal control by becoming meticulously clean. One can see no reasons why the measurement of body cleanliness attitudes cannot be rather easily accomplished. The pertinent data should be available by direct observation of the subject's appearance and also from self reports.

Numerous dimensions have been listed above as apparently or potentially significant in understanding how the "body image" operates. Are they relatively independent? Or do they represent different facets of a complex system which is actually unified in its functioning? It is too early to say much in response to such questions. One can say that measures presumably tapping each of the dimensions have been found in most studies not to be significantly correlated. For example, measures of body awareness do not consistently relate to measures of body anxiety. Or measures of boundary definiteness do not consistently correlate with indices which evaluate ability to perceive one's position in space accurately. Statistically, they seem quite independent.

However, this does not rule out the possibility that the various dimensions represent different aspects of a highly complicated, but yet coordinated, system. Illustratively, there may be stress situations in which an increase in body awareness may mobilize increased body anxiety and this may in turn produce boundary disturbance. But in a non-stressful setting a shift in body awareness may have no repercussions for level of body anxiety or boundary differentiation. That is, the relationships among the dimensions may turn out to be a function of stress level and many other variables like sex, age, presence of physical illness, availability of means for comforting one's body, degree of social isolation, and so forth. Until it has been possible to conduct many more studies in which measures are taken under a variety of conditions, it is too early to arrive at conclusions about how the major known body image dimensions "hold together".

Another useful way to look at the work reviewed in this chapter concerns the techniques which have been developed for measuring body image variables. The last ten years have produced an impressive expansion of "body image" technology. New measurement techniques have proliferated and one now has a respectable range of choice in deciding how to quantify body image variables that seem important. Let us enumerate the types of measures available.

Consider how many procedures have been devised for measuring body size estimates. Illustratively, they include moving tabs on a measuring rod, judging relative sizes of pictured representations of body parts, drawing lines on strips of paper to designate a given dimension, adjusting the size of a projected picture, indicating preferences for schematic human figures which vary in the magnitude of their proportions, designating on an exterior surface the equivalent of the distance between two points stimulated on one's body, and assembling dolls with body parts that vary in size.

Tests related to spatial aspects of the body image embrace judging the vertical, adjusting one's body to specific positions, decoding double simultaneous stimulation, and placing figures properly in miniature spatial settings.

Body awareness and evaluation, both with respect to total body and specific body sectors, has been approached via number of body references in TAT stories, spontaneous listings of body parts, body homonym associations, body area designations (as indicated by the subject pointing) made in response to stimulus themes, gender terms applied to various body regions, and manner of depicting specific body parts in figure drawings.

Anxiety about one's body has been measured by means of figure drawing indices, aniseikonic lens behavior, associations to homonyms with body and non-body meanings, self ratings, analysis of content elicited by projective stimuli, response to pictures with pain themes, interpretations of tachistoscopically exposed pictures with mutilation themes, responses to disarranged sentences containing body themes, and ratings of pictures depicting different forms of body disablement.

Boundary phenomena have been scanned with analysis of ink blot responses, drawings, measures of accuracy and style of making spatial judgments, and judgments indicative of preferred distance from others ("buffer zone").

Multiple aspects of the process of perceiving one's own appearance have been studied in terms of mirror behavior, unconscious reactions to self representations, patterns of change in one's mirror image when it is viewed aniseikonically, characteristics ascribed to human figures in one's dreams, and questionnaire responses.

Numerous other examples could be added to those cited above. The technology for measuring body image variables has been exuberant in its expansion in the last decade.

One detects in the literature a sharpened realization that body attitudes are often the resultant and reflection of interpersonal relationships. There is more interest in viewing the individual's body image as an outgrowth of social experience. One finds fewer instances in which it is tacitly accepted that body attitudes pertain simply to the literal characteristics of the body. The interpersonal basis of the body scheme has been particularly dramatized by such findings as the fact that it seems to change during psychotherapy; by the demonstration that its evaluation is affected by previous success or failure experiences; by the observation that it is correlated with various personality indices; and by the fact that even its alterations consequent upon brain damage are colored by the previous personality of the individual concerned. The decision to view body attitudes as evolving from the same socialization matrix as other kinds of significant values and standards which have concerned behavioral researchers has a noteworthy implication. It leads quite logically to the idea that information about an individual's body image may be used as an indirect means for finding out things about his psychological functioning. The possibility should be seriously considered that batteries of body image tests may ultimately become available which will enable indirect measurement of a range of significant personality parameters.

Considerable data have accumulated which paradoxically highlight the simultaneous plasticity and rigidity of the body image. It is known that gross alterations in body perception may be induced in normal persons by such agents as LSD, hypnotism, relatively brief periods of sensory isolation, and anxiety. Similarly, there are many everyday events like falling asleep or ascending in an elevator which can produce noticeable and sometimes disturbing changes in body experience. But at the other extreme, one finds situations in which massive body alterations are repudiated to the point of illusion and even delusion. The patient manifesting anosognosia in his denial of an obvious hemiplegic incapacitation or the amputee who continues to experience an absent limb as if it were still present or the individual who will not accept the changes in his appearance produced by plastic surgery illustrate this extreme. In the same vein, several studies have referred to the way in which the polio patient clings to his old body concept; and there have been analogous reports regarding other types of body crippling. It becomes an important problem to disentangle the variables that facilitate and those that inhibit body schema shift. If one embarks upon such a quest, all kinds of difficult questions present themselves. What is a real body image change? If a subject reports in an experimental setting that his head seems slightly larger than usual, is this a "real" change? If he reports that his body feels "strange", does this indicate a change process? Or are such "strange" sensations fairly common occurrences in the daily body experiences of the average individual? General confusion concerning the nature of body image plasticity has been indirectly evidenced in the literature by the fact that some (e.g., Head, Schilder, Wapner) have defined body image in a way which points up its transitory qualities; whereas others (Fisher and Cleveland, Greenacre) have focused on its long-term persisting characteristics.

The data and observations we have concerning what happens to the body image when a person is deeply troubled and develops neurotic or schizophrenic symptoms do not crystallize into simple structures. It is hoped that studies completed by the present writer, to be presented in later chapters, will help to clarify some of the confusion. But in any case, what can one say from the literature reviewed above concerning the relationship of body image and personality disorganization? First of all, we know absolutely nothing about cause and effect. There are a myriad of observations indicating that troubled people have troubled body experiences. But one does not know whether disturbances in body perception play a role in setting off generalized disorganization or whether they are reflections of a general breakdown in function. This means that we badly need studies in which body image dimensions and patterns of experience are measured in non-symptomatic children and adults to determine whether such measures will predict those who later develop serious psychiatric problems. This would be a beginning in evaluating whether there are body image forerunners of later disturbance. Another approach to this problem might involve taking sequential body image measures at various stages during a patient's recovery from acute disturbance (i.e., acute phase, midway in recovery process, final recovery). One could then ask whether these measures change in a fashion parallel with improvement in overt behavior. Do they lag behind? Or do they precede them?

As defined by published reports, the vicissitudes of body experience in the maladjusted are truly startling to behold. Patients are described who feel disjointed, literally falling to pieces, changing shape, being transformed in their sex, experiencing fantastic alterations in the sizes of certain body parts, and so forth. A reading of such reports might lead one to believe that strange and bizarre body feelings are typical of the seriously disturbed. However, this may not be an accurate impression. It is possible that the reports in the literature are selective insofar as only particularly interesting or sensational symptom pictures are offered for publication. Actually, there are indications that this may be so. Systematic studies of body image distortions in psychiatric patients and normal controls which have only recently been undertaken indicate that it is quite difficult to differentiate such groups on the basis of how often they report distorted body experiences in a variety of categories. Consistent differences have appeared in only a relatively few areas. This matter awaits additional investigation.

Body image research shows every sign of flourishing and expanding. New ideas and techniques have continued to appear in many different quarters. There has been a particularly marked increase in studies which observe standards of objectivity and scientific control. At the same time, a significant matrix of less objective, but not less significant, clinical observations has further evolved. The importance of this matrix becomes evident when one looks back and notes that some of the speculations of Head, Schilder, and Freud were eventually resolved into operational research terms and substantiated.

II

THE BOUNDARY: DEMARCATION OF ONE'S BODY LIMITS FROM THE WORLD

6
Introduction

Many of the core concepts underlying the studies to be presented in this book evolved from previous work by the author (collaboratively with Sidney Cleveland) relating to the nature of the body image boundary. This work was described in a monograph (*Body Image and Personality*) which proposed that a fundamental aspect of the body image is the manner in which the individual experiences the limits of his body. It was shown that there is considerable variation in the firmness or definiteness persons ascribe to their body boundaries. At one extreme is the individual who views his body as clearly and sharply bounded, with a high degree of differentiation from non-self objects, and at the opposite pole is the person who regards his body as lacking demarcation or differentiation from what is "out there." Sharply differing concepts may exist as to how the space encompassed by one's body is separated from the surrounding non-body space.

The fact that there is variation in how the body boundary is perceived is difficult to grasp because in the ordinary course of events most persons seem to know quite adequately where they end and the outer world begins. There are few, if any, apparent indications that persons experience their boundaries differentially or that this may play a real part in their behavior. However, in certain pathological states the existence and functions of the boundary do become apparent. It has long been noted that the disorganizing impact of brain damage or psychopathology (e.g., schizophrenia) may result in confusion about whether particular events are occurring in the body or non-body space. Instances have been cited of brain damaged patients who, when asked with their eyes closed to localize a stimulus applied to the skin, respond by pointing to a locus outside of the body. Apparently, without visual prompting they literally do not know the limits of their own bodies. Relatedly, schizophrenic patients have been observed who are unable to distinguish whether hallucinatory voices come from "outside" or "inside" (Hollender and Boszormenyi-Nagy, 1958). It is not uncommon for schizophrenics to indicate that they have difficulty in maintaining distance between themselves and even chance occurrences in their vicinity. Neighboring events are experienced as if they could actually intrude upon one's body. Apropos of this point, Schilder (1935) remarked that the schizophrenic often feels as if his body were "spread over the world." Loss of awareness of boundaries, with its accompanying precipitous anxiety and perceptual alterations, has also been reported by normal subjects while under the influence of psychotomimetic drugs (Savage, 1955), during hypnotic procedures (Gill and Brenman, 1959), and in sensory isolation (Solomon, et al., 1961).

In first discussing the possible importance of the body boundary, the writer (and Cleveland) speculated (1968, p. 56):

> . . . people show wide differences in the degree to which they experience their body boundaries as definite and firm versus indefinite and vague. One could conceive of each individual as equating his body with a "base of operations," a segment of the world that is specially his. His body would encompass his private domain and be the cumulative site for all of his past integrated experiences. It could be regarded as bounding and containing a complex system which has been developed to deal with the world. It would encompass a structure which the individual has built up in his attempts to make life satisfying for himself. Therefore, would one not expect that the sort of boundaries which the individual attributes to his body would tell a good deal about his over-all life building operations? Would one not assume that the person who sees his body as an area highly differentiated from the rest of the world and girded by definite boundaries has constructed a different type of "base of operations" from that of the person who regards his body as an area with indefinite boundaries?

There is considerable precedent for regarding the boundary as representing an important parameter. Freud (1927), Federn (1952), Klein (1932), Jung (1931, 1944), Reich (1949), and many others (Rose, 1966; Woodbury, 1966) had pointed out that variations in boundary states are linked with significant psychological events.[1]

The full potential of a concept like the body image boundary was recognized by the writer (and S. Cleveland) in the course of examining the correlates of how individuals structure the boundary regions of their imaginative elaborations of ink blots. It had been discovered (Fisher and Cleveland, 1968) that when subjects were asked to describe a series of ink blots they varied considerably in the characteristics they ascribed to the peripheries of their percepts. There were marked differences in the frequency with which definite structure, definite substance, and definite surface qualities were attributed to the periphery. These differences were found to be correlated

---

[1] A review of previous boundary formulations may be found in Chapter 1.

with various direct and indirect measures of body feeling and body sensation. A good deal of evidence accumulated that the way in which an individual depicts the boundaries of his ink blot responses mirrors how he feels about his own body boundaries. The more he views his own boundaries as firm and well articulated the more likely he is to visualize ink blot configurations as definitively bounded. It was shown that indices of boundary definiteness derived from ink blot responses were meaningfully related to such diverse body phenomena as the relative perceptual prominence of the body surface as compared to the body interior in the body schema; intensity of concern about the vulnerability of the body exterior; the distribution of psychosomatic symptoms at exterior versus interior body sites; and differences in physiological reactivity between exterior and interior sectors of the body. This material provided a rationale for regarding the ink blot responses as closely linked with body events and more specifically with the psychological and physiological differentiation between exterior and interior regions of one's body.

It would be well at this point to specify in more detail the nature of the ink blot indices which were developed for measuring body image boundary definiteness. Responses such as the following were found to represent an expression of definite boundaries: cave with rocky walls, man in armor, animal with striped skin, turtle with shell, mummy wrapped up, woman in fancy costume. These are percepts whose content positively highlights the boundary in some way. They were labeled "Barrier" responses. In each Barrier response the surface is characterized by a protective, enclosing, decorative, concealing, or substantive connotation. The Barrier category diversely embraces references to clothing, animals with unusual skins, overhanging or protective surfaces, buildings, vehicles, animals with container characteristics (e.g., kangaroo), and enclosing geographical formations (e.g., valley, lake surrounded by land). A second boundary index was also formulated which concerns percepts that emphasize the weakness, lack of substance, and penetrability of persons and objects. The term "Penetration response" was applied to them; and some examples follow: mashed bug, person bleeding, broken body, torn coat, body seen through a fluoroscope. In this category are included also representations of openings (e.g., door, vagina), degenerative processes (e.g., withering skin), and states of insubstantial existence (e.g., ghost, shadow). The detailed criteria used for scoring Barrier and Penetration responses in ink blot protocols may be found in Appendix A.[2] In most samples studied, Barrier scores have been normally distributed. While Penetration scores are also usually normal in character, there are more instances in which they were fairly seriously skewed.

Typically, the measurement of Barrier and Penetration scores has

---

[2] Several changes in scoring procedures adopted since AV: 1958 are described in this appendix. It should also be noted that Moseley, Gorham, and Hill (1963) have devised a technique for computer scoring of Barrier and Penetration.

Table 6.1
Summary of Representative Studies of Scoring Objectivity
for Barrier and Penetration

1. Ramer (1963)	For Barrier: Ramer vs. Fisher = .96 Fisher vs. Judge 2 = .81 Judge 2 vs. Ramer = .90
2. Dorsey (1965)	For Barrier: .96 between 2 independent scorers
3. Allardice and Dole (1966)	For Barrier: .95 between graduate student and author .86 between another graduate student and author For Penetration: .93 between graduate student and author .84 between another graduate student and author
4. Eigenbrode and Shipman (1960)	For Barrier: Correlations in the .80's between different scorers
5. Leeds (1965)	For Barrier: Average of .86 for six samples between independent scorers
6. Sieracki (1963)	For Barrier: Judge B Judge C Judge A vs. .89 .94 Judge B vs. .95
7. Megargee (1965)	For Barrier: Megargee vs. independent judge = .86
8. Sherick (1964)	For Barrier: .86 Sherick vs. Fisher For Penetration: .87 Sherick vs. Fisher
9. Bachelis (1965)	For Barrier: .85 between independent judges For Penetration: .95 between independent judges
10. Shontz (unpublished)	For Barrier: .87 independent judge vs. Fisher For Penetration: .90 independent judge vs. Fisher

involved the administration of an ink blot series (e.g., Rorschach cards) to subjects either on an individual basis or in a group where the blots were projected on a screen. It has been established that these scores are both significantly correlated with the total number of responses given by an individual to a set of ink blot stimuli. Therefore, it is necessary to control for response total by requesting that subjects produce a uniform number of percepts for each blot. The number requested for the ten blot Rorschach series has ranged in various studies from 20 to 30, but usually has been around 25. When evaluating a particular protocol containing a series of responses, each Barrier or Penetration percept is given a value of 1. The Barrier score is then equal to the sum of Barrier responses; and the Penetration score is equal to the sum of Penetration responses. The interscorer reliability for evaluating Barrier and Penetration percepts has proven in a succession of earlier studies to vary from .82 [3] to .97, with most values clustering in the high 80's and low 90's (e.g., Fisher and Cleveland, 1968).

Table 6.1 summarizes the results of ten more recent representative studies dealing with scoring objectivity. One can see that the reports unanimously indicate high agreement among independent scorers in their decisions about what constitutes a Barrier or a Penetration response.

The reliability of the Barrier and Penetration scores over time has been examined in several contexts. There have been seven test-retest studies.

Table 6.2
Summary of Reliability Studies

Investigation	Type of Study	Population	Reliability Barrier	Penetration
McConnell and Daston	Test-retest (60 days)	20 medical patients	.89	.80
Cleveland (R. Fisher data)	Test-retest (5 days)	50 schizophrenics	.65	.89
Fisher and Renik	Test-retest (30 min.) equivalent forms	20 normals	.85	.83
	Test-retest (30 min.)	15 normals	.87	.85
Holtzman	Test-retest (3 weeks to 1 year)	Normals	.40	—
Koschene	Test-retest (pre- and post-surgery)	11 surgical patients	.78	.18
Lerner	Test-retest (2 days: one group following sleep deprivation and another following placebo)	20 normals	.87	.63
		20 normals	.83	.83
Holtzman	Odd-even	Normals	.70	.65–.70
Holtzman	Odd-even	Schizophrenics	.70	.80
Dorsey	Split-half	26 normals	.67	—
Dorsey	Split-half	47 normals	.43	—

McConnell and Daston (1961) evaluated the reliability of the Barrier and Penetration scores by obtaining test-retest Rorschach protocols (with an intervening two months period) from 20 male Veterans Administration patients hospitalized with long-term physical disorders. The reliability of the Barrier score was about .89 and that for the Penetration score .80. From such

[3] Unless otherwise stated, all correlations are product-moment.

data it was concluded that both of the scores were sufficiently stable over time to be employed in test-retest designs.

Cleveland (1960A) noted after an analysis of Rorschach test-retest protocols (five days intervening) collected by Rhoda Fisher (1958) on 50 schizophrenic women that the reliability for Barrier was .65 and that for Penetration .89.

Fisher and Renik (1966) administered Form B of the Holtzman blots to 20 normal women and following a 15 minute interview administered Form A. A test-retest correlation of .85 was found for Barrier and a correlation of .83 for Penetration.

Renik and Fisher (1968) in a study exactly duplicating that just described, except that the subjects consisted of 15 men, observed a test-retest correlation for Barrier of .87. For Penetration the correlation was .85.

Koschene (1965) studied Barrier and Penetration changes in patients who underwent kidney transplant surgery. The Rorschach was administered pre- and post-surgery; and it was established that the reliability value for Barrier was .78, while that for Penetration was .18. Incidentally, the low correlation for Penetration had been anticipated in view of previous findings that it is sensitive to the kinds of situational effects that would be presumably linked with undergoing surgery.

Data were available from test-retest studies completed by Barbara Lerner (1966).[4] Twenty college students (ten male, ten female) responded with two percepts to each of the 22 odd-number Holtzman A blots; ingested 15 milligrams of d-amphetamine sulphate which reduced dream time for two nights; and responded on the third day to the 22 even-number Holtzman cards. An equivalent group of 20 college students were likewise tested and retested, but in the intervening time ingested only a placebo. It should be emphasized that the protocols were obtained on an individual basis and with unusual care to standardizing test conditions. All of the protocols were scored blindly for Barrier and Penetration. It was found that the test-retest coefficient for Barrier in the sleep deprived group was .87. In the placebo group it was .83. The respective test-retest coefficients for Penetration were .63 and .83.

Holtzman, et al. (1961) obtained generally low levels of retest reliability for Barrier and Penetration when using equivalent forms of his ink blot test repeated after intervals ranging from three weeks to one year. The reliability coefficients under such conditions cluster in the .40's. These are the lowest test-retest values reported and contrast with the studies cited above in which Barrier coefficients have been variously .89, .65, .85, .78, and .87; and Penetration coefficients in the .60's and .70's.

Holtzman, et al. (1961) also found that in normal adults the odd-even reliabilities of Barrier cluster around .70 and of Penetration around .65–.70. In schizophrenic groups the corresponding reliabilities were in the .70's and

[4] I am grateful to Dr. Lerner for making her records available for scoring.

low .80's. Dorsey (1965) found a split-half reliability of .67 for Barrier in one group of 26 college students and a value of .43 in another group of 47 students.

There seems to be quite a range of Barrier and Penetration reliabilities reported. While some are definitely lower than desirable, it is fair to say that most of those in the test-retest category, which are after all of prime importance in defining the stability of measurement, are of acceptable magnitude.

Apropos of the issue of stability, it is of interest that Megargee, et al. (1966) found that examiner differences and conditions of test administration (viz., neutral, positive, negative) did not significantly affect Barrier production. Also, Hamilton and Robertson (1966) did not detect appreciable effects upon the Barrier score as the result of examiners assuming either a "cold" or "warm" attitude toward subjects.[5]

The relationships of the Barrier and Penetration scores to basic parameters like verbal productivity, intelligence, and other indices of ink blot response have been presented in detail in a previous publication (Fisher and Cleveland, 1968). It has been shown in numerous studies that neither of the scores is correlated with intelligence in normal adults. Similarly, Hunt [6] has more recently found in a group of children in the 11–17 range that the boundary scores are not correlated with intelligence measures derived from the California Test of Mental Maturity or the Otis Beta Quick Scoring Mental Abilities Test. Rhoda Fisher [7] found no relationships between Barrier and intelligence (as measured by the California Test of Mental Maturity) in a sample of 24 fifth-grade boys and 31 fifth-grade girls. It is true that a few scattered reports of significant correlations between Barrier and intellectual measures have appeared. Holtzman (1965) observed a low order, but significant, positive correlation in a sample of 370 children between WISC vocabulary and Barrier. Andrews (1968) found a significant low positive correlation (.30) between IQ and Barrier in a sample of girls in the six–seven year age range; but the relationship was non-significant in a sample of boys of the same age. In neither group was Barrier related to facility in drawing the Bender-Gestalt figures. Cardone (1967) detected in a chronic schizophrenic population a significant positive correlation (average $r = .35$) between Barrier and IQ derived from the Ammons Full Range Picture Vocabulary test.

It is of interest that Bachelis (1965) has established in a male college population ($N = 84$) that Barrier is not related to cognitive measures of originality (e.g., Associational Fluency test, Alternate Uses test).[8] Kerna-

---

[5] Tangential to this matter, it is of interest that Holtzman, et al. (1963) did discover that individual administration of the Holtzman blots resulted in higher Barrier scores than group administration.

[6] Unpublished data.

[7] Unpublished data.

[8] But Clark, Veldman, and Thorpe (1965) found a significant positive correlation between Penetration and scores on Guilford's tests of divergent thinking.

leguen (1968) and Richter and Winter (1966) obtained similar negative results.

Incidentally, Philip Miller [9] has shown in male (N = 39) and female (N = 29) college student samples that Barrier is not related to a variety of social desirability measures (e.g., Crowne and Marlowe, 1964; MMPI K scale). That is, the kinds of test taking attitudes which affect responses to "paper and pencil" tests do not affect the production of Barrier percepts. The present author has similarly found chance correlations between Barrier and a variety of response set indices.

Some disagreement exists as to whether the Barrier score is influenced by the number of words in the protocol from which it is derived. Appleby (1956) and Megargee (1965) have shown correlations of the order of .46–.56 between Barrier and word count. Other studies (Fisher and Cleveland, 1968) have shown only chance relationships between these variables. It is not clear why such variations occur. Actually, of course, the relationship between projective indices and the word count of the protocols from which they are computed has been a problem for other investigators. For example, the McClelland, et al. (1953) measure of achievement motivation (n Ach) derived from Thematic Apperception test stories has in some instances turned out to be positively correlated with the length of the stories. There are methods suggested for correcting n Ach so as to eliminate the effects of word count; but a dilemma arises in applying them because one can argue that word count differences are merely expressions of the fact that those with high achievement drive will be more productive on almost any task than will those with low achievement drive. That is, the difference in word count is perhaps not the cause of n Ach score variation, but merely a reflection of it. By the same token, the Barrier score has also been shown to be positively correlated with achievement drive and the need to complete tasks. It is therefore logical that the high Barrier subject should approach the ink blot task in such a fashion as to produce longer and more complete responses than the low Barrier subject. To "correct for" length of protocol might simply eliminate some of the meaningful variance of the Barrier index. In any case, it is reassuring to note that in the above referred-to study in which Megargee found Barrier and word count to be significantly correlated, he was able to duplicate his Barrier results even when he compared segments of his sample which did not differ in word count.

However, to seek further clarification of this problem other studies have been conducted.

First of all, the relationship between Barrier and word count was examined by the present writer in four new samples of subjects (N = 26, N = 43, N = 25, N = 20). Barrier was positively and significantly correlated with word count in two samples ($r = .33$, $p < .05$; $r = .27$,

---

[9] Unpublished data.

$p < .05$) but not so in two others. It is clear, then, that there are samples in which Barrier differences appear which cannot be traced to differences in word productivity.

Another approach to the issue which was undertaken by the writer involved comparing within an individual's own protocol the number of words occurring in Barrier versus non-Barrier responses. In this way it is possible to determine if, for each individual, the production of a Barrier response is a function of word count. In a sample of 40 subjects the mean number of words comprising Barrier responses was 8.6 and that for non-Barrier responses 6.4. The difference was not statistically significant. In a second sample of 20 subjects the mean number of words comprising Barrier responses was 8.8 and that for non-Barrier responses 7.2. This difference too was not significant. As defined by results from two samples, variation in Barrier production from blot to blot within the individual's own response sequence could not be accounted for in terms of verbal productivity.

Perhaps an ideal way to learn more about the problem would be to expose individuals to conditions which would theoretically be expected to alter their boundary experiences and then to determine whether Barrier shifts occur; and, if so, whether these shifts are in any way a resultant of changes in word productivity. If gross Barrier changes can occur without correlated shifts in word productivity, this would constitute convincing evidence that productivity itself does not play a causal role in the formation of Barrier images. The opportunity to apply such a paradigm presented itself in a study by Fisher and Renik (1966) which will be described in considerable detail at a later point. It will suffice for the moment to indicate that the study involved 20 normal women who were tested with Holtzman blots; exposed to a series of tasks designed to focus their attention on their exterior body regions and therefore to increase Boundary definiteness; and retested with a second series of Holtzman blots. The test-retest increase in Barrier scores in this group was significantly higher than in suitable control groups. There were shifts in Barrier ranging from -4 to $+6$. When these shifts were correlated with test-retest changes in word productivity (ranging from -13 to $+600$), a chance coefficient was found. Gross changes in Barrier occurred which were completely independent of the word productivity variable.

In another study completed by the writer, 26 female college students were tested with one form of the Holtzman blots; exposed to 15 minutes of stress (produced by performing embarrassing tasks before "judges"); and retested with another series of Holtzman blots. The correlation between the change in Barrier and change in word count from test to retest was of a chance order.

If one looks back at earlier studies by Fisher and Cleveland (1968) of Barrier and word productivity, one finds that it was originally established that in 69 percent of all instances the decision as to whether a response should be scored Barrier could be reduced to the presence of a single word, in 75 percent to the presence of two words or less, in 93 percent to three words or less, and in 99 percent to four words or less. The great majority of Barrier responses potentially involve using only three or four words in describing each blot. This means that even a person who used only three or four words per response is capable, in terms of productivity alone, of offering a Barrier percept for each. In view of this fact, it is really not surprising that radical test-retest changes in Barrier can take place without accompanying variations in word totals. It requires at most the alteration of three or four words in a response to change it from Barrier to non-Barrier or vice versa.

Some have raised the question whether the Barrier score is merely a reflection of one of the more conventional ink blot determinants. There have been instances in which it correlated significantly with such conventional scores as form quality, color, movement and shading. However, there has been no real consistency in the reported literature. For example, Barrier has sometimes been positively related to form quality, sometimes negatively, and more often not at all. Correlations with shading,[10] color, and approach have been rare. In ten different samples of college students and two samples of psychiatric patients studied by the present author, it was not possible to detect consistent correlations (with one exception) between Barrier and the usual determinant scores. The only exception involved the relation of Barrier to number of human Movement responses. In the 12 samples studied there were six instances of significant positive coefficients (averaging about .30).

Reports by others (e.g., Landau, 1960; Compton, 1964; Shipman, et al., 1964; Holtzman, et al., 1961) have also described significant positive correlations (of the order of .30–.45) between Barrier and Movement. If one considers the accumulated findings which demonstrate that human Movement responses are predictive of level of muscle tonus and the ability to contain tension in the musculature (e.g., Meltzoff, Singer, and Korchin, 1953) and also that the same predictive power is shown by Barrier responses (e.g., Shipman, et al., 1964), it becomes possible to discern a possible explanation as to why the two types of percepts are found to overlap. Apparently, they are both sensitive to variables which are associated with the individual's habitual degree of muscular activation and kinesthetic awareness. To some degree, they both reflect the impact of kinesthetic experience upon the perceptual-imaginative process involved in the production of ink blot responses. A detailed discussion regarding the possible mechanisms whereby body experiences gain representation in ink blot percepts will be presented at a later point.

It should be emphasized again that the Movement score is the only conventional ink blot index to be consistently related to Barrier. Even this relationship has typically been of a fairly low magnitude.

[10] Incidentally, Schiebel (1965) has described an interesting positive relationship between the production of Barrier and certain types of texture percepts with tactual implications in schizophrenic subjects when responding to Holtzman blots.

Early studies with the Barrier dimension indicated that it was related to an unexpectedly large number of events in different bands of the behavior spectrum. The individual's concept of his body limits was linked with such diverse variables as ability to behave independently and autonomously; degree of personality disorganization; conduct in small group situations; stress tolerance; and patterning of physiological response. Most of these relationships were first fully described in a monograph entitled *Body Image and Personality* which was published in 1958 (re-issued in a second edition in 1968 by Dover Press). Since that time a variety of other studies have been carried out which made it possible to cross-validate and extend the original formulations.

The remainder of this chapter will be taken up with presenting the newer work that has been accomplished. Various topical areas will be outlined in turn. The past findings pertinent to each will be described and followed by accounts of more recent studies that are applicable.

Before launching into a presentation of the aggregate results that have been accumulated, it would be well to provide a brief general orientation concerning the manner in which persons with definite boundaries were originally found to differ from those with indefinite boundaries. There were broad differences between them in personality, values, and style of behavior. Those with definite boundaries proved to be relatively more autonomous and "self steering." They were more likely to have high achievement motivation and to seek task completion than the poorly bounded. They were less suggestible and also less likely to be blocked or disturbed when confronted by stressful frustration. The definite bounded individual displayed more independence in group interaction, but in such a manner as to facilitate rather than interfere with group objectives. He was better able to persist at tasks. In his general outlook he was more oriented toward interaction with others. He was more interested in communication; and literally had a greater preference for human contact. The vaguely bounded person was, contrastingly, characterized by interests in activities and vocations that minimized the human factor. In illustration of this last point, one may cite the fact that high Barrier subjects were found to be attracted to disciplines concerned with human behavior (e.g., anthropology and psychology); whereas low Barrier subjects showed a preference for impersonal fields like physics and chemistry.

Rephrasing the above, it may be said that the possession of definite boundaries was found to be accompanied by well structured individuality; concern with accomplishment; enhanced ability to maintain poise in difficult situations; and a special investment in communicative interaction. These traits, attitudes, and skills turned out to be aspects of even broader organizing configurations which were represented also at physiological and sensory levels.

The possibility of a relationship between boundary definiteness and physiological response was first suggested by studies of persons with psychosomatic symptoms. It was noted that patients with symptoms involving the skin or musculature (e.g., neurodermatitis and rheumatoid arthritis) were more likely to produce clearly bounded percepts than patients with symptoms in the body interior (e.g., duodenal ulcer, colitis). This stimulated the hypothesis that the individual with definite boundaries tends to channel [11] excitation to the outer layers of the body (viz., skin and muscle); whereas by contrast the individual with indefinite boundaries channels excitation to interior body sectors.

A number of studies were carried out with this hypothesis in mind. It was shown that in normal subjects and also in patients with psychosomatic symptoms there was a significant trend for those with definite boundaries to manifest relatively high physiological reactivity in the skin and muscle (as defined by GSR, muscle potential, vasoconstriction) and relatively low reactivity in the body interior (as measured by heart response). However, those with indefinite boundaries displayed just the converse of this pattern. It was therefore conjectured that the manner in which an individual's body image boundary is organized may result in long-term excitation patterns characterized by differential arousal of body exterior as compared to body interior sites. More broadly speaking, it appeared that the various styles of life characterizing persons with different boundary attributes were repre-sented also in differences at the physiological level.

With this introductory briefing concerning the more prominent observed correlates of the boundary scores, attention may be turned to a detailed analysis of newer findings.

[11] The term "channel" is used in the same sense that Lacey (1950) does. That is, it refers to the fact that each individual tends to show greater response in one physiological system than in others over a range of stimulus situations.

7
The Boundary and Body Experience

PREVIOUS CONSIDERATIONS AND OBSERVATIONS

When the Barrier and Penetration concepts were originally formulated, they were considered to have direct reference to the body image. It was assumed that at some level they represented experiences, fantasies, or sensations referrable to the body. But on the face of it, there are no compelling reasons for assuming that the characteristics ascribed by an individual to the boundary regions of ink blot percepts are related to how he perceives his body. In fact, some observers (e.g., Wylie, 1961) have suggested that although the boundary scores may be interesting ink blot indices, there is little evidence that they reflect how one actually experiences one's body. The validity of this criticism is debatable and depends on how one evaluates previous work which has dealt with the matter. The fact is that a number of attempts were originally made to demonstrate that the Barrier score is logically correlated with indices of body experience. Most of these attempts were indirect in the sense that they involved relating the Barrier score not to immediate indicators of body sensation but to presumed derived measures. The detailed findings have been described elsewhere (Fisher and Cleveland, 1968). However, a quick overview will help to clarify the work to be presented in this section.

Several of the earlier studies were simply designed to show in a general way that the Barrier score could predict phenomena with obvious body image significance. It was possible to establish that there was a significant negative relationship between the Barrier score and the following variables:

1. Degree of anxious concern about one's body as measured by the Secord Homonym test (1953) which is based on the number of references to body functions in an individual's associations to words having both body and non-body meanings.

2. Difficulty in adjusting to amputation as manifested by delay in the regression or disappearance of the phantom limb.

3. Preoccupation with themes of body destruction when responding to the Projective Movement Sequence test which consists of moving pictures of unstructured patterns changing in form (Lundin, 1949).

It was apparent from these three studies that the more definite an individual's boundaries the less likely he was to manifest signs of anxiety or disturbance with respect to his body.

Two other studies were also originally reported in which there was a closer approach to exploring the relationship of the Barrier score to body experiences that have specific boundary implications. One was based on the prediction that the individual who conceptualizes his boundary as vague and insubstantial would have greater anxiety about the bounding or exterior regions of his body (viz., skin and muscle) than the individual whose boundary is well articulated. Responses to a series of incomplete sentences concerning the skin (e.g., "My skin is . . ."; "When I think of my skin . . .") were used to measure anxiety about this body region. As predicted, the Barrier score proved to be significantly negatively related to such anxiety. A second study looked even more directly at the relation of the Barrier score to body experiences classified within a boundary context. It involved an analysis of the number of body exterior versus interior perceptions reported by subjects with differing boundary attributes when they were asked to monitor their own body sensations during a brief period. There were trends in the predicted direction for those with high Barrier scores to report more exterior (skin and muscle) and fewer interior (stomach and heart) sensations than those with low Barrier scores. However, the differences were largely not significant.

NEW STUDIES

The results of the previous studies just cited were encouraging but hardly satisfying. They served mainly to confirm some suppositions regarding the relationship of the Barrier score to various indices of body image disturbance. Also, they pointed up the possibility that there were exterior-interior differences in patterns of body sensation which are a function of degree of boundary definiteness.

With this background in mind, a number of new studies were undertaken to examine in varied contexts the relationship between body experiences and the Barrier score. The guiding assumption of this work was that if the Barrier score is anchored in real body experiences there should be body sensation analogues for boundary definiteness. If the Barrier score reflects properties that one ascribes to the boundary regions of one's body, it should be possible to find their sensory duplicates. It was hypothesized that the higher an individual's Barrier score the more perceptually prominent should be the boundary regions of his body (viz., skin and muscle) in relation to interior sectors (e.g., stomach and heart).

A number of projects will be outlined which approach this hypothesis from quite diverse perspectives and with radically different methodologies.

Study 1

The first study dealt with the relationship between the Barrier score and the individual's observations of his body in a relatively relaxed state. Subjects were seen in large groups in a classroom situation. They were told nothing about the purpose of the study and simply asked to cooperate on the basis of "helping out" with a research project. The group Rorschach was the first procedure administered. In order to control for response total, instructions were given to produce three responses for each of five cards (1, 2, 3, 8, 10) and two responses for each of the other five cards. Upon completion of the Rorschach, the subjects were given a sheet of paper on which were listed the names of four body sectors or organs in the following order: skin, stomach, muscle, heart. They were told that when a signal was given they were to focus their attention upon their bodies. Then, each time a prominent sensation occurred in any of the four body areas listed on the sheet they were to place a check next to the appropriate designation. The experimenter then said "Start"; and after a five-minute interval signalled "Stop." The body sensation reports obtained were scored by determining the sum of exterior perceptions (skin and muscle) and subtracting the sum of interior perceptions (stomach and heart). This score was considered to represent the relative prominence of sensations in the exterior body layers as compared with non-exterior body regions.

Two samples of subjects were studied. The first consisted of 64 college students in two undergraduate psychology courses. Fifty were female and 14 male. The second comprised 51 students in an undergraduate psychology class, of whom 35 were female and 16 male. The median age in both groups was 20.

Table 7.1
Rank Order Correlations Between Barrier Score and Difference Between Sum of Exterior and Sum of Interior Body Sensations (Ext-Int)

	Sample 1 (N = 64)	Sample 2 (N = 51)
Correlation	.33	.33
Significance Level	<.01[a]	<.01

[a] One-tailed tests have been used in view of the specific directional predictions made.

In both samples 1 and 2 the median Barrier score was 6. Likewise, in both samples the median difference between the sum of exterior (skin plus muscle) sensations and the sum of interior (stomach plus heart) sensations (Ext-Int) was such that the exterior exceeded the interior by 4. The fact that this same median difference appeared in both groups is rather noteworthy considering the loosely controlled conditions under which the body associations were obtained. No sex differences in any of the median body sensation values appeared.

Table 7.1 summarizes in terms of rank order correlations the relationships between the Barrier score and the Ext-Int indices in the two samples. Incidentally, rank order correlations were used because the Ext-Int distributions were extremely skewed. It is apparent that the Barrier score was consistently related in the predicted direction to Ext-Int sensations. In sample 1 the correlation was .33 and it was likewise .33 in sample 2. These coefficients are both significant at the $<.01$ level. One can say with confidence that there is a positive relationship between the Barrier score and a tendency for exterior body sensations to predominate over interior sensations.

The relationship of the Barrier score to the total number of body associations recorded was not significant in either sample.

Study 2

A second study extended the subject's observation of his body beyond the immediate testing situation. The question was whether the Barrier score would be related in the predicted direction to the difference between the number of interior and exterior sensations (Ext-Int) reported by the subject in his retrospective appraisal of his body reactions in past circumstances.

The subjects were seen in groups, both in classroom and laboratory settings. Barrier scores were derived from their responses to the Rorschach which was administered in the same fashion as described in Study 1. A new measure of exterior vs. interior body perception was used which posed for the subject the task of recalling a series of past experiences and indicating his memory of what body sensations each had evoked in him. The instructions were as follows:

"Below are listed a number of experiences or feelings. In each instance will you think back to the last time you had such a feeling or experience. Then try to recall how your body felt at the time. Were the main body sensations at the time in your skin? In your stomach? In your muscles? In your heart? Make your decision and indicate it by placing an X in the proper column to the right of each of the listed experiences. Whenever you are not sure, just guess."

The subject was asked to respond to a list of 30 different situations (e.g., When you are angry; When you are very tired; When you are afraid; When you feel very successful). An Ext-Int score was computed by subtracting the sum of stomach and heart responses from the sum of skin and muscle responses.

Two samples were evaluated. One consisted of 79 undergraduate college students of whom 29 were male and 50 females. The second was composed of 20 college students (17 female, three male). The median age in both groups was 20. All were paid a fee for their participation.[1]

The median Barrier score was 6 in sample 1. The median Ext-Int difference was —4. That is, the median tendency was to designate more interior than exterior sites as foci of body response in the 30 situations described. No sex differences in Ext-Int responses were evident. In sample 2 the median Barrier score was 7; and the median Ext-Int difference was —6.

Rank order correlations were employed to relate the Barrier score to the Ext-Int index.

Table 7.2
Rank Order Correlations Between Barrier Score and Ext-Int Index
Based on Recall of One's Reactions to Previous Experiences

	Sample 1 (N = 79)	Sample 2 (N = 20)
Correlation	.15 [a]	.47
Significance Level	<.20	<.01 [b]

[a] A chi-square analysis of the same data resulted in the following distribution:

	HB [c]	LB
H Ext-Int [d]	24	20
L Ext-Int	12	23

$$\chi^2 = 3.2 \ (<.05 \ ^b)$$

[b] = One-tailed test.
[c] = HB = Above median. LB = At median or below.
[d] = H Ext-Int = Above median. L Ext-Int = At median or below.

One can see in Table 7.2 that a correlation of .15 was obtained in sample 1 between the Barrier scores and the Ext-Int scores. This falls short of the .05 level of significance. However, a chi square analysis of the same data resulted in a χ^2 value of 3.2 which is significant at the <.05 level (one-tailed test). In the second sample a rank order correlation of .47 was obtained between the Barrier scores and Ext-Int scores, which is significant at the <.01 level. The results from the two samples indicate modest support for the hypothesis under consideration.

Study 3

The intent of the third study was to look at the hypothesized relationship

[1] Unless otherwise stated, it may be assumed from this point that all normal samples were recruited by payment of a fee.

between the Barrier score and Ext-Int sensations in a stressful context. More specifically, a situation was created in which the subject was made to feel that his body was threatened by an unknown drug he had ingested. The question was whether his exterior vs. interior body sensations (symptoms) under such circumstances would relate to his boundary attributes in the expected direction. The experimental procedure was as follows. Subjects were given the Rorschach in small groups, with the same control on response total as was described in Study 1. Individual appointments were then made for them. When the subject came for his individual session, he was told by the experimenter that he was to participate in a drug study which involved swallowing a pill containing a small quantity of a drug. He was informed that the drug was completely harmless but that it could produce a variety of symptoms and sensations. Only two of the total population of over 100 subjects who were asked refused to take the drug. When the subject indicated his assent to taking the drug, an electrode connected to a polygraph was attached to his finger and it was mentioned that his physiological reactions would be measured. Actually, the polygraph did not take any recordings. Its presence was intended to enhance the dramatic qualities of the situation. After the attachment of the electrode, the subject was requested to swallow a large (placebo) capsule with the aid of a small glass of water. Thereupon, he was told to lean back in his chair and to begin reporting the effects of the drug upon his body. Nothing more was said to him unless he gave no report for two minutes. In that case he was asked, "Do you notice anything?" If there was no report after four minutes he was told that he was now approaching the period when the drug would have its maximum effect and that he should therefore "get set" to describe his body experiences. At the end of 15 minutes he was presented with a checklist of body symptoms upon which he was to indicate how the drug had affected him. The checklist contained 16 items which consisted of four clusters of four items each. One cluster concerned the skin (e.g., My skin itched); another the muscles (e.g., My muscles felt tight); a third the stomach (e.g., My stomach contracted); and a fourth the heart (e.g., My heart beat faster).

The subjects consisted of 118 college students, of whom 46 were men and 72 women. Their average age was 20.

It should be initially indicated that with only a few exceptions all subjects responded to the placebo with symptoms of varying magnitude. The majority of reactions were of a mild order (e.g., itching, sensations of being cold, muscle stiffness); but about 20 percent of the group had dramatic responses. These dramatic responses ranged widely: sensations of dizziness, nausea, uncomfortable pain, concern about losing control of oneself, headache.

The Barrier score median in the group was 5. The median difference between the sum of exterior (skin and muscle) symptoms and the sum of interior (stomach and heart) symptoms (Ext-Int) were such that Ext exceeded Int by 1. No sex differences in median scores were observed.

Table 7.3
Rank Order Correlations Between Barrier Score
and Indices of Ext-Int Body Perception During Drug Condition

	Male (N = 46)	Female (N = 72)
Correlation	.33	.11
Significance Level	<.01[a]	NS [b]

[a] One-tailed test
[b] NS = Not significant

However, inspection of the data indicated that there were sex differences in the relationships of the Barrier score to the Ext-Int symptoms elicited by the placebo. It can be seen in Table 7.3 that in the female group the Barrier score is not significantly related to the Ext-Int symptom index. Whereas in the male group, one notes that the Barrier score is related in the predicted direction to the Ext-Int index as defined by the checklist (rho = .33; $p < .01$ level). In general, it may be said that in the male group increasing boundary definiteness is accompanied by a relatively greater focus upon boundary region symptoms than upon body interior symptoms in the course of reacting to a placebo.

Incidentally, no relationships were found between the Barrier score and total number of symptoms reported. Also, the number of Ext symptoms experienced was not significantly related to the number of Int symptoms.

Study 4

The fourth study was rather indirect in its approach to the hypothesis. It was based upon the premise that if selective perception of one's body chronically occurs, there should be a corresponding selectivity in one's immediate recall of verbal material consisting of references to exterior and interior body sensations. If the high Barrier individual exceeds the low Barrier individual in the degree to which he is attuned to boundary as compared to interior sensations, should there not be an analogous difference reflected in their learning and recall of material which is saturated with exterior and interior body references? Should the persisting contrast in exterior and interior body sensations not serve as a context which would differentially focus attention upon and reinforce a series of references to exterior and interior body sensations presented to the subject for memorization? Previous work in the area of selective perception and memory (Blake and Ramsey, 1951; Allport, 1955) would seem to make this a tenable expectation.

The Barrier score was determined in the usual manner. Measures of differential Ext-Int recall were obtained in the following fashion. Subjects (in groups of four to six) were told that they would be shown a list of phrases and then immediately afterwards asked to recall as many of these phrases as possible. There were 20 phrases which consisted of four clusters of five items each: skin items (e.g., skin itch, skin cold); muscle items (e.g., muscle stiff, muscle relax); stomach items (e.g., stomach pain, stomach full); and heart items (heart pound, heart beat). They were listed in random order (in two columns of ten) on an 8–1/2 by 11 sheet of unlined paper. At a given signal the subject was told to pick up and study this list which had been lying face down in front of him. He was allowed to do so for one minute. The signal was then given to put the sheet aside and to write on a blank page all the phrases he could remember. A recall period of five minutes was provided. In scoring a subject's recall, the total number of Int phrases remembered was subtracted from the total of Ext phrases.

Two samples were studied. Forty-eight undergraduate students comprised sample 1, of whom 8 were male and 40 female. Sample 2 consisted of 46 undergraduate students, of whom 19 were male and 27 female. The average age in both samples was 20.

The median Barrier score in sample 1 was 5, but was 6 in sample 2. In both samples the median difference in Ext-Int recall was —1 which indicated a slight tendency for the interior sensation phrases to predominate over exterior phrases in recall.

Table 7.4
Rank Order Correlations Between Barrier Score and Difference
Between Sum of Exterior and Sum of Interior Body Sensations Recalled

	Sample 1 (N = 48)	Sample 2 (N = 46)
Correlation	.52	.38
Significance Level	<.001[a]	<.01[a]

[a] One-tailed test

Table 7.4 indicates that the Barrier score and the Ext-Int recall index were significantly related in the fashion that was predicted. In sample 1 the rank order correlation equaled .52 ($p < .001$); and in sample 2 it was .38 ($p < .01$). Clearly, the high Barrier subjects recalled a greater proportion of exterior and a lower proportion of interior body sensation references than did the low Barrier subjects.

The results from the four studies were convincingly supportive of the original hypothesis. It turned out, as predicted, that the individual's Barrier score was linked with his perception of the relative prominence of exterior vs. interior sensations in his body. The higher his Barrier score the greater the likelihood he would report sensations from the boundary regions of his body (skin and muscle) rather than from its interior (stomach and heart). Multiple strategies demonstrated that the relationship between the Barrier score and the body exterior-interior differentiation is sufficiently strong to manifest itself in various levels of behavior. This relationship appeared in the context of immediate self observation; retrospective self observation; reported "symptoms" evoked by a fictitious drug; and selective recall of verbal material. Of course, recognition must be given to the fact that for the third of the four studies just mentioned statistical significance was attained in only one sex group. There was in Study 3 a significant trend in the male group for the Barrier score to be positively related to the Ext-Int symptom difference; but only a chance relationship appeared in the female group.

It is interesting that the relationship between the Barrier score and Ext-Int sensations manifested itself in simple and non-contrived situations. This relationship has shown itself even when subjects have been merely asked to report prominent sensations they experience in any of four body regions during a five-minute period—and with no attempt to create a special set, or to exclude extraneous stimuli, or to induce particular body states. Apparently, the exterior-interior differentiation in body perception which is related to the Barrier score is not a phenomenon that needs to be isolated under rarified conditions. It seems to be available to observation in the circumstances of merely sitting quietly in a classroom situation and agreeing to examine one's body sensations for a five-minute period at the behest of a comparative stranger who asks for cooperation in the name of a research venture. It tends to be available to observation also when the subject is asked under similar circumstances to think about his body sensations in past situations.

The results from the placebo study, while less consistent than those in Studies 1 and 2, are still rather striking. They indicate that the body sensations produced by a placebo are in many instances not of a chance order and not of a gross undifferentiated character. When the male subjects responded to the placebo there was a meaningful differentiation in whether they experienced more symptoms on the body surface or in the body interior.

The results pertaining to selective memory for Ext vs. Int body sensation phrases raise all kinds of issues.[2] They strongly imply that the body schema may function to produce selective effects during the sequence involved in perceiving, memorizing, and reproducing a set of stimuli with body connotations. There is no way of determining from the data whether the selective effects occur primarily in the perceptual, memory, or reproducing phases of the process. But somehow the relative prominence of the body image boundary (with the attendant differences in sensation patterns) does play a significant role. In principle, this phenomenon is quite analogous to that observed in previous studies which have noted relationships between selective

[2] Corroboratively, Andrews (1968) found in a sample of boys and girls (ages six–seven) that the Barrier score was positively correlated with learning words with exterior body connotations faster than words with interior implications. The relationship was considerably stronger for the girls than the boys. A borderline trend was also observed for Barrier to be positively correlated with learning action words relatively faster than non-action words.

perception and memory and various personality and attitudinal parameters (Blake and Ramsey, 1951; Allport, 1955). The perceptual highlighting or minimizing of certain body areas can apparently result in effects similar to those produced by other kinds of attitudinal and motivational states. The possibility that body schema variables might affect memory functions was suggested by Schilder (1935) and even considered by Gerstmann to be illustrated by the behavior of certain patients with organic brain pathology (1942).

If, generally speaking, it is accepted that the data are supportive of the original hypothesis which was proposed, what may one conclude? Of course the major implication is that the Barrier score is not simply an abstracted index of how the individual perceives ink blots, but rather is closely tied in with his actual body experiences. It would appear that there is a meaningful connection between the properties ascribed by an individual to the peripheral regions of images he produces when responding to ink blots and the relative frequency of sensations he experiences in the exterior vs. interior regions of his body. This relationship between the Barrier score and patterns of interior-exterior body perception may be regarded as a derivative of two factors:

1. As described in detail elsewhere (Fisher and Cleveland, 1968) there is evidence that the person with definite boundaries learns in the course of his socialization to assign importance in his body scheme to the boundary regions of his body (particularly the musculature) because they take on special significance for him as a means of contacting and coping in an active, independent, and "voluntary" fashion with the outside environment. Contrastingly, the person with indefinite boundaries who is less actively and independently oriented assigns smaller importance to his body exterior and more to the interior.[3] This difference may be presumed to result in focusing

---

[3] A quotation from *Body Image and Personality* (Fisher and Cleveland, 1968) will help to clarify this view (pp. 312–313). ". . . the individual has rather contrasting psychological experiences with his body exterior as compared to his interior. His body exterior is that part of his body which serves as the contact point with the environment. It touches the outside world in contrast to the body interior which is protected by the body wall from direct outside contact. Furthermore, the individual can better visualize the exterior part of his body than the interior. He has a detailed image of his outer aspects, whereas the interior is something hazy or ill-defined. But most important of all, the activities of the exterior body layers are much more subject to voluntary control than are those of the body interior. The individual can embellish or change the appearance of his skin; and he exerts controlling force over his striated musculature. His body interior, however, is influenced, by and large, by involuntary autonomic centers. Consequently, it may be presumed that the body interior comes to represent the realm of involuntary response. . . . One might picture the voluntary zone of the high Barrier individual's body as being chronically in a relatively high state of preparatory activation and thus more likely than other body areas to be triggered into response by stimuli. Conversely, it may be conjectured that the low Barrier person grows up in an atmosphere in which self steering is minimized and the surrender to forces and persons greater than oneself is encouraged. A set toward voluntary response is discouraged and so activation of the voluntary zone of the body is held to a minimum."

differential attention upon the areas in question. The high Barrier person whose boundary region is of relatively high importance to him would scan it with particular attentiveness; and the low Barrier person would be analogously sensitive to sensations in his body interior.

2. There is, as already mentioned, a substantial basis for considering that the high Barrier exceeds the low Barrier person in the degree of physiological activation of exterior body areas (Davis, 1960; Fisher and Cleveland, 1968; Fisher, 1959C). Conversely, the low Barrier individual manifests higher activation of body interior regions than the high Barrier individual. Such a difference in reactivity probably produces a differential intensity of sensations at the body sites in question. Therefore, at least partially, the correlation of the Barrier score with body sensation patterns would be a function of the contrast in actual reactivity levels of the body exterior and interior. One may also speculate that the sensation differences between exterior and interior which are related to the physiological factors and which persist over time acquire an influence of their own in reinforcing the psychological importance of the exterior or interior in the body schema. Obviously, a persisting dominance of sensation from one body locale could in its own right make that locale an important body schema landmark.

To summarize, the contrast between high and low Barrier persons in their relative perceptual focus upon the body exterior vs. interior may be attributed to the basic differences in significance they early assign to body exterior and interior; the differential physiological reactivity they experience at exterior and interior sites; and the experiential reinforcement they derive regarding the importance of body exterior and interior from the persisting physiological difference.

Going beyond the specific body boundary implications of the data, it may be said that they give promise that consistent individual variations in body sensation experiences can be predicted from a knowledge of how the body scheme is organized. It would appear that the mass of body sensations perceived at any given time by an individual is not a "blooming confusion", but rather a differentiated field. Persistent directive influences associated with the body image would seem to serve as organizing forces capable of sharpening or minimizing sensations from different body sectors.[4]

---

[4] The Penetration score was not significantly correlated with any of the indices of body experience and perception which were utilized in the series of studies. This raises a serious dilemma as to the meaning to assign to it. As will be seen, it does behave in a variety of studies as if it were a measure of some aspect of boundary definiteness. It often seems to tap the obverse of the Barrier score. However, the fact remains that it cannot be experimentally linked with patterns of inside-outside body experience. It will therefore be treated as an exploratory measure whose basic meaning is still a matter of uncertainty.

One may speculate as to why the Penetration index has proven more difficult to define consistently than the Barrier score. There are suggestions that it is considerably more sensitive to immediate situational factors than the Barrier score. It has, for example, been found to be

PERCEPTUAL SELECTIVITY

A study by Cassell (1966) further documents the body anchorage of the
Barrier score by pointing up its relationship to selective perception of
tachistoscopically presented pictures of exterior vs. interior body regions.
Cassell predicted that the higher an individual's Barrier score the more
quickly he would perceive pictures depicting the exterior aspects of the body,
but conversely the less quickly he would perceive pictures of the body interior.
This prediction derived, of course, from findings already cited which indicate
that the person with definite boundaries is relatively highly aware of the
exterior of his body but only limitedly so of his body interior; with the
converse holding true for the individual with vague boundaries. Presumably,

---

influenced by the familiarity of the subject with the ink blots and his set toward the whole task
of responding to them (Herron, 1964).

It seems to reflect not only body attitudes, as such, but also special sets (e.g., achievement
motivation, fearful anticipation) elicited by specific situations. One would from this viewpoint
expect to find that the relative variances contributed to it by body and situational sets
fluctuated as the contexts changed. Looking back over previous studies involving the Penetration score, there are indications that it has behaved most like a body boundary index in
hospitalized populations of patients with psychosomatic symptoms. In such populations it has
been consistently related, as predicted, to the exterior-interior sites of symptoms in a manner
which is the obverse of the relationship of the Barrier score to such symptom sites. Why this
should be so is not readily apparent. Perhaps body attitudes in patients with psychosomatic
symptoms are so sharply crystallized and so prominently pervasive that they far outweigh
any immediate situational variables that might influence the Penetration score. By contrast,
the Penetration score seems particularly sensitive to the influence of situational variables
when college students without gross body symptomatology have served as subjects.

The difficulty of applying any simple explanatory scheme to the Penetration score is
shown by two recent sets of findings in normal groups by the present writer. In one study,
subjects (N = 77) were asked to describe their appearance in a mirror while wearing a series
of humanoid masks. There proved to be a significant positive relationship between an
individual's Penetration score and the number of times he referred to the masks as looking
mutilated, scarred, or physically distorted ($\chi^2 = 5.7, p > .02$). Also should be mentioned a
series of projects by Fisher (1965B) in which it was shown that normal subjects with high
Penetration scores show selectively poorer recall for words referring to body mutilation and
death than do those with low Penetration scores. So, one is confronted with instances in which
the Penetration score is positively related in normal subjects to indices clearly involving body
image variables.

Cassell (1964) has suggested a modification of the Penetration score which includes only
responses referring either to the interior of the body or modes of entry to the interior. It
excludes all non-body percepts (e.g., shadow, doorway) which are part of the usual Penetration scoring. This score is considered by Cassell to be an index of awareness of one's body
interior regions. It is an interesting index which, in a logical sense, perhaps has more promise
than the Penetration score because it has proven to be significantly negatively related to the
Barrier score in a normal sample. The Penetration score is not negatively related to the
Barrier score in most normal samples.

the greater the awareness of, and familiarity with, a given body region the easier it would be to recognize pictures of such regions. This assumption, states Cassell, is consistent with previous findings (e.g., Solomon and Howes, 1951; Postman and Schneider, 1951) that familiarity with a word or concept facilitates its tachistoscopic perception.

A population of 104 college students (male = 61, female = 43) was studied. Barrier scores were based upon group administered Rorschach protocols. Twenty-five responses had been obtained from each subject.

Fifteen pictures in the tachistoscopic series portrayed the body exterior in a social or human context. That is, they presented exterior views of the bodies of persons engaged in social transactions, expressing emotions, or responding meaningfully (e.g., girl swimming, baby on a blanket, woman at a desk). A second series of 13 photographs depicted parts of the body exterior (e.g., eye, ear, finger, forehead) in an isolated anatomical fashion. Seven photographs represented body interior regions (e.g., heart, stomach, kidney). In addition, there were 54 non-body "filler" pictures (e.g., hat, dog, tree) which served to disguise the primary theme of the tachistoscopic presentations. All photographs were initially presented on the tachistoscope at .01 seconds. Those recognized were dropped from the series and the procedure was repeated again for .02, .03, .04, and .05 second exposure times.

It was shown that high Barrier subjects were faster than low Barrier subjects in perceiving the body exterior pictures with social meanings (p .001) and also the isolated "anatomical" representations of exterior body parts (p .01). When it was discovered that the men perceived pictures of internal organs faster than the women, the data relating to recognition of body interior parts were analysed separately by sex. In the male group the Barrier score was, as predicted, negatively correlated with ability to recognize body interior representations. But the relationship was of a chance order in the female sample. It was considered by Cassell that the tenor of his findings reinforced the formulation that the Barrier score reflects relative awareness of the exterior vs. interior aspects of one's body.

INDUCTION OF BODY IMAGE BOUNDARY CHANGES

Obviously, the most convincing evidence regarding the role of exterior and interior body sensations in the production of Barrier images would be to induce Barrier changes by actual manipulation of body sensations. Several attempts in this direction have been undertaken.

In an initial exploratory study (Fisher and Renik, 1966) it was formally hypothesized that increasing an individual's awareness of the boundary regions of his body would increase his Barrier score; whereas intensifying his awareness of interior body regions would decrease his Barrier score. The following specific possibilities were suggested:

1. Persons who are aroused to an intensified awareness of their muscles and skin (boundary) will show a larger increment in Barrier than those who are stimulated to a greater awareness of their body interior or those whose awareness of body exterior and interior is unchanged.

2. Subjects stimulated to become more aware of their body interior regions will register a greater decrement in Barrier than subjects who have not been influenced to change their body experience patterns.

The three procedures utilized for evaluating the hypotheses are described below.

Exterior

In order to appraise the effects upon the Barrier score of directing attention to skin and musculature, those in one group were first shown 25 blots of Form B of the Holtzman series and then during, and following, a series of body concentration "exercises" were shown 25 blots of Holtzman Form A. To give the subject intensified awareness of his skin and musculature he was first told, "The purpose of this experiment is to determine how much people can and do feel from the exteriors of their bodies, particularly the skin and body musculature. The first thing I would like you to do is to concentrate your attention on your skin. Each time you have any sensation from your skin, report it to me and I will note it down—any sensation of itching, touch, tickling, etc.—any sensation whatsoever. Beginning when I tell you, concentrate your attention on your skin, on the outside of your body. Describe each sensation briefly, in one or two words, so as not to interrupt your concentration on your skin. If you have the same sensation more than once, report it more than once. Is that clear? Ready? Begin.

"The next thing I would like you to do is similar, only it involves the body musculature. The muscles of the body are continuously making tiny movements, of which we are ordinarily unaware. Beginning when I tell you, I would like you to concentrate your entire attention on the muscles of the outside of your body and report to me each time you feel a muscle movement. As before, be brief so as not to interrupt your concentration. Just one or two words, saying what part of the body musculature is involved—arm, hand, neck, etc. Again, if you feel the same muscle movement more than once, report it more than once. Ready? Begin.

"The next part of the experiment involves the skin again. I am going to mention a number of sensations to you which involve the skin. Some of them will be familiar; in that case, I would like you to concentrate for 30 seconds, and see if you can remember what the sensation I name is like. See if you can feel it in your memory, so to speak. If the sensation I name is unfamiliar, I would like you to concentrate your attention on your skin for 30 seconds and tell me if you can imagine what the sensation *would* be like. The first thing I would like you to feel is your skin as cold. Ready? Begin. (Repeat for: 'skin itching', 'skin as very soft', 'skin the way it feels when a breeze blows over it', 'skin as tight', 'skin as hot', 'skin as wet', 'skin as stiff or hard', 'tickling sensation on the skin', 'skin as loose.')"

Here, Holtzman Blots 1–12 of Form A were shown to the subject.

"Now I would like you to do a few more things pertaining to sensations from the exterior of your body. These are six strips of paper. I would like you to rub each of them across the back of your hand and then arrange them on the table in order from the roughest to the smoothest. You may rub each one across the back of your hand as many times are you like. Ready? Begin.

"Now I am going to place before you these five bristles at the ends of five handles. By touching them to the skin of your palm—again, as many times each as you like—please arrange them on the table in order from the stiffest to the most flexible.

"Which did you find it easier to distinguish, the papers or the bristles?"

Holtzman Blots 13–25 were then shown to the subject.

The duration of the body attention procedures was restricted to 15 minutes. This was similarly done for all of the other experimental conditions to be outlined below.

Interior

Similar methods were used to focus the subject's attention upon her body interior. Subsequent to responding to the first series of Holtzman blots, she was instructed: "The purpose of this study is to find out how much people can and do feel from the insides of their bodies. I think you can understand that this is of some importance, medically. First of all, I'm going to show you some pictures of the inside of the human body. You can see the lungs, stomach, gall bladder, pancreas, large intestine, small intestines, heart, kidneys, great vessels inside the body—aorta, pulmonary artery, and so forth. (Organs are pointed out while named.)

"I am going to mention to you the names of a number of organs inside your own body. What I'd like for you to do is focus your attention inside your body on the organ I name. I will give you 30 seconds after each one, and tell me if you are able to receive any physical sensation from it: any feeling of movement, weight, size, shape . . . any physical sensation whatsoever. Is that clear? The first organ will be your heart. For 30 seconds, beginning when I tell you, concentrate all your attention inside your body on your heart, and tell me—I will ask you after the 30 seconds are up—whether you could feel any physical sensation from your heart. (Wait 30 seconds.) All right: were you able to receive any physical sensations from your heart? (Repeat for stomach, lungs, intestines, liver, and kidneys.)

"The next thing I'm going to do is mention a number of bodily processes to you. These are events which people may feel take place inside their bodies. Some of them will be familiar to you; you will have felt them take place inside your own body in the past. What I would like you to do is for 30 seconds—I will give you 30 seconds after each event I name—to concentrate on the sensation which I have mentioned. Even if you are not feeling it now, try to re-create the sensation; try to remember the feeling I name, and concentrate on it for 30 seconds. All right? Others will not be familiar to you. You may never have felt them take place inside your body. In that case, what I'd like you to do is concentrate your attention on the organ or part of the inside of your body involved and tell me if you can imagine what it *would* be like to feel the sensation I have named, if you did feel it. Is that clear? All right, the first thing I'd like you to feel is your stomach as very empty. Ready. Begin now. (Wait 30 seconds.) All right; were you able to feel that? (If subject is unsure, elicit any positive response and mark it down as 'yes'.) (Repeat for 'heart producing an extra heavy beat, deep inside your body'; 'a tickling sensation, deep in your chest'; 'intestinal movement, a feeling of movement in your intestines'; 'the blood flowing through the arteries and veins, deep inside your body'; 'your stomach contracted'; 'your liver working, your liver functioning'; 'a sensation from deep inside your bones, deep in your body'; 'a filled feeling, deep in your abdomen'.)

"The next thing you are going to be doing is monitoring sensations from your own heart. I am going to give you a pad and a pencil. What I want you to do is for two minutes—beginning when I tell you—to again concentrate all your attention on your heart. Each time you receive any physical sensation from your heart—any beat, any feeling of movement, weight, size, or shape—make a mark on the pad with the pencil. Make a mark for each sensation you have. All right? And during these two minutes, try to concentrate also on what the sensations feel like, because when the two minutes are over, I'm going to ask you to describe them to me. Ready? Begin now. (Wait two minutes.) All right, what sorts of sensations did you have?"

Responses to 12 of the Holtzman blots were obtained at this point. Following this, the subject was told: "Now I'd like you to do some more observation of the inside of your body. I'm going to give you some of this water in a cup. (Water very cold.) Take one mouthful and swallow it very slowly, concentrating on everything you can feel inside your body while you are swallowing it and after you swallow it. Then, when you are ready, describe to me what you could feel."

(Pour water of room temperature into a cup.) "Now I'd like you to repeat that, paying particular attention to the last things you could feel—where you felt the water last, and for how long you could feel it. (Question until two minutes have expired.)

"Now think over the various parts of the insides of your body, and tell me from what particular part you ordinarily receive the most sensation. Once again, think over the various parts of the insides of your body and tell me from which particular part you ordinarily receive the least sensation."

Holtzman Blots 13–25 were presented.

Control (Non-Body)

A "non-body" control procedure was also used. It involved test-retest with the Holtzman blots, with intervening subject-experimenter interactions of the same length as that occurring during the Exterior and Interior procedures. But the experimenter made no references to the subject's body. After the first administration of the Holtzman blots, the subject was instructed:

"I am going to show you some pictures in this book (24 pictures of various landscapes and non-human objects). I would like you to study each one for 20 seconds. When the 20 seconds are up, simply tell me whether you have ever before seen anything similar to what is shown in the picture. A response of 'yes' or 'no' will be sufficient. Then turn to the next picture. In other words, I will indicate to you when 20 seconds have elapsed, and you will say 'yes' or 'no' and turn to the next picture.

"During the next three minutes, beginning when I tell you, I would like you to name all the cities, towns or villages you can remember ever having been in, in your life. If you are still naming at the end of three minutes, I will ask you to stop.

"I am going to ask you your favorites in a number of categories. Some of these may be difficult for you, in that you may never have thought of having a favorite; or, you may have a number of favorites. In any case, I'd like you to decide on one thing in each category that you like as well or better than any other you can think of right now. Consider your choice; I don't necessarily want your first impression. The first thing I'd like you to tell me is your favorite musical instrument." (Repeat for color, composer, artist, author, song, book, movie, flower.)

Cards 1–12 of the next Holtzman set were shown to the subject. She was then told: "I'd like you to go through this stack of cards (abstract designs), one card at a time. Arrange the cards into two piles: in one pile put the cards you like, in the other, the cards you don't like.

"I'd like you to consider a moment and tell me the best course you've ever taken in school. (Or best job, if subject has had no recent schooling.) Now would you tell me a little bit about why you liked it?"

At this point, Holtzman blots 13–25 were administered.

Scoring of the Holtzman protocols was done without knowing whether they were derived from first or second testings.

There were 20, 21, and 20 women in the Exterior, Interior, and Control groups respectively. Corresponding median ages in the samples were 20, 20, and 21; and median educational attainments 15, 15, and 16 years. The experimenter was a male.

Table 7.5
Means and Standard Deviations for Test-Retest Barrier Scores
in Female Exterior, Interior, and Control Groups

Groups	Initial M	Barrier σ	Retest M	Barrier σ	Diff.
Exterior (N = 20)	5.00	2.10	6.60	3.20	+1.60
Interior (N = 21)	5.90	3.28	5.70	3.03	−.20
Control (N = 20)	5.45	3.14	5.70	2.76	+.25

The Barrier means in the Exterior, Interior, and Control groups prior to experimental manipulation were respectively 5.0, 5.9, and 5.5. They do not differ significantly from each other. Analysis of variance of the change scores for the three treatment conditions indicated a non-significant F (2.0). Comparisons of individual treatment conditions also indicated lack of significance for Exterior versus Control and Interior versus Control. However, the F value (5.16, $p < .05$) for Exterior versus Interior was significant.[5] The Exterior condition shifted Barrier in a positive direction and the Interior condition moved it slightly in a negative direction. Neither condition by itself was significantly different from the Control condition, but the slight opposing effects associated with each combined significantly. It is noteworthy that the Interior group was the only one to show a test-retest decrease in Barrier.

While significant effects were obtained only for the Exterior versus Interior procedures, the results were sufficiently promising to encourage further studies. A second project was undertaken in which the design was exactly like that just described, except that the experimenter was female instead of male. The subjects were female college students. Fifteen were exposed to the Exterior procedure and 15 to the Interior procedure. The change value from the Control group (N = 20) used in the first study was used again in the present study.

The means in the Exterior and Interior groups prior to experimental manipulation were respectively 6.5 ($\sigma = 2.7$) and 5.9 ($\sigma = 3.4$). They did not differ significantly from each other.

Analysis of variance indicated that the overall treatment effects were significant (F = 19.4, $p < .001$). Also significant were the Exterior versus Interior effect (F = 38.7, $p < .001$), the Exterior versus Control effect

[5] Klepper (1968) has used the body attention focusing procedures to determine if altered exterior or interior awareness affect one's ability to judge the vertical—as defined by the Witkin, et al. (1954) procedure for measuring degree of field independence. In a sample of college women (N = 60), an increase in body exterior awareness produced a significant increment in ability to judge the vertical accurately. A condition which augmented awareness of the body interior and a non-body control condition did not have significant effects upon judgments of the vertical.

(F = 15.6, p < .001), and the Interior versus Control effect (F = 7.2, p < .01).

The impact of the body attention focusing procedures was clearly as had been predicted. Those who focused their attention on the boundary regions

Table 7.6
Means and Standard Deviations for Test-Retest Barrier Scores
in Female Exterior and Interior Groups

Groups	Initial M	Barrier σ	Retest M	Barrier σ	Diff.
Exterior [a] (N = 15)	6.5	4.7	9.5	1.9	+3.0
Interior (N = 15)	5.9	3.4	7.4	4.1	−1.5

[a] The Control condition was represented by the +.25 change in Barrier found in the original group of female subjects who experienced a non-body oriented interview in the interval between Holtzman test and retest.

of their bodies increased their Barrier scores. Those who directed their attention to interior body sites showed a decrease in Barrier. These findings indicated grossly that the Barrier score does mirror the manner in which an individual distributes his attention to exterior versus interior body sectors.

INDUCTION OF BOUNDARY CHANGES IN MALES

Another study of boundary alteration was attempted which was concerned with replicating the above, but with a sample of males instead of females. In all respects, save that the subjects were male, the experimental procedure was identical with that described in detail in the previous study. Each subject was shown a series of 25 Holtzman blots (Form B) and a baseline or initial Barrier score was obtained. One group then directed their attention to the interiors of their bodies; and a second group concentrated upon their body exteriors. The control group was not asked to alter body attention patterns in any way. The procedures used required a total of 15 minutes in each group.

Subjects were all men. There were 16, 15 and 15 in the Exterior, Interior, and Control groups respectively. The corresponding median ages in the groups were 21, 20 and 20; and the mean educational levels 16, 15 and 15 years.

The experimenter was male.

Mean initial Barrier scores in the Control, Exterior and Interior groups were 4.6, 4.2 and 5.2 respectively. None of these means differed significantly from the others.

Table 7.7
Means and Standard Deviations for Test-Retest Barrier Scores
in the Male Exterior, Interior, and Control Groups

Groups	Initial M	Barrier σ	Retest M	Barrier σ	Diff.
Interior (N = 15)	5.20	2.21	3.40	2.19	−1.8
Exterior (N = 16)	4.20	1.86	4.89	3.36	+.69
Control (N = 15)	4.60	2.22	4.87	1.99	+.27

Analysis of variance indicated that the overall treatment effects were significant (F = 3.9, p .05). Also, the Exterior versus Interior condition comparison was highly significant (F = 6.9, $p < .01$); and the Interior versus Control comparison was significant (F = 4.6, $p < .05$). The Exterior versus Control comparison was not significant.

While the results were not as clearcut as those found in the second female sample described above, they were largely congruent with expectation. In general, they may be viewed as buttressing the proposition that exterior and interior attention focusing have opposing and predicted effects upon the Barrier score.[6]

INDUCTION OF BOUNDARY CHANGES IN SCHIZOPHRENICS

Two further inquiries were conducted to determine whether the success of the boundary altering procedures with normal subjects could be duplicated with schizophrenic patients. This was done to test the generality of the procedures and also to explore possible unique responses to boundary versus non-boundary experiences in schizophrenic subjects.

The first study involved a sample of schizophrenics, 20 of whom were administered the body exterior focusing procedure; 20 the interior procedure; and 20 of whom were controls. All subjects were female; had been diagnosed as schizophrenic; but were sufficiently cooperative to respond with apparent understanding to instructions. About 60 percent were on various tranquilizing medications, but they were distributed randomly among the three groups. About half of the subjects in each group were seen by a male examiner and half by a female. With minor exceptions the experimental techniques

---

[6] A study of tattooed prisoners by Mosher, et al. (1967) showed them to have significantly higher Barrier scores than prisoners without tattoos. One can view such findings as indicating that the presence of tattoos served to make the experience of the skin more vivid. It is also possible, of course, that those with high Barrier scores were most likely to seek tattoos.

employed duplicated those described above in the studies of change in normals. Median age was 39 and median education level 11 years; and the three procedural groups did not differ significantly in these respects. They also were similar in representation of various diagnostic categories.

Analysis of the data revealed a mean change in Barrier score of —.6 for the Exterior condition subjects, +.4 for the Interior group, and —1.15 for the Controls. None of these change scores were significantly different from each other. One could not discern that the three conditions had differential effects upon the boundary. In appraising these chance findings, the question arose whether they might reflect the difficulties involved in interesting schizophrenic patients in a complex task. There was a very wide range of change scores (—7 to +7) and an erratic inconsistency which looked quite unlike the change score distributions obtained in the normal samples. This suggested the need to do a more controlled study in which the examiners would be particularly carefully trained, and especially concerned with maintaining rapport with the patients during the experimental procedures.

A second project was therefore undertaken. It involved 29 subjects (14 male, 15 female) exposed to the Exterior condition; 22 (7 male, 15 female) to the Interior condition; and 20 Controls (15 male, 5 female). About 70 percent of the patients were taking tranquilizing medication; but they were randomly distributed among the three procedural groups. About half were tested by one male examiner and the other half by another male. The examiners were trained with unusual care. Particular emphasis was put upon the need for establishing initial rapport and presenting the body awareness procedures in a vivid ego involving fashion. The median age of the sample was 36 and the median educational level 11 years; and the three subsamples did not differ significantly from each other with references to these variables. They also did not differ in representation of diagnostic categories.

Table 7.8
Medians and Ranges of Test-Retest Changes
in Barrier in Schizophrenic Sample

Group	Test-Retest Change
Exterior (N = 29)	+ 1.0 (—5 to +6)
Interior (N = 22)	0 (—3 to +9)
Control (N = 20)	0 (—3 to +3)

Because of the presence of extreme skewing of scores, it was decided to analyze the data by means of the Median Test. The median change in Barrier in the Exterior group was +1.0 (range —5 to +6); in the Interior group 0 (range —3 to +9); and in the Controls 0 (range —3 to +3). The overall Median Test was not significant ($X^2 = 4.5$, df = 2, $p > .10$). But the

Exterior group was found to exceed the Interior group in amount of increase in Barrier ($X^2 = 3.4$, df = 1, $p < .05$, one-tail test). Also, the Exterior group exceeded the Controls in this respect ($X^2 = 3.4$, df = 1, $p < .05$, one-tail test). The Interior and Control groups did not differ.

It was possible in this sample of schizophrenic patients to produce, by means of the techniques for intensifying skin and muscle awareness, an increase in boundary definiteness significantly greater than the changes resulting from the Interior or Control conditions. Despite the problems related to motivating schizophrenic patients to participate in the body awareness tasks, the Exterior procedure evidently did make an impact. It remains an unanswered question as to why the Interior condition did not produce an equivalent decline in boundary definiteness. Obviously, a good deal more work with psychiatric populations needs to be done in order to establish how personality disorganization influences boundary altering processes.

The fact that fairly brief body attention focusing procedures can produce detectable changes in the boundary inevitably raises a question about the meaningfulness of regarding a given degree of boundary definiteness as typical of an individual over time. However, it does not really follow that because change can be produced in a specific aspect of an individual's behavior by creating special "change" conditions, that this aspect of his behavior does not have a *typical* long term level or pattern. If one is able to make a subject express strong hostility in a laboratory situation by means of unusually frustrating conditions, this does not indicate that he may not have difficulty in expressing anger in most life situations. Consider also that, while it has now been shown that the Witkin, et al. (1954, 1962) measure of field independence based upon ability to adjust a rod to the vertical is influenced by sensory isolation (Jacobson, 1966) and body attention focusing procedures (Klepper, 1968), it is still true that Witkin, et al. observed considerable stability in field independence in subjects who were followed developmentally for many years. Relatedly, one may note that the test-retest coefficients for Barrier in a number of studies have demonstrated moderate stability.

CORROBORATIVE FINDINGS

The experiments described above in which direct experimental manipulation of exterior and interior body sensations produced predicted effects upon the Barrier score have been exceedingly well supported by the recent work of Van De Mark and Neuringer (1969). They instituted a study which proceeded in two steps. First, each of 48 college students (24 male, 24 female) were assigned to one of six conditions concerned with the arousal of exterior versus interior body regions:

Internal Focus Arousal

There were two categories of Internal Arousal.

One involved actual stimulation of the body. Thus, subjects were asked to swallow dry ice; sniff Bar-B-Q smoke; listen to their own heart beat; and drink warm cola.

A second category of internal arousal was based on asking the subject to imagine doing each of the interior stimulating tasks.

External Focus Arousal

There were two types of External Arousal.

One was based on direct stimulation of the body. It included using one's muscles strenuously; holding one's hands in cold water; and experiencing vibration applied to the skin.

The second type was ideational. Subjects were merely asked to imagine doing each of the tasks just mentioned.

Neutral Focus Arousal

One of two Neutral conditions requested the subject to view maps, pictures, and listen to music.

A second requested that he imagine doing such tasks.

Following any given condition, the subject responded to the Secord (1953) Homonym test and also to a measure devised by Fisher (1965B) for ascertaining one's relative awareness of body interior versus body exterior regions. The last mentioned measure is based on the frequency with which heart, stomach, skin, and muscle sensations are reported during a period of time.

Analysis of the exterior-interior body reports subsequent to each of the six conditions indicated that the exterior body arousal procedure resulted in a significantly greater awareness of the body exterior than did the interior body arousal or neutral procedures. Interior body stimulation resulted in greater interior awareness than did the exterior body stimulation or neutral procedures. Also, the direct body stimulation effects tended to be greater than those resulting from merely imagining that one had performed the exterior or interior arousal tasks.

Having demonstrated that the body stimulation conditions had measurable effects upon exterior versus interior body awareness, Van De Mark and Neuringer undertook the second phase of their study which involved 120 college students (60 male, 60 female) who were randomly assigned to one of the six stimulation conditions. Immediately after a given arousal condition, the subject was administered the Rorschach blots (with response total controlled). It was predicted that augmenting exterior body awareness would stimulate Barrier responses to a greater degree than would any of the other experimental conditions. Further, it was hypothesized that intensifying interior body awareness would result in higher Penetration scores than would any of the other conditions.

It was found, as expected, that the subjects exposed to external somatic stimulation produced significantly higher Barrier scores than those exposed to the interior or neutral conditions. Once again as expected, the results indicated that Penetration was significantly higher in those who experienced the somatic interior focusing condition than those in the exterior or neutral conditions. However, the differential effects resulting from the body stimulation conditions were generally not more powerful than those elicited by the body imagination procedures. The authors note, "When the interiors of the body are experimentally stimulated, there is a concomitant rise in interior physical locus responses on the Rorschach. It is not even necessary to physically stimulate the two body image sectors. These effects are so powerful that even instructions to think about the interior and exterior parts of the body can mediate differential perception on the Rorschach test (p. 464)."

The Van De Mark and Neuringer data offer persuasive confirmation of the view that the Barrier percept is the resultant of sensations and feelings linked with the body exterior. They also provide the first direct evidence that the Penetration score is linked with a focus upon body interior experiences.

INK BLOT PERCEPTION AND BODY SENSATIONS

The almost isomorphic correspondence that has been observed in some of the above studies between body sensation patterns and the images elicited by ink blot stimuli is actually not an isolated finding. There have been previous reports by others which suggest that responses to ink blots may directly or indirectly pertain to body tensions and experiences. Most impressive in this respect is the considerable literature that has accumulated which indicates that the number of percepts depicting human movement which an individual produces may be an index of the level of activation of his musculature (e.g., Shipman, et al., 1964; Singer, et al., 1952). Indeed, Herman Rorschach (1921) himself speculated that human movement responses to the Rorschach blots were based on the projection of kinesthetic sensations to the framework of the blot. Not unrelatedly, it should be mentioned that Wapner and Werner have shown in several studies (1965) that tonus configurations induced in an individual's body may influence the patterning of his responses to unstructured perceptual stimuli (e.g., reversible figures).

The individual's own body probably provides him with one of the most prominent sources of stimulation and information when he finds himself in a poorly defined situation. Witkin, et al. (1954) have emphasized this point

with regard to the special types of unstructured perceptual situations to which
they expose their subjects. The typical setting in which ink blot responses are
obtained is one in which all external stimulation aside from the blots themselves is minimized. When a subject is asked to interpret a series of ink blots
he usually sits quietly for about an hour with one or more other persons who
give him a minimum of information. He is offered no guidance and only the
vaguest definition of his task; and actually the very novelty of the task
requirement makes him feel that his customary modes of thought and anchors
are inappropriate. One may conjecture that in such a situation the importance of his own body is magnified and its consequent prominence in the
perceptual field is probably enhanced. From this perspective it is not far-
fetched to assume that when one is experiencing one's body as an object with
heavily contoured boundaries (as does the high Barrier person) that this
pattern may impose itself as a patent in attempting to structure a vague ink
blot. Similarly, if one were receiving strong kinesthetic sensations, with their
obvious connotations of activity and movement, they might suggest a theme
to be found when searching an ink blot for meaning. In short, the possibility
exists that patterns of body sensation (whether they relate to one's shape,
size, boundedness, or muscle tensions) may become sufficiently prominent in
unstructured situations to impose themselves as frames of reference upon the
perceptual field. The fact that "background" information can influence
perception in this fashion is well documented by the work of Klein, et al.
(1958), Eagle (1959), and Allison (1963). It is pertinent to note also that
Fisher (1965B) was able to show a positive relationship between degree of
awareness of one's own body and selective superiority in the learning and
recall of words having body reference as compared to words with non-body
meaning.

If it is true that ink blot perception may become the carrier for body
experiences, it should be possible to demonstrate this fact with other classes
of body sensations besides those linked with degree of boundary definiteness.
Such a demonstration would seem to be important in firmly establishing that
the process considered to underlie the expression of boundary sensations in
the boundary characteristics of ink blot percepts is not an *ad hoc* contrivance,
but rather a phenomenon of generalized import.

A study [7] will now be presented whose purpose was to test further the
hypothesis that one's body experiences may find representation in interpretations of unstructured material. A specific prediction was made that the
greater the prominence of a subject's stomach in his body scheme the more
likely he is to perceive themes relating to nutritive processes when asked to
describe imaginatively a series of ink blots. That is, the more prominent the
representation of one's stomach in the body scheme the more is it presumed

---

[7] The essentials of this study were published by the writer as a paper entitled "Body
Sensations and Perception of Projective Stimuli" in the *Journal of Consulting Psychology*, 1965,
29, 135–138.

to intrude into the total perceptual field and to stimulate a set to perceive that which is associated with the stomach and its functioning.

The prominence of the subject's stomach in his body scheme was measured by means of a technique which involves his comparing the degree of awareness of his stomach with his degree of awareness of a number of other body areas. An instrument has been developed, Body Focus Questionnaire (BFQ), which presents him with a list of paired references to body sectors (e.g., stomach vs. arm, stomach vs. heart, head vs. leg, arm vs. neck). He is asked to turn his attention upon his body and to indicate for each pair of body parts which he is "most conscious of or aware of right now". Fourteen of the comparisons involve the stomach versus various non-stomach areas. The remaining items can be scored for other body dimensions, but in the present study served merely as filler to conceal from subjects that the measurement process was concerned only with the stomach concept. Administration of the BFQ took place in a group setting, with two to five subjects typically participating.

The Rorschach ink blots, which were also administered on a group basis, were used to obtain a sample of ink blot responses which could be analyzed for frequency of stomach related themes. The Rorschach protocols were scored blindly for nutritive themes in terms of the following criteria.

    1. All direct references to food (e.g., cake, apple, ice cream).

    2. All direct descriptions of eating or drinking (e.g., swallowing something, drinking beer, digesting food).

    3. All images of oral activities that have indirect nutritive implications (e.g., smoking, biting, chewing gum).

Each such reference was counted as one unit; and they were summed to arrive at a total score. No more than one unit was given for any one response. Two judges who independently scored 50 protocols showed 91 percent agreement in applying the scoring criteria.

All the subjects were seen either within one hour after breakfast or lunch in order to minimize the effects of hunger upon the responses obtained. Two separate studies were carried out with these procedures and they will be separately described.

Study 1

This study involved 52 men and 50 women. They were college students. Their median age was 21 years.

The median BFQ stomach score was 7, with a range from 0 to 14. The median ink blot nutritive score was 0, with a range from 0 to 3. No sex differences were apparent for either of the scores.

The highly skewed character of the nutritive scores required a nonparametric analysis of the data. Therefore, the BFQ and nutritive scores were related by means of chi-square. It can be seen in Table 7.9 that when

Table 7.9
Chi-Square Analysis of Relationship of Stomach Awareness
to Ink Blot Nutritive Responses in Study 1

	Low Stomach Awareness [a] (0–5)	Medium Stomach Awareness (6–9)	High Stomach Awareness (10–14)
High Nutritive (1 or more)	7	14	17
Low Nutritive (0)	24	27	13
	$\chi^2 = 7.9$ (df $= 2$); $p = .02$		

[a] The distribution of stomach awareness scores was divided into as nearly equal thirds as possible.

the subjects with above median nutritive scores and those with median or below scores are compared in terms of a trichotomy of stomach awareness scores, there is a significant relationship in the predicted direction [$\chi^2 = 7.9$, df $= 2$, p .01]. The higher a subject's stomach prominence scores the greater is the number of nutritive responses that he gives to the ink blots.

Study 2

The subjects consisted of 51 men and 42 women who were college students recruited by payment of a fee. Their median age was 21 years.

Table 7.10
Chi-Square Analysis of Relationship of Stomach Awareness
to Ink Blot Nutritive Responses in Study 2

	Low Stomach Awareness [a] (0–5)	Medium Stomach Awareness (6–8)	High Stomach Awareness (9–14)
High Nutritive (1 or more)	8	15	14
Low Nutritive (0)	25	15	16
	$\chi^2 = 5.2$ (df $= 2$); $p < .10$		

[a] The distribution of stomach awareness scores was divided into as nearly equal thirds as possible.

The median stomach prominence score was 7 (range 0–14) and the median nutritive ink blot score was 0 (range 0–3). No sex differences emerged.

Analysis of the data by chi-square in the same fashion as was done in Study 1 reveals borderline confirmation for the hypothesis. As shown in Table 7.10, there was a relationship in the predicted direction between the stomach awareness and ink blot nutritive variables [$\chi^2 = 5.2$, (df = 2), $p = <.10$], but it attained only the $<.10$ level of significance.

Despite the rather limited distributions of ink blot nutritive responses obtained, it was possible in two different studies to find support for the hypothesis tested. Further evidence is thus provided that the individual's body experiences (body image) may play a role in his perception of an unstructured stimulus like an inkblot. It has already been shown that there are meaningful relations between muscle tension and the perception of human movement in ink blots and between the focus of attention on the boundary layers of one's body and the attribution of clear boundaries to ink blot percepts.

The importance of one's body as a matrix of sensations which selectively influences the perception of sensations from "out there" has not been sufficiently recognized. It has been particularly neglected in situations where the "outer" stimulus is a poorly defined configuration with relatively less structure than that represented by the existing pattern of body sensations. Allison (1963) has recently shown that relatively poorly organized cognitive structures are likely to register the influence of even minimal extraneous stimulus inputs. The implications of a body image framework for interpreting responses to projective targets like ink blots need to be seriously examined. The results of the present study and the work with the Barrier score represent two successful demonstrations of this potential.

VERBAL REPRESENTATION OF BOUNDARY DEFINITENESS

Past attempts have been made to measure boundary definiteness with techniques involving other than ink blot responses. None have been particularly encouraging, although some minor success was attained in showing a positive relation between the Barrier score and certain forms of elaboration in drawings of a house (e.g., amount of decorative facade). It is a matter of interest whether other forms of expression besides ink blot constructions reflect Barrier qualities. If so, not only would the generality of the Barrier orientation be extended but also possible new approaches to its measurement might be provided.

Hartley (1964) set himself the task of differentiating persons of varying boundary definiteness in terms of the responses to words with two or more meanings (homonyms). In a preliminary study he determined Barrier scores in a sample of 57 college (30 male, 27 female) students; and obtained the "first word you think of" in response to 375 words (e.g., jam, rash, sling) administered over a period of days. The words had been impressionistically chosen by Hartley as having the potential to differentiate high and low Barrier persons. The issue was whether high and low Barrier persons would interpret the homonyms differently and therefore offer different types of responses to them. Because it was discovered that the females had significantly higher Barrier scores than the males, the data were analyzed separately for the two sexes. Those words which discriminated successfully within each sex group were then applied to a second sample (33 males, 50 females). Eleven homonyms survived this selection process for males and eight for females. The 11 words which were discriminating for the males were as follows:

> peer—pier (read as one word to the subject)
> cell—sell
> band—banned
> pail—pale
> tag
> berry—bury
> design
> sling
> waist—waste
> vain—vane—vein
> box

For the females the eight words were:

> rash
> cell—sell
> been—bin
> pail—pale
> vanity
> sling
> vain—vane—vein
> temple

A homonym score could be computed for each individual indicating the number of times his word associations were typical of those found in high Barrier subjects. A correlation of .80 ($p < .001$) was found between this homonym Barrier score and the usual Barrier score in the male group. The equivalent correlation for the females was .56 ($p < .001$). Apparently, there are differences in set or attitude toward stimulus words which go along with variations in boundary definiteness. It is difficult from Hartley's data to discern the nature of these differences. Quite impressionistically, one notes, after examining the detailed responses presented in his data, that in the female group high Barrier subjects exceeded the low Barrier in the frequency with which their word associations referred to the body. For the male group, there was perhaps a trend in the opposite direction.

SEX DIFFERENCES

Some of the sex differences in Hartley's data described above lead quite appropriately into the present discussion of sex differences in boundary characteristics. Although it had been accepted on the basis of earlier studies that there were no adult sex differences in boundary definiteness, hints began to accumulate that small but consistent differences might be present when careful controls were imposed to obtain an equal number of responses from men and women with similar educational and socio-economic backgrounds. A study designed to test this possibility definitively was undertaken by the present writer in a large sample of college students (male = 274, female = 290). Rorschach ink blot responses were obtained on a group basis, with the usual control of the number of responses to be given to each blot. The median Barrier and Penetration scores in the male group were, respectively, 6 (range 0–16) and 3 (range 0–12). The respective medians in the female group were 7 (range 1–18) and 2 (range 0–12). The Barrier difference was highly significant [$\chi^2 = 11.5$, df = 1, $p < .001$] and this was also true of the Penetration difference [$\chi^2 = 13.6$, df = 1, $p < .001$]. These findings state clearly that the males have lower Barrier and higher Penetration scores than the females.

Other studies have been completed which point in the same direction. Jacobson (1965) noted in a population of college students (male = 75, female = 61) that the males had significantly lower Barrier scores than the females ($p < .02$). As already referred to, Hartley (1964) found in one sample of college students (male = 30, female = 27) that the males had lower Barrier scores than the females ($p < .05$); and he obtained similar results ($p < .01$) in a second sample of students (male = 33, female = 50). A potentially important sidelight of Hartley's study was the discovery that Barrier is correlated with a measure of masculinity-femininity based on the classification of subjects' associations to words. He found a significant trend ($p < .02$) in a male group for those with medium Barrier values to be high on masculinity, while those with extreme Barrier values (low or high) tended toward femininity. In a female group the medium Barrier subjects were characterized as feminine and the high or low extreme Barrier subjects as masculine ($p < .10$).

Sex differences in Barrier have also been detected in children. Joyce Morton (1965) reported on the basis of group administered Rorschach protocols that girls had higher Barrier scores than boys in a sample of 12-year-olds ($p < .01$), in a sample of 13-year-olds ($p .02$), and in a sample of 14-year-olds ($p < .05$). The totals of subjects in each of these samples were respectively 27, 22, and 33.

Gail Gordon (1964) examined 360 normal children with individually administered Holtzman blots. The children comprised three different age groups: six years, nine years, 12 years. Each group contained an equal number of boys and girls. Girls scored higher on Barrier and lower on Penetration than did boys at all age levels. Analysis of variance indicated that the overall sex effect was significant (p .05).

Five different studies, involving both adults and children, have affirmed the fact that females possess more definite boundaries than males.[8]

It is not a simple matter to account for the greater degree of boundary definiteness displayed by the females. This represents a contradiction of stereotypes which portray the male as superior to the female with regard to such variables as self-definition, clarity of body concept, and body security. A view emphasizing male superiority in this respect was especially fostered by Witkin, et al. (1954) who found that men were better able than women to utilize body cues in making spatial judgments, and who therefore concluded that men have a more secure and effective body concept. Actually, when one examines Witkin's work, it becomes apparent that his conclusions regarding body concept differences between the sexes are deductions from the fact that women performed more poorly than men in using kinesthetic cues to make spatial judgments when they also have the choice of using visual cues for the same purpose. The fact which is usually overlooked is that when women were placed in situations in which they were forced to rely on their own kinesthetic resources, they proved to be just as accurate in their spatial judgments as men. It is not logical to interpret Witkin's work as demonstrating that women cannot utilize body cues as efficiently as men. Interestingly, one may note further that when he analyzed sex differences in body concept as defined by figure drawing indexes he was unable to detect any superiority for the male.

Other studies have provided information which suggests not only that the female devotes more attention to her body than the male, but also that she more quickly arrives at an articulated and realistic concept of it. Katcher and Levin (1955) observed that girls arrive at a realistic concept of their body size at an earlier age than boys. Swenson and Newton (1955) and Wieder and Noller (1950, 1953) reported that girls attain earlier than boys a sexual definition of self as measured by the frequency with which they portray a

---

[8] An analysis was also undertaken by the author to determine if the differences in Barrier between males and females could be traced to one or two particular categories of content. For example, were the differences a specific function of females producing more references to clothing or decorative objects than the males? All responses in a sample of 53 males and 54 females were classified into four different categories (viz., clothing, skins, man-made structures, geographical formations). It was found that the elevated Barrier scores of the females were not due to the special contribution of any one or two categories.

figure of the same sex as self when asked to draw a picture of a person. They noted too that girls earlier incorporated details into their drawings which clearly distinguished the sex of the figure. Machover (1953) after analyzing the drawings of 1,000 children from ages five–11 indicated that girls seemed to have less difficulty than boys in evolving a comfortable body concept.

It is possible, then, that the relatively greater boundary definiteness exhibited by the women in the present study represents a clearer articulation of the body concept. Perhaps women exceed men in the clarity with which they perceive their bodies as differentiated and individualized. One could argue that the culture encourages the female to be more interested in her body than it does the man.[9] Also, her role as a woman is more explicitly identified with her body and its functioning than is true of the man. The man's role and status are typically defined in terms of his accomplishments and attainments rather than in terms of his body attributes, but for the woman her role is still largely defined in relation to the attractiveness of her body to the male and her ability to bear children. She learns rather early that her body will be her most important means for the attainment of a meaningful role. It is true that the male is given various messages about the importance of having a strong masculine body, but it becomes evident to him that his success as a man will have little to do in the long run with his body attributes. Only an athlete can see a direct equation between his body strength and success in life. A woman probably more nearly equates self with body. She has a clearer concept than a man of the role her body will play in her life. It is quite apropos to point out further that one of the prime eventual goals of most women involves the conversion of her body into a "container" or protective enclosure for the production of children. Does not the successful conceptualization of one's body as a containing, protective form necessarily mean that it must be experienced as having clear and dependable boundaries?

A further, more detailed discussion of the significance of sex differences in boundary attributes will occur at a later point.

ANALYSIS OF BOUNDARY ALTERING CONDITIONS

Earlier, evidence was offered that the boundary may be altered by procedures which cause an individual to focus differentially upon exterior or interior sectors of his body. It is a matter of importance to ascertain what

[9] Relatedly, Mordkoff (1966) studied reports of autonomic changes in one's body in male and female samples. He found that females reported more such changes than men. Degree of reported awareness of somatic changes was positively correlated with indices of maladjustment in the males but not in the females.

other specific stimulus input conditions [10] may change the boundary. Toward this end a variety of investigations were carried out. Typically, Holtzman ink blots were administered; a well defined stimulus situation introduced; and a second Holtzman was administered either during or after the special condition introduced in order to detect its impact upon the boundary.

EFFECT OF DISTORTED MIRROR IMAGE
UPON BOUNDARY

The first investigation to be described sought to determine the effect upon one's boundary of being confronted with a grossly distorted visual image of one's body. If an individual responds to ink blot stimuli while he is perceiving a seriously distorted visual representation of himself, will this produce a decrement in Barrier type responses? That is, will the visually distorted image intrude upon the existing body concept in a disorganizing fashion and be reflected in boundary dissolution?

Fifteen female college students participated in this study. The first 25 blots of Form B of the Holtzman Ink Blot test were administered while the subject sat in front of an ordinary full-length mirror which produced no distortion in her image. This mirror was introduced to control for the presence of a distorting mirror in the subsequent retest condition. All responses were taken down verbatim by an examiner whose image was not visible in the mirror. No special reason was given to the subject for the introduction of the mirror. Following the completion of the 25 blots, she was asked to fill out a questionnaire which required 15 to 20 minutes. Then, she was asked to sit in front of a full-length "carnival" mirror with marked concave and convex distortions which grossly altered her image (e.g., shortening, widening, creating disparities in size of body areas along the vertical axis). After observing herself, she was further asked to describe the various ways in which the mirror changed her appearance. This was done to encourage awareness of, and involvement with, the mirror distortions. The first 25 cards of Form A of the Holtzman blots were administered, but after every third blot, a brief inquiry was made as to other distortions the subject might have noticed in her mirror image (e.g., "Do your arms look different?", "Do your legs look different?"). This was part of a continuing attempt to maintain the subject's involvement with the mirrored alterations. All protocols were scored blindly for Barrier.

---

[10] This term "stimulus input conditions" was intended to refer to specific situational attributes—in distinction to broad and more vague factors with boundary modifying connotations like pregnancy, schizophrenic disorganization, or sensory isolation which will be described at a later point.

The mean test-retest change in Barrier was $+.07$ ($\sigma = 3.7$). This value was not significantly different from that observed in a female control group in the earlier cited study concerned with boundary alteration via focusing of attention upon exterior versus interior body sites. This control group, which experienced an interview involving no body references in between test and retest with the Holtzman blots, had shown a small Barrier increase of $+.25$. One may therefore conclude that the distorting mirror did not have an appreciable impact upon the Barrier score.

IMPACT OF DISTORTED KINESTHETIC EXPERIENCE UPON BOUNDARY

As a next step in defining what alters the boundary, attention was turned to the effects of gross distortion of an individual's usual kinesthetic experiences upon his retest Barrier score. If one is exposed to stimuli which markedly change one's pattern of kinesthetic awareness, might this have a disorganizing effect on the body concept which would then be translated into a decrease in boundary definiteness?

Thirty-one female college students were studied with reference to this problem. Each subject was initially asked to respond to the first 25 cards of Form B of the Holtzman Ink Blot test. A questionnaire was then administered which required approximately 15 to 20 minutes. At this point, three vibrators [11] were attached to the subject: one on the middle of each arm and one on the sole of the left foot. The combined pattern of vibration they produced was intense and pervasive and largely "covered over" the individual's usual way of experiencing her body. However, it was not so discomforting as to interfere seriously with thinking or verbalization. Just before turning the vibrators on it was explained to the subject that the purpose of the next phase of the procedure was to evaluate her ability to give ink blot responses while being distracted by vibration. With the vibrators running, each subject then responded to the first 25 cards of Form A of the Holtzman test.

Scoring of Barrier was done blindly. The mean Barrier change was -1.0 ($\sigma = 3.0$). That is, there was a trend for the gross vibration to result in a decrease in boundary definiteness. When the mean Barrier decline in the vibration group was compared with the change score of $+.25$ obtained in the female control group in the earlier mentioned study concerned with boundary alteration by means of focusing of body attention, the difference proved not to be significant. The vibration experience apparently did not alter the boundary appreciably.

---

[11] The vibrator on the foot was an Oster vibrator massage unit. The vibrators on the arms weighed about two ounces each and were actually made of small model motors whose shafts were eccentric.

One can only presume that the externally imposed kinesthetic experience, while rather intense, was not able to disrupt seriously the existing patterns of exterior-interior differentiation. Also, it obviously did not reinforce awareness of the boundary region.

PERCEPTION OF MUTILATION THEMES AND BOUNDARY

The effect upon the boundary of exposure to a film with mutilation themes was next considered. If an individual is confronted with vividly presented images and themes concerning death and body destruction, will this have a negative effect upon his body image and result in boundary disturbance? A dramatic and powerful film (Signal 30)[12] was employed to test the possibility. This film was produced to warn drivers of the dangers to be encountered on the highway. An attempt is made to frighten the viewer into being a safe driver by providing many gory examples of the consequences of carelessness. There are repeated close-ups of blood and mutilated bodies and shattered cars. Also, the sound track carries the moans and screams of the dying. The total impact of the film is such as to make the average viewer anxious, queasy, and hopeful of "getting it over with."

The effect of viewing the film was studied in a sample of 25 female college students. Each subject was asked to respond to the first 25 cards of Form B of the Holtzman Ink Blot test. A ten-minute segment of the film was shown; the first 13 cards of Form A of the Holtzman blots were administered; five more minutes of the film shown; and 12 more blots administered. The entire procedure was explained to the subject as concerned with evaluating the effects of the "safety" film on imaginative responses.

Scoring for Barrier was done blindly. The mean Barrier shift as a consequence of viewing the film was $-.33$ ($\sigma = 3.2$). This value did not differ significantly from the mean shift for the female control group in the previously described study concerned with boundary alteration via focusing of attention upon exterior versus interior body sites. Obviously, there was little consistency in the direction of shift. Although there was intense communication of mutilation imagery during the experimental condition, no evidence of a general reduction in boundary definiteness presented itself.

One cannot but be impressed with the fact that such a psychologically threatening procedure produced no decline in Barrier, whereas a relatively non-threatening method like inducing increased awareness of the interior of one's body did result in a Barrier decrease. This reinforces the specific

[12] Highway Safety Foundation, Inc., P. O. Box 1563, Mansfield, Ohio. This film has already been shown by Boyar (1964) to intensify anxiety about death.

importance of the factor of selective awareness of exterior versus interior body sites in determining boundary delineation.

ANALYSIS OF BOUNDARY CHANGES RESULTING FROM REMOVAL OF CLOTHING

A unique opportunity presented itself to consider the effect upon the individual's boundary of removing his clothing. The clothing that an individual wears covers the outside of his body and might be thought of as easily incorporated into what he considers to be his boundary regions. It is not mere speculation that clothing and other forms of body decoration may be "used" in an attempt to reinforce one's boundary. Compton (1964) has shown with reference to schizophrenic women that those with the poorest boundaries prefer clothes with bright, outstanding patterns which presumably give special visibility (with the hope for increased substantiality?) to the boundary. Relatedly, Mosher, et al. (1967) reported that prisoners with tattoos (that embellish the skin) have higher Barrier scores than prisoners without tattoos. At the same time that one speculates about the potential boundary reinforcing effects of clothing, one needs to consider the possible boundary reinforcing impact of removing one's clothing. When an individual removes his clothes he is more forcefully confronted with his body as a perceptual object. This is particularly true of his skin which, upon being uncovered, becomes a massive source of new sensations and experiences. The result could be enhanced feelings of boundary definiteness.

Weighing the above views, it was speculated that while in normal persons clothing would be experienced as part of the boundary, the reinforcing effect would be relatively small as compared to sensations which would be aroused in the actual boundary regions of the body (i.e., skin and muscle) when the clothing was removed. Therefore, the act of removing one's clothing should more often result in enhancing than diminishing boundary definiteness.

This hypothesis was evaluated in a sample of 42 women (mean age = 26.5) who were participating in a study of the personality correlates of sexual responsivity (Fisher and Osofsky, 1967). During a first session each subject wrote her own responses to the first 25 cards of Form B of the Holtzman blots. Five days later each subject participated in a series of gynecological and physiological evaluations which necessitated removing all of her clothing. Subsequent to these evaluations, which were of about 30 minutes duration, she was asked, with only a gown and sheet covering her, to write out her responses to the first 25 cards of Form A of the Holtzman blots. Although subjects were not in a state of complete nudity during this time, it is clear that they experienced themselves as being without clothing and were unusually aware of their bodies. This intensified body awareness was actually documented by increases in Body Prominence scores which were obtained during the unclothed as compared to the clothed sessions. The Body Prominence score, which will be described in considerable detail at a later point, is derived from the subject's response when asked to list "twenty things that you are aware of or conscious of right now." It is based on the number of references to one's body and clothing. A significant increase in Body Prominence occurred from session 1 to 2 ($t = 5.3$, $p < .001$).

The mean shift in Barrier score from the dressed to nude state was $+.6$ ($\sigma = 2.8$). This shift was in the expected direction, but not significantly so. It also did not differ from the amount of change ($+.25$) typifying a female control group in the earlier described study concerned with the effects of exterior versus interior attention focusing upon the boundary. Removing one's clothing did not produce a consistent kind of boundary alteration. Although it anticipates a later presentation of material pertinent to the relationship of Barrier to sexual responsivity, it should be incidentally mentioned that the degree to which the subject's Barrier score shifted positively from the clothed to nude states was correlated with reported sexual responsiveness. The more her Barrier score increased the more likely she was to depict herself as deriving satisfaction from intercourse, as defined by self ratings of sexual responsiveness.

A striking finding, apropos of the determinants of boundary change, was the demonstration of a significant positive correlation ($r = .37$, $p < .05$, $N = 37$) between increase in Barrier and reported increase in skin sensations and experiences. During the clothed and unclothed sessions the subject had been asked to respond to the Body Distortion Questionnaire (Fisher, 1964C, 1966B) which contains, among other scales, one comprising 10 items which inquires concerning the presence of a variety of skin experiences. The subject answered Yes, No, or Uncertain with regard to whether she was aware of such skin sensations as the following: itching, tickle, cold, warmth, tightness. It was found that the greater the increase in skin experiences produced by nudity the larger was the increment in Barrier. This represents an unusually clear demonstration at a correlational level that intensity of skin awareness and boundary definiteness are meaningfully linked in the fashion expected by the exterior-interior model.[13]

OTHER CHANGE CONDITIONS

To learn more about the conditions capable of producing boundary changes, a number of other studies were conducted. They examined numerous factors

---

[13] Another change score derived from the BDQ (viz., feelings of pertaining to one's body being dirty) was also correlated with change in Barrier. The greater the increase in reported sensations of being dirty (from the clothed to the nude state) the smaller was the increase in Barrier from test to retest ($r = -.40$, $N = 37$, $p < .025$).

that might potentially affect the boundary. As will be seen, they all failed to provoke significant shifts in test-retest Barrier scores. The typical design, in each study, was the same as that outlined for the previously described boundary change experiments. Form B of the Holtzman blots would be administered; the experimental condition would then be introduced; and finally Form A of the Holtzman blots administered. All subjects were female college students. The experimenter was always a female.

The special experimental conditions that were introduced, each with a test-retest design, will be briefly enumerated below.

1. Subjects (N = 15) were exposed to 15 minutes of quiet soothing music which they listened to while lying on a couch. The question was whether the relaxed state, with its presumed decrease in muscle tonus, would affect the boundary.

2. In another instance, subjects (N = 16) listened to 15 minutes of rousing march music; and actually marched to it for brief periods. The effect of the presumed increase in muscle tonus was considered. There was particular interest in comparing the effects of the soothing and rousing types of music.

3. An exciting stimulus situation was created by having subjects (N = 20) watch a 15 minute film of a car race. The film depicted speed, competition, and potential danger—but no accidents or injuries were portrayed.

4. The racing film was contrasted with another experimental condition in which the subjects (N = 14) watched 20 minutes of film which were selected because of their boring and uninteresting content (viz., instructions concerning how to use a quantitative balance in chemistry experiments). It was intended to determine if boredom and excitement had differential boundary effects.

5. The impact of a special form of stress was evaluated by placing subjects (N = 26) in a situation in which they were told that a group of experts would be watching and photographing their behavior while they performed a series of embarrassing tasks. They were actually shown the "experts" who were standing behind a one-way mirror. In addition, electrodes were attached to them and they were informed that their physiological responses were to be recorded. Fifteen minutes of such "stress" intervened between test-retest with the Holtzman blots.

The mean amount of Barrier change elicited by each condition is shown below:

Soothing music	−.4	($\sigma = 2.3$)
March music	+.6	($\sigma = 2.5$)
Film of car race	−1.3	($\sigma = 3.1$)
Boring film	+.3	($\sigma = 3.2$)
Stress condition	−.6	($\sigma = 2.7$)

None of these change values differed significantly from the mean of +.25 obtained for the previously mentioned control group of women who were tested and retested, with an intervening interview that did not attempt to manipulate body experience.

Further, the change values for soothing and rousing march music did not differ significantly. The change values for the boring and exciting films did not differ significantly.

One can see that the experimental conditions were largely ineffective in altering the boundary. Boredom, excitement, relaxing rhythm, rousing rhythm, and stress all failed to produce measurable Barrier shifts. The boundary proved to be relatively resistant to alteration. This contrasts with the boundary effects that resulted from specifically directing attention to exterior or interior body sites.

8

The Boundary
and Various Levels of Behavior

Multiple and complex correlates of the boundary scores have been turned up since 1958 by way of cross validational and predictive studies and also exploratory undertakings. These studies have served to strengthen the original framework of the theory which was erected with regard to the function of the boundary in regulating behavior. They have also permitted some extensions of the theoretical framework.

PSYCHOPHYSIOLOGICAL PATTERNS

Psychophysiological patterns were among the first correlates of boundary definiteness to be observed. It had been initially established that patients with rheumatoid arthritis, neurodermatitis and conversion symptoms involving the musculature were characterized by higher Barrier and lower Penetration scores than patients with stomach ulcers or spastic colitis. From such findings the notion evolved that persons with definite boundaries who develop psychosomatic symptoms under stress tend to do so in the exterior body layers (viz., skin and muscle),[1] whereas persons with indefinite boundaries tend to manifest such symptoms in the interior body regions (viz., stomach, gut, and other internal organs). This exterior-interior model was later extended to persons in the normal range by findings which indicated that normal subjects with definite boundaries manifest relatively high

[1] A definition of what is meant by the terms body exterior and body interior is important at this point. Body exterior is meant to include the skin, the striate musculature, and the vascular components of these two systems. Body interior is considered to include all the internal viscera. This definition of body exterior versus body interior is intended to have purely locational or geographical implications and is not concerned with the embryonic origins of various body areas.

reactivity in the muscles and skin (e.g., in terms of Galvanic Skin Reflex [2] and Muscle Action Potential) and low reactivity at interior sites (exemplified by heart rate); but with just the obverse pattern appearing for those with indefinite boundaries. These findings were viewed as indicating that although a stream of excitation may be triggered by certain centers (e.g., the hypothalamus), there may be differential degrees of response to it in the body interior versus the body exterior. The similarity of this perspective to Lacey's (1959) concept of autonomic channeling is obvious. It is important to note that the differentiation between exterior and interior response introduces the concept that body reactivity can be viewed not only in terms of organ systems and conventional categorizations like "sympathetic–parasympathetic" but also in relation to the spatial properties of the body itself.

Previous encouragement for pursuing physiological response patterns within the exterior-interior spatial context of the body had already been provided by early observations and studies which have been summarized elsewhere (Fisher and Cleveland, 1968). A brief overview of the more prominent of these studies follows.

Burton and Edholm (1955) had reported that the maintenance of temperature homeostasis in the body could be schematized as involving a "central deep 'core' of the body of uniform regulated temperature, surrounded by a 'shell' of cooler peripheral tissues, whose temperature moreover is dependent on that of the environment as well as on physiological factors."

Kleitman (1939) proposed an "evolutionary theory of consciousness" which underscored the contrasting effects upon consciousness of stimuli arising in the viscera and stimuli from more exterior sites, particularly proprioceptive in character.

Lorr, Rubenstein, and Jenkins (1953) factor analyzed the ratings made by psychotherapists of various aspects of the behavior and somatic symptomatology of patients; and found that those ratings could be reduced to clusters analogous to various layers of the body [e.g., endodermal, mesodermal, cerebrotonic (focused upon skin complaints)]. Similarly, Wenger (1941, 1948) and also Sanford, et al. (1943) reported that analyses of a variety of physiological measures revealed clusters that could be conceptualized as involving particular layers of the body. For example, Wenger described a factor "representing certain functions of the skin and peripheral blood vessels".

Considerable work was done with adrenaline and non-adrenaline which indicated that they acted differentially and perhaps in opposing ways upon interior (e.g., heart) and exterior (e.g., peripheral vessels) body sites. Thus, Goldenberg (cited by Funkenstein, et al., 1954) ascertained that intravenous non-adrenaline produced heightened blood pressure as the result of increased

[2] The GSR is considered to be an exterior measure simply because it relates to potential changes which occur in end organs of the skin.

peripheral resistance, while adrenaline effected a blood pressure rise chiefly by means of increased cardiac output.

There were also a fair number of specific physiological findings in the literature concerning patients with "psychosomatic" symptoms which were congruent with the exterior-interior model. These studies seemed to indicate that the exterior or interior character of the symptom was matched by corresponding patterns of general exterior-interior reactivity. Karush, Hiatt, and Daniels (1955) discovered trends for patients with ulcerative colitis (interior symptoms) to respond to stressful stimuli with the colon, but to manifest relatively little response to such stimuli in terms of peripheral vascular changes. Lewinsohn (1954) detected significantly lowered skin reactivity (as defined by skin resistance) in ulcer patients who may be classified as a group with an interior symptom. Van der Valk and Groen (1950) and Little (1950) reported findings which similarly depicted ulcer patients as having limited reactivity in the skin and peripheral vasculature. Little also observed that his ulcer group was unusually reactive in terms of heart rate. Graham (cited in Wolff, 1950) showed that patients with psychosomatic skin disorders had greater skin responses to histamine or pilocarpine than did subjects in a control group.

The existence of such support, as fragmentary as it was, helped to crystallize experimental tests of the exterior-interior model. These tests proved to be consistent with the model. Davis (1960) attempted the first formal study in which it was applied to a prediction of reactivity patterns in normal subjects. He compared a number of physiological indices obtained under stress and rest from 25 men with unusually high and 25 men with unusually low Barrier scores. Measures of skin resistance, muscle potential, and total resistance of peripheral blood vessels were secured to represent body exterior reactivity. Measures of heart response were taken as samples of body interior reactivity. As predicted, the low Barrier subjects proved in general to be more responsive in terms of indices of heart reactivity than the high Barrier subjects. Furthermore, the high Barrier subjects exceeded the low Barrier subjects in muscle reactivity at a significant level; and at a borderline level exceeded them in reactivity as defined by total peripheral vascular resistance and basal skin resistance.

Two other sources of data concerning reactivity of normal subjects proved at this time to be congruent with the outside-inside model. An analysis of material collected by Herring (1956) indicated, as predicted, that there was a significant negative correlation between the Barrier score and minimum heart rate in a group of 25 men while undergoing surgery. Similarly, it was shown in an analysis of data collected by Funkenstein, King and Drolette (1954) on 51 males exposed to a frustrating situation that the Barrier score was negatively related to indices of heart reactivity, and positively so (at a borderline level) to total resistance of the peripheral vascular system.

Such was the state of the evidence concerning the exterior-interior hypothesis at the time that *Body Image and Personality* was published. It remained for further work to arrive at a broader collection of pertinent information.

One of the first efforts in this direction was undertaken by Fisher and Cleveland (1960). They considered it of primary importance to repeat their work with rheumatoid arthritics and patients with duodenal ulcers which had provided them with the original stimulus for speculating that there was a relationship between boundary definiteness and degree of exterior vs. interior reactivity. The rheumatoid arthritics were viewed, of course, as representing a group with exterior symptoms and the ulcer patients a group with interior symptoms. The arthritics were placed in the exterior symptom category because of the prominences of muscle and joint stiffness which is regarded as occurring in what are psychologically outer layers of the body. By contrast, the ulcer symptom occurs in a region which is psychologically very much the interior of the body. Fisher and Cleveland studied 26 male arthritics and 34 male patients with duodenal ulcers who were being treated in a Veterans Administration hospital. The mean age of the arthritics was 36.8 years and that of the ulcer patients 34.6 years. The mean duration of symptoms for the arthritics was 10.9 years and for the ulcer patients 7.7 years. These patients were intensively interviewed and blots from the Holtzman Ink Blot test were used to obtain a sample of 25 responses which were scored for the Barrier and Penetration indices. In addition, each subject was monitored for GSR (exterior) and heart rate (interior) responsivity in a stress situation and a subsequent rest condition. The stress was created by dropping a heavy iron bar on the floor next to the subject. It was found, as predicted, that the arthritics had significantly higher Barrier scores ($p < .001$) and lower Penetration scores ($p < .10$) at a borderline level than the ulcer patients. The trends for the physiological measures taken during stress were also significantly in the predicted direction. The arthritic group was characterized by a larger number of GSR responses ($p < .01$, one-tailed test) and a lower heart rate ($p < .001$, one-tailed test) than the ulcer group. Clear-cut differences between the groups did not appear during the rest condition. It is parenthetically interesting that in concordance with previous findings the arthritics were also observed to be more interested in athletic muscular expression than the ulcer patients and less tolerant of open, uninhibited displays of anger.[3]

A follow-up of this and related studies was then undertaken by Williams (1962). He contrasted 20 arthritics and 20 patients with peptic ulcers with respect to their boundary scores and also their physiological reactivity under several conditions. The mean age of the ulcer group was 38.6

---

[3] Moos and Solomon (1965A, B) have reaffirmed in a female population that arthritics have particular difficulty in expressing anger in a direct form.

years and that of the arthritics 42.7 years. Barrier and Penetration scores were derived from responses to the Rorschach ink blots. Physiological recordings of GSR, heart rate, and muscle potential were taken under conditions of rest, stress, recovery, and reassurance. In addition, recordings were secured during conditioning trials which involved a buzzer as the conditioned stimulus and an electric shock as the unconditioned stimulus. It was found that the arthritics produced more Barrier responses ($p < .10$) and fewer Penetration responses (p .001) than the peptic ulcer patients. The results involving the physiological data were rather complex in pattern and can best be presented by quoting from Williams' (1962) own summary: "Another prediction was made that Rheumatoid Arthritic and Peptic Ulcer patients could be differentiated on the basis of specific and non-specific GSR's, heart rate, and muscle activity under restful, stressful, recovery and reassurance conditions. The prediction received partial confirmation in demonstrating that Ulcer patients when compared to Arthritic patients tended to manifest higher heart rates while Arthritics tended to manifest higher muscle activity than the Ulcer group. GSR proved to be a poor discriminator of either interior or exterior physiological activity. It was conjectured that the criterion employed for evaluating GSR might have been too gross and too insensitive to reflect differences between the groups" (p. 114).

"The Barrier variable was used to divide the subjects into High Barrier (HB) and Low Barrier (LB) groups. The prediction was that HB patients would manifest more reactivity in terms of muscle activity and galvanic skin responses, whereas LB patients would manifest more reactivity in terms of heart rate. This prediction received partial corroboration in that the HB group was found to display higher muscle activity under activating conditions; LB patients were found to show higher heart rates under stressful conditions" (p. 115).

The results for the adaptation and conditioning procedures used by Williams were variable and difficult to summarize. One can say that there were some significant trends for the arthritics to manifest greater muscle response than the ulcer patients during adaptation and conditioning. Also, the ulcer patients manifested a "tenuous" trend to be higher than the arthritics in heart rate during adaptation, but not during the conditioning itself. No significant GSR results emerged. When the subjects were categorized not by medical diagnosis, but rather by their Barrier score, it was found that there were tendencies for GSR and muscle response values during adaptation and conditioning to go in a direction congruent with an exterior-interior model, but not significantly so. Some of the values for heart rate were significantly differentiating in the predicted direction. It should be noted that the difficulties involved in interpreting Williams' data were enhanced by the shrinkage of his ulcer group to as few as ten subjects in most analyses and also by deficiencies in some of his recording procedures and methods for eliciting physiological response.

Cleveland, Snyder, and Williams (1965) looked further at the issue of boundary differences in groups with exterior vs. interior symptoms. In one instance 18 males with rheumatoid arthritis proved to have higher Barrier (p .001) and lower Penetration scores (p .10) than 20 males with ulcerative colitis or peptic ulcer. In a second investigation 20 male arthritics had higher Barrier (p .001) and lower Penetration scores (p .02) than 20 males with peptic ulcers. All patients studied were from Veterans Administration hospitals.

Shultz (1966) was able to confirm previous findings regarding differences between patients with skin symptoms and those with stomach symptoms. He compared 20 males with eczematoid dermatitis with 20 males with duodenal ulcers. All were patients in a V.A. hospital. The dermatitis patients had higher Barrier ($p < .05$) and lower Penetration ($p < .10$) scores than the ulcer patients. This represents the first independent confirmation of Fisher and Cleveland's original reportthat certain types of skin symptomatology are linked with elevated Barrier scores.

Moos and Engel (1962) compared a group of 12 rheumatoid arthritics and 12 hypertensives for GSR, muscle potential, heart rate, and blood pressure reactivity during a series of conditioning trials. While the original purpose of their study was not to test the exterior-interior model, they considered that they could examine it from the viewpoint that the arthritics were high and the hypertensives perhaps relatively low in the Barrier score range. The gist of their findings on this issue may be conveyed by the following quotation from their paper (p. 239):

The results are also pertinent to the body image schema developed by Fisher and Cleveland. The facts that the rheumatoid arthritics (high Barrier scorers) had higher levels of muscle potential in the symptomatic muscle, reacted more in both muscles, showed higher GSR levels and reacted more in GSR than the hypertensives are all consistent with their theory. Muscle tension and GSR are both exterior body reactivity indicators and the arthritics should show both higher levels and higher reactivity in these measures. Systolic blood pressure, another indicator of body interior reactivity, was higher in their low barrier score group. Therefore, the systolic blood pressure results also seem consistent with their theory; i.e., they would probably predict that hypertensives who should have low barrier scores would show sustained elevations in systolic pressure.

The heart rate results, however, are not consistent. It should be clear that Fisher and Cleveland have not made any explicit predictions about differences between hypertensives and arthritics; however, we believe it is a logical extrapolation from their theory to predict that arthritics would have lower heart rate reactivity than hypertensives. Heart rate is a body interior measure and arthritics are body exterior reactors. Our results show that arthritics have higher heart rate levels than hypertensives and tend, although not specifically, to show greater initial heart rate reactivity.

These heart rate findings are consistent with . . . findings that hypertensives show slower heart rate reactivities than normotensives. They suggest that this lower reactivity in hypertensives is a compensatory mechanism to prevent even greater rises

in blood pressure by lessening increases in cardiac output. This would suggest that
Fisher and Cleveland will have to expand their body image schema to take account
of the interactions between the physiological measures they utilize.

This analysis of the differences between the arthritics and hypertensives
must, of course, remain speculative until it is demonstrated that hypertensives
are actually low Barrier. But even so, it is of prime importance to give
consideration to the idea offered by Moos and Engel that a given autonomic
response may be unusually elevated or depressed in a direction opposite to
that predicted by the exterior-interior model simply because of compensatory
forces generated by some other autonomic reactions. As studies are done with
increasing numbers of autonomic measures, it will be necessary to make
predictions about exterior and interior responses which anticipate the
consequences of interaction between systems.

Fitzgerald (1961) investigated children with Legg-Perthes-Calve disease
(LPC). This "disease", whose etiology remains vague, produces damage to
the hip joint; and resembles in some ways the symptomatology of rheumatoid
arthritis. Using a body image frame of reference, Fitzgerald examined 20
boys (ages five–12) with LPC and 15 controls. The control group consisted
of boys with disabling difficulties resulting from such causes as poliomyelitis
and traumatic injury. A third minor control group (N = 5) was studied
which was comprised of boys diagnosed as "hyperactive". Barrier and
Penetration scores were obtained from all subjects by means of the Rorschach
ink blots. In addition, the Wechsler Intelligence Scale for Children (WISC)
was administered. A questionnaire consisting of 125 items, which was filled
out by the subject's parents, tapped such variables as the child's early background, his behavior at home, and his degree of investment in muscular
activities. The results for the boundary scores supported the notion that the
LPC children would have more definite boundaries than the controls.
Fitzgerald used the difference between the Barrier and Penetration scores as
his prime index of boundary definiteness; and reported that the LPC group
was significantly higher (.001 level) than the controls in this respect. For the
Barrier score alone the LPC group exceeded the principal control group at the
.10 level and the "hyperactive" controls at the .05 level. In view of previous
findings that persons with higher Barrier scores are unusually inclined to
channel tension to the musculature, it is interesting that the LPC group was
observed to have displayed significantly more muscular activity during the
administration of the ink blots than the controls. Parental reports also indicated that the LPC children had been unusually active in outdoor play and
particularly likely to suffer serious falls from a height. Quite apropos of the
matter of muscular expression was the further finding that the LPC children
attained significantly higher (.001 level) Performance than Verbal scores on
the WISC. They did better on those tasks which involve actual motor
manipulation of objects than on those in which the response required was

purely verbal. The controls did not show such a difference. If one thinks of the Performance items of the WISC as requiring more skill in muscular movement and response than do the Verbal items, it would follow that LPC children are characterized not only by a high level of muscular expressiveness but also by relatively more developed muscle-oriented than verbal skills. It was an incidental finding of the study that the Barrier score was correlated .64 (.001 level) in the LPC group with an index of social mobility based on the difference between the father and the paternal grandfather in number of years of formal education.

Cleveland, Reitman, and Brewer (1965) have discerned behavior patterns in a group of 30 juvenile rheumatoid arthritics (14 male, 16 female) which sound surprisingly similar to those described by Fitzgerald. When questioned, the mothers of the arthritic children described them as physically more active than the average child prior to the onset of the arthritis. Also, on the Wechsler Intelligence Scale the arthritic children scored significantly higher on the Performance than on the Verbal subtests. This difference between Verbal and Performance scores was not found in a control group of asthmatic children. As predicted, the arthritic children proved to have significantly higher Barrier scores (.01 level) than the asthmatic controls. However, the two groups did not differ in terms of number of Penetration responses. One may say that the Cleveland, et al. data support Fitzgerald's work with reference to the child with joint disease in several respects: by indicating that the arthritic child is unusually physically active before the onset of his clinical symptoms; by demonstrating the superior development of the arthritic child's motor (performance) as compared to his verbal skills; and by establishing that the arthritic child perceives his body boundaries as particularly clear and well defined.

An unique approach to exterior-interior symptom differentiation is represented in the work of Ueno (1967). He was interested in boundary differences among Japanese patients with hypochondriacal complaints occurring at exterior versus interior sites. He compared seven patients with exterior complaints (e.g., skin itchy, joint aches, hands benumbed) with six with interior complaints (e.g., heart throbs, stomach aches); and found that the former had, as predicted, significantly higher Barrier scores ($p < .05$). In a further novel exploration, Ueno compared six patients with headache symptoms who attributed their symptoms to an "exterior" cause (e.g., accidental trauma) and 15 with headaches who felt they were of internal origin (e.g., brain tumor); and he detected no Barrier differences of significance between the groups. However, the use of the term "exterior" to refer to headaches which are thought to be caused by an external trauma seems somewhat strained. After all, the patient probably still thought that the trauma had produced damage inside of his head. But in any case, the fact that patients with explicit exterior versus interior hypochondriacal complaints could be distinguished in terms of their Barrier responses suggests that additional work with choice of complaint site in hypochondriasis may have fertile possibilities.

Several studies which have apparently not been supportive of the exterior-interior symptom differentiation scheme should now be considered.

Sherick (1964) was not able to establish a boundary difference between arthritic and ulcer patients. Twenty-one male arthritics and 21 males with peptic ulcer symptoms who were patients in a Veterans Administration hospital were evaluated with a battery of procedures which included the Rorschach blots. Neither the Barrier nor Penetration scores significantly distinguished the groups. When one examines the conditions which prevailed in the Sherick study, certain discrepancies come to light which raise questions concerning its reliability.

1. First of all, the subjects were obtained by approaching them and formally asking whether they would be willing to volunteer to participate in a research project. A larger percent of the ulcer than the arthritic patients who were contacted refused to take the test. Such differential rates of volunteering were not allowed to occur in previous studies reported involving arthritic and ulcer patients. This becomes a matter of real importance if one considers that the ulcer patients who did not wish to participate were probably the most threatened and disturbed by the prospect of a new experience and therefore, by the same token, likely to be persons with poorly articulated boundaries. In other words, there is a possibility that the volunteering process may have eliminated an important low Barrier segment of the ulcer symptom group.

2. A second matter of importance is that many of the ulcer patients (but not the arthritics) were taking a prescribed dose of a tranquilizer at the time they were evaluated. Cleveland (1960A) has shown that tranquilizers increase boundary definiteness in persons who are disturbed or disorganized. From this view, there is a genuine possibility that the boundaries of the ulcer patients were artificially bolstered; whereas this was not true for the arthritics.

3. There are also a number of subsidiary factors of unknown importance which complicate defining the actual characteristics of the ulcer group. One discovers that two of the "ulcer patients" proved ultimately not to have verifiable ulcer pathology. Further, one is informed that six of the ulcer patients were Negroes, while none of the arthritics were Negroes.

Overall, it is apparent that the arthritic and ulcer patients differed in so many other respects besides their symptomatology that the conditions probably did not provide a fair test of the hypothesis.

Another negative study was carried out by Eigenbrode and Shipman (1960). It failed to replicate the boundary distinction between psychosomatic patients with interior as opposed to exterior symptoms. Eigenbrode and Shipman examined the Rorschach protocols of 54 patients with "psychosomatic skin disorders" (exterior) and 29 patients with internal disorders (e.g., stomach ulcer, genito-urinary disease). Their scorings for the Barrier index failed to show significant differences between the two groups. One critical question that may be raised concerning this study relates to the fact that the Rorschach protocols had been collected by more than seven different examiners (many of whom were students) who perhaps varied sufficiently in their methods of obtaining descriptive responses from the patients to have introduced serious unreliability into the measurement process. Eigenbrode and Shipman considered and rejected this possibility on the basis of an analysis of variance of the scores obtained by the seven examiners who had tested 78 percent of the cases. However, such an analysis is inconclusive in view of the fact that it did not include 22 percent of the sample of the examiners. It is interesting that Shipman, et al. in a subsequent study, shortly to be described, obtained results which, rather than contradicting the exterior-interior model, clearly supported it.

Barendregt (1961) compared the Barrier scores of 18 women with rheumatoid arthritis, 20 women with asthma, and 20 normal women without any illnesses. He particularly expected that the arthritics (exterior) would have more definite boundaries than the asthmatics (interior). Response total was not controlled and so the Barrier scores were expressed as percentages of the number of responses in each protocol. The arthritics were found not to have significantly higher Barrier percents than the asthmatics. They also did not differ from the normals.

A final negative study was carried out by Hirt, Ross, and Kurtz (1967). The Barrier and Penetration scores of 20 patients with exterior symptoms (10 dermatological and 10 rheumatoid arthritis) were compared with those of 20 with interior symptoms (10 cardiac pathology and 10 bronchial asthma). Neither Barrier nor Penetration successfully discriminated between the symptom groups. An analysis of covariance which controlled for ego strength in terms of the Holtzman Integration score revealed similar chance differences in Barrier and Penetration between the groups. Another phase of this investigation involved a "physician experienced in both psychiatry and internal medicine" examining the charts of numerous hospitalized patients and selecting eight with consistent exterior symptoms (mainly arthritis and dermatitis), eight with consistent interior symptoms (mainly heart difficulties) and eight with histories of both the exterior and interior types. No differences in Barrier among the groups were obtained. But a significant difference for Penetration opposite to that expected by the exterior-interior model was shown.

As one scans the negative findings just cited and also the previously enumerated positive ones concerning the relationship of Barrier to exterior versus interior clinical symptoms, it is apparent that some questions and contradictions have arisen which need to be clarified. While most of the data presented have been supportive of the exterior-interior model, there have been exceptions. These exceptions could be dismissed as representing the usual degree of contradiction and failure to replicate which occurs when any hypothesis is widely checked by a variety of investigators. That is, one could argue that the contradictory studies constitute a small minority which are inevitable when there are so many opportunities for unknown differences in design and subject characteristics and also chance factors to intrude.

However, in examining the studies which really seem to contradict the exterior-interior model (viz., Eigenbrode and Shipman, 1960; Hirt, et al., 1967; Barendregt, 1961) one cannot help but be impressed that they involve illnesses different from those represented in studies which have been supportive of the model. Past supportive work has made use of the following categories of exterior symptomatology: juvenile and adult arthritis, various dermatological difficulties, conversion hysteria, Legg-Calve-Perthes disease, muscle stiffness, muscle tics; and the following interior categories have been considered: stomach ulcers, colitis, vomiting. The non-supportive studies have included the same exterior categories, but for their interior representation have largely utilized asthmatics and patients with coronary disease and to a more minor degree patients with urinary and lung symptoms. The heavy representation of asthmatics in the two most directly negative studies cited above (viz., Barendregt and Hirt, et al.) could mean that asthmatics constitute an exception to the exterior-interior model. They are not typified by the low Barrier scores one would expect in those with interior symptoms. Why this should be so is not now apparent. Of course, the etiology of asthma is still largely unknown; and future observations may clarify why it does not classify as "interior." For example, Leigh, et al. (1967) and Schwartz (1952) present evidence that a strong hereditary factor may be involved in the etiology of asthma. If this were so, one could hardly approach its etiology in terms of an exterior-interior scheme. One could also raise questions about whether such factors as the physiological effects (e.g., neuromuscular reactions, tremor) of the sympathomimetic type drugs typically used to treat asthma or the unusual tensing and special mobilization of auxiliary muscles to assist in the asthmatic's breathing might not accentuate feedback from boundary sectors—thereby artificially enhancing the sense of boundary definiteness which would be reflected in an arbitrary elevation of Barrier scores.

The other major interior symptom group which has not been "correctly" classified in terms of Barrier score are patients with coronaries. Hirt, et al. (1967) failed to find low Barrier scores in coronary patients. Because of the multiple physical variables known to correlate with the occurrence of coronary symptoms (e.g., age, sex, smoking, weight, diet) this syndrome illustrates particularly well one of the chief complications that arises in viewing body illness from the perspective of the exterior versus interior differentiation. This complication grows out of the original intent to eliminate from the exterior versus interior classification those illnesses directly due to physical trauma or specific environmental substances which produce malfunction. For example, if a man's skin is damaged by a chemical he cannot meaningfully be said to have developed an exterior "symptom." Or if he swallows a poisonous substance and it damages his stomach he could not meaningfully be said to have an "interior" symptom. The terms "exterior" and "interior" were meant to indicate not only the body locale of a symptom, but even more importantly were intended to convey the idea of an etiological process derived from an organized mode of physiological channeling which in turn was related to a particular psychological orientation. It was fairly explicit in the original exterior-interior concept that only those illnesses should be considered within the scheme that seem to have a significant "psychosomatic" component. Otherwise, there would be no opportunity for the exterior versus interior response tendencies presumably linked with definite versus indefinite boundaries to be expressed. If an illness is due to heredity, a specific physical trauma to tissue, a poison or toxin introduced at a given time from the environment, or a designated infectious agent, it cannot sensibly be used to test the exterior-interior formulation. Of course, there is great difficulty in applying these criteria operationally because the etiologies of many illnesses remain vague or unknown and one cannot truly ascertain whether they are characterized by a substantial "psychosomatic" component. This is so even of a number of the illnesses which have conformed well to the exterior-interior model (e.g., rheumatoid arthritis, Legg-Calve-Perthes disease). The temptation arises, of course, to argue that any illness which does not conform to exterior-interior expectations does not have a sufficient psychosomatic component to make it a valid candidate for exterior-interior classification; and to urge the obverse for those that do conform well to the model. There is in this respect an ambiguity about the exterior-interior model which is unfortunate. One must acknowledge that this ambiguity limits one's ability to define its validity. However, the dilemma can only in part be attributed to deficiencies in the exterior-interior formulation. A significant part is simply due to our lack of knowledge concerning the causation of many major illnesses.

Are we in a position to assert fairly definitely that some illnesses provide a poor test of the exterior-interior concept because they are so strongly influenced by specific non-psychosomatic factors? Perhaps with careful study several such illnesses can be specified. For example, the role of smoking and diet in coronaries seem sufficiently specific to raise a question about the suitability of this syndrome. Longstanding heart disease (e.g., valve defects) due to rheumatic fever would likewise seem unsuitable. Liver difficulties due to alcohol or toxins, kidney symptoms due to hypertension or toxins; and perhaps most other illnesses highly correlated with advanced aging might offer further negative examples. Investigators should keep this perspective in mind when attempting to test exterior-interior hypotheses.

When all the facts are in, it may also turn out that the exterior-interior model can best be described as not merely valid or invalid but rather as applicable to some classes of psychosomatic phenomena and not to others.

For example, one could conceive of illnesses in which the psychosomatic component was due to psychological factors which were introduced very early in the individual's life; while the psychosomatic factor in other classes of illnesses might, on the contrary, be the result of psychological stresses which occur only after adulthood has been attained. Perhaps the exterior-interior differentiation would be meaningful for the first category of illnesses and not the second. Or it may eventually be observed that the exterior-interior differentiation applies for particular illnesses in one social class or culture but not in others. With increasing knowledge, the placing of such limitations upon the generality of a theoretical model is almost inevitable.

The exterior-interior model defines only one variable involved in "choice" of symptom site. There are undoubtedly many variables which typically interact in the final determination of such a site. Because the exterior-interior vector is merely one among many involved, it should rarely be expected to account for more than a small part of the determining variance.

AUTONOMIC MEASURES IN NORMAL SUBJECTS

It is probably of import that studies which have evaluated the exterior-interior model within the context of autonomic response patterns in normal subjects have given more consistently positive support to it than have observations pertaining to symptoms in clinically ill psychosomatic groups. Perhaps this relatively higher level of success is due to the fact that exterior-interior channeling of autonomic responses in normals is not camouflaged by the grossly disorganizing and complicating processes often associated with the development of clinical symptomatology.

A range of studies pertinent to exterior-interior autonomic reactivity in normal subjects will now be reviewed:

Shipman, Oken, Grinker, and Goldstein (1964) appraised exterior versus interior response in 15 patients hospitalized for depressive symptoms. They measured muscle tension, heart rate, and blood pressure. The measures of muscle tension were uniquely detailed in that they were taken from seven different sites simultaneously (viz., frontalis, right neck extensions, right trapezius, right biceps, right forearm flexors, left quadriceps, and left gastrocnemius). Four separate periods of recording of physiological reactivity were secured. One involved a stress interview to arouse intense affect. Another was aimed at encouraging the subject "to pull himself together" and to exert strong self-control over himself. There were also two conditions which were intended to produce states of neutral relaxation. In addition, a variety of projective and questionnaire measures were taken, among which was the Barrier score. Analysis of the data indicated that the Barrier score, along with several other indices, was significantly and positively predictive of general level of muscle activation. Indeed, the Barrier score proved to be a better predictor in this respect than a large array of personality indices. Furthermore, as would be anticipated, the Barrier score was negatively related to heart rate. Shipman, et al. observed that the predicted pattern of relationship between Barrier and muscle tension and heart rate was maximized during the neutral relaxed conditions but minimized during the affect arousal sessions; and suggested that the unity of this particular "trait-physiology" pattern might be susceptible to disruption by special or unique affect mobilizations. This is an interesting possibility which may eventually help to clarify why the Barrier-exterior-interior reactivity cluster has been most sharply apparent under certain conditions in some experiments and under apparently different conditions in other experiments. Intercorrelations among the various measures revealed that the Barrier score was part of a cluster (including emotional stability and Rorschach movement) which was specifically predictive of muscle tension level. This cluster was defined as encompassing (p. 26) "the ability to moderate emotional reactions, the ability to delay action through the use of inner fantasy, the ability to remain associatively open with a clear sense of body limits, and the ability to keep trait anxiety reduced. . . . Thus, we tend to think of the . . . cluster as signifying the presence of a characterological strength in which ideation and clearer sense of self have been developed."

In a subsequent study Heath, Oken, and Shipman (1967) reconsidered muscle tension patterns in 44 non-psychotic patients who had applied for treatment in an outpatient psychiatric clinic. Electromyograms were secured from seven different muscle sites during five experimental conditions: rest, white noise, recovery, psychological stress, and a second recovery. No correlations of significance were found between Barrier and the electromyogram values. This was not congruent with the more positive results obtained by Shipman, et al. in their analysis of the relation of Barrier to muscle reactivity in the previously cited investigation of depressed patients. Likewise, none of the other psychological variables (e.g., Rorschach Movement) they had previously studied were correlated with the electromyogram values. It was concluded from the data and an analysis of the literature dealing with muscle tension and personality that the "relations between muscle tension and personality factors vary as a function of the type of individual being studied, and that findings concerning depressives do not necessarily apply to other patient groups" (p. 726).

Attention may now be turned to a careful appraisal of the exterior-interior scheme which was undertaken by Armstrong in a normal population (1968). He predicted that there would be differential conditioning of outer and inner autonomic responses in high and low Barrier subjects. The GSR was selected as an outside and heart rate as an inside response. Twenty male subjects in the upper 40 percent and 20 in the lower 40 percent of the usual Barrier score range were studied. They were conditioned to heart rate and

GSR responses simultaneously according to a partial reinforcement differential conditioning procedure. The unconditioned stimulus was a shock which was paired with a tone that served as the conditioned stimulus. Another tone was also introduced into the conditioning design in order to control for pseudo-conditioning. Measures of conditioning for each of the autonomic responses were devised in terms of differences between the magnitude of the control responses and the magnitude of the conditioned responses. When the GSR and heart rate responsivity of each subject for the last three conditioning trials were ranked and related to Barrier scores by means of analysis of variance, a significant F for the Barrier X conditioning interaction was found. It was established that the high Barrier subjects showed higher levels of GSR conditioning than the low Barrier subjects, with the obverse holding true for heart rate conditioning. No differences in extinction rates for the conditioned responses could be detected between the high and low Barrier groups. Armstrong felt that the results provided (p. 61) "considerable support for Fisher and Cleveland's general hypothesis that the body image Barrier concept is meaningfully related to events at the physiological level." However, there were aspects of the data which led him to speculate that the response differences between the high and low Barrier subjects were not so much a function of "reactivity" or "conditionability" as due to differential rates of adaptation of the two autonomic modalities to the series of repetitive conditioned and control stimuli.

Zimny (1965) checked the exterior-interior model in terms of skin resistance and heart rate reactivity in a sample of 24 college girls. The physiological measures were recorded for each individual just prior to (anticipatory phase) and during performance of a five-minute rotary pursuit task. For the group as a whole, the Barrier score was significantly correlated only with anticipatory reactions as defined by a skin resistance index of activation ($r = .44, p < .02$, one-tail test). When the eight subjects with the highest and the eight with the lowest Barrier scores were compared, it was found that during the anticipatory phase the high Barrier subgroup showed significantly greater skin activation ($p = .005$, one-tail test) and lower heart activation ($p = .03$, one-tail test) than the low Barrier subgroup. Significant differences for the performance phase of the experiment were not obtained. Zimny suggested that more meaningful results were found for the anticipatory than the performance phases because the performance phase measurement tapped not only the subject's stress reaction but also responses set off by the sheer physical effort involved in the rotary pursuit task. The anticipatory measurements, which correlated with Barrier, were presumably not confounded by the effect of sheer physical exertion.

Roessler, Burch, and Childers (1966) appraised GSR responsivity to five intensities of sound and light on four different occasions in 32 medical and dental students who were selected so that at one extreme were those concordantly high on both Barrier and the Barron Ego Strength scale and at the other extreme those concordantly low on Barrier and Ego Strength scores. It was predicted that the highs would manifest more GSR reactivity than the lows. This proved to be true in all but two of 80 comparisons. The prediction was significantly supported.

Fisher and Osofsky (1967) studied the relationship of the Barrier score to GSR frequency and heart rate in a sample of women (N = 25) during a variety of conditions. Each subject was seen on two separate occasions with a week intervening. Measures were taken during several rest periods and stress conditions (undergoing a gynecological examination, doing difficult arithmetic problems). Total mean GSR and heart rate values for the two sessions combined were computed. The subjects were then ranked for their degree of GSR responsivity (1 = high responsivity) and also ranked in terms of heart rate (1 = highest heart rate). An exterior-interior reactivity index was determined for each subject which equaled her GSR rank minus her heart rate rank. The greater the positive numerical value of the index the relatively higher was the indicated interior as compared to exterior reactivity. When the Barrier score, based on 50 Holtzman blots (derived from Forms A and B), was related to the exterior-interior index, a correlation of —.32 was obtained (p .05, one-tail test). That is, the higher the Barrier score the relatively greater was the exterior as contrasted to interior response. The finding was, of course, in harmony with theoretical expectation.

Fisher (1959C) extended the exterior-interior hypothesis to a group of normal, largely adolescent girls. This group comprised 30 girls in the age range nine–15. Fifteen of them were 14 years of age. Individual Rorschach protocols were obtained from which Barrier scores were derived. The frequency of GSR response was chosen as a measure of exterior reactivity and heart rate was selected as an indicator of interior responsivity. Physiological recordings were taken during an initial "anxiety phase" which was elicited by kicking over a chair and sounding a large iron gong and also during a subsequent "rest phase." It was found, as predicted, that the Barrier score was positively correlated (rho = .46, p .01) with GSR frequency and negatively correlated (—.51, p < .01) with heart rate during stress. While similar respective positive and negative correlational trends were found during the rest phase, they attained only the <.10 level for GSR and fell well short of significance for heart rate. This was the first study to demonstrate that the exterior-interior reactivity model could apply to normal subjects outside of the adult range.

Malev (1966) made use of the exterior-interior concept in designing a study of physiological response in normal children who fell into even younger age categories than those in the Fisher project. His study included 34 male six-year-old and 31 male eight-year-old children whose physiological responses (GSR, heart rate, blood pressure) were monitored during rest and stress. Stress was produced at the onset of the physiological recording period by banging a metal bar behind the subject and simultaneously emitting a loud groan. A sample of "rest" reactivity was secured later in the session after the subject had been asked about his reaction to the stress and reassured "I won't scare you again." The mothers of the children were also interviewed to ascertain the frequency with which each child had in the past been characterized by exterior versus interior symptoms. Exterior symptoms comprised such manifestations as twitching of the face, muscle pain, and skin rashes; whereas interior symptoms were exemplified by complaints like vomiting and diarrhea. The results indicated that at age six the number of outside symptoms was positively related to the Barrier score ($p < .05$). Also the ratio of Barrier to Penetration scores [4] was positively related to number of outside symptoms ($p < .01$) and to the ratio of exterior to interior symptoms ($p < .01$). In the eight-year-old group the Barrier score was positively linked with the ratio of outside to inside symptoms (.02 level) and also with the number of outside symptoms alone (.10 level). In both age groups the relationship of boundary definiteness to frequency of exterior and interior body symptoms seemed to conform moderately well to the pattern that would be expected in terms of the exterior-interior model as it has been defined in adults.

However, the findings with regard to the autonomic measures were more complex and less consistent. Number of GSR responses in the six-year-old group was not related to boundary definiteness. But "stress" and "no stress" heart rates were both positively related to the Penetration score ($<.02$ and $<.01$ levels respectively). The Barrier score was not related to stress heart rate but was negatively so to "no stress" heart rate ($p < .10$). Systolic blood pressure was observed to be significantly and positively related to the Barrier score, as was diastolic blood pressure. This same trend was noted for the relationships of the Barrier-Penetration ratio to systolic and diastolic blood pressures.

The patterns of results in the eight-year-old group indicated that the Barrier score was positively related to all the indices of autonomic response ($p < .10$ level with stress GSR frequency; $p < .02$ level with stress heart rate; $p < .10$ level with stress diastolic pressure). No relationships of significance appeared between the Penetration score and the autonomic indices.

To some degree, the autonomic results in the six-year-old population resemble the outside-inside pattern found in adults. However, the results in the eight-year-old group indicate that high Barrier subjects generally exceeded low Barrier subjects in all autonomic channels. There was in this instance no exterior-interior selectivity in the responses manifested. Malev had no ready explanation as to why the data in the six-year-old group should tend to conform to the exterior-interior model while that of the eight-year-olds should not. However, he noted that the symptom patterns which mothers

---

[4] Malev devised an overall index of boundary definiteness based on the following ratio: $\dfrac{\text{Barrier score}}{\text{Penetration score}}$. The larger the ratio the greater is the presumed boundary definiteness.

described were correlated with the boundary scores in both the six- and eight-year-old subjects in the same manner that characterizes adults. He therefore suggested that symptom reports by mothers about their children may be more representative of their usual autonomic patterning than are limited time samples of physiological responsiveness as observed in an artificial laboratory context.

RESPONSE TO SKIN IRRITANTS

Brown (1959) applied the Barrier and Penetration indices to the discrimination of 20 college students with contact dermatitis from 20 controls. He cited previous studies which suggested that emotional and personality factors might possibly play a predisposing role in sensitizing the individual to skin contactants. His own findings indicated a borderline tendency ($p < .20$) for the dermatitis cases to have higher Barrier and lower Penetration scores than the controls. There was a more significant difference for Barrier between the dermatitis and control subjects ($p < .02$) when only those classified as introverts (in terms of questionnaire scores) were compared in each group. The introversive dermatitis cases had higher Barrier scores than the introversive controls. Brown pointed out that the experimental and control groups were "impure" insofar as the former probably contained people "exposed to powerful allergens" and the latter "young adults who may yet develop contact dermatitis."

Brown and Young (1965) made a second attempt to investigate the contact dermatitis problem. They did not find gross differences in Barrier between an experimental group of men (N = 21) who had shown sensitization in a chemical plant to dinitrocholorobenzene and 19 control men (N = 19) who had not developed such sensitization. However, following the lead regarding the potential importance of extroversion-introversion as a modifying variable suggested in the initial Brown study cited above (1959), an analysis was conducted which considered not only the experimental-control variable but also the subject's degree of extroversion-introversion, measured by the Maudsley Personality Inventory and Guilford's STDCR inventory. As predicted on the basis of the earlier exploratory finding, the experimental subjects who were introverts tended to score higher on Barrier than the control introverts (p .10, one-tail test). Brown and Young concluded that extroversion-introversion should be treated as significant modifiers of Barrier differences between groups with exterior vs. interior symptoms. They speculated that if one symptom group happened to be largely composed of extroverts and another of introverts, the Barrier differences between them would be so confounded by this fact that differences related to symptoms themselves would not be detected. One sidelight of this study was the demonstration within the control group of a significantly higher Barrier score for subjects with low neuroticism scores (derived from Maudsley Personality Inventory) than for subjects with high neuroticism scores. This difference did not hold true within the experimental group.

Relevant to Brown's interests in skin response to chemical agents is a study by Cassell and Fisher (1963) which hypothesized that skin response to histamine should be positively related to boundary definiteness. It was anticipated in terms of the exterior-interior model that the more definite an individual's boundary the greater would be his response to the stimulus of histamine injected into his skin. When histamine is introduced into the skin it typically results in a local dilation of the capillaries and wheal formation, followed by a localized erythema which is due to the dilatation of the arterioles (Lewis' triple reaction). Cassell and Fisher measured the magnitude of this skin reaction both with reference to its degree of redness and its spatial extent. The subjects consisted of 55 male and 45 female normal college students. In the female group it was shown that the higher the Barrier score the more intense was the skin reaction. This proved to be true whether the criterion of skin response was degree of erythema (rho = .42, p = .001, one-tailed test) or its spatial extent (rho = .31, p .01, one-tailed test). No relationships were apparent between the Penetration score and the indices of skin reactivity. However, the Barrier minus Penetration score was positively related to erythema color (rho = .31, p = .01, one-tailed test). In the male group only chance associations appeared between the boundary parameters and histamine reactivity. One exception to this was a significant tendency for the Barrier minus Penetration score to be positively linked with duration of histamine flare (χ^2 = 5.3, df = 1, p < .01, one-tail test). There was no ready explanation for the marked differences in results obtained for the female as compared to the male group. In speculating about the findings which were significant, Cassell and Fisher noted that previous reports by other investigators suggested that histamine response was augmented when the individual was expressive and communicative and that such response was minimized when withdrawal from interaction from others was prominent. Thus, persons in the process of communicating strong affect manifest high histamine response; whereas withdrawn schizophrenics react minimally. But the Barrier score too has been shown to be positively correlated with a set to communicate. This parallel in the communication factor between the Barrier score and histamine skin response suggested to Cassell and Fisher the possibility that both are sensitive to some meaningful relationship between the boundary characteristics of an individual and his readiness to communicate with others.

EXTERIOR–INTERIOR SYMPTOM DIFFERENCES IN NORMAL SUBJECTS

When the connection between exterior-interior symptomatology and boundary definiteness had been shown for patients with serious symptoms (e.g., arthritis, colitis), the same paradigm was applied to normal subjects. The question was asked whether the relative exterior vs. interior occurrence of the minor symptoms present in normal healthy subjects would likewise prove to be related to boundary definiteness. In the first reported study of this issue which involved 87 college students (Fisher and Cleveland, 1968) it was found, as predicted, that high Barrier subjects experienced more exterior symptoms than low Barrier subjects (p .02). The difference for interior symptoms was in the expected direction, but not significant. The occurrence of exterior and interior symptoms was determined by asking each subject to indicate the frequency with which he had had symptoms at exterior (e.g., muscle pain, skin rash) and interior sites (e.g., stomach pain, heart pain).

Subsequently, a number of similar investigations have been undertaken. Although, as will be seen, the results have been mixed, the underlying trend conformed to the exterior-interior model. Minor difficulties arise in comparing various studies because, despite the fact that they have largely employed the same symptom questionnaire, they vary with respect to the indices devised to represent the exterior-interior symptom dichotomy. For example, some simply use an exterior symptom percent and an interior symptom percent; others compute the difference between number of exterior and interior symptoms; and so forth. Unless otherwise indicated, the questionnaire actually employed to obtain symptom information from the subject inquired concerning 15 different exterior and 13 interior symptoms. These items were embedded among 45 other symptom items designed to camouflage interest in the exterior-interior dimension. The subject was asked to check the frequency (never, one–two, three–five, six–ten times) with which he had experienced each symptom during the previous three years.

The results for a number of studies will now be reviewed.

Cassell [5] noted in a group of 47 male college students a significant negative relationship ($p < .02$) between Barrier and percent of interior symptoms $\left(\dfrac{\text{total interior symptoms}}{\text{total symptoms}} \right)$; but the relationship involving percent of exterior symptoms was not significant. Cassell also found in a sample of 47

---

[5] Personal communication. Cassell has found in two samples low but significant negative relationships between percent of exterior and interior symptoms reported. One of the samples was composed of more than a thousand college students. Fisher has similarly observed significant negative correlations in two groups. There is a small but definite trend for exterior and interior symptom occurrence to be antithetical.

female college students a significant positive link between Barrier and percent of exterior symptoms ($p < .05$), but with reference to interior symptoms the results were chance.

Osofsky and Fisher [6] were able in a population of 64 female nursing students to demonstrate a significant positive correlation ($r = .21$, p .05, one-tail test) between Barrier and the difference between number of exterior and interior symptoms (E-I).

Fisher and Bialos [7] obtained data for 41 women who had come to a Planned Parenthood center for contraceptive advice. The Barrier score was positively related to the E-I difference but not significantly so ($p < .20$).

It was already reported earlier in this book that the Barrier score proved to be positively and significantly correlated in a normal male group (N = 46) with the tendency, after ingesting a placebo, to develop more unusual sensations and "symptoms" in exterior than in interior body sites. This result with the males was not duplicated in the female group (N = 72).

The findings of Malev (1966) which have already been mentioned should also be reiterated. He showed that the Barrier scores of six-year-old normal boys (N = 30) were positively and significantly correlated with the E-I difference reported by their mothers as typifying them. This same significant correlation appeared for a group of normal eight-year-old boys (N = 30).

More recently, Fisher and Fisher,[8] using the same symptom checklist described by Malev, were able to demonstrate in a population of 99 normal children (age range seven–16) that their Barrier scores are positively correlated ($r = .20$, $p < .025$, one-tail test) with their mothers' judgments concerning the degree to which exterior symptoms predominated over interior symptoms in past illnesses. The correlation between Barrier and fathers' symptom judgments was not significant. The correlation between father and mother judgments of exterior vs. interior symptoms (E-I) was significant ($r = .22$, $p < .05$), but of low magnitude.[9]

While the trends cited above were largely in the anticipated direction, there were also unexpected variations and difficulties in replication. A project was therefore designed by the author to provide a more detailed perspective on the variables which possibly dilute the relationship between Barrier and exterior-interior symptom differences. This project was particularly concerned with analyzing more minutely the importance of various parameters of the symptom reports. Subjects were asked not only to indicate the frequencies with which they had experienced various exterior and interior

[6] Unpublished data.

[7] Unpublished data.

[8] Unpublished data.

[9] It should be incidentally mentioned that exploratory efforts have been made to relate the Barrier score to obesity. Masling (unpublished data) found in a sample consisting largely of Israeli women (N = 20) that the grossly obese had significantly higher Barrier scores than non-obese controls. However, Maher (1968) noted only a chance correlation in an American sample between Barrier and obesity.

symptoms in the previous six months, but also to supply the following information about each symptom: degree of discomfort produced, how often it recurred during their life, whether its cause was known or unknown, and whether it was the result of a direct injury. Using this information, a number of exterior minus interior symptom indices were constructed which were weighted differentially for such factors as frequency, chronicity, and degree of associated subjective distress. Fifty-six male and 59 female college students were evaluated.

The data indicated that the exterior-interior symptom difference is not as simple and straightforward as one might assume. The correlations between reports of old and more recent E-I symptoms were significant, but at a low level (viz., .20–.30). There were also unexpected divergences between E-I reports for symptoms that had occurred frequently and those which were infrequent. In the male group E-I of 1–2 (during three-year period) frequency had a chance link with E-I of 3–5 frequency. Even more strikingly, in the female sample E-I of 1–2 frequency was *negatively* related to E-I of 3–5 frequency ($r = -.47$, $p < .001$). One could also cite other complicating factors, such as the low correlation between E-I differences involving symptoms of known cause and those of unknown cause and the limited relationship between E-I differences involving symptoms that have high discomfort and those with low discomfort.

The Barrier score itself was largely unrelated in both groups to the special E-I indices constructed. In the female group it did have a borderline positive relationship [$\chi^2 = 4.8$, df $= 2$, $p < .10$] with the E-I differences based on symptoms that had been experienced with a frequency of six–ten times. Further, it was significantly and positively correlated with the difference between total muscle symptoms and heart symptoms ($r = .25$, $p < .05$) and also the difference between total skin symptoms and heart symptoms ($r = .25$, $p < .05$). One can see that clearer results emerged in the female group for E-I differences involving special exterior and interior sub-categories than for gross categories in which various exterior or interior systems were lumped together.

It is of even greater interest that a relationship between Barrier and exterior-interior symptom locus was demonstrated in the combined male and female groups in terms of responses to the following inquiry which had been included in the symptom questionnaire: "Describe the one symptom, no matter how slight, which has reappeared most consistently during your life." There were 49 responses in the total male and female samples that clearly involved either skin, muscle, joints, heart, stomach, or intestines. On this basis 28 were classified as exterior and 21 as interior. Sixty-six of the original responses (e.g., colds, eye strain, headaches) could not be classified as exterior or interior. A chi-square analysis indicated that outer symptoms were relatively more frequent in the high Barrier group than in the low Barrier group and the converse was true for interior symptoms ($\chi^2 - 3.8$, df $- 1$,

$p < .05$, one-tail test). While the results just described are far from definitive, they suggest that the Barrier score is more likely to be related to E-I differences involving symptoms of long rather than short duration. The brief transient symptom may be due to accidental or incidental factors which do not represent basic exterior versus interior channeling processes.

EXTERIOR–INTERIOR SYMPTOMS AND PERSONAL–ENVIRONMENTAL EXPECTATIONS

Richman (1966) has taken a careful look at some of the trait and attitudinal correlates of the degree to which an individual is typified by exterior as compared to interior symptomatology. His findings are intensely interesting because they provide a glimpse of the potentially wide-ranging fashion in which one's exterior-interior symptom differentiation pattern may mesh with one's perceptions and expectations of the world.

He analyzed data from a 78 item checklist of physical symptoms administered (by Wilfred Cassell) to an incoming freshman class at Syracuse University. Sixteen of the symptoms were of the Exterior type; 13 were of the Interior category; and the remainder simply served as "filler." The instructions were to indicate whether each symptom had in the "last three years been experienced: never, one–two times, three–five times, six–ten times, more than ten times, serious enough to require medical treatment." A total of 1234 males and 1252 female students were evaluated. In the male sample 142 with extreme tendencies toward exterior as compared to interior symptoms were chosen; and conversely 115 at the interior extreme were identified. In the female group 81 at the exterior extreme and 61 at the internal extreme were selected. All subjects had been administered Stern's Activities Index (Stern, 1963) and also the Stern College Characteristics Index (Stern, 1963). The Activities Index is a self report inventory which measures intensity of various needs (in the Murray [1938] sense). The College Characteristics Index tapped the students' (all freshmen) expectations of what the Syracuse college environment would be like.

In the male sample, there were significant differences between the extreme exterior and interior symptom groups for two of the 12 Activities Index first order factors. The exterior symptom group scored higher on Audacity (Audacity-Timidity) and Sensuousness. Richman interpreted the results as follows: "Individuals with external symptomatology were found to enjoy indulging themselves in thoughts of future fame and achievement. They think of themselves as being tough in mind and body and aggressive in physical activity. This group is also found to be rather sensuous, seeking physical gratifications that can be easily obtained through the senses" (p. 8).

In the female sample, there were significant differentiations between the exterior and interior groups on five of the first order and two of the second order factors of the Activities Index. The interpretation of the differences offered by Richman was as follows:

> . . . the major difference between these two groups is that the females with external symptomatology score consistently higher on the Achievement Orientation factors. These females are more audacious, have greater intellectual and applied interests, and are more motivated than girls with internal symptomatology. . . . Like their male counterparts, these girls are found to be more sensuous than those with internal symptomatology. In addition, the females with external symptomatology are seen to show a greater interest in achieving success in practical endeavors. (p. 9.)

With regard to the results derived from the College Characteristics Index, it was ascertained that males with internal symptoms exceeded males with external symptoms in expecting the college environment to be well-ordered, scheduled, providing mutually supportive group activities for students, and essentially non-intellectual. As for the female subjects, there were trends for those with internal symptoms to exceed those with external symptoms in expecting the college environment to be supportive, fair and kind, not requiring any activities that are physically dangerous, and considerate of their physical and mental welfare.

Richman, in reviewing his findings, concluded that they paralleled those obtained by Fisher and Cleveland in the investigation of the exterior-interior symptom correlates of the Barrier score. The parallel lies in the fact that the exterior symptom groups in the Richman study manifested traits and attitudes found in high Barrier persons and the interior symptom groups were characterized by an orientation found in low Barrier persons. Thus, the exterior symptom male and female groups were particularly achievement oriented. At the same time, the interior symptom groups were unusually expectant that the environment should provide them with support and structure. Such achievement drive and the contrasting need for support from the world were originally found to characterize high and low Barrier individuals respectively.

It is encouraging that this first attempt to map out attitudinal correlates of exterior-interior symptoms in a normal sample should fit well with theoretical expectations based on the original Barrier findings.

GENERAL CONSIDERATION
OF EXTERIOR–INTERIOR REACTIVITY MODELS

Aside from the projects described above which were specifically undertaken to examine the exterior-interior concept, there have been other more indirectly pertinent studies. In line with the distinction made in the exterior-interior model between skin reactivity (as defined by skin resistance level or GSR) and heart reactivity, it is interesting that an increasing number of reports have appeared which distinguish the import of skin resistance and heart rate levels or analogous indices.

Lacey (1959) has been particularly explicit in making such a distinction. On the basis of experiments performed by both himself and others he suggested that increased skin conductance is characteristic of states when the individual is "open" to the environment and "ready to react to it"; whereas cardiac acceleration is likely to be associated with states of shutting out or "rejecting the environment." He proposes that "skin conductance increase is excitatory, whereas increase of cardiac rate is inhibitory of this simple transaction of the organism with the environment" (p. 205). Lacey notes that Darrow had relatedly discovered that stimuli not requiring "extensive association of ideas" (perhaps encouraging a receptive attitude toward the environment) produced heart rate deceleration, while stimuli that were unpleasant or requiring "associative processes" (perhaps stimulating a non-receptive set) resulted in heart rate acceleration. Darrow had also stated that "sensory stimuli" tended more than "ideational stimuli" to set off "peripheral changes" as defined by skin resistance and vasoconstriction. Lacey further pointed out that Wundt had defined pleasant stimuli as initiatory of cardiac deceleration and unpleasant stimuli of just the obverse. If one thinks of "pleasant" and "unpleasant" stimuli as respectively arousing receptive and non-receptive attitudes, Wundt's formation obviously shares elements in common with those of Darrow and Lacey.

It is apparent that such formulations are congruent with the inside-outside model which would expect skin conductance and heart rate to be opposite to each other in the way they relate to boundary definiteness. The congruence becomes clearer if one notes that the well bounded person who is typified by high skin conductance and low heart rate is more sensitively attuned to his environs than the person with vague boundaries. That is, clear definition of boundaries has proven in various studies to be accompanied by special interest in interacting with others and generally fostering active interchange with them. High and low Barrier individuals may of course be contrasted in the receptivity or defensiveness they display in their stances vis-à-vis the environs. This attitudinal difference does indeed sound remarkably like the receptivity dimension suggested by Lacey.

Paul Obrist (1962) has followed up the Lacey formulation vigorously. In one project he observed 28 male subjects who were asked to deal successively with six different stimulus conditions: two noxious stimuli (viz., intense cold and white noise), complex mental arithmetic problems, and three tasks involving close attention to environmental inputs (e.g., finding hidden faces of people in a drawing). Shifts in heart rate, systolic blood pressure, peripheral blood flow, skin resistance, and respiration were determined between a basal period preceding stimulation and during the stimulus. There was a consistent trend for heart rate deceleration to occur when the subject was paying attention to environmental inputs. Contrastingly, the noxious stimuli and the arithmetic task were accompanied by heart rate acceleration. The skin resistance changes were not consistently correlated with whether the subject was focusing upon an environmental input. Obrist interpreted his findings as indicating good support for the proposition that there is a link between direction of attention and mode of cardiovascular response. He also theorized on the basis of the patterning of the various autonomic measures he had obtained that the cardiovascular responses during different attention states are cortically derived.

In subsequent research he and his collaborators (Obrist, Hallman, and Wood, 1963) tested the hypothesis that speed of response on perceptual and sensory-motor tasks would be positively related to degree of activation as measured by skin resistance and inversely correlated with heart rate. Fifty-four males were asked to engage in one task which involved fine judgmental discriminations between pairs of pictures. There was also a second task which called for tracing a pattern that could be viewed only in a mirror. Skin resistance, GSR, and heart rate were recorded during task performance. The hypothesis under study was rather consistently supported by the correlations between the performance times on the tasks and the levels of activation for each of the autonomic variables.

It must also be acknowledged that one study by Campos and Johnson (1966) was completely unable to demonstrate a relationship between direction of attention and heart rate or skin resistance changes. Indeed, these investigators established that heart rate changes were often associated with whether subjects had been asked to verbalize. Heart rate decrement accompanied non-verbalization and heart rate increase typified the verbalization condition. The concept of verbalizing versus non-verbalizing seemed to explain the findings much better than Lacey's concept of environmental intake versus environmental rejection. It was suggested by Campos and Johnson that Lacey's original findings might have been unknowingly contaminated by the influence of the verbalization variable.

In any case, other accounts of physiological patterns which seem to have outside-inside implications (although less explicitly so) have not been a rarity. Kagan and Moss (1962) investigated the physiological response patterns of male subjects ($N = 30$) who were exposed to a series of stimuli designed to elicit a gamut of attitudes and emotions. They generalized from their results that "heart rate and palmar conductance behaved differently to different kinds of inputs. When the experimental task required sustained attention to simple incoming signals, heart rate showed a deceleration while palmar conductance increased" (p. 284). That is, when the subject was prepared to "receive" input he showed heightened skin reactivity and diminished heart response.

Davis, Buchwald, and Frankmann (1955) examined the patterning of physiological reactivity of 24 subjects to selected pictures (e.g., landscape, nude female figure, geometrical abstraction). They recorded 12 different response parameters (e.g., GSR, heart rate, muscle potential). Here is one of the basic conclusions they derived from the findings:

> In the response to all the picture stimuli there is an increase of muscular tension and sweat-gland activity, an "activation" one might say; a decrease in the activity of the others is very common. . . . There is a clear contrast between the heightened activity of skin and muscle and the lowered action of all the other variables, which are circulatory and respiratory. (p. 51.)

Gendlin and Berlin (1961) found that skin activation, as defined by skin resistance and GSR reactivity, was significantly lower when subjects were asked to concentrate continuously on an internal experience than when turning their attention to external objects or discontinuously to internal events.

Wenger (1957) uncovered what he calls the "B pattern" of autonomic response in the course of his analysis of multiple autonomic indices. This "B pattern" is represented by high heart rate, high systolic blood pressure, low salivary output, high finger temperature, and low palmar conductance. What is of special interest from the view of the outside-inside concept is the fact that high heart rate and low palmar conductance were both simultaneously included as a part of the same cluster. It is this contrast of heart rate and skin reactivity which tends to characterize the individual with indefinite boundaries.

In the same vein, one could go on in considerably more detail to describe the work of Blumberg and Gonik (1962), Mandler and Mandler (1962) and others who have reported differences in the conditions that elicit GSR versus heart rate response and also heart deceleration versus acceleration. Most of the findings of these studies seem supportive of the idea that different classes of psychological stimuli may be involved in GSR as compared to heart response and also in heart acceleration versus deceleration.

Although, as will be seen later in the chapter, it has been difficult to show by means of the Barrier score that schizophrenics have less definite boundaries than normals, it is of interest that there have been reports suggesting that schizophrenics manifest relatively more interior than exterior physiological activation. Scattered indications have appeared that schizophrenics have a higher heart rate and lower skin reactivity than normal subjects. Jurko, Jost, and Hill (1952) published a paper which referred to heart rate as being generally higher in a schizophrenic than in neurotic or normal samples. Conversely, skin reactivity as defined by GSR and basal resistance proved overall to be less in the schizophrenic than in the other two groups. Jurko, et al. pointed up the relatively low skin reactivity of the schizophrenic sample and cited past studies with similar findings. They enumerated, for example, Syz (1926), Hoch, Kubis and Rouke (1944), and

Sherman and Jost (1942) as having found diminished GSR responsivity in schizophrenics.

Reese, Dykman, and Galbrecht (1961) demonstrated some significant trends for psychiatric patients to be more activated in terms of heart rate and less so with respect to skin resistance level than normal subjects (in a situation involving adaptation to tones and questions). The schizophrenic segment of the psychiatric sample likewise tended toward higher heart and lower skin response than the non-psychotic segment of the sample.

Ingram (1962) did not discern any heart rate differences between schizophrenic and non-schizophrenic subjects; but he did find the former to have significantly higher skin resistance levels (i.e., lower degree of skin activation).

Berger (1964) found that schizophrenics manifested a higher heart rate during rest than did normals. But the normals manifested significantly higher GSR response than the schizophrenics during stress.

Reviewing the existing pertinent literature, Buss and Lang (1965) concluded that high heart activation is characteristic of schizophrenic patients. A slight trend toward relatively high skin resistance was also tentatively noted. Further, a relatively high level of muscle activation was considered to typify schizophrenics. The conclusions concerning heart and skin activation tend to be harmonious with the exterior-interior formulation, but that relating to muscle activation is obviously contradictory.

DRUG EFFECTS

In a still vague and unfocused fashion there is evidence emerging that some drugs may produce patterned effects which have outside-inside implications.

Davis and Williams (1960) observed quite a range of autonomic responses in normal subjects to a series of drugs varying in tranquilizing and activating effects. These responses could not be easily classified in terms of broad categories like sympathetic or parasympathetic. One drug, Marplan, which has "activating" effects, simultaneously produced increased heart rate and heightened skin resistance. That is, it activated the heart but diminished skin responsivity.

Wenger (1957) refers to a study by Sherry which demonstrated that the B pattern response (which includes low skin and high heart activation) occurred with unusually high frequency in a population of schizophrenics taking chlorpromazine.

Klerman, DiMascio, Greenblatt and Rinkel (1959) explored in normal males the relationship between certain personality variables and response patterns to a number of drugs (e.g., reserpine, phenyltoloxamine). They discovered that subjects who had a history of muscular expression and who de-emphasized intellectual and artistic endeavor could be distinguished in their drug reactions from subjects with limited athletic interests and a strong intellectual orientation. A sedative drug which reduced muscle tonus was disturbing to the former but not the latter. However, reserpine proved to have disturbing effects in a fashion which was just the reverse of this pattern. It is particularly striking that during placebo administration the non-athletic group exhibited a reduction in muscle tension, whereas the athletic group evidenced a *rise* in muscle tension and a *decrease* in heart rate. The outside versus inside reactivity implications of this pattern are obvious.

9
Perceptual Vividness
of the Environment

Some of the experimental evidence presented above argues fairly convincingly that specific attitudes toward the reception of information from one's environs are probably accompanied by corresponding patterns of autonomic response. When a person is "tuned in" for environmental input his skin tends to become relatively highly activated and his heart to decelerate. It is this pattern which is typically exhibited by the individual with definite boundaries. He is usually mobilized to receive input; whereas the individual with indefinite boundaries is in a state of poor tuning for reception from his surroundings. The contrasts in behavior which derive, at least in part, from this differential tuning will be highlighted by material to be presented in this section which demonstrates that high Barrier persons experience the environment more vividly than do those with low Barrier scores.

The high Barrier individual chronically manifests a physiological activation pattern equivalent to the preparation for perceiving what is "out there." The boundary appears to function as a sensitive interface between the individual and the outer world. It serves to individuate him but at the same time permits him to "tune" outwardly in an alert fashion. With the above perspective, it was hypothesized that the boundary functions to heighten receptivity and therefore to increase the vividness of stimuli. The person with definite boundaries may be assumed to experience what impinges upon him with more perceptual intensity than does the person with indefinite boundaries.

Central to testing such an hypothesis is finding a means for measuring perceptual vividness. The technique finally chosen involved the Ames Thereness and Thatness Table (T-T) (Kilpatrick, 1952). It consists of two viewing tunnels which are side by side. The tunnel on the right, which is completely dark, contains no cues for distance and therefore none for size.

The stimulus to which the subject responds is projected on a screen set up in this tunnel at a distance of two meters from him, and it is viewed monocularly. In the left tunnel, viewed binocularly, there are five lucite rods (each lighted by a 15-watt incandescent lamp) at 65-centimeter intervals. A Clason projector, on the right side of the apparatus and shielded from the subject's view, is used to project the image of a picture on the screen in the tunnel on the right. This projector can alter the size of the projected image over a wide range without significantly changing its clarity or brightness. As the image size is increased the picture seems to move toward the subject, and as it is decreased it appears to move away. It is therefore possible to present the subject with a judgmental task which seems to involve the spatial placement of a picture but which actually revolves about altering its size on the screen. The experimental task was one in which the subject was asked to view (with his head in a headrest) a projected picture in the right-side tunnel and told that he could, by means of a knob, move it forward or backwards on a track in order to line it up with rods in the left-side tunnel. The instructions were as follows:

"You will be looking at various pictures of objects which you will see in front of you. On your left you will see some lighted rods. Your job will be to turn the knob with your right hand and make the object line up with the rod I name. I want you to move the picture back and forth until it is even with the rod I name."

The size setting made with the knob could be read from a pointer attached to the lens holder that moved as the subject turned the knob. A scale from 1 to 13 was used, with larger values indicating a larger image and by implication closer optical placement. The voltage on the bulb in the Clason projector was kept at a maximum reading of 120 volts by means of an auto transformer, thus controlling its 4,250 lumen output.

In a first study, six pictures were presented (front view of clothed male, front view of female nude, rhombus-shaped geometric figure, ice cream parfait, front view of clothed female, and rear view of male nude). They were all line drawings of the same height and width; and presented in the sequence just enumerated.

In a second study, seven pictures were used. They consisted of photographs of a man being shot, a tree, a fetus lying in some mud, a skull, a vulture sitting on a dead deer, a boy, and an unsightly leg ulcer. The pictures of the tree and boy were chosen to represent pleasant themes and the others were selected for their unpleasant impact. This distinction was made in order to be able to determine if there were special boundary screening effects associated with the pleasant-unpleasant distinction.

Judgments of all pictures were obtained under six different conditions. Each picture was first presented at the apparent furthest position from the subject and he was asked to line it up with the rod second closest to him. A second series of trials involved telling the subject to move the picture from the closest possible position to the position of the fourth rod. Thirdly, the picture was to be shifted from midway (half-way point on size scale) to the fifth rod. Fourth in sequence was the task of moving the picture from the apparent closest position to the fifth rod. Next, the picture was to be moved from midway to the second rod position. Finally, the subject manipulated the picture from the farthest position to the apparent position of the third rod. A total score was derived equal to the mean of the Clason settings for all pictures for all trials.

Prior to the experiment the subjects were tested for visual acuity and astigmatism, respectively, by means of a Snellen chart and an astigma sunburst chart. Only those with 20–20 vision and no astigmatic defects went on to participate. Five minutes of dark adaptation were allowed before the T-T task.

The logic of using the T-T technique for measuring perceptual vividness was derived from previous work involving this technique by Ittelson (in Kilpatrick, 1952) and Hastorf (1950). He demonstrated that a picture presented in the T-T apparatus which is more vivid than another requires a smaller or "further away" setting in order to be lined up with a spatial reference point. The less vivid a picture the greater the "magnification" it requires in order to match the standard of how one would expect it to look at a given distance. In terms of the hypothesis underlying the present study, it was anticipated that the Barrier score would be negatively correlated with Clason setting. That is, the more definite an individual's boundaries the more intense the picture would appear to him and therefore the greater the likelihood he would place it so as to reduce its apparent size.

Barrier scores were obtained by means of the Rorschach blots which were administered in the usual fashion designed to control for number of responses.

The subjects in Study 1 consisted of 70 male college students. Their median age was 20.

The subjects in Study 2 were 39 female college students. Their median age was 20.

Study 1

The median Barrier score was 5 (range 0–14). The median of the means of each subject's total Clason settings was 8.3 (range 2.5–11.8).

Because of the skewed character of the Clason distribution, chi-square was employed for the analysis of the data. When the dichotomized Barrier scores were related to the trichotomized (into as equal thirds as possible) Clason scores, a significant relationship in the predicted direction was found $(\chi^2 = 7.4, [df = 2], p < .02)$. No special differences in relationship were observed between Barrier and the individual pictures as a function of their specific content.

Table 9.1
Chi-Square Analyses of Relation of Barrier Scores
to Thereness-Thatness Clason Setting Scores

| | | Study 1 | | |
| | | | Clason Setting | |
		Far (2.5–7.5)	Medium (7.6–9.1)	Near (9.2–11.8)
Barrier	High (6–14)	13	15	7
	Low (0–5)	13	6	16
	$\chi^2 = 7.4$ (df $= 2$), $p < .02$			

| | | Study 2 | | |
| | | | Barrier | |
		High [b] (9–14)	Median (4–8)	Low (1–3)
Clason Setting	Near [a] (7.5–11.0)	1[c]	9	9
	Far (3.2–7.4)	9	5	6
	$\chi^2 = 8.3$ (df $= 2$), $p < .02$			

[a] High = Above median
   Low = At median or below
[b] Trichotomized into as equal thirds as possible.
[c] As defined by Walker and Lev (1953), for χ^2 distributions involving 2 or more degrees of freedom, the calculations made for these cell values give an adequate approximation of an exact probabilities computation.

Study 2

The median Barrier score was 6 (range 1–14). The median Clason score was 7.4 (range 3.2–11.0).

Chi-square was used to relate the dichotomized Clason scores to the trichotomized Barrier scores. A significant relationship in the predicted direction was shown ($\chi^2 = 8.3$, [df $= 2$], $p < .02$). The Clason settings of the pleasant and unpleasant pictures did not differ in their relationships to the Barrier scores.

The findings from both of the studies were supportive of the hypothesis under consideration. When an individual views a stimulus in the T-T situation, its apparent vividness is significantly a function of his boundary attributes. This is generally true across a range of stimuli and does not seem to be a function of the pleasant or unpleasant attributes of the stimulus. The more definite an individual's boundaries the more do his T-T judgments reflect a perceptually intensified impression of the stimulus. Apparently, the stimulus does "pass through" the boundary and is affected by the process. But what does one mean when one refers to a stimulus as "passing through" the boundary? At one level is meant that incoming sensory information interacts with a central attitude or set toward reception of what is "out there". With increasing boundary delineation, there is a demonstrated greater interest in communication and readiness to invest energy in perceptual receptivity. This orientation imparts increased subjective intensity to experience. Similar augmenting effects of focused attention upon stimuli have been well documented in other studies (Haber, 1966).

One can speculate that the boundary intensification of experience occurs partially at peripheral sites. It is known that the Barrier score is positively correlated with degree of activation of muscles and skin and peripheral vasculature sites which constitute the bounding or peripheral regions of the body. Contrastingly, the Barrier score is negatively correlated with activation of inner sites or organs like the heart. Relatedly, it has been shown that the Barrier score is positively correlated with density of sensations experienced in the skin and musculature and negatively so with density of sensations in more interior sites like the heart and stomach. Since the sense organs, e.g., eyes, ears, touch receptors, do constitute a part of the body periphery, it is possible that they share in the activation and heightened awareness of the periphery which characterizes the existence of a well-defined boundary. Such activation could serve to increase sensitivity and therefore to augment intensity. Analogous increases in peripheral acuity as the result of activation of the sense organ itself have been described (Granit, 1955).

The present findings indicate that a fundamental parameter like the perceptual vividness of meaningful stimuli is related to the state of one's boundaries. The importance of this fact could be considerable. Perhaps degree of perceptual vividness contributes to how lively, stimulating, and interesting the "outer world" appears. The individual with definite boundaries who from day to day sees the world relatively vividly may therefore find it more exciting and provocative and demanding of self investment than does the individual with indefinite boundaries whose perceptual experiences are muted. It should be noted that Federn (1952) suggested a similar view in his formulation that the apparent realness of external objects depends upon their passing through a "cathected" boundary.

10
Response to Stress

In the monograph *Body Image and Personality* (Fisher and Cleveland, 1968) it was proposed that the possession of definite boundaries permits the individual to deal relatively efficiently with stress. The following quotation conveys the view that was taken:

... the real test of one's ability to be self-steering occurs in stress situations. It is not difficult for many individuals to maintain an appearance of mastery and forcefulness when they are in easy circumstances; but when problems and complications develop which are threatening, there is a considerable reduction in the number that are able to show mastery behavior. Our model of the high Barrier individual suggests that he would have particularly good facility for maintaining his equilibrium in the midst of stress. His well-defined boundaries provide him with protection and a base of operations, as it were. The low Barrier person would, on the contrary, be expected to be vulnerable to stress and to find it difficult to maintain his own course through the complications and confusion associated with the stress. It would follow, then, that high Barrier people would show better performance on stress tasks than low Barrier people. (p. 137.)

A series of studies was originally carried out to test this proposition in various ways. Two experiments involved the relationship of the Barrier score to performance on a task requiring the subject to trace a pattern which he could observe only in a mirror that rotated the visual field. While tracing the pattern, he was exposed to distracting and stressful stimuli. Errors in performance were counted in terms of the number of times the sides of the pattern were touched or crossed. In both studies persons with definite boundaries made significantly fewer errors than those with indefinite boundaries. However, the Barrier score had only chance relationships to the total time required to complete the tracings.

Another of the stress studies dealt with responses to a situation in which subjects were first allowed to succeed in a test of hand steadiness and then systematically made to fail. Just before each hand steadiness trial the subject was asked to estimate how well he could perform on the succeeding trial. It was established that high Barrier individuals more realistically modified such estimates downward in the face of failure than did low Barrier individuals.

Rather complex relationships were found between the Barrier score and decrement under stress in performance on the Digit Symbol subtest of the Wechsler Bellevue Intelligence Scale. It should be clarified that decrement in Digit Symbol performance refers to the decline produced by a stress after the subject has attained a stable level through practice. In one study where decrement in performance seemed to be a function of anxiety and instability the Barrier score and decrement were negatively related; while in another study where decrement seemed to be due to lack of concern or arousal about the experimental threat it was positively correlated with the Barrier score. That is, the Barrier relation to decrement seemed to be a function of whether anxiety was acting to facilitate or interfere with performance.

A different order of stress was evaluated in a project which dealt with adjustment to the disablement of one's body resulting from poliomyelitis. The manner in which the problem of the study was conceptualized is conveyed by the following quotation: "Every individual who becomes infected with poliomyelitis and who is hospitalized for treatment of this disease is undoubtedly exposed to tremendous stress. He is faced with possible death, with severe physical incapacitation, with separation from his family and friends, and with inability to care for himself. Can the individual's reaction to this stress be predicted from the Barrier score?" (Fisher and Cleveland, 1968, p. 146). A series of patients recovering from polio in a hospital were rated with regard to whether they were "poorly" or "well" adjusting and these ratings were related to their Barrier scores. The results indicated that there was a significant positive relationship between boundary definiteness and judged adequacy of adjustment to the disablement.

The power of the Barrier score to estimate adequacy of response to body disablement was exemplified in a second earlier study that concerned amputees. It is known that after an individual has had a limb amputated he continues to experience a "phantom" representation of it as if it were still present. The phantom is first felt to be outside the stump; but as adjustment to the loss proceeds, the phantom decreases in apparent size and retracts. Finally, before completely vanishing it may appear to be inside the stump. The perception of the position of the phantom in relation to the stump may be used roughly as an index of the degree to which readjustment to the amputation has proceeded. The study which is presently referred to involved a group of amputees who had been asked by Haber (1956) to draw pictures of their phantoms. An analysis of these pictures demonstrated that those who still conceived the phantom as outside the stump had significantly lower Barrier scores than those portraying the phantom as inside the stump. On this basis it seemed reasonable to conclude that the more definite a subject's body boundaries the less his difficulty in rebuilding the body concept that had been disrupted by the destruction of a portion of his body.

As just cited, there appeared to be evidence that reaction to the stress of body disablement was less severe in the definite than indefinite bounded individual. Adequacy of adjustment to polio disablement and also amputation seemed to be promisingly correlated with the Barrier score. Since the publication of these findings, further studies have been undertaken which bear on their validity and generality.

Landau (1960) organized an elaborate appraisal of both body image attitudes and adjustment to disability in a population of 40 male paraplegics who had been incapacitated for a median period of ten weeks. The following body image parameters were considered: (1) boundary scores; (2) index of body concern as reflected by responses to the Secord Homonym test of Bodily Concern (1953); and a measure of dissatisfaction with one's body as depicted by the Secord-Jourard Body Cathexis Score. The subject's adjustment to his disability was evaluated by means of two instruments. One was the Psycho-Social Rating Scale which required raters who were familiar with each patient to judge adequacy of adjustment in terms of such variables as motivation, somatic preoccupation, dependency, acceptance of disability, and behavior on the ward. A second evaluation procedure involved the Berger Sentence Completion test which was constructed to obtain the patient's own expressed feelings about his disability. Each patient was asked to complete a series of incomplete sentences (e.g., "Every man . . ."; "The loss of . . ."); and these responses were rated by three psychologists as to the degree of adjustment-maladjustment they apparently revealed.

The Barrier score was clearly predictive of adequacy of adjustment $(r = .51, p < .001)$ as defined by an overall index computed from the Psycho-Social ratings and the Berger Sentence Completion evaluations. However, the Penetration score had only a chance relationship to this criterion. The Body Cathexis index was in general not able to differentiate successful from unsuccessful adjustment, but the Secord Homonym test did significantly do so $(r = .35, p .025)$. In this last instance the finding was that the greater the body concern registered in response to the Secord homonyms the less adequate the adjustment to the disability. It is interesting that the Barrier score correlated better with the adjustment criterion than did any of the other body image indices used or, indeed, did any combination of conventional Rorschach determinant scores (e.g., W, M, F + %).[1] Landau

[1] Landau also found that the Barrier score was positively and significantly correlated with the social class of the subject as defined by occupational level. The Penetration score was not correlated with social class. However, it should be noted that Holtzman has found Penetration responses to occur significantly more often (.001 level) in low than high social class subjects. It may be recalled too that Fitzgerald (1961) reported a significant positive correlation between the Barrier score and an index of upward social mobility. Such findings can be interpreted as supportive of the view that need for achievement is positively related to the Barrier score. There are obviously other implications to the findings which remain to be explored.

emphasized the fact that the Barrier score was not significantly linked with the duration of the patient's disablement. This is congruent with a previous study in which the Barrier score proved not to be correlated with the amount or duration of disablement produced by polio (Ware, Fisher, Cleveland). Relatedly, Fisher (1959A) has reported that the decline in physique associated with advanced aging is not accompanied by lowered Barrier scores. He compared a group of individuals with a median age of 67 with a group of younger persons whose median age was 36 and who had been chosen on a matching basis from the immediate families of the aged subjects. Barrier score differences between these two groups were wholly non-significant.[2]

Even firmer substantiation of the tie between boundary attributes and reaction to the disablement of one's body was reported by Sieracki (1963). He studied 50 white males in a Veterans Administration hospital who had serious physical defects. Half of the group had visible disabilities of the type associated with paraplegia, amputation, and poliomyelitis. The other half had non-visible disabilities such as are present in pulmonary tuberculosis and rheumatic heart fever. The division into visibly and non-visibly disabled groups was a unique feature of this project. An evaluation was made of each patient's degree of acceptance of his disability by means of the Berger Sentence Completion test and a rating scale pertaining to his ward behavior. The results indicated that in both the visibly and non-visibly disabled groups degree of acceptance of the disability was positively and significantly related to the Barrier score. The demonstration that the Barrier score provides meaningful information about acceptance of non-visible as well as visible disabilities represents an important extension of previous findings. No correlation was observed, as expected, between the Barrier score and age, duration of illness, or gross level of anxiety. Another aspect of this study involved relating the Barrier score to the subject's scores on the Kuder Preference test. It was anticipated that high Barrier individuals would manifest relatively greater preferences for people-oriented activities (e.g., social service) than low Barrier individuals; and that the converse would be true for non-people oriented preferences (e.g., computational). The findings in this instance did not support the hypothesis.

McConnell and Daston (1961) attempted a novel test of the concept that boundary definiteness may play a role in reactions to body threatening experiences. They appraised the reactions of 28 women to the stress arising from their pregnancies. Each subject was seen twice. The first evaluation occurred during the eighth or ninth month of pregnancy. At this time the Rorschach test and the Osgood Semantic Differential were administered; and also an interview was obtained which dealt with attitude toward the pregnancy (e.g., was it planned or unplanned, did it elicit feelings of happi-

[2] The Penetration score was also found not to be significantly different between the younger and older groups.

ness or unhappiness). The Osgood Semantic Differential required the subject to rate her own body in terms of 17 scales (e.g., beautiful-ugly, hard-soft, active-passive). Three days after delivery a second evaluation was made of the patient. At that time the Rorschach and Semantic Differential[3] were administered again.

The Barrier score proved to be positively correlated with the favorableness of the subject's attitude toward her pregnancy, as ascertained from interview material. One should add that the Penetration score declined significantly from the pregnancy to post-pregnancy testing periods. This suggested that concern about body vulnerability, which is probably prominent during the pregnancy, decreased after delivery had been successfully completed. The Barrier score did not shift from first to second testing; and this was viewed by McConnell and Daston as congruent with earlier observations in the literature which indicate that it is not influenced by generalized changes in the body itself.

Some of the results derived from the Semantic Differential responses alone proved to have stimulating implications. The Evaluative scores shifted in a direction of more positive self appraisal from pre- to post-pregnancy. Apparently the subjects in general regarded their bodies as more devalued and ugly during pregnancy than after delivery. However, another interesting trend was that women with positive evaluative attitudes toward their bodies during pregnancy tended to shift in a more negative direction after delivery; whereas women with negative attitudes during pregnancy shifted to the more positive pole afterwards. This trend was statistically significant (p .05). McConnell and Daston suggested that the subject shifting from a negative to a positive attitude might be one who was threatened by the pregnancy and then relieved when delivery had occurred. The subject changing from a positive to a negative orientation would be one "relatively happy with the prospect of an addition" but experiencing after delivery a "loss of some of the esteem which attends pregnancy and a shifting of the center of attention from her to the neonate."

The Barrier score has also been applied to the prediction of amenorrhea in girls experiencing the stress of leaving home to attend school. Osofsky and Fisher (1967) followed the menstrual patterns of 66 girls in a freshman class entering nursing school. Rorschach protocols were obtained during the week of their arrival. Each subject kept a "menstrual calendar" for the first four months of school which provided information concerning the regularity of her menstrual periods. The Barrier score was, as predicted, significantly negatively correlated with the interval between the last period prior to, and the first period after, school entry ($r = -.27$, $p < .02$, one-tail test). It was also negatively correlated with the largest delay in menses ($r = -.27$,

---

[3] Barts (1959) has failed to find any direct meaningful relationships between the boundary indices and Semantic Differential ratings of one's own body.

$p < .05$, one-tail test) during the four months of observation and with amount of delay in first menses in school in relation to when expected ($r = -.22$, $p = .05$, one-tail test). Here one can see that the Barrier score was able to predict the development of a menstrual symptom in girls exposed to the stress of separation from home. The correlations between Barrier and the indices of amenorrhea were not reduced when several subjects who had previously had serious amenorrhea were dropped from the analysis. Indices relating to previous illness, age of onset of menses, body size, and developmental attributes were not correlated with the symptoms of amenorrhea.

Fisher and Bialos [4] determined whether the Barrier score would predict disturbed response to a gynecological examination which is often experienced as stressful and embarrassing. The subjects were 49 women who received a pelvic examination as part of the procedure involved in obtaining contraceptives from a Planned Parenthood clinic. The examining physician rated each subject on a five-point scale with regard to degree of anxiety manifested. Barrier scores were derived from responses to the Holtzman blots. They were negatively related ($r = -.26$, $p < .05$, one-tail test) to the degree of anxiety. The higher a subject's Barrier score the less anxiety she manifested during the pelvic examination. Those with well articulated boundaries apparently found the examination less stressful than those with vague boundaries.

Masson (1963) has made an opening wedge into the question of whether one's reactions to viewing others whose bodies are disabled are related to boundary definiteness. He theorized that when an individual sees the body of another who has been mutilated or crippled this constitutes a threatening stimulus which conveys to the perceiver the information that the same thing might happen to him. There is the implication that the perceiver's body could be similarly breached or damaged. With this viewpoint, Masson hypothesized that the less definite an individual's body boundaries the more disturbed will he be by the perception of body disablement in another. In other words, the greater his sense of body vulnerability the more intense the potential threat conveyed by the sight of body damage. Masson studied 100 college students. Their attitudes toward the disabled were measured by asking them to compose TAT type stories about six pictures representing different forms of body damage. One picture represented facial disfigurement, one wheelchair confinement, three arm amputation, and one leg amputation. In addition, a neutral picture not involving a mutilation theme was included. This was shown first in the series. The subjects' stories were rated by judges in terms of degree of negative feeling expressed toward disabled figures. Also, the stories were analyzed with regard to the number of themes expressing anxiety and discomfort (Discomfort-Relief Quotient). No relationship was detected between boundary definiteness and simple degree of acceptance of the disabled figures in the stories. When the level of anxiety

[4] Unpublished data.

and discomfort expressed in the story elicited by the neutral picture was compared to that manifested in the story evoked by the first body disablement picture, it turned out that low Barrier subjects were significantly more likely than high Barrier subjects to show an increase in anxiety to the disablement picture. However, this was true only if one excluded those cases in which the individual's anxiety in reaction to the neutral picture was already at the maximum possible level and therefore incapable of registering an increase for the disablement picture that followed in the series. Masson's work indicated that boundary definiteness might have promise as a predictor of disturbance aroused by the sight of mutilation in others.

Another approach to the issue was attempted by Cormack (1966). He tested the hypothesis that the less definite an individual's boundaries the more threatened he would be by the sight of human figures that were mutilated. It was presumed that those with poor boundaries would be particularly threatened by such a sight because of their heightened sense of body vulnerability. The subjects were 20 male college students who represented extremes of feeling secure or insecure about one's body as defined by the Barrier score, the Secord Homonym test (1953), and the Jourard and Secord (1955) Body Cathexis scale. Their reactions to representation of mutilation were evaluated by having them view through a series of aniseikonic lenses a life size male manikin with obvious mutilations (arm amputation and eye injury) and another without mutilations. A determination was made of the power of aniseikonic lenses required (on a 13 point scale) before the subject perceived a change in the appearance of the manikins. Using the model proposed by Wittreich and Radcliffe (1955), it was assumed that the greater the "resistance" shown by a subject to perceiving aniseikonic distortion the greater the anxiety aroused by the given stimulus. An index involving the difference in aniseikonic distortion thresholds between the mutilated and non-mutilated manikins defined the degree of threat posed by the mutilation. Incidentally, it was observed, as anticipated by Wittreich and Radcliffe's work, that the threshold for perceiving distortion in the mutilated figure was higher than that for the non-mutilated figure. A significant relationship in the predicted direction was found between Barrier and the degree of threat apparently represented by the mutilated manikin. This relationship was demonstrated by cubing each subject's Barrier score and plotting it against the threat criterion. It resembled a hyperbola. That is, subjects with very low Barrier scores felt very threatened by the mutilation. But as Barrier scores increased the apparent threat quickly decreased. A similar analysis showed no relationship between either the Body Cathexis scores or the Homonym scores and the aniseikonic threat index. Cormack, in referring to the Barrier results, concluded (p. 58): "These findings further suggest that the relation between body image and the perception of physical disability may be viewed in terms of the degree of differentiation of the body from the environment. A poorly differentiated body concept implies a feeling of threat when confronted with the stimulus of physical disability. A high differentiated body image, on the other hand, indicates that physical disability is not a threatening stimulus." [5]

Attention may now be turned to the surprising outcome of a line of inquiry pursued by Hammerschlag, Fisher, DeCosse, and Kaplan (1964). They involved themselves with the general question of how an individual reacts to the stress of discovering serious body symptomatology in himself. The group studied consisted of women with breast tumor or cancer symptoms. The specific question posed about the women in this group concerned the relationship of their boundary scores to the degree to which they delayed in seeking medical consultation after observing their breast symptoms. It was initially conjectured that the higher a woman's Barrier score the less would she be threatened by the discovery of her symptoms and therefore the more quickly would she proceed on a rational basis to seek medical consultation and treatment. The low Barrier woman was regarded as likely to be so threatened by her symptoms that she would try to deny their significance and therefore irrationally delay seeking medical evaluation. In a preliminary sample of 15 cases the converse of the above expectations proved to be true. It was the high rather than low Barrier woman who delayed the longest in going to a physician. This finding led to a reconsideration of the variables involved in patient delay in obtaining medical consultation. There were a number of previous studies which suggested that perhaps the largest factor in delay was not fear but rather reluctance to become involved in a relationship which is seen as requiring submission to an authority figure. To become a patient is often experienced as surrendering one's independence and putting oneself "into the hands" of the doctor.

From this perspective, it became clear why the high Barrier person who builds his identity around independence and self assertion might be more reluctant to go to a physician than the low Barrier person who does not emphasize individuality and self direction. A formal hypothesis to this effect was formulated; and a new sample of 26 women with breast symptoms was collected in order to check it out. Barrier scores computed from Holtzman blots significantly (p .05) supported the hypothesis. The high Barrier woman behaves more irrationally than the low Barrier woman with regard to the matter of seeking help for body symptomatology. Perhaps this is a function not only of differing attitudes toward authority figures (viz., the physician) but also less intense motivating anxiety upon discovery of the body defect.

It should be mentioned that the MMPI L, K, and Repression scales which were also employed in this study had only chance relationships to delay behavior. However, interestingly, the L (Lie) scale was negatively and significantly related to the Barrier score. The high Barrier subjects apparently

___

[5] It is pertinent that Siller and Chipman (1967) found that an inkblot score developed by Landis (1963) which presumably taps permeability of the ego boundary was related to attitudes toward the disabled. The greater an individual's boundary permeability the more unfavorable were certain of his perceptions of the disabled.

had less need to put on a false protective front in responding to the MMPI questions. This constitutes a replication of the same finding reported by Mausner (1961).[6]

The results pertaining to Barrier and delay behavior were tested in a further study by Fisher (1967A) involving female patients with cancer. The design was exactly the same as in the Hammerschlag, et al. (1964) work except that in addition to a sample of women with cancer of the breast (N = 28) there was a sample with cancer of the cervix (N = 34). It was shown that the Barrier score was positively and significantly related to number of weeks delay in seeking medical consultation in the breast sample ($p < .05$) and in the cervix sample ($p < .05$). Delay was not related to education, age, or marital status. These findings added substantial confirmation to the original observations of Hammerschlag, et al. (1964). For reasons already suggested, the woman with definite boundaries has great difficulty in relating herself as a patient vis-à-vis a physician.

Aside from its correlation with tolerance for body disability the Barrier score also previously demonstrated itself to be positively linked with the ability of subjects to tolerate other types of stress, e.g., such as is produced by a mirror drawing task under frustrating conditions. More recently, Brodie (1959) pursued the issue further by studying the Barrier score, among other measures, as a predictor of response to stressors. The subjects consisted of 30 male and 30 female college students who were exposed to two stress tasks: (1) The first involved reading several paragraphs while listening to one's own voice which was fed back through earphones after an arbitrary delay that resulted in frustrating confusion; (2) a second task required one to hold a metal rod as steadily as possible in a small hole while being repeatedly shocked. The responses to stress were appraised from immediate behavioral ratings by the subject and the experimenter and also from tape recordings of the subject's expressed feelings about the stress demands. All of the indices of stress reaction were organized in terms of the following dimensions: self blame versus blame of others for failure; degree of emotional expressivity; aggressiveness versus passivity; and tenacity in persevering at task goals.

The Barrier score had a puzzling series of relationships with the stress indices. It correlated negatively and significantly with emotional expressivity during stress. The results indicated too that the high Barrier subjects were more often labeled as "controlled" and "guarded", while low Barrier subjects were described as "uninhibited" or "impulsive." Further, the Barrier score was positively linked with being perceived by raters as "happy" and negatively with being perceived as "angry" and "assertive." In women, the Barrier score was positively related at a borderline level with being rated as tenacious in dealing with a hand steadiness task. At a subjective level, the high Barrier subjects seemed to find the stresses more discomforting than did

---

[6] Unpublished progress report entitled "Experimental Studies of Social Interaction", 1961, National Institute of Mental Health, Grant No. M–2836.

the low Barrier subjects. However, they showed a significantly greater decrease in anxiety as the experiment progressed. These data do not easily fall into a meaningful pattern. They do suggest that the Barrier score and certain aspects of how stress is experienced are interrelated; but do not permit more specific conclusions.

Shipman (1965) studied, in a population of 40 neurotic outpatients (20 male, 20 female), the relationship between Barrier and performance on the Stroop Color Naming test which is a measure of the ability to read words designating given colors but printed in colors which differ from those mentioned. The Stroop test has been shown in numerous studies to be a measure of the ability to perform in the face of interference of stressful distraction. It was found that Barrier and successful performance were positively correlated ($r = .46$, $p < .01$). The individual with the greatest boundary definiteness was likely to show relatively greatest efficiency in dealing with the stress of this cognitive task.

The Barrier score has shown itself to have some value in predicting the ability of Peace Corps volunteers to adapt adequately to the somewhat stressful rigors of a field assignment in a foreign country. Holtzman, Santos, Bouquet, and Barth (1966) reported the outcome of a project concerned with forecasting the adjustment of Peace Corps volunteers ($N = 92$) assigned to a program in rural Brazil. The Barrier score, obtained from responses to Holtzman blots prior to field assignment, added meaningful variance to a combination of variables which significantly predicted work effectiveness of the volunteers. The Barrier score did not relate meaningfully to other criterion variables like amount of warmth displayed toward Brazilians or ability to get along with other volunteers.

Another approach to the stress problem is presented in the work of Shultz (1966). He exposed his subjects (20 male duodenal ulcer and 20 male eczematoid dermatitis patients) to distractions while they were performing on four Scrambled Word tests. Two levels of stress were achieved by varying the intensity of disruptive sound stimulation and disruptive visual stimulation (photic stimulator). The stresses were not applied until the fourth Scrambled Word task. An interactive relationship was found, such that the low Barrier subjects performed more adequately under low stress and the high Barrier subjects more adequately under high stress ($p = .05$). The possibility of such relativity has already been implied in an earlier report by Fisher and Cleveland (1968). They analyzed data from two separate studies in which the Barrier score was correlated with decrement in Digit Symbol performance under stress. In one instance, those with definite boundaries showed relatively less decline in performance than did those with indefinite boundaries; whereas in a second study just the opposite pattern occurred. Interestingly, in the first case decline in performance had also been found to be proportional to the subject's anxiety level; and in the second case performance decrement was, quite contrastingly, inverse to degree of neuroticism.

That is, the Barrier score was negatively related to performance decrement in a situation in which the most anxious subjects manifested the greatest decrement; and it was positively correlated with performance deterioration in a setting in which the most neurotic subjects declined the least. Obviously, then, one needs to know the meaning of a stress situation to a subject before one can predict how his boundary attributes will influence his response to it. One may conjecture from Shultz' data that if the stress is peripheral and calls forth mobilization only from those who are easily stirred to anxiety, the Barrier score will be inverse to performance effectiveness. Only the more anxious will be aroused to put extra effort into their performance. But if the stress is intense and represents a generalized threat to efficiency, the well bounded individual will prove better able to cope with it than the poorly bounded. This last point may explain why studies involving the relation between Barrier and severe body disablement have uniformly turned out in a simple unidirectional manner. The stress imposed by real life body crippling is always sufficiently great to be analogous to stress situations in which there is intense generalized threat.

Stress effects resulting from pain, which is simultaneously a body threat and stimulus to general anxiety, have been correlated with boundary attributes by Nichols and Tursky (1967). They predicted that the ability to tolerate pain would be positively related to the Barrier score. Thirty male college students served as subjects. Each individual was seated in a reclining chair and an electrode was attached to his right forearm. A series of shocks were administered to him and four levels of intensity were identified:

1. The point at which he perceived the shock as "uncomfortable."
2. The level at which it appeared to him as "painful."
3. The intensity at which he requested that the stimulation be discontinued in response to the instruction, "We'll gradually make it stronger until you tell us you don't want to go any higher."
4. The point at which he refused to go any higher in response to the question, "Would you be willing to go one step higher?"

The results generally indicated that the more definite the subject's boundaries the greater his tolerance for the shock pain. Barrier and pain tolerance were positively correlated for each of the four levels of intensity, although only the coefficients for the last three enumerated above were significant (respectively $p < .05$, $p < .005$, $p < .05$). Nichols and Tursky interpreted their findings to mean (p. 108): "the individual who attains a high Barrier score is able to perceive a painful shock stimulus in its appropriate context and assume that although the shock hurts, it won't result in any permanent damage. The low Barrier individual, on the other hand, experiences his body as highly vulnerable and the electric shock stimulus as highly threatening to the integrity of his body."

The Secord Homonym test which was included in this study was not related to shock tolerance. An index of anxiety derived from the Holtzman blots was inversely related to pain tolerance for two of the shock conditions.

Looking broadly at the stress studies outlined above, what can one say? It would seem reasonable to regard them as reaffirming that adequacy of adjustment to the stress of body disablement is positively correlated with the Barrier score. The Barrier score seems to provide meaningful information about adaptation to amputation, poliomyelitis, paraplegia, pregnancy, and other special body states. It offers a cogent framework within which to anticipate how an individual will cope with gross alterations in his body. There is also new supporting information which indicates that the boundary is involved in response to stresses other than those arising from body disablement. It would appear that if a situational stress is such that it strains an individual's resources, his adequacy in dealing with it will be partially a function of his boundary strength.

11
Trait Patterns

The trait picture of the person with definite boundaries which figured prominently in previous work embraced such related characteristics as high achievement drive, clear formulation of goals, and a need to complete tasks. It was considered that the more definite an individual's boundaries the greater was his dedication to taking an active, "self steering", accomplishing stance toward his environs. The identification of well articulated boundaries with an achieving attitude was originally demonstrated by Fisher and Cleveland primarily in terms of TAT imagery (e.g., McClelland n Achievement score). There was also some evidence with respect to this issue derived from observations of achievement behavior in school and classroom situations.

Further opportunity to check the relationship between the Barrier score and achievement orientation has since presented itself in terms of results obtained with the Edwards Preference Schedule (1954). Three studies have been completed pertaining to the relationship between the Barrier index and an Achievement score which is one of the subscales of the Edwards Preference Schedule. A high score on the Achievement subscale is obtained by endorsement of such statements as the following:

- I like to do my very best in whatever I undertake.
- I would like to accomplish something of great significance.
- I would like to write a great play or novel.
- I like to be successful in things undertaken.
- I like to solve puzzles and problems that other people have difficulty with.

It can be seen in Table 11.1 that the Barrier index and Edwards Achievement were consistently related in the predicted direction, but of the six comparisons one was at a borderline level of significance and two were of a chance order. Inspection of the distributions of scores in the three studies did not reveal any apparent reason why the results in Study 3 fell short of significance; whereas those in Studies 1 and 2 were generally supportive of

Table 11.1
Relationship of Barrier to Achievement Scores of Edwards Preference
Schedule

	Study 1		
Male (N = 50)		Female (N = 50)	
Chi Square	Signif. Level	Chi Square	Signif. Level
4.0	<.02 [a]	9.7	<.001

	Study 2		
Male (N = 52)		Female (N = 48)	
Chi Square	Signif. Level	Chi Square	Signif. Level
4.3	<.02	2.7	.10

	Study 3		
Male (N = 53)		Female (N = 54)	
Product-Moment Correlation	Signif. Level	Product-Moment Correlation	Signif. Level
+.18	NS [b]	+.10	NS [b]

[a] All findings were in the predicted direction.
[b] NS = Not significant.

the hypothesis. The findings do indicate a trend for increasing degree of boundary definiteness to be accompanied by correspondingly more intense achievement wishes as defined by self reports.

However, in a study reported by Shipman (1965) involving 40 neurotic outpatients (20 male and 20 female) the Barrier score was not significantly correlated with Edwards' Achievement. When the Barrier scores of these patients were also related to the frequency with which they chose achievement oriented words (e.g., ambitious, determined) from an adjective check list as being characteristic of themselves, a positive correlation was found ($r = .36$, p .05). Actually, if one considers each sex group separately, the correlation for the males was .62 and that for the females .02.

Rhoda Fisher (1966A) has looked further at this issue in a group of 49 white sixth grade children (boys = 30, girls = 19). Barrier scores were determined from responses to group administered Rorschach plates. An index of relative achievement was derived for each child by determining the difference between his class rank in I.Q. and his class rank for average final report card grades. Another achievement pertinent index was obtained by asking the classroom teacher to indicate on a checklist containing ten achievement oriented adjectives (e.g., energetic, determined) and ten non-achievement adjectives (e.g., lazy, unambitious) the ten best typifying each student. Total number of achievement adjectives chosen was used as an indicator of the degree of achievement drive visibly manifested by the student to the teacher. Analysis of the data revealed that the Barrier score was positively related to the amount of "overachievement" shown, as defined by obtaining higher grades than would be anticipated from I.Q. level ($p < .01$, one-tail test). Also, the Barrier scores of the boys were positively linked with the number of achievement adjectives chosen by the teacher to describe them ($p < .001$, one-tail test). In the female group the relationship was in the expected direction, but not significant. The fact that achievement traits, as defined by adjectives, have proven in both this study and Shipman's not to be related to the Barrier scores of female subjects is actually congruent with multiple published observations indicating that achievement drive does not manifest itself at a social level in the same overt manner in women as it does in men.

Still another approach to the issue was taken in terms of selective memory. Fisher and Osofsky,[1] in the course of a study of pregnancy, administered 25 cards of Form B of the Holtzman blots and a memory task involving achievement and non-achievement words to a sample of 38 pregnant women. These women were variously in the second through sixth month of pregnancy. Their mean age was 22.3 and mean educational level 10.4 years.

While responding to a variety of procedures, they were asked to learn a list of 20 words, ten of which referred to achievement themes and ten of which were neutral. The two classes of words were matched for length and placed in equivalent positions in the list. The following was the list employed:

Think	Best *
First *	Light
Ride	Sing
Try *	Win *
Chief *	Master *
Play	Buy
Honor *	Goal *
Agree	Round
Word	Prize*
Excel *	Turn

[* Achievement words]

Each subject was told to learn the list of words which was shown to her for

[1] Unpublished data.

one minute typed on a sheet of paper. She was then given five minutes to write all the words she could recall. A score was computed which equaled the number of achievement minus non-achievement words recalled. The use of this technique was based on the assumption that the greater the importance of achievement to an individual the greater would be his tendency to learn and recall words with achievement significance in a selectively superior fashion.

In this sample a correlation of .32 ($p < .05$) was obtained between Barrier and the achievement minus non-achievement word recall score. The more definite the subject's boundary the relatively larger proportion of achievement as compared to non-achievement words she recalled. Barrier was not correlated with the total of all words recalled.

In a subsequent study [2] Rhoda Fisher sought to duplicate this work in a group of 25 fifth grade children. The design was exactly the same, except that the word list learned was projected on a screen in a group setting. The correlation between Barrier and the achievement minus non-achievement word recall index was, however, not significant. It was not possible to duplicate in the child sample the results found in the adult female sample.

The term "self steering" has often been suggested as characteristic of the person with well articulated boundaries. It is intended to designate an orientation which underscores the importance of autonomy and making one's own decisions. Shultz (1966) sought, in the course of a larger study, to determine if the degree to which an individual adopts a "self steering" attitude toward a stress situation is correlated with the definiteness of his boundaries. The subjects he studied consisted of 20 males with duodenal ulcers and 20 with eczematoid dermatitis who were undergoing treatment for their symptoms at a Veterans Administration facility. After completing a series of tasks under stress which involved word constructions, they were asked to look at a series of 45 pairs of cartoons and to choose the one in each case that best described their feeling about the stress and what to do about it. The cartoons were originally developed by Grace and Graham (1952) to represent characteristic attitudes toward life (which presumably were basic to the development of specific psychosomatic symptoms). These cartoons had been submitted by Shultz to 20 judges with training in psychology who had been asked to rank them in terms of how well they expressed the idea of "self steering" as originally defined in the Fisher-Cleveland model. Each cartoon, therefore, had a judged self steering stimulus value. When the Barrier scores of the 40 subjects were related to their cartoon choices, it was demonstrated significantly that with increasing boundary definiteness there was a greater "self steering" orientation.

The finding may be graphically illustrated by noting that high Barrier

[2] Unpublished data.

subjects endorsed strongly a cartoon expressing the view that they ". . . felt threatened with harm and had to be ready for anything". But the low Barrier subjects favored a cartoon depicting the view that they ". . . felt humiliated and wished that the situation was over and done with."

12
Personal Interaction

SMALL GROUP BEHAVIOR

Behavior in a social context should be influenced by how individuated one feels. One would logically expect that an index portraying how a person delimits himself from his surroundings should contain useful information about how he contacts and reacts to others. A number of studies were originally reported by Fisher and Cleveland (1968) which indicated that high and low Barrier individuals do behave differently in small group situations. The earliest of these studies involved the formation of "pure" groups of high Barrier individuals and "pure" groups of low Barrier individuals which were then observed while they performed various tasks such as cooperatively creating stories or discussing particular issues and arriving at group decisions about them. It was ascertained in the course of this work that groups composed entirely of high Barrier subjects were more concerned with achievement and the attainment of goals than groups composed entirely of low Barrier subjects. It was also informally observed that interactions in the high Barrier group were relatively more spontaneous and equalitarian. Another interesting finding was that high Barrier groups endorsed the view that the individual and his own efforts determine his fate; whereas the low Barrier groups were identified with the position that "human relations are relatively unimportant and that human behavior is regulated by external and impersonal forces" (p. 208).

Fisher and Cleveland explored too the behavior of individual high and low Barrier subjects in small group contexts. This was done primarily by having members of a closely interacting group rate each other with respect to various behaviors (e.g., Who influences the other group members the most? Who is most active in resolving group differences?) Evidence was obtained that the Barrier score was positively correlated with the following variables in group situations: spontaneous expressiveness, independence, facilitating group objectives, warmth and friendliness, and ability to cope with aggression. One discerned from such data that the person with well articulated boundaries tried to support group goals, but that he simultaneously maintained his own independence. Somehow the high Barrier person is relatively more autonomous than the low Barrier person in his orientation and yet also more interested in facilitating the effectiveness of group functioning.

A test of these findings was undertaken by Cleveland and Morton (1962). They studied 70 psychiatric patients in a therapy program based on group interaction. The patients were asked in the final week of a four week period to fill out a sociometric questionnaire requesting nominations of group members who had been characterized by various types of behavior. High Barrier group participants received significantly more nominations than the low Barrier participants for the following: ability to influence other group members; high acceptance by the group at large; ability to operate effectively without direction and support from a leader; the inclination to put group above personal goals; the desire to get something accomplished; helping to resolve differences that arise between other group members; trying hard to keep the group "on the ball"; being the one to whom other group members prefer to talk. These results represent a cross-validation of most of the previous findings which have been cited. They depict the individual with definite boundaries as striving to motivate the group to accomplishment; maintaining self identity in the midst of group interaction; and simultaneously serving as an integrating and supportive force for the group process.

Joyce Morton (1965) explored in an adolescent population the relation between boundary attributes and one's role in the group. She obtained Barrier scores for 46 boys and 41 girls in grades seven–nine of a junior high school in Canada. In addition, several sociometric questions were administered which inquired concerning first, second, and third choices of friends with whom one would prefer to eat lunch, to accompany in a move to another classroom, and to participate with in favorite in-school and out-of-school activities. The Barrier score proved not to be correlated with the number of positive sociometric choices received by each individual. In appraising this finding, Morton reasoned that while the interest in communication and interaction which characterizes the high Barrier person might be expected to result in his forming many friendships, it is also true that his autonomous assertive stance might just as well antagonize others. This is perhaps true, but the question remains as to why the present results differ from previous studies just cited in which the individual's Barrier score was typically positively correlated with the number of favorable nominations he received from the group. Perhaps the dynamics of positive choices differ in an adolescent as compared to adult groups? Another consideration is that all previous sociometric studies have involved persons who were interacting in a therapeutic or quasi-therapeutic context. The personal qualities which elicit positive choices in a therapeutic endeavor (e.g., forthrightness, direct communicative stance, ability to keep the group "on the ball") may not be endearing to one's classmates in school.

An additional analysis was conducted by Morton to determine the relationship between the Barrier scores of sociometric choosers and those whom they choose. It turned out to be significantly positive. The higher an individual's Barrier score the more likely he was to award his sociometric choices to someone with equally as definite boundaries. The relationship was particularly strong in terms of high Barrier subjects making reciprocal choices. No sex differences were observed in the patterning of the results. Morton wondered whether the special tendency of high Barrier subjects to make reciprocal choices did not reflect "the greater empathy attributed to the high Barrier—the ability to recognize in certain others a greater interest in people than in things and their own need for affection and interpersonal relationships could lead the high Barrier subjects to find attractive other high Barrier people" (p. 47).

This is the first instance in which mutual friendship choices have been evaluated with reference to boundary attributes. There seems to be initial promise in pursuing the matter further.

Ramer (1963) completed a particularly well controlled analysis of how boundary definiteness affects communication between individuals in a group situation. He hypothesized that the high Barrier person would exceed the low Barrier person:

1. In initiating interpersonal communications.
2. In communicating committal, directive, and disagreeing statements rather than self depreciating ones.

He studied 96 female college students (in groups of four) in a setting in which each was isolated from the others by a screen. Instructions were given to write a story about several pictures and then to communicate with a partner, who was actually fictitious, about the story by composing notes which would presumably be delivered by the experimenter. One-third of the subjects were given no responses to the messages they sent; another third were given unfriendly replies from the fictitious partner; and the remaining third were given friendly replies. The communications written by subjects were analyzed with reference to their quantity and also their content as defined by specific interaction categories [e.g., giving directions, giving opinion and orientation, asking for orientation and opinions, self deprecia- tion]. It turned out that high Barrier subjects sent more messages (p .01) and more units of communication (p .05) than the low Barrier subjects. With regard to the content of the messages written, the high Barrier subjects issued more opinions and clarifying, orienting statements than the low Barrier group. They also tended, though not significantly, to give more directions for action and to manifest less self depreciation. It is of interest that there were no indications that the stress of receiving negative replies to a message enhanced the behavioral differences between the high and low Barrier subjects. The general tenor of Ramer's findings was consonant with the idea that the individual with definite boundaries is more likely than the individual with indefinite boundaries to act communicatively in group situations and also to pitch his messages at a self assertive rather than self depreciating level.

A study by Rosenbluh (1967) should be presented at this point because it suggests that the difference in communicativeness associated with high versus low boundary definiteness may be modified complexly by situational factors. Male (N = 64) and female (N = 64) college students were individually evaluated as they attempted to identify the concept underlying a series of words presented to them. The words referred to various parts of the body;[1] and the differentiating concept was the fact that some pertained to the upper and some to the lower aspects of the body. The design was such that half of the subjects were seen by an experimenter of like sex and half by one of the opposite sex. One of the measures taken during the experiment was the amount of time the subject talked. Examination of this "talk time" data indicated, at a significant level, that when the experimenter was the same sex as the subject, those persons with high Barrier scores increased the amount of time they talked and those with low Barrier scores decreased in this respect. When the experimenter was opposite in sex to the subject, a trend was found for the high Barrier individual to decrease "talk time" and the low Barrier person to increase it. Rosenbluh states (p. 47): "Highs (i.e., high Barrier), possibly due to their supposedly higher awareness of their surroundings, were somewhat subdued in their talking with the opposite sex experimenter present, whereas Lows, with less of an apparent interest in the external . . . did not allow the presence of the opposite sex experimenter to lessen their talk time. . . . With regard to talk activity, Lows seem to have been drawn out of their 'shells' by the opposite sex experimenter." Incidentally, the level of efficiency displayed by subjects in discerning the concept underlying the words presented to them showed significant interactions with Barrier and sex of the experimenter. High Barrier men arrived at solutions significantly faster than low Barrier men when the experimenter was a male. But when female subjects were matched with male experimenters, the reverse trend was observed.

The Rosenbluh results are, indeed, intriguing. They suggest an important factor, related to the sex of the person with whom one is interacting, which moderates the role of boundary definiteness in communicativeness. This moderating process may apparently even produce reversals—so that the very

[1] One cannot resist mentioning that previous work by Pishkin and Blanchard (1964) and Pishkin and Shurley (1965) concerned with concept identification indicated that women were particularly superior to men when the concept involved differentiating a right and left body site (right ear versus left ear). It was speculated by Pishkin, et al. that women were more sensitive than men to cues with body connotations.

set which facilitates interaction with one sex interferes with interaction with the other sex. If these observations can be cross-validated, they will invite a careful analysis of the differential response to males and females by those with definite and indefinite boundaries.

The set to make contact with the world which generally typifies the person with well articulated boundaries was found by Twente (1964) to show through even in behavior associated with waking up in the morning. He arranged for 30 individual male subjects to respond immediately upon awakening in the morning to a 73 item questionnaire which inquired concerning their sensations and experiences during the waking-up period. The questionnaire offered them such statements as the following to endorse or reject as characteristic of their waking-up behavior:

- I look out the window at the weather.
- I roll over and look around the room.
- I turn on the radio.
- I look at the sky.
- I smoke a cigarette.
- I notice my legs.

One cluster of items, which seemed to reflect awakening behavior aimed at communicating with other people, was positively and significantly correlated with the Barrier score. Another cluster apparently pertaining to behavior motivated by the wish to increase sensory contact with one's environs, was likewise positively linked with the Barrier score. Twente characterized the wakening behavior of the high Barrier individuals as follows (p. 13):

He is interested in talking to others, turning on the radio and focusing his attention on the outside sounds, sights and smells of reality.

An indirect demonstration of the link between boundary definiteness and social closeness has been provided by Frede, Gautney and Baxter (1968), using an indirect means for evaluating how subjects (30 college students) would portray social interaction. A miniature stage-setting was provided and also 67 cardboard figures on bases depicting a range of characters. Five different backgrounds were provided for the stage (living room, street scene, doctor's office, bedroom, blank). The subject was asked to place figures of his choice in the various stage settings and to create stories about them (which were tape recorded). These stories were analyzed in terms of the frequency with which the characters moved toward, against, or away from each other. The exact location of all figures chosen and placed on the stage by the subject was also recorded. While no differences between high and low Barrier subjects could be discerned with reference to how often the figures in their stories moved toward, away, or against each other, there was a significant trend (p .05) for the total amount of interaction to be positively related to Barrier. The higher the Barrier the greater the amount of interaction. Also, it was established that the Barrier score was negatively and significantly related (p .05) to the average distance between figures placed in the stage settings. The individual with definite boundaries was inclined to place the figures closer together than the individual with indefinite boundaries. One sees in these results an affirmation that preference for communication and close interaction goes along with the well articulated boundary.

RESPONSE TO SUGGESTION

As the active, rather forceful interpersonal stance associated with clear boundaries was highlighted in various studies, one could guess that it would be difficult to put a high Barrier person into a passively accepting role. He would not be likely to take well to expectations that he respond acquiescently. By implication, this should mean that submissiveness and suggestibility would be negatively related to boundary definiteness. Fisher and Cleveland (1968) first tested the validity of this proposition by considering the relationship of the Barrier score to several measures of suggestibility (e.g., willingness to accept inappropriate ink blot percepts as correct, amount of body sway produced by the suggestion that one's body is not steady). Significant support for the proposition was found with reference to two of the three suggestibility indices which were used.

Additional support came from the earlier mentioned study by Cleveland and Morton (1962) which involved 70 psychiatric patients. As part of their study, they asked the subjects to view a movie in which the action focused on a jury involved in a murder trial. This jury was depicted as initially casting one vote for acquittal and the remainder for conviction; and it ultimately shifted to a unanimous decision of "not guilty." The film was shown up to the point where the second ballot was about to begin. The subjects were then told that by the end of the story the jury votes would change unanimously to acquittal. Their task was to list the jurors in the rank order in which they might be expected to change their votes. Next, they formed into small groups that were instructed to arrive at unanimous group decisions with respect to the same ranking procedure. Later, after the group decisions were completed, the individual subject was again asked to rank the jurors in the order in which they would change their minds. It was therefore possible to compute an index of suggestibility in terms of how much the individual had, as the result of the group experience, altered his second as compared to his first rank list. This index of suggestibility turned out to be negatively and significantly (p .01) correlated with the Barrier score.

Preliminary findings by Mausner [2] are also pertinent to report. He

[2] Mausner, unpublished progress report entitled "Experimental Studies of Social Interaction", 1961, National Institute of Mental Health, Grant No. M–2836.

constructed a situation in which subjects judged how many dots were briefly exposed. As they rendered their judgments, they were receiving reports of the same phenomena from a partner. Although the partner's statements seemed to emanate directly from him, they were actually manipulated by the experimenter so as to appear to contradict the subject's reports. Each subject's responses to the contradictions were evaluated. It was found that the higher the Barrier score the greater the likelihood that the subject would consider his own judgments, rather than his partner's, to be correct. Also, the Barrier score was positively correlated with how satisfied the subject was with his own performance and negatively related to his degree of anxiety. However, there was no relation between Barrier and the actual degree to which the subject changed his judgments under the impact of the false information fed to him. Incidentally, the Barrier score was significantly and negatively related to the Lie score on the Minnesota Multiphasic test. This implies that the individual with definite boundaries has less need to present an exaggerated favorable picture of himself than does one who is vaguely bounded. Hammerschlag, et al. (1964) have more recently reported the same negative correlation between the Barrier index and the Lie score.

A particularly carefully designed study of the relation of Barrier to yielding behavior was carried out by Dorsey (1965). He conducted a preliminary and a subsequent major investigation of the influence of boundary definiteness and several other body image variables upon behavior in an Asch type conformity situation. The Asch situation was set up in such a fashion that the subject was asked to make a series of perceptual judgments while in a group containing "pseudosubjects" who were confederates of the experimenter and who tried to influence judgments in an arbitrary direction. The subject was asked to evaluate a variety of spatial and size stimuli projected on a screen. He judged relative object sizes, object heights, linear distances, and so forth. His decisions were given verbally after hearing those of three of the experimenters' confederates and his response was in turn followed by that of a fourth confederate. The confederates (two male, two female) had been carefully trained as to how to express their judgments and were instructed to look disapprovingly or questioningly at the subject when his estimates differed from their own. In the preliminary group of 26 college women the Barrier score was positively correlated ($r = .40$, $p < .05$) with nonconformity to the group pressure. Similarly, in the subsequent major study involving 46 college men Barrier was also positively correlated ($r = .48$, $p < .001$) with nonconformity to the group expectation. Dorsey indicated that the findings directly supported the view that boundary definiteness is related to the ability to be "self steering" and to behave independently of direct group pressure.

The Secord Homonyms test, the Secord and Jourard Body Cathexis Questionnaire, and a Q-sort of 65 statements (24 of which are body related) were used to tap other body image dimensions. None of these measures were able to predict in a straightforward fashion the amount of nonconformity shown. Also, none were significantly correlated with the Barrier score.

Dorsey proposed on the basis of the correlation between Barrier and nonconformity that a sense of body substantiveness may be a prerequisite for being able to resist the group. In a novel vein, he conjectured that such a feeling of body substantiveness is particularly required for nonconformity when one's body is under direct visual focus of the group members during the disagreement. He wondered whether the low Barrier person might not find it easier to "give in" because, "Conformity to group pressure results in a reduction of the intensity of group focus (on a physical self which is perceived as inadequate)" (p. 145).

Dorsey's results have been supported by B. Rothschild and J. Masling.[3] Forty-four male college students were evaluated in a yielding type situation. Each subject was seated alone in a room and listened to what he thought were telephone reports from other subjects of their estimates of the numbers of clicks in a series of sequences which were presented. The sequences were actually pre-recorded on tape and the subject gave his estimates after listening to the reports of four other pseudosubjects. Barrier scores were determined from responses to the Rorschach. Because response total was not controlled, the Barrier score was divided by the response total and expressed as a percent value. A chi-square analysis confirmed, as anticipated, that yielding was negatively related to boundary definiteness $[\chi^2 = 9.0, \text{df} = 1, p < .005]$.[4]

One of the more extreme forms of suggestion which has been investigated within the framework of the boundary concept is hypnotic susceptibility. Fisher (1963A) predicted that hypnotic susceptibility would be negatively correlated with boundary definiteness. Twenty-five male and 42 female college students constituted the experimental sample. Their hypnotic susceptibility was measured by means of the Stanford Hypnotic Susceptibility Scale. This scale involves a standard hypnotic induction followed by a series of suggestions. A subject's score is defined as equal to the number of instances in which he responds positively to 12 suggestion tasks. The hypnotist in this study was a male, but there was also an observer present during each

---

[3] I am grateful to Dr. Bertram Rothschild for making these data available.

[4] It is of related interest that a simple report of the individual's relative awareness of sensations from the exterior as compared to the interior sectors of his body is correlated with a measure of acquiescence, which one may conceptualize as tapping a dimension analogous to yielding. In terms of previous findings, it would be expected that persons with a predominance of exterior sensations (i.e., possessing a perceptually clear boundary) would be relatively self-assertive and therefore nonacquiescent. Fifty-one males and 54 females were asked to report their body sensations from two exterior and two interior sites for a five-minute period (Fisher, 1965A). As predicted, scores equal to the sum of exterior minus the sum of interior sensations were significantly and negatively related to acquiescence scores derived from the Bass Social Acquiescence Scale (Bass, 1956) which involves agreeing or disagreeing with a series of proverbs. The greater the perceptual prominence of the body boundary regions the less the acquiescence displayed when indicating agreement or disagreement with the proverbs.

Table 12.1
Rank Order Correlations Between Body Image Indices
and Hypnotic Susceptibility in Males and Females

Variables	Males (N = 25)		Females (N = 42)	
	Rho	Significance Level	Rho	Significance Level
Hypnotic susceptibility versus				
Barrier	−.23	NS [a]	−.01	NS
Penetration	.42	<.05	.15	NS
Barrier minus Penetration	−.47	<.02	.15	NS

[a] NS = Not significant. Does not even attain .10 level of significance.

hypnotic session who was the same sex as the subject. Table 12.1 presents the rank order correlations between various boundary scores and hypnotic susceptibility in the two sex groups. It can be seen that no relationships of significance occurred in the female group. The pattern in the male groups was congruent with expectation, but only if one considers both the Barrier and Penetration scores. The Barrier score was negatively correlated with hypnotic susceptibility, though not significantly so. The Penetration score was positively linked with susceptibility ($p < .05$ level); and a combined Barrier minus Penetration score, which other investigators have used (e.g., Conquest, 1963), was rather strongly and negatively correlated ($p < .02$ level) with susceptibility. These findings obviously need to be replicated and clarified. It is puzzling why meaningful trends were found for the males but not the females.

INTERVIEWER IMPRESSIONS OF PERSONS VARYING IN BOUNDARY DEFINITENESS

It would appear that boundary attributes do play a part in how the individual conducts himself in personal interactions. This has been particularly well shown with reference to behavior in small groups. However, the question arises whether boundary characteristics are sufficiently reflected in immediate behavior so that an interviewer could detect some of the traits and modes of response which are presumably linked with relatively high versus low boundary definiteness. From various sources of data a picture has emerged of the well-bounded individual as one who has a clear awareness of his identity or self and also the social context in which he is participating. The well-bounded person seems to be in sensitive communication with himself and also with others. He seems to be aware of his own motives and goals and at the same time visibly aware of the expectations and attitudes of others. He knows who he is and how others are responding to him. Of course, the obverse picture typifies the poorly bounded individual.

The question is whether in the course of spontaneous interaction with persons varying in boundary definiteness it would be possible to pick up cues which would differentiate them in terms of a constellation of traits relating to clarity of communication with self and others. A study was instituted to answer this question.

The subjects consisted of 123 men and 72 women participating in a ten week training course at Syracuse University. The median age was 23 years and the median educational level 16 years.

The apparent ability of subjects to communicate with self and others was judged by means of an interview. Ten interviewers were recruited. They were paid for their services. Seven had Ph.D.'s in clinical psychology and at least three years of clinical work; and three were M.D.'s with at least four years of background in psychiatry. Each interviewer saw from 10–25 subjects. He was instructed to conduct an unstructured 50 minute interview; and subsequently to make ratings with reference to the following three issues: [5]

How communicative did you find this person to be in his interview with you?

1. Very difficult to communicate with.
2. Slightly more difficult than average to communicate with.
3. About average to communicate with.
4. Unusually easy to communicate with.

How much insight into, and understanding of, his own behavior does this person manifest?

1. Seems grossly unaware of his own motivations.
2. Not as aware of own motives as average.
3. About average.
4. Unusually thoughtful and perceptive regarding own motives.

How clearly has this individual worked out his identity?

1. Rather hazy and indefinite sense of identity.
2. Average sense of identity.
3. More definite and clear-cut sense of identity than average.

It was assumed that these three rating categories would broadly define the behavioral pattern under investigation.

---

[5] The interviewers were also asked to make several other ratings for purposes of a training program in which the subjects were involved. These ratings were not pertinent to the present study.

Interviewers were instructed to use their own previous interview experiences as a basis for their judgments. One matter of definition raised by the interviewers concerned the term "identity" as it was used in the question "How clearly has this individual worked out his identity?" "Identity" was therefore defined as referring to how clearly the individual had set goals for himself and arrived at definite values and standards. The interviewers generally found their rating tasks not to be unreasonable in terms of the information they obtained from the 50 minute interaction.

The Barrier score was obtained on a group basis in the usual fashion. As can be seen in Table 12.2 the Barrier score was related to all of the

Table 12.2
Chi-Square Analysis of Relationship of Barrier Score
to Interview Ratings

Variables		Barrier Scores H [a]	L	χ^2	Significance Level
Communication with Others	4	50	31		
	3	42	32	6.5 (df = 2)	<.05
	1–2	15	25		
Self Insight	4	30	15		
	3	59	49	4.9 (df = 2)	<.10
	1–2	18	24		
Clarity of Identity	3	44	25		
	2	46	41	4.9 (df = 2)	<.10
	1	16	22		
Average of Evaluations [b]	H	55	31	5.4 (df = 1)	.02
	L	51	57		

[a] H = Above median
    L = At median or below
[b] = The N is 194 instead of 195 because one interviewer omitted his third rating
of one subject.

interview variables in the predicted direction—although in some instances at a borderline level. Subjects with higher Barrier scores exceeded those with lower scores in their ability to communicate with others ($p < .05$); in their apparent insight into their own motives and behavior ($p < .10$); in their manifest clarity of identity [6] ($p < .10$); and in overall communication with

[6] There are findings which indicate that in men one aspect of such clarity may involve a distinct sense of being masculine. It has been shown in four samples of male subjects that the Barrier score is positively and significantly correlated with an index reflecting the relative predominance of male as compared to female imagery in ink blot productions. The index is equal to the sum of all human figures in a protocol labeled as male minus the sum of those

self and others as defined by the average of the three interview evaluations (p .02).

The three interview rating variables all proved, in terms of chi-square, to be positively and significantly interrelated with each other at the .001 level or better. It is not clear whether this is due to halo effect or the intrinsic relatedness of the rated behaviors.

Interviewers tended to judge that those with definite boundaries exceeded those with indefinite boundaries in communicativeness, awareness and understanding of their own behavior, and clarity of self definition. One may or may not choose to view these relationships as embracing a common behavioral category involving the ability to communicate with self and others. However, it is apparent that individuals who differ in boundary definiteness make unlike impressions in a face-to-face interaction with regard to meaningful behavioral dimensions. The findings concerning clarity of identity are especially noteworthy because they reaffirm the view stated else-where (Fisher and Cleveland, 1968) that degree of boundary articulation reflects the consistency and definiteness of goals and values that have been interiorized. In general, it is of interest that differences in the body image boundary are accompanied by perceptible differences in conduct in a face-to-face interaction.

SEXUAL RESPONSIVENESS

Males

Since high and low Barrier individuals differ in the way they interact with others, might one expect their sexual behavior to differ? Sexual behavior involves an extreme form of intimate personal interaction. Therefore, one might anticipate that the high Barrier person would be more sexually expressive and more spontaneously interested in sexual contacts than the low Barrier person. An attempt was first made to test such an hypothesis with reference to the behavior of men.[7] An opportunity to do so arose in terms

---

referred to as female (M-F). Perhaps a man is best able to experience himself as a differentiated entity when his identifications and imagery are uni-directionally and unambivalently masculine in character. One may speculate that a self concept sharply developed around masculine values would find expression in imagery with high masculine content. To have a close balance of masculine and feminine values might prevent the unified self feeling that is perhaps required for well articulated boundaries. If this formulation is correct, it applies only to males because no consistent relationships have been observed between Barrier and M-F in female samples.

[7] A substantial portion of this study was originally published by Fisher and Cleveland in the *Journal of Psychology*, 1958, *45*, 207–211.

of data which had already been collected by Epstein and Smith [8] (1957).

Epstein and Smith studied the relationship of projective measures of sex drive to other measures of sex drive. They secured group Rorschach protocols; and so it was possible to score the protocols to establish the Barrier score of each subject. The following indices concerned with sexual response, which they obtained, were used as criteria measures.

1. Need Sex

This measure was based on stories given by subjects to eight TAT type pictures. Epstein and Smith describe it as follows (p. 474):

> This score was adapted from the Murray scoring system. . . . Need sex is defined as the need "to seek and enjoy the company of the opposite sex. To have sexual relations. To fall in love, to get married". . . . A basic weight of 1 was assigned to the slightest indication of romance (e.g., "They are man and wife"), of 2 when a direct reference to romance was made or when some secondary physical contact was indicated (e.g., "They love each other." "He would like to kiss her.") and of 3 when sexual intercourse was implied (e.g., "She has become pregnant, and they are wondering what to do"). The basic weight was then modified by taking into account centrality, frequency, and duration.

2. Sex Drive Questionnaire

Subjects responded to a questionnaire under a presumed anonymous condition. They were to respond to three check lists which requested: "(a) day of last orgasm, with a range of 'today' to 'more than seven days ago'; (b) average rate of orgasm during the past two months, with a range from

Table 12.3
Chi-Square Analyses of Differences in Various Sexual Indices
Between High Barrier and Low Barrier Subjects

Sex Scores	Group with Higher Score	Level of Significance
TAT need sex	H.B.[a]	<.05
Orgasm rate	H.B.	.05
Orgasm recency	H.B.	N.S.[c]
Subjective rating of sex drive	N.D.[b]	—
Picture ratings	H.B.	N.S.

[a] H.B. = High Barrier
[b] N.D. = No difference
[c] N.S. = Not significant

[8] The kindness of Dr. Seymour Epstein in making the data available is acknowledged with gratitude.

o to 22 or more times per week; and (c) subjective rating of sex drive at the moment, with a range from 'no sexual desire at all' to 'intense sexual desire'."

3. Ratings of Pictures

Subjects were instructed also "to rate on a 5-point scale the sex appeal of three women whose pictures were successively projected on the screen. The first was of an attractive young woman in a bathing suit; the second was of a woman in a night gown who was lying seductively on a bed; the third was of a model wearing a low cut dress."

Fifty-three men in an introductory psychology class served as subjects.

The differences between above median and below median Barrier score subjects, in relation to the sex indices, were in the expected direction. The high Barrier subjects were characterized by significantly higher TAT need sex scores and orgasm rate scores than the low Barrier subjects. The above median Barrier subjects were higher (not significantly) in orgasm recency and picture rating scores. The groups did not differ with reference to the subjective ratings of sex drive. Generally, subjects with well delineated boundaries were more sexually active and expressive than those with vague boundaries. These results offer another instance in which a form of close and intimate social interaction is linked with the state of the boundary.

Females

The opportunity also presented itself to determine how boundary definiteness was related to sexual responsiveness in a female population. Fisher and Osofsky (1967) obtained Barrier scores and a number of measures of sexual responsiveness from a sample of 42 women (mean age = 26.5) who had been paid a substantial fee to volunteer as subjects for a study of "menstrual and reproductive functions."

Twenty-five blots of Form B of the Holtzman series were administered on a first occasion. A week later 25 blots of Form A were administered after the subject had removed all of her clothing (to prepare for a gynecological examination) and was covered only with a sheet. As already described in detail earlier, the purpose of this procedure was to evaluate the effect upon the Barrier score of removing one's clothing. Since clothing so obviously is involved with boundary experiences, one would expect their removal to affect boundary delineation.

Self report measures were used to evaluate sexual responsiveness. Subjects were asked to rate their usual degree of sexual responsiveness (5-point scale) and orgasm consistency (6-point scale) and also estimate intercourse frequency per week. In addition, they were asked to rank one list of ten phrases (e.g., unsatisfied, weak, as if I would burst) in terms of how aptly they described their subjective feelings during intercourse and another list of ten phrases (e.g., unsatisfied, tired) with reference to feelings experienced post-orgasm. The term "unsatisfied" was included in both lists and was the only one which directly concerned amount of enjoyment obtained from intercourse. Only this term was considered to be specifically pertinent to the topic of inquiry in the present section.

As previously indicated, there was a significant trend for the degree of Barrier increase from the clothed to the nude state to be positively correlated with reported degree of sexual responsiveness $(r = .27, p < .05,$ one-tail test). It was not correlated, however, with orgasm consistency, frequency of intercourse, or the degree to which the term "unsatisfied" was rejected as descriptive of feelings during and following intercourse. The one positive finding involving sexual responsiveness was interpreted as indicating that the ability to experience one's nude body (with all of the sexuality implied) not as a threatening but rather as an enhancing stimulus may play a role in being able to enjoy sexual interaction.

The Barrier score based on the initial Holtzman series alone was not significantly correlated with self rated sexual responsiveness, orgasm consistency, or intercourse frequency. It was positively correlated $(r = .32, p < .05)$ with the degree to which subjects rejected the term "unsatisficd" as descriptive of their feelings post-orgasm; and showed a trend $(r = .24, p > .10)$ to be positively correlated with rejection of "unsatisfied" as applied to the period of intercourse previous to orgasm. The Barrier score derived from the second Holtzman series had only a chance relationship with the various indices of sexual responsiveness. One can see that the Barrier score was of limited effectiveness in predicting sexual responsivity and enjoyment of sexual experience. Indeed, it was able to predict significantly only the degree of satisfaction experienced shortly after orgasm. It did not relate to frequency of intercourse or ability to have orgasm consistently. Of special interest is the fact that the one significant correlation that did emerge involved a completely subjective variable.

Generally, the data for the female sample were less convincing than those for the earlier described male sample in indicating a link between boundary definiteness and sexual responsiveness. However, a few promising leads emerged which invite further consideration.

13
Psychopathology

DOES SCHIZOPHRENIA PRODUCE BOUNDARY LOSS?

The loss of the ability to define oneself and to distinguish one's personal space from that which is non-self has often been associated with neurotic and psychotic disturbance. As already indicated, it has been widely conjectured that schizophrenic breakdown is marked by a dissolution of boundaries and a failure to distinguish between signals originating within oneself and those impinging from outside sources (e.g., Schilder, 1935; Fenichel, 1945). Several writers (e.g., Des Lauriers, 1962) have speculatively pinpointed loss of boundaries as the fundamental defect in schizophrenia and even developed psychotherapeutic techniques based upon dramatizing the existence of the patient's body periphery—thereby hoping to restore the lost boundary.

However, it has been difficult to muster straightforward, empirical support for the proposition that boundary defects characteristically accompany psychopathology. In the 1958 monograph, *Body Image and Personality*, it was shown that normal and neurotic subjects as a group obtained significantly higher Barrier and lower Penetration scores than schizophrenic subjects. But normal persons could not be distinguished in terms of Barrier or Penetration scores from patients diagnosed as neurotic. Somewhat qualitatively, it was also observed that the schizophrenics produced relatively numerous Penetration responses which floridly depicted violations of the body (e.g., "a body torn open", "scalped head", "a bloody dripping nose"). Finally, it should be mentioned that visible but not significant trends were present for paranoid schizophrenics to manifest greater boundary definiteness than non-paranoid schizophrenics. Such trends had been speculatively anticipated in terms of the idea that the paranoid defense involves not a breakdown in boundaries but rather tight, rigid self encapsulation. It might have been expected too in view of the fact that paranoid schizophrenics usually display less breakdown than other schizophrenics in their ability to deal with various motor and perceptual tasks (e.g., Witkin, et al., 1954). That is, the paranoid apparently functions in a relatively less disorganized fashion.

Following the publication of the work just summarized, a considerable array of new projects was initiated by various investigators. These ranged from attempts to distinguish diagnostic groups on the basis of boundary scores to analyses of boundary score fluctuations in patients undergoing treatment.

It might be well to begin the survey of these new studies with an account of the Holtzman, et al. (1961) findings. The Holtzman ink blots were administered to numerous normal and pathological groups; and the results indicated that the Barrier score was higher and the Penetration score lower in normals than in chronic schizophrenics.[1] The difference involving Penetration was significant (p .01); but that for Barrier was not. The intercorrelations of 23 indices (including Barrier and Penetration) based upon the ink blot responses obtained in 16 different samples of subjects were factor analyzed. It was observed that the Barrier score consistently loaded high on a factor associated with "well organized, ideational activity, awareness of conventional concepts" (p. 171). As for the Penetration score, it loaded high on several factors related to disturbance (e.g., indices of immaturity, body concern, and poor reality testing). Such findings placed the Barrier and Penetration scores at the opposite ends of an adaptive–maladaptive continuum.

Similar results were obtained by Holtzman, Gorham, and Moran (1964) in a factor analysis of a battery of tests that had been administered to 99 chronic schizophrenic men. The battery included the Holtzman ink blots, proverbs, tests of word meaning, and sorting tasks. The Barrier score loaded highly on a factor defining the ability to be ideationally integrated. The Penetration score was part of a factor indicative of conceptual autism and psychopathology. It was also associated with a factor in which production of blatant sexual ink blot responses was prominent.

Jaskar and Reed (1963) compared the boundary scores of a group of women who were patients in a state psychiatric hospital with those of a group of normal controls. The hospitalized patients comprised 19 schizophrenics and 11 individuals who were in the neurotic category. The control group was obtained from applicants for employment at the hospital. Neither the Barrier nor Penetration scores differentiated the two groups. These scores also did not distinguish the neurotics and schizophrenics within the patient sample. Jaskar and Reed obtained a battery of other body image measures (viz., Secord Homonym Word Association test, Body Cathexis test, and the Franck-Rosen Drawing Completion test) from the subjects. All were ineffec-

---

[1] Portions of this material appeared in a review by the present writer entitled "A Further Appraisal of the Body Boundary Concept", *Journal of Consulting Psychology*, 1963, 27, 62–74.

tual in separating the groups except the Secord-Jourard Body Cathexis test which depicted the controls as more satisfied with their bodies than the patients.

Reitman (1962) compared in a male V.A. patient group the boundary scores of 40 who were hospitalized for neurotic symptoms and 40 hospitalized as schizophrenics. There was a non-significant trend for the schizophrenics to have lower Barrier scores than the neurotics; and a significant trend (.05 level) for the schizophrenics to have higher Penetration scores than the neurotics.

Cardone (1967) could detect no Barrier or Penetration differences between a group of male chronic schizophrenics (N = 42) and a control group of normal men (N = 10) working as attendants in a state psychiatric hospital.

Vinck (1967) compared 23 schizophrenics and 34 non-schizophrenics; and reported that the two groups did not differ in Barrier. However, Penetration was significantly higher in the former than in the latter sample.

A major effort has been made by Conquest (1963) to clarify the issue of whether the paranoid schizophrenic has a more clearly articulated body boundary than the non-paranoid schizophrenic. It may be recalled that Fisher and Cleveland detected trends for relatively definite boundaries to be present in the paranoid individual; but these trends were not of significant proportions. Conquest designed an analysis of the body image characteristics of 40 male schizophrenics. Half of the group was diagnosed as paranoid; and the other half was composed of those with non-paranoid diagnostic labels. The following battery of procedures was administered: Holtzman ink blots (for Barrier and Penetration); Secord Homonym Word Association test; Draw-A-Person test [scored for field independence-dependence as defined by Witkin, et al. (1954)], and the Body Cathexis test. In addition, each patient's degree of paranoia was rated by means of the paranoid-morbidity scale from the Lorr Inpatient Multidimensional Psychiatric Scale. As predicted, the Barrier score proved to be significantly higher and the Penetration score significantly lower in the paranoid than the non-paranoid group. The Barrier minus Penetration score exceeded either of these scores alone in the effectiveness with which it designated the paranoids as having more articulated boundaries than the non-paranoids. However, the Barrier minus Penetration index was not correlated with the Lorr paranoid-morbidity score. The Penetration score was likewise not linked with the Lorr scale; but the Barrier score was positively and significantly correlated with it. Conquest found the various body image tests in his battery of procedures to be essentially uncorrelated with each other. Only the Barrier score and degree of positive evaluation of one's body (Body Cathexis) proved to be significantly positively related. There was also a borderline negative relationship between Barrier and degree of field dependence as measured by figure drawing criteria.

A factor analysis of the data disclosed two factors:

1. One was labeled "Body as a Reference Point." It loaded positively on Barrier, body interest, positive Body Cathexis, and Penetration but negatively on field dependence. Conquest summarized his interpretation of the factor as follows (p. 122): "The factor shows itself to be composed of variables having to do with the body as a stable reference point, the relatively stable aspects of the body's boundaries, and a positively-oriented interest in the body."

2. A second factor, "Body-boundary Gestalt", loaded positively with Barrier, negatively with Penetration and also negatively with the ability to perceive ink blot stimuli as total gestalts. It was speculated that there may be an interdependent tie between possessing well articulated boundaries and the ability to grasp gestalt qualities of the perceptual field.

Of the various findings, those concerning the differentiation of paranoid from non-paranoid are of special import for the immediate topic of this section. The Barrier score proved to be more effective than any of the other body image measures for demarcating the paranoid from the non-paranoid schizophrenics. This would suggest that the body image differences between the two categories of patients may be relatively specific to the matter of boundary definiteness.

The reliability of Conquest's results was moderately affirmed by Fisher (1964C) who compared the boundary scores of 24 paranoid (ten male, 14 female) and 18 non-paranoid (seven male, 11 female) schizophrenics who did not differ significantly in age, education, cooperativeness, or length of hospitalization. The paranoids manifested a trend to have higher Barrier scores (p .10, one-tail test) than the non-paranoids. The paranoids were not lower on Penetration; but the combined Barrier minus Penetration score was significantly higher for the paranoids than the non-paranoids ($p < .01$, one-tail test).

The fact that paranoid schizophrenics can obtain relatively high Barrier scores and the further fact that some schizophrenic samples do not have lower scores than neurotic and normal control groups forces one to conclude that schizophrenic symptomatology may occur without gross boundary disruption. In considering this matter and attempting to formulate some generalization about the determinants of boundary breakdown in schizophrenia, Fisher (1966B) took a special cue from the relatively greater boundary definiteness found in paranoids as compared to non-paranoids. He suggested that the boundary is best maintained in those schizophrenics who, like the paranoid, continue to see themselves as playing an individualistic and important role. That is, one of the prime distinctions of the paranoid is that he has reconstructed the world in such a way as to give himself a position which is of central importance by virtue of either straightforward grandiose exaggeration of his power or exaggerated fantasies regarding the unique concentration of evil forces arrayed against him. The paranoid, as contrasted to the non-paranoid, has constructed a good "cover story" which gives him a sense of significance and prominence even in the midst of his disorganization and retreat from reality. Conceivably, past observed differences in boundary definiteness between paranoids and non-paranoids could be a function of the "cover story" effect rather than paranoia as such. Thus, schizophrenic or psychotic disturbance would not necessarily result in loss of boundaries. Rather, such loss would occur only when there is an inability to imagine or fabricate a role in which one feels a sense of individual significance. Boundedness would be associated with a sense of self significance, no matter how bizarre the assumptions underlying it.

With this rationale, Fisher (1966B) undertook a study in which it was predicted that the Barrier score in schizophrenic subjects would be positively related to their apparent degree of self-importance and also their amount of paranoia. The prime factor in boundary maintenance in schizophrenia was considered to revolve about a feeling of significance rather than degree of objectively defined disorganization. The subjects consisted of 45 male and 46 female hospitalized schizophrenics who were in an 18–45 age range; had completed at least eight grades; and received no shock treatment prior to being evaluated. Fifty-six had been diagnosed as paranoid and 35 as non-paranoid. Twenty male and 20 female neurotics were also included so as to make possible further comparisons of the Barrier scores of schizophrenics and non-schizophrenics.

Individually administered Holtzman blots were used to measure Barrier. The person who administered the Holtzman and a battery of other tests rated the patient on the abbreviated form of the Lorr, et al. (1963) Inpatient Multidimensional Psychiatric Scale. It was particularly anticipated in terms of the hypothesis cited above that scores for two of the Lorr subscales (Grandiose Expansiveness and Paranoid Projection) would be positively correlated with Barrier. Grandiose Expansiveness, which involves ratings of feelings of superiority and of possessing unusual powers, was regarded as a direct index of how much importance the patient ascribes to himself.

Similar to the results in several past studies, the schizophrenic samples did not display lower Barrier or higher Penetration scores than their respective neurotic samples. In fact, the female schizophrenics had significantly higher Barrier scores than the female neurotics ($p < .05$). This may be taken as an additional indication that schizophrenics as a group do not necessarily have less definite boundaries than non-psychotic persons.

When the Barrier scores of those schizophrenics diagnosed as paranoid were compared with those of the non-paranoids, the paranoids were found to be significantly higher ($\chi^2 = 4.7$, $p < .05$). No difference could be detected for Penetration. The Lorr Paranoid Projection score was not correlated significantly with Barrier in either the male or female schizophrenic groups. But there was, as predicted, a significant positive correlation between Barrier and Lorr Grandiose Expansiveness in the female schizophrenics ($r = .32$, $p < .05$) and a borderline positive one ($p < .10$) in the male schizophrenics.

Subsequently, an additional schizophrenic sample consisting of 20 males and 23 females (median age = 32, median educational level = 11 years) was obtained from a number of state hospitals. About 60 percent of the group were taking tranquilizers, but none had received shock therapy within six months of being studied. Twenty-five responses to Form B of the Holtzman blots were secured from each individually. In order to evaluate the patient's feelings about himself (i.e., positive or grandiose versus negative or non-grandiose) he was asked to rate himself on a series of 14 continua. Some samples of these continua follow: successful-unsuccessful, powerful-weak, healthy-sick. Other tests were administered which are not pertinent to the present hypothesis. In addition, the physician treating each patient was asked to rate his degree of grandiosity (among other variables) on a five-point scale.

The median grandiosity rating was found to be 1 (little or no grandiosity) and the range was 1–5. When the trichotomized Barrier scores (as equal thirds as possible) were related by means of chi-square to the dichotomized (at the median) grandiosity ratings, a borderline positive relationship was found ($\chi^2 = 4.7$, df = 2, $p < .10$). The greater the patient's Barrier score the higher was his level of grandiosity judged to be. This, of course, offered a bit more support for the hypothesis concerning the role of grandiosity in maintaining boundaries in the midst of schizophrenic disorganization.

The average self ratings of the patients showed only a chance relationship with the Barrier score. That is, as defined by the patient's publicly stated view of himself, his feelings concerning his own effectiveness and comfort were not correlated with the character of his boundaries. Whether this lack of support for the hypothesis resulted from a defect in one of its aspects or whether it was a function of defensiveness and camouflage maneuvers associated with being asked to describe oneself publicly remains to be seen. Another possibility to consider is that while a schizophrenic may manufacture a grandiose "cover story" for himself pertaining to a particular role (e.g., that he is a person of great importance), he may simultaneously be aware of discomforts and deficiencies in himself (not pertinent to the "cover story" role) which will find expression if he is asked to rate himself in a variety of areas.

The findings from the last two studies described do support previous reports that schizophrenics diagnosed as paranoids have more definite boundaries than those diagnosed as non-paranoids.[2] Furthermore, the positive

---

[2] The potential of the boundary scores for measuring other kinds of maladjustment aside from that in the category of psychosis is pointed up by Miner and DeVos' (1960) finding that urban Arabs who are conflicted about their identity produce significantly higher Penetration scores (.05 level) than oasis Arabs who have not yet been exposed to such extreme identity conflict. This, by the way, is confirmatory of previous data (Fisher and Cleveland, 1968) which demonstrated that Japanese-American men who were struggling to adapt to United States life had less definite boundaries than native Japanese not beset by such identity problems.

A brief reference is in order too concerning an attempt to use the Penetration score, among a series of others that were derived from the Holtzman blots, to discriminate a group of

correlations between Barrier and Grandiose Expansiveness are encouraging with regard to the principal hypothesis that was tested. There does seem to be a basis for asserting that the boundary definiteness of a schizophrenic individual is related to how well he is able, in the midst of his breakdown, to manufacture a role or "cover story" which continues to portray him as a person whose existence has import and meaning in the world. It is thought provoking to consider that boundary differentiation can perhaps be maintained on the basis of assumptions and modes of thought which are illogical and even bizarre.

It is an interesting matter to speculate how a feeling of being "special" or important might get translated into a sense of boundary definiteness. Does a feeling of significance perhaps increase muscle tonus and thereby intensify boundary sensations? Does a feeling of insignificance result in responses which encourage muscle flaccidity and thereby diminish feedback from the muscle sheath of the body? Does feeling worthless result in a turning away from what is "out there" and consequently produce (in the process of turning inward) increased awareness of one's body interior which in turn decreases the ratio of exterior to interior sensations experienced? The alternatives proposed are all possible. It will be necessary to analyze patterns of body experience and physiological response in passive versus active and failure versus mastery situations in order to obtain clarification.

A dissertation by Francis (1968) has more recently raised the question whether an adequate understanding of the role of self concept (feeling about one's importance) in maintaining boundary definiteness in the schizophrenic individual may not require a rather complex model which simultaneously considers not only degree of experienced self-importance, but also amount of disorganization that has occurred.

Francis related the Barrier scores of 46 male schizophrenics to their degree of acceptance of their disability (as measured by self ratings on the Tennessee Self Concept Scale) and ward behavior (as determined by nurses' ratings). The results indicated that Barrier was not significantly related to how favorably patients rated themselves. These ratings encompassed such dimensions as level of self-satisfaction and feelings about oneself in a moral-ethical sense. The lack of relation between Barrier and such self ratings duplicated the observation by Fisher just cited above. But data derived from nurses' ratings of patients indicated that Barrier was positively correlated with degree of adjustment to the ward situation. Also, a significant interaction was found in an analysis of variance between Barrier scores, self ratings, and nurses' ratings. The trends indicated that those judged to be well adjusted by the nurses and who rated themselves in a similarly positive way had the

---

patients with brain damage from a control group. Barnes (1963) found that the Penetration score was one of several ink blot indices which contributed significantly to distinguishing 50 brain damaged from 50 control subjects.

highest Barrier scores. But those who were judged to be poorly adjusted by the nurses and who rated themselves as well adjusted had the lowest Barrier scores. This relationship had been predicted by Francis. He anticipated that poor boundaries would characterize those whose self evaluations were most contradicted by evaluations made by others—particularly at the extreme of poor adjustment. The significant interaction of self ratings, nurses' ratings, and Barrier may mean that the Fisher formulation described above is too oversimplified when it looks for straightforward correlations between grandiosity and boundary definiteness.

Perhaps grandiosity serves as a protective mechanism only when the amount of personal disturbance or regression has not exceeded certain limits. The grossly disorganized patient with hebephrenic response modes whose thinking logic has deteriorated in wide areas may not be able to maintain his boundaries no matter how great his grandiosity. But the individual who retains a moderate amount of integration may best be able to protect his sense of boundedness and to guard his individuality by adopting a grandiose identity.

The existence of apparently intact boundaries in those with a deviant life adjustment is not confined to the schizophrenic category. Another example of societally defined deviant adjustment which is accompanied by no detectable disturbance in the boundary has been provided by Hooker.[3] She probed the possibility of distinguishing a male homosexual sample ($N = 30$) from non-homosexual controls ($N = 30$) in terms of boundary qualities. The homosexuals were unique in that they were persons who showed no signs of being disturbed by their homosexuality and who had in other respects made quite adequate life adjustments. They were not the usual homosexual sample which is recruited largely from psychiatric sources. It was found that their Barrier and Penetration scores were not significantly different from those of the control group. Such results would seem to indicate that a homosexual mode of sexual expression does not per se carry with it a breakdown in one's sense of body articulation or integrity. It would appear that if a homosexual works out an adequate, successfully structured life role for himself his sense of individuation and boundedness need not be impaired.[4]

BOUNDARY CHANGE PHENOMENA

Cleveland (1960A) made use of test-retest scores derived from the Holtzman ink blots to determine whether the boundaries of schizophrenics changed as they became less disorganized. The study embraced 25 male schizophrenics

---

[3] Personal communication.

[4] Similarly, Witkin, et al. (1962) found that homosexuals could not be distinguished from normal controls in terms of degree of field independence.

whose clinical symptomatology was rated upon first entering the hospital and after five and 13 weeks of treatment with tranquilizers. Whether the patient attained sufficient recovery to be judged capable of leaving the hospital was also ascertained. Decrement in Penetration from the first testing to that at the fifth week was positively and significantly correlated with rated improvement in symptomatology. This was analogously true for the interval from first testing to retest at the 13th week. Also, patients who were able to leave the hospital had significantly lower Penetration scores than non-discharged patients. Barrier had only chance relationships with the indices of clinical recovery.

Another aspect of this project involved 45 schizophrenics who responded to the Rorschach blots when they were first admitted to the hospital and a second time before discharge. Psychiatric ratings of clinical symptomatology were made at equivalent times. Decline in Penetration was positively and significantly linked with being rated as improved or markedly improved. Barrier shifted significantly only in the instance of the markedly improved. This shift was in a positive direction. Cleveland interpreted his results as indicating a "firming up" of boundaries in the schizophrenic who improved clinically. Of course, this "firming up" was almost entirely reflected in Penetration rather than Barrier changes.

Cardone (1967) sought to evaluate the effects of a tranquilizer (chlorpromazine) upon the boundaries of male chronic schizophrenics. He administered the Rorschach (to obtain Barrier and Penetration scores) and also other body image measures to a number of groups previous to, and following, specified conditions. For one group (chronic schizophrenics, $N = 16$) the condition involved taking a placebo for 30 days. A second group (chronic schizophrenics, $N = 16$) received chlorpromazine for 30 days. A third group (chronic schizophrenics, $N = 10$) received no treatment; and a fourth (normal psychiatric aides, $N = 10$) also received no treatment from pre- to post-testing. Clinical status of patients was initially measured by means of ratings by staff personnel. These ratings were used to equate the groups. The results indicated that chlorpromazine did not significantly change Barrier or Penetration scores. Indeed, it did not alter any of the body image measures employed, viz., Secord and Jourard Body Cathexis technique (1953); Fisher Body Distortion Questionnaire (1964C); Adjustable Body-distorting Mirror (Traub and Orbach, 1964). Cardone's failure to find a shift in Penetration in his patients receiving chlorpromazine treatment may possibly not be congruent with Cleveland's report in which such a shift was shown in patients receiving tranquilizers. It is difficult to say because Cardone does not indicate whether his treated patients significantly improved. In the Cleveland study the decrease in Penetration was associated with significant improvement in clinical symptomatology.

The process of boundary change in psychiatric patients was subjected to an unusually careful scrutiny by Reitman and Cleveland (1964). They observed 20 male neurotics and 20 male schizophrenics who, on the average, were exposed to about three hours of sensory isolation. Responses to Holtzman ink blots, measures of tactile sensitivity, figure drawings, estimates of body size, and Bender-Gestalt drawings were obtained just before and shortly after the isolation experience. A control group was also tested and retested, but did not undergo sensory isolation. No significant shifts in the test-retest scores for this group were detected, but a number were observed for the experimental subjects. Thus, the neurotics obtained higher Penetration and lower Barrier scores. The schizophrenics were characterized by a shift toward lower Penetration and higher Barrier scores. That is, sensory isolation seemed to result in less boundary articulation for the neurotics and more articulation for the schizophrenics. It was assumed by Reitman and Cleveland that this was a resultant of the fact that the sensory isolation minimized environmental input which, for the schizophrenic, is threatening and disruptive. But for the neurotic it decreased a form of stimulation which is utilized to support the boundary.

What was really impressive was that the test-retest results for the tactile sensitivity and body size estimation tasks were also in the opposite direction in the neurotic and schizophrenic samples; and the direction of the difference was congruent with the boundary data. In the neurotic group tactile sensitivity declined from pre- to post-sensory isolation; and estimates of body size increased.[5] On the other hand, the data for the schizophrenics indicated a shift toward greater tactile sensitivity and a decreased concept of body size. Such findings can be seen as congruent with the boundary findings if one considers previous observations by Wapner, Werner, and Comalli (1958). They found that increasing the sensory prominence of the boundary of the head (by physically touching it) resulted in a diminished sense of head size. They proposed that perceived size of a body region tends to be decreased as its boundaries become more definite. With this perspective, the test-retest shift of the schizophrenics toward a sense of decreased body size could be a resultant of increased boundary articulation; and the size shift in the neurotics a function of decreased articulation. Such boundary shifts did, indeed, occur —at least as measured by the Barrier and Penetration changes.

One sees here simultaneously that the schizophrenics increase in boundary definiteness and also decrease in perceived body size; whereas the neurotics decrease in boundary definiteness and increase in perceived body size. The force of these observations is even further reinforced if one notes that the presumed sharpening of the schizophrenics' boundaries was also accompanied by an increase in tactual sensitivity, and the diffusion of the neurotics' boundaries by diminished tactual sensitivity. It would seem logical to expect (in view of the relation of Barrier to sensory vividness) that the more articu-

[5] Kitamura (1964) reports that following 48 hours of sensory deprivation normal subjects overestimate their heights significantly more than do control subjects.

lated boundary would have greater sensitivity. The above findings represent a rare congruence among three measures of change in two contrasting groups. Incidentally, significant changes in size perception did not occur for non-body objects (e.g., baseball). Meaningful shifts as the result of the sensory isolation appeared only when some form of body perception was involved.

Another study involving the relation of the boundary to sensory isolation should be cited at this point, although the subjects were normals rather than psychiatric patients. Jacobson (1965) obtained from a pool of 136 college students, 20 males and 20 females, half of whom had unusually high and half unusually low Barrier scores. They were distributed equally, in terms of Barrier and sex, to experimental and control conditions. The experimental group experienced an hour of sensory deprivation while the controls spent an hour alone, with a radio playing and magazines available to read. Pre- and post-Barrier scores were obtained. Gross differences in Barrier changes between the experimental and control groups could not be detected. It is true that sensory deprivation did result in low Barrier subjects changing significantly more (upward) than did high Barrier subjects (downward). But the same significant pattern of change was found in the control group—with the females changing more than the males. Looking at the combined experimental and control groups, it was found that low Barrier subjects gained more Barrier responses than high Barrier subjects lost; and females evidenced greater change than males. Jacobson suggests that the increase in Barrier which occurred in those with vague boundaries is quite analogous to the Reitman and Cleveland observation that sensory deprivation firms up the boundaries of schizophrenics (whom he presumed could be classified as low Barrier). He goes on to note that field dependent persons who perhaps resemble low Barrier subjects to some degree are more restless (anxious) during sensory deprivation than the field independent (high Barrier) and move around more. He adds that such movement during sensory deprivation "might serve to supply the subject with enough tactual and kinesthetic stimulation to increase his awareness of the boundary layers of the body" (p. 50) and therefore increase his post-deprivation Barrier score. From this perspective, the increased Barrier scores of the schizophrenics in the Reitman-Cleveland project and the increased Barrier scores of the poorly bounded normals in the Jacobson experiment might both be due to the augmented muscle feedback in these groups from heightened motoric restlessness.

The greater Barrier changes found by Jacobson in the female as compared to male subjects were interpreted by him as meaning, at one level, that males have a closer identity between body and self than do females and therefore their body perceptions (among which is the sense of boundedness) would be less vulnerable to alteration by sensory deprivation. This interpretation is highly speculative and stands in sharp opposition to Fisher's findings, described elsewhere in this book, which depict the average woman as having a more meaningful identity with her body than does the average man.

Jacobson's findings that normals exposed to sensory deprivation do not differ grossly from controls in pre-post Barrier changes was reaffirmed by Rosenzweig and Gardner (1966). Ten male subjects responded to 22 cards of Form A of the Holtzman ink blots; experienced eight hours of sensory deprivation while listening to white noise; and then responded to 22 cards of Form B of the blots. Ten controls followed the same paradigm, except that they listened to taped jokes and stories during their eight hours of isolation. Ten other controls duplicated the process, but they listened to the taped stories and jokes played backwards. Pre-post difference scores for Barrier and also Penetration were not significantly different among the three conditions. Indeed, only two of the 21 scores that can be derived from the Holtzman (form appropriateness, human) gave significant results in this respect.

Related to this matter of attempting to induce changes in the boundary is a study by Ohzama (1964) in which the effects of alcohol consumption upon the boundaries of normal Japanese students were analyzed. Test-retest Rorschach records were obtained from 39 subjects, such that the first test sometimes occurred during intoxication and the second after recovery from intoxication; or with a reversal of this sequence. Twelve controls were tested and retested without consuming any alcohol. While the results of this study are difficult to determine from the data presented, it would appear that during the alcohol condition Barrier was significantly lower than during the non-alcoholic condition. The Penetration score did not differentiate the two conditions.

McGlothlin, Cohen, and McGlothlin (1966) have offered some data concerning the boundary effects of taking LSD. They were interested in the long-term impact upon normal subjects ($N = 24$ males) of experiencing three sessions during which they were under the influence of 200 mcg. of LSD. Among various other measures used, 30 Holtzman blots were administered prior to the three LSD sessions; 30 more two weeks after the LSD sessions; and 30 more six months later. Analogous blot measures were taken for one group of subjects who experienced three sessions in which they had ingested only 20 mcg. of LSD and for another group which experienced three sessions in which 20 mg. of amphetamine were ingested. Analysis of the data indicated that in the experimental group the shift in Barrier from the pre-LSD test to the test two weeks post-LSD was not significant. However, the shift from pre-LSD to six months post-LSD was significant ($p < .05$). A significant increase in Barrier occurred during this period. McGlothlin, et al. considered this increase, with its presumed implication of greater adaptive strength, to go along with other findings which indicated increased ability to tolerate stress as the result of the LSD experience. For example, it was demonstrated that six months post-LSD there was less GSR response to stress stimuli than there had been during the pre-LSD period. No significant changes in Barrier occurred during the control conditions; and Penetration did not shift significantly during the experimental or control conditions.

DELINQUENCY

Attempts have been made to determine whether boundary disturbance is present in other forms of behavior deviation besides the neurotic and schizophrenic syndromes. Particularly interesting findings have emerged with reference to delinquency and acting-out behavior.

Rhoda Fisher (1966B) contrasted the boundary attributes of 45 normal white boys with those of 46 white boys in a special school program because of their inability to adjust to regular classroom conditions. Inability to adjust was primarily evident in impulsive and aggressive behavior, with associated failure to attain minimum achievement standards. The normal and acting-out groups did not differ significantly in age or religious affiliation. Barrier was measured by means of the Rorschach blots. It was shown that the normal boys had significantly higher Barrier scores than the boys in the special class ($p < .01$).

Similar trends were reported by Megargee (1965). He obtained responses to the Holtzman ink blots from 75 male juvenile delinquents who were in custody. Forty-five were Negro and 30 white. Mean age was 15 and mean IQ 96. The mean Barrier score of the group was significantly lower ($p < .001$) than that of two normal groups collected by Holtzman, et al. (1961). In addition, when the Barrier scores of 28 of the delinquent boys who had been judged as most extreme in terms of constituting a serious threat to the community were compared with the scores of the 44 other boys who were less serious threats, the first were noted to be significantly lower ($p < .001$). During the time that the delinquents were in custody they were rated by two counselors with respect to the amounts and kinds of aggression they displayed. A significant trend was found ($p < .05$) for the Barrier score to be inversely related to aggressiveness. Megargee raised the question whether this result and the fact that delinquents who are overtly so aggressive have lower Barrier scores than normals did not contradict Fisher and Cleveland's original report that high Barrier college students expressed anger outwardly in a frustrating laboratory situation, while low Barrier students expressed it inwardly. That is, why should Barrier be positively linked with aggressive expression in one situation and negatively so in another? Megargee sought to resolve the apparent conflict by pointing out that, "If . . . the Barrier score is regarded as an index of adjustment or fitness rather than as an index of anger, or aggression, the contradiction becomes understandable. It is appropriate for an . . . undergraduate who has been subjected to a deliberately provocative laboratory situation to express anger outwardly in an interview where self-expression is encouraged. On the other hand, it is not adaptive for a juvenile delinquent to express all of his frustrations through socially disapproved aggression up to and including homicide" (p. 310).

Also, Megargee had an interesting point to make in relation to the view that the Barrier score taps an aspect of ego integration which is probably strongly influenced by body feelings and experiences. He indicates that normal adolescents who are typically confused about their identities, particularly as a result of the radical changes occurring in their bodies, have been found in several of Holtzman, et al. studies (1961) to have unusually low Barrier scores. Their scores are actually lower than those of any other non-clinical group. It is a striking coincidence that those who are most caught up in the process of identity transformation and body change should be characterized by the least definite boundaries.

Leeds (1965) hoped, on the basis of boundary differences, to distinguish adolescent male narcotic addicts (N = 30) from adolescent male non-addicted delinquents (N = 30) and adolescent male normal controls (N = 30). All of the subjects he studied were white and their IQ's were within an 80–120 range. A variety of intellectual and personality measures were taken. Barrier scores were determined from responses to individually administered Rorschach blots. The addict group obtained lower Barrier scores than either of the other two groups, but only the difference with reference to the normal controls was statistically significant ($p < .0001$). Further, the non-addicted delinquent group had significantly lower Barrier scores than the normals ($p < .001$). As an additional phase of his study, Leeds secured data from the mothers of all of the adolescent subjects. He reported that the Barrier score medians were of increasing magnitude as one proceeds from the mothers of the addicts (N = 30) to the mothers of the delinquents (N = 30) and then to the mothers of the normals (N = 30). This pattern of Barrier differentiation among the mothers was significant in terms of a Median Test ($p < .05$).

The Barrier scores of the mothers were correlated within each group with the Barrier scores of their sons. The correlation in the addict group was .06; in the delinquent group .30; and in the normal group .28. None of these coefficients are significant. Although with one-tail tests, which might be justified in terms of the fact that Leeds had predicted positive correlations from previous findings by Fisher and Cleveland (1968), the .30 value would be significant at the .05 level and the .28 value would be just short of such significance. Further data and discussion pertinent to child-parent similarities in boundary definiteness will be presented at a later point.

Norma Compton [6] has reported the only data permitting an evaluation of the boundary attributes of delinquent girls. She administered the Rorschach individually to 22 girls in the Utah State Industrial School for delinquents and to a group of normal high school girls matched for age, IQ, economic and ethnic background. Because she had not controlled for response total, she found it necessary to do so by dividing the Barrier scores in each protocol by the total number of responses in that protocol. The Barrier percent scores

---

[6] Personal communication.

so obtained proved not to differentiate significantly between the delinquents and normals. It is of incidental interest that when the preferences of the delinquent girls for various fabrics were measured, it was discovered that those favoring warm colors had significantly lower Barrier scores than those favoring cold colors. One is reminded that McClelland (1961) found need achievement to be positively correlated with preferences for colors in the "cool" spectrum. This is pertinent because Barrier is positively correlated with achievement drive and is in the present instance also positively associated with liking for the cool part of the color spectrum.

Another study by Compton should be described at this point because, apropos of the color preference data just mentioned, it includes information about the relation of the Barrier score to clothing preferences.

Using a group of 30 hospitalized women (23 diagnosed as schizophrenic) Compton (1964) examined the relationship between boundary scores and clothing preferences. She speculated that an individual's clothing may represent an aspect of his body image. She states (p. 40): "Clothing may be considered an extension of the self and can serve as a means of reinforcing body walls or of transforming the body image entirely." It was predicted that (p. 400) "women with concepts of their body boundaries as weak and indefinite may attempt to define these boundaries through clothing choices emphasizing such aspects as large fabric designs, strong figure-ground contrasts, bright colors, rough textures, and maximum body coverage." Clothing and design preferences were determined by showing to individual subjects a series of 93 cards, each containing two 5 in. × 7 in. fabric swatches or dress designs. The subject chose the fabric or design on each card that she would prefer for clothing for herself. The Barrier score (expressed as a per centage of the total number of responses) was negatively and significantly correlated with the choice of bright, saturated clothing colors (p .05) and also clothing fabrics with strong figure contrasts (p .01). Positive and significant correlations appeared between the Penetration percentage and choice of warm color clothing (p .05 level) and also clothing with large designs (p .05 level). Such data led Compton to the following interpretative conclusion (p. 42): "The results of the Clothing Fabric and Design Preference Test indicate that women with low Barrier percentages preferred brighter, more highly saturated colors and stronger figure-ground contrasts in selecting clothing fabrics than women with high percentage of Barrier scores. These results are consistent with the report of Fisher and Cleveland who say that some of their data suggest that in the absence of a body-image capable of supplying a minimum constancy in new situations, the individual finds it necessary to create exterior conditions which will artificially provide a substitute boundary." That is, the choice of clothes with colorful, well articulated designs is seen as an attempt to define and reinforce weak body boundaries.[7]

---

[7] An incidental outcome of this study was the discovery that the subjects' Barrier scores were positively and significantly correlated with their weight-height ratios. The higher the

Further verification of the possible role of clothing in reinforcing the boundary has come from Kernaleguen (1968). She found in a sample of female college students (N = 68) that the Barrier score was negatively and significantly correlated with the degree to which one was regarded by one's peers as a fashion leader. She concluded that low Barrier women used fashionable clothing to bolster weak body boundaries.

Looking back at the studies concerned with delinquency, one can say that there is a consistent trend for male children and adolescents with school adjustment, delinquent, or acting-out problems to manifest poorer boundaries than normal controls. This has been shown in terms of the data collected by R. Fisher on children with school adjustment difficulties, the results presented by Megargee on delinquents in custody, and the Leeds results on adolescent addicts and delinquents. Only the findings for the female delinquents were not consistent with expectation. It is important to ask why more consistent differences were obtained in differentiating male acting-out children and adolescents from normal controls than in distinguishing adult schizophrenics and neurotics from normal controls. One possibility is that disturbance of the acting-out variety, such as characterized the children, is basically more linked with the state of the boundary than is neurotic or schizophrenic disturbance. Perhaps the inability to contain oneself motorically is particularly associated with poorly differentiated boundaries. One could argue that consistent distinguishing results would be found for adults if acting-out criminal groups were compared with normals. This remains to be seen. In any case, one cannot help but be impressed that the acting-out child or adolescent, who lacks the rationalized protection of a rigid delusional system or neurotic pattern, is in a position where he is forcefully given the message that he is a failure and that the culture does not have a meaningful role for him as long as he persists in his "delinquency." In this setting he is unable to muster a sense of real self-importance and this may be a deficit which grossly interferes with boundary formation and maintenance.

MISCELLANEOUS PSYCHOPATHOLOGICAL PHENOMENA

Lester (1967) investigated the hypothesis that psychiatric patients who have attempted suicide would have lower Barrier and higher Penetration scores

---

Barrier score the relatively greater was the body weight in relation to height. Compton pointed out that this was contradictory to the original Fisher-Cleveland work in which Barrier and body type classification had only a chance inter-relationship. However, the fact that her finding was derived from a psychotic rather than normal sample raises questions about its generality. One might wonder whether it was a result of some factor such as the tendency of the more disorganized patients (and perhaps possessing poorer boundaries) to eat less and be more poorly nourished.

than psychiatric patients who were not suicidal. He derived this hypothesis from the assumption that suicide represents directing anger inward against self; whereas the individual with well articulated boundaries seems to be inclined to express anger outwardly. Twenty suicidal patients were matched with 20 non-suicidal patients for sex, age, and psychiatric diagnosis. While the Barrier and Penetration differences between the two groups were in the predicted direction, they did not attain statistical significance. In reviewing the findings, Lester was inclined, on the basis of the existing literature, to conclude that there is no solid evidence that suicides are more likely than others to be typified by a "turning inward" of hostility upon themselves.

Differences in boundary characteristics between high and low anxious normal children have been described by Swartz (1965). Such differences related to anxiety would seem to be pertinent to issues of personality disturbance and psychopathology. Swartz administered the Holtzman blots to 20 pairs of children matched for grade, sex, and IQ. One of each pair was in the lower third of scores on Sarason's Test Anxiety Scale for Children and the other member of the pair was in the upper third. The high anxiety children were found to have significantly lower Barrier scores than the low anxiety children ($p < .05$). Penetration did not distinguish the groups. In a second study Swartz [8] obtained Holtzman blot responses from 60 high and 60 low anxiety children (as defined by the Sarason Test Anxiety Scale for Children) who were once again matched for age, sex, and IQ. Using one-tailed tests, which would be justified in a cross-validation effort, it was found that the high anxiety children had significantly lower Barrier and higher Penetration scores than the low anxiety children. The consistency of the findings over two studies is noteworthy.

Epstein [9] compared the boundary scores of a group of 13 English children with school phobias with those of a group of normal controls. The children with school phobias had lower Barrier ($p < .05$) and higher Penetration scores ($p < .10$) than the normals. Epstein also noted that the school phobia group had higher body awareness (as defined by the Secord Homonym test) than the normals ($p < .001$).

Exploratory attention has been directed to boundary phenomena in alcoholics. Cleveland and Sikes (1966) assessed Barrier and Penetration score differences between 70 male chronic alcoholics in a Veterans Administration hospital treatment program and 50 non-alcoholic, non-psychotic psychiatric patients at the same hospital. The Barrier score did not distinguish them; but Penetration was significantly higher (p .02) in the alcoholics than non-alcoholics. Following a 90 day treatment program which focused on group therapy, no changes in Barrier or Penetration occurred.

[8] Personal communication.
[9] Personal communication from Edward Epstein.

In a second study Cleveland and Sikes [10] found that in a sample of 146 alcoholics who participated in a 90 day group therapy oriented program there was a significant increase (p .001) in Barrier from pre- to post-therapy. The varying results of the two studies just cited do not suggest consistency in the relationship of Barrier to alcoholic behavior.

[10] Personal communication from Sidney Cleveland.

14
Parental Characteristics and Boundary Definiteness

INTRODUCTION

Having isolated a meaningful personality variable, one is drawn to the quest of determining how it evolves developmentally. One would like to know what experiences in the process of growing up are most influential in boundary formation. If it is assumed that the child's interactions with his parents play the major role in shaping him, it becomes a matter of importance to trace and define how his boundary characteristics are related to the attributes of his parents.

Previous attempts have been made in this direction. Fisher and Cleveland (1968) looked at two pertinent issues: (1) the extent of Barrier similarity among family members; (2) the correlations between certain parent attributes and the Barrier scores of their children. Similarities in Barrier among family members proved to be limited. A low positive relationship was found between spouses in a psychiatric population (rho = .25, N = 54, p < .10). Similarly, in this population a low borderline relationship (rho = .42, N = 16, p < .10) was observed between the average of mother and father Barrier scores and the Barrier scores of their adolescent (ages 11–17) children. Correlations between the parental Barrier scores and the scores of their pre-adolescent (ages four–ten) chidren were of a chance order. The Barrier scores of the children in the sample were also studied with reference to certain indices derived from Rorschach and TAT protocols obtained from their parents. The indices included measures of personal maladjustment and rigidity based on Rorschach patterns [Fisher Maladjustment and Rigidity Scores (Fisher, 1950)] and evaluations of achievement orientation and feelings about family closeness as judged from TAT productions. The mothers of children with definite boundaries were shown to exceed significantly the mothers of children with indefinite boundaries in personal integration, flexibility, achievement orientation, and sense of family closeness. Results involving the fathers were not differentiating.

From these findings and also certain qualitative aspects of the children's projective responses it was concluded that poor boundary formation was most likely to occur when an individual had parents (particularly mothers) who were not only poorly integrated and rigid but who, in addition, chronically conveyed the intent of intruding upon him in a "threatening, destructive, and disrupting" fashion.

FURTHER FAMILY RESEARCH

Since the completion of the work just described, Fisher and Fisher (1967) collected from a series of families data which are pertinent to the matter of how parents' attitudes may influence the boundaries of their children. These data were a by-product of a large project concerned with two prime problems: similarities in personality and body image among family members (e.g., sib versus sib, mother versus father); parental attributes predictive of offspring characteristics. Entire families living in Syracuse, New York, were studied. In each family the father, mother, and children were evaluated. They were recruited by offering sums of money to such organizations as church groups and boy scout and girl scout troops. Special efforts were made to reduce volunteering effects by giving bonuses if a large proportion of an organization participated. Forty-five Jewish and 73 Protestant families participated. The parents were seen in group sessions typically involving five–eight couples. All children in the age range seven–11 were evaluated individually, but those in the 12–17 range were seen in groups varying in size from three to eight. The children's Barrier scores were obtained by asking them to produce two percepts for each Rorschach blot. Response total was limited to 20 because many of the younger subjects had difficulty in producing a greater number. Parental Barrier scores were based on the usual sample of 25 Rorschach responses. Aside from the ink blots, there was administered to each child the Secord Homonym test (designed to tap body awareness) and measures of accuracy in estimating the size of one's own body.[1] There was administered to each parent (in addition to the ink blots) procedures intended to scan a spectrum of personal variables which might possibly play a part in the child's boundary formation. These procedures included: Parental Attitude Research Instrument [2] which presumably evaluates child rearing attitudes (Schaefer

---

[1] Only the Barrier results will be considered here.

[2] This was a modification of the PARI Chorost (1962) designed so that it could be administered to both mothers and fathers.

and Bell, 1958); the Allport-Vernon-Lindzey (1960) Study of Values which determines the intensity of one's values in six different areas (e.g., Religious, Theoretical, Economic); and the Thurstone (1953) Temperament Schedule which involves self evaluation in relation to seven trait dimensions (e.g., Impulsivity, Vigor, Dominance).

SPOUSE AND SIB SIMILARITIES IN BOUNDARY DEFINITENESS

The correlation between Barrier scores of spouses was found to be of the same low order as previously observed. For all spouses in the total sample the coefficient was .13. In the Jewish sample (N = 45) the correlation was .36 ($p < .03$), but in the Protestant sample (N = 73) it was non-significant (.08).

When, for all possible families (N = 59) in which there were multiple children of the required ages, the Barrier score of the youngest child in the seven–11 range was correlated with the score of the youngest in the 12–17 range, the coefficient was .02. A more detailed analysis within sex groups indicated a correlation of .47 ($p < .10$) for boys seven–11 versus boys 12–17 (N = 12). The equivalent correlation for girls (N = 26) was −.13. Apparently, sib similarity in boundary definiteness is, with the exception of the borderline relationship cited for brothers, largely negligible.

PARENT–CHILD RELATIONSHIPS

The Barrier scores of the mothers were not significantly correlated with those of their male or female children at either of the two different age levels (i.e., seven–11 and 12–17).[3] However, the fathers' scores tended to be positively correlated with those of their sons in the seven–11 range ($r = .21, p > .10$) and with those of their daughters in the seven–11 group ($r = .26, p < .05$). None of the other correlations involving fathers and children were significant. These results go along with the previously reported Fisher-Cleveland finding of rather low correlations between parents and child for Barrier.

Similar low relationships have been described by Leeds (1965) who examined Barrier similarities between mothers and their adolescent sons who were classified into three groups: drug addicts (N = 30), delinquents (N = 30), and normals (N = 30). The correlations between mothers and

---

[3] Whenever reference is made in this section to a sample of children of a given age level, this means that the sample is composed of the youngest child in each family who falls within that age level.

sons were not statistically significant in any of the groups. Two of the correlations did approach significance. In the delinquent group the rho correlation was .30 (p =.10) and in the normal group it was .28, which is just short of the .10 level.

Also, Rhoda Fisher [4] found in a sample of 26 boys with severe school

Table 14.1
Correlations of Barrier Scores Among Family Members

	Total Group
Father vs. Mother	.13
Father vs.	
Son (7–11) (N = 47)	.21
Son (12–17) (N = 46)	−.06
Daughter (7–11) (N = 60)	.26 (p < .05)
Daughter (12–17) (N = 62)	−.14
All Children Combined	
Youngest child (7–11) (N = 93)	.24 (p .025)
Youngest child (12–17) (N = 80)	−.11
Mother vs.	
Son (7–11) (N = 47)	−.03
Son (12–17) (N = 46)	−.02
Daughter (7–11) (N = 60)	.13
Daughter (12–17) (N = 62)	−.07
All Children Combined	
Youngest child (7–11) (N = 93)	.10
Youngest child (12–17) (N = 80)	−.03
Sibs 7–11 vs. Sibs 12–17 (N = 59)	.02
Male Sibs 7–11 vs. Male Sibs 12–17 (N = 12)	.47 (p < .10)
Female Sibs 7–11 vs. Female Sibs 12–17 (N = 26)	−.13
Father–Mother Average vs.	
Son (7–11) (N = 47)	.10
Son (12–17) (N = 46)	−.06
Daughter (7–11) (N = 60)	.23 (p < .10)
Daughter (12–17) (N = 62)	−.11
All Children Combined	
Youngest child (7–11) (N = 93)	.20 (p .05)
Youngest child (12–17) (N = 80)	−.08

adjustment problems that their Barrier scores were not significantly correlated with those of the mothers (r = −.03).

When the data in the present study are considered with reference to the Leeds and the Fisher results just cited and also the earlier Fisher and Cleveland findings, it seems rather well demonstrated that, in a broad sense, the Barrier attributes of a child cannot be predicted from those of his parents. There are trends for positive relationships to exist, but they are slight.

[4] Unpublished data.

STUDY OF VALUES

Some of the parental Study of Value measures were predictive of Barrier

Table 14.2
Correlation of Mother and Father Study of Value Scores with their Children's Barrier Scores

	Theoretical	Economic	Aesthetic	Social	Political	Religious
Father vs.						
Boys 7–11 (N = 43)	−.13	−.20	.47 ***	.09	.04	−.18
Boys 12–17 (N = 46)	.28 *	−.11	.13	.04	−.01	−.10
Girls 7–11 (N = 55)	.05	.05	.04	−.14	.04	−.06
Girls 12–17 (N = 55)	−.08	−.17	.06	.06	.05	.08
Mother vs.						
Boys 7–11 (N = 44)	−.30 **	−.31 **	.28	.30 **	.00	.02
Boys 12–17 (N = 49)	.22	−.26	.21	.03	−.10	−.12
Girls 7–11 (N = 60)	.03	.13	.11	.07	−.04	−.18
Girls 12–17 (N = 55)	.03	−.12	.20	.06	−.08	−.07
Average of Mother and Father vs.						
Boys 7–11 (N = 42)	−.32 **	−.32 **	.45 ***	.22	.02	−.07
Boys 12–17 (N = 46)	.29 **	−.19	.20	.07	−.08	−.10
Girls 7–11 (N = 53)	.10	.08	.12	−.05	−.04	−.13
Girls 12–17 (N = 52)	−.08	−.14	.13	.06	−.09	.04

     * p .05
    ** $p < .05$
   *** $p < .01$

levels in their children. This was primarily true in terms of correlations between parents' scores and those of their sons in the seven–11 age range. The father's Aesthetic score was positively correlated ($r = .47, p < .001$) with his son's (age seven–11) Barrier score; and the mother's Aesthetic score was likewise correlated with her son's Barrier ($r = .28, p < .10$). The average of the mother and father Aesthetic scores was correlated .45 ($p < .01$) with son's Barrier. In addition, mother's Theoretical and Economic scores were negatively correlated ($−.30, p < .05; −.31, p < .05$) and her Social score positively correlated ($r = .30, p < .05$) with son's Barrier. The average of mother and father's Theoretical scores and also the average of their Economic scores were negatively related to son's Barrier ($r = −.32, p < .05; r = −.32, p < .05$).

The data for the boys 12–17 revealed much less of significance. Father's Theoretical score was positively correlated with the boy's Barrier ($r = .28, p$ .05); mother's Theoretical was likewise correlated, but the coefficient was only .22. An average of mother and father Theoretical scores was clearly related to child's Barrier ($r = .29$, p .05). Also, a borderline negative relationship between mother's Economic and boy's Barrier ($r = -.26$, $p < .10$) appeared.

None of the father or mother Study of Value scores were significantly correlated with daughter's Barrier at either the seven–11 or 12–17 age levels.

What has emerged most clearly from the data is the fact that the greater the Aesthetic interests of mothers and fathers the greater is the boundary definiteness of their sons in the seven–11 range. But the greater their Theoretical or Economic interests the less definite are their sons' boundaries. To appraise the implications of these findings it would be well to review the definitions of the Study of Value dimensions involved.

The person with a high Aesthetic score is considered to be one who is interested in "grace, symmetry, or fitness." He finds his "chief interest in the artistic episodes of life." He is dedicated to beauty and the enjoyment of impressions. For the Theoretical person the "dominant interest . . . is the discovery of truth. . . . He takes a cognitive attitude . . . he is necessarily an intellectualist. . . . His chief aim in life is to order and systematize his knowledge." Finally, the Economic man is "interested in what is *useful*. . . . This type is thoroughly 'practical' and conforms well to the prevailing stereotype of the average American businessman" (Allport, Vernon, Lindzey, 1960, pp. 4–5). It is pertinent to note that Allport, Vernon, and Lindzey regard both the Economic and Theoretical orientations as opposed to the Aesthetic position.

If one integrates these definitions, it would appear that parents with strong interests in cognitive abstractions and the economic uses of objects and materials have sons (seven–11) with poor boundaries; whereas parents with interests in the artistic and all that is linked with the term have sons who possess well articulated boundaries. Such a pattern is congruent with previous studies by Fisher and Cleveland (1968) in which it was observed that persons with indefinite boundaries tend to be particularly interested in things and abstractions and those with definite boundaries to be strongly oriented toward persons, communication with others, and the appreciation of artistic-aesthetic experiences. That is, when qualities previously found associated with definite or indefinite boundaries occurred in parents they were accompanied by correspondingly definite or indefinite boundaries in the parents' children. Within the limits of the relationship between parents and their seven–11 year old sons these facts fit together well; and offer a picture in which basic parental value orientations pertaining to the personal vs. impersonal possibly influence the boundary characteristics of their sons.

But, unfortunately, some of the other findings indicate that such a simple formulation is incomplete. One is confronted with the fact that for boys 12–17 the Barrier score is positively correlated with fathers' and mothers' Theoretical scores. This is a reversal of what would be expected. The occurrence of the reversal for both mothers and fathers argues against it being a chance phenomenon. Of course, an additional complication is that parental values do not predict Barrier levels in their daughters at any age. It is possible that the principles governing the influence of parents upon their children's boundaries differ for sons and daughters. Even further, it is possible that parental traits which affect the child's boundary in one direction during pre-adolescence have the opposite impact in the adolescent phase. We have no way of knowing until further information accumulates.

THURSTONE TEMPERAMENT SCALE

Scores derived from the Thurstone Temperament Scale which had been administered to the parents proved to have largely chance relationships with the Barrier scores of their children. This represents one more instance in which personality or trait measures derived from paper and pencil techniques have failed to be meaningfully related to boundary variables.

MOVEMENT RESPONSES

One index, aside from Barrier, was derived from all parents' Rorschach protocols. It was the human movement score (M). The M score was selected because it is the only Rorschach determinant which has consistently shown itself to be positively related to the Barrier index. Quite convincing evidence has accumulated that M is a measure of the ability to delay motor response and to postpone immediate gratification; and it has actually been demonstrated in one study to be positively correlated with build-up of muscular tension as measured by muscle potential levels (Shipman, et al., 1964). The fact that M is associated with Barrier and also with muscle potential level, which is one of the most dependable physiological correlates of Barrier, suggested that it might represent a factor relevant to boundary formation. One could specu-late, for example, that a parent with high M, who would presumably tend to delay response rather than act impulsively and who could tolerate heightened muscle activation rather than seeking quick release, would provide for his children a model of response delay and monitored self containment of tension in the musculature. Since the musculature contributes an important part of the feeling of body boundedness, learning such a pattern of tolerance for muscle activation might serve to highlight and emphasize the child's boundaries.

In the family data one finds that father's M was positively correlated ($r = .29$, $p = .05$) with his son's Barrier score in the seven–11 age range; and there was a similar correlation between mother's M and son's Barrier ($r = .35$, $p < .03$). The average of mother's and father's M was correlated

.40 ($p < .01$) with son's Barrier. However, neither father's nor mother's M was related to Barrier in sons 12–17 or in daughters of any age level. The expectation regarding parent M and the child's Barrier score was supported only with reference to boys seven–11. Within this limited group the support was strong because significant results were obtained for the relation of both mother's and father's M scores to the child's Barrier.

These findings are interesting but fragmentary. They only whet one's appetite and raise the same troublesome questions that appeared with reference to the relationships of parents' Study of Value scores to their children's Barrier scores. Once again one must ask why there are significant correlations only when one considers boys in the seven–11 range and why no results of significance appear for either of the daughter samples.

PARENTAL ATTITUDE RESEARCH INSTRUMENT

A modification by Chorost (1962) of the Parental Attitude Research Instrument (PARI) was administered to each parent. It is a 115 item forced-choice questionnaire which was devised to measure child rearing attitudes and to be applicable to both mothers and fathers. In adapting the original PARI scale, care was taken to minimize any style or content changes. The respondent was asked to answer each item with one of four alternative choices: strongly agree, mildly agree, mildly disagree, strongly disagree.

Two basic factor scores were derived in terms of previous findings (Zuckerman, Barrett-Ribback, and Monashkin, 1958; Schaefer and Bell, 1957; Schaefer, 1959). The first, labeled Authoritarian Control, was determined from responses to the following ten subscales (each containing five statements):

1. Excluding Outside Influences
2. Deification of the Parent
3. Intrusiveness
4. Suppression of Sex
5. Breaking the Will
6. Approval of Activity
7. Fostering Dependency
8. Suppression of Aggression
9. Avoidance of Communication
10. Ascendancy of Parent

The second factor score, Parental Warmth, was represented by two subscales:

1. Irritability
2. Marital Conflict

The factor scores permit an evaluation, based on self reporting, of how authoritarian and also how cold the parent is in his dealings with his children. There are a number of limitations of this approach to measuring child rearing attitudes, one of the chief of which is the fact that test taking attitudes (e.g., social desirability) may significantly affect patterns of response.

Neither the mother's nor father's Authoritarian and Coldness scores were related to son's Barrier at any age level.[5] Mother's Authoritarian and Coldness scores were also unrelated to daughter's Barrier at any age level.

Table 14.3
Correlations of Parents' PARI Scores with Children's Barrier Scores

	Authoritarian	Cold
Father vs.		
Boys 7–11 (N = 48)	−.20	.06
Boys 12–17 (N = 47)	−.07	−.06
Girls 7–11 (N = 61)	−.20	−.01
Girls 12–17 (N = 62)	−.23 *	.19
Mother vs.		
Boys 7–11 (N = 49)	−.04	−.10
Boys 12–17 (N = 50)	−.11	−.14
Girls 7–11 (N = 63)	−.03	.17
Girls 12–17 (N = 67)	.09	.08
Mother and Father vs.		
Boys 7–11 (N = 48)	−.16	−.04
Boys 12–17 (N = 47)	−.12	−.18
Girls 7–11 (N = 61)	−.13	.10
Girls 12–17 (N = 62)	−.09	.19

$* p < .10$

While father's Coldness score was not correlated with daughter's Barrier, his Authoritarian score was negatively correlated with it both at the seven–11 and 12–17 age levels ($r = -.20$, $p < .10$; $r = -.23$, $p < .10$). These correlations are borderline but worth noting because they both involve father and daughter.

An appraisal was also made of the relationships between the parents' PARI subscale scores and their children's Barrier scores. Since there are 26 PARI subscales, a large array of correlations is involved. To simplify the survey of results, only those findings will be mentioned which have the same

[5] Tolor and Jalowiec (1968) asked male college students to respond to the PARI "as you think your mother would have rated it"; and found that the resultant scores had only chance correlations with Barrier. They also reported that the Rotter (1966) Internal-External scale, which presumably taps beliefs concerning whether rewards or reinforcements are contingent upon one's own behavior or are independent of it, was not significantly correlated with Barrier.

significant (or nearly so) directionality in at least two of the eight possible correlational categories.

Few significant correlations are to be found between the Barrier scores of boys and the PARI subscores of their parents. There was a trend for the Foster Dependency subscore to be correlated negatively with the Barrier scores of boys in the seven–11 range. For father vs. son the correlation was —.46 ($p <$ .001) and for mother vs. son it was —.22 (just short of .10 level). The Foster Dependency category is exemplified by statements like "A parent should do his best to avoid any disappointment for his child" and "A child should be protected from jobs which might be too tiring or hard on him." Parents who endorsed the view that children should be carefully protected had sons with relatively low Barrier scores. One other trend observed with reference to the seven–11 boys involved a negative relationship between their Barrier scores and fathers' Suppression of Sex PARI score ($r =$ —.30, $p <$ .05). For the 12–17 boys there was an analogous borderline correlation with mother's Suppression of Sex score ($r =$ —.24, $p =$ .10). Those parents who endorsed statements like "A young child should be protected from hearing about sex" had sons with vague boundaries. Of course, these few significant results and others to be described below could easily be due to chance. They are mainly cited as possible leads for future exploration.

Several consistencies in results were observed with reference to the girls. Father's Avoidance of Affection PARI scores were negatively correlated with Barrier scores of daughters seven–11 ($r =$ —.32, $p =$ .01) and also daughters 12–17 ($r =$ —.29, $p =$ .03). Daughters with low Barrier scores were likely to have fathers who supported such statements as the following: "Kissing and tender treatment of children should be kept within limits if children are to develop properly" and "It's quite possible for a parent to overdo love and affection for children."

Daughters' Barrier scores were negatively related to fathers' Deification PARI scores. For the seven–11 category the correlation was —.24 ($p <$ .05) and for the 12–17 category it was —.27 ($p <$ .03). The more that fathers supported the following statements the less definite were the boundaries of their daughters: "More parents should teach their children to have unquestioning loyalty to them" and "A child soon learns that there is no greater wisdom than that of his parents."

Daughters' Barrier scores were also negatively related to Fathers' Excluding Outside Influences PARI scores. With respect to the seven–11 category the correlation was —.21 ($p =$ .10); and for the 12–17 group it was —.25 ($p =$ .05). The less definite a daughter's boundaries the more her father endorsed the following sorts of sentiments: "It's best for the child if he never gets started wondering whether his parents' views are right" and "There is no excusing someone who upsets the confidence a child has in his parents' way of doing things."

There was one other trend involving girls and their fathers which should

be mentioned. Barrier scores of girls seven–11 were negatively and significantly correlated with their fathers' Martyrdom scores ($r = -.30, p = .03$);
while Barrier scores of girls 12–17 were also negatively, although not significantly, related to Fathers' Martyrdom scores ($r = -.18, p > .10$). Fathers
of low Barrier girls tended to agree with such statements as "Children should
realize how much parents have to give up for them" and "A parent must
expect to give up his own happiness for that of his child."

Strangely, the mothers' individual PARI scores showed no consistency
in their relationships to their children's Barrier scores. Only with reference
to the PARI variable, Encouraging Verbalization, was there more than one
significant correlation. Mothers' scores for this variable were positively
correlated with sons' Barrier in the 12–17 category ($r = .28, p < .05$) and
also daughters' Barrier in the 12–17 range ($r = .23, p = .05$). Children with
definite boundaries had mothers who agreed with statements such as:
"Children should be allowed to disagree with their parents if they feel their
own ideas are better" and "Children should be encouraged to tell parents
about it whenever they feel family rules are unreasonable."

While all of the findings described above could be attributed to chance,
it is worth while to consider their tenor. Most of the statistically significant
results involved comparisons of fathers and their daughters. The father who
favors a non-authoritarian, affectionate approach to one's children which
allows them full access to outside views and does not expect them to feel
unusually obligated to, or in awe of, their parents is perhaps the one most
likely to encourage clear boundaries in his daughter. Poor boundaries in a
daughter seem to go along with a father who is controlling and impersonal
and who wants to relate in terms of his own special right to expect obedience
or feelings of obligation. The other results which were cited have similar
implications. That is, the Barrier scores of sons in the seven–11 category
were negatively related to how much the parents favored treating them
in a dependent, over-protective fashion; and the Barrier scores of boys
in the 12–17 range were negatively related to the degree to which the parents
felt they should be protected against obtaining sexual information. Finally,
there was a trend for children in the 12–17 category to have high Barrier
scores if their mothers felt they should have the right to disagree with their
parents.

COMMENTS

Despite a major effort to determine how parents' traits and attitudes
possibly influence their children's boundary attributes, limited clarification
has emerged. There are hints and leads but few solid generalizations. Most of
the significant findings have involved relationships between parents and boys

in the seven–11 age range. A tendency was also observed for fathers' scores to be more correlated with those of their children than is true of mothers'.

Cutting across sex and age groupings, one may say that there are trends for the parent with definite boundaries, high M, high Aesthetic interests, low Economic interests, and low degree of Authoritarianism in child rearing practices to have children with the most definite boundaries. As earlier mentioned, these trends resemble findings in previous exploratory studies in which parents of children with definite boundaries were noted to be particularly oriented toward personal human contact and free non-rigid modes of response.[6]

[6] Rhoda Fisher (1966C) has indirectly reinforced the probable existence of a link between the state of the child's boundary and his parents' characteristics by showing that boundary changes in children undergoing a therapeutic experience were related to the hostility levels of their mothers. Nineteen male children with severe school adjustment problems who were of elementary school age were studied. They were enrolled in a special program designed to provide them with support, therapeutic contact, and individual classroom attention. The Rorschach (two responses per card) was administered individually at the outset of the program and again one year later. At the outset, the mothers of these children were also seen and their responses to the Buss-Durkee Hostility Scale were obtained. When the total hostility score of the mother was related to change in Barrier shown by her son during the therapy process, a correlation of $-.59$ ($p < .01$) was found. The more hostile the child's mother the less likely he was to develop firmer boundaries. One could interpret this finding to mean that when a mother is typified by an angry aggressive attitude she interferes with any boundary reinforcement her child receives from a special therapeutic milieu. However, since the mother's hostility score was not related to the child's initial Barrier score, one cannot assume a simple model in which the child's boundary articulation is inverse to his mother's aggression level. One can only say that when a disturbed child is provided with therapeutic conditions his ability to "repair" his boundaries will be negatively influenced if his mother is an angry (and presumably an attacking and disruptive) person.

15
Negative Results

In the process of looking for new areas of application for the Barrier score, the present author has correlated it with a number of variables which proved not to be meaningfully related. Such negative results will be briefly reviewed in order to caution those who might contemplate work on similar problems.

The possibility has been investigated that the boundary plays a role in the individual's perception of his body size. It was originally conjectured that those with vague boundaries might feel without "limits" or "spread out" and therefore inclined to overestimate their size. However, the Barrier score did not turn out to be consistently correlated (in normal or schizophrenic subjects) with estimates of self height, shoulder width, hip width, stomach size, head width, and mouth width. Shontz [1] has reported similar negative findings.

It should be noted too that the size dimensions of human figure drawings have failed to be consistently correlated with Barrier.

The hypothesis was evaluated that persons who smoke heavily might be seeking oral reassurance to counter feelings of body inadequacy and vulnerability. In a series of ten samples of normal subjects the Barrier score has on three occasions been negatively correlated with number of cigarettes smoked per day. However, in the other seven samples the coefficients were of a chance order.

Rhoda Fisher (1966B) has shown in a sample of children that the Kagan Conceptual vs. Reflective Cognitive categories are not related to Barrier.

No relationships have been observed by the author between Barrier and the following: ethnic background, religious affiliation, degree of religious interest, frequency of church attendance, frequency of church attendance of one's parents.

It has been a temptation to isolate a particular "problem area" or

---

[1] Shontz, F. C. Unpublished final progress report (for grants RD814P and RD1590P, Department of Health, Education and Welfare) entitled "Perception of Distance on the Body."

psychodynamic theme which would distinguish the well bounded from the poorly bounded. One would like to be able to say that conflict about a given issue (e.g., dependency, hostility) plays an important role in how a person structures his boundaries. There are clinical papers which propose such possibilities. Several studies involving normal subjects have been completed by the author in which the Barrier score was correlated with thresholds for perception of tachistoscopically presented pictures of themes relating to hostility, dependency, heterosexuality, and homosexuality. Similar studies have been done in which the same pictures have been presented to subjects in the Ames Thereness-Thatness apparatus (Hastorf, 1950) which measures emotional response in terms of the sizes assigned to pictures. Consistent correlations between Barrier and responses to given dynamic themes could not be demonstrated. These results add weight to other findings which indicate more and more that multiple factors influence boundary attributes.

16
Review, Formulation, and Speculation

GENERAL REVIEW

About ten years have intervened since the first presentation of the Barrier concept. These years have seen a rapid accumulation of information concerning its validity and utility. With only limited exceptions, the new research findings have corroborated previous reports and formulations. The nature of the body image boundary has come into increasingly clearer focus. Its properties have been precisely defined; subjected to careful measurement; and related to numerous meaningful parameters.

Let us review some of the chief accomplishments of the work that has been described in this chapter. There is now an abundance of evidence that the Barrier index can be scored with high objectivity and that it is acceptably stable over time. Major progress has occurred in pinpointing the immediate "origin" of the Barrier type percept. Contrary to speculations that it might be an expression of "response style" or other variables without body image significance, converging experiments have shown that it is a function of the clarity with which the individual experiences the boundary regions of his body. The fact that the Barrier score is anchored in body experience is reaffirmed by several lines of observation. It is (1) correlated with reports of the relative frequencies of sensations at exterior and interior body sites; (2) related to selective memory for words referring to exterior versus interior sensations; (3) apparently influential in determining the occurrence of placebo-induced exterior versus interior symptoms; (4) correlated with differential ability to distinguish pictures of exterior and interior body regions presented tachistoscopically; and (5) systematically alterable by changing the individual's usual patterns of attention to his body. More indirectly, the pertinence of body phenomena to Barrier has been pointed up by its correlations with body anxiety, body awareness, and exterior versus interior differences in physiological reactivity and psychosomatic symptom formation. It is also a matter of related interest that while Barrier predicts tolerance for various types of stress, it has been particularly successful in predicting reactions to stress associated with the disablement of one's own body. Few, if any, other indices are intimately linked with body response at so many different levels.

Despite an abundance of data indicating that the Barrier score is linked to body experience phenomena, some have continued to speculate that it can be explained in terms that do not involve body perception. They seek a simple cognitive or "response style" variable as a prime explanatory concept. Kagan, et al. (1964), for example, indicated the belief that the Barrier response was only an expression of a more general tendency to give clear, well articulated responses. In fact, they specified that it represented the same sort of articulated mode of response that they had found to be associated with a specific cognitive approach (Reflective). However, R. Fisher (1966B) found a chance correlation between the Kagan, et al. Reflective measure and the Barrier score. It is worth repeating for emphasis that Barrier has not shown consistent relationships with any response style or cognitive measure. The burden of proof therefore rests strongly upon those who would assert the existence of such relationships.

The accumulated findings have also reaffirmed the original view regarding the trait structure and general personal orientation of those with well versus poorly articulated boundaries. In terms of earlier work, it had been proposed that with increasing boundary definiteness a person can more clearly see himself as an individual possessing differentiated identity and can act in a more autonomous "self steering" fashion. Those with definite boundaries were depicted as having special interest in attainment; strong intent to preserve independence; and enhanced ability to function adequately under difficult circumstances. This portrayal has been supported by data indicating that the Barrier score is positively correlated with achievement drive in both adults and children; positively related to clarity of identity as defined by interviewer evaluations; negatively correlated with measures of yielding, suggestibility, and hypnotic susceptibility; and positively related to effectiveness in coping with stress in laboratory and real life situations. Almost paradoxical in the face of this association between boundary definiteness and self affirmation is the continuing demonstration that the Barrier score is correlated with being communicative and sensitive to the needs of others in small group situations. As already described, there are several new studies in which it has been ascertained that boundary definiteness is positively related to frequency of initiating messages to others in a group, communicativeness in an interview setting, and acceptance by other group members. The person with clear boundaries seems to take the initiative in group interchange and to seek an integrative role.

Speaking broadly, it would appear that as boundary delineation becomes sharper there is corresponding individuation which has protective functions, but not in the sense of sealing oneself off from others or retiring behind a heavy fortified line of defense. There is individuation which provides self-confidence and the ability to function as an independent unit, but at the same time it encourages sensitivity to, and interest in, others. Perhaps the very fact of feeling clearly bounded provides the security needed to communicate easily and to initiate contacts spontaneously.

The well articulated boundary seems to make for alert receptivity toward one's environs. This is true in terms of responsiveness to others and perhaps at simpler sensory levels, such as exemplified by the earlier described fact that Barrier is positively correlated with the ability to make fine discriminations among color hues. Findings from the use of the Thereness-Thatness technique indicate too that with increased boundary definiteness perceptual events are experienced with greater vividness. Results from several sources have demonstrated that there is a physiological analogue for boundary differentiation; and this analogue offers assistance in understanding the alert receptivity apparently associated with the clearly defined boundary. The Barrier score has shown itself to be positively related to arousal levels in those body areas most directly in contact with, and involved in communication with, the environment. It is positively linked with measures of activation of skin, muscle, and peripheral vasculature (e.g., GSR, muscle potential). By contrast, it is negatively related to indices of internal activation (e.g., heart rate). One may presume that the arousal of "exterior" body layers results in an intensified "tuning in" on what is occurring in one's vicinity. Actually, support for this statement is provided by the work of Lacey (in Rubenstein and Parloff, 1959), Obrist, et al. (1963), and others which indicates that during the time an individual is oriented to receive information from "outside" he manifests heightened skin and diminished heart activity; but when his attention is turned inward the physiological pattern is of a reversed character. It has been proposed that the physiological events themselves may serve to facilitate or inhibit sensory input. If so, one can take the view that the state of an individual's boundaries, with its accompanying exterior versus interior physiological levels of arousal, fosters chronic positive or negative conditions for receiving "outside" information.

The physiological differences associated with boundary variation have manifested themselves in adults, adolescents, and even in one sample of children. They have been detected in spontaneous autonomic patterns, conditioned responses, and reactions to specific chemical agents (e.g., histamine). They have at various times been picked up via heart response, blood pressure, peripheral vascular changes, GSR, and muscle potential measured at numerous sites. Relatedly, correlations between Barrier and outside versus inside psychosomatic symptom patterns have been reported in both children and adults. These correlations have appeared for minor complaints in the normal range and serious syndromes of an incapacitating intensity. Such symptoms as the following have been investigated in this context: rheumatoid arthritis, Legg-Calve-Perthes disease, eczema, stomach ulcers, colitis, and contact dermatitis. While it is true that a number of studies have not confirmed the relationship between Barrier and exterior vs. interior reactivity and symptom occurrence, the large majority have been supportive. But at the same time, the negative exceptions should not be dismissed. They may indicate weakness or limitations in the exterior-interior model. Only further work can clarify this matter.

Within the normal range, the Barrier score seems to have potential for predicting response to demanding stress. Indeed, the more severe the stress condition the more does boundary definiteness mediate adequacy of coping behavior. Ability to adjust to one of the most traumatic of life stresses, viz., the serious incapacitation of one's own body, has been consistently correlated with boundary definiteness in four different studies. The equation of clear boundaries with stress tolerance easily leads to the thought that there should be a meaningful correspondence between the state of the boundary and personal disorganization as represented by neurotic and schizophrenic symptomatology. However, while there are trends for those who are psychiatric patients to have relatively poorly articulated boundaries, there are also abundant examples of patients who demonstrate well structured boundaries, even as they grossly distort reality.[1] This is particularly true of paranoid schizophrenics and those with symptoms of grandiosity. It was this fact which suggested that boundary maintenance need not be based on attitudes or perceptions which are consensually validated. Apparently, if a person feels that he is significant and can see importance for himself in the scheme of things, e.g., as defined by a paranoid construction, this provides him with the security required for boundary maintenance, even if the assumptions underlying the sense of importance are bizarre to others.

There are hints here and there that the boundary may be further involved in such diversity as: response to separation from home, anxiety generated by a medical examination, capacity to tolerate pain, willingness to seek medical attention, behavior upon awakening in the morning, clothing preferences, willingness to reveal information about oneself, understanding of one's own motives, choice of friends, masculinity-femininity, manner in which one's emotions are experienced, and so forth. Each of these areas is

---

[1] Witkin, et al. (1954) have relatedly pointed out that individuation and "developed differentiation," as measured by their techniques, may occur in patients who are so disturbed that they require hospitalization.

One should also note that Federn (1952), in his formulations concerning ego boundaries in schizophrenia, suggested that while such boundaries may become very fluid during the early stages of regression, they could at later points of the regressive process be re-established in a rigid, firm fashion—but encompassing a smaller area of the individual's self structure.

worth further exploration and thought. In their diversity they dramatize the pervasive influence of the boundary. Without doubt, the way in which an individual delimits the area of space occupied by his body will have continuing consequences for him. The clarity with which he can experience a line of demarcation between his body and the contiguous world will color many facets of his life. We know that it will affect the sensory "quality" of his body, the experiential prominence of various body sectors, and probably how secure he feels about the capacity of his body to resist intrusion and damage. We also know that it will exert selective effects upon perception of the outside world and the vigor with which one engages other persons and objects. Further, we can speculate that it will influence the manner in which excitation is channeled to different body areas and the probability that psychosomatic symptoms will develop at certain body sites. There are few levels of experience and overt behavior that are not at least tangentially influenced by boundary conditions.

ISSUES AND PROBLEMS

What is the Boundary?

Boundary definiteness is measured in terms of certain qualities of ink blot images. But how does the boundary actually exist? Is it a pattern of body experiences? Is it a set of attitudes about one's relationship to the world? Is it a derivative of the way in which specific body regions are physiologically activated?

   Originally it was proposed that the clarity of an individual's boundaries was a reflection of the values and characteristics of significant figures that had been internalized. In referring to "internalization," Parsons and Bales (1955) state (p. 54): "the primary structure of the human personality *as a system of action* is organized about the internalization of *systems* of social objects . . . in which the individual has come to be integrated in the course of his life history." They regard the program of interiorization which underlies an individual's socialization to be initiated with the internalization of the simple interaction pattern with his mother and to progress to the internalizations of complex systems revolving about multiple interacting relationships with other family members. They describe internalization systems as varying in stability, differentiation, and boundary clarity. With this perspective as a framework, the following formulation was offered in 1958 (Fisher and Cleveland, pp. 353–354) regarding the nature of the body image boundary:

  . . . we conceptualize each interiorized system as possessing formal boundary properties. These boundary properties may be viewed as varying relative to the nature of the relationships that were the prototype for the system. For example, if an individual's interactions with the mother figure have been such that she had a series of meaningful, clear-cut, and stable expectations of him and he in turn developed similar patterns of expectation of her, one would assume that the interiorized systems growing out of the relationship would have definite, well articulated boundaries. If, however, the mother's expectations have been experienced as not meaningful or as erratic and inconsistent, it would make for a poorly organized interior system with ill-defined boundaries. Degree of boundary definiteness of the system may be equated with the degree to which the relationship between the self and the prototype for the interiorization helped to make the world look meaningful and capable of being dealt with effectively. It is hypothesized that the qualities of the boundaries one ascribes to one's body reflect the predominance of either poorly or well-bounded internalizations. It is suggested that . . . the body-image boundary almost isomorphically (mirrors) the overall boundary characteristics of these systems.

The added assumption was made that the "boundary attributes of the primary interiorizations are projected to the body-image boundary" and that "the actual body locus identified with the boundary responds with a pattern of excitation equivalent to the boundary attributes" (pp. 358–359). To be more specific, it was speculated that interiorized systems are expectancies or sets which imply a readiness to respond to the world in certain ways. These expectancies may be paraphrased in terms like: "I can achieve," "I can be effective by getting things done," "I can be an individual and people will continue to be my allies and friends," "There is meaning and consistency in my relationships with others." They are sets with action significance. They imply getting things done, dealing actively with one's environs, and being interested in involvement with others. Presumably, as a result, areas of the body most in contact with the world and used for action "outward" (e.g., muscle, skin) would be activated in preparation for fulfilling the underlying expectancies. Another quote from Fisher and Cleveland's 1958 formulation is pertinent to this point (p. 358): ". . . the exterior layers of the body (particularly the musculature) tend to be equated with voluntary, reality-coping behavior, whereas the body interior is equated with involuntary response. The orientation of the high Barrier person is therefore translated into a persistently high level of activation of the exterior body layers. There is a set to respond with this region of the body which is manifested in a long-term pattern of preparatory excitation."

The above formulation equates the boundary with a series of expectancies which are translated into activation of tissue in the "outer" layers of the body. While it was also suggested as part of this formulation that the activation of "outer" body sectors might "feed back" to central expectancy systems and therefore create a self reinforcing circuit, little was made of this possibility. However, newer findings suggest that the actual experience of the activated boundary may, in itself, be an important contribution to a sense of boundary definiteness. This is certainly indicated by the Fisher and Renik

(1966) and Renik and Fisher (1968) studies which demonstrated that intensifying an individual's awareness of the skin and muscle regions of his body increased his Barrier score. Similar implications derive from the Reitman and Cleveland (1964) findings that sensory isolation alters boundary definiteness. To receive a stream of sensations of a particular intensity from the boundary of one's body may serve to reinforce one's sense of being delimited from what is "out there."[2] It may provide a feeling of being "contained" and protected which augments such feelings as they are derived from past socialization interactions. Compton's (1964) work on clothing choices in disturbed women and Kernaleguen's (1968) work concerned with clothing choices of normal women indicate too that there may even be "clothing strategies" which are adopted in an attempt to give one's boundaries a visual vividness or solidity otherwise felt to be lacking. Perhaps we will discover in time that there are other techniques (e.g., self touching, tight clothing, preferences for temperature extremes) which are used as a means of increasing the sensory intensity and therefore the clarity of the boundary. The body image boundary in an adult individual can best be pictured as a phenomenon reflecting both long term assumptions about people and objects and also sensory feedback from the body periphery. The sensory experience associated with the physiological activation of the periphery probably becomes an integral part of boundary maintenance. A more detailed formulation will be offered later regarding the manner in which persistent body sensations which are part of the organized body image help to maintain its organization and also selective attitudes toward the world.

The above discussion compromises in its attempt to discern the relative contribution of body sensation and social attitude variables to boundary maintenance. But there is a temptation to conceptualize the body boundary either primarily as a function of body experience or else as a resultant of certain general attitudes toward the world. One looks for closure as to whether the body boundary is or is not something quite specially founded upon body phenomena. It is confusing to talk about a "body boundary," but at the same time to refer to its functions in relation to non-body variables like "identity" and "social role." This confusion reflects the fact that we have, in the past, thought of the body and its functioning as a separate category apart from phenomena like the self concept or social role. But in actual fact, one's

[2] Strangely, boundary sensations produced by physical symptomatology do not seem to influence the Barrier score. This is evident from the fact that Barrier does not differ for patients with either exterior or interior symptoms of varying intensity or duration (Fisher and Cleveland, 1968; Landau, 1960). If Barrier were influenced by the sensory feedback from a symptom, one would certainly expect persons with skin (e.g., neurodermatitis) or muscle symptoms (arthritis) of many years duration to differ in Barrier from those who have had their symptoms for only a few weeks. Such differences have not been found. But one must reserve final judgment on this matter until studies involving more complex designs (e.g., simultaneously considering severity, duration, and amount of sensory awareness of the diseased areas) have been employed.

body is, almost from the beginning, a social object. It becomes inextricably a component of identity and the individual's social world. Social role, self concept, body experience, and fantasies about one's body represent shifting perspectives on an underlying self organization process.

Source of the Boundary

Intimately a part of the issues discussed above is the question whether it is possible to specify what socialization experiences affect boundary formation. Despite considerable work devoted to this question, we can still respond to it only meagerly. The single thread of continuity running through the diverse observations which have been made relates to the matter of having positive facilitating personal interactions. From several different sources there is evidence that the parent showing sensitivity to feeling and stimulus subtlety and oriented toward engagement with others is likely to encourage a clear sense of boundedness in his children. One could paraphrase this by saying that the parent who is open to experience and communication, particularly as it emerges from contact with others, provides boundary enhancing conditions. Apparently, under such conditions a child can more easily feel that there is interest in responding to him as a person and that his communications are received and treated as meaningful. To be attended to and meaningfully perceived rather than ignored, rejected, or attacked may be the underlying factor which promotes the experience of being a delineated person. The actual empirical findings do not clearly demonstrate this view, but they point roughly in the same direction.

We can also entertain the possibility that at any time during an individual's life his sense of boundedness will be increased by the feeling that he is a focus of interested attention and communication. Possibly this would occur most often in a setting where one was admired or assigned special positive status. But there are also clues that it can occur as a result of the unreal centrality which the paranoid or grandiose schizophrenic can create for himself by means of his delusional system. The enhancement of self, which accompanies the belief that one is a focus of attention and a maker of widely significant decisions, apparently bolsters boundary delineation. In view of this fact and also the fact that children do not generally have lower Barrier scores than adults one must conclude that boundary firmness is not a function of developmental maturity. It is a function of certain feelings and attitudes which can be influenced by past experiences with one's parents; present relationships; fantasies, myths, and delusions; and patterns of body sensation. Perhaps it is the complexity of factors contributing to the state of the boundary which makes it so difficult to isolate clear consistent correlations between an individual's Barrier score and the attributes of his parents. It will be recalled that in the major study, earlier described, which examined the parental antecedents of children's boundary characteristics, the greatest number of relationships were found between parents and children in the seven–11 age range. Fewer relationships showed up for parents and children in the 12–17 range. Possibly by the time a child has attained the 12–17 level he has become involved with many groups and sources of influence outside of the family which have boundary modifying impact and consequently the state of his boundaries is less directly a reflection of parental influences.

It should be mentioned parenthetically that while a firm boundary provides an individual with a "safe base of operations" and therefore assists him in facing up to stress demands, it may also encourage irrational behavior. In the case of the paranoid it may provide the security to act out a delusional system. In normal subjects it has already been shown (e.g., Hammerschlag, et al., 1964) to encourage ignoring certain body dysfunctions and therefore delaying in seeking medical treatment. That is, the sense of security associated with the well delineated boundary may result in under-rating the significance of body symptoms and assuming unrealistically that one's body can cope with the disturbance without outside help. There may be other analogous situations, e.g., confrontation by a difficult psychological conflict, when delay in seeking outside help might prove seriously disadvantageous.

Boundary Building and Body Security

There are obvious analogies between the establishment of a body boundary and the multifarious other ways in which people build structures to shelter, protect, and separate themselves. A tremendous amount of energy goes into constructing houses, fences, forts, walls, and various lines of demarcation. There are also many strategies used to protect and set one's body off from others. These range from the wearing of armor and heavy clothing to the use of uniforms, badges, and other insignia. One could argue that most persons do not feel safe unless they have taken measures to shield and contain themselves from the space bordering upon them. They seem to require assurance of a protective boundary, which is literally constructed or symbolically designated, in order to feel in control of their environs. The body boundary may likewise be viewed as an attempt to shield the body space and to provide security for the highly valued anatomical and symbolic things contained within the body (e.g., ego, self, heart, procreative ability).

It is logical to speculate that one's sense of security was originally closely dependent upon how secure one felt about one's body. The child's feeling tone is probably heavily influenced by how adequately he has been fed, allowed to assume comfortable postures, protected from pain, provided with the proper amount of body contact, and so forth. Danger is for him linked with signals indicating malfunctioning of, or painful intrusion upon, his body. Of course, as he grows older his perceptions become more complex and he is able to anticipate danger in terms of events that have no direct relevance for his body functioning. But the question arises whether the early body oriented definition of security does not continue to play an important role. It is possible that the adult persists, at some level, to perceive all forms of danger (whether they be economic, reputational, or political) as having potentiality for injuring his body. There is perhaps an historical "pull" to translate threats into the "body language" prototype of an earlier developmental phase. Kagan and Moss (1962) have made some interesting observations indicating that early childhood anxiety about one's body may persist into adulthood and affect behavior in a number of areas.

The above perspective could help to explain the generalized importance of the body boundary as a source of security and self stabilization. The original process of boundary formulation would be a basic step in building up a feeling of security about one's body. For the individual to experience his body as separated from the contiguous space would permit him to perceive it as enclosed, protected, and not easily intruded upon. Without adequate boundary development he would have minimal confidence in the trustworthiness of his body. If therefore it were true that many types of threats which the individual encounters during his life get translated into the language of possible body damage, those lacking adequate boundaries would be particularly sensitive to such threats. They would be inordinately aroused by danger because of its body destructive implications. They would lack the sense of body security which may be fundamental to all security.[3]

At present there are no data to give a sound empirical footing to the formulation that non-body threats can be translated into body threats. The supporting observations are largely clinical and unsystematic. Of course, there is a massive psychoanalytic literature which cites numerous clinical examples of neurotic or schizophrenic patients who have apparently reacted to life crises or threatening figures not in terms of their realistic consequences but rather as if they could produce "castration" or severe body damage. It is indirectly pertinent too that Pitcher and Prelinger (1963) have shown that fantasies of body destruction are very common in children; and Gottschalk, et al. (1964) has shown that this is similarly true for adults. Because such fantasies can be commonly detected even in healthy persons without apparent body defects, one might reason that they are responses to a variety of stressful life situations and not just those related to specific body difficulties.

Merleau-Ponty (1962) has done a masterful job of pointing out how one's body becomes an important experiential context which introduces order and meaning into our relationships with other objects. He conceives of the individual's body as a highly organized sector of space which is the only consistent background for experience and the only anchor providing a continuing line of stability for perception. The body with its ability to sustain purposeful movement "superimposes upon physical space a potential or

[3] This view is related to Freud's idea that body experience is the nucleus of the formation of the ego.

human space" (p. 111). From Merleau-Ponty's view, there is a clearly articulated area of space called "my body" in which I can experience identity and a sense of existence. The question arises whether it is possible for the delimiting of one's body space to be so vague that one has difficulty in experiencing one's body as an anchoring context and a source of perceptual continuity. Certainly there are individuals with central nervous system damage who seem to have lost a considerable part of their ability to use body experience in such a fashion. What of the non-damaged individual whose boundaries are extremely vague? Does he have difficulty in sustaining a feeling of clear existence and individualized spatiality? We know that in some instances (e.g., after LSD, sensory deprivation, flying for sustained periods at high altitudes) the individual may suddenly feel a loss of existence and spatiality. He may feel that he is "losing" his body. Perhaps those with vague boundaries chronically struggle with muted sensations of the same character. They might, therefore, have special difficulty in seeing the world as stable or dependable and as capable of being modified by their own intent. Without a clear boundary, one is but an extension of a much larger impersonal space.

Advantage of Boundary Articulation

Let us appraise some of the obvious and also not so obvious advantages that may accrue to the individual from a clearly delineated boundary. The sense of protection and security provided has already been underscored. However, the focus has been entirely upon security against "outside" threat. It is possible that a firm boundary also provides reassurance about one's ability to control one's own impulses. We know that fears about loss of self-control and inappropriate impulsivity are common. One of the important sources of body anxiety and sensations of body vulnerability in our culture derives from fear of loss of body control, particularly with reference to the sphincters. To feel that he is well "enclosed" may bolster an individual's assurance that nothing will "leak out" or "break out." To feel that he is enclosed may serve as a signal that self-restraints are available to prevent flagrant impulsivity. Kaufman and Heims (1958) reported many fantasies of gross breakdown in body boundaries in delinquents who could not control their own impulsive acting-out; and it has already been shown that the Barrier score is consistently low in delinquent samples. Another fact to consider is that when the well bounded person channels excitation to outer rather than interior sectors this may bolster feelings of self-control because it minimizes heart and visceral sensations which are particularly likely to be experienced as amorphous turmoil within oneself pressing for undisciplined release.[4] Consider too that if

---

[4] Of course, a high degree of interior excitation could be experienced not only as an "interior" threat. It could be "projected" outward and serve to intensify the apparent danger

wish-derived impulses are channeled to "voluntary" rather than "involuntary" body sectors the individual may have increased opportunity to understand their intent or content. He probably has greater skill in "decoding" the implications of certain patterns of muscle activation than he does of diffuse visceral patterns. The "intent" of interior excitation is likely to remain unclear or "unconscious" and therefore more threatening because it is difficult to subject to rational decision making.

The support provided by the boundary in containing impulses may not be merely subjective. It may derive too from the demonstrated fact that the clear boundary involves the ability to maintain a persistent heightened level of muscular activation. Such ability signifies a capacity to "hold in" and delay response and to tolerate build-up of tension. The individual with articulated boundaries would actually have special capabilities for tolerating tension and restraining himself until the "proper" opportunity for response presents itself.

In maintaining a relatively large ratio of exterior to interior activation the high Barrier person probably has response advantages over the low Barrier person who manifests an activation ratio of an obverse character. He may derive advantages in response efficiency. Exterior arousal with its alerting of the voluntary musculature indicates a readiness for action. It means being "set" to release energy at the periphery where it has problem solving potential. But interior arousal means activation of organ systems which have few, if any, direct problem solving capabilities. It is even possible that the arousal of interior organs has a negative effect upon efficiency of response insofar as it creates diffuse sensations which are distracting and pull attention away from what is significant "out there." The fact that the high Barrier individual is physiologically more set for action than the low Barrier individual can, at another level, be viewed as representing a more active stance toward incoming stimuli. This "active" stance, as already indicated, involves a series of attitudes about the feasibility of impressing and controlling the environment. It particularly involves crystallized standards about how far one will allow the "outside" to intrude upon one's autonomy. In that sense, the individual with definite boundaries is set to "filter" what impinges upon him and to modulate the impact of what comes in his direction. He possesses a screen of "sets" which permits him to be selective in what he will "take" and accept. There is increasing evidence (Shakow, 1963) that those who cannot adopt such "filtering" sets are characterized by serious adjustment difficulties (e.g., schizophrenic breakdown [5]). The activated exterior represents an efficient recognition of the fact that there is an important geographic component to

---

of the outer world. Schachter's experiment (e.g., Schachter and Wheeler, 1962) dealing with the effects produced by adrenalin under special conditions illustrates the possibility of directing visceral arousal toward differential targets. He demonstrated that adrenalin could enhance the effects of stimuli with quite different significances.

[5] Such sets may be related to what Freud labeled the "Reizschutz" or barrier against stimuli.

one's relationship to the world. The individual is prepared for action at the line where his body makes maximum contact with what is "non-self."

Although a demarcated boundary may create favorable conditions for efficient transactions with what is outside of oneself, it should be acknowledged that it does not appear to be particularly potent in fostering the cognitive and fantasy processes which constitute creativity. The work by Bachelis, which was earlier referred to, indicated few correlations between Barrier and scores on a battery of creativity tests. Also, Fisher and Cleveland (1968) reported that there were no Barrier differences between individuals in certain disciplines who had attained great success because of their originality and those who had not attained such success. One could even guess that the loose, apparently aimless trial and error fantasy associated with certain kinds of creativity might be hindered by a high Barrier orientation. This could be especially true for fantasy that had no discernible action implications. Insofar as keeping a goal in mind or having a need for task completion are antagonistic to creativity, the firmly bounded person would be at a disadvantage. He might also be at a disadvantage if a given form of creativity required "opening" oneself freely and without anticipatory assumptions to a variety of "outside" experiences.

Relationships to Other Body Image Dimensions

In numerous studies the Barrier score has proven not to be consistently related to other conventional body image measures currently used. It is not meaningfully correlated with scores from the Secord-Jourard Body Cathexis test, degree of over- or under-estimation of one's body size, or response to aniseikonic distortion of one's mirror image. Although it has manifested a positive relationship with scores from the Secord Homonym test on two different occasions, it has failed to do so in several other instances. Variable results have appeared too with reference to Witkin, et al. measures of "body articulation." As noted in their book (1962), the Barrier score has shown itself to be positively correlated with field independence in some samples (particularly female), but not in others (particularly male). Jacobson's (1965) results also showed a positive correlation between Barrier and field independence in one sample but not in another. While there is overlap between Witkin's articulation formulation and the boundary definiteness concept, it is small and inconsistent. The major differences between the approaches are truly highlighted by two facts: (1) From Witkin's view the male has a more articulated body concept than the female; whereas Barrier findings suggest just the opposite. (2) Witkin's data indicate that certain intellectual and cognitive abilities are closely linked with body articulation, but the Barrier score has evidenced few relationships with intellectual measures.

The fact that the Barrier score is not correlated with most conventional body image measures and that, indeed, they are not intercorrelated with each other has been lamented by some commentators. They worry that such lack of relationship reflects inconsistency or limited unity in the concept of body image. However, it is clear, as one surveys the body image literature, that the term "body image" is analogous to the term "personality." That is, it refers to a general class of phenomena which embraces many separate subsystems. The variables entering into the organization of body experience are manifold and some are quite independent of others. Another familiar problem to keep in mind is that the various body image measures which have been devised tap in at different levels of awareness. Some, for example the Secord and Jourard Body Cathexis technique, involve the subject making evaluative statements about his own body and are probably much influenced by social desirability attitudes. Others, such as the Barrier index or the Secord Homonym test, depend upon response samples which are much less susceptible to conscious control and censorship. It would be quite surprising if body image measures based on such differing response samples were consistently correlated.

17
Final Perspective

The scaffolding of the boundary concept with its associated model of exterior-interior differentiation has been erected. One can look back over a profusion of efforts and trace with fair clarity the major ways in which the boundary seems to enter into behavior. It is unnecessary to detail further the many successful corroborations which have accumulated. But one must acknowledge that some defects and strains in the boundary model have shown up. This has been particularly true in two areas. First, it has been difficult to apply the concept of exterior versus interior psychosomatic symptom localization with complete consistency to a wide range of illnesses. Problems of definition and specificity have arisen which currently limit the validity of the concept. Secondly, as already abundantly discussed, it has been necessary to give up previous simple formulations which equate degree of boundary definiteness with ego soundness. The new formulation with respect to this matter accepts the notion that the boundary can remain well delineated if a disorganizing or regressive process does not destroy an individual's sense of having meaningful worth or importance. But it remains difficult to accept that the boundary of a grandiose schizophrenic does not really differ from that of a person who is successfully testing and adjusting to reality. One would guess that the Barrier score is in this instance telling only a part of a more complicated story that we have yet to learn.

Obviously, both of the areas in which the exterior-interior model has shown limitations should have priority in further research. What other areas should have priority? Some thoughts concerning this matter will be reviewed.

Little has been done to cross validate and extend earlier leads which indicated that the well bounded individual is relatively more interested in people and less interested in things than the vaguely bounded person. Further work should be done in which the Barrier score is related to formal measures of interest patterns and also the actual occupational choices which individuals have made.

318

The whole issue of what can change the boundary needs to be appraised from many new directions. We need to know how the first experience of leaving home (e.g., beginning regular attendance at kindergarten) affects the boundary. What about the effect of the first camp experience away from home? How is the boundary affected by the loss of a parent; or a good friend? What does the new intimacy of a marriage relationship do to one's boundary? What is the impact of extended periods of success or failure (e.g., in school work)? What is the effect of major body changes associated with adolescent growth? Does the first menstrual experience produce detectable alterations? These are just a few of the problems that need to be explored in naturalistic situations. If they can be meaningfully approached, they may well give us the clearest ideas about how the boundary is involved in major life adjustments and crises.

There is much yet to learn about how the boundary influences the quality of experience of the outside world. Initial leads do indicate that stimuli are more vivid in those with more articulated boundaries. But how does this apply to the range from simple sensory attributes to complex physiognomic perceptions? Are simple colors, for example, perceived with differential vividness? Are the emotional expressions of others experienced differentially?

One would like to learn about the family and developmental variables which control boundary formation. Is it the intrusive, hostile parent who is most likely to limit boundary articulation in his child? Or is it the parent who too much encourages passivity? Do mother and father have equal or different degrees of influence on the child's boundary? And how is this related to the sex of the child?

To what extent can methods be fabricated for artificially bolstering the boundary? Can exercises which increase muscle and skin experiences result, over a period of time, in appreciable bolstering of the boundary? If so, does the method have any potential for helping certain classes of schizophrenics or others struggling with problems in which the inability to define oneself vis à vis the world is an important component?

Many other issues could, in all likelihood, be profitably examined. Quite randomly, one could consider the relationship of the Barrier score to:

1. Individual differences in drug responses.
2. Rate of recovery from various illnesses (e.g., cold, mononucleosis).
3. Motor skills.
4. Sex role.
5. Ability to adapt to long-continued decrease or increase in sensory input.
6. Susceptibility to conditioning.
7. Feelings about self.
8. Attitudes toward death.

9. Need for new experience.
10. Sexual responsiveness.
11. Clothing preferences.
12. Style of response to psychotherapy.

It will be interesting to see whether the next ten years will witness as great an accumulation of new knowledge about the boundary as occurred in the last ten.

III

BODY AWARENESS IN MEN

18
Back Awareness in Men and the "Anal Character"

INTRODUCTION

This chapter is the first of several to be concerned with the subjective, experiential aspects of the body image.

Previously described findings concerning the body image boundary indicated that part of the process of establishing a boundary involves differentiating exterior from interior body sensations. The individual who has definite boundaries is relatively more aware of sensations from bounding regions like skin and muscle than from interior organs (e.g., stomach, heart). The obverse is true for the individual with vague, poorly articulated boundaries. Somehow, the act of self-definition and distinguishing one's body as an independent entity is linked with intensified or dampened awareness of certain exterior versus interior body regions. The question logically follows whether the experiential accentuation or blurring of other body sectors might also prove to be related to adjustment strategies or personality variables. Aside from the distinction between exterior and interior, are there additional experiential differentiations? Are there patterns such that individuals habitually focus their attention upon specific body sectors and not others? Are there, among the shifting currents of body experience, certain persisting ones which become landmarks? If so, what is their function? Much of the material in this chapter and others that follow seeks to cope with these questions.

From a scientific view, the subjective aspects of body experience have proven to be an elusive phenomenon. Despite the fact that each of us has an infinite number of body sensations and experiences to draw upon and ponder, it has been difficult to order them into schemas or continua which would help to clarify behavior, aside from those at the simplest sensory or motor levels. Actually, considerable skepticism has prevailed within psychology as to whether the body experiential matrix has much to offer in the way of explanatory concepts. One does note a relatively active period from about 1910–1930 when the possibility was seriously considered that body sensations play an important role in affective response, judgments and attitudes. The publications of Yokoyama (1921), Nafe (1927), Nakoshima (1909), Warren (1922), Young (1927), and Hunt (1932) exemplify a heavy investment in questions relating to the influence of body sensations on broad cognitive and affective variables. It was proposed that sensations from highly specific body areas could be distinguished in their effects upon psychological processes. For example, in one instance (Hunt, 1932) pleasant and unpleasant experiences were equated respectively with "bright pressure" sensations in the upper chest and "dull pressure" sensations in the abdomen and lower trunk. Within this same period James and Lange (1922) formulated the view that peripheral sensory experience was the core of what we call an emotion. But with the upthrust of behaviorism, which vociferously opposed all subjective reports of experience and the attacks upon the James-Lange formulations by Cannon who emphasized central factors in emotion (1939), the study of body sensations as a psychological phenomenon fell off sharply. Reports about body sensations became identified with introspection and as such rather disreputable. Since that time body experience phenomena have been taken up by psychologists only spasmodically and in quite specialized contexts.

Here and there on the recent scene body sensation experiences have been given importance in theoretical statements or as experimental variables. A significant tangent of interest is represented in the work of Witkin and his group (1954). The concept of field independence-dependence which has sustained their efforts is constructed around measures of how well an individual is presumably able to utilize orienting sensations from his own body in order to make accurate spatial judgments when he is confronted with kinesthetic and visual cues which are spatially conflicting. Degree of accuracy in making such spatial judgments has proved to be linked with a variety of personality parameters. Witkin suggested on the basis of his findings that there are parallels between the manner in which an individual experiences his body and also his perceptions of other persons and objects. He indicates that, at one level, an individual's ways of using and interpreting his own body sensations mirror his characteristic ways of perceiving and interpreting non-self objects.

The Werner-Wapner sensori-tonic group (1949), which has been concerned with response to spatial vectors, also assigns considerable import to body sensations and experiences in its explanatory concepts. When describing how one perceives directional stimuli (e.g., an arrow pointing to the right), they propose that the directional stimulus results in corresponding muscle activation gradients which either balance or accentuate it. That is, a visual directional stimulus excites a positively or negatively isomorphic muscle arousal pattern (e.g., right side more activated than left) which presumably provides sensory information permitting compensatory adjustments in response. It is assumed that sensory input is continuously matched by body sensation experiences which feed back centrally and serve to modify it. Such body sensation "matches" are seen as having prime import in maintaining organismic equilibrium.

The Witkin and Werner-Wapner statements represent the most active current attempts to give the body sensory context some meaningful roles in psychological processes. There are other scattered efforts with the same intent that may be mentioned. Helson (see Allport, 1955), in his adaptation-level theory, refers to the background of body experience as one variable which consistently influences judgments and decision making. However, he does not really offer a model of how such influence is exerted. Mason (1961) reported in several studies that when persons are exposed to a stimulus with focused emotional content it arouses similar circumscribed body sensations in most of them. Thus, anger arousing material resulted in a "spread" of sensations over the "upper-front-torso areas"; and fear was experienced mainly in the "back body areas" (p. 399). Quite relatedly, Gemelli (1949) observed that special localized body sensations typify particular affective states. Both Mason and Gemelli hoped to be able to represent and categorize psychological response in terms of the individual's perception of his "internal" rather than "external" environment.

It is outside of formal psychological circles that the principal interest in the body sensation matrix has been shown. Primarily in psychoanalytic theory does one find a heavy investment in understanding why certain body areas are prominently in awareness, others ignored, and still others characterized by pain or unusual sensations. Psychoanalysts have been concerned with explaining each individual's unique subjective body geography. Freud set the example for such interest with his developmental theory which emphasizes shifts of libido from one body region to another in the course of attaining maturity. As he conceptualized it, there is a sequence of investment of energy and attention in oral, anal, and genital body sectors as the individual progressively moves through the socialization process. This means that certain body regions are highlighted and become objects of intensified attention as a function of how adequately the individual masters specified psychological conflicts. Indeed, Freud proposed that if a person could not deal adequately with crucial problems he would remain "fixated" at a level below full maturity and there would be a corresponding "fixation of libido" in given body sectors. For example, if problems relating to dependence and incorporation were not resolved one would come to manifest the traits of the "oral character," with a corresponding chronic investment of libido in the oral body areas (e.g., mouth, teeth, stomach) which would occupy an exaggerated enlarged place in the body experiential field. Freud offered an analogous formulation for the "anal character" and there have been subsequent analytic statements about the "urethral character," the "phallic character" (Fenichel, 1945) and so forth. Freud's (1924, 1938) descriptions of the oral and anal character types depict an explicit relationship between investment of energy in certain body sectors and the existence of focal conflicts (with their associated personality defenses). Related equations have been proposed by Schilder (1935), Reich (1949), Alexander (1948), Deutsch (1953) and others (Fenichel, 1945). Reich was so impressed with the mutually reinforcing link between body experience patterns and personality defenses that he asserted it was necessary in the process of psychotherapy not only to deal with psychological conflicts, as such, but also to alter directly the body sensation experiences bound to them.

The most detailed observations and speculations concerning the variables that contribute to the sensory prominence of various body areas have been offered by Schilder (1935). He accepts Freud's paradigm about the importance of the oral, anal, and genital zones as erogenous (libido) foci providing a basic framework within which to organize body experience. He interprets various phenomena that involve either extreme hyper- or hypo-awareness of body parts in terms of such parts symbolically representing erogenous zones. Presumably, they are avoided or focused upon as a way of rejecting or gaining indirect satisfaction of urges or wishes associated with the zones with which they are symbolically equated. But there are many aspects of body awareness which Schilder interprets outside of the libido scheme. It is worth while to scan the range of his observations in this respect. He points out the tendency for right-handed persons to be more aware of the right than left body sides because they use the right side more often. He notes that skin areas which are stretched over bone (e.g., over knuckles and cheek-bones) take on special prominence. In another instance, he observes that the persisting pull of gravity may be particularly experienced in the legs, or the lower part of the abdomen, or at the base of the skull. As part of his interest in the influence of others upon one's body image, he remarks that association with a significant person who has a body deformity or who is concerned about a particular body area may result in becoming anxiously focused upon an analogous area of one's own body. He discusses too the way individuals use clothing to draw both their own and the attention of others to a body feature (e.g., the appearance or the pressure of a piece of clothing may cause a body region to be perceptually enhanced). His clinical observations had informed him well of the diversity of personalistic and situational factors which simultaneously impinge to shape awareness priorities among body regions.

There is a superabundance of papers in the current psychoanalytic literature which attempt to trace via clinical and psychotherapy material the manner in which special attitudes toward body areas evolve from unconscious needs. Hyper- or hypo-awareness (associated with pain, paresthesia, anesthesia) of regions like the nose, eyes, throat, and total body has been traced to sexual conflicts. Similar awareness problems with regard to mouth, throat, stomach, and gastrointestinal tract have been conceptualized as deriving from conflictual oral wishes. Other exaggerations in body awareness have been variously ascribed to anal conflicts, repressed hostility, exhibitionism, Oedipal difficulties, mourning needs, and so forth. One cannot but be impressed with the sheer number of cases which have accumulated in which clinicians believe they can demonstrate causal ties between pinpointed unconscious conflicts and unusual body awareness experiences. They converge on the common proposition that when an individual is unusually attuned to, or avoidant of, a body area this may be an expression of personal conflicts or adjustment strategies.

But why should one expect to find parallels between body awareness patterns and the psychological problems which engage an individual? Aside from the previously referred to psychoanalytic rationale for such parallels, there are two general possibilities to consider that are at least implicit in the existing body image literature.

First, it has been suggested that in the course of socialization the child acquires certain response patterns (e.g., traits) because of crucial experiences he has with his parents; and these experiences in turn often revolve about body functions linked with specific areas of his body and may therefore result in his placing special valuations upon these areas. Illustratively, his style of sexual behavior might be influenced by the orientation he adopts from his parents toward the sexual regions of his body (e.g., lower half of body). Consequently, there would be a correlation between his attitudes toward sexual expression and his attitudes toward the sectors of his body having sexual functions.

Another consideration which has been noted is the unique closeness of the individual's body to himself as a perceiver. His body is the only object in his perceptual field which he simultaneously perceives and is also a part of himself. Its special closeness to himself (ego, identity) maximizes the likelihood that it will reflect and share in his most important preoccupations. Like all ego significant objects it can become a convenient "screen" upon which are projected one's most salient concerns. An illustration of such projection would be provided in the case of the individual who feels unimportant and inferior and then presumably transfers this view to some part of his body by perceiving it as smaller than it is. Indeed, Popper (1957) and also Wapner and Krus (1959) have shown that failure experiences result in subjects perceiving themselves as relatively shorter in stature.

The program of research to be presented in the following pages, dealing with the significance of particular modes of subjective body experience, evolved over a period of years. During initial stages it was largely unsuccessful; but the frequency, logic, and consistency of previous clinical reports regarding the significance of subjective body experience provided the incentive to continue exploration until meaningful results began to emerge.

Early in the course of this work it became evident that there are distinct sex differences. A pattern of body awareness in men usually had entirely different personality correlates than did the same pattern in women. For this reason all results will be reported separately for each sex.

The broad objectives of the studies to be described were to determine whether there are consistent individual differences in body experiences and whether such differences are related to style of life and personality defenses. If someone is consistently aware or unaware of a particular part of his body, does this tell us something meaningful about him as a person? Operationally, this question was conceptualized as requiring the measurement of how the individual distributes his attention to a number of major dimensions of his body and then ascertaining if the specific distribution was predictive of various attitudes, values, and modes of defense which we roughly place under the rubric of "personality."

Embedded in the background of this work was the speculative hope that body experience data might prove to be a worth-while source of information about an individual's personality. If there were a variety of body experiential "landmarks" and if each were tied to fairly circumscribed traits or defense modes, a potentially rich array of predictors would become available. Presumably, instead of measuring personality traits directly, one might be able to appraise them via their body experience representations. As will be seen, the results turned out to be moderately encouraging in this respect.

BODY FOCUS QUESTIONNAIRE

One prime technique has been utilized in the studies to be described below for measuring the manner in which an individual distributes his attention to the various regions of his body. It is called the Body Focus Questionnaire (BFQ) (Appendix B) and was designed to evaluate a variety of body experience dimensions. The basic format of the BFQ involves presenting the subject with a series of verbal references to paired body regions and asking him to indicate which of the two constituting each pair stands out most clearly in his awareness. For example, he might be confronted with the choice of indicating whether he is more aware of the back of his head or the front of his head; or in another instance whether he is more aware of his right or his left arm. The finalized version of the BFQ requests 108 such judgments. It comprises eight scales: Front-Back, Right-Left, Heart, Stomach, Eyes, Mouth, Head, and Arms.[1] The number of items per scale varies from 11 to

---

[1] The Arms items, while theoretically existing as a scale, have not consistently or meaningfully correlated with other psychological measures; and will therefore not be discussed in later chapters.

19. The average time required to respond to the 108 items is about 20–30 minutes. When the BFQ is administered, the following instructions are given:

"Turn your attention upon yourself. Concentrate on your body. Below is a list in which different areas of your body are listed in pairs. In each case pick the area or part which is at the moment most clear in your awareness."

Choices are indicated by marking an IBM answer sheet. A score for a given dimension (e.g., Back) is simply equal to the number of times it is chosen as being more clearly in awareness than the other body areas with which it is compared. The entire series of BFQ items is presented in the Appendix. In order to conceal the fact that specific dimensions of body experience are under scrutiny, the items comprising the various scales are distributed randomly through the list of comparisons.

The BFQ represents a compromise between the intent to obtain meaningful samples of certain subjective aspects of body experience and the need to be able to express such information in easily quantifiable terms. Earlier preliminary studies had indicated that there are great difficulties involved in coding an individual's free, spontaneous qualitative reports of his body experiences and using such information to define how he allocates his attention to his body. Other more disciplined kinds of reports were also explored, such as asking the individual to indicate the frequency of sensations at a few restricted body sites (e.g., stomach vs. skin) for a given period of time. Certain of these approaches were partially successful: but their over-all reliability proved to be low. The technique finally incorporated into the BFQ captures some of the straightforward reporting of body sensations which is to be found in spontaneous elaborations; but reduces the complexity of the judgments required by focusing upon narrow and rather easily managed bits of perceptual information. Rarely are there complaints that the judgments required by the BFQ are too difficult; and even children as young as age seven have managed them adequately.

The specific scales assembled were chosen on the basis of previous anecdotal and clinical reports which suggested that certain body areas were particularly likely to become symbolically linked with psychological conflicts and attitudes. The language used to refer to body parts and areas in the BFQ was kept as simple and non-technical as possible. Information concerning matters of test-retest reliability will be presented in the sections to follow which deal with each of the BFQ scales. Also, in these sections will be described data concerning the correlations of the BFQ indices with alternate measures of body awareness.

An important question to be raised about any scale is whether it is seriously influenced by variables like acquiescence and social desirability. As will be shown, such variables play an insignificant part in BFQ judgments.

The BFQ has been successfully administered in both individual and group settings. No perceptible differences in mean values have occurred as a function of individual versus group conditions.

It should be reiterated that sex differences were highly significant in defining the significance of particular BFQ dimensions. Therefore, BFQ findings will be presented separately for men and women. In the immediate pages that follow the data pertinent to men will be described. Then, in subsequent chapters, the data derived from female samples will be appraised.

BACK AWARENESS
AND THE "ANAL CHARACTER"

The first major body experience dimension to be described is that relating to the differentiation between the front and the back of one's body. If measurement of the relative awareness of the front versus back body regions were undertaken, would one find that there are consistent individual differences? Do some focus most of their attention on the back of the body; whereas others concern themselves primarily with the front? If there are such consistencies, what are their origins and how do they impinge on other aspects of behavior?

REVIEW OF "ANAL CHARACTER" CONCEPT

The distinction between the front and back of the body has been widely considered psychoanalytically, but rarely experimentally. Freud (1924, 1938), Abraham (1927), Ferenczi (1955), Fenichel (1945), Tausk (1933), Schilder (1935) and others have theorized that the back of one's body is largely associated with anal functions. Of course, Freud originated the idea. He developed the concept of an "anal personality" who is unconsciously preoccupied with anal sensations (linked with the back of the body) as the result of conflicts experienced during the period of childhood when control of the anal sphincter is learned. He proposed that the conflicts faced by the child during the anal period center on issues of obedience and passivity versus opposition and self assertion. At a more elementary level, they presumably relate to control versus lack of control of a body function which is considered to be dirty and socially unacceptable. The "anal personality" is portrayed as having great anxiety about displeasing his parents in terms of possible loss of control of his anal sphincter and the associated implications of disobedience and soiling aggression. He is therefore said to be defensively strict with himself about being spontaneous or impulsive. Also, he is defensively clean, orderly, and obedient. But it is theorized that while he exercises such restraint over himself he has an underlying resentment about being controlled which permeates his behavior in the form of negativism and stubbornness. Many other traits, presumably deriving from his special mode of defense, may be found listed in the literature, e.g., ambivalence, perfectionism, punctuality, miserliness, rigidity, conscientiousness, perseverance, and aloofness. It should be acknowledged that more recent ego oriented versions of psychoanalytic theory have not been especially enthusiastic about Freud's original developmental model with its emphasis upon the importance of body experience and the investment of energy (libido) in primary erogenous zones. Such concepts are regarded as too biological and instinct oriented. They are sometimes dismissed as "old-fashioned."

There have been efforts to study the "anal character" formulation empirically. Questionnaires and projective tests have been used to evaluate the meaningfulness of "anality" as a trait. Sears (1936), Beloff (1957), Barnes (1952), Krout and Tabin (1954), Stagner, Lawson, and Moffitt (1955), Couch and Keniston (1960), Schlesinger (1963), Lazare, Klerman, and Armor (1966), Mandel (1957), Finney (1961), and Gottheil (1965) have shown that questionnaire items presumably sampling anal attitudes can be formulated which are coherent statistically and in relation to the Freudian "anal stage" model. Also, Blum (1949) and Miller and Stine (1951) have findings indicating that projective responses to pictures and story completions can be reliably analyzed for anal themes.

In recent years, interest in the anal character concept has grown sufficiently among researchers to stimulate a number of attempts to evaluate its validity in an experimental context. The results have been mixed, but generally encouraging. Because the anal character formulation will play a substantial role in some of the work which is to be presented, it would be well to review the tenor of relevant empirical findings.

There is, first of all, a cluster of studies which is concerned, quite literally, with relating anal personality traits in an individual to the severity of his toilet training. The hypothesis typically tested was that anal character traits would be most prominent in those who had had the harshest toilet training discipline. Beloff (1957) found no relationship between male college students' degree of anal character orientation, as defined by questionnaire responses, and the severity of their toilet training as determined from their mothers' reports. But he did discover that the students' anality trait scores were positively and significantly correlated with the anality trait scores of their mothers who had responded to the same questionnaire. Bernstein (1955) could find no indications in a group of young male and female children that anal traits like collecting, constipation, or pleasure in smearing were linked to coerciveness of toilet training which was defined by mothers' reports. However, amount of negativistic behavior (which is supposedly anal in origin) observed in a controlled play situation was positively correlated with toilet training coerciveness. Hetherington and Brackbill (1963) discerned little evidence in a group of male and female children that the anal traits of obstinacy, orderliness, and parsimony, as manifested in a series of situational tests, were correlated with mothers' statements regarding the time and manner of toilet training. Significant positive correlations were reported between girls' degree of obstinacy, orderliness, and parsimony and the corresponding traits in their mothers. For boys and their fathers the relationships were largely of a chance order. Whiting and Child (1953) surveyed the toilet training practices applied to children in a number of cultures and could find few consistent correlates or consequences as defined by the behavior of adults in such cultures. Finally, it may be parenthetically mentioned that Beller (1957) noted in a group of children varying in age from two to six that those with poorest control over their anal functions were rated by observers as particularly dependent and lacking in achievement motivation. Generally, the studies cited indicate that anal character traits cannot be attributed to a special category of parent behavior called "toilet training." There does seem to be evidence, though, for asserting that anal traits are likely to reflect the existence of similar characterological tendencies in one's parents.

A novel perspective regarding the anal character typology has been developed by Couch and Keniston (1960). They view anal attitudes as contributing to the general tendency to agree or disagree with others ("yeasaying" versus "naysaying"). They measured the extent to which subjects in a number of samples said "yes" or "no" to a lengthy list of questionnaire statements. Scores derived in this way were then related to attitudes about anal themes. Anal attitudes were evaluated by asking subjects to express their like or dislike for activities which have anal significance insofar as they involve dirt and messiness (e.g., smelling offensive odors, saying dirty things, exploring dirty slums and alleys). Other questionnaire and interview derived measures were also taken that tapped impulse control, feelings about parents, conventionality, and so forth. Significant trends were noted for the yeasayer to feel comfortable about anal expression and impulses; to have poorly internalized the injunctions of his parents about anal and other types of control; to have sought externally defined guide lines for his conduct; and to be generally impulsive. The naysayer was found to avoid activities with anal connotations; to be self-controlled; and to have internalized parental injunctions strongly. In referring to the contrast between yeasayers and naysayers, Couch and Keniston state that, "During their early socialization period they tend toward opposite resolutions of the 'anal' problems around control of impulses. The passive and receptive egos of yeasayers seem to be an outgrowth of their lack of internalization of parental control" (p. 173). "The naysayers' retentive or suppressive resolution of anal problems shows many manifestations of their internalization of parental demands for control and of their subsequent aversion for 'anally expressive' impulses" (p. 172).

A paradoxical blend of psychoanalytic theory and operant conditioning methodology has proven, in the work of Noblin (1962) and Timmons and Noblin (1963), to be an unexpected source of support for the anal character model. Noblin studied a group of male psychiatric patients who had been classified as anal or oral characters in terms of ward behavior, diagnosis, and responses to the Blacky test. He predicted that in an operant conditioning situation the anals would condition best to the reinforcing effect of pennies and the orals would condition best to gumball rewards. The choice of pennies to reinforce the anals was based on the psychoanalytic equation between feces and money—with the implication that money would therefore have special import to one with anal concerns. The conditioning task related to the choice of first person versus second or third person pronouns in a series of sentences. Noblin's predictions were clearly supported by the data. Money was a more effective reinforcer for the anal character than gumballs; and the obverse was true for the orals.

Timmons and Noblin (1963) anticipated that, since the anal character is obstinate and "resistant" and the oral character is supposedly compliant, a positive verbal reinforcer would decrease a given response category (use of first person versus second or third person pronouns) for anals but increase it for orals. This hypothesis was solidly upheld in a population of 30 subjects who had been selected in terms of their responses to the Blacky Test. No difference was found between anals and orals in their ability to verbalize the purpose of the conditioning procedure, although it had been considered that the anals, because of their supposedly more obsessive and precise orientation, might have been superior in this respect. Subsequently, Noblin, Timmons, and Kael (1966) went further and not only predicted that positive verbal reinforcement would decrease a response category for anals and increase it for orals, but also proposed that negative verbal reinforcement would have the obverse effect for each of the two character types. The positive reinforcer used was of a mild affirmatory form such as "Good" or "O.K." The negative verbal reinforcement was expressed in terms like "Um-no" or "You can do better." Twenty-four anals and 24 orals were selected for study from a college population on the basis of Blacky Test criteria. Their responses under affirmatory and negative reinforcing conditions conformed significantly to the hypothesis. An obvious similarity presents itself between these findings and the report of Couch and Keniston (1960) indicating that the anal character is a naysayer rather than a yeasayer.

The results of a study by Bishop (1967) bear further on the matter of response of "anals" to negative and positive conditions. Using a sample of 67 men consisting of subgroups high and low on anal hoarding tendencies (as defined by the Grygier (1956) Dynamic Personality Inventory) she evaluated their responses to two boring tasks under two contrasting conditions. For one condition they were led to expect a large reward for their participation and were then deprived of it. For a second condition they received their expected reward. It was predicted and found that in the deprivation situation the high anals expressed more dislike for the boring tasks than the low anals; whereas in the non-deprivation condition the high anals liked the tasks more than the low anals. One of the original predictions was made in terms of the theoretical view that the anal character is unusually motivated to "hold on" to and "keep back" what he has obtained and will therefore respond with acute frustration and disappointment if it is taken from him. In the deprivation condition of this experiment the subject was led to believe that he had a sum of money in his grasp and then it was "taken" from him. The second of the predictions (favorable response of anals to boring task under reward conditions) was based on the idea that the anal character would be particularly gratified by a monetary reward. It is also of interest that there was a trend for the high anals to adopt a more negativistic and independent stance in their judgments and responses than the low anals.

Rosenwald, Mendelsohn, Fontana, and Portz (1966) have looked somewhat more directly than usual at behavior elicited by stimuli with anal connotations. They employed an "action" oriented approach which involved confronting subjects with direct, literal representations of anal material rather than symbolic forms. In studying 48 male subjects, they determined the efficiency of each individual in making a series of tactual form discriminations while his arm was immersed in water and compared it with his efficiency in doing so when his arm was immersed in a "dirty and odorous" mixture of oil and flour simulating fecal matter. The disparity in his amount of time per correct judgment for the water versus "anal" conditions was used as an index of his inability to cope with conflict resulting from anal stimulation. The anal coping difficulty index proved to be positively correlated with indecisiveness in a dot estimation task and "anal anxiety" as measured by questionnaire responses. But, surprisingly, it was positively correlated with *good* performance in creatively conceptualizing the relationships among clusters of words with anal meanings. Rosenwald, et al. speculated that this last result might be due to the fact that the individual who is "sensitive" to anal stimuli (and therefore "captivated" or "hindered" by the anal action test) would also be "alert to the opportunity for a symbolic anal response such as provided by word clusters with complex anal connotations." These results hint that predicting the effects of anal conflict on cognitive efficiency is difficult, with unexpected sensitization and repression variables making an appearance. Incidentally, anal coping difficulty was not correlated with the presence of anal character traits tapped by questionnaire responses.

A similar "action oriented" approach to the study of response to anal stimuli was adopted by Rapaport (1963). He was interested in the differential reactions of oral and anal (obsessive-compulsive) characters to oral and anal experiences likely to arouse anxiety. For his oral characters he chose hospitalized drug addicts (N = 40) who also manifested oral traits like accentuated interest in food, dependence, and impulsivity. The anal characters were hospitalized psychiatric patients (N = 40) who manifested "anal" traits like stubbornness, orderliness, and mistrust. From the pool of subjects, two anal and two oral groups (each numbering 20) were set up. Subjects in one of the anal groups and one of the oral groups were told that they were going to participate in a physiological experiment which involved measuring their reactions to the placement of suppositories in the anus. Those in the other oral and anal groups were led to expect that they would participate in a study concerned with their physiological reactions to sucking various objects (e.g., nipple). The degree of anxiety aroused in subjects by their anticipated anal or oral experiences and also their preferences for waiting "alone" or "in a group" previous to the anticipated session with the anal and oral stimuli were dependent variables. It was found that anal characters manifested more anxiety when confronted with anal than when faced with oral stimulation. Such differentiation between the effects of oral and anal stimuli was not detected for the oral characters. As anticipated by the observation that anal characters tend to use "isolating" defenses, they were found to prefer waiting alone to a significantly greater extent than did the oral subjects. It is important that this study was able to establish that anal characters react selectively to anal versus oral stimuli.

Carpenter (1965) examined the relationship between "anal-erotic" conflict and ability to perform a cognitive abstraction task involving definitions of the similarities between words with anal, aggressive, and neutral connotations. Intensity of anal conflict was assessed with a true-false Anality Questionnaire which inquired concerning anal anxieties (e.g., "Being unable to wash my hands after using the toilet upsets me") and anal character traits (e.g., "When I lend someone money I feel uneasy"). Abstraction performance was evaluated from responses to 30 word pairs, ten with anal references, ten with aggressive implications, and ten neutral. Forty-four males were studied. Contrary to expectation, the subjects with high anal conflict showed less impairment in abstraction of anal and aggressive words, as compared to abstraction of neutral words, than did those subjects with low anal conflict. This difference was shown to be largely due to the fact that the high anals performed more poorly than the low anals when specifying similarities between neutral words. In explanation, it was speculated that the individual with high anal conflict invests considerable energy in maintaining rigid defenses over a wide range of situations so as to be prepared to deal with anal threat if it should appear. But such defensive preparation is inappropriate for dealing with neutral stimuli and therefore interferes with the high anal's ability to do so adequately. In any case, Carpenter's findings failed to establish a link between anal conflict and efficiency in dealing cognitively with words that have anal or aggressive significance.

Other aspects of cognitive functioning, related to memory, have been studied within the context of the anal character typology. Adelson and Redmond (1958) measured anal expulsive and anal retentive tendencies with the Blacky test in a female sample. They also measured immediate and delayed memory for passages with "innocuous" and "disturbing" content. Subjects who were high on anal retention did significantly better on the memory tasks than subjects who were high on anal expulsion. In a follow-up to this work, Pedersen and Marlowe (1960) appraised similar memory behavior in 70 males who had been classified as anal expulsive or retentive in terms of Blacky responses. The results proved not to be confirmatory of Adelson and Redmond's data. Actually, they tended to go in directions opposite to prediction. It is of interest that a measure of n-achievement showed no relation to either of the anal variables.

Campos proposed that anal retentive personality traits result in an overevaluative "saving" attitude toward time, with the consequence that time passage is overestimated. He developed a 10-item "Retentive Personality Scale" which requests responses to such statements as "I believe in being thrifty" and "I believe in striving for perfection". In an initial project (1963) he established a significant positive correlation between retentive anal traits and a "retentive way of expending time" as measured by a 10-item scale of time expenditure (p. 60, Campos). Subsequently, he studied (1966) in a group of 100 males the degree to which retentive anality seemed to affect their estimates of how long it had taken them to fill out the anality questionnaire. His hypothesis was supported by the fact that those with the highest anality scores did most overestimate the time elapsed.

The anal character concept has also been applied to understanding occupational choice. Schlesinger (1963) anticipated that such occupations as accounting and chemical engineering would provide opportunity for the gratification of anal traits because of their emphasis on orderliness, regularity, and reliability. Contrastingly, she anticipated that an occupation like educational psychology would not provide such opportunity. A factor-analytically constructed questionnaire to measure anal traits was administered to students in accounting (N = 22), chemical engineering (N = 28), and educational psychology (N = 22). The psychologists were found to be less retentive than the accountants and engineers "in relation to a variety of objects such as money or ideas . . ." (p. 75). A similar pattern of differences was found for the trait of orderliness; but unfortunately social desirability effects seemed to play a large part in the differences.

One of the traits said to be associated with accentuation of anal character formation is an interest in collecting (presumably as a sublimation of the wish to retain and control valued feces). Lerner (1961) sought to test this aspect of the anal character model by comparing sensitivity to anal stimuli in a group of stamp collectors and a group of non-collectors. The stamp collecting sample consisted of 30 boys in the 11–16 year range. The control subjects were matched for sex, age, grade, reading ability, and vocabulary level. Two procedures were used to measure sensitivity to anal stimuli. One involved subjects attempting to identify a series of words, typed on sheets of paper, which varied in their readability. Half of the words had anal meaning and half were neutral. A second procedure was quite analogous except that subjects were asked to identify the anal and neutral words, varying in audibility, from a tape recording.

A criterion of sensitivity to anal themes was used which was based on differences in ability to identify anal as compared to neutral words. It was found that the stamp collectors were significantly more sensitive to anal references than the controls when listening to the tape recorded words, but this was not true for the condition involving the visually presented words. The results, while not completely consistent, do lend support to the psychoanalytic notion that collecting behavior is part of a cluster of attitudes tied in with the anal character typology.

Gordon (1966) has extended the use of the anal character construct to predicting the behavior of psychologists when interpreting various kinds of test and clinical protocols. In one sample she measured the presence of anal traits by means of the Grygier (1956) Dynamic Personality Inventory. The subjects were asked to interpret a Rorschach protocol of a patient by indicating agreement or disagreement with a series of statements. It had been predicted that high anal subjects would be less confident of their interpretations than low anal. This derived from the psychoanalytic view that anality involves vacillation, indecision, and lack of confidence. The data supported the expectation. A second hypothesis had stated that high anals would make fewer specific as compared to general predictions about the patient than low anals. The source of this hypothesis was the psychoanalytic formulation that anality involves a tendency to generalize and not to make specific commitments. It too was confirmed by the data. A third prediction had indicated that high anals would find less pathology in the patient than low anals. A rationale for this statement was derived from the perspective that since anality is paralleled by denial of hostility and, indeed, by reaction formation in the opposite direction, there would be a tendency to see the "good" healthy aspects of patients and to minimize their pathology. Significant support for this hypothesis was found.

In a second study (1967) involving a sample of 44 psychologists the same design was followed, with two exceptions: (1) Instead of interpreting a Rorschach protocol the subject read and made judgments about a transcript of what was supposed to be an initial interview with a patient; (2) Two levels of patient anality were introduced, insofar as one transcript was constructed to depict a patient with many anal defenses and complaints and a second transcript depicted a patient without any anal attributes. This was done to see if intensification of the anal significance of material to be judged would elicit intensified defensiveness in high anal psychologists. The overall findings confirmed the three hypotheses from the first study concerning the interaction between a psychologist's anality and the confidence, generality, and degree of attribution of pathology characterizing his clinical interpretations. However, the interactions between patient anality and psychologist anality for the three interpretative variables were not significant.

An anal orientation is apparently able to influence and modify the complex interpretative judgments which take place when test or interview data are appraised by a psychologist. Such influence may manifest itself diversely in the generality and level of confidence of interpretations which are made and also in the amount of pathology ascribed to a patient.

Miller and Stine (1951) scored the story completions of children in the age range seven–14 for various psychoanalytically defined pregenital impulse expressions and related these scores to indices of sociometric status. One of the pregenital scores computed was labeled "anality" and involved all references to smearing, cleanliness, retention, and money. A borderline tendency was observed for those children who were popular with their peers to have higher anality scores than those rejected by their peers. This was contrary to expectations. However, Fisher (1966A) later affirmed that popularity with peers probably was characteristic of the individual with an anal orientation.

Two attempts have been made to check out psychoanalytic speculations that stuttering is a symbolic expression of anal conflicts. The mouth has been viewed in such instances as having some of the significance of the anal sphincter (Fenichel, 1945). Keisman (1958) administered a check list of anal and non-anal self-descriptive items to stutterers, persons with other types of speech defects, and a group with no speech defects. No differences pertinent to anality were detected among the groups. Carp (1962) obtained Blacky test responses from a group of stutterers (N = 20) and matched non-stutterers (N = 20). There was a significant trend for stutterers to score lower than non-stutterers on Anal Expulsiveness, but the difference for Anal Retentiveness was not significant.

Even more tangential applications of the anal trait concept are to be found in the work of Farber (1955) who has shown a positive relationship between anality and aggressive political attitudes and in the exploratory findings of McNeil and Blum (1952) who reported correlations between anal retentive traits (as defined by the Blacky test) and certain handwriting characteristics.

The above review reveals that a surprisingly large number of attempts have been made to check the validity of propositions derived from Freud's anal character typology. They have ranged from correlational studies to direct experimental tests. It is impressive that the direct experimental studies (e.g., Rosenwald, et al.; Noblin; Noblin, et al.) have turned up the most convincing support. What conclusions can be reasonably drawn from the findings cited? The following seem to be appropriate generalizations:

1. As defined by questionnaire responses, there are clusters of attitudes and traits which are statistically coherent and also congruent with the anal character typology.

2. Specific forms of toilet training do not seem to be related to the development of anal traits. But the existence of anal traits in a mother increases the probability of their occurrence in her daughter and perhaps also in her son.

3. The anal character is likely to be carefully self-controlled; a naysayer; obstinate; and relatively more responsive to negative than positive reinforcement. He is also particularly responsive to money as a reinforcer.

4. It is an unresolved matter as to whether "anal erotic conflict" results in cognitive impairment when dealing with stimuli that have anal significance.

5. Similarly, the evidence is not yet clear whether anal character traits play a role in learning and recall.

6. There are exploratory hints that anal traits may influence career choice, perception of time, popularity in a peer group, interest in collecting, political aggressivity, and handwriting characteristics.

7. The evidence is not very promising that anal traits are involved in, or expressed via, the symptom of stuttering.

The aggregate reports invite serious consideration of the anal character concept. They encouraged the writer to apply it to understanding individual differences in relative awareness of front versus back regions of one's body. In the course of multiple studies of this problem it has proven to be more reasonable and more productive of verifiable hypotheses than any of the other explanatory concepts which were considered.

INVESTIGATION OF FRONT–BACK AWARENESS

Exploratory Studies

The guiding theme in the program of research undertaken with regard to front-back awareness was that the more closely an individual's behavior conforms to the pattern of the anal character the greater will be his awareness of the back as compared to the front of his body. As previously mentioned, the anal character is portrayed in psychoanalytic theory as one who has height-ened anxiety about the potential loss of control of his anal sphincter and the associated implications of disobedience and soiling aggression. In these terms, his anal region takes on exaggerated importance to him. He needs to control and regulate it; and consequently might be expected to devote a good deal of energy to monitoring the sensations emanating therefrom. It may be assumed that because the anal region is located in back of the body there is a tendency to identify it with the back; and so the anal character's concern about his anal region would become generalized to the entire back of his body. In our culture, the term "back" has obviously become almost synonymous with "backside," "buttocks," and anal functions.

Hypotheses

The first exploratory experimental attempts to relate front versus back awareness to anal character attributes revolved about the following issues:

1. A basic assumption about the anal character is that he has considerable anxiety about losing control of himself and possibly allowing bad, objectionable things to "spill out." As a result, he is presumably careful, restrained and avoids spontaneity. Couch and Keniston (1960) provided supporting evidence in their finding that the "anal retentive character" is prominently characterized by self-control and restraint over impulsive expression. With this view, it was anticipated that the greater a man's awareness of the back versus front of his body the more he would conduct himself in a controlled fashion that avoided spontaneity or "spur-of-the-moment" impulsivity.

2. Another frequent speculation about the anal character is that he associates hostility and aggression with that which is anal and dirty. He is portrayed as denying aggressive impulses, but seeking indirect outlet for them in negativism and obstinacy. Therefore, it seemed reasonable to propose that the higher a man's back awareness the stronger would be his tendency to avoid direct aggressive expression and instead to make use of negativism.

3. A central theme in formulations about the anal character is that he is made anxious by stimuli with anal connotations. If so, degree of back awareness should be positively correlated with amount of anxiety aroused by perception of stimuli with anal references.

4. It is difficult to find a clear statement regarding the kinds of traits and modes of behavior most likely to typify parents whose sons fit the anal character pattern. But two previous studies (Beloff, 1957; Hetherington and Brackbill, 1963) have hinted that parents with anal traits may foster similar traits in their children. Since the denial and control of aggressive soiling impulses is said to be a key defensive need for the anal character, it might be logical to assume that his parents would have similar needs. This could be translated into the expectation that his parents would have difficulty in being openly aggressive or hostile. Taking such a view, it was hypothesized that back awareness would be positively correlated with the extent to which one recalls one's parents as providing a model of behavior that minimized the direct expression of aggressive impulses.

5. A fifth, somewhat tangential, hypothesis was derived from work by Miller and Stine (1951) in which it was observed that children whose fantasies were typified by anal themes were, in terms of sociometric criteria, unusually popular with their peers. Miller and Stine speculated that the controlled traits of the "anal character" might impress others as a sign of being steadfast and orderly and elicit favorable evaluations. Relatedly, Couch and Keniston (1960) concluded from their data that for the "anal retentive": "The necessity of friction and aggressiveness in competitive situations is strongly denied, and replaced consciously by reactive trust and tolerance for others" (p. 172). From two different perspectives there seemed to be evidence that the anal character is proficient in pleasing rather than antagonizing others in group settings. It was therefore hypothesized that degree of back

awareness would be positively correlated with the individual's interest in group participation and also his popularity in such group situations.

BFQ Parameters

The measurement of back awareness which is required by all of the above hypotheses was accomplished by means of the Body Focus Questionnaire (BFQ) Back scale which in most instances [2] consisted of 19 items scattered through the 108-item total BFQ. In a variety of normal populations the mean BFQ Back score has fluctuated in the vicinity of 7.7. The trend is to be slightly more aware of the front than the back of one's body. Table 18.1 indicates

Table 18.1
Means and Standard Deviations of BFQ Back Scores

Mean	σ	N
6.4	3.5	45
8.0	4.1	50
7.5	4.2	48
7.5	4.3	57
8.0	3.9	45
8.5	4.2	47
8.7	4.2	51
7.1	3.8	51
7.6	3.9	50
7.6	4.0	53

typical mean values obtained in a range of male college student populations. Distributions were, with rare exceptions, quite normal in character.

In a population of 57 males the test-retest reliability [3] of the BFQ Back score, with a week intervening, was found to be .74.[4] In a second sample of 52 males the test-retest reliability with a week intervening was .82. Finally, in a third sample (N = 51) with a week intervening, the coefficient was .75.

It should also be noted that in a sample of 51 men BFQ Back had chance correlations with the MMPI K and L scales, the Marlowe-Crowne Social Desirability scale (1964), and the Bass Acquiescence scale (1956).

No significant correlations with measures of intelligence have been found in college student or children samples. This lack of relationship with

[2] In some of the earlier studies, which will be specified, a briefer BFQ Back scale consisting of only six items was used because it was first thought that the front-back BFQ comparisons necessarily had to involve sites that were perfectly homologous and there were few such sites that could be clearly defined verbally.

[3] For an earlier, brief six-item version of the Back score a test-retest (one week intervening) correlation of .44 ($p < .01$) was found for 52 male subjects.

[4] All correlation coefficients are product-moment unless otherwise specified.

intelligence has typified all of the BFQ dimensions which have been studied.

Most of the BFQ scales are relatively independent of each other. The nature of the intercorrelations of BFQ Back with the other scales is best conveyed by summarizing the results for ten different male populations (average N = 50). There were two significant negative correlations with BFQ Stomach (−.27, −.28); three significant negative correlations with BFQ Heart (−.30, −.40, −.27); three significant negative correlations with BFQ Right (−.28, −.35, −.34); and four significant negative correlations with BFQ Head (−.33, −.34, −.35, −.28). It can be seen that none of the relationships are really consistent and those that do occur are largely in the .20's and .30's. For all practical purposes, BFQ Back stands as an independent variable among the other BFQ scales.[5]

Questions can, of course, be raised as to the validity of a scale like BFQ Back. How does one know that BFQ reports actually reflect the way in which the individual habitually perceives the front versus back regions of his body? There are no single operations which would suffice to demonstrate such validity. But, on the positive side, one can point to the direct nature of the observations requested by the BFQ of the subject; their relative judgmental simplicity; and their lack of correlation with distorting variables like acquiescence and social desirability. The force of the argument here is that it would seem to be within the capability of the average individual to report his relative awareness of one body area as compared to another; and, furthermore, he would seem to have little motivation for concealing his actual judgments in public reports.

In an attempt to evaluate the generality of the information contained in a BFQ Back score, a number of studies were undertaken to compare the BFQ approach with another. These studies involved a design in which subjects were asked early in an experimental session to respond to the BFQ, and then, following intervals of one to two hours, during which they filled in various questionnaires, to report the occurrence of all sensations at two front and back sites over a five-minute period. Reports were made by placing checks under four headings (front of head, back of head, front of body, back of body) listed on a sheet of paper.

Four separate samples were studied by means of this procedure. Three consisted of male college students (N = 48, N = 50, N = 44) and one of male schizophrenic patients (N = 30). The respective correlations of BFQ Back with the number of back minus number of front sensations reported for the three normal samples were .28 ($p = .05$), .26 ($p < .10$), and .34 ($p < .05$). The correlation in the schizophrenic sample was .33 ($p < .10$). It would appear that the two methods for obtaining measures of relative front-back awareness were consistently, although modestly related.

---

[5] In relation to the work earlier presented, it should be observed that BFQ Back has not shown consistent relationships with the Barrier score.

Testing Hypotheses
Study A

Returning now to the hypotheses concerning the relation of BFQ Back to anal character traits, it will be recalled that the first predicted an inverse relation between degree of focus on one's back and behavioral spontaneity.

In testing [6] it, the following procedure was used:

The intensity of a subject's attention to his back was measured with an early version of the Body Focus Questionnaire (BFQ) containing references to six paired front-back body sites (e.g., front of head versus back of head, front of neck versus back of neck); and the subject indicated in each case whether he was more aware of the front or the back site. His score could range from 0 through 6.

The Impulsive scale, one of seven contained in the Thurstone Temperament Schedule (1953) was chosen to ascertain how much spontaneity typified the subject. Thurstone states, "High scores in this category indicate a happy-go-lucky, daredevil, carefree, acting-on-the-spur-of-the-moment disposition." The Impulsive score is based on the subject's reports concerning his own behavior, as indicated by responding Yes, No or ? to a series of statements.

In dealing with the spontaneity variable, an unpublished Anal Orderliness scale developed by Henry Murray was also administered to one sample. This scale contains ten items which inquire concerning compulsive and perfectionistic behavior (e.g., "I do things more slowly and carefully than others"; "I am generally methodical and systematic in the way I go about things"). The subject indicates his degree of agreement on a five point scale.

The Order scale of the Edwards (1954) Personal Preference Schedule was also applied to a sample. It was intended to measure the degree to which one keeps things neat and orderly and systematically organized.

Three different samples of subjects were studied with the Thurstone scale. They consisted respectively of 40, 51, and 60 male college students. The median age in each of the groups was 20. A fourth sample of 52 students (median age 20) was studied with the Murray Anal Orderliness scale. A fifth sample of college students (N = 51, median age 20) was evaluated with the Order scale of the Edwards Preference Schedule.

The BFQ Back median [7] in sample 1 was 2 (range 0 through 6). The

---

[6] As will be seen, highly diverse methods have been used to evaluate the validity of BFQ formulations. In some instances the methods involve overt behavior whose validity implications are clear. In other instances they are much less clear. The strategy has been adopted, whenever possible, of using varied methods whose results can be compared to ascertain if they add up in a convincingly consistent manner.

[7] BFQ Back values will be given only for major studies or in instances when they are atypical.

Impulsive median was 9 (range 5 through 17). Chi square [8] was used to examine the relationship between the variables because the Impulsive scores were seriously skewed. When the trichotomized Back scores were related to the dichotomized (at the median) Impulsive scores, it was found that they were negatively linked at a borderline level ($\chi^2 = 4.6$, df $= 2$, p .10).

In sample 2 the mean BFQ Back score was 3.1 ($\sigma = 1.8$). For the Impulsive scores the mean was 10.6 ($\sigma = 2.7$). A product-moment correlation of —.24 was found between the Back and Impulsive scores. With a one-tailed test, which was used because this was a cross-validation attempt, the coefficient is significant at the .05 level.

In sample 3 the mean Back score was 2.5 ($\sigma = 1.7$). The mean Impulse score was 10.6 ($\sigma = 3.5$). A significant negative correlation of —.26 ($p < .05$, one-tailed test) was found between the two sets of scores.

The results for sample 4 in which the Murray Anal Orderliness scale was employed indicated that Orderliness was significantly and positively correlated with BFQ Back ($r = .36$, $p < .01$, two-tail test), as predicted. The mean Orderliness score was 16.2 ($\sigma = 5.6$).

In sample 5 the mean BFQ Back score was 3.1 ($\sigma = 1.8$) and the mean Edwards Order score was 48.6 ($\sigma = 30.8$). BFQ Back and Order were correlated only .09.

The data from four of the five samples fitted the expectation that the greater a man's awareness of his back the more likely he is to avoid responses which are not carefully controlled. None of the individual relationships were large but their consistent directionality over four samples was encouraging. Since anxiety about loss of impulse control is a prominent difficulty ascribed to the "anal personality," the above finding added weight to the notion that attention to one's back and "anality" have overlapping significance.

Study B

Other exploratory studies were undertaken to determine whether the relationships of BFQ Back to several of the other anal trait variables were in the predicted direction.

A second hypothesis stated that back awareness would be negatively correlated with open aggressiveness and positively so with stubbornness or negativism. Two subscales of the Buss-Durkee Inventory (Buss and Durkee, 1957) were employed to get at the anger variables: (A) 10-item Assaultive scale which is typified by assertions like "Whoever insults me or my family is asking for it," "If I have to resort to physical violence to defend my right, I will." The subject responds by answering Yes or No to each item. (B) 5-item Negativism scale which is represented by a statement like "When someone is bossy, I do the opposite of what he asks." Of course, back awareness was

---

[8] Yates correction has been applied whenever the theoretical value in a cell is 5 or less.

measured in this case and in relation to the other hypotheses that follow by means of the BFQ.

The hypothesis that back awareness would be positively correlated with anxiety about stimuli with anal significance was explored via responses to the Blacky pictures (Blum, 1949). More specifically, in terms of responses to one Blacky picture labeled Anal Sadism which depicts the dog named Blacky in a position where his anus is visible and it is apparent that he has just defecated.

The Blacky pictures consist of 11 scenes in which a dog is portrayed as engaged in activities illustrating crucial developmental problems in the psychoanalytic scheme (e.g., Oral Eroticism, Castration Anxiety). A new approach to measuring response to the pictures was attempted. The subject is presented with the 11 pictures arranged in the order in which they are usually administered. He is told that in a later session he will be asked to compose stories about some of them. In preparation for this, he is to examine the pictures and put them in rank order, with the one he would most prefer to elaborate upon first in sequence and the one he would least prefer to describe last in sequence. It was assumed the greater the anxiety aroused in a subject by a picture the more motivated he would be to evade involvement with it by assigning it a low rank order. Only the reactions to the picture specifically related to an anal theme were considered pertinent for the present study.

Table 18.2
Product-Moment Correlations of BFQ Back
with "Anal Character" Variables

BFQ Back versus	r	Significance Level
Buss-Durkee Assaultive	−.13	
	(N = 52) [a]	n.s.[b]
Buss-Durkee Negativism	.27	
	(N = 52)	<.05
Blacky Anal Sadism	.26	
	(N = 51)	<.10
Father anger	−.38	
	(N = 50)	<.01
Mother anger	.06	
	(N = 52)	n.s.
Total affiliation with organizations	.21	
	(N = 55)	>.10
Total elective offices held	.27	
	(N = 55)	<.05

[a] N varies because the subjects gave incomplete responses to some procedures or else misunderstood the instructions. In the case of parental ratings there were instances in which a father or mother had died when the subject was still a young child and therefore could not be recalled.

[b] Does not even attain .20 level.

Another hypothesis had predicted that BFQ Back would be negatively correlated with the subject's perception of how openly his parents expressed anger. Therefore, he was asked to indicate on a three point scale the degree to which each of ten statements concerned with behavior expressive of anger applied first to his mother and then to his father. Examples of the statements follow: Likes a fight; Expresses anger openly and directly; Good at telling people off. The responses Not at all true; Slightly true; and Very true were weighted respectively 0, 1, 2. Total scores could range from 0 through 20.

The subjects were 55 male college students. Their median age was 20. The BFQ Back score mean for the subjects who completed the Buss-Durkee scales was 2.4 ($\sigma = 1.6$). The mean for the Buss-Durkee Assaultive scale was 5.2 ($\sigma = 2.4$); and for the Negativism scale it was 1.9 ($\sigma = 1.4$). One can see in Table 18.2 that BFQ Back had a chance relation to Assaultive, but that it was significantly correlated with Negativism in the predicted direction ($r = .27$, $p < .05$). Back awareness was not correlated with self reports of overt aggression, but it was positively so with such reports of negativisitic behavior. However, in a subsequent study involving a new sample of college students ($N = 48$), BFQ Back was not significantly correlated with the Negativism score or any of the other Buss-Durkee scales.

The Blacky picture data were supportive of the proposition that back awareness is positively correlated with the level of anxiety aroused by representations of anal function. Table 18.2 shows that BFQ Back is correlated .26 ($p < .10$) with the rank order placement of the Anal Sadism picture. The higher the BFQ Back score the less willing was the subject to compose a story about the Anal Sadism picture. But in a series of other samples this borderline relationship was not consistently supported. Indeed, evidence emerged that the Blacky ranking procedure was quite unreliable and its use was abandoned. Although it was applied in the early stages of several studies dealing with other BFQ variables, space will not be taken in subsequent chapters to report the largely negative and unstable results that were obtained.

One notes, with reference to the hypothesis concerned with degree of parental anger, that the mean anger score attributed to mother was 7.9 ($\sigma = 3.7$) and to father 5.6 ($\sigma = 2.6$). Table 18.2 indicates that BFQ Back was, as predicted, negatively correlated with Father Anger ($r = -.38$, $p < .01$). It had only a chance correlation with Mother Anger. The hypothesis was supported in terms of father's recalled traits but not in terms of mother's.

The fifth hypothesis proposed that BFQ Back would be positively correlated with degree of participation in group activities and also one's popularity in such groups. To obtain an index of the subject's amount of participation in groups, he was asked to list the organizations to which he had belonged in high school and his first year in college. His popularity in these groups was estimated by asking him to list the elective offices he had held in each.

The BFQ score in this study was based on the enlarged number of 19 items.

The subjects were 55 male college students whose median age was 20.

The data dealing with the relation of BFQ Back to group participation were mildly favorable to the proposed hypothesis. There was a trend for the predicted positive correlation between BFQ Back and Total Affiliation with Organizations, although it was not significant ($r = .21$, $p < .10$). Further, the relationship between BFQ Back and Total Elective Offices Held was significantly positive, as predicted ($r = .27$, $p < .05$). One could say that those with relatively greater back awareness were those who most frequently reported election to office in the organizations to which they belonged.

It should be added that in a subsequent corroborative follow-up to this study involving another sample of 51 college men (median age = 20), subjects were asked to report all of the organizations to which they had belonged in high school and also to designate those in which they had held elective office. BFQ Back scores proved to be correlated .25 ($p < .10$) with Total Affiliation with Organizations and .37 ($p < .01$) with Total Elective Offices Held.

The concept of a link between back awareness and anal character traits was mildly supported in the above exploratory studies. The most discouraging findings were those related to the use of the Blacky pictures. However, encouragement was offered by the Thurstone Impulsive scale data and the Murray Anal Orderliness scale findings which indicated that the individual who focuses attention on his back is also one who restricts impulsive expression and behaves with compulsive care. The related assumption that such an individual would also avoid direct expression of aggression and rely instead on indirect forms of stubbornness was only partially confirmed. BFQ Back turned out not to be correlated with Buss-Durkee Assaultive, but positively so with Negativism. However, the Negativism finding did not hold up in a subsequent study. There was partial confirmation of the hypothesis that back awareness is negatively correlated with the degree to which one's parents are recalled as openly showing anger. The confirmation was only partial because, while the data involving recall of the father's behavior were congruent with expectation, those pertaining to mother were not. It was speculated that the mother's style of anger expression might be less important than father's in providing a model for a son.

The most tangential prediction made assumed that an individual's degree of back focus would be positively linked with how involved he was in group activities and also how popular he was in such groups. The results affirmed the expectation about back awareness and popularity in organized groups but indicated only a non-significant trend in the predicted direction for group participation. A subsequent study successfully cross-validated these findings. However, they should be cautiously interpreted because subjects' reports of their own group behavior were used rather than more objective observations. But, it is also true that the significant findings are congruent with the work of Miller and Stine (1951) in which preoccupation with anal themes in children was found to be related to their group popularity. The anal orientation presumably basic to back awareness did seem to make for popularity with one's peers. This could possibly be regarded as a function of modulated self-control or "reactive trust and tolerance for others" (Couch and Keniston, 1960) which might have a pleasing conciliatory effect. It was speculated too that the negativism usually ascribed to an anal orientation might not be prominent in peer interactions; and that it might be more common in encounters with authority figures.

PARANOID DEFENSE

The early exploratory attempts to tie in back awareness with anal conflicts also led to an investigation of the relationship between such awareness and paranoid symptomatology.

Freud (1911) and other analytic theorists (e.g., Ferenczi, 1911) underscored the importance of "anal fixation" in the formulation of the paranoid delusion. It was considered that the paranoid delusion represents an attempt to disown and project outwardly passive-receptive (homosexual) aims derived from fixation on anal-erogenous zones. Tausk (1933), Starcke (1920), and Von Ophuijsen (1920) attempted to demonstrate that the persecutor in the delusion is assigned attributes associated with anal sensations and the buttocks. Aronson (1952) and Meketon, Griffith, Taylor, and Wiedeman (1962) have tested the concept of paranoia as a defense against passive-feminine homosexual impulses by comparing the frequency of "homosexual signs" in the Rorschach responses of paranoid as contrasted to non-paranoid schizophrenics. The results have largely supported the concept. Moore and Seltzer (1963) have shown that in terms of clinical reports homosexual conflicts are more prominent in the paranoid than the non-paranoid schizophrenic. Both clinical and experimental observations tend to concur with the psychoanalytic formulation that the paranoid system is to some degree a defense against homosexual fantasies linked with passive anal-receptive attitudes.

If the paranoid delusion is correlated with anxiety about fantasies with anal reference, it should follow from the front-back awareness work which has been described that the paranoid would have relatively high awareness of his back. That is, disturbance about anal issues would be accompanied by intensified back concern. Operationally, this was considered to mean that the paranoid schizophrenic should have greater back awareness than the non-paranoid schizophrenic.

A study was undertaken to test this proposition.

Back awareness was measured with a 19-item front-back subscale embedded in a Body Focus Questionnaire containing 108 items. Subjects were seen individually. An observer rated their level of cooperation on a 3-point scale. Forty-four male schizophrenics were evaluated (paranoid, 27; non-paranoid, 17). They had not received shock therapy up to at least six months prior to the test session. The median ages in the paranoid and non-paranoid groups were, respectively, 33 (range 22–47) and 35 (range 18–43). This difference is not significant. In both groups the median years of education was 12. Ratings for cooperation were not significantly different for the two groups. Equal proportions (67%) of each group were receiving tranquilizing medication; and the dosage levels were not significantly different.

The mean BFQ Back score for the paranoids was 8.7 ($\sigma = 3.2$) and for the non-paranoids 6.5 ($\sigma = 3.4$). A t-test indicated that, as predicted, the difference between the groups was significant at the $<.05$ level ($t = 2.1$).

A follow-up on these findings was attempted in a second sample of male schizophrenic patients (paranoid, 16; non-paranoid, 17). The median ages in the paranoid and non-paranoid samples were respectively 34 (range 21–49) and 36 (range 19–49); and they did not differ significantly. Median number of years of education in both groups was 12. Approximately equal proportions (50–60%) of each group were receiving tranquilizing medication. The mean Back score for the Paranoids was 7.9 ($\sigma = 3.0$) and that for the non-paranoids was 7.5 ($\sigma = 3.3$). These means were not significantly different.

Support for the hypothesis was received in the first study but not in the second. This leaves the issue in doubt. A major problem encountered in investigating this matter relates to the obvious unreliability of the paranoid and non-paranoid diagnostic categories. Patients were seen in several different hospitals and it was apparent that definitions of "paranoid schizophrenia" were often only vaguely similar.

CROSS VALIDATION AND EXTENSION OF FINDINGS

Despite mixed results, there were sufficient positive findings to encourage further studies to clarify the relationship of anal character concepts to front-back awareness. This work will be reviewed below in functional clusters.

Response to Stimuli with Anal Meaning

As earlier indicated, one would expect variations in back awareness to be paralleled by degrees of selectivity in responding to stimuli with anal connotations. If back awareness is a function of feelings about anal matters, it should be meaningfully related to how an individual reacts when he is asked to perceive and cope with anal references. Anal references will be defined as pertaining either directly to defecation or to frequently associated derivatives described by terms like "dirty," "messy," and "smelly."

Tachistoscopically Presented Blacky Anal Sadism Picture

An effort was made to relate back awareness to differential response to the Blacky Anal Sadism picture when presented tachistoscopically. It was expected, of course, that selective attitudes toward the representation of the dog Blacky defecating would be evidenced in how much difficulty was encountered in perceiving it accurately. A population of 41 college men served as subjects. The BFQ was administered to them individually. Subsequently, they were brought into a darkened room; dark adapted for one minute; and then instructed how to observe a picture (of a pencil) presented tachistoscopically. Six Blacky pictures (Anal Sadism, Castration Anxiety, Masturbation Guilt, Oral Sadism, Oral Eroticism, and Sibling Rivalry) were pointed out to them, taped to a surface, and it was noted that each was designated by a number. They were instructed that each picture would be shown several times at high speed on the tachistoscope and each time they were to report the number of the one they identified it as being. Each picture was shown six times in the course of six randomized sequences. The exposure times for each sequence were as follows: 2.3, 2.5, 3.0, 3.5, 4.0, 4.5 m sec. For each picture there was determined the number of times it was correctly identified and also the fastest speed at which it was identified. Each was converted to a rank relative to the respective values for the other five Blacky pictures.

BFQ Back proved to have a chance correlation with the rank of the number of times Anal Sadism was correctly identified. However, it had a significant positive correlation with rank of the first speed at which it was correctly perceived ($r = .36$, $p < .025$). The higher the back awareness the longer was required to make the first accurate identification. Apparently, the Anal Sadism picture was more likely to arouse an inhibitory reaction in those with high back awareness. BFQ Back was not significantly correlated with any of the tachistoscopic indices concerned with the other five Blacky pictures.

The results derived from the tachistoscopic procedure indicate a selective response to the Anal Sadism picture which parallels back awareness.

Cleaning Behavior

A major assumption regarding the anal character is that he has strong impulses to soil and be dirty and finds it necessary to defend himself against such impulses by demonstrating that he is a very "clean" unsoiled person. With this point in mind, the question then arises whether BFQ Back is related to the way in which the individual habitually reacts to the dirt he encounters in his environment. One would assume that the need to engage in anti-dirt (cleaning) activities would be positively correlated with intensity of back awareness. This is essentially a prediction that with increasing back awareness there is a defensive sensitivity to dirt stimuli because of their anal significance. In order to investigate this proposition, male college students (N = 56) were asked to write a description of how they spent an average week. Their specific instructions were as follows: "Describe a typical week in your life. Give an account of the routine aspects of it as well as some of the high spots. Go into detail. You will have 15 minutes to write. Be sure to fill two pages." The descriptions obtained in this manner were blindly coded for every reference to the following kinds of categories:

> Cleaning activities
> Eating or oral gratification
> Work oriented behavior
> Sports activities
> Seeking entertainment
> Seeking interaction with other persons

Cleaning activities included any references to washing or cleansing one's body, clothes, or other possessions (e.g., "I wash my hair," "I clean my room," "I polish my car," "I take my clothes to the laundry"). The number of references in each category was expressed as a percentage of the total number in all categories. This was done to control for the length of each subject's description. Two raters who scored 20 protocols attained 91 percent agreement on number of references coded as belonging to the "cleaning" category. Agreement for the other categories ranged from 78 to 92 percent.

The mean percent of references to cleaning activities was .4; and the range was from .2 to 1.6.

The correlation between BFQ Back and % Cleaning Reference was .29, which is significant at the <.05 level. Those individuals with the greatest back awareness reported engaging in the largest percent of anti-dirt activities. None of the other categories of subjects' descriptions of their average week were significantly correlated with BFQ Back. This finding represents direct evidence that back awareness and sensitivity to dirt are related in a way which would be predicted by the "anal character" model.

Further exploration of this issue was attempted by examining the number of references to dirt and cleanliness made by subjects in a free spontaneously expressive situation. A sample of 41 male college students served as subjects. BFQ forms were administered to them individually. They were also asked on two occasions, a week apart, to list on a sheet of paper "20 things that you are aware of or conscious of right now." Each protocol was scored for the number of references to dirt or cleanliness. Some examples of scorable responses follow:

> The blotter is dirty.
> My shoes are dirty.
> There are erasure specks here.
> I need to do my laundry.
> My hands are dirty.
> The ash tray is clean.
> There is dust here.

Two judges, each independently scoring 20 protocols, attained 93 percent agreement.

It was anticipated, of course, that the greater an individual's back awareness the more likely he was to become concerned with matters of dirt and cleanliness during his spontaneous expressions.

The relationship between BFQ Back and number of dirt references was examined by means of chi-square.

The median number of dirt references for the two protocols combined was 2 (range 0–6). A chi-square analysis indicated that BFQ Back scores were, as predicted, significantly and positively related to the number of dirt references ($\chi^2 = 5.0$, df = 1, $p < .05$). This constitutes firm affirmation of the results described above based on the number of references to cleaning activities in subjects' descriptions of how they spend an average week.

Memory for Words with Anal Significance

Sets or attitudes can sometimes be detected by their impact upon learning and recall (e.g., Rapaport, 1942). The possibility was therefore considered that the relation between back awareness and anal attitudes might be traced via learning measures. If an individual is especially activated or is made anxious by stimuli with anal meaning, should this not register in a selective pattern of recall of words with anal connotations which he has learned? In order to evaluate this possibility a list of 20 words was constructed. Ten dealt directly or indirectly with themes or terms associated with defecation and the anal regions of the body. Ten were neutral words which were matched to be of the same average length as the anal words. The total list is shown below as it was presented to subjects for learning.

Seat *	Poem
Climb	Gas *
Smell *	Think
Decide	Regular *

Back *	Magical
Simple	Bottom *
Strain *	Radio
Retain *	Expel *
Sign	Wood
Bat	Rear *

[* Anal words]

It was presumed that anal anxieties or concerns would result, during learning, in selective awareness of the anal words which could be measured in later recall. There was no clear basis for deciding whether such selectivity would have a facilitative or repressive form. One might expect a repressive effect; but there are previous studies, e.g., Rosenwald, et al. (1966), in which anal anxiety actually facilitated efficiency in manipulating words with anal connotations. Therefore, it was predicted only that degree of back awareness would be associated with some form of selectivity in the learning and recall of the anal words.

A sample of male college students (N = 61) was studied. They were seen in small groups. Their BFQ Back scores were obtained in the usual fashion. To measure selective recall, they were asked to learn the 20 word list, containing the anal words, which was projected upon a screen for one minute. Immediately afterwards they were given five minutes to write down as many of the words as they could recall. A selectivity index was computed equal to the sum of anal words minus the sum of non-anal words recalled. The mean selectivity score was .7, indicating that on the average subjects recalled almost one more anal than non-anal words. A correlation of .22 was found between BFQ Back and the tendency to recall more anal than non-anal words. This value falls at the <.10 level, which is of borderline significance.

Frugality and Thrift

One of the traits frequently mentioned in the literature (e.g., Fenichel, 1945) as characteristic of the anal character is that of thrift or frugality. It is theorized that the sense of obligation to control and retain feces is generalized to a feeling that one ought to retain objects and possessions. Barnes (1952) has devised two scales which presumably measure frugality (8 items) and thrift (5 items) respectively. The subject is asked to answer Yes or No to a series of questions pertaining to how motivated one is to save, accumulate, and not expend. In two samples of male college students (N = 50, N = 51) BFQ Back was found not to be significantly related to either the Frugality or Thrift scales.

Chain Associations

A "chain association" method for evaluating responses to various themes, which has been described by Story (1963), was used to ascertain the relationship of back awareness to sensitivity to words with anal connotations. Subjects were asked to give the first ten words that "come to mind" as each of 14 stimulus words were presented to them. The words, in the actual sequence of presentation, were as follows:

House	Sky
Taste	Stab
Mess	Rear
Hit	Swallow
Suicide	Shoot
Suck	Stink
	Hurtself

Three of the words were anal (mess, rear, stink); three oral; three aggressive; three masochistic; and two neutral. All associations were taken down verbatim; and the time required in each instance to produce ten responses was recorded.

The associations given to each stimulus word were scored in terms of how directly they pertained to the original meaning of the word. Each response was classified as directly, indirectly, or not at all related to the stimulus word. A response was considered to be directly related if it was a clear example of the class denoted by the stimulus words. For example, words like "garbage," "mud," "feces" and "dirt" would be "direct" responses to the word "mess." A response was classified as indirectly related if it referred to feelings, affects, or reactions that might typically be linked with the content of the stimulus word. For example, responses like "unpleasant," "annoying," and "repugnant" were classified as indirect. Words like "sky," "man," or "swim" given in reaction to "mess" would exemplify the category of being unrelated to the stimulus. Two judges working independently with 20 protocols attained an overall average agreement of 84 percent in classifying degree of directness of associations.

A weight of 2 was given for each direct association, 1 for each indirect association, and 0 for each unrelated association. Scores could, therefore, range from 0 to 20 for the ten associations produced for a stimulus word. The mean for each cluster of words was computed; and means for time scores were similarly determined.

It was presumed that if the theme or issue denoted by a cluster of stimulus words were of special significance to a subject it would be evidenced in one or both of the following ways: (1) unusually short or long time scores for producing associations; (2) particularly high or low scores for directness of associations. That is, the subject could be delayed and inhibited or alerted and loosened.

When the BFQ Back scores of a group of male college students (N = 43) were related to the rank order of the time required to produce a quota of associations to the anal words as compared to the time for producing such quotas for the other themes, a significant negative correlation was noted ($r = -.32$, $p < .05$). That is, the higher the back awareness the more quickly were the required numbers of associations to the anal words given. There were no other correlations of significance between BFQ Back and the other rank order time scores. That for the Anal words was unique.

BFQ Back was not significantly correlated with the Anal score or any of the other scores denoting directness of associations.

Only in terms of the time score was back awareness linked with selectivity in responding to the anal theme. Interestingly, the selectivity took the form not of slowed up but rather speeded up response. One is reminded that Rosenwald, et al. (1966) found "anal characters" to show special facility in dealing with verbal material with anal connotations.

Humor

Weiss (1954) devised a humor test which was intended to tap attitudes pertaining to five psychodynamic themes:

> Oral Eroticism (six jokes)
> Oral Sadism (seven jokes)
> Anal Expulsiveness (four jokes)
> Oedipal Intensity (five jokes)
> Castration Anxiety (four jokes)

Presumably, degree of liking or disliking of jokes with a common theme provides clues as to the individual's attitude toward that theme. A version of the Weiss test was constructed which instructed subjects to indicate on a six-point scale how enjoyable they find each of a series of jokes in which the five themes are randomly distributed. The numbers of jokes dealing with each theme are shown in parentheses next to each category listed above. As indicated by Weiss, it is still unclear whether anxiety and conflict about a specific theme are most likely to result in extreme high or low ratings of pertinent jokes—or both. In the present study, it was decided to consider only degree of favorableness or unfavorableness of response; and to conceptualize high or low ratings as indicative of selective response rather than of the presence or absence of anxiety.

Each subject's mean rating of the jokes in each category was computed; and the means were assigned ranks (rank 1 = least enjoyable).

It was expected, of course, that BFQ Back would be significantly related to ratings of the Anal Expulsive jokes, but not to the jokes in other categories. The following is an example of an Anal Expulsive joke.

An agitated mother rushed into a drug store, screaming that the infant in her arms had just swallowed a .22 calibre bullet.
"What shall I do?" she cried.
"Give him the contents of this bottle of castor oil," replied the druggist, "but don't point him at anybody!"

In a sample of 47 male college students, the mean Anal Expulsive rank was 3.0 ($\sigma = 1.4$). BFQ Back proved to be correlated .28 ($p < .05$) with the Anal Expulsive ranks. The greater an individual's awareness of his back the greater was his relative enjoyment of the jokes with anal content. None of the correlations of BFQ Back with the ranks of the other joke categories was significant.

The findings established an interconnection between back awareness and selective response to anal jokes.

EFFECT OF PERIPHERAL STIMULATION OF FRONT–BACK SITES

Initial Testing of a Theory

It is necessary at this point to make a major digression in order to outline a theory concerning the functioning of "body landmarks" (such as represented by one's relative awareness of the front versus back of one's body) in guiding behavior. The theory to be described became a prime source of ideas for many of the studies to be presented in this book. It resulted in experiments which demonstrated quite directly that the sensory prominence of a body area can influence cognitive processes selectively.

The incentive to develop this theory came from several sources. First of all, one finds an accumulation of work by other investigators which indicates that body sensations, as such, provide an influential context in judging and evaluating what is "out there." For example, it has been shown that the position of one's body (viz., lying down versus sitting up) may affect the mood of TAT stories (Beigel, 1952). Secondly, as already described, there are a number of studies pertinent to boundary definiteness which indicate that the state of the boundary probably plays a role in certain types of selective memory (Chapter 7). Thus, a significant positive correlation was found between the individual's Barrier score and his tendency to recall a predominance of verbal references to exterior body sensations (e.g., skin itches) as compared to interior sensations (e.g., heart beats) which he had learned. Selectivity in learning was, in this instance, an apparent function of a pattern of body experience. It appeared as if the relative predominance of exterior versus interior sensations in the individual's own body was reflected in a similar ratio of recall of verbal references to exterior versus interior body experiences. Analogously, it was demonstrated in another study (Fisher, 1965C) that the greater an individual's awareness of his stomach prior to responding to a series of ink blots the more likely he was to produce images referring to eating, food, and other oral themes. These and similar findings suggested that degree of awareness of a region of one's own body could be a significant force in the perceptual field—helping to shape its properties.

A further incentive to theory construction about the role of peripheral body cues in cognitive-judgmental processes came from the initially promising results derived from the application of the Body Focus Questionnaire. A range of evidence emerged, which will be described later in greater detail, that individuals do distribute their attention consistently over time to certain major body locales and that the highlighting or minimizing of a locale is linked with specific traits or conflicts. Such apparent significance in degree of awareness of a body region and the previously mentioned observations that the relative sensory prominence of a region is associated with selective perceptual and learning effects seemed to call for theoretical investigation. Was there a way of synthesizing the observations that a perceptually highlighted body sector was simultaneously representative of certain wishes and sets and perhaps also a source of selective influence upon cognitive activities?

Sketched broadly, the following line of thought was taken. It was considered that relative awareness of a body sector represents, in part, an expression of an important attitude and exerts a significant force itself in guiding behavior. Somehow, during socialization one probably learns to associate certain wishes and conflicts with specified regions of one's body. This would be exemplified by the way in which the back becomes associated with anal functioning and anal conflicts. But the idea was rejected that the enhanced awareness of a body region related to a particular wish or conflict is a mere epiphenomenon or by-product. Rather, there seemed to be excellent hints from some of the selective memory findings, already cited above, that the awareness itself played a regulatory role. Indeed, the idea presented itself that the awareness might influence (in an excitatory or inhibitory manner) the set or conflict with which it was associated. Perhaps the perceptual prominence of a body region linked with a specific set or wish could, in turn, have a feedback influence upon the set. The clear position was taken that the relative vividness of various body areas in the body scheme serves as an organized system of peripheral cues designed to play a role in regulating response. This idea may be compared to the homely analogy of the child who remembers to buy a certain article at the store because his mother tied a string to his finger to remind him of it. Just so, it was presumed, may an

individual develop on the basis of his socialization experiences a variety of
"attached strings" (i.e., perceptually highlighted body areas) which become
persistent sources of signals that modify judgments and responses.

More formally, the theory may be presented as follows:

The body scheme, considered as a series of landmarks with differential
sensory prominence, may be conceptualized as a representation in body
experience terms of attitudes the individual has adopted. These are experiences coded as patterns of body awareness (e.g., involving muscle, stomach).
It may be presumed that the patterns of body awareness exist as circuits based
on the following sequence: perceptual focus upon a body area because of its
utility or significance or activation in relation to a goal; increased physiological and also sensory arousal of the area as a consequence of its special
prominence; further feedback from such arousal to the subsystem in the CNS
involved in the original highlighting of the area. Thus, the individual's body
scheme contains landmarks which reiterate to him that certain things are
important and others are not. Just as a contracting stomach is a signal to seek
food. the perceptual prominence of certain muscles maintained at high tonus
may be a reminder to attend or not to attend to some class of objects. In this
sense, the individual with relatively high awareness of his back would be
reminded by this persistent "back" sensory signal to avoid situations which
stimulate the kinds of conflicts found in the "anal character." It could
function also to inhibit and dampen the central "anal" conflict.

The possibility that body sensations might function to modify perception
and cognition in this fashion has been considered at length by Solley and
Murphy (1960). They noted that Solomon and Wynne (1954) had found that
avoidance conditioning in dogs was influenced by amount of visceral autonomic feedback. Solomon and Wynne had actually concluded that "at least
some of the afferent feedback impulses from the viscera have the properties of
stimuli and so are capable of becoming conditioned stimuli and drive stimuli"
(p. 369). Solley and Murphy indicated that proprioceptive feedback might
function similarly; and proposed that a percept could get linked or locked to
proprioceptive and autonomic feedback mechanisms "so that the percept and
the feedback mechanisms are mutually excitatory" (p. 243). Illustratively, it
was suggested that the continuous tightening of certain muscles might act
chronically to inhibit specific anxiety arousing memories. "The painful
memories are 'locked' in a state of unawareness by the incessant feedback
from the tightened muscles" (p. 244). Quite analogously, other investigators
have found that cues derived from body sensations may influence perception
and learning. Level of muscle tonus, asymmetry of tonus, position of body in
space, body deformity, amount of autonomic arousal, and body sensations
derived from drug effects have all proven to be variables that significantly
affect cognitive processes. The body image emerges in the model just described
as a framework of meanings assigned to body areas which in turn are accompanied by sensory signals that have a selective impact upon perception and

cognition. In assigning such importance to body signals outside of the CNS, one swings back in the direction of peripheral theories of thought and affect which were supported vigorously at one time by Titchener (1924), Washburn (1916), James (1892), Jacobsen (1929), Freeman (1948A, B), Guthrie (1952) and others. While theories emphasizing central factors are currently more acceptable and in vogue, it has been observed by several reviewers (e.g., Gellhorn, 1964) that the contribution of peripheral factors has not yet been adequately evaluated.

If the theory proposed is a valid one, it should be possible to influence cognitive processes selectively by changing the sensory prominence of given body areas. That is, if a specified level of awareness of the back of one's body influences response to situations with anal connotation (e.g., involving dirt), it should be possible to alter selective responses to such situations by changing the individual's relative awareness of his back.

The first experimental attempt to test the theory was actually made with respect to front versus back awareness. Since the back seems to mean "anal" or dirty and front just the opposite, it was anticipated that increasing the experiential prominence of either should have opposite selective effects upon memory referring to dirt themes.[9]

The following list presenting ten dirt and ten non-dirt words, developed for an earlier study, was employed to evaluate selective memory effects. [The dirt words are marked with an asterisk.]

Line	Brick
Neat *	Dirt *
For	Smear *
Odor *	Plant
Dealt	Mess *
Mud *	High
Inch	Clean *
Foul *	Print
Trip	Putrid *
Impure *	Table

The mean length of the two sets of words is equal and they are spaced equivalently through the list.

The subject was asked to learn and recall this list under one of three conditions. In one condition he was told that he was to participate in a study of the effect of distraction upon learning. A vibrator (Oster Massaget, Model 212, 35 watts, weight 2 lb., 4 ounces) was strapped on top of a piece of sponge

---

[9] Without real reason, the idea was initially favored that back stimulation would enhance and front stimulation would inhibit recall of dirt words. But a series of studies subsequently pointed up the difficulty of predicting the specific directionality of peripheral stimulation effects.

material to his back and turned on for one minute so that he could "get used to the vibration." The list of words, typed on a sheet of paper, was then presented to him and he was asked to learn it. After one minute the list was removed and he was given five minutes to write down all of the words he could recall.

The second experimental condition was exactly the same except that the vibrator was strapped to the left forearm and the subject placed his hand in a comfortable position with the palm down. In this position the vibrator produced a vibration which was distinctly experienced as involving the entire front of the body.

A third experimental condition duplicated the same procedure except that the learning task was presented without a vibrator being attached to the subject's body.

The recall of each subject was scored by subtracting the sum of non-dirt words recalled from the sum of dirt words recalled.

Sixteen male college students served as subjects for the front vibration condition; 16 for the back vibration condition; and 16 for the neutral condition. Male examiners collected the data. Median age in all three groups was 20 years and the median educational level in all was 15 years.

The mean dirt–non-dirt recall score for the front vibration condition was —.43; and for the back vibration condition it was +1.37. For the neutral condition the mean was +1.31. Back vibration resulted in greatest selective superiority in recall for dirt words. Front vibration produced the greatest selective deficit in recall for dirt words; and the neutral condition gave results similar to those for the back condition.

Analysis of variance indicated that the overall differences among the conditions were significant ($F = 4.4$, $p < .05$). The difference between the back and front stimulation conditions was significant ($F = 6.9$, $p < .01$), and also that between front and neutral ($F = 6.5$, $p < .01$). The difference between the back and neutral conditions was not significant. One can see from the pattern of results that the differences produced by vibration were largely a function of the front condition which seemed to inhibit the learning of dirt words.

Incidentally, the total numbers of words recalled under each of the conditions did not differ significantly.

The results of the studies did indicate that peripheral stimulation of front versus back body sites had different effects upon the selective learning of dirt words. Therefore, they support the theory that peripheral signals, which are experienced as differential awareness of body regions, may play a role in regulating central attitudes.

Considerably more data supportive of the theory will be cited in various chapters to follow which deal with awareness of other body areas (e.g., right versus left, eyes, mouth).

In any case, one of the reasons for citing the front-back vibrator experiments in the present section was because they show in direct experimental terms that variations in front-back body experiences also influence the selective perception of stimuli with anal significance. They affirm what has emerged with several more indirect procedures, namely, that front-back awareness is linked with anal variables. Actually, if one looks back at the other results in this section, it seems fair to say that despite the fact that a number were of borderline significance, they do display encouraging consistency in the predicted direction. There was conformance with expectation for: the Blacky tachistoscopic results; the cleanliness score derived from subjects' descriptions of how they spend an average week; the findings pertaining to dirt and cleanliness in spontaneous self expression; chain associations to anal words; reactions to anal jokes; and the selective anal memory data.

HOMOSEXUAL CONFLICTS

It was pointed out that Freud (1924) and others (e.g., Fenichel, 1945) thought of the anal character as struggling to defend himself against passive receptive (feminine) aims. The original concept was that "fixation" on the anal zone represented in part a retreat from heterosexual genitality and an identification with a passive (non-aggressive) orientation bearing some resemblance to a feminine stance. The investment in a body opening (anus) rather than a body projection (penis) was thought to be paralleled by intensified unconscious feminine receptive fantasies having homosexual intent. Such homosexual intent was presumably ego alien and aroused anxiety which triggered defense strategies aimed at repression and denial. The formation of a paranoid delusion was depicted as one of the more extreme forms of these defensive strategies. It was said that the paranoid delusion provided a means for "projecting out" the unacceptable homosexual wishes. The implied link between paranoia and the "anal character" conflict about homosexual wishes led to the earlier study described above in which an attempt was made to demonstrate that back awareness is higher in paranoid than non-paranoid schizophrenics.

If the anal character model regarding back awareness is valid, it should be possible to show that degree of back awareness is positively correlated with anxiety and conflict about homosexual themes.

Perceptual Selectivity in Terms of the Ames Thereness-Thatness Apparatus

One approach to linking back awareness to anxiety about homosexual issues was undertaken in terms of selective response to a picture with homosexual implications which was presented on the Ames Thereness and Thatness Table (T-T) (Kilpatrick, 1952).

The Ames T-T can be used to create an ambiguous perceptual situation in which the value or emotional significance of a stimulus (e.g., picture) can be determined in terms of size or distance characteristics ascribed to it (Hastings, 1952; Hastorf, 1950; Kilpatrick, 1952). It was anticipated that if an individual were asked to make a judgment in the T-T setting about a homosexual stimulus he would display sensitivity to that stimulus. The assumption was made that the higher an individual's back awareness the greater the probability he would display an exaggerated or selective response to a picture portraying a nude male from the rear which has obvious homosexual implications.

The Thereness-Thatness technique which was employed for measuring perceptual response consists of two viewing tunnels which are side by side. The tunnel on the right, which is completely dark, contains no cues for distance and therefore none for size. The stimulus to which the subject responds is projected on a screen set up in this tunnel at a distance of two meters from him, and it is viewed monocularly. In the left tunnel, viewed binocularly, there are five lucite rods (each lighted by a 15-watt incandescent lamp) at 65-centimeter intervals. A Clason projector, on the right side of the apparatus and shielded from the subject's view, was used to project the image of a picture on the screen in the tunnel on the right. This projector can alter the size of the projected image over a wide range without significantly changing its clarity or brightness. As the image size is increased the picture seems to move toward the subject, and as it is decreased it appears to move away. It is therefore possible to present the subject with a judgmental task which seems to involve the spatial placement of a picture but which actually revolves about altering its size on the screen. The experimental task was one in which the subject was asked to view (with his head in a headrest) a projected picture in the right-side tunnel and told that he could, by means of a knob, move it forward or backwards on a track in order to line it up with rods in the left-side tunnel. The instructions were as follows:

> You will be looking at various pictures of objects which you will see in front of you. On your left you will see some lighted rods. Your job will be to turn the knob with your right hand and make the object line up with the rod I name. I want you to move the picture back and forth until it is even with the rod I name.

The size setting made with the knob could be read from a pointer attached to the lens holder that moved as the subject turned the knob. A scale from 1 to 13 was used, with larger values indicating a larger image and by implication closer optical placement. The voltage on the bulb in the Clason projector was kept at a maximum reading of 120 volts by means of an auto transformer, thus controlling its 4,250 lumen output.

Six pictures were presented (front view of clothed male, front view of female nude, rhombus-shaped geometric figure, ice cream parfait, front view of clothed female, and rear view of male nude). They were all line drawings of the same height and width; and presented in the sequence just enumerated.[10] Judgments of the pictures were obtained under six different conditions. Each picture was first presented at the apparent furthest position from the subject, and he was asked to line it up with the rod second closest to him. A second series of trials involved telling the subject to move the picture from the closest possible position to the position of the fourth rod. Thirdly, the picture was to be shifted from midway (halfway point on size scale) to the fifth rod. Fourth in sequence was the task of moving the picture from the apparent closest position to the fifth rod. Next, the picture was to be moved from midway to the second rod position. Finally, the subject manipulated the picture from the farthest position to the apparent position of the third rod.

Prior to the experiments the subjects were tested for visual acuity and astigmatism, respectively, by means of a Snellen chart and an astigma sunburst chart. Only those with 20–20 vision and no astigmatic defects went on to participate. Five minutes of dark adaptation were allowed before the T-T task. Following the T-T trials the subject was asked to recall the pictures he had seen. He then undertook several other tasks. At the end of the session he was again asked to recall the T-T pictures.

The mean size setting of each picture for the six trials was computed. Also, the mean rank (Rank 1 = largest or "closest" setting) of each picture in relation to the other five pictures in the series was determined. The number of pictures the subject forgot or described with error in the two recall tasks was tabulated. Since six errors were possible for each recall, scores could range from 0–12. The purpose of this index was to ascertain the degree to which the subject seemed to be dealing repressively with the themes in the T-T pictures.

The analysis of the data was complicated by issues of "defensive style" which have already been described in previous T-T studies. Shellow (1956) found the subjects manifesting anxious involvement in the T-T task made pictures relatively large (i.e., apparently closer to themselves). Those without such involvement made pictures relatively small (i.e., apparently farther away). Analogous results were obtained by Hastings (1952) who noted that insecurity was positively correlated with setting pictures relatively "close." Also, Kaufer (in Ittelson and Kutash, 1961) reported that persons characterized by an anxious "moving away" from people put emotional pictures "closer" to themselves. This contrasted with subjects typified by a "moving toward" others orientation who put such pictures "farther away." In terms of

---

[10] The drawings pertaining to other than the homosexual theme were used to measure attitudes linked with other BFQ variables; and the derived results will be presented at a later point.

previous experiments by Ittelson (in Kilpatrick, 1952) and Hastorf (1950) it is known that a picture presented in the T-T apparatus which is more vivid than another requires a smaller or "farther away" setting in order to be lined up with a spatial reference point. It is therefore likely that the anxiously involved subjects who put specific T-T pictures relatively "close" to themselves do so because they defensively minimize their intensity. An evasive orientation under the T-T viewing conditions results in the pictures being set larger or "closer" because they appear subjectively less intense. The pictures require extra "magnification" to match the standard of how large one would expect them to be at a given distance.

The two memory tasks included in the present T-T procedure provided a means for determining whether the subject took a repressing attitude toward the T-T pictures. They made it possible to evaluate whether his anxiety was sufficiently intense to intrude repressively upon his cognitive functioning. The analysis of the T-T data was based on a separation of subjects into those manifesting repression in their recall and those dealing non-repressively with the pictures. This approach was encouraged by exploratory observations indicating that the relationships between BFQ scores and T-T settings were frequently reversed in the two groups. Thus, as anticipated, specific BFQ scores in the repression group tended to be positively correlated with setting given pictures larger (apparently closer); while in the non-repression group the relations between such BFQ scores and T-T settings were in the opposite direction.

The subjects consisted of 54 male college students. Their median age was 20.

A division was made between subjects who evidenced no errors in their recall of the T-T pictures and those with two or more errors. Four subjects who made only one error were not included in the analysis in order to have a clear cutting point between the error and no error groups. This categorization derived from the formulation that a repressing (forgetting) response to the pictures should be expressed in a different mode of perceptual defense than a non-repressing response. Twenty-five of the subjects proved to be Repressors and 29 Non-repressors.

Mean BFQ Back scores were respectively 7.2 (σ = 3.5) and 7.8 (σ = 4.5) in the Repression and Non-repression groups.

The T-T index to which the BFQ Back score was related involved the difference in rank between the female nude setting and the male nude setting. This index evaluates the difference in the way the subject responded to a heterosexual as compared to a homosexual theme. The coding of the rank difference scores was such that the more negative they were the larger (closer) was the heterosexual compared to the homosexual setting.

In the Repression sample a significant chi-square was found between BFQ Back and the tendency to make the male nude larger (closer) than the female nude (χ^2 = 7.4, df = 2, p = .025). The equivalent relationship in the Non-repression sample was not significant. The results were supportive of the hypothesis in one instance but not in the other.

Tachistoscopic Response

Selective response to tachistoscopically presented words was also employed for detecting anxiety about homosexual stimuli. A list of 14 words was compiled. Three were words with common homosexual connotations (homo, sissy, rear). Three dealt with hostility themes (shoot, hate, kill); three others had oral significance (food, candy, suck); and three related to heterosexuality (love, kiss, flirt). Two words were included with narcissistic reference (self, mine). They were all widely used four or five letter words, and the average length of those in the various categories was equivalent. Subjects were asked to view each word (arranged in a random order) five times consecutively at increasing exposures (3.3, 3.4, 3.6, 4.0, 4.5, milliseconds) and to report repeatedly what they perceived. The earliest speed at which a given word was correctly recognized was determined. Values ranging from 1 (recognition at 3.3 milliseconds) to 7 (non-complete recognition) were assigned and they were averaged to arrive at an overall index for each category of words. The only prediction that was made was that BFQ Back would be correlated with a selective response to the homosexual words. Whether the selectivity would take the form of inhibition or facilitation could not be anticipated.

Forty-five male college students were studied who responded to the BFQ and to the tachistoscopic series.

It was found that BFQ Back was positively correlated ($r = .28, p < .05$) with the average tachistoscopic threshold value. That is, the greater the individual's awareness of his back the more difficult it was for him to recognize the homosexual words. This result, of course, demonstrated the selectivity that had been predicted. None of the other word category threshold values, besides hostility, were significantly correlated with BFQ Back. The hostility finding will be discussed shortly in a section dealing with modes of disposition of anger in those varying in back awareness.

One week after the completion of the tachistoscopic task the subjects returned to participate in another session. At that time they were asked to write down all of the words they could recall having previously seen tachistoscopically. A determination was then made of the percentage of the words actually recalled which fell into each content category. BFQ Back was negatively and significantly correlated with percent of homosexual words recalled ($r = -.43, p < .01$). Correlations of BFQ Back with the other recall categories were all of a chance order. It is striking that the more intense the individual's back awareness the more likely he was to forget selectively those words with homosexual connotations.

A second tachistoscopic study was instituted in which selective response to a series of pictures was evaluated. The pictures dealt with the following themes: achievement (person climbing mountain), nurturance (person holding baby), homosexual (two male figures holding hands), heterosexual (two figures kissing), rejection (one figure rejecting an overture from another), and narcissism (person looking at self in mirror). Each theme was represented in terms of scenes involving stick figures that had been successfully used in a previous study by Forrest and Lee (1962). Pictures were shown six times consecutively (in the order listed above) at the following speeds: .008, .01, .025, .05, .075, and .125 seconds. The earliest speed of recognition of each picture was determined; and its rank order with reference to all of the other recognition thresholds computed.

A sample of 45 male college students was used. In addition to the tachistoscopic data, BFQ responses were also obtained.

When BFQ Back was related to the rank order of the Homosexual picture threshold, a correlation of $-.30$ ($p < .05$) was found. The higher the individual's back awareness the more quickly he perceived the Homosexual theme. BFQ Back was not significantly correlated with the values for the other pictures.

These findings, when considered in conjunction with the data for the tachistoscopically presented homosexual words, indicate that variations in back awareness are linked with selective perceptual response to homosexual references. However, the selectivity may take the form of either heightened sensitivity to, or inhibitory shutting out of, the stimulus.

Vague Sex Pictures

Homosexual conflict, such as apparently associated with high back awareness, would be expected to evidence itself in a sense of indecisive vagueness about one's sexual identity. There should be anxious concern and alarm about not being able to experience self as possessing an unambiguous sexual role. One might therefore conjecture that the greater an individual's amount of back awareness the more defensively he will react to stimuli designed to highlight sex role vagueness. An opportunity to pursue this formulation was offered by a series of 15 pictures of human figures adapted from a larger number developed by Doidge and Holtzman (1960) to study homosexuals. The figures portrayed were originally taken from drawings, paintings, and statues photographically produced so as to make the sex ambiguous. The lack of specification of sex in the pictures was regarded as likely to evoke particular anxiety in those with sex role conflicts and therefore likely to evoke defensive maneuvers which would result in negative attitudes toward the pictures (e.g., analogous to that described by Murray, 1938). With this rationale, a procedure was devised to involve the subject judgmentally with each of the pictured figures and to record his reactions via ratings.

Each picture was projected in a semidarkened room for 15 seconds. The subject was asked to decide whether the figure was male or female and to indicate on a 5-point scale its apparent degree of masculinity-femininity. These judgments were obtained to ensure there would be direct confrontation with the threatening, poorly defined sexual attributes of each figure. In order to measure the amount of defensive negative affect aroused, two ratings of each figure were obtained. One was an evaluation of the attractiveness of the figures on a 5-point scale ranging from "good looking" to "ugly" and the other was a rating of the friendliness of the figures on a 5-point scale ranging from "friendly" to "unfriendly." Three indexes of defensive negative response were computed:

1. Sum of the 15 ratings of degree of Ugliness.
2. Sum of the 15 ratings of degree of Unfriendliness.
3. A total score equal to the sum of the Ugliness and Unfriendliness ratings.

Two samples of college males were studied (N = 48, N = 56). BFQ Back proved in both studies to have only chance correlations with the various indexes of defensive response to the vague sex pictures. If unusual anxiety about sexual identity was aroused by the pictures in those with high back awareness, it was not detected by the rating procedure.

References to Male Interaction

If the back aware individual is anxious about homosexual wishes, he might be expected to be reluctant about relating to other men. Such relating would be threatening insofar as it would create situations which might tempt him to express feelings and attitudes that were previously confined to a fantasy level. Going a step further, one might also anticipate that homosexual anxieties would inhibit explicit thought and imagery involving male interaction. If so, those who are most back aware should be characterized by a reduction in imagery involving male figures. This hypothesis was tested in two samples of male college students (N = 51, N = 24).

The procedure used for measuring the density of imagery relating to male figures was based on obtaining a direct introspective sample of the stream of thought at a given time. Each subject was asked to list on a sheet of paper "20 things that you are conscious of or aware of right now." He was also told to use more than one word in describing each of the "20 things." The presence or absence of a reference to a male figure was determined for each statement. Some examples of statements that are scored [11] as male references follow:

> I am thinking of John.
> I wonder how Charley is feeling today.
> There are two workmen outside.
> My fraternity is giving a party.
> We played poker in the dormitory last night.

Two judges, independently scoring 30 protocols, correlated .93 in their evaluations.

In one sample (N = 51) the dichotomized (at median) BFQ Back scores were negatively and significantly related to the trichotomized (equal thirds as possible) number of male references (χ^2 = 6.3, df = 2, p < .05).

In a second sample (N = 24) BFQ Back was again negatively and significantly related to number of male references (χ^2 = 6.2, df = 1, p < .02). These findings affirm that the greater an individual's back awareness the less likely he is to focus upon male interaction in his conscious stream of thought. It is assumed that such avoidance of male themes represents a defensive maneuver motivated by homosexual anxiety.[12]

Comment

Rather convincing corroboration has been secured for the formulation, based on the anal character concept, which associates back awareness in men with homosexual anxieties and conflicts about relating to other males. Selective response sets toward homosexual stimuli which were presented in the Ames Thereness-Thatness apparatus and also tachistoscopically have proven to be related to BFQ Back, as predicted. Meaningful support for the homosexual formulation has come too from data concerning the density of one's images about other men. Responses to pictures with vague sexual identity have not conformed to expectation. While most of the supportive relationships described were of a low order, they were consistent and encouraging.

---

[11] I am indebted to Owen Renik for devising the scoring system and also for originating the idea upon which the data in this section are based.

[12] Despite the apparent presence of homosexual anxiety in those with high back awareness, no indications of decreased heterosexual activity or unusual anxiety in the face of heterosexual stimuli could be detected in them. BFQ Back has not been consistently related to various measures of heterosexual activity and interest (e.g., amount of dating, ability to perceive heterosexual stimuli exposed tachistoscopically) which will be described in later chapters. The individual with a high Back score seems to be specifically disturbed about homosexual rather than heterosexual issues. Further, no evidence has appeared that measures of the two types of anxiety or concern are consistently related. Perhaps in the normal individual the two classes of anxiety involve fairly separate domains.

DISPOSITION OF HOSTILITY

In the preliminary findings pertaining to BFQ Back which were earlier cited it was reported that back awareness was not correlated with the Assaultive subscale of the Buss-Durkee Inventory, but was positively and significantly so with the Negativism subscale. However, in a subsequent study the Negativism finding was not reaffirmed. Back awareness did turn out to be negatively and significantly correlated with how angry one recalled one's father to have been, but had a chance relationship with mother's reported anger. These results (based upon self reports) did not support the supposition that the high back aware person inhibits direct aggressive behavior, as the anal character is presumed to do. Nor did they support the idea that back awareness is associated with the supposed negativism of the anal character. They were partially congruent with the supposition that difficulty in expressing hostility would typify the parents of individuals with greatest back awareness.

To broaden these preliminary observations, studies were undertaken in which BFQ Back was related to a spectrum of hostility indices, derived at one extreme from self reports and at the other from responses only minimally vulnerable to conscious manipulation.

The question whether Negativism is related to back awareness was examined further by means of a 10-item scale of Negativism developed by Finney (1961). This scale included items like "I sometimes keep on at a thing until others lose their patience with me" and "I frequently find it necessary to stand up for what I think is right." In a sample of college men (N = 51) this Negativism score was not significantly related to BFQ Back.

An attempt was also made to investigate a level of hostility response less open to direct self manipulation than the self reports characteristic of the Buss-Durkee and Finney scales. This was done in a sample of 59 college men by administering two tests: (1) the Bass Famous Sayings Test (1958) which provides an Aggression index, and (2) a word construction task. The Bass measure involves the subject agreeing or disagreeing with a series of 90 proverbs. His responses to 30 specifically dealing with hostility themes are taken as an indicator of degree of hostility. High hostility scores are obtained by those who agree with proverbs stating that most people enjoy being aggressive; that it is preferable to do things by oneself; that one should avoid joining organizations; that one should be wary of false friends; and that one should reject people of low ability.

The word construction technique was based on the number of hostile words produced when the subject was given a sheet with an array of blank lines, each preceded by a letter, and instructed as follows: "Below are a series of blanks and each is preceded by a letter. As quickly as you can, think of a word beginning with each letter and write in the rest of the word." A word was scored as hostile if it overtly referred to an act of aggression (e.g., hit, punch, war), hostile feeling (e.g., angry, mad, irritated), or means of attack (e.g., gun, sword, tank). Two scorers, working independently with a sample of 30 protocols, attained 90 percent agreement in their judgments.

BFQ Back correlated .24 ($p < .10$) with the Bass Proverb hostility score. When the dichotomized (at median) Bass scores were related by means of chi-square to the trichotomized (as equal thirds as possible) BFQ Back scores, a significant positive relation was found [$\chi^2 = 7.4$, df $= 2$, $p = .025$]. Also, BFQ Back correlated .25 ($p = .05$) with number of hostile word completions. Using the proverb and word completion measures, which are rather covert approaches that do not pretend to be evaluations of how the individual habitually expresses anger and which may be regarded as simply methods for sampling the existence of hostile tensions, one finds a trend for those most back aware to be characterized by the most angry responses. Back awareness, in these terms, is related to the existence of anger, without definition of whether it is overt or concealed.

The chain association method, earlier described, was also applied to examine the relationship of back awareness to response to stimuli with hostility connotations. It will be recalled that the chain association method involved asking subjects to give ten associations to a series of words tapping various themes (hostile, anal, oral, masochistic, and neutral). The hostile theme was represented by three words (hit, stab, shoot) and the masochistic by two words or phrases (hurt self, suicide). There was computed for each cluster of words comprising a theme the average time required to produce ten associations. Also, the average directness versus indirectness of the associations given to the stimulus words was determined. In a sample of 40 college men the BFQ Back score was not related to either the time or directness of association indices derived for the hostile words. BFQ Back was, however, positively correlated ($r = .30$, p .05) with the rank of the average time required to produce the masochistic word associations (as compared to the times for the other themes). That is, the higher the subject's back awareness the longer he required to give his quota of associations to the masochistic words. The BFQ Back score was not significantly correlated with the index denoting degree of directness of associations to the masochistic words.

These findings provided little clarification of the problem under consideration. They did not indicate a link between back awareness and response to directly hostile words. They did point to a tendency for increased back awareness to be accompanied by a selective response (as defined by the time index) to masochistic words.

Exploration of the hostility issue was pursued at still another level in terms of perception of tachistoscopically presented hostile words. One may regard such a tachistoscopic measure as providing information about reactions to hostile themes in a setting where conscious manipulation of the response is held to a minimum. The study to be described embraced the same sample of 45 males and the same methodology as referred to in the previous section dealing with the relation of BFQ Back to words with homosexual connotations. It will be recalled that subjects viewed 14 words in the tachistoscope, each at five consecutive speeds (3.3, 3.4, 3.6, 4.0, 4.5 milliseconds); and their thresholds for correctly identifying those with specific themes were determined. Among the 14 words were three (shoot, hate, kill) dealing with hostility. BFQ Back was found to be correlated .28 ($p = .05$) with the average threshold for correctly perceiving these three words. That is, the greater the individual's back awareness the more difficulty he displayed in identifying the hostile words.

Another study was undertaken with a sample of 49 male college students in which BFQ Back was related to the speed of accurate tachistoscopic identification of a line drawing of two men fighting. Included in the series of pictures presented was one dealing with an achievement theme, one dealing with dependency, and two with masochistic import (man shooting self, man stabbing self). All the pictures had been drawn so as to be of uniform area and line definiteness. Each picture was shown successively at six speeds (.008, .01, .025, .05, .075, .125 seconds). BFQ Back proved to have only a chance correlation with the threshold at which the hostility theme was correctly perceived. It was also not correlated with the thresholds for the masochistic pictures.[13]

A third opportunity to evaluate the relationship of BFQ Back to perception of tachistoscopically presented hostile stimuli was provided by data collected by Rhoda Fisher.[14] She studied a group of 23 boys (mean age = 9.8 years) who were in a special program for those unable to adjust adequately to a regular school classroom situation. BFQ responses were obtained individually from each; and also each was asked to describe a series of nine stick-figure drawings presented tachistoscopically. Three dealt with hostility (two people shooting at each other; two people sword fighting; one person hitting another). Two portrayed narcissistic themes; two dealt with nurturance; and two with social interaction. A picture was presented four times consecutively at increasing speeds (.01, .03, .05, and .10 seconds). The tachistoscopic scores obtained for the hostility pictures were analyzed by chi square. When the dichotomized (at median) BFQ Back scores were related to the

---

[13] The relationship of BFQ Back to ability to deal with masochistic themes has been appraised with two other procedures (described in detail in Chapter 22). One of these procedures involved determining whether there was selective response to proverbs with masochistic versus non-masochistic content. Another was based on examining responses to masochistic versus non-masochistic words presented tachistoscopically. There was a trend in both instances for BFQ Back to be positively correlated with responding faster to the masochistic than the neutral themes; but statistical significance was not achieved. In general, most of the pertinent data suggest that BFQ Back and masochism are not linked.

[14] I am indebted to my wife for making these data available.

trichotomized (in equal thirds as possible) scores representing the sum of the rank orders of the thresholds for correct identification of the hostile pictures, a borderline positive relationship was found ($\chi^2 = 5.4$, df $= 2$, $p < .10$). The results indicated that with increasing back awareness there was a trend to have greater difficulty in perceiving the hostile pictures accurately. Although the relationship was not a strong one, it did add some support to the findings pertaining to BFQ Back and threshold for perception of hostility which were observed in the first college sample.

The findings involving the various studies reported which were actually statistically significant (viz., proverb, word completion, chain associations, and tachistoscopic scores) do not easily mesh. One can only suggest that back awareness is positively correlated with the intensity of some kinds of angry tension and with difficulty in *directly* facing up to angry feelings or fantasies.

OVERVIEW

Several goals have been achieved by the work dealing with BFQ Back. First of all, it has been possible to demonstrate that back versus front awareness can be objectively and reliably measured. Secondly, the anal character model concerning the variables that contribute to back awareness has been shown to be reasonable. This model has successfully predicted relationships between BFQ Back and the following: sensitivity to stimuli with anal connotations, negative attitudes toward dirt, measures of self-control and orderliness, and homosexual anxiety. It should be noted that the anal character model was not successful in predicting attitudes about frugality or modes of hostility disposition.

The response selectivity associated with elevated back awareness sometimes took unexpected directions. It is, for example, not clear why BFQ Back was negatively correlated with an index indicating amount of time required to give associations to anal words. Why should the man with high back awareness give his associations faster to these words than the person with low back awareness? Similarly, one does not discern why BFQ Back was positively related to degree of enjoyment of anal jokes. In view of other instances in which BFQ was correlated with a tendency to shut out stimuli with anal significance (e.g., response to tachistoscopically presented Anal Sadism picture), one wonders at the fact that the high back aware individual turned out to enjoy jokes with blatant anal content. It is of parallel interest that in one context BFQ Back was positively correlated with ability to perceive stimuli with homosexual connotations and in another negatively related to such ability. Apparently, the anal character orientation can manifest itself in multiple ways that seem in some instances to have opposite implications, at least on the surface.

The effectiveness of the anal character concept in pinpointing personality and attitudinal factors pertinent to back awareness[15] adds support to previous findings concerning its meaningfulness. A number of Freud's original statements about the role of anal attitudes in personality formation are indirectly supported. The findings are of particular import insofar as they indicate that the manner in which an individual distributes his attention to a major spatial dimension of his body is not a random matter. The distribution process seems to be part of a larger response system related to a cluster of focused conflicts, wishes, and defenses.

In some fashion, not yet evident, the anal character learns a special sensitivity to sensations from the back of his body (presumably equated with anal sensations). This seems to be part of a broader pattern involving a perspective which underscores the need to behave in a well controlled fashion that will minimize possibilities of soiling or "messing up." The awareness of back which is part of the anal character pattern has been depicted as a guiding and inhibitory function. It seems to provide a peripheral sensory signal which the individual carries into many situations and which fosters response selectivity aimed at facilitating certain defenses.

The validity of the BFQ Back findings and of those to be reported in future chapters dealing with BFQ phenomena depends upon the extent to which one accepts the logic of the studies which have been carried out. In large part, these studies are based on the assumption that selectivity in perception and learning can be used as an indicator of the existence of underlying attitudes and adjustment strategies. However, it should be added that in most instances results derived from selective response patterns have also been buttressed by findings from conventional measures of personality traits and self reports concerning one's typical behavior in life situations.

[15] BFQ Back was not consistently related to other clusters of measures involving heterosexual behavior, orality, religiosity, and so forth.

19
The Right-Left Body Division
in Men and Sex Role

INTRODUCTION

Another major aspect of body experience chosen for study relates to the differentiation between right and left. It concerns the degree to which the individual focuses his attention upon the right as compared to the left side of his body.

There has been extended interest in the fact that different values and functions are often assigned to apparently symmetrical areas on either side of the midline of the body. The right and left sides obviously share in a division of labor which has been the subject of a tremendous literature dealing with such topics as handedness, eye dominance, and right-left differentiation (Jasper and Raney, 1937; Schoen and Scofield, 1935; Benton, 1959; Takala, 1951). Also, there have been numerous speculations concerning the differences in symbolic value attributed to the right and left body sides (Fenichel, 1945; Hertz, 1960; Schilder, 1935). It has been variously proposed that the right side is associated with strength, masculinity, and goodness; whereas the left is linked with weakness, femininity, and badness. Such speculations have been often inspired by clinical observations of psychiatric and neurological patients who manifest delusions and unusual ideas about the two body sides. These patients may, in the course of their disorganization, emphasize one side and completely deny the existence of the other; label one as masculine and the other as feminine; see each as representing entirely different identities; and so forth. Reports concerning phenomena of this sort have been sufficiently numerous to suggest that gross distinctions are indeed habitually made in the meanings assigned to the right and left sides. Another stimulus for assuming that there are right-left differences is the frequency with which cultures adhere to beliefs and modes of expression that point up a contrasting conception of what right and left mean. Blau (1946) and Hertz (1960) have described these cultural beliefs and definitions at some length. Particularly pertinent is the following quotation from Blau (p. 63):

> The ethical halo surrounding laterality is best illustrated by language. Language offers an excellent key to the understanding of cultural patterns, since it is a unique representation of the composite cultural background of a people. . . .
>
> In many, if not all languages, a distinct dualism in words seems to exist for right and left. . . . The right represents permanence, force, power, strength, grace, dexterity, dispatch, godliness, rectitude, truth, goodness, and sanctity. The left represents the opposite, the reverse, the lack, the negation of all the traits and characteristics attributed to the right hand. The distinctions between right and left are not confined to simple objective orientation but are extensively enmeshed with moral, ethical, and religious values.

The obvious division of function between the two body sides, coupled with the widespread manner in which right and left have been symbolically and culturally distinguished, raised the possibility that there was a corresponding body image dimension of significance.

The present studies were based on the view that the relative prominence of the right and left sides in an individual's body scheme (as defined by focus of attention) would be correlated with indices of sexual adjustment and sexual identification. Such correlates were anticipated because of the anecdotal and clinical observations cited above in which the right-left concept has been associated with issues related to masculinity and femininity. However, the specific link of masculinity with right and femininity with left, which has been so widely assumed, was not accepted because the few empirical studies which have been done do not support such a simple equation (e.g., Fisher, 1965D; Fisher, 1960B; Fisher, 1962B).

BFQ Parameters

A scale of 15 items was constructed to measure degree of right versus left awareness. It was embedded randomly in the larger context of the total array of BFQ items. Subjects were asked to indicate their right or left choices when presented with paired comparisons of the following order: right arm versus left arm, left leg versus right leg, right ear versus left ear, left eye versus right eye. The total number of right choices constituted the final score. It could range from 0 through 15. The mean number of right choices found in a range of normal populations has clustered in the vicinity of 9.0. The average tendency is to be more aware of one's right than left side.

In a sample of 57 college men, the 15-item BFQ Right scale has shown a test-retest (one week intervening) reliability of .62.[1] In another sample

[1] All correlations are product-moment unless otherwise stated.

Table 19.1
Means and Standard Deviations of BFQ Right Scores

Mean	σ	N
9.4	3.0	45
8.8	3.5	50
9.2	3.4	48
9.0	3.6	57
9.3	3.2	45
8.9	2.7	47
8.1	3.4	51
9.8	3.5	51
8.3	2.8	50
9.0	3.5	53

(N = 51), with a week intervening, the test-retest coefficient was .58. In another sample of college men (N = 52) the test-retest coefficient after a week was .71.

Table 19.1 depicts the means and standard deviations for BFQ Right occurring in ten different samples of male college students. In general, the distributions of scores have been normal in character.

The BFQ Right scale has turned out to be largely independent of other BFQ scales. One finds in a series of ten studies (average N = 50) that there were three significant correlations with BFQ Back (—.28, —.35, —.34); two with BFQ Stomach (.28, .29); one with BFQ Mouth ($r = .35$); one with BFQ Eyes (.35); three with BFQ Heart (.35, .34, .40); and two with BFQ Head (.32, .46). These correlations are obviously not large or consistent.[2]

Chance correlations have been found between BFQ Right and the MMPI K and L scales, the Bass Acquiescence Scale (1956), and the Marlowe-Crowne (1964) Social Desirability scale. Apparently, none of the usual response set variables are involved in the right-left judgments.

The generality of the BFQ Right score was tested by means of a method similar to that used in relation to BFQ Back. Subjects were asked to respond to the BFQ and then, about an hour later, assigned the task of reporting the occurrence of all sensations at two right and two left body sites during a five-minute period. They gave their reports by assigning checks to four headings (right side of head, left hand, left side of head, right hand) listed on a sheet of paper. Two studies were carried out with this procedure. In two samples of male college students (N = 53, N = 57) BFQ Right was positively and significantly correlated with the number of right minus the number of left sensations ($r = .36$, $p < .01$; $r = .39$, $p < .01$) reported. These results

[2] No consistent correlations between BFQ Right and the Barrier score have been observed.

clearly demonstrate a similarity in the right-left judgments obtained by the two different techniques.

EXPLORATORY STUDIES

Initial Hypothesis

In first approaching the possible correlates of the distribution of attention to the right and left body sides, an exploratory study was undertaken which involved relating a right-left attention index to a gross measure of the individual's sexual orientation, that is, his level of heterosexual interest. Two questions were under consideration: (a) Is the degree of right versus left attention correlated with heterosexual interest? (b) If so, what variations in such interest accompany greater focus on the right as compared to the left sides?

The version of the right-left BFQ scale used in this study was an early one consisting of nine items. A score was derived equal to the total number of times the right side was designated as being more perceptually prominent than the left.

The Edwards (1954) Personal Preference Schedule was administered to obtain responses to the Heterosexuality scale which inquires concerning the degree to which the subject considers heterosexual activities (e.g., being in love, kissing the opposite sex) to play an important part in his own behavior.

The subjects were 51 male college students who were paid a fee for participating. Their median age was 20. They were all right-handed in order to eliminate the possible effects of handedness upon the distribution of right-left attention.[3]

The mean Body Focus Questionnaire Right [4] score was 5.5 ($\sigma = 2.3$). The mean Edwards Heterosexuality percentile score was 53.6 ($\sigma = 30.1$). There proved to be a product-moment correlation of $-.27$ ($p = .05$) between the Right score and the Heterosexuality score. The greater the attention an individual focused on the right side of his body the less was his apparent heterosexual orientation as defined by the Heterosexual scale. This provided initial support for the view that the right-left dimension of the body image reflects aspects of the individual's sex role and sexual adjustment. It was an intriguing question as to why focus of attention on the right rather than the left side should denote a reduced level of heterosexual response. Discussion of this issue will be postponed until a later point.

---

[3] In all studies to be described involving the right-left dimension, handedness has been similarly controlled.

[4] BFQ Right values will largely be given only for major studies or in instances in which they are atypical.

Further Hypotheses

An attempt was made to generalize from the initial findings by formulating the following hypotheses which specify disturbance in various levels of one's sexual behavior as correlated with increasing focus of attention upon the right side of the body:

The greater the focus of a man's attention upon the right side of his body:

1. The less active will be his general level of heterosexual behavior.

2. The more defensive he will be when confronted with stimuli that arouse anxiety about sexual identity.

3. The more anxious he will be in responding to symbolic representations of sexual problems and threats.

The early abbreviated version of the BFQ was used to determine the subject's right-left distribution of attention. To increase the reliability of the measure it was administered on two separate occasions, with an average of seven days intervening. A total Right score was derived equal to the sum of the right-side sites chosen on the two different occasions. The product-moment correlation between the test and retest Right scores from this early abbreviated scale was .58.

Multiple procedures[5] were employed to get at the sexual role variables referred to in the hypotheses.

Heterosexual activity level was appraised directly by means of a questionnaire inquiring concerning the subject's present and past sexual interaction with girls. He was asked to indicate the age at which he began dating; the average number of dates he had during each of the four years of high school and also currently; and the number of times he had "gone steady" or been engaged. The following scores were derived from this information:

1. Age at which began dating.
2. Average of number of dates per week for the four years of high school.
3. Average number of dates per week in current life.
4. A "serious dating" index equal to the number of times has "gone steady" (maximum of 2) plus a credit of 1 for currently going steady plus a credit of 2 for being currently engaged.

Responses to pictures with vague sexual identity (as described in Chapter 18) were used to determine the subject's reactions to stimuli intended to arouse anxiety about sexual identity. One would conjecture that those who have difficulty in heterosexual adjustment would have problems related to sex role identity. However, it was presumed that men with high right

---

[5] One technique, involving recall of father's and mother's sexual expressiveness, which was used will not be reported because it proved in retest studies to be highly unreliable.

awareness would have sex role difficulties not as a function of homosexual [6] conflicts, as is true of men with high back awareness, but rather as a result of other factors to be discussed at a later point. In any case, it was expected that an individual's lack of assurance concerning his ability to be heterosexually effective would color his responses to stimuli with sex role conflict connotations. The stimuli which subjects were asked to respond to were 15 pictures of human figures from a series developed by Doidge and Holtzman (1960). As earlier indicated, the figures were taken from drawings, paintings, and statues photographically reproduced so as to make the sex ambiguous. It was assumed that the greater an individual's uncertainty about his sexual identity the more disturbing he would find such pictures and therefore the more defensive negative affect they would arouse in him (e.g., as suggested by Murray, 1938). With this rationale, a procedure was devised to involve the subject judgmentally with each of the pictured figures and to record his reactions via ratings.

Each picture was projected in a semidarkened room for 15 seconds. The subject was asked to decide whether the figure was male or female and to indicate on a 5-point scale its apparent degree of masculinity-femininity. These judgments were obtained to ensure there would be direct confrontation with the threatening, poorly defined sexual attributes of each figure. In order to measure the amount of defensive negative affect aroused, two other ratings of each picture were obtained. One was an evaluation of the attractiveness of the figures on a 5-point scale ranging from "good looking" to "ugly" and the other was a rating of the friendliness of the figures on a 5-point scale ranging from "friendly" to "unfriendly." From the ratings three indexes of defensive negative response were computed:

1. Sum of the 15 ratings of degree of Ugliness.
2. Sum of the 15 ratings of degree of Unfriendliness.
3. A total score equal to the sum of the Ugliness and Unfriendliness ratings.

Another procedure was used to determine how easily the individual verbalizes sexual thoughts in a free expressive situation. It was presumed that the greater his anxiety about sexual matters the more difficult it would be for him to make sexual references. The opportunity for free expression of thoughts and images was provided by asking him to list on a sheet of paper "20 things you are conscious of or aware of right now." Responses were obtained on two occasions, with a week intervening. Sexual references were defined to include only direct statements about heterosexual interests or activities (e.g., "I would like to kiss a girl," "I am going on a date tonight").

[6] In fact, BFQ Right has shown itself not to have consistent relationships with any of the measures of homosexual conflict described in the chapter dealing with back awareness. It was similarly not related to clusters of variables (viz., anxiety about incorporation, anal concern, sensitivity to hostility) associated with the other major BFQ dimensions.

Two judges achieved 91 percent agreement in their scoring of 40 protocols. The Sex Reference score equaled the sum of sexual references in the two samples of responses and could range from 0 to 40. It was anticipated that BFQ Right would be negatively related to the Sex Reference score.

The subjects consisted of 52 male college students with a median age of 20. The BFQ Right score was determined by means of the finalized revised scale comprising 15 items instead of nine.

Table 19.2
Means and Standard Deviations for BFQ Right Scores,
Indexes of Heterosexual Behavior,
Vague Sex Picture Ratings, and Sexual Reference Scores

Variable	Mean	σ	N
BFQ Right	10.5	4.1	49 [a]
Heterosexual behavior			
Age began dating	14.7	1.7	50
Dates in high school	.8	.5	52
Current dates	1.7	1.3	49
Serious dating score	2.3	1.7	51
Vague sex pictures			
Ugly ratings	44.0	5.5	48
Unfriendly ratings	43.7	4.7	48
Unfriendly plus Ugly	87.9	8.5	48
Sexual references	1.8	1.3	49

[a] Variations in N are a function of subjects either missing certain tests or not answering specific questions in a given test.

Table 19.3
Product-Moment Correlations of BFQ Right Scores
with Heterosexual Activity Indexes

BFQ Right versus	r	Significance Level
Age began dating	.30 (N = 50)	<.05
Average number dates per week in high school	−.21 (N = 52)	>.10
Average number of dates per week currently	−.39 (N = 49)	<.01
Score for serious dating	−.29 (N = 51)	<.05

The BFQ Right score proved to be correlated in the predicted direction with the subject's reports of heterosexually motivated behavior. As shown in Table 19.3, the higher his BFQ score the later the age at which he began to date girls ($r = .30, p < .05$); the less his current amount of dating per week ($r = -.39, p < .01$); and the lower his score for serious dating as defined by "going steady" and being engaged ($r = -.29, p < .05$). There was also a correlation of $-.21$ between BFQ Right and amount of dating in high school which is in the predicted direction, but not significant ($p > .10$).

Table 19.4
Product-Moment Correlations of BFQ Right Scores
with Indicators of Negative Response to Vague Sex Pictures

BFQ Right versus	r	Significance Level
Sum of Ugly ratings	.30 (N = 48)	<.05
Sum of Unfriendly ratings	.30 (N = 48)	<.05
Unfriendly and Ugly	.36 (N = 48)	.01

When one examines the relationships between BFQ Right and the Vague Sex Picture rating, it is apparent that they are supportive of the hypothesis under consideration. Table 19.4 indicates that each of the Vague Sex Picture ratings (Ugly and Unfriendly) is correlated .30 with BFQ Right ($p < .05$) and that the combined Ugly and Unfriendly ratings attain a correlation of .36 ($p .01$) with BFQ Right.

Table 19.5
Product-Moment Correlations of BFQ Right Scores
with Sex Reference Scores

BFQ Right versus	r	Significance Level
Sex reference		
Set 1	−.30 (N = 50)	<.05
Set 2	−.38 (N = 50)	<.01
Sum	−.39 (N = 50)	<.01

Correlations between BFQ Right and the Sex Reference scores were significant in the predicted direction. BFQ Right had a correlation of $-.30$ ($p < .05$) with Sex References in the first set of responses; $-.38$ ($p < .01$) with Sex References in the second set of responses; and $-.39$ ($p < .01$) with the sum of Sex References in both sets.

The findings supported the proposition that the greater a man's focus of attention upon the right as contrasted to the left side of his body the more likely he is to be characterized by inhibition in his heterosexual behavior, anxiety about his sexual role, and difficulty in expressing ideas with sexual reference.

CROSS–VALIDATION AND EXTENSION

Following the success of the above studies in tracing the sex role correlates of right versus left awareness, additional inquiries were launched. These efforts will be described in the following sections.

Reported Sexual Behavior

One of the first undertakings was a cross-validation effort concerned with the relation of BFQ Right to reported frequency of heterosexual interaction. The previous indices of heterosexual interaction used had largely involved asking subjects to recall and estimate how frequently they dated in high school and also currently and to indicate degree of "serious" dating as exemplified by "going steady" or being engaged. One of the obvious problems in using recalled average frequency of dating is that it involves a rather hazy computation which is probably quite vulnerable to wishful distortion. In order to deal with this problem, it was decided to use an index of heterosexuality activity based on reports of clearly specified behaviors that would be quite difficult to distort on a wishful basis alone. The index chosen was the "serious dating" index previously described which is equal to the number of times the subject has "gone steady" (maximum of 2) plus a credit of 1 for currently going steady plus a credit of 2 for being currently engaged. The limit to a credit of 2 for having "gone steady" was originally introduced to deal with the possibility that an anxious or disturbed attitude toward heterosexuality might be expressed in a defensive, compensatory pattern of repeatedly setting up apparently serious relations and then terminating them.

The relationship of BFQ Right to the serious dating index was examined in three new samples of male college students ($N = 61$, $N = 51$, $N = 50$). Rather skewed distributions were obtained for the dating index; and so the results are reported in terms of chi-square values. The BFQ Right values in all the samples were not remarkably different from those previously listed for other groups of college males. The median serious dating scores were respectively 1, 2, and 2. In sample 1, when the dichotomized (at median) BFQ Right scores were related to the trichotomized (as equal thirds as possible) dating scores, the predicted negative relationship was found

($\chi^2 = 7.1$, df $= 2$, $p < .05$). In sample 2, an analogous result was obtained ($\chi^2 = 3.5$, df $= 1$, $p < .05$, one-tail test); [7] and also in sample 3 ($\chi^2 = 6.0$, df $= 2$, p .05). The results were consistent and indicate that serious involvement with women tends to be inverse to the degree to which the individual focuses his attention on the right side of his body.

Perceptual Selectivity in Terms of Ames Thereness-Thatness Apparatus

The same earlier described Ames Thereness-Thatness (T-T) procedure used to evaluate response selectivity with reference to BFQ Back was also used to test an hypothesis pertinent to right awareness and selective response to heterosexual stimuli. It will be recalled that the T-T technique involves the subject viewing pictures in a darkened ambiguous perceptual situation and apparently adjusting them to line up with a series of rods, but in fact altering the size of an image projected on a screen. That is, while the task seems to require the spatial placement of a picture, it actually involves altering its projected size on a screen. The size judgment made in this fashion has been shown to be sensitive to the evaluative response evoked in an individual by the content of a stimulus picture.

In the present study six pictures were presented (front view of clothed male, front view of female nude, rhombus-shaped geometric figure, ice cream parfait, front view of clothed female, and rear view of male nude). They were all line drawings of the same height and width; and were responded to in the sequence just enumerated. Details concerning the mode of presentation may be found in the section dealing with BFQ Back.

In the original sample of 54 college men who served as subjects, a distinction was made between those who dealt with the pictures in a Repressive versus non-Repressive fashion. This was done by asking each subject to recall, at two points subsequent to the T-T task, as many of the pictures as possible. Those making two or more recall errors were labeled as Repressors (N = 25) and those making no errors as non-Repressors (N = 29). It was expected that BFQ Right would be significantly related to accentuated response to the picture with heterosexual content (viz., the nude female). The actual T-T index to which the Right scores were related involved the difference in rank between the female nude setting and the male nude setting. This index was chosen because it evaluates the degree to which the subject responds selectively to a heterosexual, as compared to a non-heterosexual, nudity theme. The coding of the rank difference scores was such that the more negative they

---

[7] Since the study was of a cross-validational nature and since the degree of freedom for the chi square analysis was 1, a one-tail test was employed.

were the larger (closer) was the female as compared to the male setting. In the Repression group the mean T-T difference score was —.1; and in the non-Repression group it was —.8.

A significant chi-square ($\chi^2 = 6.8$, df = 2, $p < .05$) was found in the Repression group between BFQ Right and the T-T female-nude-rank- male-nude-rank difference. That is, the higher the subject's Right score the greater was his tendency to make the female nude picture larger (closer) than the male nude picture. The chi-square between BFQ Right and the female-nude-rank–male-nude-rank difference was not significant for the non-Repression subjects. In one of two instances, then, the prediction was supported that a differential response to a heterosexual theme would accompany variations in right awareness. The result in the Repression sample indicated that with increasing BFQ Right scores there is a corresponding trend to dampen or defensively minimize the intensity of the female nude as compared to the male nude. One may regard this as congruent with other indications that the male who has high right awareness is relatively uncomfortable when dealing with heterosexual matters.

Vague Sex Pictures

Data were available which made it possible to consider in another sample the previously mentioned results indicating that degree of defensiveness aroused by pictures of persons with vague sexual identity was positively related to degree of right awareness. Subjects (N = 56) were shown 15 pictures with vague sexual identity and asked to rate each of the figures on a 5-point scale in terms of attractiveness (good looking–ugly) and also apparent friendliness. It had been assumed that degree of anxiety aroused would be reflected in defensive behavior as defined by the extent to which negative qualities were ascribed to the figures. BFQ Right was found to be correlated .25 ($p < .05$, one-tail test) with the degree to which the figures were seen as ugly. But the correlation of BFQ Right with amount of unfriendliness attributed to the figures was only .08. The findings supported the previously reported observations that right awareness was linked with ratings of attractiveness of the vague sex pictures; but they were not supportive of the data involving ratings of the friendliness of the figures.

Tachistoscopic Selectivity

Selective response to heterosexual themes was pursued further in relation to perception of such themes presented tachistoscopically. The study to be described is the same as that earlier outlined in the BFQ Back section in which back awareness was correlated with perceptual thresholds for words with homosexual implications. It may be recalled that subjects were asked to identify 14 words, of which three dealt with homosexuality, three with hostility, two with narcissism, three with orality, and three (love, kiss, flirt) with heterosexuality. The words were each randomly presented at five consecutively increasing time exposures (3.3, 3.4, 3.6, 4.0, 4.5 milliseconds); and the earliest speed at which they could be recognized was noted. In the present instance an average threshold value for the heterosexual words was computed.

The sample consisted of 45 male college students.

BFQ Right proved to have a chance relationship with the rank of the average tachistoscopic threshold value for the three heterosexual words ($r = .07$). It was also not significantly correlated with any of the ranks of the average threshold values for the other content categories.[8]

In a second session, one week later, the subjects were asked to write down all the words they could remember having previously seen tachistoscopically. The percentages of words recalled falling into each of the content categories were then computed. For heterosexual words the mean percentage was 38.5 ($\sigma = 18.4$). It was found that BFQ Right was, as anticipated, negatively correlated with the percentage of heterosexual words recalled ($r = -.36$, $p < .03$). That is, the greater the individual's awareness of the right side of his body the more he selectively forgot ("repressed") the words with heterosexual reference. None of the correlations of BFQ Right with the percentages of words recalled in other categories even approached significance.

The tachistoscopic responses themselves did not demonstrate that selectivity in perception of heterosexual words is linked to the BFQ Right parameter. But the subsequent recall data indicated that somehow the perceived heterosexual words were assimilated in an unlike fashion by those differing in degree of right awareness.

Another sample of men (N = 45) was studied in which BFQ Right was correlated with threshold for perception of a pictured heterosexual theme (man and woman kissing). The details of the procedure have already been described in the section dealing with the relation of BFQ Back to thresholds for perceiving tachistoscopically presented homosexual stimuli. It may simply be noted that six different pictures were presented (each six times); and the point of accurate identification of the theme determined. BFQ Right proved to have a chance correlation with the rank order of the threshold for perception of the heterosexual picture. This finding is congruent with that described above in indicating that the heterosexual attitudes associated with variations in right awareness do not seem to produce a selective attitude toward heterosexual themes presented tachistoscopically.

---

[8] In a study in which BFQ Right was related to speed of perception of six Blacky pictures (Castration Anxiety, Oral Eroticism, Oral Sadism, Sibling Rivalry, Anal Sadism, Masturbation Guilt) presented tachistoscopically, only chance relationships occurred.

Early Memories

The heterosexual difficulty presumed to typify those with high right awareness implies an inability to identify with the usual phallic role. This further implies difficulty in identifying with phallic concepts and modes of expression. Erikson (1951) and also others have shown that the male is more likely than the female to construct or draw forms which are phallic, elevated, or intrusive. It was therefore hypothesized that degree of right awareness should be negatively related to the presence of phallic imagery. In order to obtain a sample of imagery which could be scored for phallic attributes, an early memory technique described by Holleman (1965) seemed especially appropriate. Subjects were asked to write down ten early memories. All are elicited by specific questions like, "What is your earliest memory of your father?", "What is your very earliest memory?", "What is your happiest or most pleasant memory of childhood?" Holleman devised a reliable scoring system for "phallic-intrusive and phallic-locomotor configurations" which in modified form was applied to the present study. The following themes were treated as having phallic significance.

1. Riding vehicles or animals (e.g., bicycle, automobile, horse).
2. Using tools or phallic-shaped objects (e.g., hammer, sword, flagpole).
3. Hunting, shooting, fishing.
4. Engaging in competitive sports.
5. Fighting other boys.
6. Wearing uniforms, medals, or other emblems of recognition.
7. Climbing.
8. Participating in initiations and strength testing rituals.

In a sample of 54 college men the median number of phallic memories was 3. As predicted, a chi-square analysis indicated that BFQ Right was negatively related to number of phallic memories ($\chi^2 = 3.0$, df = 1, $p < .05$, one-tail test). A one-tail test was considered justified in view of the specific directionality of the prediction made.

The greater the individual's right awareness the less frequently did his early memories contain references to the kinds of phallic configurations which have been found to be associated with a sense of manliness and masculine aspirations.

Female Nudity

The question was considered whether the variations in attitudes toward heterosexuality accompanying differences in right awareness might be expressed in reactions to nude female figures. One might expect that the greater an individual's BFQ Right score the less attractive he would find female nudity. Data were available from a sample of 45 college men who were asked to rate nine drawings of women, six of which were nude and three clothed. Each picture was rated on a 5-point scale of "sex appeal" (5 = highest score). The median sex appeal rating of the nude pictures was 3 and that for the non-nudes 2. BFQ Right was found to be negatively, but not significantly, related to the sex appeal ratings of the nudes ($\chi^2 = 4.1$, df = 2, $p < .20$). The relationship of BFQ Right with the ratings of the clothed figures did not even approach the .20 level. A slight trend in the anticipated direction appeared for the ratings of the nudes, but it was not statistically significant.

RIGHT–LEFT AWARENESS AND THE PERIPHERAL STIMULATION THEORY

One of the most direct efforts to test the relationship between right awareness and reactions to stimuli with heterosexual significance involved an attempt to alter response to sexual words by stimulating the right and left body sides. This experiment grew out of the earlier described theory (Chapter 18) which proposed that a body area which is associated with a given wish or set is part of a system in which it can, via its degree of perceptual prominence, produce selective effects in cognition which are related to the given wish or set. By way of illustration, it may be recalled that stimulation of front and back body sites with a vibrator produced selective effects in the learning and recall of "dirt" words presumably having anal connotations.

If it is actually true that the right and left body sides are associated with opposite attitudes toward heterosexual matters, it should be possible to show that stimulation of right versus left sites results in opposite forms of selectivity when dealing with heterosexual stimuli. This was expressed operationally in the hypothesis that the application of a vibrator to the right hand would have an opposite effect upon the learning and recall of words with sexual connotations than would a vibrator placed on the left hand.

A list containing ten sexual and ten non-sexual words, developed earlier, was used to evaluate the selective memory parameter. The list is shown below.

Plan	Caress *	Feel *	Kiss *
Touch *	Train	Build	Twist *
Debate	Listen	Flirt *	Skate
Run	Perfume *	Dust	Hug *
Dance *	Write	Date *	Color

[Sex words are indicated with an asterisk]

The two sets of words were equated for length and spaced equivalently throughout the list.

Learning of the list occurred under three conditions. In one instance, each individual was told that he would memorize a number of words while experiencing an interfering distraction. A vibrator (Oster Massaget, Model 212, 35 watts) was strapped to the subject's right arm and he was told to "get used to the vibration" for one minute. Then, with the vibrator still operating, he was asked to learn the list of words which was presented on a typed sheet for one minute; and finally, when the list was removed, he was given five minutes to write down as many of the words as he could recall. A second experimental condition duplicated the first in all respects except that the vibrator was placed on the left arm instead of the right. For the third experimental condition the list was learned without a vibrator attached to the subject's body.

A score was computed for each subject equal to the number of sex words minus non-sex words recalled.

The right-arm vibration, left-arm vibration, and neutral condition samples consisted respectively of 28, 21, and 48 male college students.

The mean sex minus non-sex recall scores were $+2.6$ for the right-vibration condition; $+1.5$ for the left-vibration condition; and $+1.5$ for the neutral procedure.

Analysis of variance indicated that the overall differences among the conditions were significant ($F = 4.2, p < .05$). Further, the right and left vibration conditions were significantly different ($F = 5.1, p < .05$); and the right versus neutral condition difference was also significant ($F = 7.7, p < .01$). The left and neutral conditions were not significantly unlike.

The means of the total numbers of words recalled were 10.4, 10.3, and 10.9 respectively for the right, left, and neutral conditions. None of these differences are significant.

In general, then, the results indicated that right vibration increased selective superior recall for sex words, as compared to both the left vibration and neutral conditions. Left vibration did not have an effect greater than the neutral procedure. Apparently, right peripheral stimulation does result in selective cognitive processes which increase the subject's probability of learning and recalling words with sexual meaning. This supports the hypothesis proposed; whereas the lack of difference between the left stimulation and neutral conditions was not supportive.

The fact that different selective memory effects in dealing with sexual words could be elicited by right versus left stimulation certainly speaks effectively for the notion that the right-left dimension has basic sexual implications.[9]

_____

[9] However, despite the successful substantiation of the hypothesis which was obtained, it should be noted that in two attempts ($N = 60$, $N = 55$) to correlate selective memory for

NARCISSISM

In an entirely exploratory fashion, evidence has been found that a right-sided focus of attention occurs in those who somehow fear or find unacceptable narcissistic investment in themselves. From this perspective, their hetero-sexual difficulties might be a function of an orientation which dictates that certain gratifications which are self-enhancing or pleasurable to self (such as sexual contact) will be negatively experienced. Perhaps they have learned to avoid that which connotes investment in self. There have been two lines of evidence relevant to this view. One concerns the reactions shown to tachisto-scopically presented representations of narcissistic behavior. Data from three studies have accumulated in which BFQ Right has been related to threshold for accurate perception of narcissistic themes.

A first study, previously cited in the section dealing with BFQ Back, involved a sample of college men (N = 45) who were asked to react to six tachistoscopically presented pictures. Each picture was shown six times consecutively. One, portraying a person looking in a mirror at his own image, was included which was intended to represent the theme of narcissism. The other themes contained in the series were heterosexual, homosexual, achieve-ment, nurturance, and hostility. It was specifically anticipated that variations in right awareness would be accompanied by selective responses to the narcissistic picture. No prediction was made whether the response would involve sensitization or inhibition. When BFQ Right was related to the rank order of the narcissism threshold with respect to the other thresholds, a borderline correlation of .26 ($p < .10$) was found. The higher the BFQ Right score the more difficult it was to perceive the narcissism theme accurately.

In another project, also previously described in the section dealing with BFQ Back, right awareness was correlated with threshold for the perception of words with narcissistic meaning. A sample of 45 male college students was studied. Words pertaining to various themes were presented tachistoscopically and thresholds for correct perception were determined. Each word was shown five times consecutively. Two of the 14 words presented (viz., self, mine) were intended to have narcissistic significance. Other themes repre-sented by the words in the series were as follows: homosexual, heterosexual, hostile, and oral. The rank order of the average threshold of the narcissistic

---

sexual words with BFQ Right in male samples, significant relationships could not be shown. That is, when the subject's usual degree of right awareness was correlated with the manner in which he learned and recalled sexual words no correlation was discerned. Why significant results were obtained with the vibrator condition but not in the usual state remains a mystery.

words (in relation to thresholds of other classes of words) had a chance correlation with BFQ Right.

There was also a third study by Rhoda Fisher, already described above with reference to BFQ Back variables, which involved tachistoscopic responses of disturbed boys (N = 23). Each subject was seen individually and asked to describe nine tachistoscopically presented stick figure pictures. Two portrayed narcissistic themes (person looking in a mirror, person on a stage); three dealt with hostility; two concerned nurturance; and two involved social interaction themes. A picture was presented four times consecutively at increasing speeds (.01, .03, .05, and .10 seconds). The sum of the rank orders of the narcissistic thresholds proved to be correlated .57 ($p < .01$) with BFQ Right. The higher the subject's right awareness the more difficult it was for him to perceive the narcissistic pictures accurately. This finding supported the first cited above in which a borderline positive relation was found between BFQ Right and difficulty in perceiving a narcissistic picture. It should be noted that one of the two narcissistic pictures used in the sample of children, viz., person looking in mirror, was also used in the other study. Taken together, these two studies, both of which used pictures as stimuli, encourage the view that variations in right awareness are linked with issues pertaining to narcissism. It is true that in the second study cited above involving tachistoscopic perception of narcissistic *words* (viz., self, mine) the threshold for accurate perception was not correlated with BFQ Right. One can only conjecture that words like "self" and "mine" did not have the same impact and defense arousing force with reference to narcissism as did the pictures with their rather flamboyant self display themes.

A second line of evidence concerning the narcissism variable is based on deductions from the nature of one's expressed dissatisfactions. He who is narcissistically invested would tend to do things for himself rather than for others. He is probably dissatisfied with roles which require him to carry burdens that detract from his personal ease and impatient with situations which do not provide him with satisfaction or comfort. If so, it might be possible to approach the question of estimating narcissism in terms of the kinds of dissatisfactions one expresses. For exploratory purposes it was assumed in the present study that narcissistic attitudes are revealed in the following classes of dissatisfactions.

1. Those which emphasize uncomfortable burdens imposed upon self by the world.

2. Those which concern situations in which one is not sufficiently entertained, stimulated, or gratified.

In order to obtain a sample of an individual's dissatisfactions, a procedure was devised which involved asking him to describe on a sheet of paper 20 things that he does not like. No further definition of the task was given, except to urge that each item on the list be described in detail. The scoring of the "things disliked" conformed to the two categories listed below.

1. All references to having unpleasant duties or obligations, burdens,

and difficult conditions to endure were determined. Examples of items in this "Burden" category are as follows: having to volunteer for a job, having to attend evening classes in school, studying for an examination, washing dishes, being obligated to do too much, going to class early in the morning.

2. A second Non-gratification category embraced all statements about disliking situations in which there is a lack of adequate stimulation or gratification. It contained the following sorts of references: dull situations, dull professors, boring classes, boring company, doing nothing, seeing a poor movie, watching a poor TV show.

Scoring of 25 protocols by two independent judges indicated 89 percent agreement for the first category and 94 percent for the second.

The mean number of "Burden" dislikes expressed was 2.3 ($\sigma = 2.3$); and the mean number of "Non-gratification" dislikes was 1.0 ($\sigma = 1.1$). BFQ Right was negatively and significantly correlated with number of "Burden" dislikes ($r = -.28, p < .05$); but had only a chance relationship to the "Non-gratification" dislikes. A second analysis of the relation of the Non-gratification scores to BFQ Right by means of chi-square was also not significant.

The prime finding, then, was that the greater an individual's right awareness the fewer the number of dissatisfactions he expresses which revolve about a sense of being imposed upon, and burdened by, the world. This was taken to mean an inverse relation between right awareness and degree of narcissism.

The results concerning narcissism and right awareness have interesting implications. A further test of them awaits the development of other methods for measuring narcissism. The data indicate that right awareness is either inverse to number of narcissistic dissatisfactions or positively linked with difficulty in perceiving narcissistic themes. It seems to go along with an orientation which minimizes investment in, and gratification of, self. Perhaps the highly right aware person has learned that he ought not please, or have high regard for, himself. If this were so, there would still be a problem in deciding the manner in which such an attitude might enter into the heterosexual difficulties associated with right awareness. It is understandable that if an individual feels that he is not entitled to self enhancement or gratification this could interfere with establishing heterosexual relationships which do promise potential gratification. But why should the interference manifest itself only with respect to heterosexual gratification? Why are other areas (e.g., oral satisfaction, pleasure in male companionship) not implicated? The answers to such questions are not apparent at present.

OVERVIEW

The BFQ Right scale offers promise. It is a relatively independent measure; manifests passable test-retest reliability; and seems capable of predicting results that cohere sensibly. Primarily, the findings indicate that the more intense a man's focus of attention upon the right side of his body the more likely he is to have problems in heterosexual adjustment. He is more likely to have reduced heterosexual interaction; to become defensive when confronted with sexual references; and to be alarmed by situations which cast doubt upon his sex role.

A prime question raised by these findings is why heterosexual difficulties are associated with a focus of attention on the right as opposed to the left body side. Two possible explanations may be offered. One derives from observations concerning the differential response characteristics of the right and left sides. The response of the right side tends to be slower and more controlled than that of the left. Schoen and Scofield (1935) reported that when the eyes of the right-eyed person are shifting from one fixation point to a new target, the left eye responds first, "snapping" to its new position and sometimes overshooting, as compared to the right eye, which moves more gradually and precisely. Similarly, Travis and Herren (1929) and Jasper and Raney (1937) noted that when right-handed individuals were asked to perform a task quickly and simultaneously with both arms, the left responded first. Such findings suggest that in right-handed persons the right side is characterized by a stable set which facilitates control but also inhibits the spontaneity of that side as compared to the non-dominant side. Jasper and Raney (1937, p. 161) specifically stated "... the tendency for the non-dominant side to lead in attempted simultaneous movement may indicate a greater cortical control ('inhibition') of the movements of the so-called dominant side which is only a counterpart of the more highly perfected coordination of movement on this side." If so, the right side could become associated with control; whereas the left would betoken spontaneity. The relationship between poor heterosexual adjustment and focus on the right could be construed as indicating that those having difficulties in heterosexual expression are also those who "ignore" the spontaneous side of their bodies and concentrate on the "controlled" side. To attend to the right could represent a set to respond in a careful, self-controlled fashion, and such a set might be antithetical to the spontaneity required for adequate heterosexuality.

A second possible explanation for the relationship between focus on the right and heterosexual role relates to the fact that the right-handed individual is aware that his right hand is stronger than his left. He might, therefore, associate the right hand with strength and power which are attributes that typically define masculinity. But the left hand would be for him the "weaker one" and in that sense less masculine or more feminine. If one were doubtful about his masculine adequacy, he might express such concern in an anxious awareness of his right side which he equates with the strength needed to be masculine. He could be thought of as anxiously watching his right side because he anticipates it will not function to provide the power he feels he needs to be manly.

It is an intriguing matter that an inverse relation was found between BFQ Right and indices of narcissism. With augmented right awareness there is an apparent diminished investment in self. This finding may eventually prove to be the best of leads concerning the meaning of the particular pattern of traits and attitudes that parallel degree of right awareness. It may be, for example, that during socialization an individual who learns to avoid self-investment may also find it particularly difficult to establish contacts which result in general self gratification.[10]

[10] This may be the factor which distinguishes the sex role disturbance associated with high back awareness from that linked with high right awareness. The sex role anxieties of the first mentioned seem to be derived from unconscious homosexual conflicts and wishes. The sex role problems of the second mentioned do not involve homosexual conflicts. Instead, they seem to grow out of inhibitions about permitting oneself a phallic identity or sensual gratification. Note also that while the sex role anxieties of those with high back awareness do not seem to affect amount of overt heterosexual activity, the conflicts of the high right aware do go along with reduced heterosexual behavior.

20
Eye Awareness in Men
and Incorporative Wishes

INTRODUCTION

The eyes have a unique role in obtaining information and also in the expressive functions of the face. Therefore, one would expect them to have great import in the body scheme. Much speculation has been stirred about their psychological and symbolic significance. Of course, folklore and superstition have been responsible for theories about the eyes as a source of power and malignance. Concepts of cursing, bewitching, and gaining control over others have often been phrased in terms of mysterious use of the eyes.

There are many clinical reports concerning hypochondriacal and delusional ideas which may develop concerning the eyes. These have given rise to a considerable literature, primarily psychoanalytic, which speculates about the nature of the unconscious fantasies that can be elaborated about one's eyes. It has been variously suggested that they are unconsciously equated with oral "taking in" processes; hostile ("evil eye") intent; wishes to see forbidden sexual scenes; and even the genital organ itself (Fenichel, 1945). Most of these speculations could be conceptualized within the category of incorporative intent. Whether they suggest oral, sexual, hostile, or non-hostile aims they depict the eyes as accomplishing these aims largely by functioning as a channel for admission and "taking in." Things are, in fantasy, destroyed, incorporated, or sexually contacted via the imagined opening (or channel) provided by the eyes. It was the emphasis in the literature on the fact that the eye is so often experienced as an opening which can "take in" which suggested the possibility that eye awareness might be linked with incorporative attitudes. But since the eyes are not truly incorporative in the way that a body opening like the mouth is, it was considered that the person who focuses on his eyes is probably one who is fearful of real incorporative wishes and therefore substitutes the sort of unreal ones exemplified by defining the eye as an oral channel. This view led to the hypothesis that degree of eye awareness is positively correlated with anxiety about incorporation (presumably via the mouth) and negatively so with indicators of free expression of incorporative wishes. The model for this formulation is provided by the Freudian concept that the use of a substitute zone for an erogenous purpose is due to anxiety which prevents use of the corresponding real erogenous zone. Specific hypotheses which were derived are listed below:

1. Degree of eye interest is inversely related to the enjoyment of eating. The greater the emphasis upon the eyes (as a substitute incorporative channel) the less does the primary oral zone (mouth) serve as a source of pleasure.

2. Also, one would expect that the greater an individual's focus upon his eyes the more anxiety he would evidence when responding to food related stimuli.

3. Quite analogously, degree of eye focus should be positively correlated with amount of anxiety evoked by symbolic references to incorporation.

4. Finally, it seemed logical to expect that eye interest would be negatively correlated with the degree to which one's parents were recalled as giving. If eye interest depicts a sense of not being able to secure oral gratification, one might anticipate that such an attitude would reflect experiences with parents who appeared to be selfish and unwilling to give of their resources.

Eye awareness was measured with the Body Focus Questionnaire (BFQ). Included in the BFQ array of paired-comparisons were 11 items in which the eyes were compared to other facial areas (e.g., eyes versus ears, eyes versus mouth, eyes versus chin). The BFQ Eye score could range from 0 to 11. It was found that the test-retest coefficient for Eye scores, with a week intervening, was .71 [1] in one group of 57 subjects. In another group (N = 52) the test-retest reliability, with a week intervening was .54. In a third group (N = 51), with a week intervening, the coefficient was .65.

Like most BFQ variables, the Eye scale is relatively independent of the other BFQ scales.[2] In a series of ten different male samples (with average N of 50), it was correlated six times significantly with BFQ Head (.39, .35, .40, .32, .31, .38); twice with BFQ Stomach (.29, .36); twice with BFQ Arms (.37, .39); twice with BFQ Right (.25, .35); twice with BFQ Heart (.27, .27); once with BFQ Mouth (.30). While there are rather consistent correlations with BFQ Head, they are largely in the .30's. None of the correlations were really substantial or consistent.

BFQ Eye scores in college male populations have clustered around 7.1. There is a tendency to be slightly more aware of one's eyes than other areas of

---

[1] All correlation coefficients are product-moment unless otherwise specified.
[2] BFQ Eyes has shown no consistent relationships with the Barrier score.

Table 20.1
Means and Standard Deviations of BFQ Eye Scores

M	σ	N
7.3	2.6	45
7.3	2.8	50
7.4	2.4	48
7.3	2.9	57
6.6	2.6	45
7.5	2.5	47
6.8	2.6	51
6.8	2.9	51
7.3	2.0	50
6.7	2.8	53

one's face. Table 20.1 presents BFQ Eye means for ten different samples of male college students. With rare exceptions, score distributions have not deviated significantly from normality.

BFQ Eyes has proven not to be consistently correlated with measures of response set like the MMPI K and L scales, the Marlowe-Crowne (1964) Social Desirability scale, and the Bass Acquiescence scale (1956).

EXPLORATORY STUDIES

The Byrne Food Attitude scale (Byrne, Golightly, and Capaldi, 1963) was used to test the hypothesis that BFQ Eyes would be negatively correlated with enjoyment of eating. This scale is composed of 221 items which inquire concerning liking for foods, pleasantness associated with past eating experiences, cooking skill of mother, and importance of food as a reward and comfort. Responses to each item are registered by the subject in terms of True and False. Only 47 of the 221 items have shown scale coherence for males and these are the items which are scored. The higher the score the more the subject is considered to have a positive attitude toward eating.

To investigate whether BFQ Eyes is positively related to anxiety when confronted with food stimuli, a selective memory procedure was used which has proven successful in other studies (Fisher, 1964A, 1965B). This procedure assumes that if a subject is asked to learn material which provokes anxiety, his recall for it will be relatively poorer than for equated material without anxiety connotations. Subjects (in small groups) were asked to view for one minute a list of 20 words projected on a screen; and they were subsequently given five minutes to write down as many of the words as they could recall. The list consisted of ten words referring to food and ten without food implications which were of the same average length and randomly distributed. The words in the list are enumerated below:

Plan	Beef *
Mint *	Road
Hall	Pair
Bun *	Broth *
View	Cream *
Raisin *	Fair
Check	Tea *
Honey *	Trace
Book	Plum *
Hash *	Stone

[Food words are starred]

A subject's score equaled the number of food words minus the number of non-food words recalled.

The question whether BFQ Eyes would prove to be related to the subject's recall of his parents' generosity required that ratings of the parents be obtained. Each subject indicated on a 3-point scale how applicable to his mother were each of nine statements concerned with generosity (e.g., "Feels we should help those weaker than ourselves"; "Considers it important to help charitable causes"). The same responses were obtained with regard to father. Weights of 0, 1 and 2 were applied respectively to the response alternatives of "Not at all true," "Slightly true," and "Very true." Total scores could range from 0 through 18.

The subjects consisted of 62 male college students recruited by payment of a fee. Their median age was 20.

The mean BFQ Eyes score was 6.4[3] ($\sigma = 2.5$). The mean Byrne Food Attitude score was 34.5 ($\sigma = 5.5$). Table 20.2 indicates that BFQ Eyes is, as predicted, significantly and negatively correlated with the Byrne index ($r = -.29$, p .03). The greater the subject's focus on his eyes the less he reports enjoyment of food-related experiences.

The mean selective food memory score was $+.2$ ($\sigma = 2.3$), indicating only a slight tendency for the group to remember more food than non-food words. A correlation of $-.29$ ($p < .05$) was found between BFQ Eyes and the memory score. It would appear, as hypothesized, that with increasing awareness of one's eyes there is a parallel tendency to show selectively poor recall for references to food.

The data involving the ratings of parental generosity indicated a mean of 5.1 ($\sigma = 2.0$) for Father and a mean of 11.7 ($\sigma = 3.4$) for Mother. Table 20.2 reveals that BFQ Eyes had a significant correlation of $-.30$ (p .03) with Father Generosity and a borderline one ($-.21$, p .10) with Mother Generosity.

In this preliminary study, eye awareness did prove to be related to anxiety about eating and food as indicated by the results involving the Byrne Food Attitude scale and the food for memory words. Evidence was found too

Table 20.2
Product-Moment Correlations of BFQ Eyes
with Incorporative Attitude Variables

BFQ Eyes versus	r	Significance Level
Byrne Food Attitude score	−.29 (N = 61)	.03
Selective food memory	−.29 (N = 59) [a]	<.05
Father generosity	−.30 (N = 57)	.03
Mother generosity	−.21 (N = 60)	.10

[a] There are variations in N because some protocols had to be discarded either as a consequence of misunderstandings of instructions or the inappropriateness of certain questions (e.g., pertaining to a father or a mother who was long deceased).

that eye awareness is significantly linked with a male subject's recall of the generosity of his father, but only at a borderline level with his recall of mother's generosity. The predictions which were supported evolved from the assumption that if an individual concentrates his attention upon a body area capable of serving as a substitute or symbolic opening he does so because he is fearful of experiences with some primary body opening. Presumably, the focus upon the symbolic opening is an indirect attempt to experience what is forbidden elsewhere in the body. This assumption is a derivative of Breuer and Freud's (1936) generalized theory concerning the mechanisms underlying conversion phenomena.

CROSS–VALIDATION AND EXTENSION

The next step in dealing with the formulation regarding the significance of eye awareness was to undertake the cross-validation of the initial findings. Descriptions of this work follow.

Food Attitude Scale

One of the important results had indicated that BFQ Eyes was inversely related to a measure (Byrne, et al., 1963) of how much satisfaction the individual derives from eating. A follow-up study was carried out which involved a sample of 57 college men. BFQ Eye scores were related to Byrne Food Attitude scale scores. The mean Byrne score was 34.1 ($\sigma = 4.6$). As predicted, degree of eye awareness and enjoyment of food related experiences proved to be negatively and significantly correlated ($r = -.22$, $p < .05$, one-tail test). A one-tail test was considered justified in view of the specific cross-validating nature of the study.

Selective Food Memory

A second finding that was re-evaluated concerned the previously obtained negative relationship between eye awareness and selective superior recall for words pertaining to food. A sample of 45 college men was appraised. The same previously described list, consisting of ten food and ten non-food words, was submitted to subjects to learn during a one-minute period and then to recall during a subsequent five-minute period. The median difference for food minus non-food words recalled was 0 (range $+4$ to -4). A chi-square analysis indicated that BFQ Eyes was, as expected, negatively and significantly related to selective superior recall for food words ($\chi^2 = 2.7$, df $= 1$, $p = .05$, one-tail test). The earlier finding was replicated.

Tachistoscopic Presentation of Blacky Pictures

The relationship between eye awareness and selective reaction to Blacky pictures was considered in a study, previously cited, which evaluated responses to six Blacky pictures presented tachistoscopically. Two of the Blacky pictures presented the Oral Eroticism and Oral Sadism themes; and the other four comprised Anal Sadism, Masturbation Guilt, Castration Anxiety, and Sibling Rivalry. Each picture was shown at six different speeds. It was for obvious reasons hypothesized that the greater an individual's eye awareness the more difficulty he would have in perceiving the Oral Eroticism and Oral Sadism themes. Data derived from a sample of 41 male college students indicated that BFQ Eyes was positively correlated at a borderline level with the rank order of the time exposure at which Oral Eroticism was first correctly identified ($r = .28$, $p < .10$). BFQ Eyes was also negatively correlated ($r = -.35$, $p < .05$) with the rank order of total number of times Oral Eroticism was correctly identified. That is, the greater the individual's eye awareness the more difficulty he had in coping with the Oral Eroticism picture. However, no relation was discerned between eye awareness and the response indices for Oral Sadism. It should be mentioned too that BFQ Eyes was negatively correlated with the rank order of the time exposure at which the Castration Anxiety ($r - -.41$, p .01) theme was correctly recognized. It was positively correlated with the rank order of the total number of times Masturbation Guilt was correctly identified ($r = .40, p < .01$). The meaning of these last correlations is not immediately evident.

Parental Generosity

As predicted by the formulation concerning the sense of oral deprivation linked with eye awareness, it had been shown that BFQ Eyes was negatively correlated with how generous and giving one recalled one's parents to have been. Confirmation was significant with respect to one's recall of father's degree of generosity but only at a borderline level with reference to one's recall of mother's generosity. To evaluate the stability of these results, the same nine-statement questionnaire concerning parental generosity (e.g., "Considers it important to help charitable causes") was used to measure recalled generosity of father and also mother. Thirty-six male college students served as subjects. The mean amount of generosity attributed to father was 8.8 ($\sigma = 3.2$) and to mother 11.3 ($\sigma = 2.8$). BFQ Eyes was negatively correlated with Mother Generosity ($r = -.24, p < .10$, one-tail test) and Father Generosity ($-.32, p = .03$, one-tail test). It is interesting that whereas in the first study the correlations found were significant for Father Generosity and borderline for Mother Generosity, the converse occurred in the present study. The trends, while weak, indicate at least a consistent directionality in the correlation between BFQ Eyes and the amount of generosity recalled as characterizing one's parents.

The cross-validating findings pertaining to the Byrne Food Attitude Scale, selective memory for food words, and recall of parental generosity were reassuring.

FURTHER STUDIES OF ORALITY AND INCORPORATION

Since the primary conflict going along with eye awareness seemed to revolve about oral wishes and fantasies, a concerted effort was made to examine the relationships between BFQ Eyes and a spectrum of orality indices.

Proverbs

Story (1963) was able to use responses to proverbs as a technique for detecting selective attitudes about oral themes. He found that alcoholics when asked to interpret a series of proverbs with oral connotations (e.g., Once in people's mouths, it is hard to get out of them; He who can lick can also bite) had more difficulty in doing so than controls. The oral proverbs presumably aroused affects which interfered with the process of restating their meaning. If eye awareness relates to oral conflicts, it should be possible to demonstrate that BFQ Eyes is correlated with patterns of response to oral proverbs.

A study involving 44 male college students was undertaken in which their BFQ Eye scores could be related to how they dealt with oral proverbs. Seven oral and seven neutral proverbs were read to the subjects individually. Examples of the oral type have already been cited above. The neutral are exemplified by the following: too many chiefs, not enough Indians; the work praises the workman. The task was to explain the meaning of each proverb. The time that it required the subject to begin his response following the presentation of each proverb was measured and also the total amount of time to give what he considered to be an adequate explanation. Two indices were computed: (1) Average initial response time for neutral proverbs minus average initial response time for oral proverbs; (2) Average total response time for neutral proverbs minus average total response time for oral proverbs. Response to neutral proverbs was used as a base in order to control for general differences in making cognitive decisions.

The mean initial neutral minus oral response time was —.18 seconds ($\sigma = .5$). The mean total neutral response time minus oral time was 8.1 seconds ($\sigma = 2.0$). BFQ Eyes was correlated —.25 ($p < .10$) with the average initial neutral time minus average initial oral time. Similarly, BFQ Eyes was correlated —.34 (p .025) with average total neutral time minus average total oral time. Both of the findings indicate that the greater the subject's eye awareness the relatively longer he required to initiate and complete response to the oral as compared to the neutral proverbs. While the result for the total time index was more clearly significant than that for initial time, the two together indicate that variations in eye awareness were accompanied by selective differences in response to the oral themes. In this instance the greater the eye awareness the more difficulty the subject seemed to have (i.e., he took longer) in coping cognitively with the oral material. One may assume that the conflicts about incorporation which seem to typify those with high eye awareness interfered with their attempts to analyze the oral proverbs.

Humor

Can the selectivity in responding to oral stimuli which apparently parallels eye awareness be shown to extend to reactions to jokes with oral content? A modification of the earlier described humor test devised by Weiss (1955) was used to investigate this question. Jokes in five different categories (Oral Eroticism, Oral Sadism, Oedipal, Anal Expulsive, Castration Anxiety) were presented to 47 male college students who were asked to indicate on a 6-point scale how much they enjoyed them. For each subject the mean rating for each joke category was computed. These means were then ranked (rank 1 = least enjoyable). It was presumed that eye awareness would be related to degree of enjoyment of the Oral Eroticism and Oral Sadism jokes, but not of the others. No prediction was made about the direction of the relationships because, as Weiss notes, it is not yet clear that high or low ratings of jokes dealing with a given theme have any fixed meaning about how comfortable or uncomfortable one is with reference to that theme.

The median Oral Eroticism rank was 3 (range 1–5) and the median for Oral Sadism was 3.5 (range 1–5). BFQ Eyes was observed to be positively and significantly related to the Oral Eroticism ranks ($\chi^2 = 7.1$, df $= 1$, $p < .01$) and also positively, but not significantly, with Oral Sadism ranks ($\chi^2 = 4.1$, df $= 2$, $p < .20$). BFQ Eyes was not related to the rank values of any of the other joke categories.

The findings indicated that the more intense an individual's eye awareness the relatively greater was his enjoyment of the Oral Eroticism jokes. A similar but slight trend appeared with reference to the Oral Sadism jokes. Once again eye awareness was associated with a special perspective toward orality.

Perceptual Selectivity in Terms of Ames Thereness-Thatness Apparatus

The opportunity to appraise selectivity in perception of oral stimuli as a parallel of degree of eye awareness was offered in the earlier described (BFQ Back section) data derived from the use of the Ames Thereness-Thatness (T-T) technique. A brief reminder concerning the manner in which these data were collected is in order. The T-T technique involves the subject viewing pictures in an ambiguous setting and apparently adjusting their spatial positions to line up with a series of rods; but actually the judgments made relate to changing their size rather than their spatial positions. Such size judgments provide meaningful information about the evaluative responses evoked by a picture's content.

As part of the design of the study T-T responses were obtained to six line drawing pictures, one of which portrayed an oral theme (ice cream parfait). It will also be recalled that a distinction was made between those who dealt with the pictures in a Repressive versus non-Repressive manner. This was done by testing at subsequent times the subject's memory of the content of the T-T pictures. Those making two or more recall errors were classified as Repressors (N = 25) and those making no errors as non-Repressors (N = 29).

The T-T index employed was the difference between the average of the ranks of the settings for the two nude figures minus the rank of the ice cream parfait setting. It was intended in this way to determine if the response to the oral stimulus was different from the response to the other two most vivid or ego-involving picture stimuli in the series. The mean difference score was $-.4$ for the Repressors and -1.2 for the non-Repressors.

In the Repression sample a borderline relationship at the $<.10$ level obtained between BFQ Eyes and the difference between the average of the nude ranks and the parfait rank ($\chi^2 = 5.3$, df $= 2$, $p < .10$). The higher the subject's Eye score the greater was the tendency to set the parfait picture relatively larger (closer) than the nude pictures.

The equivalent relationship in the non-Repression group was of a chance order. However, it should be reported that in this sample BFQ Eyes was positively and significantly correlated with the rank of the sum of T-T values for the parfait picture ($r = .35$, p .05). That is, the greater the eye awareness the greater was the tendency for the subjects in the non-Repression sample to perceive the parfait as small (far away). This pattern of response may be considered to represent defensiveness on the part of the non-Repressive individual. The presumed hyperalertness or sensitivity to the picture on the part of the non-Repressors results in defensively making it smaller (putting it at a distance to diminish its intensity).

The borderline trends in both the Repression and non-Repression groups should be kept in mind to be considered in the context of related results.

Early Memory

A previously described Early Memory technique similar to that developed by Holleman (1965) was used to sample the existence of oral imagery. Subjects, in response to a series of specific questions (e.g., "What is your earliest memory?") were asked to write down ten early memories. The following themes were designated as having oral significance.

1. References to eating or drinking.
2. Wishes for food or drink.
3. Descriptions of any figure as engaged in buying, securing, or preparing food.
4. References to illness caused by food.

Agreement between two independent judges for 25 protocols was 96 percent.

It was expected that the greater an individual's eye awareness the more he would produce memories containing either very few or many references to oral themes. That is, degree of eye awareness should be associated with selectivity in recall of oral themes. There was difficulty in spelling out a more directional hypothesis because it is not clear from the existing literature whether anxiety about incorporation is likely to be accompanied by a high or low amount of oral imagery and fantasy.

A sample of 54 college men was studied. The mean number of oral memories produced was 1.0 (σ = .9). BFQ Eyes was found to correlate .25 (p < .10) with number of oral memories. One sees here a borderline trend for the amount of Early Memory oral imagery to be positively related to intensity of eye awareness. Once again the finding, while not strictly significant, was suggestive.

Average Week

When BFQ Eyes was related in a sample of college men (N = 56) to the number of references to eating in an individual's account of how he spends an average week, the association was of a chance order. The Average Week measure, earlier described, involves the subject writing for a 15-minute period and depicting in detail his routine of living during an average week in his life. All references to eating, preparing, or buying food were scored. The total number of food references divided by the total of all scored activities included in other categories (e.g., Cleaning, Entertainment) was taken as an index of interest in food. Before applying the food reference score, it was shown that two independent raters were able to evaluate 25 protocols and attain 90 percent agreement. However, as stated, it proved not to be correlated significantly with BFQ Eyes.

Tachistoscopic Perception

One of the tachistoscopic studies earlier described had involved subjects (45 male college students) trying to identify 14 words randomly presented tachistoscopically. Each word was shown at five consecutively increasing time exposures (3.3, 3.4, 3.6, 4.0, 4.5 milliseconds); and the earliest speed at which it could be identified was ascertained. Three of the words referred to homosexuality; three dealt with heterosexual themes; three with hostility; two with narcissism; and three with orality (food, candy, suck). The rank order (relative to other word categories) of the average of the three oral word threshold values was determined. When these rank values were dichotomized (at median) and related by means of chi-square to the trichotomized (into as equal thirds as possible) BFQ Eyes scores, a borderline negative relationship was noted (χ^2 = 4.8, df = 2, p < .10). The higher the BFQ Eye scores the more quickly were the oral words recognized. Thus, there was a sensitized rather than inhibited orientation toward oral references on the part of those with high eye awareness. BFQ Eyes was not significantly correlated with any of the other tachistoscopic rank values.

When the subjects in the tachistoscopic study were asked a week later to recall all of the words they had perceived, there were chance correlations between BFQ Eyes and the percentages of the total words recalled which were in the oral category.

Chain Associations

The "chain association" technique, previously described, provided data of interest concerning the relationship between eye awareness and associative responses to words with oral meaning. It will be recalled that this technique involved asking subjects to give ten associations to each of 13 words. Three of the words (taste, suck and swallow) dealt with oral activities; and the others variously presented anal, aggressive, masochistic, and neutral themes. All associations were written down verbatim by the experimenter; and the time taken to complete ten associations to each was recorded. The mean of the total time taken to respond to each cluster of words was determined; and the means were ranked. Assignment of rank 1 to a theme indicated that the smallest amount of time was required to complete response to words in that theme group. The associations given to each stimulus word were scored in terms of how directly they adhered to its actual meaning. This was done with the intent of determining how motivated the subject was to evade dealing with specific themes. It was anticipated that the greater an individual's eye awareness the more he would display selective response to the oral words.

In a sample of 43 male college students BFQ Eyes was found to be negatively correlated ($r = -.29$, p .05) with the rank (relative to other word themes) of the average amount of time required to complete associations to the oral words. The greater the eye awareness the more quickly were the associations to the oral words completed. There was one other significant finding which indicated that the higher the eye awareness score the longer was required to complete associations to the hostile words ($r = .29$, p .05).

No correlations of significance appeared between BFQ Eyes and the indices indicating how directly the associations which had been produced adhered to their respective stimulus words.

The results are not impressive. But they once more indicate a trend for variations in eye awareness to be paralleled by selectivity in response to oral stimuli. It is of interest that the selectivity takes the form of increased speed of response (sensitization?) to such stimuli with intensified eye awareness.

PERIPHERAL STIMULATION: EFFECT OF INTENSIFYING EYE AWARENESS

As was analogously true for other body awareness dimensions earlier considered (e.g., front-back, right-left), one of the most direct ways of testing the presumed association of oral conflicts with eye awareness was via observations of the selective cognitive effects resulting from peripheral eye stimulation. The general theory has already been outlined which proposed that a body landmark related to a particular wish or set is part of a system in which it can have feedback effects on the wish or set and also become a source of semiautonomous signals capable of influencing cognitive processes. Some evidence in support of the theory has been presented in terms of the effects of front versus back and right versus left stimulation on memory for words.

In view of the relationship between eye awareness and incorporative wishes, it was hypothesized that increasing an individual's awareness of his eyes would selectively influence his ability to learn and recall words referring to food. It was expected that directing an individual's attention to his eyes would significantly increase or decrease his recall of food as compared to non-food words.

The list for evaluating selective memory consisted of ten words pertaining to food and ten without food reference. It is shown below.

Plan	Beef *
Mint *	Road
Hall	Pair
Bun *	Broth *
View	Cream *
Raisin *	Fair
Check	Tea *
Honey *	Trace
Book	Plum *
Hash *	Stone

[Food words are starred]

The average number of letters in the food and non-food words was the same and the positions of the two types of words in the list were equivalent.

Learning and recall were studied under three conditions. The first was concerned with the effect of intensified eye awareness. In order to create such eye awareness, each subject was instructed as follows: "I am interested in the sensations which you experience within your eyes. I would like to have you look at the wall, stare at it, and tell me in detail what you are now experiencing within your eyes." After a minute of such reporting of eye sensations, the subject was told that he would be shown a list of words to learn and "while you are doing this I will be watching your eyes to determine any special eye movements that occur." The list was then presented for one minute and the subject had five minutes to write down as many of the words as he could recall. During the entire learning and recall period the experimenter kept his eyes fixed on the subject's eyes.

One of the control conditions which was set up involved the subject learning the word list while his awareness of his mouth, rather than his eyes, was increased. In order to draw his attention to his mouth he was asked prior to, and during the learning and recall process, to hold a tongue depressor in his mouth. In other words, the procedure duplicated that for the experimental condition except the subject's mouth rather than his eyes was highlighted. In another control condition the list was learned in the usual fashion, but without accompanying body stimulation of any kind.

It was expected that the eye awareness condition would produce effects different from each of the two control conditions. But it was not anticipated that the two control conditions would have unlike effects.

For each subject, a score was computed equal to the sum of food words minus the sum of non-food words recalled.

Subjects for the eye awareness, mouth awareness, and neutral conditions consisted respectively of 29, 20, and 52 male college students.

The mean food minus non-food recall scores were $+2.9$ ($\sigma = 2.1$), $+1.6$ ($\sigma = 1.9$) and $+1.1$ ($\sigma = 2.0$) for the eye, mouth, and neutral conditions respectively. Analysis of the data indicated that the difference between the eye and mouth conditions was significant ($t = 2.3$, $p < .05$), as was the difference between the eye and neutral conditions ($t = 3.8$, $p < .001$). Congruent with expectation, the difference between the two control conditions (i.e., mouth versus neutral) was not significant.

The means of the total numbers of words recalled (viz., 11.4, 11.5, and 11.1 respectively for the eye, mouth, and neutral conditions) did not differ significantly from each other.

As hypothesized, the eye enhancement condition resulted in selective learning and recall with reference to the food words. The direction of the selectivity was to facilitate recall of the food words. This selectivity was supported both in relation to the control mouth enhancement and control neutral procedures. Further, as expected, there was no difference between the two control conditions.

OVERVIEW

Some consistent, although not high, relationships between BFQ Eyes and indices of oral behavior have been ascertained. An individual's awareness of his eyes is clearly negatively correlated with his enjoyment of eating. Similarly, it is negatively related to how well he is able to learn and recall words pertaining to food. The trends have also been definite with respect to the fact that differences in eye awareness among individuals go along with apparent trait differences in their parents. BFQ Eyes was negatively correlated with how generous subjects recalled their parents to have been. Anxiety about incorporation which parallels eye awareness is perhaps derived from interactions with parents who are not generous or giving and who somehow communicate that it is wrong to expect to be "fed" or gratified in those ways which we loosely encompass under the rubric "oral."

In an attempt to strengthen the formulation that eye awareness is proportional to concern about oral issues, multiple approaches have been employed. Studies were undertaken which variously have made use of tachistoscopic perception, Thereness-Thatness placement of pictures, early memories, proverb interpretation, selective enjoyment of jokes, and so forth. Most of the results obtained were repeatedly in the predicted direction, but often of borderline statistical significance.

There is a good deal more to do in clarifying the implications of eye awareness, but some excellent leads have been brought to light.

It is of interest that many of the beliefs and theories to be found both in folklore and the psychoanalytic literature which identify the eyes as having "taking in" and incorporative-like significance seem to be supported by the empirical data.

21
Heart Awareness in Men, Religiosity, and Guilt

INTRODUCTION

Unrealistic concern with one's heart has been reported often as a neurotic symptom (Fenichel, 1945; Schneider, 1954). It has been conjectured that such concern reflects factors like repressed sexual excitement, unexpressed rage, and fear of death. In scanning the statements in the literature about what characterizes the person who focuses upon his heart, one finds their diversity difficult to integrate. Little agreement exists as to which affects or impulses might preoccupy the heart-conscious individual. However, there are intriguing references to the idea that the heart, because of its special importance and its unique prominence as a source of body sensations and rhythms, may easily become involved with the individual's fantasies and conflicts. Perhaps it offers a convenient focus for feelings and anxieties about oneself.

Heart awareness seemed from the very beginning of the BFQ work to be worth serious study, but there was little material available from which to derive plausible hypotheses about its possible personality relationships. Therefore, the decision was made to undertake, first of all, some general exploratory efforts. This work was based on the use of a 15-item scale which sampled the individual's degree of awareness of his heart. A number of widely scanning studies were pursued with BFQ Heart to ascertain its relationships with personality measures (e.g., Edwards Preference Schedule) and social variables (e.g., social class, religion), but the results were largely of a chance order. It would serve little purpose to describe them. One of the few promising trends that did emerge was the observation that an individual's heart awareness is positively related to his ratings of religiosity of his parents and also himself. This finding seemed noteworthy in light of previous reports that persons with anxiety about their hearts are unusually conscientious (Ross, 1945). In fact, a study by Wittkower, Rodger, and Wilson (1941) portrays such persons as puritanical, with a strong sense of duty and morality. One could, on the basis of such a perspective, discern an initial rationale for regarding heart awareness as related to issues of morality, religiosity, and virtuous conformity. The possibility presented itself that heart awareness would be positively correlated with an approach to life emphasizing religious commitment, with its accompanying concern about issues of right and wrong. The hypotheses which were formulated on the basis of this perspective will be presented shortly.

Table 21.1
Means and Standard Deviations of BFQ Heart Scores

M	σ	N
6.5	4.1	45
4.9	3.1	50
4.5	3.9	48
6.2	4.4	57
5.8	4.3	45
4.8	3.8	47
4.7	3.9	51
5.9	4.5	51
7.1	4.0	50
5.3	4.3	53

In the studies to be described in this chapter, heart awareness was measured with the 15-item Heart subscale of the BFQ. This scale inquires concerning the relative awareness of heart as compared to a series of other body areas (e.g., heart vs. muscles, heart vs. stomach, lungs vs. heart, feet vs. heart). Mean values have fluctuated in the vicinity of 5.6. Apparently, the average individual tends to have low awareness of his heart in relation to other body areas. Table 21.1 presents the means and standard deviations of BFQ Heart in a range of male college student samples. It has been rare to find distributions which were seriously skewed.

The independence of the BFQ Heart scale was evaluated by correlating it with the other BFQ scales in ten different samples (average N = 50). The results showed three significant correlations with BFQ Back (−.30, −.40, −.27); three with BFQ Right (.39, .34, .42); two with BFQ Eyes (.27, .27); two with BFQ Mouth (.30, .35); and one with BFQ Stomach (.29). As has been true of previous results pertaining to interrelations of BFQ variables cited, the correlations were neither consistent nor indicative of appreciable overlap between BFQ Heart and the other BFQ scales.[1]

---

[1] No consistent relationships between BFQ Heart and the Barrier score have been observed. This is not surprising if one considers that BFQ Heart is based on a comparison of heart with not only body exterior but also interior sectors.

It should further be indicated that BFQ Heart has proven to have chance relationships with the MMPI K scale, the Bass Acquiescence scale (1956) and also the Marlowe-Crowne (1964) Social Desirability scale. However, it was highly negatively correlated with the MMPI L scale ($r = -.48$, $p < .001$, $N = 54$). These results are a bit puzzling. They indicate no relationship between BFQ Heart and the need to make a socially desirable impression as defined by K and the Crowne-Marlowe measure, but a strongly inverse one with the need to be grossly dissimulating as measured by the L scale. Further comments on this matter will be offered at a later point.

Three appraisals of the test-retest reliability of BFQ Heart have been completed. In all instances a week intervened between test and retest. The reliability coefficient in one sample ($N = 51$) of college men was .62 ($p < .001$); in another ($N = 57$) the coefficient was .77 ($p < .001$); and in a third ($N = 52$) it was .68.

EXPLORATORY STUDIES

Proceeding from the view, earlier mentioned, that heart awareness may somehow be linked with a religious moralistic approach to life, the following hypotheses were initially ventured:

1. The greater an individual's awareness of his heart the more religious will be his orientation.

2. A derived assumption is that his degree of heart focus would be positively related to the amount of religiosity he ascribes to his parents.

3. With increasing heart awareness there should be enhanced concern and guilt about wrongdoing.

4. Degree of heart focus should be positively linked with anxiety about sexual expression, since sexual behavior is among the most stringently regulated by religious standards. This was formally entertained as an hypothesis despite the fact that data already available from other studies indicated that BFQ Heart was not significantly correlated with a variety of indices of heterosexual interest and response.

5. A more tangential prediction was also made about the relationship between heart awareness and openness to aesthetic experiences. This prediction was made because among the few significant relationships observed in earlier exploratory studies was a negative correlation between BFQ Heart and the Aesthetic subscale of the Allport-Vernon-Lindzey Study of Values ($r = -.28$, $p < .05$, $N = 50$).[2] This suggested that the more aware an individual is of his heart the less is his interest in, and sensitivity to, artistic and imaginative representations. The pertinence of this hypothesis to the tentatively formulated religious-oriented picture of the heart-oriented person

---

[2] All correlation coefficients are product-moment unless otherwise specified.

was enhanced by the fact that previous studies (Allen, 1955) reported a trend for religiosity and aesthetic interest to be negatively correlated.

Several procedures were employed to evaluate religiosity, which was hypothesized to be one of the important correlates of heart awareness.

1. The subject estimated the average number of times per month he currently attended church.

2. He rated his own level of religiosity on a 5-point scale.

3. His score on the Religious subscale of the Allport-Vernon-Lindzey Study of Values was determined.

The religiosity ascribed by the subject to his parents was evaluated by obtaining his estimates of how often each, on the average, attends church per month. Also, he indicated on a 5-point scale his response to the following question: How important a part did religion play in your family when you were growing up?

Measurement of guilt and anxiety about wrongdoing, which also played an important role in the hypotheses formulated, was approached via a selective memory task. It was anticipated that the higher an individual's sense of guilt the more he would selectively forget words he had learned which referred to guilt themes. The following list of words was exposed on a screen in a group setting.

Round	Honest *
Fault *	Sight
Judge *	Happy
Across	Bible *
Book	Forge *
Steal *	Worker
Ready	Law *
Rule *	Paint
Bark	Wrong *
Verdict *	Clerk

[Guilt words are starred]

The subject was told to study the list. After he had done so for one minute, he was given five minutes to write on a sheet as many of the words as he could recall. Ten of the words in the list refer directly or indirectly to guilt linked ideas; and ten are neutral. The mean length of the two sets of words is equivalent. A selective memory score was derived equal to the number of guilt words minus the number of non-guilt words recalled.

Several different procedures were utilized to examine the subject's orientation toward a sexual role and sexual expression.

1. Amount of heterosexual activity was taken as one criterion of freedom to be sexually expressive. It was appraised by means of the same, earlier described, questionnaire which inquires concerning dating behavior.

2. Selective memory for sexual words served as another index of anxiety

about sexual issues. Subjects viewed the following lists of words for one minute and were then given five minutes to recall them.

Plan	Caress*
Touch *	Train
Debate	Listen
Run	Perfume *
Dance *	Write
Feel *	Kiss *
Build	Twist *
Flirt *	Skate
Dust	Hug *
Date *	Color

[Sexual words are starred]

Ten of the words have sexual connotations. The other ten are neutral and of the same average length as the sexual ones. A memory score was computed equal to the number of sexual minus the number of non-sexual words recalled. It was considered that the greater the subject's anxiety about sexual matters the more he would show selectively poor recall for the sexual words.

3. Still another approach to the matter of sexual orientation was attempted by means of the Vague Sex Pictures earlier described. These are the pictures which, by virtue of their vague definition of the sex of the human figures shown, are intended to arouse anxiety in those who have poorly defined concepts of their own sex roles. Degree of anxiety aroused by these pictures is evaluated in terms of the amount of negative affect they evoke, as evidenced in ratings of the attractiveness and friendliness of the figures.

Motivation for seeking out and opening oneself to aesthetic experiences was measured with the Aesthetic score of the Allport-Vernon-Lindzey Study of Values. This is the index which has already been mentioned as having been related to BFQ Heart in an earlier exploratory study.

Sixty-one male students participated as subjects (median age 21).

The mean BFQ Heart score was 5.3 (σ = 4.3). Table 21.2 indicates some support for the hypothesis that BFQ Heart is positively correlated with degree of religiosity. One finds BFQ Heart positively related at a borderline level with estimate of frequency of church attendance and also self-rating of religiosity. When church attendance frequency and self-rating of religiosity were simply summed for each subject, this combined index was positively and significantly related to BFQ Heart (r = .34, p < .01). A relationship of .40 (p < .005) was found between BFQ Heart and the Study of Values Religious score.

Table 21.2 demonstrates too that there are trends for the subject's BFQ Heart score to be positively linked with the level of religiosity he attributes to his family. It is positively correlated (r = .38, p < .01) with estimates of frequency of mother's church attendance and ratings of importance of

Table 21.2
Product-Moment Correlations of BFQ Heart with Religious Variables

BFQ Heart versus	r	Significance Level
Estimate of frequency of church attendance per month	.23 (N = 61)	<.10
Self-rating of religiosity	.24 (N = 61)	<.10
Study of Values Religious score	.40 (N = 58)	<.01
Estimate of frequency of father's church attendance per month	.15 (N = 56)	n.s.[a]
Estimate of frequency of mother's church attendance per month	.38 (N = 60)	<.01
Estimate of importance of religion in family	.24 (N = 61)	<.10

[a] Not significant

religion in the family $(r = .24, p < .10)$. While it is positively correlated with estimates of the frequency of father's church attendance, the coefficient was not significant.

The idea that BFQ Heart is tied in with a sense of guilt about wrongdoing was slightly reinforced by its borderline negative correlation $(r = -.22, p < .10)$ with selective memory for words referring to guilt themes. This

Table 21.3
Product-Moment Correlations of BFQ Heart with Sexual Indices

	r	Significance Level
Heterosexual behavior		
Average number of dates per month in high school	.08 (N = 61)	n.s.[a]
Average number of dates per month in college	−.02 (N = 58)	n.s.
Index of serious dating	−.03[b] (N = 60)	n.s.
Sexual memory	−.23 (N = 61)	<.10
Vague sex pictures		
Ugly ratings	.28 (N = 56)	<.05
Unfriendly ratings	−.11 (N = 56)	n.s.

[a] Not significant
[b] Also not significant by chi square analysis

relationship was examined further by means of chi-square. The trichotomized (as equal thirds as possible) Heart scores were compared with the dichotomized (at median) memory scores. A χ^2 of 9.1 (df = 2) was found which is significant at the <.02 level.

The findings for the sexual behavior variables were, as expected, largely negative.[3] Table 21.3 shows that BFQ Heart had only a chance relationship to average number of dates per week in high school and college and also to the index of serious dating. This reaffirmed what had been observed in other samples.

A borderline negative correlation in the predicted direction was observed between BFQ Heart and selective recall for sexual words (r = —.23, p < .10). But it should be indicated that in another study involving 55 male college students this correlation was not reaffirmed. BFQ Heart was correlated .28 (p < .05) with the degree to which the Vague Sex Pictures were perceived as Ugly. The correlation of BFQ Heart with how Unfriendly the Vague Sex Picture figures were judged to be was not significant. The significant result involving the Ugly ratings was not, however, supported in another sample. Results from 48 male college students indicated that BFQ Heart was not significantly related to either the Ugly or Unfriendly ratings.

A final result to be mentioned is the fact that there was an encouraging correlation of —.31 (p < .03) in the predicted direction between BFQ Heart and the Aesthetic scale of the Study of Values.

The results embracing religiosity of self and recalled religiosity of one's parents concurred with the hypothesis that the more aware an individual is of his heart the greater his current and past commitment to religious values. The correlations between BFQ Heart and religious parameters (e.g., frequency of church attendance and self-rating of religiosity) carry weight because they represent cross-validations of the same relationships which were observed in an earlier study.

The hypothesis concerning the association of guilt about wrong-doing with heart awareness was supported by the findings involving selective memory for guilt words. These results seem to be worth further study. They not only attained statistical significance, but have an attractive pertinence to the concept of heart awareness as being a function of a religious, moralistic orientation.

There was no sign of a relationship between BFQ Heart and reported frequency of heterosexual behavior. Heart awareness showed a borderline inverse relationship to the ability to recall sexual words that had been learned; but, as indicated, another study did not support the finding.

A significant positive correlation was found between BFQ Heart and

---

[3] Note also that BFQ Heart has been found not to be significantly related to the perception of six tachistoscopically presented Blacky pictures, some of which have sexual connotations (e.g., Castration Anxiety, Masturbation Guilt).

ratings of Ugliness of the Vague Sex Pictures; but this relationship, too, was not supported in another sample.

As expected the results for the various sexual variables were largely negative. They indicated that heart awareness is probably not related to sexual behavior in any generalized sense.

Cross-validation was obtained of the original finding that heart awareness is inverse to interest in aesthetic experience. If one conceptualizes aesthetic interest as indicating openness to novel representations and fantasy productions, it would follow that the heart-focused individual tends to seal himself off from such stimuli. This finding can be used as a keynote to integrate much of the data. Focusing upon one's heart may be regarded as part of a way of life which revolves about a closed-off world defined by religious precept and perhaps also guilt. It may be an important part of this way of life to feel guilt and anxiety about certain forms of fantasy, particularly those expressing sexual wishes or the urge to do what is wrong.[4]

CROSS-VALIDATION AND EXTENSION

Two aspects of the above findings seemed particularly important to verify further. They pertain to the relationship of heart awareness to religiosity and also aesthetic interests. These may be viewed as key variables in establishing a bridge between amount of heart awareness and degree of adherence to a "closed-off" religious orientation. Several pertinent studies will be outlined.

Religiosity

The dependability of the original finding that BFQ Heart is positively linked with religiosity was evaluated in a new sample of college men (N = 42). BFQ Heart scores were correlated with subjects' self-ratings (on a 5-point scale) of how religious they consider themselves to be. These variables proved to be positively and significantly related ($r = .29$, $p < .05$, one-tail test); which reaffirmed again the trend of previously obtained results. In this same sample the subjects were asked to rate (on a 5-point scale) the importance of religion in their family and to estimate the frequency with which each of their parents attended church per month. BFQ Heart was found to be correlated .21 ($p < .20$, one-tail test) with rated importance of religion

---

[4] Parenthetically, it should be noted that the earlier mentioned negative correlation between BFQ Heart and the Lie scale from the MMPI could be due to the reluctance of one who is moralistically oriented to fabricate or make lying statements about himself.

in family; .30 (p < .05, one-tail test) with estimates of father's and .30 (p < .05, one-tail test) with estimates of mother's frequency of church attendance.

Another study was carried out which sought to compare heart awareness in two groups representing extremes of self-rated religiosity. From a pool of 350 male college students who had evaluated their own religiosity on a 5-point scale, 68 were secured who perceived themselves in the lowest category of no religious interest at all and 70 who considered that they were either in the highest (5) or next to highest (4) categories of religiosity. It was originally intended to limit the high religious group to those who rated themselves with the extreme designation of 5; but only eight subjects fell into this extreme group. Therefore, those in the 4th category were added to the 5th. BFQ Heart scores were obtained from all of the subjects. A chi-square analysis was made of the relationship of the two groupings of religiosity ratings to the trichotomized (as equal thirds as possible) BFQ Heart scores. The anticipated positive relationship was found to be present (χ^2 = 6.4, df = 2, p <. 05).

An attempt was also made to cross-validate the original positive link found between heart awareness and religiosity as defined by the Allport-Vernon-Lindzey Study of Values. A new sample of 45 male college students was obtained and the Study of Values administered. The median Religious score was 35 (range 11–52). When the dichotomized (at median) BFQ Heart scores were related by means of chi-square to the trichotomized (as equal thirds as possible) Religious scores, a significant positive relationship in the predicted direction was found (χ^2 = 6.9, df = 2, p < .05).

Working within the limitations of the rather narrow range of religiosity to be found in a college population, it has been possible to demonstrate with consistency that the greater an individual's investment in religion the more intensely he is aware of his heart. A similar demonstration has been possible for the relationship between the estimated religiosity of the individual's parents and his own heart awareness. It would, of course, be logical and of considerable interest to measure heart awareness in extreme groups with a proven commitment to religion (e.g., priests, theological students). One would expect the results just described to be duplicated with increased clarity.

Aesthetic Orientation

In two previously cited instances BFQ Heart was negatively correlated with amount of aesthetic interest as defined by the Aesthetic score of the Allport-Vernon-Lindzey Study of Values. It was decided to follow up on these results by investigating the relationship between BFQ Heart and another index tapping interest in the aesthetic. The Artistic score from the Kuder Preference Record (Kuder, 1956) was chosen as a rough equivalent of the

Study of Values measure. It was expected that BFQ Heart would be negatively correlated with the Artistic score. When, in a sample of 51 male college
students, the Kuder Preference Record was administered, a correlation of
—.30 (p < .05) was found between BFQ Heart and the Artistic score. A
non-significant negative correlation with the Literary scale was also noted.
It should be mentioned that heart awareness was not correlated with any of
the other Kuder scores. One may conclude that there is dependability in the
observation that the intensity of one's heart awareness is negatively related
to how strongly one is invested in an artistic-aesthetic orientation toward the
world.

Devotion to Work

One might expect other attitudes, often associated with religiosity, to characterize those with heightened heart awareness. For example they might be
expected to emphasize devotion to duty, propriety, and rejection of that
which is frivolous. Fromm (1941) particularly noted the association of a "hard
work" orientation with certain forms of religiosity, in the course of his discussion of the Protestant ethic. It was this matter of degree of devotion to work
which was investigated with reference to heart awareness. It seemed reasonable to hypothesize that the greater an individual's heart awareness the more
importance he would ascribe to work activities and the less he would value
"non-work" ways of spending time. The opportunity for evaluating this
proposition was provided by a technique, previously described, which is
based upon having subjects indicate how they spend an average week. The
specific instructions given are as follows: "Describe a typical week in your
life. Give an account of the routine aspects of it as well as some of the high
spots. Go into detail. You will have 15 minutes to write. Be sure to fill two
pages." The material obtained is blindly coded for a number of categories
(e.g., cleaning activities, eating, social interaction). However, there are two
of special interest for present purposes which pertain to Work and Entertainment. The Work category includes any references to working at a job,
studying, going to class, and taking examinations. Incidentally, the heavy
representation of school activities in this category reflects the fact that the
"average week" technique has been applied only to college students. As for
the Entertainment rubric, it embraces all references to being a spectator at
athletic or artistic events, watching TV or listening to the radio, reading for
relaxation, and attending parties. The number of references in each category
was expressed as a percentage of the total number in all categories. It was
intended that a percentage expression would correct for differences in the
length of each subject's description. Reliability values of 92 percent and 90
percent were attained between two independent judges in scoring respectively
the Work and Entertainment dimensions.

A sample of 56 male college students was studied to determine if the anticipated positive relationship between BFQ Heart and % Work and the negative relationship between BFQ Heart and % Entertainment could be ascertained. The mean Work score was 3.3 (σ = 1.0) and that for Entertainment .6 (σ = .5). A correlation of .29 (p < .05) was found between BFQ Heart and the Work score; and one of $-$.25 (p < .10) between BFQ Heart and Entertainment. As predicted, degree of heart awareness was positively correlated with investment in Work and negatively so with interest in Entertainment. However, the finding with reference to Entertainment held true only at a borderline level of significance.

An opportunity to learn more about work investment in relation to heart awareness was provided by the Tomkins-Horn Picture Arrangement Experiment (Tomkins and Miner 1957). As originally devised, this technique consists of 25 sets of line drawings—each presenting three scenes which can be arranged in a sequence to form a meaningful story. The pictorial material seemed especially appropriate for present purposes because a large number of the scenes depict men in work situations and therefore provide ample opportunity to place active work interpretations upon their activities. Beneath each set of drawings are three lines and the subject, after deciding the proper sequence for the three scenes, writes a one-sentence account of what is happening in each. Tomkins and Horn have elaborated a complex scoring scheme involving many personality and mood variables for dealing with the scene arrangements that subjects produce. However, in the present study the scoring was simply based on the number of times scenes were perceived as centering upon the performance of active work. Work themes would be exemplified by statements that a story character is working, preparing to work, or had just completed his work. There were 75 statements given by each subject and so his Work score could vary from 0 to 75. In the sample of college men studies, the mean Tomkins-Horn Work score was 14.5 (σ = 1.8). Analysis of the results indicated that BFQ Heart was correlated .25 (p < .10) with the Work score. The result was in the expected direction, but of borderline significance.

The combined results suggest tentatively that amount of investment in work activities, as contrasted to interest in entertainment seeking, is greatest in those with enhanced heart awareness. The religiosity accompanying high heart awareness may be one aspect of a general dedication to that which is considered to be serious and virtuous.

Ames Thereness-Thatness Apparatus (Response to Nudity)

Initial studies, previously cited, indicated that BFQ Heart was not convincingly related to measures concerned with sexual interest or sex role. These results did not match the original assumption that sexual interest, because it is disapproved in many religious systems, would be negatively correlated with heart awareness which is positively associated with religiosity. Subsequent studies in which BFQ Heart has been correlated with amount of serious dating, response to tachistoscopically presented sexual themes, and other indices of sexual behavior have continued to give non-significant findings. Heart awareness and sexual parameters do not co-vary.

There has been only one instance in which heart awareness seemed to have a solid relationship with a sexual variable. This occurred in the earlier cited work concerned with response to pictures presented in the Ames Thereness-Thatness (T-T) apparatus. It will be reiterated for purposes of clarity that the T-T procedure involves asking the subject to make a series of judgments which seem to concern the spatial placement of the pictures, but which actually are based on varying their apparent size. Size attributes assigned to stimuli in this way have proven to be indicative of the kinds of evaluative responses they elicit. In the present instance, the T-T experiment obtained reactions to six pictures, one of which portrayed a nude female and another a clothed female (matched for size and shading). It will be recalled that a distinction was made with reference to whether subjects deal with pictures in a Repressive or non-Repressive fashion. The distinction was based on the subject's ability to recall the content of the T-T pictures at a subsequent time. Repressors ($N = 25$) were those making two or more recall errors; and non-Repressors ($N = 29$) made no errors.

It was predicted that BFQ Heart would be positively correlated wth accentuated response to the nude female picture because it represents a theme of flagrant sexuality. The hypothesis derived, of course, from the idea that an open display of sexuality, as exemplified in a nude female, is reprehensible in religious and puritanical systems.

The T-T index chosen to tap the subject's reaction to a theme of openly displayed sexuality was the difference between the rank of his setting of the nude female picture and the rank of his setting of the clothed female picture. His response to a minimally sexualized clothed female figure could be compared with that to a nude maximally sexualized female figure. In the Repression category the mean T-T index was $-.4$ ($\sigma = 3.1$) and for the non-Repressors it was $+.1$ ($\sigma = 2.7$). The chi-square describing the relation of BFQ Heart and the difference between nude female and clothed female ranks was significant ($\chi^2 = 4.9$, df $= 1$, $p < .05$). The higher the subject's Heart score the more likely he was to set the nude female larger (closer) than the clothed female. In the non-Repression group the equivalent relationship was also significant ($\chi^2 = 6.0$, df $= 2$, $p = .05$); and, as anticipated, it was in the opposite direction. Contrasting with the trend for the Repressors, it turned out that the greater the Heart awareness the smaller (further away) the nude was set as compared to the clothed female.

Of all the T-T results obtained in relation to BFQ variables, those for

BFQ Heart are most impressive because they are the only ones to be significant in both the Repression and non-Repression samples. It was therefore puzzling that other sexual measures did not correlate consistently with heart awareness. One possible explanation to be considered is that the T-T sexual index used (Clason setting for nude female minus that for clothed female) does not simply tap heterosexual attitudes, but perhaps, more specifically, feelings about the open display of sexuality which would be represented by a nude female body. It is known that groups which do not differ in amount of sexual behavior may still differ in how much they disapprove of open nudity in the course of sexual interaction. Kinsey, et al. (1948) have documented this point in comparing lower and upper socio-economic groups. Perhaps, then, degree of heart awareness might be related to a specific aspect of heterosexual orientation, viz., feelings about female nudity. One might expect those with a religious orientation to be especially negative about open display of female nudity.

This possibility was examined by use of a series of drawings of women six of which were nude and three clothed. Male college students ($N = 45$) were individually asked to look at the pictures and to rate each on a 5-point scale of "sex appeal" ($5 =$ highest score). It was presumed that the greater the anxiety and disapproval aroused by the nudity of the female figures the lower they would be rated in "sex appeal." The mean sex appeal rating of the nude pictures was 2.6 ($\sigma = .9$) and that for the non-nudes 1.7 ($\sigma = .6$). BFQ Heart was found to be negatively and significantly correlated with sex appeal ratings of the nudes ($r = -.28$, $p = .05$), but it had a completely chance correlation with the ratings of the clothed figures ($r = -.07$). That is, high heart awareness was paralleled by a somewhat negative evaluation of the nude figures. But within the limits of the low reliability imposed by having only three clothed female figures, an analogous relationship was not found for heart awareness versus response to non-nude female representations. While far from decisive, such data do suggest that heart awareness may be connected with a specific kind of sexual concern such as represented by display of female nudity.

PERIPHERAL STIMULATION: EFFECTS UPON MEMORY FOR GUILT WORDS

Manipulation of degree of heart awareness was used to ascertain whether selectivity could be produced in dealing with a theme that might logically be expected to be influenced by such awareness. This approach was, of course, motivated by the more general interest in testing the theory that signals from peripheral body landmarks are capable of exerting effects upon central cognitive processes.

Heart awareness seems to be associated with variables involving religiosity, moralism, and devotion to work. It was conjectured that a theme common to these variables is guilt.[5] A good case can certainly be made out for the importance of guilt in religious and moralistic attitudes. Indeed, it has already been shown that the greater an individual's heart awareness the more he is inclined to forget selectively words that portray guilt themes. It was with this view that an experiment was designed to study the effects of increasing heart awareness upon memory for words with guilt connotations. It was hypothesized that increasing an individual's heart awareness would selectively affect his memory for guilt words; whereas control conditions would not result in such a selective impact.

The list of words used to test the hypothesis was as follows:

Round	Honest *
Fault *	Sight
Judge *	Happy
Across	Bible *
Book	Forge *
Steal *	Worker
Ready	Law *
Rule *	Paint
Bark	Wrong *
Verdict *	Clerk

[Guilt words are starred]

One sample of subjects learned the list in a situation which enhanced heart awareness. In order to intensify heart awareness, they were asked to monitor and count their own heart rates for two successive one-minute periods. They were then asked to observe their hearts for another one-minute period, during which they were to record on a sheet of paper each time that they became aware of a specific sensation (e.g., thumping) in that region. Finally, they were asked to learn the list of words (one minute exposure), but to focus awareness upon their hearts during the process and to be prepared to describe what heart sensations they had experienced. After the one-minute learning period, subjects were given five minutes to write down as many of the words as they could recall. A score was computed which equaled the number of guilt words minus non-guilt words recalled.

A second, control sample learned the same word list under conditions designed to maximize skin rather than heart awareness. The subject was told to focus his attention upon the skin of his left arm and for one minute he placed a check on a sheet of paper each time that he had a distinct skin sensation. Next, he was asked to stroke the skin of his arm for 15 seconds with a piece of cotton and to describe the entire experience. Finally, he was told

[5] Despite its link with guilt, BFQ Heart has shown only chance relationships with measures of response to masochistic themes.

that he was to learn a list of words, but was instructed to monitor his skin sensations in the process and to be prepared to describe them.

A third control group learned the word list without any body stimulation.

It was anticipated that the heart awareness condition would differ from the two control conditions but it was not expected that the controls would differ from each other.

The subjects were male college students. There were 21, 23, and 51 men respectively in the heart awareness, skin awareness, and non-body stimulation samples.

The mean guilt–non-guilt mean recall score for the heart awareness group was $+.28$ ($\sigma = 1.0$); for the skin awareness sample $+1.3$ ($\sigma = 2.0$); and for the non-body stimulation sample $+1.6$ ($\sigma = 2.0$). The difference between the heart and skin awareness groups was significant ($t = 2.2$, $p > .05$); and likewise the difference between the heart awareness and non-body stimulation group was significant ($t = 3.7$, $p < .001$). The means for the two control samples did not differ significantly.

There were no significant differences in the total number of words recalled under the three conditions.

The findings indicate that intensifying heart awareness produced a significant decline in selective memory for guilt words, as compared to the two control conditions. There was a smaller proportion of guilt words recalled in the heart awareness sample than in either the skin awareness or non-body stimulation samples. These findings demonstrate specificity in the association of guilt concern with heart awareness. They also supply a bit more confirmation of the general theory that the perceptual prominence of a body region is a significant variable in itself in influencing cognitive processes.

OVERVIEW

The information which has been gleaned about heart awareness indicates that the original hypotheses which tied it to matters of morality and religion are fairly sound. Likewise, there is evidence that heart awareness is greatest in those who are non-aesthetic and non-artistic in their interests and who therefore presumably have a limited amount of certain types of experiences (e.g., imaginative fantasy, emotional response to artistic productions, physiognomic perception). A picture emerges which would link intensity of heart awareness with the extent to which an individual has adopted a way of life based on religiosity; conformance to what is considered proper and virtuous; and the dampening down of experiences that have to do with the aesthetic or artistic.[6]

[6] Note that BFQ Heart was not consistently correlated with any of the clusters of variables (e.g., anal, oral) associated with other BFQ dimensions.

One's curiosity is indeed stirred as to why an individual's intensity of attention to his heart should be linked with such an orientation. One could pursue Fenichel's (1945) suggestion that the heart, because of its rhythmic pulsation and its growing larger–growing smaller qualities, is easily associated with sexual experience. As such, devotion of attention to one's heart could represent an anxious concern with an organ symbolizing illicit excitement incompatible with a religious, virtuous orientation. Of course, an argument against this formulation would be the fact that BFQ Heart has had few consistent relationships with the sexual variables which were studied.

Another speculation could go to the opposite extreme and suggest that the heart is one of the morally "safest" body organs to which one can direct one's attention. There are no taboos about referring or attending to one's heart. This contrasts with the fact that overtones of sex, dirt, and other embarrassing topics apply to many other major body sectors (e.g., gut, genitals). Perhaps the individual raised in a moralistic atmosphere which contains taboos about looking at, or touching, "bad" body regions would find his heart one of the few safe allowable body experiences. In focusing upon his heart he could experience awareness of his body, but without showing interest in the "bad" side of himself.

22
Mouth and Stomach Awareness in Men—Sensitivity to Hostility

INTRODUCTION

This chapter will concern itself with the correlates of mouth and stomach awareness in men. Both mouth and stomach awareness have been considered, in the studies to be described, as separate dimensions and measured with individual scales. However, they were found to be sufficiently similar to encourage parallel treatment. As will be seen, there are certain basic similarities in the configuration of variables with which they are correlated.

The obvious incorporative and nutritive functions of the mouth and stomach have led to much theorizing concerning the role of such areas in the development of attitudes about incorporation, giving and taking, and being self-sufficient. Freud (1910, 1923), Abraham (1927), Erikson (1950), and others have proposed ties between the nature of one's experiences with one's mouth and stomach and traits like dependence, passivity, aggressivity, and optimism. It is of interest that the psychosomatic views of Alexander (1948) first gained prominence with respect to the presumed origin of stomach ulcers in the association of stomach activation with passive fantasies (viz. the desire to be fed).

Over the years, empirical findings have been obtained which tentatively indicate that specific personality traits may be related to socialization experiences involving the mouth and stomach. For example, Goldman (1948, 1950) found that "oral" optimism and pessimism were significantly correlated with age of weaning. Blum and Miller (1952) reported that certain of an individual's traits are correlated with the frequency of his mouth movements. Beller (1957) observed in children that dependency was significantly related to "oral" behaviors such as manner and amount of eating and frequency of mouth movements. Whiting and Child (1953) found that cultures with a negative orientation toward incorporation (e.g., characterized by early weaning) were inclined to explain illness as due to incorporation of something "bad". It should also be acknowledged that other researchers have failed to detect meaningful correlations between traits and measures descriptive of experiences with mouth or stomach (e.g., Orlansky, 1949). But the literature confronts one with interesting observations which invite investigation and elaboration.

The appraisal of possible correlates of mouth and stomach awareness in men was guided by the premise that so-called oral traits and conflicts should be prominently involved. It was expected that an individual's awareness of his mouth and stomach would be, at least partially, a function of how giving and bountiful versus stingy and depriving he perceived the world to be. For an individual to be particularly focused upon his mouth or stomach seemed to be a possible indicator of underlying anxiety about securing supplies and "nourishment" from the world.

Measurement of mouth awareness was undertaken with an 11-item BFQ Mouth scale. It involves, in each instance, a comparison of mouth awareness with degree of awareness of a number of other head areas (e.g., eyes, ears, hair). Test-retest reliability, with a week intervening, was .63 in one sample of male college students (N = 57). In another sample (N = 52), with a week intervening, the test-retest reliability was .73. In a third example (N = 51), with a similar intervening period, the test-retest reliability was .70. There were no indications of significant relationships between BFQ Mouth and the MMPI K and L scales, the Crowne-Marlowe (1964) Social Desirability scale, and the Bass Acquiescence scale (1956).

Table 22.1
Means and Standard Deviations for BFQ Mouth and BFQ Stomach

| | Mouth | | | Stomach | |
M	σ	N	M	σ	N
7.3	2.3	45	7.7	3.4	45
7.4	2.5	50	6.7	3.8	50
7.6	2.4	48	7.3	3.4	48
7.2	2.9	57	8.1	3.1	57
7.2	2.1	45	7.5	2.8	45
7.0	2.4	47	6.5	3.4	47
7.5	2.7	51	7.7	3.7	51
7.4	2.8	51	6.7	3.2	51
7.1	2.3	50	7.8	3.4	50
7.6	2.7	53	8.1	3.5	53

Table 22.1 presents various mean values for BFQ Mouth obtained in college male populations. A typical value is 7.3, indicating a slight tendency

to be more aware of the mouth than other facial areas. Score distributions have typically been normal.

In a series of ten different male samples, with an average N of 50, BFQ Mouth was positively correlated with BFQ Stomach eight times. The average correlation was about .24, which falls at the .10 level of significance. The two variables are consistently related, but at a low order of magnitude. BFQ Mouth was also correlated once with BFQ Right (.38); once with BFQ Eyes (.30); twice with BFQ Heart (.30, .35); and twice with BFQ Head (.28, .39).

BFQ Stomach was measured with a 14-item scale which involved comparing stomach awareness with awareness for diverse other body sites. The mean of the ten different samples shown in Table 22.1 is 7.4. Score distributions have been largely normal. In one sample of male college students (N = 57) BFQ Stomach displayed a test-retest reliability (one week intervening) of .57. The test-retest coefficient was .66 in a second sample (N = 52); and .69 in a third sample (N = 51). As already indicated, BFQ Stomach had a consistent, but quite low, positive correlation with BFQ Mouth in eight of ten different normal samples (average N = 50). It also had one significant correlation with BFQ Heart (.29); two with BFQ Eyes (.29, .27); two with BFQ Right (.28, .29); and two with BFQ Back (.27, −.28).

It did not correlate significantly with the MMPI K and L scales, the Marlowe-Crowne (1964) Social Desirability scale,[1] or the Bass (1956) Acquiescence scale.

EXPLORATION OF ORAL VARIABLES

The first efforts to understand mouth and stomach awareness were, as dictated by the existing literature, largely concerned with variables having to do with incorporation, eating, and orality. It was presumed that the degree to which an individual focused upon his mouth or stomach would be paralleled by selective responses to various kinds of oral stimuli.

A repertoire of techniques for measuring response to stimuli with oral meaning was employed. These techniques actually duplicate the battery of procedures for measuring incorporative attitudes already described in the earlier chapter dealing with eye awareness.

When they were applied, the results obtained were largely not promising. Both BFQ Mouth and BFQ Stomach [2] were discovered to be unrelated to the following measures:

---

[1] BFQ Mouth and BFQ Stomach have shown non-consistent correlations with the Barrier Score.

[2] Means for BFQ Mouth and BFQ Stomach will be given only for major studies or when they are atypical.

1. Byrne Food Attitude Scale:

This is a scale which inquires how positively the individual feels about eating, early eating experiences, and a list of specific foods.

2. Blacky Pictures:

It is a measure based on the subject's ability to identify correctly the two Blacky oral pictures (Oral Eroticism, Oral Sadism) when they are presented tachistoscopically.

3. Early Memory:

This procedure evaluates the amount of oral imagery in a series of early memories produced by the subject.

4. Average Week:

A count is made of the number of references to eating and food in a free, spontaneous description of how one spends an average week.

5. Tachistoscopic Perception of Oral Words:

Degree of selectivity is determined in accurately perceiving oral words (viz., food, candy, suck) as compared to other categories of words tachistoscopically presented.

6. Parental Generosity:

Responses are obtained to a nine-statement questionnaire concerning parental altruism and generosity.

7. Thereness-Thatness Apparatus:

Selective reaction to a picture of an oral theme is measured in terms of the size ascribed to it in an ambiguous perceptual context.

A review of the results obtained from these procedures indicated Mouth and Stomach awareness were both unrelated to attitudes toward food, selective response to oral stimuli, and feelings concerning the generosity versus selfishness of one's parents.

Contrasting with these negative findings, there were two instances in which BFQ Mouth was observed to be meaningfully linked to orality indices. A brief account of these results follows.

Selective Food Memory

One of the methods for tapping attitudes toward oral themes, which has already been described, is based on degree of selective response to food words presented in a learning task. During a one-minute period subjects learn 20 words, ten of which refer to food and ten of which are neutral. From a subsequent five-minute recall period there is tabulated a score equal to the number of food words minus non-food words correctly remembered.

BFQ Mouth proved in two samples (N = 62, N = 45) to be negatively and significantly correlated ($r = -.28$, $p < .05$; $r = -.29$, $p = .05$) with the selective memory index. That is, the greater the subject's mouth awareness the more likely he was to forget selectively words pertaining to food.

BFQ Stomach had only a chance correlation with memory for food words.

Chain Associations

Another procedure for exploring oral attitudes makes use of the subject's responses when he is asked to give ten associations to each of 13 words (Story, 1963). Three of the words deal with oral activities (taste, suck, and swallow). Scores are derived which depict the amount of time required to produce the quota of ten responses and also the directness with which the associations adhere to the original meaning of the stimulus words.

In a sample of 44 men, BFQ Mouth was positively correlated (.46, $p < .01$) with the directness of the associations given to the oral words, but not with the directness of the associations to other categories of stimulus words (e.g., hostile, anal). The greater an individual's awareness of his mouth the more directly he was able to respond to the oral stimulus words. No relation was found between BFQ Mouth and time required to give a quota of oral associations.

BFQ Stomach was not related to any of the association indices relevant to orality.

The few significant findings enumerated were not impressive against the background of the major proportion of results which failed to exceed chance expectancy. It does not look as if either mouth or stomach awareness have a great deal to do with special attitudes or modes of response to oral themes. Quite paradoxically, an individual's intensity of awareness of two body regions which are functionally central to eating and incorporation seems to have limited direct import with respect to oral concerns and conflicts. This contrasts with the fact that awareness of one's eyes, which have no specialized oral functions, is closely interwoven with oral attitudes.

HOSTILITY

The failure to find a connection between either mouth or stomach awareness and selective response to oral stimuli led to further search. Since incorporative function has been considered by many to have not only nutritive but also biting, destructive significance, the relationships of hostility measures to mouth and stomach awareness were investigated.

In several samples an attempt was made to relate BFQ Mouth and BFQ Stomach to self report measures of hostility like the Buss-Durkee Hostility scale, the Murray Oral Aggression scale, and the Edwards Aggression scale. They were also related to hostility indices derived from semi-projective approaches, such as exemplified by the Bass (1958) Hostility scale and a word construction procedure. No consistent or meaningful trends could be detected in the data.

However, noteworthy trends emerged when the BFQ Mouth and BFQ Stomach measures were related to responses to tachistoscopically presented hostility themes. There were three studies, whose methodology has been previously described, in which BFQ Stomach and BFQ Mouth were correlated with thresholds for accurate perception of hostile stimuli.

One involved a sample of 45 male college students who were asked to identify 14 different words presented tachistoscopically. Three of the words dealt with hostility (shoot, hate, kill) and the others referred variously to heterosexual, oral, and narcissistic themes. Each word was shown at five consecutively increasing time exposures (3.3, 3.4, 3.6, 4.0, 4.5 milliseconds); and the average earliest speed at which the three hostile words could be identified was determined. BFQ Stomach was found to correlate $-.28$ ($p < .05$) with the rank order (relative to other themes) of the average hostility threshold. The greater the individual's stomach awareness the more quickly he recognized the hostile words. Furthermore, when subjects were asked a week later to recall all of the words that had been tachistoscopically exposed, a correlation of .40 ($p < .01$) was found between BFQ Stomach and the percent of words recalled in the hostile category. With increasing stomach awareness there was recall of a greater percent of hostile words.

As for BFQ Mouth, it proved to be correlated $-.25$ ($p < .10$) with the rank of the hostility threshold and at a chance level with the percent of hostile words recalled. Neither BFQ Stomach nor BFQ Mouth were correlated with the percents of other categories of words (e.g., oral, homosexual) recalled. They were also not correlated with the threshold scores for any of the word themes, aside from hostile, which were presented.

In another study, male college students ($N = 49$) were asked to respond to a series of five pictures presented tachistoscopically. The pictures were sketches in which area and line definiteness had been controlled so as to render them uniform. They represented the following themes: hostility (two men fighting), achievement, dependency, and masochism (two pictures: man shooting self, man stabbing self). Each was shown successively at six speeds (.008, .01, .025, .05, .075, .125 seconds). BFQ Stomach was correlated .29 ($p < .05$) with the recognition threshold for the hostile picture. The greater the stomach awareness the longer it required to perceive the hostility picture accurately. BFQ Mouth was correlated $-.24$ ($p < .10$) with the hostility threshold. At a borderline level, there was a trend for those most mouth aware to perceive the hostile picture most quickly.

Significant findings also emerged with reference to the masochistic pictures. BFQ Mouth was correlated $-.41$ ($p < .01$) with the average of the thresholds required to perceive the two masochistic pictures accurately. The greater the mouth awareness the more quickly were the masochistic pictures recognized. As for BFQ Stomach, it was not significantly correlated with the average of the two masochistic thresholds, but was significantly so ($r = -.39$, $p < .01$) with the threshold for the picture depicting a person shooting himself. This result, for one picture, was in the same direction as the findings just noted for BFQ Mouth. Neither BFQ Stomach nor BFQ Mouth were correlated significantly with threshold values for the non-hostility themes.

In a third instance which involved a sample of disturbed boys (N = 23, mean age 9.8) studied by Rhoda Fisher,[3] reactions to a series of nine tachistoscopically presented stick figure pictures were secured. Three of the pictures portrayed hostility (two people shooting at each other; two people sword fighting; one person hitting another); two dealt with narcissism; two with nurturance; and two with social interaction. Each picture was presented four times consecutively at increasing speeds (.01, .03, .05, and .10 seconds). BFQ Stomach correlated $-.29$ ($p > .10$) with the sum of the hostility thresholds; and BFQ Mouth had a purely chance relationship with this sum. They were not correlated with the threshold values for the other pictures.

A second set of results pertinent to hostility and masochism presented itself in an earlier referred to study involving chain associations to stimulus words. Subjects (N = 43) were asked to give ten associations to each of 13 words or phrases. Aside from the oral, anal, and neutral words represented, there were two masochistic references (suicide, kill self) and, in addition, three hostile references (hit, stab, shoot). All associations were written down verbatim by the experimenter; and the time required to provide ten associations to each was recorded. Also, the associations given to each stimulus word were scored with reference to how directly they conformed to its basic meaning. The intent of this scoring procedure was to ascertain the degree to which the subject had sought to evade dealing with specific themes.

BFQ Stomach was found to be correlated .43 ($p < .01$) with the rank (relative to other themes) of the average amount of time needed to produce ten associations for the masochistic references. It was not significantly related to the score indicating how directly the associations adhered to the meanings of the stimulus words. Similarly, BFQ Mouth was positively correlated with the rank of the amount of time needed to produce the response quotas for the masochistic references ($r = .30$, $p < .05$), but not significantly so with the scores indicating directness of associations. Therefore, in terms of the time scores, there was selectivity in response to the masochistic words which paralleled variations in both stomach and mouth awareness. As for the hostile words, it was found that BFQ Stomach was not significantly correlated with any of the indices (viz., time and directness of association scores) indicating mode of response to them. BFQ Mouth was correlated $-.27$ ($p < .10$) with the rank of the average time required to complete associations to the hostile words. The greater the mouth awareness the more quickly were

[3] I am indebted to my wife for making these data available.

the associations delivered. Mouth awareness was not related to the directness of the associations elicited by the hostile words. Neither BFQ Stomach nor BFQ Mouth were significantly related with indices pertaining to responses to the non-hostile and non-masochistic words.

The relatively consistent correlations with masochistic measures of both BFQ Mouth and BFQ Stomach encouraged additional follow-up in the same vein. A study was designed which appraised the differential responses to stimuli with masochistic connotations of men varying in mouth and stomach awareness. Thirty-two male college students served as subjects. Each subject responded to two tasks:

1. One involved identifying words presented tachistoscopically. Each subject was shown the following terms (in the same sequence): suicide, ceiling, kill self, dress up. Two were neutral and two were considered to have masochistic significance. Each word was shown at the following successively increasing speeds: 33, 34, 36, 40, and 45 milliseconds. An index was computed equal to the average time required to identify the neutral words minus the average time required to identify the masochistic terms. The higher the score the relatively less difficulty the subject had in perceiving the masochistic as compared to the neutral terms.

2. A second task was a variant of the proverb technique. Subjects were asked to explain the meaning of each of 14 proverbs. In alternate order seven masochistic and neutral proverbs were presented. Examples of masochistic proverbs are as follows:

If you sing before breakfast, you'll cry before night.
It is better to suffer an injury than to commit one.

Examples of the neutral proverbs are as follows:

You tickle me and I'll tickle you.
The printing press is the mother of errors.

The total time required to explain each proverb was determined. An index was computed which equaled the average time to explain the neutral proverbs minus the average time required to explain the masochistic proverbs.

The tachistoscopic data were found to be strongly skewed. Therefore, a chi-square analysis was undertaken of the relationships of BFQ Stomach and BFQ Mouth to the neutral minus masochistic time scores. BFQ Stomach was found to be negatively related ($\chi^2 = 2.8$, $p < .10$) at a borderline level to this index. When the dichotomized (at median) neutral minus masochistic time scores were related to the trichotomized (equal thirds as possible) BFQ Mouth scores, a borderline negative relationship appeared ($\chi^2 = 4.6$, df $= 2$, p 10). Heightened awareness of the stomach or mouth was accompanied by a trend to require a relatively longer time for accurate perception of the masochistic as compared to neutral terms.

Analysis of the proverb data indicated that BFQ Stomach was correlated —.18 with the neutral minus masochistic proverb time score; and BFQ Mouth was correlated —.35 ($p < .05$) with this score. In both instances, the greater the awareness of the given body area the longer was required to explain the masochistic as compared to neutral proverbs. However, only in the case of BFQ Mouth was the correlation statistically significant.

One may conclude that the data indicate a tendency for both BFQ Mouth and BFQ Stomach to be linked with selective response to masochistic themes. The direction of the findings implies that the greater the awareness of the areas in question the more inhibition and blocking are manifested when confronted by masochistic references.

The apparent tie between the body awareness variables and measures of hostile and masochistic feelings led to a consideration of how BFQ Mouth and BFQ Stomach might be related to degree of hostility attributed to one's parents. Could the sensitivity to hostility found in those high in mouth and stomach awareness be somehow a function of feelings that one's parents were either very hostile or else incapable of expressing hostility? Each of 55 male college students had been asked to indicate on a 3-point scale the degree to which ten statements concerned with behavior expressive of anger applied first to his mother and then his father. Examples of the statements follow: "Likes a fight." "Expresses anger openly and directly." "Good at telling people off." The responses (not at all true, slightly true and very true) were weighted respectively 0, 1, 2. Total scores could range from 0 through 20. The data obtained indicated that BFQ Stomach was correlated .28 ($p < .05$ $N = 52$) with the amount of hostility recalled as characterizing mother, but had only a chance correlation with the hostility attributed to father. Similarly, BFQ Mouth was correlated .29 ($p < .05$ $N = 52$) with how hostile mother was rated, but had a chance relationship with the ratings of father. It is striking that both of the BFQ measures were positively related to recalled hostility of mother—but not to that of father. An angry, aggressive orientation on the part of mother may possibly play a role in mouth and stomach awareness and their associated sensitivity to hostility.

The findings indicate that BFQ Stomach has fairly consistent correlations with measures pertaining to hostile and masochistic impulses. The equivalent relationships for BFQ Mouth are barely borderline. One can merely say that they suggestively resemble those found for BFQ Stomach. It is important to point out that better than chance correlations between BFQ variables and hostility indices did not occur when the latter were of the self report type. Meaningful results emerged only when responses to hostility themes were measured in a setting designed to minimize the influence of conscious manipulation and social desirability sets upon reactions.

On the basis of the results presented, it seems reasonable to speculate that the individual with high stomach awareness (perhaps this applies to high mouth awareness too) is selectively concerned about anger and aggression. He is "tuned in" on the potential hostility in the world.

EFFECT OF MOUTH STIMULATION UPON SELECTIVE MEMORY FOR HOSTILE WORDS

It was decided to test the presumed tie between mouth and stomach awareness and attitudes toward hostile themes by ascertaining whether mouth
stimulation could influence these attitudes. This test was derived from the
model, already earlier described, which depicts the degree of awareness of a
body area as serving to reinforce the prime attitude associated with that area.
According to this model, if a selective attitude is associated with a body area,
changing the perceptual prominence of the sector will alter the attitude. The
mouth rather than stomach was chosen as a test site because it is more easily
available for direct stimulation which can alter its sensory prominence. The
specific proposition was evaluated that if an individual's awareness of his
mouth were changed, this would affect his mode of response to hostile stimuli.
No prediction was made about the direction of the change to be expected.
That is, there was no logical basis for predicting whether increasing awareness
of the mouth would sensitize or inhibit perception of hostile stimuli.

The experimental design for testing the proposition involved the study of
how a list of ten hostile and ten non-hostile words was learned and recalled
under three conditions. The list was as follows:

Read	Tease *
Push *	Drive
Plan	Count
Sift	Snub *
Hit *	Plant
Refuse *	Reject *
Roll	Kill *
Grab *	Raise
Swim	Curse *
Hurt *	Paint

[Hostile words are starred]

The hostile and non-hostile words were of equal average length and distributed
equivalently throughout the list.

In one sample (22 male college students), each subject was individually
asked to put a tongue depressor in his mouth; to concentrate on learning the
list of words which was exposed typed on a sheet of paper for one minute; and
to write down during a subsequent five-minute period as many of the words
as he could recall. This condition was directed, of course, at evaluating the
effect of intensified mouth awareness upon the selective learning of the hostile
words. A second sample (21 male college students) followed exactly the same

procedure. But the tongue depressor was taped to the subject's forehead instead of being held in his mouth. This served as a control condition, providing stimulation of a body area other than the mouth. A third sample (50 male college students) learned the list in identical fashion, except that no body stimulation was introduced. It provided a second control condition.

In each instance a score was computed which equaled the number of hostile words minus the number of non-hostile words recalled.

It was anticipated that the mouth stimulation condition would differ from the two control conditions, but that the control conditions would not differ from each other.

The median scores for the mouth stimulation, forehead stimulation, and non-stimulation were respectively 0 (range +5 to −5), +1.0 (range +3 to −5), and +1.0 (+5 to −6). Chi-square was used to compare the three groups because the score distributions were seriously skewed.

The mouth stimulation scores were found to be significantly lower than the forehead stimulation scores ($\chi^2 = 3.9$, $p < .05$). That is, mouth stimulation resulted in a tendency to recall selectively fewer hostile words than was the case with forehead stimulation. Similarly, the mouth stimulation scores were significantly lower than the non-stimulation scores ($\chi^2 = 4.0$, $p < .05$). The forehead and non-stimulation condition scores did not differ from each other. The total number of words learned under each condition did not differ significantly from each other.

The data conformed to expectation. Mouth stimulation resulted in a degree of inhibition of response to the hostile words which was not duplicated by the forehead stimulation or non-stimulation procedures. Using the originally presented correlational findings as a basis, it was possible to conceptualize a basic attitude linked with mouth awareness and then to test the meaningfulness of the formulation by evaluating the effect of sensory accentuation of the mouth upon selective memory for hostile words. The results derived from the experiment were more clearcut than most of the correlational findings. This is especially true of the correlational findings obtained with reference to BFQ Mouth which have been barely of marginal significance.

OVERVIEW

Mouth and stomach awareness seem to be more related to hostility than to oral variables. That is, they are more pertinent to matters of anger and aggression than they are to matters of incorporation and oral gratification. The greater the individual's mouth or stomach awareness the more he is sensitized to, and probably conflicted about, anger. In speculating why the mouth and stomach should have such an association, one may go back to the fact that many of the individual's early relationships (e.g., with mother) are importantly defined in terms of eating transactions. Friendly versus hostile attitudes on the part of important figures could often be communicated in the language of feeding. Although an individual might be well fed (even over-fed) by a parent, he could learn from that parent's behavior that there was underlying unfriendliness and anger. The way in which food is conveyed to the child probably tells him a good deal about how friendly the world is. It is interesting in this respect that both BFQ Mouth and BFQ Stomach were positively correlated with a perception of mother as angry and aggressive. Perhaps an unfriendly mother arouses persistent expectations of encountering anger and aggression and this, in turn, is linked with gastrointestinal sectors like the mouth and stomach because such sectors are so prominently involved in mother-child interchange. To be sensitized to aggression may also repre-sent an underlying feeling that one is inevitably going to be a victim and get hurt. One carefully scans for aggression because attack of some sort seems inevitable. Such anticipation implies a sense of being without adequate protective power and also points to an identification with the role of the victim. It is this last kind of identification which may account for the correlations found between BFQ Mouth and BFQ Stomach and various measures of masochism.

23
Head Awareness in Men and Anality

The matter of head awareness will be considered with reference to several different issues. First of all, material will be presented which deals with trait and defense correlates of variations in head awareness. In addition, because of special circumstances to be described later, it has been possible to utilize head perception as a context within which to examine some determinants of the frequency with which an individual touches a given sector of his body and also to consider the factors which influence the susceptibility of a sector to visual alteration when viewed through distorting lenses.

The head is a prominent part of the total body configuration and is a focal point for much interest and attention. It would be expected to assume a good deal of importance in the body scheme because it is the location of the major senses, the locale of the face which is the presenting representation of self, and the area associated with intellectual, logical functions. A fair number of statements are to be found in the literature, particularly from psycho-analytic sources, concerning the special psychological significances assigned to the head (e.g., Fenichel, 1945; Schilder, 1935; Mason, 1961). These diversely underscore its intellectual and controlling connotations, its symbolic phallic meaning, and its function as a target for upward displacement of unacceptable feelings and wishes associated with the functioning of the lower areas of the body.

The empirical study of head awareness in men was approached by means of a 12-item scale contained in the Body Focus Questionnaire. This scale comprises a series of comparisons in which degree of awareness of one's head is matched against amount of awareness of a number of other (non-head) body areas (e.g., legs, heart, arms). In ten different male samples (average N = 50) BFQ Head values have clustered around 7.4. There tends to be slightly greater awareness of one's head than of non-head areas. BFQ Head scores have, in general, been normally distributed.

Table 23.1
Means and Standard Deviations for BFQ Head

M	σ	N
7.7	3.6	45
7.6	2.8	50
7.7	2.9	48
7.4	2.9	57
6.9	3.4	45
7.4	2.9	47
6.9	2.7	51
7.1	2.8	51
7.7	3.0	50
7.5	3.2	53

BFQ Head was observed in ten different samples (average $N = 50$) to be significantly correlated with other BFQ variables in the following fashion: BFQ Eyes (.39, .35, .40, .32, .31, .38), BFQ Mouth (.28, .39), BFQ Back (−.33, −.34, −.35, −.28), and BFQ Right (.32, .46).[1] It was correlated positively with BFQ Eyes six times and negatively with BFQ Back four times. As indicated, these correlations were typically in the .30's. Only scattered relationships with BFQ Mouth and BFQ Right appeared and there were none with the other BFQ scores.

Test-retest reliability coefficients for BFQ Head have been obtained in several samples of male college students. In three different instances ($N = 57$, $N = 51$, $N = 52$) the respective coefficients after an intervening week were .60, .52, and .74.

Data have accumulated indicating that BFQ Head is not consistently related to such measures of response set as the K and L scales of the MMPI, the Bass Acquiescence Scale (1956) and the Marlowe-Crowne Social Desirability scale (1964).[2]

The comparability of the BFQ Head scale with another approach to measurement of head awareness was evaluated. This was done in several samples by correlating BFQ Head scores with indexes depicting the relative density of sensations at head versus non-head sites. It was presumed that the greater an individual's head awareness, as defined by BFQ Head, the higher would be the relative density of the head sensations he experienced. In three samples the difference in occurrence of head versus non-head sensations was ascertained by asking subjects to indicate over a five-minute period each time definite sensations were felt at four different sites (viz., front of head, back of head, front of body, back of body). The subject recorded his experiences by

[1] All correlations are product-moment unless otherwise specified.
[2] The Barrier score has shown largely chance correlations with BFQ Head.

placing checks under the appropriate headings listed on a sheet of paper. A score was computed which equalled the total number of head minus non-head sensations. In one sample (N = 50) this score was found to be correlated .35 with BFQ Head (p .01). In a second sample (N = 48) the equivalent correlation was .23 ($p < .10$); and in a third (N = 44) the correlation was .30 ($p < .05$). In two other studies the identical procedure was employed, except that the four observed body sites were right side of head, left side of head, right side of body, and left side of body. The head minus non-head sensation score which was derived correlated .25 ($p < .10$) with BFQ Head in one sample (N = 53) and in a second (N = 57) the correlation was .28 ($p < .05$). Consistent relations in the predicted direction were confirmed.

Trait and Defense Correlates

Specification of the traits and defenses that are most probably associated with differences in head awareness in men was guided by the fact that BFQ Head turned out to be correlated with a considerable number of the anality measures described in the previous chapter dealing with back awareness. Actually, BFQ Head was observed to be correlated with several clusters of anal measures, but not at all with others. These correlational patterns will now be reviewed. They were empirically detected and were not resultants of hypothesis testing.

Selective Response to Anal Stimuli

First of all will be considered a range of findings [3] indicating that head awareness is linked with selective response to stimuli with anal connotations.

Cleanliness Behavior

The "anal character" typology derives from the concept that special defenses are developed in the process of learning to control anal functions and associated impulses to soil and dirty. Since dirt represents soiling, it presumably has anal significance. One index of anal attitudes which has been devised by the writer concerns the degree to which an individual devotes energy to the control and removal of dirt in his environs. The Average Week technique, earlier described, has been used for this purpose. A determination is made of the percent of references to cleaning behavior (washing or cleaning of self, clothes, and possessions) occurring in an individual's 15-minute

---

[3] BFQ Head values will be given only for major studies or in instances in which they are unusual.

written description of how he spends an average week in his life. Adequate scoring objectivity has been demonstrated. In a sample of 56 college men the % Cleaning References [4] scores were found to be correlated —.27 ($p < .05$) with BFQ Head scores. The more attention an individual directs to his head the less energy he devotes to banishing dirt. The direction of this relationship, as is true of a number of others to be cited, is the opposite of that found for BFQ Back.

Spontaneous Dirt References

Another means for evaluating selective interest in "anal" stimuli was based on the frequency with which persons mentioned dirt themes when given the opportunity to be freely expressive. A sample of 41 male college students were asked on two occasions, a week apart, to list on a sheet of paper "twenty things that you are aware of or conscious of right now." Each protocol was scored for the number of references to dirt or cleanliness (e.g., "I need to do my laundry," "There is dirt here"). Adequate scoring objectivity has been shown. The sum of the number of dirt references from the two protocols obtained was found to be correlated —.30 ($p < .05$) with BFQ Head. The more aware an individual was of his head the less often he referred to dirt and cleanliness in his spontaneous statements. This too was opposite to the pattern observed for BFQ Back.

Chain Associations

The chain association method also provided pertinent data. It will be recalled that this procedure requires the subject to give a series of ten free associations to each of 13 stimulus words. Three of the words are anal (mess, rear, stink); three oral; three aggressive; three masochistic; and two neutral. The mean times required to complete ten responses to each of the clusters of words were determined and rank ordered. Further, the associations given were rated with reference to how much their meanings departed from those of the original stimulus words; and an average score was established for each category of words. In a sample of male college students (N = 43) BFQ Head was correlated at a borderline level (.26, $p < .10$) with the rank of the anal time. The greater an individual's head awareness the relatively longer he tended to take to complete his associations to the anal words. This result reversed that reported in the BFQ Back chapter. Incidentally, BFQ Head was not correlated with the rank orders of the time scores for any of the other themes. It was in addition not related to the scores indicating the degree to

---

[4] Mean values for the various anality indices to be cited in this chapter are to be found in the BFQ Back chapter.

which the associations deviated from the meanings of the stimulus words that had elicited them.

Jokes

Head awareness was appraised with reference to selective response to anal jokes. Using a modification of a procedure devised by Weiss (1955), responses to jokes in five different categories (Anal Expulsive, Oral Erotic, Oral Sadistic, Castration, Oedipal) were obtained. The subject was asked to indicate (on a 6-point scale) how much he liked each joke. The mean ratings of jokes in each category were computed and rank ordered (rank 1 = least liked). In a sample of male college students (N = 47) the rank order of the Anal Expulsive jokes was correlated —.29 (p < .05) with BFQ Head. Correlations involving the other joke categories were not significant. The findings indicated that the more aware a subject was of his head the relatively less he enjoyed the Anal Expulsive jokes. This was the opposite of the result observed with reference to BFQ Back.

Blacky Pictures Presented Tachistoscopically

Another approach concerned selective response to the Blacky Anal Sadism picture (Blum, 1949) when presented tachistoscopically. As outlined previously, a technique was devised which involves showing each of six Blacky pictures (Anal Sadism, Oral Eroticism, Oral Sadism, Castration Anxiety, Masturbation Guilt, Sibling Rivalry) in random order at six successively increasing time exposures. Scores are computed which indicate the first speed at which each picture is correctly identified and also the total number of times it is accurately perceived. These scores are converted to ranks. In a sample of male college students (N = 41) BFQ Head was correlated —.38 (p < .025) with the rank of the number of times the Anal Sadism picture was correctly perceived. The correlation with the rank of the first time Anal Sadism was accurately identified was at a chance level. The more intense an individual's awareness of his head the more often he accurately identified the Anal Sadism theme. This result was the opposite of that found for BFQ Back.

It should be mentioned too that BFQ Head was significantly correlated (r = .30, p < .05) with the rank of the number of times Masturbation Guilt was correctly perceived.

Memory for Words with Anal Significance

Ten words with anal connotations (e.g., gas, expel, seat, regular) and ten with non-anal significance (e.g., bat, poem, radio) had been combined into a list which subjects were asked to learn and which served to detect selective response to anal themes. The list was shown for one minute to subjects and they were given five minutes to write down as many of the words as they could recall. A score was computed which equalled the number of anal minus non-anal words recalled. When the learning list was administered to a sample of male college students (N = 61), a correlation of .21 (p .10) was found between BFQ Head and the recall index. There was a borderline trend for degree of head awareness to be positively related to relatively superior recall of anal as compared to non-anal words. This was the first instance in which a result was in the same direction as that found for BFQ Back.

OVERVIEW

The data presented to this point suggested that degree of head awareness is paralleled by selective attitudes toward stimuli with dirt or anal connotations. These selective attitudes seem to be the opposite of those associated with back awareness. They involve, in most instances, a less defensive response to anal themes.

When an analysis was further undertaken of the relationships of BFQ Head to a variety of the indicators of homosexual anxiety and conflict which had been found to be correlated with degree of back awareness, largely chance coefficients were found. BFQ Head was not correlated with responses to a homosexual theme presented in the Ames Thereness-Thatness apparatus; number of references to male interaction in spontaneous expressions; thresholds for tachistoscopically presented homosexual words; and ratings of pictures with vague sexual identity. Relatedly, BFQ Head did not differentiate paranoid (in whom homosexual conflict is presumably heightened) from non-paranoid schizophrenics.

Other variables (originally related to BFQ Back), such as sensitivity to hostile themes, frugality, and thrift were not correlated with head awareness. It is interesting too that BFQ Head was not correlated with impulsivity (as measured by the Impulsivity scale of the Thurstone Temperament Schedule) which, as earlier mentioned, was consistently linked with the back awareness dimension.

A special connection exists between BFQ Head and a selective attitude toward anality.[5] However, there are many aspects of the anal character orientation (pertaining to homosexual conflict, hostility, and self-control) which do not seem to bear on head awareness. As a matter of fact, the large number of negative findings raises questions whether some of the significant

---

[5] BFQ Head did not correlate consistently with any of the other clusters of variables (e.g., heterosexual, incorporative) related to other BFQ dimensions.

results cited above were due to chance. One is a bit reassured by the fact that the significant results cluster in a common area pertaining to sensitivity to anal stimuli. In any case, the findings need to be viewed as tentative.[6]

Why should head awareness and anal attitudes be related? One possibility is that head is primarily identified with face which is perhaps more strongly equated with the front of oneself than any other body sector. In that sense, the head would be the obverse of the back; and it is true that the correlations of BFQ Head with anal indexes were obverse to those characterizing BFQ Back. One may also recall that BFQ Head and BFQ Back were found in several instances to be negatively correlated. Another explanatory possibility is that the head, because of its position, is particularly well suited to represent the antithesis of the lower area of one's body, which so commonly has anal significance. Anal functions take place "down there," but not "up there." Still further, psychoanalytic theorists (e.g., Fenichel, 1945) have proposed that because thinking and the use of words (e.g., via obsessiveness and intellectualized self-imposed constraints) seem to play such an important role in the control of anal impulses, the head takes on anal meaning symbolically.

A PERSPECTIVE FOR INTERPRETING SELECTIVE SELF TOUCHING AND LENS INDUCED SELF IMAGE CHANGES

The BFQ Head dimension offered opportunities for bridging between an individual's amount of awareness of a body sector, the frequency with which he touches it, and his likelihood of seeing it as changed when viewed in the unstable perceptual field created by distorting lenses. It enabled consideration of some of the special ways one may treat and perceive a specific body region in relation to how vividly it is experienced. Why the head dimension is particularly well suited for this purpose will become clearer as detailed pertinent findings are presented. However, it may be said that one of the main reasons is that the head, perhaps because of its distinct part in the body configuration, is the target for responses (from oneself) which are sufficiently distinct and frequent to be measurable. This was in contrast to the difficulty encountered in identifying differentiated responses (as defined by self touching and lens induced distortions) to other body areas like right versus left, back versus front, eyes, and, of course, those with an interior location.

[6] This is especially true because the opportunity did not present itself for directly evaluating the effect of head stimulation upon selective learning of words with anal significance. This is partially due to the difficulty in stimulating *increased* general awareness of one's head without simultaneously arousing awareness of *specific* areas of one's head like the eyes or mouth.

Self Touching

Casual observation reveals that people are constantly touching themselves. It is also easy to discern that they touch some body areas and not others and further that total rates of self touching may vary considerably. We know little about motivations for self touching, aside from the obvious instances in which itching, pain, and similar sensory experiences act as instigators. Does self touching serve any specific purposes? Is it a way of highlighting a particular body area? Is it a substitute means for providing sensory input? Is it a way of comforting self? Does it help to delineate the boundary? Is it primarily a way of feeling and experiencing one's body or of stimulating it? Many such questions come to mind. Psychoanalytic observers (e.g., Deutsch, 1952) of patients on the couch have concluded that they may touch a specific body area because it symbolically represents an unconscious conflict or issue of concern. It has also been suggested by some (Fenichel, 1945) that self touching of certain body parts by psychiatric patients represents reassurance against their·anticipated loss.

There have been a fair number of studies of body expressive behavior (e.g., Krout, 1954) but with minor exceptions they have not been concerned with self touching, as such. A study by Moos (in press) is noteworthy. It found that psychiatric patients, who were asked to wear a small radio transmitter so that their interactions with others could be recorded, touched themselves less while outfitted with the transmitter than when not so outfitted. The sense of being observed seemed to inhibit self touching.

Self touching should represent a significant form of behavior. Because of the taboo against talking to oneself, it is one of the few observable forms of action in which the individual responds directly to himself. It conceivably provides a series of overt representations of an individual's "transactions" with himself. Also, since self touching is action directed to one's own body, one would expect it to be influenced by body attitudes. Indeed, it might possibly play a role in the maintenance of body scheme patterns. Perhaps the need to highlight a certain body area in the body scheme stimulates intensified touching of that area. Or the need to minimize an area might inhibit such touching. It appeared important to explore possible ways in which self touching contributes to the process of integrating body experience. One of the first tasks in the process of investigating self touching was to find a means of classifying its occurrence. After considerable informal study of self touching in various persons, the following observational categories were developed.

> Number of touches to head (neck or higher).
> Number of touches to trunk (below neck to waist).
> Number of touches to lower body area (below waist to toes).

The touching of one arm by the other or one leg by the other was not counted because it was not clear whether such behavior in which a body part touches a similar one would have the same significance as when one body part touches another which is dissimilar. It was found that observers could maintain judgmental accuracy most optimally for five-minute periods; and this was adopted as the unit period. But a minimum of three such five-minute units were typically obtained when self touching phenomena were to be related to other variables.

In one sample of 20 male college students who (while sitting quietly) were observed by two judges for ten minutes, it was found that inter-judge correlations for the various categories were as follows:

Head	.91
Trunk	.88
Lower Body	.93
Total	.94

In a second sample of 15 male college students observed under similar circumstances by two judges the inter-judge correlations were as follows:

Head	.93
Trunk	.87
Lower Body	.90
Total	.92

How stable over time are the touch patterns of an individual? One project undertaken to answer this question involved taking three five-minute samples (initially, 30 minutes later, and again after 30 minutes). This same procedure was repeated seven days later. Observations were made through a one-way mirror. All the time samples occurred while subjects (42 male college students) were sitting alone at a desk and answering various questionnaires.

When self touch values for the first combined 15-minute sample were correlated with those of the retest 15-minute sample, the following relationships were noted. The total number of self touches in session 1 correlated .45 ($p < .01$) with the total for session 2. Total head touches during session 1 correlated .31 ($p < .05$) with total head touches during session 2. For trunk contacts, the test-retest coefficient was .33 ($p < .05$); and for lower body contacts it was —.23. There was a significant degree of continuity between sessions 1 and 2 for all of the self touch variables except number of lower body touches; but it was of a very low order.

Correlations were also computed among the three five-minute self touch scores for each session. In session 1, sample 1 correlated .39 (p .01) with sample 2 and .08 with sample 3. Sample 2 correlated —.19 with sample 3.

During session 2, sample 1 correlated .61 ($p < $.001) with sample 2 and .21 with sample 3. Sample 2 correlated .34 ($p < $.05) with sample 3.

Sample 1 of session 1 correlated .37 ($p < $.025) with sample 1 of session 2, .49 ($p = $.001) with sample 2 of session 2, and .07 with sample 3 of session 2. Sample 2 of session 1 did not correlate significantly with any of the samples of session 2. Sample 3 of session 1 correlated .48 ($p < $.01) with sample 2 of session 2, but was not significantly related to any of the other samples of session 2.

In a second test-retest study self touch observations were made on male patients (N = 20) just prior to (one day) minor surgery and again within a day or two after such surgery. The observations were obtained by a male while seated in the same hospital room as the patient, who was usually sitting in a chair and writing responses to questionnaires on a clip board. The period of observation prior to surgery was five minutes and that post-surgery was ten minutes. The correlation between the pre- and post-total scores was .67 ($p < $.001). Test-retest values for the head were correlated .60 ($p < $.001). Those for the trunk and lower body could not be computed because they were too skewed.

An analysis of the frequency of self touching with reference to different body areas is shown in Table 23.2. The values presented apply to situations. in which the subject does not know he is being observed.

Table 23.2
Means and Standard Deviations of Self Touch Values

	Sample [a] 1 (N = 44)		Sample 2 (N = 45)	
	M	σ	M	σ
Head	13.1	8.4	14.8	9.1
Trunk	1.0	1.7	3.1	2.4
Lower	.9	1.3	1.9	2.2
Total	15.0	9.7	19.9	10.6

[a] All subjects were male college students observed through a one-way mirror.

One can see that the majority of self touches are to the head. The number of head touches tends to be five or six times as great as that occurring at trunk or lower body sites.

Little has been done as yet to investigate the situational factors which influence the rate of self touching. But some evidence was obtained that the presence of an observer in the same room as the subject results in a decrease in self touching. In a sample of 44 male college students whose self touching was observed by a man in the same room the self touch score was 8.5 ($\sigma = $5.8).

This contrasts with mean self touch scores of 15.0 ($\sigma = 9.7$) and 19.9 ($\sigma = 10.6$) respectively in samples of 44 and 45 male college students who were similarly observed, but through a one-way mirror. Both of the sets of differences were significant ($t = 3.8$, $p < .001$, $t = 6.3$, $p < .001$). This reminds one of the Moos (in press) study earlier mentioned in which it was found that psychiatric patients who felt they were being observed manifested a reduction in amount of self touching.

These were the first exploratory bits of knowledge which were assembled concerning self touching. Despite the obvious instability of the phenomenon, it was decided to examine it further from other perspectives.

Head Awareness and Head Touching

One of the basic questions pursued was whether an individual's rate of head touching is linked to how aware he is of his head. It was difficult, in the absence of information concerning the function of self touching, to predict the possible character of its relationship to head awareness. If self touching of an area were a function of its perceptual prominence, one might expect a positive correlation between awareness and self touch measures. But if self touching contributed to awareness, varying relationships might be expected as a function of the amount of the contribution. Consider, for example, what the variations might be if self touching were one of several variables influencing awareness. When its influence was primary, a positive correlation would be expected. However, when other variables exerted major influence, the relationship might become zero and even negative.

Three studies have been undertaken in which BFQ Head was related to amount of head touching. All involved male college students ($N = 44$, $N = 32$, $N = 45$) who were observed through a one-way mirror while responding to a series of questionnaires.[7] Five-minute samples of self touching were recorded at approximately the following points: initially; 30 minutes later; and again after 30 minutes. Scores were computed which represented the sum of the 15 minutes of sample observations. Mean number of head contacts in the first study was 13.1 ($\sigma = 8.4$). BFQ Head scores were found to be correlated .29 (p .05) with the head touch score. In the second sample the mean head touch score was 7.4 ($\sigma = 2.8$), and the correlation between BFQ Head and head touching was $-.12$. In the third sample the mean head touch score was 14.8 ($\sigma = 9.1$); and the correlation between BFQ Head and head touching was .27 ($p < .10$).[8] In two of the three samples, then, head

[7] Barrier scores and measures of body awareness (Body Prominence) were also obtained from the subjects in a few samples. They both proved to be unrelated to self touching.

[8] In later studies of male psychiatric patients BFQ Head and amount of head touching were not significantly correlated. As will be seen, this may be a function of the fact that special compensatory processes influence self touching in psychiatric patients.

awareness and head touching were positively correlated. One of the positive correlations was clearly significant and one was borderline.

BFQ Head was not significantly correlated with number of self touches to the trunk or lower body in the three samples; and none of the other BFQ variables were consistently correlated with self touch scores. It should be pointed out that it was really impossible to relate the trunk self touching score to any BFQ score which would be as analogously circumscribed as the BFQ Head measure in its area of body designation. This was also true with reference to the lower body self touch score which is a composite of touches to pelvic, thigh, and leg areas. No BFQ score embraces this combination of areas.[9] The results pertaining to the correlations between head awareness and head touching are provocative. They suggest that the two variables may have an underlying relationship, but they also indicate that it is an unstable one. Perhaps uncontrolled variables like temperature, fatigue, and degree of hunger play an as yet undefined role in stimulating head touching; and the demonstration of a relationship between BFQ Head and head touching may depend upon a proper balance among these variables. For example, on a cold day the subject could arrive at the experimental session with the exposed skin of his face chilled or his nose running; and therefore direct an unusual amount of touching to his head. This rate of head touching could be considerably higher than he would typically display. There may be a "usual" tempo of head touching which is correlated with degree of head awareness, but which can be sharply elevated or reduced by special situational factors.

If it eventually turns out that the usual tempo of head touching is positively correlated with head awareness, there are several interpretations that could be made. One could speculate that self touching provides a means for controlling and altering the prominence of an area in the body scheme; or that the varying experiential prominence of body sectors controls the touch input to such sectors by the individual. Or there may be a more complex system in which self touching is regulated by degree of awareness of an area and in turn influences the perceptual prominence of that area.

LENS INDUCED CHANGES IN APPEARANCE OF BODY PARTS

The self touching data just reviewed had permitted a look at the relationship of two variables: the amount of attention an individual focuses on a sector of his body and how he treats it motorically as defined by the frequency with

---

[9] A series of items referring specifically to the legs and feet was extracted to determine if awareness of this region would correlate with amount of lower body self touching. But chance findings emerged.

which he touches it. By use of a lens distortion technique it was also possible to examine the relationship between awareness of a body area and how an individual reacts to that area in an unstable perceptual field. It is this work which will be described in the present section.

A number of studies occur in the literature which deal with body image phenomena via the individual's response to seeing his body as it is apparently altered by aniseikonic [10] lenses. The majority of these studies have been concerned with sex differences in lens induced responses (e.g., Wittreich and Grace, 1955; Fisher, 1964E); and they will be described in detail later. The few others published have been primarily concerned with the individual's reaction to the sight of mutilation when viewed through aniseikonic lenses. Moderately convincing evidence exists (Wittreich and Radcliffe, 1955; Cormack, 1966) that when looking through aniseikonic lenses it is more difficult to perceive changes in the appearance of someone who is mutilated (e.g., amputee) than in the appearance of someone who is not mutilated. Such data have been interpreted as indicating that normal perceptual changes produced by aniseikonic lenses will be inhibited or minimized if the perceptual target is anxiety provoking. The presence of danger apparently motivates the individual to "hold on" to the usual attributes of perceptual objects and to avoid change.

Really, what has emerged from the lens studies is the fact that within a range where lens distortion is not too compelling, the nature of the changes experienced by an individual will be affected by his level of anxiety and also selective sets. The influence exerted by selective sets is illustrated by the finding (Wittreich and Grace, 1955) that men are more likely than women to experience their legs as altered when viewing themselves aniseikonically in a mirror—with the converse being true for alteration of the head. This sex difference has been speculatively traced to differing attitudes on the part of men and women toward the lower and upper regions of their bodies. It was the potential for eliciting differential responses of this type to various sectors of one's body which led to the use of distorting lenses in the work shortly to be described.

Two studies were devoted to appraising, among other things, the relationship between the amount of lens induced alteration attributed by an individual to a specific area of his body and his relative awareness of that area. The design, in each study, involved obtaining BFQ scores on one occasion and then, a week later, measuring responses to various lenses. The lens procedure was as follows. Each subject was asked to stand five feet from a full-length mirror and to put on a pair of aniseikonic lenses (right = 5% @ 90°, left = plano). He was told to look around the room and to describe

[10] Aniseikonic lenses result in the image of an object which is formed in one eye differing in size and shape from the image of the same object formed in the other eye. They often produce tilting of the perceptual field and can alter one's mirror image in innumerable ways.

apparent changes produced by the lenses. When he became aware of some of the obvious aniseikonic distortions (e.g., walls tilted), he was requested to examine his image in the mirror and to describe all changes he could detect. This description was written down as verbatim as possible. Next, the subject was asked to judge which of three body areas (viz., head, arms, legs) was most changed in appearance and which least changed. This same procedure was repeated with each of the following sequences of lenses:

> Lens 2: Right: 14% @ 90°
>   Left: 14% @ 90°
> [Produces a widening effect]
>
> Lens 3: Right: 10% @ 45°
>   Left: 10% @ 45°
> [Aniseikonic]
>
> Lens 4: Right: 10% @ 135°
>   Left: 10% @ 135°
> [Aniseikonic]
>
> Lens 5: Right: 14% @ 180°
>   Left: 14% @ 180°
> [Produces lengthening effect]
>
> Lens 6: Right: plano
>   Left: plano
> [Produces no distortions. Introduced as a control]

The judgments regarding head, arm, and leg changes were coded so that a value of 3 was assigned for each trial to the body area considered most changed, 1 to the area regarded as least changed, and 2 for the remaining area which was intermediate.

A sum of scores was computed separately for each of the three body areas on the basis of responses to the first five sets of lenses. Scores for an area could range from 5 (little change) to 15 (most change). The sixth set of lenses, which were ordinary glass, elicited distortion responses from only three or four subjects in the total array of subjects; and demonstrated that distortion reports for the other lenses were stimulated by their optical properties.

In addition to the scoring system just described, another was evolved which was based on the verbalized reports of change in response to the following instruction repeated before each trial: "Look at your image in the mirror and tell me what is changed or different about it." Reports elicited by the first five sets of lenses were analyzed for the following categories:

Head changes
Arm changes
Leg changes [11]

---

[11] Other categories were also scored which are not pertinent to present considerations.

A maximum of 1 point was given for any category for any trial. The score for a category could range from 0–5. Scoring objectivity was determined by comparing independent scorings for the categories by two judges in a sample of 39 college males. Inter-scorer agreement did not fall below 95 percent for any of the lens change variables.

Data for two samples of male college students (N = 39, N = 35) were available.[12]

Table 23.3
Means and Standard Deviations of Lens Alteration Scores

| | Study 1 | | Study 2 | |
	M	σ	M	σ
Head Rating	2.0	.5	1.8	.5
Arm Rating	1.9	.4	2.1	.3
Leg Rating	2.0	.4	2.1	.6
Head Content	2.7	1.2	1.5	1.3
Arm Content	1.5	1.2	1.5	1.0
Leg Content	3.1	1.2	2.4	1.4
Total Change	15.6	3.5	10.3	3.0

Table 23.4
Intercorrelations of Lens Variables

| | Study 1 (N = 35) | | | | | | |
	1	2	3	4	5	6	7
Head rating (1)		−.64	−.60	.50	−.12	−.36	.22
Arm rating (2)			−.23	−.23	.19	.12	−.08
Leg rating (3)				−.39	−.05	.34	−.16
Head content (4)					.25	.18	.57
Arm content (5)						.14	.48
Leg content (6)							.43
Total change (7)							

One can see that in Study 1 (Table 23.4) the Head lens rating score was correlated .50 ($p < .01$) with the Head lens content score; the Arm lens rating score was correlated .19 with the Arm lens content score; and the Leg lens rating score was correlated .34 ($p < .05$) with the Leg lens content score. In Study 2 (Table 23.5) the respective correlations were .35 ($p < .05$), .37 ($p < .025$), and .53 ($p < .001$). With the exception of the correlation between the Arm lens rating and Arm lens content scores for Study 1, all

[12] Barrier scores and body awareness scores (Body Prominence) were available for subjects in one sample and they were found to be unrelated to any of the lens alteration scores.

Table 23.5
Intercorrelations of Lens Variables

| | Study 2 (N = 39) | | | | | | |
	1	2	3	4	5	6	7
Head rating (1)		−.06	−.79	.35	.00	−.42	.05
Arm rating (2)			−.57	−.18	.37	−.31	−.02
Leg rating (3)				−.18	−.21	.53	−.03
Head content (4)					.21	.06	.42
Arm content (5)						.18	.38
Leg content (6)							.48
Total change (7)							

coefficients were significant. The two methods for eliciting reports of lens induced changes in specific body locales were parallel in their results. An analysis was undertaken of the relationships of BFQ variables to the lens scores indicating amount of change experienced at specific body locales. Of course, the BFQ Head and BFQ Arms scores were the only ones directly pertinent to the Head and Arms lens change scores. In order to provide a BFQ index comparable to the Leg lens change category, a special scale was constructed which involved 16 comparisons of legs and feet with other body areas (e.g., head, neck, stomach, heart, arms).

There was no basis for predicting the direction of relationships between BFQ scores and their corresponding lens change scores. It was simply anticipated that the BFQ and lens variables would be selectively linked. High awareness of an area might be paralleled by either high or low lens induced alteration of that area.

The data for Study 1 indicated that BFQ Head was correlated .30 (just fractionally short of the .05 level) with the Head lens rating score and .35 ($p < .05$) with the Head lens content score. In Study 2 BFQ Head was correlated −.28 (p .10) with the Head lens rating score and −.01 with the Head lens content score.

BFQ Arms in both Studies 1 and 2 was not significantly correlated with any of the Arm lens change scores.

The special BFQ Leg scale which was devised correlated −.23 ($p > .20$) with the Leg lens rating score and −.46 ($p < .01$) with the Leg lens content score in Study 1. For Study 2, the corresponding correlations were .16 ($p > .20$) and .30 ($p < .10$).

None of the three BFQ scores in question (viz., Head, Arms, Legs) were correlated with the lens scores descriptive of changes in the other two non-related body areas. It is also true that the remainder of the BFQ dimensions (viz., Right-Left, Back, Heart, Stomach, Mouth, Eyes) were not correlated with any of the lens change scores.

The findings portrayed a borderline, but discernible trend for head awareness and lens induced head changes to be linked. It is true that in Study 1 the link was positive and in Study 2 it was negative in direction. At the moment there are no clues as to the circumstances which encourage a positive rather than a negative relationship. One can only speak of the existence of a relationship. This was found to be similarly true when BFQ Legs and the Leg lens scores were considered. In Study 1, BFQ Legs tended to be positively correlated with Leg lens changes; and in Study 2 the direction shifted in the opposite direction. BFQ Arms was not at all related to Arms lens alterations in either of the two studies.

At this point it would be of interest to look at the relationships of lens change scores for a body locale and the self touch scores for that locale. The head is the only sector which permits such a comparison straightforwardly, since the two types of scores are not available for arms or legs specifically. In Study 1 the Head lens rating score was correlated .30 ($p < .10$) with the Head self touch score; but the latter score had a chance correlation with the Head lens content score. As for Study 2, the Head lens rating score was correlated .18 with Head self touch and the Head lens content score was correlated .29 ($p < .10$) with Head self touch. There was only a minimal tendency for frequency of head touching to be positively correlated with degree of head lens distortion experienced.

OVERVIEW

Results for two of the three body sites studied raise a possibility that with improved methodology information can be derived concerning awareness of a body sector which would predict one's likelihood of perceiving it as differentially altered when viewed through distorting lenses. If one considers the lens distortion and self touching data in conjunction, those for the head sector are especially noteworthy. The amount of attention an individual directs to his head seems to have a low order but significant relationship to how he responds to it motorically in terms of self touch and also how he experiences it in the unstable perceptual context created by lens distortion. Such findings offer a glimmer of hope that BFQ dimensions will provide access to an organized system which monitors and controls the manner in which major body sectors become "objects" of perception and action. Analogous to organized attitudes which determine how an individual will focus upon, and "make contact with," certain objects in his environs, there are probably regulatory processes which guide him in his dealings with the regions of his body. It is possible to ask speculatively whether there may not be a wide gamut of selectively directed body activities which are a function of the awareness levels of various body sectors. Does the way an individual clothes or decorates a body area reflect its relative prominence in the body scheme? Will one assign a bright color to one area and a neutral one to another as a function of how relatively aware one is of them? Compton's (1964) work, which has already shown a significant correlation in a female schizophrenic population between boundary definiteness and the color patterns preferred for one's clothing, suggests that such a possibility is not terribly far-fetched. Also, what about the distributions of other kinds of body decoration and "treatment," such as tattoos, jewelry, cosmetics,[13] plastic surgery, tight garments, and so forth? How are they tied in to the differentiated way in which the individual experiences his body?

[13] Systematic studies of self touching and lens distortion phenomena in women have not yet been undertaken. However, in the one sample of female college students ($N = 34$) whose self touching behavior was observed BFQ Head and head touching had a negative relationship ($r = -.21$, $p > .20$). A similar negative correlation ($r = -.30$, p .05) was found in one ($N = 40$) of two female schizophrenic samples observed. It may turn out, as is true for so many body experience phenomena, that the nature of the relationship between head awareness and head touching is quite different in women than it is in men.

24

Back Awareness in Women
and Anality

INTRODUCTION

Since it was possible to make psychological sense out of the way a man distributes his attention to his body, similar inquiries were attempted with regard to women. In the earliest studies involving the Body Focus Questionnaire, both men and women were studied; but it became obvious that results for the two sexes were different and often opposite in character. The analysis of body attention patterns in women was consequently made a separate enterprise and was not seriously undertaken until the major findings concerning men had been assembled. It proved to be a relatively difficult matter. For one thing, women show less consistency than men in their degree of awareness of specified body sectors. Their test-retest reliabilities for most sectors tend to be lower than those found for men; and in some instances are so minimal as to discourage further investigation. But beyond this, it has simply turned out to be more arduous to demonstrate in women that degree of awareness of a body area is associated with specific traits or defenses. Why this should be so will be discussed at a later point. Perhaps what has just been said is too broadly negative in its implications. In actual fact, it was possible to construct reasonably satisfying accounts concerning the significance of several body awareness dimensions in women. This work will now be reviewed.

When considering variations in back awareness among women, it was logical to ask if they are understandable with reference to the "anal character" model. That is, since the model served so well in explaining back awareness patterns in men, it seemed potentially applicable to women. Would one find, as was the case for men, that the woman with high back awareness was typified by anxiety about anal themes, fear of loss of control, homosexual conflicts, difficulty in coping with hostile impulses, and perception of her parents as loath to express anger?

Table 24.1
Means and Standard Deviations of BFQ Back Scores

M	σ	N
8.1	3.3	47
7.5	3.1	51
8.2	4.2	54
8.9	3.8	48
8.7	4.3	50
8.2	3.4	50
9.0	4.7	40
7.6	4.1	55
7.3	3.8	52
8.5	3.6	49

Before proceeding to review the studies which dealt with these and related questions, a word should be said about the properties of the BFQ Back scale, as manifested in relation to women. The same 19-item scale which was applied to men was employed for women. BFQ values in many samples of female college students (as shown in Table 24.1) have tended to average about 8.2. This is higher (but not significantly so) than the 7.7 value found for men. Distributions of scores have been largely normal in character.

The test-retest reliability of the BFQ Back scale (seven days intervening) proved to be .60 in one sample of college women (N = 49). In a second sample of college women (N = 40), with a week similarly intervening, the test-retest coefficient was .73.

When relationships of BFQ Back with other BFQ scales were reviewed in ten different samples of women (average N = 50), they proved to be largely chance or inconsequentially low. The one exception involved the correlations with BFQ Heart. These were consistently negative (viz., —.42, —.27, —.13, —.22, —.31, —.41, —.40, —.36, —.09, —.30). Seven of these coefficients are significant *at least* at the .05 level and four at the .01 level or better. But only three attained .40 or more; and so one may consider the two scales to be largely independent.

In several studies the K and L scales of the MMPI and the Marlowe-Crowne (1964) Social Desirability scale have not shown consistent, statistically significant relationships to BFQ Back. Social desirability sets do not play a role in BFQ Back judgments.

It should further be indicated that the relationship between BFQ Back scores and relative densities of back versus front body sensations was ascertained in three samples of college women. Such studies were intended to evaluate further whether the BFQ Back score parallels other indices which concern back versus front sensory experiences. As previously described, a method for determining frequencies of back and front sensations has been developed which is based on subjects reporting for a five-minute period each time they feel a definite sensation at two front (front of head, front of body) and two back (back of head, back of body) sites. Reports are made by checking appropriate designations on a sheet of paper. A score is then computed equal to the number of back minus front sensations experienced. In one sample of women (N = 50) a correlation of .34 ($p < .025$) between BFQ Back and the back minus front sensation frequency score was found. In a second sample (N = 52) the correlation was .26 ($p < .10$); and in a third sample (N = 51) it was .31 ($p < .05$). All of the correlations were in the predicted direction; and two were statistically significant.

Preliminary Studies

The first study of the correlates of back awareness in women which was undertaken was designed to evaluate whether they were comparable to those found in men. It was therefore asked whether BFQ Back was related to the following variables:

1. Need for self-control

This was measured by means of the Impulsivity scale of the Thurstone (1953) Temperament Scale. It will be recalled that in men BFQ Back was negatively related to Impulsivity. Back awareness in men was associated with a need for careful self-control.

2. Characteristic ways of expressing anger

The Buss-Durkee (1957) Hostility scale was employed on an exploratory basis to examine several aspects of hostility expression. Particular interest was focused on whether the Negativism scale would be correlated with back awareness—since stubbornness is one of the presumed attributes of the anal character.

3. Homosexual conflict

Homosexual conflict proved to be typical of men with intensified back awareness. The question was whether this would also be true for women.

One measure utilized to evaluate possible homosexual difficulties was the same as that previously applied to men. It basically involves counting the number of references to relationships with women spontaneously produced when an individual is asked to list "20 things you are aware of or conscious of right now." The rationale for this technique has been discussed in detail in the previous section on back awareness in men. It is assumed that the greater the anxiety about homosexual contacts the fewer the references to like sex contacts will be made.

A second technique was concerned with differential response to a nude male and nude female figure presented in the Ames Thereness-Thatness apparatus. Other figures included were a clothed male and a clothed female. The question was whether back awareness in women would be associated with a selective response to the nude female figure.

4. Perceived ease of parents in showing anger

Since men with high back awareness were characterized by the view that their parents had been reluctant and inhibited about expressing anger, inquiry was undertaken of whether this was analogously true for women. Subjects were asked to fill out a 10-item scale in which they indicated their recall of how overtly their parents expressed anger. Some sample items in the scale are as follows: Expresses anger openly and directly; Good at telling people off. The subject indicated the degree to which such statements applied to each of her parents.

To evaluate the above possibilities, a sample of 53 female college students was studied.

The BFQ Back scores proved to be unrelated to most of the dependent measures. Back awareness had only chance correlations with the Impulsivity score (Thurstone Temperament Scale), the two measures of homosexual [1] anxiety, and amount of hostile behavior attributed to each of the parents.

It was positively correlated (.39, $p < .01$) with the Negativism score of the Buss-Durkee but not with any of the other Buss-Durkee scales. This finding pertaining to Negativism was the only significant lead that emerged from the study. An attempt to cross-validate it was undertaken. In a sample of 50 female college students the BFQ and the Buss-Durkee Hostility inventory were administered. BFQ Back proved to be correlated .23 ($p < .05$, one-tail test) with Buss-Durkee Negativism, and .41 ($p < .01$) with the Buss-Durkee Assaultive scale. This finding indicated that back awareness was positively correlated with Negativism and also the tendency to express open, forceful aggression. The Negativism result confirmed that previously observed; and together they suggest that the anal trait of stubbornness (as Freud con-

---

[1] It is pertinent to this lack of relationship between BFQ Back and homosexual anxiety, that in two samples of schizophrenic women no differences were found between paranoids and non-paranoids with reference to amount of back awareness. As indicated, Freud considered homosexual conflict basic to the development of the paranoid delusion.

ceptualized it) is, indeed, related to degree of back awareness in women. One complication presented by the data from the second study was the fact that the Assaultive score was also positively correlated with back awareness. However, since this finding did not appear in the first study involving the Buss-Durkee, one can regard it skeptically. Incidentally, more data pertinent to negativism will be presented later in this section.

ATTITUDES TOWARD DIRT

Aside from the Negativism findings, the others were not encouraging. However, the possibility was considered that the particular pattern of anal variables related to back awareness in women might be quite different from those associated with back awareness in men.

It was decided to shift the investigatory strategy and to focus on the simple question whether back awareness in women is somehow related to feelings and attitudes about dirt. One of the fundamental parameters in the anal character formulation is the idea that selective attitudes toward anal functions (e.g., feces) become generalized into special feelings about dirt. The anal character is presumably concerned about dirt; sensitive to it; and motivated to remove or minimize it. Several studies of the dirt variable will now be described.

Awareness of Dirt

One technique previously used to study dirt attitudes in men was based on the number of spontaneous references to dirt and cleanliness themes made by an individual in a free expressive situation. Subjects are asked to list on a sheet of paper "20 things that you are aware of or conscious of right now." Each protocol is then scored for the number of references to dirt or cleanliness it contains. Several examples follow of the types of statements scored:

> My shoes are dirty.
> I need to do my laundry.
> The ash tray is clean.

As described earlier, adequate scoring reliability has been demonstrated. The assumption underlying the procedure is that the greater an individual's concern about dirt the more it will intrude into his spontaneous observations and thoughts.

It was anticipated that BFQ Back in women would be positively correlated with number of dirt and cleanliness themes. A sample of 37 women (median age 26; median education 12 years) were individually studied. BFQ and spontaneous awareness reports (blindly scored) were obtained from each. The median number of dirt themes produced was 0 (range 0–3). A chi-square analysis indicated that BFQ Back was positively and significantly related to number of dirt themes ($\chi^2 = 9.7$, df $= 1$, $p < .001$). The greater the subject's back awareness the more likely she was to evidence concern with dirt themes. This same result was previously found to be true for men.

Cleaning Behavior

A second study concerned with back awareness and attitudes toward dirt was based on a procedure previously outlined which evaluates how much energy the individual typically invests in anti-dirt activities. If heightened back awareness betokens concern about anal conflicts, it should be reflected in a need to minimize or "fight" the dirt in one's environment. In order to test this idea, a procedure was used which had also been applied to men. Fifty-two college women were individually requested to write a description of how they spend an average week. They were specifically told: "Describe a typical week in your life. Give an account of the routine aspects as well as some of the high spots. You will have 15 minutes to write. Be sure to fill two pages."

As previously described in the section dealing with back awareness in men, a content analysis of such descriptions, involving a range of categories, can be made with adequate objectivity. One of the categories concerns cleaning activities. It includes any references to washing or cleansing one's body, clothes, or other possessions (e.g., "I polish my car," "I take my clothes to the laundry," "I clean my room"). The number of cleaning references in a subject's description is expressed as a percentage of the total number of references to activities embraced by the entire range of six scoring categories used (e.g., eating, work, sports). In the present sample the median percent of cleaning references was 5 (range 0–20). When the dichotomized (at median) cleaning reference percents were related by means of chi square to the trichotomized (as equal thirds as possible) BFQ Back scores, a significant positive relationship was observed ($\chi^2 = 9.8$, df $= 2$, $p < .01$). The more vivid a woman's back awareness the greater the amount of energy she apparently devotes to keeping herself and her surroundings clean.

Memory for Words with Anal Significance

Selective memory for words with anal significance was also used to examine the relationship of back awareness to attitudes toward anal stimuli. It was considered that if back awareness is linked with specific anal attitudes it should be possible to show that BFQ Back is significantly related to selective memory for words with anal connotations. Fifty-six female college students were studied. They were seen in small groups of five or six. Selective memory for anal words was measured by exposing on a screen for one minute a list of words comprising ten with anal and ten with non-anal connotations; and subsequently giving subjects five minutes to write down as many as they could recall. A score was derived equal to the number of anal minus non-anal words remembered. The actual list used was as follows:

Seat *	Poem
Climb	Gas *
Smell *	Think
Decide	Regular *
Back *	Magical
Simple	Bottom *
Strain *	Radio
Retain *	Expel *
Sign	Wood
Bet	Rear *

* Anal words

As was true when this list was applied to the study of back awareness in men, no prediction was made concerning the direction of selectivity because previous work (e.g., Rosenwald, et al., 1966) indicated that anal concerns may have variable effects upon efficiency in manipulating words with anal meaning.

In the present sample the mean anal minus non-anal word score was .9 which is similar to that previously found in men. The BFQ Back scores were correlated at a borderline level (.23, $p < .10$) with the anal word selective memory scores. The greater the woman's back awareness the larger was the predominance of anal words she recalled. This same pattern was observed when BFQ Back and anal memory scores were correlated in a male sample. In both instances increasing back awareness seemed to be associated with a facilitation of recall for anal references.

EFFECT OF FRONT-BACK STIMULATION UPON MEMORY FOR DIRT WORDS

As suggested in a number of previous chapters, one of the more definitive tests of the link between awareness of a specific body sector and concern with a particular problem or issue is the demonstration that altering awareness of the sector selectively affects response to stimuli pertinent to the presumably associated issue. It was earlier shown that in male subjects the selective recall for words with dirt themes may be differentially influenced as a function of whether the front or back of the subject's body is stimulated during the learning process. Back stimulation resulted in recall of a greater proportion of dirt words than did front stimulation.

Analogously, it was anticipated that if front versus back awareness in women plays a role in response to dirt stimuli, it should be possible to influence selective learning of dirt words by stimulating front and back body sites. No specific directional hypotheses were made. It was simply proposed that front and back stimulation would have opposite effects upon memory referring to dirt themes.[2]

The following list presenting ten dirt and ten non-dirt words, developed for an earlier study, was employed to evaluate selective memory effects. (The dirt words are marked with an asterisk.)

Line	Brick
Neat *	Dirt *
For	Smear *
Odor *	Plant
Dealt	Mess *
Mud *	High
Inch	Clean *
Foul *	Print
Trip	Putrid *
Impure *	Table

The mean length of the two sets of words is equal and they are spaced equivalently through the list.

The subject was asked to learn and recall this list under one of three conditions. In one condition she was told that she was to participate in a study of the effect of distraction upon learning. A vibrator (Oster Massaget, Model 212) was strapped on top of a piece of sponge material to her back and turned on for one minute so that she could "get used to the vibration." The list of words, typed on a sheet of paper, was then presented to her and she was asked to learn it. After one minute the list was removed and she was given five minutes to write down all of the words she could recall.

The second experimental condition was exactly the same except that the vibrator was strapped to the left forearm and the subject placed her hand in a comfortable position with the palm down. In this position the vibrator produced a vibration which was distinctly experienced as involving the entire front of the body.

A third experimental condition duplicated the same procedure except

---

[2] Without real reason, the idea was initially favored that back stimulation would enhance and front stimulation would inhibit recall of dirt words. But a series of studies subsequently pointed up the difficulty of predicting the specific directionality of peripheral stimulation effects.

that the learning task was presented without a vibrator being attached to the subject's body.

The recall of each subject was scored by subtracting the sum of non-dirt words recalled from the sum of dirt words recalled.

Twenty-one women served as subjects for the front vibration condition; and there were also 21 for the back vibration condition. The subjects for the neutral condition comprised 57 women. The same male experimenter obtained the data for the front and back conditions, but a different male experimenter obtained it for the neutral condition. All of the subjects were female college students.

The mean dirt–non-dirt recall score for the front vibration condition was +.1; and for the back vibration condition it was +2.3. For the neutral condition the mean was +1.7. Back vibration resulted in greatest selective superiority in recall for dirt words. Front vibration produced the greatest selective deficit in recall for dirt words; and the neutral condition gave results in between the front and back extremes.

Analysis of variance indicated that the three conditions differed significantly from each other ($F = 5.6, p < .05$). In addition, the back versus front difference was significant ($F = 10.0, p < .01$); and the front versus neutral difference was significant ($F = 7.7, p < .01$). The back versus neutral condition difference was not significant.

The total number of words recalled for the front vibration condition was 11.9; and for the back vibration condition 12.4; and for the neutral condition 12.3. None of these values differ from each other significantly.

The results of the studies did indicate that peripheral stimulation of front versus back body sites had different effects upon the selective learning of dirt words.

If one considers these results in conjunction with those already cited which show that back awareness in women is related to memory for anal words, amount of energy devoted to keeping one's environs clean, and number of references to dirt themes in a spontaneous expressive situation, they form a convincing aggregate. They justify stating that back awareness in women is related to attitudes about dirt and, by implication, anal matters. Women display a particularized response to dirt and anal themes which goes along with the amount of attention they direct to the back.

NEGATIVISM

In trying to understand what other aspects of the anal character complex are relevant to back awareness in women, the original finding cited earlier concerning the positive correlation between BFQ Back and Negativism was further considered. While negativism did not turn out to be one of the anal character traits linked with back awareness in men, there did seem to be such a possibility in the case of women. In two female samples earlier cited BFQ Back was positively correlated with the Buss-Durkee Negativism score.

To consider this issue from another perspective, a project was initiated in which negativisitic behavior, as judged by raters well acquainted with each other, was related to back awareness. Forty members of a college sorority who had known each other for at least a year were paid a fee to participate in a study in which they responded to several tests, including the BFQ, and also rated each other (on a 5-point scale) with respect to 12 traits listed below:

Neatness	Sympathy
Aggression	How Comfortable with Women
Stubbornness	Self-control
Generosity	Fear of Being Hurt
Ambition	Suspiciousness
Exhibitionism	How Comfortable with Men

They were seen in one large group session. The rating category dealing with stubbornness was intended to be synonymous with negativism. The other rating categories were included on a purely exploratory basis to determine if they might be associated with back awareness. It was particularly anticipated, in terms of the anal character typology, that Neatness, Suspiciousness, and Generosity might be related to back awareness. For each subject, a score was computed for each trait which was the average of the 39 ratings made by others.

The mean Stubbornness rating was 3.2 ($\sigma = .5$), indicating a judgment that the amount of stubbornness was about average. BFQ Back was correlated .18 with the Stubbornness variable. However, because the distribution of Stubbornness ratings was quite skewed a chi-square analysis was undertaken which indicated a significant positive relationship ($\chi^2 = 3.8$, df $= 1$, $p < .03$, one-tail test). The greater the individual's back awareness the more stubborn she was judged to be by the other members of her sorority. This result was, of course, congruent with the previously observed positive relationship between BFQ Back and Buss-Durkee Negativism. It is pertinent that BFQ Back was not related to a form of more directly expressed hostility represented by the rating category Aggression. The only other significant findings to emerge were a negative correlation ($-.35$, p .025) between BFQ Back and Generosity and a negative correlation ($-.33$, $p < .05$) between BFQ Back and Sympathy. That is, the greater the individual's back awareness the less generous and less sympathetic she was perceived to be by her peers. The finding with regard to Generosity was particularly noteworthy because stinginess and frugality have been described by Freud as characteristic of the anal character. As will be seen, this lead was followed up in another study.

Although magnitude of the relationship between back awareness and rated stubbornness was not impressive, it does represent a third consistent instance of significant findings in this area.

FRUGALITY

An attempt was made to look further at the above cited observation that rated degree of Generosity was inverse to BFQ Back. An 8-item Frugality scale developed by Barnes (as cited by Schlesinger, 1963) was used to measure the general dimension of behavior related to generosity, willingness to give, and frugality. Some of the items included in the scale (answered as True or False) were as follows:

You hate to discard your old clothing.
You readily lend your things to others.
You accumulate a great many things because you rarely throw anything away.

It was expected that the greater a woman's back awareness the more frugal would be her orientation.

A sample of 43 college women were seen in small groups. They responded to the BFQ and the Frugality scale. The mean Frugality score in the sample was 5.4 ($\sigma = 1.7$); and it proved to be correlated .34 ($p < .025$, one-tail test) with BFQ Back. The hypothesis was supported that Frugality is positively related to degree of back awareness.

OVERVIEW

The accumulating evidence argues persuasively that back awareness in women is somehow a function of attitudes concerned with anal functions [3] and a derivative of the kind of defense system which Freud referred to in his discussion of the anal character. One finds that the greater the amount of attention a woman focuses on her back the more likely she is to manifest special sensitivity to dirt and anal stimuli; to be inclined to behave in a negativistic or stubborn fashion; and to be characterized by stingy or frugal attitudes. She does not, as might be anticipated by the anal character model and also the results obtained for men, display special attributes related to homosexual conflicts or anxiety with reference to possible loss of self-control. It is not clear why different aspects of the anal character cluster are related to back awareness in women as compared to men. This may be due to

---

[3] BFQ Back was not correlated consistently with any of the clusters of variables which are related to other major BFQ dimensions.

differences in the traits and defenses elicited by anal conflicts in men and women. The psychoanalytic literature is not very explicit about such possible differences, but observers have periodically remarked that they might be expected in view of the obvious divergent socialization patterns for males and females in our culture. Perhaps anal conflicts in men elicit defenses primarily related to self-control and homosexual anxiety; whereas in women they are expressed via the kinds of mechanisms implied in stubbornness and frugality.

25

Right-Left Awareness in Women and Identification with Others

INTRODUCTION

The tendency to focus more attention on the right than the left side of one's body was found to occur in men who had an unusual amount of anxiety about heterosexual stimuli and who avoided heterosexual interaction. It was this finding which provided the initial paradigm for investigating the significance of variations in right-left awareness in women.

Before describing the work concerned with the meaning of right-left awareness in woman, a few words should be said concerning the measurement scale employed. The same 15-item BFQ Right scale described for men was used in the evaluation of women. The test-retest reliability (one week intervening) in one sample (N = 49) of college women was found to be .60;[1] and in a similar sample (N = 40) under equivalent conditions it was .44. These test-retest values are certainly low. They are difficult to explain because the test-retest coefficients for men with the identical scale were a good deal higher. As will be discussed at a later point, it is possible that women have less consistent modes of distributing attention to their bodies than men; and this might account for their relative lack of judgmental consistency concerning focal body experiences over time.

In ten female samples (average N = 50) BFQ Right was significantly correlated seven times with BFQ Heart (.43, .28, .29, .36, .29, .28, .36), five times with BFQ Stomach (.39, .27, .28, .29, .38), and five times with BFQ Mouth (.42, .44, .46, .35, .34). As will be seen, the rather consistent correlations with BFQ Heart mirror the fact that the two dimensions overlap in their attitudinal implications. Such similarity in the significance of right and heart awareness was not observed for men.

---

[1] All correlations are product-moment unless otherwise stated.

Table 25.1
Means and Standard Deviations of BFQ Right Scores

M	σ	N
7.6	3.5	47
8.4	3.1	51
9.4	3.7	54
8.4	3.3	48
9.8	3.3	50
8.5	3.6	50
7.9	3.6	40
7.5	3.9	55
9.2	2.7	52
9.3	3.3	49

BFQ Right values in a variety of female college student samples have clustered about 8.6, which is slightly smaller than that found for males. Score distributions have generally been normal in character.

BFQ Right has shown itself to be unrelated to measures of response set (e.g., MMPI K and L scales, Marlowe-Crowne Social Desirability scale [1964]) in several female samples.[2]

The generality of the BFQ approach to measuring right-left awareness was evaluated by correlating BFQ Right with an index based on the relative density of sensations from the right and left sides of one's body. Two samples of college women (N = 51, N = 40) were studied. They were seen in small groups. BFQ measures were taken and subsequently they were asked to report for a five-minute period each time they experienced a distinct sensation at any of four sites: right side of face, left side of face, right side of body, left side of body. These sites were listed on a sheet of paper and the subject placed a check beneath the appropriate heading each time that a sensation was experienced. A score was computed which equalled the sum of the right-side sensations minus the sum of the left-side sensations. In sample 1 this score was correlated .40 ($p < .01$) with BFQ Right and in sample 2 it was correlated .43 ($p < .01$). The greater the relative density of sensations on the right side the larger was the BFQ Right score.

HETEROSEXUAL VARIABLES

As stated above, the first strategy in trying to understand the significance of right awareness in women was to ascertain whether it was linked with heterosexual attitudes and behavior in the same fashion that characterized men.

[2] BFQ Right has not been consistently correlated with the Barrier score.

This involved a study of 53 female college students. Several procedures were used to evaluate heterosexual orientation. One pertained to apparent degree of heterosexual interest, as measured with the Heterosexual scale of the Edwards Preference Schedule (1954). The tenor of the Heterosexual scale may be illustrated by noting that it inquires concerning such matters as the individual's interest in going out with members of the opposite sex, kissing those of the opposite sex, and reading books with sexual themes. Another procedure requested subjects to respond to a brief questionnaire which inquired concerning frequency of dating in high school and college and number of serious relationships (viz., "going steady" and being engaged). Further, subjects were asked to write down "20 things you are conscious of or aware of"; and these statements were analyzed for the number of explicit references to themes with sexual significance (e.g., "I had a date last night," "My boyfriend kissed me"). Other tests were administered which were not pertinent to right-left differentiation.

It was found that BFQ Right and Heterosexuality had only a chance relationship. However, BFQ Right [3] proved to be positively correlated with the Edwards Deference ($r = .29$, $p < .05$) and Intraception ($r = .31$, $p .025$) scales and negatively so with Achievement ($r = -.30$, $p < .05$), Autonomy ($r = -.28$, $p < .05$), and Aggression ($r = -.27$, $p < .05$). BFQ Right had only chance correlations with the reports of previous dating behavior [4] and also number of sexual references in a free expressive situation.

The pattern of the findings involving the Edwards scales suggested that those with high right awareness were inclined to be non-aggressive, non-forceful and to be especially interested in understanding and identifying with others. This last attribute seemed to be indicated by the fact that the highest correlation found was between BFQ Right and Intraception ($r = .31$). The Intraception scale inquires concerning the individual's investment in observing others, understanding how others feel about problems, putting oneself in another's place, analyzing the motives of others, and predicting how others will act.

INTRACEPTION

To check the stability of these findings a new study was undertaken in which the BFQ and the Edwards Preference Schedule were administered to a

---

[3] Mean BFQ Right values will be given only for major studies or in instances in which they are atypical.

[4] The fact that BFQ Right has chance relationships with self reported dating behavior has been substantiated in several different samples.

The Allport-Vernon-Lindzey study of values (1960) was also administered, but the results will be described at a later point.

sample of 49 college women who were seen in small groups. Once again BFQ Right proved to be positively and significantly correlated ($r = .33$, p .025) with Intraception. However, it was not related to any of the other scales with which it had been significantly correlated in the previous study.

To obtain further corroboration of this finding, the BFQ and the Edwards Preference Schedule were administered to a new sample of college women ($N = 59$) who were seen in small groups. Once again, BFQ Right and Intraception were positively correlated ($r = .19$, $p > .10$), but not significantly so. In two of three studies, then, right awareness and self reported degree of intraception were positively correlated. The high right aware woman seems to be interested in "getting inside" of others and trying to experience the world as they do. In some ways this is reminiscent of the fact that men with high right awareness were low in narcissism. However, in the studies concerned with right awareness in men only the Heterosexuality scale of the Edwards Preference Schedule was related (negatively) to BFQ Right. The relationship involving the Intraception scale was observed to be entirely of a chance order. While the high right aware male was low in narcissism, he did not seem to be particularly motivated to identify with or "get inside of" others (as defined by the Edwards' Intraception score). But it is just this attitude that the Intraception findings seem to suggest with regard to women.

A question that logically arises is whether the intraceptive orientation of the high right aware woman also manifests itself in a desire to play roles which involve sympathetic identification with others and offer the opportunity to behave in ways which maximize possibilities for psychological closeness. This would be exemplified at one level in roles focused upon serving, helping, and understanding others. A negative answer to the question would seem to be in order if one reviews the correlations of BFQ Right with the Edwards Nurturance scale, which was designed to measure interest in such activities as helping friends when they are in trouble, assisting others less fortunate, forgiving others, and showing a great deal of affection toward others. In three different studies BFQ Right was not significantly correlated with Nurturance. However, despite these findings, it was decided to evaluate the relation of BFQ Right to motivation for playing a sympathetic, helping role as defined by formal interest measures. Most interest scales contain a dimension or category defining roles in which one is sympathetic to and helps others (e.g., social worker, counselor, Red Cross worker). A measure of the strength of interest in this type of activity is one which might be expected to be positively correlated with right awareness in women. Two studies were carried out to test this view. In one instance the BFQ and the Kuder (1956) Vocational Preference Record were administered individually to a sample of 56 college women. The Kuder contains nine categories (e.g., Mechanical, Artistic) besides the one (viz., Social Service) considered pertinent to the hypothesis. It was found that BFQ Right was positively correlated ($r = .32, p < .025$) with the Social Service score. Incidentally, it also had a negative correlation with the Literary score ($r = -.30, p .025$) and a positive one with the Musical score ($r = .29, p < .05$). In a second study the BFQ and the Thurstone (1947) Interest Schedule were administered individually to a sample of 51 college women; and it was predicted that BFQ would be positively related to the score indicating amount of interest in Humanitarian occupations. As expected, BFQ Right was positively correlated with the Humanitarian score ($r = .25, p < .05$, one-tail test). A one-tail test was considered justified because this represented an attempt to cross-validate the results obtained with the Kuder Social Service measure. BFQ Right was not significantly related to any of the other Thurstone scores (e.g., Physical Science, Musical, Artistic, Literary).

Two samples were also studied in which BFQ Right was related to the Social score of the Allport-Vernon-Lindzey Study of Values (1960). This score is presumed to measure how much one loves people. It is said to reflect the degree to which an individual's orientation is kind, sympathetic, and unselfish. One would therefore expect that degree of right awareness would be positively correlated with the Social score. The BFQ and the Study of Values were administered on a group basis to two samples of college women ($N = 51, N = 39$). In the first sample BFQ Right was positively correlated with Social ($r = .25, p < .05$, one-tail test), and in the second the correlation was also positive ($.23, p > .10$, one-tail test). No consistent correlations were observed between BFQ Right and any of the other Study of Values scores. While the results involving right awareness and the Social score were of borderline significance, they were consistently in the predicted direction. One may cautiously say that the greater the subject's awareness of the right side of her body the more likely she is to be portrayed as unselfish and sympathetic by the Social score. It is puzzling why right awareness was correlated with a sympathetic "I want to help others" orientation, as defined by the Study of Values Social index and the formal interest measures, but not with such an orientation as measured by the Edwards Nurturance score. Perhaps the difference is a function of the fact that the Nurturance scale includes, among others, behaviors related to displaying affection, which is not a prime component of the Humanitarian, Social Service, and Social dimensions.

If one considers the findings from the interest and value tests in conjunction with those pertaining to Intraception, it would appear that a woman's degree of right awareness is, in fact, linked with how invested she professes to be in understanding and sympathizing and identifying with others.

Another approach to this matter was undertaken by means of the Sociable scale of the Thurstone Temperament Schedule. This self report scale ascertains the degree to which an individual enjoys the company of others, makes friends easily, and is sympathetic and cooperative in his relations with others. Presumably, the special social orientation which has been ascribed to the woman with high right awareness should evidence itself in elevated Sociable scores. Three samples of college women (N = 60, N = 50, N = 34) were studied. BFQ Right was correlated .25 (p .05), .31 ($p < $.05), and .19 ($p > $.20) respectively with Sociable in the three samples. All the correlations were positive and two were significant. No consistent relationships with the other Thurstone Temperament Schedule variables were noted. The findings with respect to the Sociable scores were in the direction anticipated.

An opportunity to look at the relationship of right awareness to social attitudes in terms of overt behavior, as observed by peers, was provided in a study, already cited earlier, in which 40 college sorority girls were asked to rate (5-point scale) each other for the following 12 characteristics: Neatness, Aggression, Stubbornness, Generosity, Ambition, Sympathy, How Comfortable with Women, How Comfortable with Men, Self-control, Fear of Being Hurt, Suspiciousness, Showing Off. Five of these characteristics were considered to be pertinent to the right awareness dimension. It was expected that right awareness would be positively correlated with Generosity and Sympathy and negatively related to Stubbornness and Suspiciousness. The possibility was also weakly entertained that right awareness might be negatively related to Aggressiveness. The rationale for anticipating a positive relationship with Generosity and Sympathy is obvious in terms of the intraception and "serving others" concept. The predictions about Stubbornness, Suspiciousness, and Aggressiveness were more indirect, but were based on the reasoning that an intraceptive "I want to identify with others" orientation involves a sense of trust in people and a desire to relate congruently rather than in an oppositional manner. Analysis of the data indicated borderline positive relationships between BFQ Right and Generosity ($\chi^2 = 3.0$, df = 1, $p < $.10) and Sympathy ($\chi^2 = 3.2$, df = 1, $p < $.10). Negative relationships were observed between BFQ Right and Stubbornness ($\chi^2 = 4.0$, df = 1, $p < $.05) and Suspiciousness ($\chi^2 = 6.9$, df = 1, $p < $.01). The relationship between BFQ Right and Aggression was not significant; and this was also true of the relationship of BFQ Right with all of the other rating variables. Generally, the pattern of results was similar to that predicted. Especially good confirmation was obtained that those with high right awareness would not be stubborn toward, or suspicious of, others. It is true that only borderline support was found with respect to the predictions for the traits of Generosity and Sympathy; whereas the intraception formulation would lead one to expect strongest support in this area.

The Kuethe social schemata method (Kuethe, 1962) provided an opportunity to consider whether right awareness was related to an indirect measure of attitudes about social closeness. This technique is based upon asking subjects to place miniature cut-out felt cloth representations of human figures upon an unstructured felt background. The subject places the figures in any way that he prefers. Measurement is taken of the distance between the figures. It has been shown that the greater the interest in, and motivation for, certain types of interactions the more closely are figures, representative of such interactions, likely to be placed near each other. Data have accumulated in the literature which suggest that persons who have difficulties in their social relationships tend to place various human representations further apart than do those without such difficulties. In view of the apparent link between right awareness and motivation to be close to others, one would expect BFQ Right to be negatively correlated with the distance between human figure placements. To test this hypothesis a sample of 31 college women were individually studied. They were asked to place each of five sets of figures upon a felt background (12 × 24 inches). The sets were as follows:

1. An adult male and adult female figure.
2. Two adult males.
3. Two adult females.
4. Woman and child.
5. Man and child.

The adults were approximately 8 inches in height and the children 4 inches. A total score was computed which equaled the average of the distances between the two figures in each set. The mean distance in the sample was 1.9 inches. A chi-square analysis (used because of the skewed Kuethe distribution) indicated a chance relationship between BFQ Right and the mean distance between the figures. This was, of course, not supportive of the hypothesis.

EFFECT OF RIGHT–LEFT PERIPHERAL STIMULATION UPON SELECTIVE LEARNING OF CLOSENESS–DISTANCE WORDS

If intraceptive attitudes are related to a woman's relative awareness of her right and left body sides, it should be possible to alter them by changing the sensory prominence of the two sides. This assumption derives from the now frequently enunciated theory that selective attitudes and the body areas with which they are linked are part of an organized system in which they mutually affect each other. This theory regards degree of awareness of a body area as having the capability of exciting or inhibiting a specific attitude toward the world; and, in turn, proposes that variations in such an attitude may find representation in alterations of awareness of the body area in question.

With this perspective, an experiment was designed in which the effects of right versus left sensory stimulation upon memory for words considered to be relevant to an intraceptive orientation could be evaluated. It was difficult to derive logically a series of words which would be pertinent to intraception. However, the idea presented itself that an intraceptive attitude is one which involves understanding and identifying with others; and in that sense may be defined in terms of getting close (at least psychologically) to them. Presumably, the more intraceptive one's attitude the more interested one would be in closeness. Therefore, a list of words was assembled which included ten referring to states of closeness and ten referring to states of distance.

The list was as follows:

Near *	Distant
Leave	Arrive *
By *	Contact *
Out	Apart
Approach *	Neighbor *
Touch *	Foreign
Far	Adjacent *
Unite *	Absent
Stranger	Depart
Away	Close *

[Closeness words are starred]

Closeness and distance words were of equal average length and spaced equivalently throughout the list.

Learning of the list occurred under three conditions. In one instance each individual was told that she would memorize a number of words while experiencing an interfering distraction. A vibrator (Oster Massaget, Model 212) was strapped to the subject's right arm and she was told to "get used to the vibration" for one minute. Then, with the vibrator still operating, she was asked to learn the list of words which was presented on a typed sheet for one minute; and finally, when the list was removed, she was given five minutes to report as many of the words as she could recall. A second experimental condition duplicated the first in all respects except that the vibrator was placed on the left arm instead of the right. For the third experimental condition the list was learned without a vibrator attached to the subject's body.

A score was computed for each subject equal to the number of closeness words minus distance words recalled.

It has not been possible in experiments directed at changing attitudes by altering body awareness landmarks to specify the direction of the changes which will be produced. In the present instance the only prediction made was that right and left vibration would result in opposite effects upon selective memory.

The right-arm vibration, left-arm vibration, and neutral condition samples consisted respectively of 18, 17 and 31 female college students.

The mean closeness minus non-closeness scores were +.72 for the right-vibration condition; —.94 for the left-vibration condition; and +.84 for the neutral procedure.

Analysis of variance indicated that the three conditions were significantly different (F = 4.9, p < .05). The right versus left difference was also of significant magnitude (F = 6.2, p < .01); and that between left and neutral was significant (F = 8.9, p < .01). The difference between right and neutral was not significant.

Differences in total numbers of words learned under the three conditions were not significant.

The results indicated that right and left vibration had opposite effects upon selective memory for closeness versus distance words. Right vibration was accompanied by a tendency to recall more closeness than distance words. Left vibration resulted in the recall of more distance than closeness words. However, one needs to consider that the right vibration and neutral conditions did not differ; whereas the left vibration and neutral conditions were significantly unlike. This indicates that the primary effect of the vibration occurred when it was applied to the left body site.

Once again support was obtained for the proposition that cognitive attitudes may be altered by stimulating focal body sites. Also, the findings support the view, derived from various other kinds of data, that the right-left body awareness dimension in women is tied in with intraceptive (closeness-distance) attitudes.

OVERVIEW

There is the usual temptation to speculate about the reason for the association between the right-left awareness dimension and an intraceptive orientation [5] in women. Why should high right awareness be accompanied by investment in understanding and identifying with others? One possibility that comes to mind derives from an earlier suggested view that since the right hand is stronger than the left (in right-handed persons) it becomes associated with power and strength. Generalizing from this fact, the entire right side of the body may be associated with force, power, and self-assertion;[6] while the left, because of its lesser strength, may take on softer, non-power oriented signifi-

---

[5] BFQ Right was not consistently correlated, with one exception, with the clusters of variables related to other BFQ dimensions. The one exception involved BFQ Heart; and this will be explained in Chapter 27.

[6] The association of right and left with power connotations had been demonstrated in one study by Fisher (1961A) in which achievement motivation was correlated with right versus left bias in perception of the directionality of autokinetic movement. Relatedly, Fisher (1965D) found that the ratio of male versus female names assigned by men to puppets placed on their right and left hands was related to their apparent need to feel superior to women.

cance. If this were so, one could regard the increased right awareness of the intraceptive woman as a way of ensuring control of the forceful side of herself. Perhaps she focuses upon the right side to be sure that its assertiveness is properly inhibited. This might be necessary to her style of relating which is based on softness and identifying with others in an accommodating fashion. Whether this view has any validity remains to be seen. One of its defects is that while the right-left differentiation between that which is strong and less strong logically relates to an assertive versus non-assertive mode of response, it does not touch on the specific quality of intraception and sympathy which distinguishes degree of right versus left awareness in women.

26
Eye Awareness in Women

When the 11-item Eye awareness scale of the BFQ was applied to women, it was discovered to have very inadequate test-retest reliability. In one sample of college women (N = 49) the reliability coefficient, with seven days intervening between test and retest, was .29 ($p < .05$); and in a second sample of women (N = 40) the coefficient, with seven days again intervening, was .38 ($p < .01$). These values indicate little consistency in how aware women are of their eyes.

Despite the low test-retest reliabilities obtained, attempts were made to ascertain if eye awareness in women was related to anxiety about incorporation in the same fashion as had been observed in men. It will be recalled that the greater a man's awareness of his eyes the greater his apparent anxiety about references to eating and other representations of incorporation. To determine whether a similar pattern applied to women, a study was done with a female sample (N = 51) in which BFQ Eyes was related to two measures concerned with incorporation: Byrne's Food Attitude Scale (Byrne, et al., 1963) and memory for food versus non-food words. The results indicated chance relationships between amount of eye awareness and these two measures.

The extremely low test-retest reliability for the BFQ Eye scale suggests that women do not integrate their eyes into their body concept in the same stable fashion that men do. While searching for clues regarding this difference, it was discovered that women obtain significantly higher BFQ Eye scores than do men. In ten different female samples the mean BFQ Eyes score was 7.8 ($\sigma = 2.4$). For men the average score for ten samples was 7.1 ($\sigma = 2.6$). The difference, as indicated by a t-test, was significant at the .001 level. That is, women tend to be more aware of their eyes than are men. There may be some cultural or socialization factor which intensifies eye awareness in women generally. The eyes are, of course, assigned great importance in determining a woman's attractiveness—as testified by the elaborate procedures that have been devised for beautifying the eye. The eyes may be so completely monopolized as a *standard* beauty representation in the body scheme of the woman that she has difficulty in consistently projecting individualized wishes and fantasies upon them.

27
Heart Awareness in Women and Sociability

INTRODUCTION

It was noted in the chapter dealing with right awareness in women, that BFQ Right was rather consistently positively correlated with degree of heart awareness. In seven of ten samples (average N = 50) significant coefficients [1] were obtained (.43, .28, .29, .36, .29, .28, .36). Most were in the high .20's and the .30's. It was the consistency of these small correlations which suggested that BFQ Heart might be linked with parameters similar to those related to BFQ Right.

Heart awareness was measured with the same 15-item scale used to evaluate heart awareness in men. The test-retest reliability (one week inter-

Table 27.1
Means and Standard Deviations for BFQ Heart

M	σ	N
6.9	5.0	47
4.2	3.1	51
5.4	4.0	54
4.2	3.6	48
5.7	3.8	50
4.2	3.2	50
5.1	3.9	40
6.0	4.6	55
3.5	3.9	52
3.6	3.8	49

[1] All correlations are product-moment unless otherwise stated.

vening) in one sample of college women (N = 49) was .75; and in a similar sample (N = 40) under equivalent conditions it was .65. These are the highest reliability values observed for women for any BFQ variables.

The mean values obtained in a number of female college student samples have averaged 4.9, indicating very low awareness of one's heart as compared to other body areas. Distributions of BFQ Heart have been normal in character. Incidentally, the mean BFQ Heart score for women tends to be lower than that found in male samples, but not significantly so.

No consistent correlations have been detected in several female samples between BFQ Heart and the MMPI K and L scales or the Marlowe-Crowne Social Desirability scale (1964).[2] That is, BFQ Heart scores do not seem to reflect the influence of social desirability response sets.

BFQ Heart was found in ten different samples (average N = 50) to be rather consistently and negatively related to BFQ Back (−.42, −.27, −.31, −.41, −.40, −.36, −.30). These seven coefficients were significant *at least* at the .05 level and four at the .01 level or better. But only three of the correlations were as high as .40. BFQ Heart was not significantly correlated with any other BFQ variables except BFQ Right (already described).

EXPLORATORY WORK

Since heart awareness was correlated with fair consistency with both back and right awareness, an appraisal was made of the relationship of BFQ Heart to the variables which were originally observed to be linked with BFQ Back and BFQ Right.

It was found that the relationships of BFQ Heart to the various anal measures associated with BFQ Back were of an entirely chance order.

Contrastingly, some interesting leads emerged when BFQ Heart was correlated with a series of variables which had been observed to be pertinent to right awareness.

Since BFQ Right was originally found to be linked with an intraceptive attitude (identifying with others), primarily as measured by the Intraception scale of the Edwards (1954) Preference Schedule, this was the first possible correlate of BFQ Heart that was examined.[3]

It was found in a sample of 53 college women that BFQ Heart was correlated only .23 ($p < .10$) with the Edwards Intraception scale. Also, it

---

[2] BFQ Heart has not shown consistent correlations with the Barrier score.

[3] Because BFQ Heart was related to religiosity in male samples, various indices of religious interest (e.g., frequency of church attendance, Allport-Vernon-Lindzey [1960] Study of Values Religious scores) were examined with reference to heart awareness in female samples. No consistent relationship could be detected.

did not correlate significantly with any of the other Edwards scores. In second (N = 49) and third (N = 59) samples of college women BFQ Heart was observed again not to be significantly related to any of the Edwards scores. It is also true that BFQ Heart was not related in other samples to the Humanitarian score of the Thurstone (1947) Interest Schedule or the Social Service score of the Kuder (1956) Preference Schedule—although both of these scores had shown themselves to be correlated with BFQ Right.

SOCIAL VALUES, SOCIABILITY, AND CLOSENESS

Since the Social score of the Allport-Vernon-Lindzey (1960) Study of Values was originally found to be positively correlated with right awareness, BFQ Heart was also related to this measure. When this was done, the first positive finding appeared. Two samples of college women were studied. In one sample (N = 51) a chi-square of 2.8 ($p < .10$, df = 1) was found, indicating that the greater the heart awareness the more were Social values endorsed. In a second sample (N = 39), chi-square revealed an even more significant positive relationship between BFQ Heart and Social scores ($\chi^2 = 7.1$, df = 1, $p < .01$). These two findings affirmed that the more vivid a woman's awareness of her heart the more likely she was to adhere to values which emphasize love of others. BFQ Heart was not consistently related to any of the other Study of Values scores, besides Social.

It was possible to look at this matter from another perspective in terms of data based on the Sociable scale of the Thurstone (1953) Temperament Scale. The Sociable scale defines how much one enjoys interacting socially with others. Persons with high Sociable scores state that they enjoy the company of others, make friends easily, and are agreeable in their relations with others.

Three samples of college women (N = 60, N = 50, N = 34) had been secured in which degree of heart awareness could be correlated with Sociable scores. The mean Sociable scores were respectively 12.4 ($\sigma = 3.7$), 13.0 ($\sigma = 3.9$), and 11.9 ($\sigma = 3.3$). BFQ Heart correlated .31 ($p < .025$), .23 ($p > .10$), and .30 ($p < .10$) respectively with the three sets of Sociable scores. All of the correlations were positive, as expected. One was statistically significant; one fell at a borderline level; and one attained the $< .10$ level. It may be said that the data weakly indicated a trend, such that the greater an individual's heart awareness the more she was interested in interacting socially with others.

A channel for looking at the relationship of BFQ Heart to overt behavior which is pertinent to liking people and being interested in social interaction was supplied by the previously described study in which members of a sorority (N = 40) rated each other for 12 characteristics: Neatness, Aggression, Stubbornness, Generosity, Ambition, Sympathy, How Comfortable with Women, How Comfortable with Men, Self-control, Fear of Being Hurt, Suspiciousness, Showing Off. It was conjectured that heart awareness should be positively correlated with Generosity, Sympathy and negatively related to Stubbornness, Suspiciousness, and Aggression. BFQ Heart was found to be positively related to Generosity ($r = .31$, $p < .05$) and Sympathy ($r = .28$, $p < .10$); although in the later instance the coefficient was of borderline significance. Two of the three negative relationships expected with reference to BFQ Heart were indeed negative (viz., $-.17$ with Stubbornness, and $-.13$ with Suspiciousness); but none were significant. In general, the data seemed to indicate that the greater the subject's heart awareness the more she was perceived by her sorority peers as generous and sympathetic. Incidentally, BFQ Heart was not correlated with any of the other trait variables which had been rated.

The Kuethe (1962) social schemata technique was used as an indirect means for ascertaining whether heart awareness and attitudes about social closeness are interrelated. As already stated, this technique is based upon the schemata constructed by subjects when asked to place figures with social meaning (e.g., person representations) upon an unstructured felt cloth background. Kuethe and others have shown that the greater the distance placed between figures the less interest there is in the type of interaction exemplified by those figures. Some evidence exists that persons who tend to be socially withdrawn place a variety of human figures in the Kuethe settings so that they are unusually far apart. In the present study the subjects (31 college women) were individually asked to place five different sets of figures (adult male and female, two adult males, two adult females, woman and child, man and child) upon the background. The average distance between the two figures in each set was computed. The mean of these values was 1.9 inches. When the social distance scores were compared by means of chi-square with the BFQ Heart scores, a significant negative relationship was found ($\chi^2 = 4.1$, df = 1, $p < .05$). With greater heart awareness, there was an increasing tendency to place the human figures closer together. The schemata concerning social interaction produced by subjects with high heart awareness depicted more closeness than did those constructed by subjects with low heart awareness.

EFFECT OF INTENSIFIED HEART AWARENESS UPON SELECTIVE LEARNING OF CLOSENESS–DISTANCE WORDS

Heart awareness seemed to be related to attitudes about being close versus distant from others. With this view, an attempt was made to determine the effect of increasing heart awareness upon memory for words differing in their closeness-distance connotations. In terms of the author's theory concerning the role of peripheral body signals in modifying central attitudes, it should be possible to influence selective learning of closeness versus distance words by altering degree of heart awareness.

The same list of words was used to test this hypothesis as was used in evaluating the effects of right-left stimulation upon memory for words with differing connotations concerning states of closeness. The list is shown below.

Near *	Distant
Leave	Arrive *
By *	Contact *
Out	Apart
Approach *	Neighbor *
Touch *	Foreign
Far	Adjacent *
Unite *	Absent
Stranger	Depart
Away	Close *

[Closeness words are starred]

Closeness and distance words were of equal average length and spaced equivalently throughout the list.

A sample of female college students (N = 30) learned the list in a situation which enhanced heart awareness. In order to intensify heart awareness, they were asked to monitor and count their own heart rates for two successive one-minute periods. They were then asked to observe their hearts for another one-minute period, during which they were to record on a sheet of paper each time that they became aware of a specific sensation (e.g., thumping) in that region. Finally, they were asked to learn the list of words (one-minute exposure); but to focus awareness upon their hearts during the process and to be prepared to describe what heart sensations they had experienced. After the one-minute learning period, subjects were given five minutes to write down as many of the words as they could recall. A score was computed which equaled the number of closeness words minus distance words recalled.

Only one control condition was used. This was the neutral sample of college women (N = 31) used in Chapter 25 who learned the closeness-distance word list without any special body awareness instructions.

No prediction was made except that the selective memory score would be different for the heart awareness and the neutral conditions.

The mean heart awareness condition score was found to be +.13 ($\sigma = 1.84$) and that for the Control condition +.84 ($\sigma = 1.92$). This difference was not significant, as defined by a t test. The enhancement of heart awareness did not have a detectable effect upon selective learning of the closeness versus distance words. Therefore, one must regard the experiment as non-supportive of the view that heart awareness in women is related to attitudes concerned with social closeness and distance.

OVERVIEW

Most of the findings suggested that the greater a woman's awareness of her heart the more she is oriented to being sociable and placing value upon close, friendly interaction with others. This proposition was rather clearly supported by findings from the Social score of the Study of Values and suggestively so by the Sociable scale of the Thurstone Temperament Schedule. Peer rating data and social distance scores derived from the Kuethe social schemata technique were also consistent with the formulation. The failure to influence selective learning of closeness-distance words by enhancing heart awareness constitutes the most serious negative evidence against the formulation. It indicates the need for a cautious interpretation of the overall findings.

If firm evidence eventually emerges that heart awareness and a "social" orientation [4] are related, one will need to learn more about how the "social" orientation of the woman with high heart awareness manifests itself. Is the apparent investment in being social largely an intellectual attitude that is registered in self report questionnaires? Does it get expressed in overt behavior? For example, does it show in the number of close friends the individual has? Is it reflected in her popularity? At the other extreme, can one expect to find that the woman with low heart awareness is an isolate? Is she considered to be cold and unfriendly? Answers to such questions will require studies of overt behavior in various social settings.

It is of interest, too, that while the sociable attitudes of the high heart aware woman resemble those of the high right aware women, they lack the particular ingredient of intraception which typifies the latter. There is an apparent desire to be close to others, but the element of wanting to identify closely with ("getting inside the skin of") others is absent.

One cannot help but see at least a faint analogy between the "sociable" attitudes of the high heart aware woman and the religious investment of the high heart aware man. To be religious implies in Western culture an identification with good-intentioned, friendly modes of relating to other persons. Similarly, a sociable orientation signifies a friendly and considerate way of relating to others. In this tangential sense, then, heart awareness may be related in both sexes to a common variable. One does not know how to label this variable. Perhaps one could say that it involves behaving in a "good," "nice" fashion.

---

[4] BFQ Heart was not consistently correlated with clusters of variables related to other (with the exception of BFQ Right) BFQ dimensions.

28

Mouth and Stomach Awareness in Women and Power Orientation

As was true for men, one finds that mouth and stomach awareness have related significance in female subjects. Therefore, the work pertinent to each will be considered together in this chapter.

Table 28.1
Means and Standard Deviations of BFQ Mouth and BFQ Stomach

BFQ Mouth			BFQ Stomach		
M	σ	N	M	σ	N
6.8	2.1	47	7.8	3.2	47
7.7	1.9	51	7.5	3.3	51
7.9	1.8	54	7.1	3.9	54
7.0	2.0	48	6.3	3.4	48
6.6	2.3	50	6.3	3.2	50
7.0	2.0	50	7.5	3.5	50
7.4	2.1	40	7.6	3.9	40
7.0	2.7	55	6.8	3.1	55
7.2	2.2	52	7.3	3.4	52
8.0	2.4	49	7.5	3.9	49

Mouth awareness was measured with an 11-item scale. The average value in numerous samples of female college students was 7.3, which is not significantly different from that observed for males. Score distributions have been largely normal in character.

Test-retest values, with seven days intervening, have been found to be .46 [1] in one female sample (N = 49) and .45 in another (N = 40). These

[1] All correlations are product-moment unless otherwise stated.

values, like others already cited for women, indicate very limited stability over time.

Stomach awareness was measured with a 14-item scale. BFQ Stomach scores in multiple samples of female college students have clustered about 7.1. This value is not significantly different from that characterizing men. Score distributions have typically been normal.

Test-retest reliability, with seven days intervening, was .54 in one sample of women (N = 49) and .66 in another (N = 40). These values are low, but more reassuring than those found for BFQ Mouth.

BFQ Mouth shows a tendency toward a positive relationship with BFQ Stomach. In ten different samples (average N = 50) it was positively correlated with BFQ Stomach five times (.25, $p < .10$, .41, $p < .01$, .24, $p < .10$, .23, p .10, .26, $p < .10$). It also showed a definite trend to be positively related to BFQ Head, with five of ten correlations attaining significance (.32, .36, .40, .25, .41). Further, it was positively and significantly related to BFQ Right five times (.42, .44, .46, .35, .34).

As for BFQ Stomach, aside from its relationships with BFQ Mouth, it was also correlated with BFQ Right. In ten different samples (average N = 50) it was positively correlated with BFQ Right five times (.39, .27, .28, .29, .38). Despite the fact that BFQ Stomach and also BFQ Mouth were apparently more clearly correlated with BFQ Right than with each other, their meanings, as defined by correlations with other classes of variables, turned out to be closer to each other than to BFQ Right.

Incidentally, while various measures of response set (e.g., MMPI L, K, and Marlowe-Crowne [1964] Social Desirability scale) were found to be unrelated to mouth awareness, there were two samples (N = 40, N = 35) of women in which BFQ Stomach was negatively correlated with L ($r = -.36$, $p < .025$; $r = -.25$, $p < .20$) and K ($r = -.47$, $p < .01$; $r = -.24$, $p > .20$).[2]

EXPLORATORY WORK

First attempts to determine possible correlates of mouth and stomach awareness involved study of oral variables. The obvious eating and incorporative functions associated with these two regions present an impelling argument for investigating oral factors. Therefore, in a sample of college women (N = 51) the BFQ, the Byrne (Byrne, et al., 1963) Food Attitude Scale and a learning task concerned with relative memory for food versus non-food words were administered on an individual basis. BFQ Mouth [3] proved not to be related

[2] Neither BFQ Mouth nor BFQ Stomach have shown consistent correlations with the Barrier score.

[3] BFQ Mouth and BFQ Stomach means will be cited only when major studies are involved or when the values are atypical.

to any of the scores pertinent to oral attitudes which were derived from these measures. This was also true for BFQ Stomach.

Since sensitivity to masochism had been observed to be linked with mouth and stomach awareness in men, an exploratory excursion into this region was also made. Data involving the BFQ and a tachistoscopic task containing two pictures with masochistic themes (and three neutral ones) were available from a sample of college women (N = 50). BFQ Mouth and BFQ Stomach both proved to have chance correlations with indices indicative of selective response to the masochism themes.

A third exploratory opportunity was provided by a sample (N = 40) of sorority women, previously described, in which BFQ variables could be related to ratings by peers for 12 different traits (e.g., Ambition, Aggression). BFQ Mouth and Stomach were not correlated with any of the rated trait variables.

POWER ORIENTATION

A fourth exploratory opportunity was available in a sample of college women (N = 53) in which the Edwards (1954) Preference Schedule and the Allport-Vernon-Lindzey (1960) Study of Values had been administered. It was found that mouth and stomach awareness were not significantly correlated with any of the Edwards scores. However, BFQ Mouth was correlated .23 ($p < .10$ N = 51) with the Study of Values Political score and BFQ Stomach was correlated .32 ($p < .025$ N = 51) with it. That is, the greater the individual's mouth or stomach awareness the stronger was her Political orientation. The Political score is defined as a measure of how interested one is in gaining power.

The next step was to determine whether the relationships of both BFQ Mouth and Stomach to the Study of Values Political score could be reaffirmed. BFQ and Political scores were available from another sample of college women (N = 39); and it was found that BFQ Mouth was positively correlated with the Political measure ($r = .31$, $p < .05$). But BFQ Stomach had only a chance correlation with it. The results held up for mouth awareness, while those for stomach awareness did not. Incidentally, BFQ Mouth and Stomach were not correlated consistently across both samples with any of the other Study of Values scores.

One might expect the kind of association that tends to exist between mouth awareness (and perhaps stomach awareness) and a Political orientation to be reflected when other measures concerned with aggression, achievement, and autonomy are applied. That is, one might expect degree of mouth or stomach awareness to be positively correlated with measures pertaining to the exercise of power, such as aggression and achievement. But, in actual fact, the Achievement, Autonomy and Aggression [4] scores of the Edwards Preference Schedule were in an earlier cited study found to be uncorrelated with BFQ Mouth or Stomach.

The same negative results appeared in another group of women (N = 49) in which the BFQ and the Edwards Preference Schedule [5] were administered.

It is true that in a sample of 40 women who were asked to write stories about five TAT cards, BFQ Mouth proved to be positively related to n Achievement scores which were derived ($\chi^2 = 5.9$, df = 1, $p < .02$). But BFQ Stomach had only a chance relation to the n Achievement scores.

As already indicated, ratings by sorority peers of an individual's aggression and achievement behavior were found to be unrelated to her mouth and stomach awareness. Incidentally, achievement was defined in terms of how ambitious the rated individual was judged to be. If there are power aspirations linked with mouth and stomach awareness, they were not apparent in overt expressive behavior as judged by one's peers.

Guided by the earlier presented evidence derived from the Study of Values, that mouth and stomach awareness might somehow be linked to attitudes about power, a study was designed to evaluate the relationship between such awareness variables and selective response to power or achievement words encountered in a learning task. The hope was that the learning task would prove to be more sensitive to the existence of special attitudes about power or achievement themes than the other techniques just described. It was anticipated that the greater a woman's mouth or stomach awareness the more likely she would be to respond selectively to words with power implications. There was no basis for predicting the direction of the selectivity. The BFQ and the following list of words were administered to a sample of women (N = 51).

Think	Best *
First *	Light
Ride	Sing
Try *	Win *
Chief *	Master *
Play	Buy
Honor *	Goal *
Agree	Round
Word	Prize *
Excel *	Turn

[Power or achievement words are starred]

The ten power or achievement words were chosen so as to refer to themes

---

[4] Correlations of BFQ Mouth and Stomach scores with the subscales of the Buss-Durkee Hostility inventory have also been observed to be largely of a chance order.

[5] BFQ Mouth and BFQ Stomach were also not related to the Dominant score of the Thurstone (1953) Temperament Schedule.

associated with attainment and competitive mastery. The non-achievement words were matched so as to contain the same number of letters and were spaced similarly in the list. The list was presented to subjects in the standard manner described in previous studies in which such learning tasks have been administered. The subject was asked to view the words, typed on a sheet of paper, for one minute; the list was then removed; and finally five minutes were provided to write down as many words as could be remembered. An index was computed equal to the number of achievement minus non-achievement words recalled.

BFQ Mouth was found to be correlated .25 ($p < .10$) with the Achievement minus non-Achievement memory score and BFQ Stomach was correlated .34 ($p < .025$) with it. In both instances the trend was for greater awareness of the body areas in question to be accompanied by selective superior recall for the power or achievement words. These results were supportive of the view that mouth and stomach awareness are tied in with special attitudes toward stimuli with power connotations. Neither of the BFQ scores was correlated with the total number of words learned.

A second pertinent study [6] was done which involved 39 girls in the fifth grade. These girls were seen in a group setting in which they responded to the BFQ and subsequently were asked to learn the list of achievement–non-achievement words under the same conditions as just described above, except that the words were projected on a screen. It was found that BFQ Stomach was correlated .45 ($p < .01$) with the Achievement minus non-Achievement memory score; but BFQ Mouth had only a chance relationship with it. No correlations of significance were found between the BFQ variables and total words recalled. These data reinforced the fact of an association between stomach awareness and selective superior recall for achievement words. However, they cast doubt upon the borderline result which had previously been obtained with reference to mouth awareness.

EFFECT OF PERIPHERAL STIMULATION OF MOUTH UPON MEMORY FOR ACHIEVEMENT WORDS

To look more closely at a possible association between mouth and stomach awareness and selective response to words with achievement (power) significance, a study was devised in which an attempt was made to influence selective recall for such words by varying the subject's awareness of her mouth. Mouth awareness rather than stomach awareness was chosen for manipulation for two reasons. First, its relation to memory for achievement

---

[6] I am grateful to my wife, Rhoda Fisher, for making these data available to me.

words was more in doubt and therefore it provided a stiffer test of the hypothesis. Secondly, the mouth is more accessible than the stomach to direct stimulation which can alter its sensory prominence. Of course, this study represented not only a test of the idea that mouth awareness is linked with selectivity toward a certain class of stimuli, but also of the general theory that stimulation of peripheral body sites can influence cognitive processes in a predictably focused manner.

Three learning conditions were studied. In one condition the intention was to appraise the effect of mouth stimulation upon recall of achievement versus non-achievement words. Each subject was asked to place a tongue depressor in her mouth; permitted to study the word list for one minute; and given five minutes to write down as many of the words as she could recall. The tongue depressor was held in her mouth throughout the entire process.

One of the control conditions used was exactly the same as that just described, except that the tongue depressor was taped to the subject's forehead, rather than being held in her mouth. This provided stimulation of a head area, but not specifically the mouth. In addition, a second neutral control condition was used which simply involved learning the word list without any special body stimulation being applied.

There was computed for each subject in each condition a score equal to the number of achievement minus non-achievement words recalled.

It was expected that the effects of the mouth stimulation condition would differ from the effects of the two control conditions. But it was not anticipated that the controls would differ from each other.

There were 22, 19, and 49 female subjects respectively in the mouth stimulation, forehead stimulation, and neutral conditions. All were college students.

The mean Achievement minus non-achievement recall scores were $+1.4$ $(\sigma = 2.3)$, $+2.5$ $(\sigma = 1.5)$, and $+2.7$ $(\sigma = 1.9)$ in the mouth, forehead, and neutral conditions respectively.

The difference between the mouth and forehead conditions was of borderline significance as defined by a t test $(t = 1.8, p < .1)$. Inspection of the two distributions indicated that one very extreme value among the mouth scores was largely responsible for the lack of formal significance. Indeed, a chi-square analysis demonstrated the presence of a significant differential $(\chi^2 = 3.9, \text{df} = 1, p < .05)$. The difference between the mouth and neutral conditions was also significant $(t = 2.3, p = .03)$. As for the forehead and non-body control procedure means, they were, as predicted, not significantly different from each other.

It was also found that the means of the total numbers of words recalled were 11.6, 12.7, and 12.1 respectively for the mouth, forehead, and neutral conditions. These values do not differ significantly.

The data demonstrate that with mouth enhancement there is a selectively diminished ability to learn and recall words pertaining to achievement (power). As expected, there were no differences in selectivity between the forehead and neutral procedures. One may say that when the mouth is stimulated in female subjects a process is initiated which inhibits recall of words with achievement meaning.

EFFECTS OF MOUTH ENHANCEMENT UPON PERCEPTION OF POWER THEMES

Another experiment was executed which considered the effect of increasing mouth awareness upon selective perception of tachistoscopically exposed pictures relating to power and aggression. Two pictures were drawn which portrayed female figures in aggressive stances or action. One depicted an aggressive looking woman in slacks holding a long pole in her hand. Another portrayed a woman with a knife held threateningly in her hand. There were also three other pictures: ice cream parfait (oral), front view of woman in dress (neutral) and man and woman embracing (sexual). All pictures were drawn so as to be of equivalent area and line quality. They were each exposed successively five times at increasingly slower speeds (.011, .027, .060, .082, .37 seconds). Their order of presentation was as follows: neutral female, man and woman, woman with pole, parfait, woman with knife.

One group of female college students (N = 14) attempted to identify the tachistoscopically exposed pictures while they were asked to hold a tongue depressor in the mouth. This was the group considered to have enhanced mouth awareness.

A control group of college women (N = 20) responded to the pictures without enhanced awareness of a specific body area.

It was predicted that the subjects in the mouth enhancement group would show a selective response to the power pictures but not to the other three. That is, the highlighting of the mouth was presumed to produce a special set toward aggressive or power stimuli. No prediction was made as to whether the selectivity would take the form of inhibition or facilitation of perception of the power pictures.

The threshold for recognition of each picture was given a value from 1 through 5 (1 = quickest recognition). Each subject's values for the five pictures were rank ordered, with rank 1 assigned to the picture most quickly recognized.

If the hypothesis were correct, the experimental and control groups would differ for the ranks assigned to each of the power pictures, but not for the three control pictures. That is, differential selectivity would occur only when a power theme was involved.

The mean rank of the first power picture (woman with the pole) in the experimental group was 3.18 (σ = .98) and the equivalent mean in the control group was 4.05 ($\sigma = 1.15$). The mean rank of the second power picture (woman with knife) was 4.32 ($\sigma = .67$) and the equivalent control mean was 3.17 ($\sigma = 1.12$).

The t for the difference involving the first power picture was 2.32 ($p < .05$); and the t for the second difference was 3.77 ($p < .001$). Thus, as predicted, both of the differences were statistically significant. It should be added that, as expected, the two groups did not differ significantly for the mean ranks of any of the three control pictures.

It is interesting that in the instance of the first power picture (woman with pole) the selectivity of the experimental group evidenced itself in facilitated (faster) perception than the controls; whereas the obverse was true for the second power picture (woman with knife). The predicted fact of a selective response to the power pictures by the group with increased mouth awareness was observed, but the nature of the selectivity shifted in terms of the position of the power picture in the presentation sequence. Such shifts in the character of the selective response as a function of serial position have been found by the writer in other tachistoscopic studies.

Overall, the data do demonstrate that enhancing mouth awareness can influence perceptual response to a power theme.

OVERVIEW

The results outlined above must be regarded as tentative. There docs seem to be an association between amount of mouth and perhaps stomach awareness and power variables.[7] However, it is not clear why this association appears only when the Study of Values Political score and selective response to achievement (power) words and tachistoscopically exposed pictures with power themes are used to evaluate power attitudes. Why does it fail to appear when the Edwards Preference Schedule or peer ratings of achievement and aggression are applied? Perhaps this is a function of the fact that one is dealing with an attitude about the value of possessing power or a sensitivity to the import of power—rather than a trait or style of behavior with power implications. One would conjecture that wishes and conflicts concerning power issues are involved, but not overt power behavior.

Why should mouth or stomach awareness be pertinent to power attitudes? One could speculate that because these body sectors are central to the process of eating and the focus of early contacts with mother in which she feeds and nurtures, they become associated with issues of passivity versus independence. It is possible that the mouth and stomach symbolize passivity and subordina-

---

[7] Neither BFQ Mouth nor BFQ Stomach were consistently correlated with clusters of variables related to other BFQ dimensions.

tion to stronger figures. If so, one can understand why BFQ Mouth and Stomach are correlated with measures concerned with power, which, in the final analysis, have to do with weak versus strong roles. One might say that the woman who is concerned about power focuses attention upon a part of herself which has strength-weakness connotations. This focusing process may represent a watchful effort to inhibit passive meanings that may be implicit in mouth and stomach sensations.

It will be recalled that in the case of men, mouth and stomach awareness seemed to be associated with sensitivity to hostile and masochistic themes. This was interpreted as representing an expectation of being attacked or becoming a victim. Obviously it represents an orientation which has power [8] implications, but opposite to that found in women. It is a statement of powerlessness insofar as it is an anticipation of being a victim of hostility.

In both men and women, the prominence of the mouth and stomach in the body scheme may have a relationship to attitudes about power (although in quite different ways).

[8] However, significant correlations between BFQ Mouth or BFQ Stomach and the Political score of the Study of Values have not been obtained in male samples.

29
Head Awareness in Women and Heterosexual Behavior

INTRODUCTION

Head awareness in women was determined with the 12-item scale used in the study of men. This scale has shown a test-retest reliability, with one week intervening, of .56 [1] in one sample of college women (N = 49); and in another similar sample (N = 40) the equivalent coefficient was .68.

Table 29.1
Means and Standard Deviations of BFQ Head Scores

M	σ	N
7.7	3.3	47
7.6	2.9	51
7.7	2.8	54
7.4	2.8	48
6.9	3.2	50
7.4	2.8	50
6.9	2.9	40
7.1	2.3	55
7.7	2.9	52
7.5	3.0	49

No consistent correlations with the MMPI K and L scales or the Marlowe-Crowne (1960) Social Desirability Scale have been observed. [2]

Table 29.1 shows the mean values for BFQ Head obtained in ten different

[1] All correlations are product-moment unless otherwise stated.
[2] No consistent correlations have been observed between BFQ Head and Barrier.

samples of college women. BFQ Head values have clustered around 7.4, which is exactly the same as that found in male samples. In general, scores have been normally distributed.

BFQ Head was found in ten different samples of female college students (average $N = 50$) to be positively and significantly correlated with BFQ Mouth five times (.32, .36, .40, .25, .41). It was not related significantly to any of the other BFQ variables.

EXPLORATORY WORK

Since head awareness in men was tied in with anal attitudes, the first analyses of the BFQ Head variables involved its correlations with a range of measures pertaining to anality (e.g., attitudes toward dirt, Negativism). However, purely chance results were obtained. Head awareness in women did not seem to have anything to do with anal attitudes.

HETEROSEXUALITY

This failure to find a relationship between head awareness and anality indices eliminated the only specific lead which logically presented itself. However, in scanning the data which were available for exploratory purposes, a rather consistent relationship was detected between BFQ Head and self-reported dating behavior. Subjects had been asked to respond to a questionnaire which inquired concerning their average frequency of dating per week during the four years of high school, their average number of dates per week in current life, and the number of times they had "gone steady" or been engaged. From the last items of information a "serious dating" index was computed which equaled the number of times has "gone steady" (maximum of 2) plus a credit of 1 for currently going steady plus a credit of 2 for being currently engaged.

Data were available for four samples of female college students ($N = 53$, $N = 57$, $N = 34$, $N = 31$) and one sample of married women ($N = 41$).

As shown in Table 29.2, almost all of the correlations were in a negative direction. BFQ Head was significantly and negatively correlated with the serious dating index in two of the four samples in which it could be computed ($r = -.34$, r .01; $r = -.49$, $p < .001$). It was similarly significantly and negatively related to frequency of current dating in two of the four samples in which it could be meaningfully ascertained ($-.33$, $p < .025$; $-.42$, p .01). None of its correlations with frequency of dating in high school were significant, but two were of borderline magnitude ($-.25$, $p < .10$; $-.27$,

Table 29.2
Correlations of BFQ Head with Self Report Dating Scores

Dating Reports	Samples				
	1 (N = 53)	2 (N = 57)	3 (N = 41)	4 (N = 34)	5 (N = 31)
Average number of dates per month in high school	−.02	−.25 *	−.27 *	−.22	.25
Average number of current dates	−.13	−.33 ***	— a	−.42 ***	.16
Index of serious dating	−.34 **	−.49 ****	— b	−.22	.22

ª All subjects in this sample were married and so the question about "current dating" was not applicable.

ᵇ For this married sample, the index of "serious dating" could not be meaningfully computed.

**** $p < .001$
*** $p < .01$
** $p < .025$
* $p < .10$

$p < .10$). Apparently, the greater a woman's head awareness the less she participated in intimate heterosexual interaction and dating. At least, such seems to be true as indicated by the individual's own self reports of dating behavior.

When the relationship of the BFQ Head score to the Heterosexuality score of the Edwards (1954) Preference Schedule was considered in three samples of female college students (N = 49, N = 51, N = 59), chance correlations were obtained. While degree of head awareness was negatively linked with amount of self reported dating behavior, it was not similarly linked to endorsing Edwards statements which express interest in doing things with sexual implications (e.g., "I like to kiss those of the opposite sex," "I like to listen to or to tell jokes involving sex," "I like to read books and plays involving sex"). Incidentally, BFQ Head was not consistently correlated with any of the other Edwards scores.

Another perspective on the relationship of head awareness to heterosexual attitudes was afforded by data concerned with the spontaneous verbalizations of two samples of college women (N = 59, N = 48). Subjects had been individually asked to list on a sheet of paper "20 things you are conscious of or aware of right now." This was done to ascertain how easily the individual verbalizes sexual thoughts in a free expressive situation. It was assumed that the presence of inhibition or anxiety about sexual matters would make it difficult to refer to sexual themes. Sexual references were defined to include only direct statements about heterosexual interests or activities (e.g., "I am going on a date tonight"; "My boyfriend is visiting me this weekend"). An index (Sex Reference) was derived equal to the number of sexual references produced. It could range from 0 to 20. Adequate inter-scorer agreement for this index has been demonstrated.

The mean Sex Reference score in sample 1 was 1.2 ($\sigma = 2.4$) and in sample 2 it was .41 ($\sigma = 1.1$). BFQ Head turned out to be negatively and significantly related to the Sex Reference scores in sample 1 ($-.34, p < .01$) and also sample 2 ($-.29, p < .05$). The more head aware the subject was the less she produced references to sexual themes.

It will be recalled that evaluations of overt behavior were available for a sample of sorority girls who had been rated for 12 different attributes (e.g., Aggression, Ambition, Neatness, How Comfortable with Women) by their peers. Unfortunately, these attributes were almost entirely not applicable to the problem under discussion. Only one rating (dealing with how comfort-able the individual is with men) was pertinent. However, BFQ Head was not significantly correlated with this variable. Indeed, it was not significantly correlated with any of the rated attributes.

OVERVIEW

It should be explicitly acknowledged that exploration of the head awareness variable has been quite inadequate. Numerous other indices pertinent to heterosexual attitudes need to be systematically related to BFQ Head. In addition, the opportunity did not present itself for determining the effect of head stimulation upon selective memory for sexual themes.[3] This is work that should have first priority in future exploration of head awareness in women.

Perhaps the available data do justify stating that head awareness in women has something to do with heterosexual attitudes.[4] While BFQ Head was not related to the Edwards Heterosexuality score, it was consistently negatively correlated with self reported frequency and intensity of hetero-sexual contacts and also freedom to verbalize heterosexual thoughts in a spontaneous expressive situation. Apparently, those who are most head aware have difficulty coping with that which has heterosexual implications. As already stated, it will require considerably more work with other measures of heterosexuality before this view can be solidly affirmed.

If head awareness in women is tied in with heterosexual attitudes and behavior, this may be a function of the favorable position of the head in functioning as a target for what psychoanalytic observers call "upward

[3] Partially, this was due to the difficulty of finding a means for increasing *general* head awareness, without producing intensified awareness of *specific* parts of the head like the mouth or the eyes.

[4] BFQ Head was not consistently correlated with any of the clusters of variables related to other BFQ dimensions.

displacement." It has been speculated that sexual wishes associated with lower body areas like the genitals may be defensively denied and associated with upwardly located body areas which are "safer" in the sense that they are well distanced from the "bad" lower areas. Perhaps it is "safer" and more acceptable to have a prominent or unusual sensation in one's head than in one's genitals. Possibly, too, the head might be particularly focused upon by those with heterosexual conflicts because it would be a way of "escaping" awareness of the body itself, with its obvious sexual significance. Head awareness would, in this sense, be a means of evading body awareness.

V
SEX DIFFERENCES IN BODY AWARENESS AND PERCEPTION

30
General Body Awareness in Men

INTRODUCTION

In previous chapters the primary goal was to understand the ways in which persons distribute their attention to circumscribed regions of their bodies. Now, the orientation will be shifted to consider the determinants of how an individual divides his attention between his body in general and non-body (non-self) objects in his world. It is possible to conceive of persons on a continuum defining how aware or preoccupied they are with their own bodies, as compared to other potential perceptual objects. At one extreme would be the individual who is typically highly invested in his own body—engrossed with its appearance, sensations, and attributes. This stance might be exemplified momentarily in the preoccupation of one looking at himself in a mirror or concerned about an unusual body sensation or symptom. At the other extreme would be the individual who is energetically absorbed in the world "out there" and only slightly invested in his own body. The quality of such an orientation might be momentarily apparent when one is devoting great attention to some demanding task or dramatic spectacle.

Little solid information is available in the past literature concerning the significance of variations in body awareness. Psychoanalytic theorists (e.g., Fenichel, 1945; Schilder, 1935) have commented on it primarily as it relates to concepts like narcissism, castration anxiety, and ego formation. Indirectly, the general psychiatric literature has been concerned with it in terms of phenomena like hypochondriasis, depersonalization, and self mutilation.

The major empirical efforts to measure variables pertinent to body awareness have involved four techniques.

1. The MMPI Hypochondriasis scale attempts to evaluate degree of

preoccupation with one's body as a "sick" or "ailing" object. A survey of the literature pertinent to this measure may be found in Chapter 4.

2. A second technique is the Van Lennep (1957) index based on the number of references to body themes and experiences introduced into stories about TAT type pictures. It has not been widely used. One particularly noteworthy finding which has emerged from its application is the fact that girls are characterized by an increased interest in their bodies as they mature beyond adolescence, whereas boys manifest a decreasing amount of such interest.

3. Mandler and Kremen (1960) and Mandler, Mandler and Uviller (1958) have developed a self report procedure which systematically inventories the amount of autonomic arousal one consciously experiences in a variety of situations. The general amount of self reported awareness of autonomic arousal in self has been shown to be significantly correlated with actual measures of autonomic response in specific settings. Interesting sex differences have been observed with this technique which will be described in more detail at a later point.

4. The most frequent approach to measuring body awareness has involved the Secord (1953) Homonym test. As already indicated, this procedure requires the subject to give his first association to a series of homonyms, each having a body and also a non-body meaning. For example, the word "beat" might elicit the association "heart" which has obvious body connotation or the association "rhythm" which does not have a body reference. Examples of other homonyms included in the Secord series are as follows: nail, index, gag, trunk, sling, organ, mole, swell. Secord originally found some evidence that those giving a large number of body associations were either narcissistic or anxious (with this last category predominating), while low scorers were apparently "over-controllers" who "rid themselves of anxious feelings by means of a self-denial mechanism and thus avoid giving bodily responses." Those scoring in the middle range were described as least anxious and most stable.

Little systematic work has been done with the Homonym score. Some evidence does exist that when degree of body awareness is evaluated by the Homonym score in female populations it is negatively related to satisfaction with one's body, as measured by the Jourard-Secord Body Cathexis scale (Secord, 1953; Secord and Jourard, 1953). That is, the higher the apparent amount of body awareness the less satisfied is the individual with her body. In male populations (e.g., Landau, 1960) such a relationship has not been established. Correlations between Homonym scores and measures of self acceptance have given largely chance results (Secord and Jourard, 1953). Fisher and Cleveland (1968) reported a negative correlation between Barrier and the Homonym score; but this observation has not held up consistently in replication studies (e.g., Conquest, 1963; Sherick, 1964). Landau (1960) found that the Homonym score was significantly negatively related to ability to adjust to body disability; but Cormack (1966) indicates that it has a chance correlation with response to the perception of body mutilation. Jaskar and Reed (1963) found that women in health oriented occupations (e.g., nursing) obtained higher Homonym scores than women in non-health oriented occupations (e.g., clerical). Sherick (1964), Jaskar and Reed (1963), and Conquest (1963) have not been able to discern meaningful relationships between Homonym scores and various indicators of ego strength and psychopathology. Dorsey (1965) reported a chance correlation between Homonym scores and yielding behavior. Epstein (1957) indicated that Homonym scores were not significantly correlated with field independence or estimates of one's body size. Boraks (1962) corroborated the negative findings with regard to body size.

In general, the most consistently established observation has been that showing a negative correlation between the Homonym score and body satisfaction in women. While further work may yet convincingly prove the validity and utility of the Homonym test, the existing findings are not encouraging. There are also difficulties in applying it which derive from the original conceptual vagueness concerning whether a high score indicates narcissism or anxiety. If one had to guess, it might be predicted that the Homonym test will eventually turn out to be sensitive to certain specific kinds of body anxiety, but that it is not a measure of *general* body concern.

A new approach to the measurement of body awareness was taken by the present author. It is based on the frequency with which an individual refers to his own body when a sample is taken of what lies within his immediate awareness. An index, referred to as "Body Prominence", is derived from his awareness reports. The actual procedure for obtaining a Body Prominence score is as follows. The subject is asked to liston a sheet of paper "20 things [1] that you are aware of or conscious of right now". He is also told to use "several words" in each of his descriptions. In the protocols so obtained, all direct or indirect references to one's body are scored. Such body references are defined so as to include explicit body designations (e.g., "My skin tingles," "My eyes are tired," "My muscles are strong"); temperature sensations (e.g., "I am cold"); kinesthetic sensations (e.g., "My muscles are relaxed," "I feel like taking a walk"); eating and other oral impulses or experiences (e.g., "I would like to eat a piece of pie," "I feel like smoking," "I am looking forward to lunch," "I am going to buy groceries for dinner"); various other body needs and experiences (e.g., "I like to sleep," "Kissing is fun"); and references to the state of one's health ("I am healthy," "My head hurts," "I am taking medication"); descriptions of one's clothing or clothing accessories (e.g., "My dress is green," "My purse is pretty," "I need to do my laundry"). References to clothing were included because they are so intimately linked to

---

[1] Any number of awareness reports may be asked for. A minimum of 20 is recommended, although in earlier studies as few as ten were obtained.

one's body.[2] See Appendix C for detailed examples of the application of the scoring scheme.

This approach is based upon the simple rationale that the greater an individual's perceptual focus upon his own body the more should it (or appropriate equivalents) find representation in his reports regarding the content of his awareness.

Scoring reliability has been evaluated in several samples. In one instance interscorer agreement for two judges for 59 protocols was 95 percent. In a second sample interscorer agreement for 50 protocols was 91 percent; and in a third involving 49 protocols amount of concordance was 93 percent. All scorers were given preliminary training with repeated examples until their judgments indicated mastery of the scoring criteria. Kutner [3] found 98 percent agreement between his scoring of 20 Prominence protocols and that by the present writer.

The test-retest stability of the Body Prominence index, when it is applied to men, has been investigated. One study involving 51 male college students (who were seen in small groups) compared Body Prominence scores after an intervening period of 21 days. The reliability coefficient was found to be .59.[4] A second study which included 50 male college students (seen in small groups) compared Body Prominence test-retest scores taken on three occasions, each time with an intervening interval of seven days. The reliability coefficient for score 1 versus score 2 was .63. The reliability coefficient for score 1 versus score 3 was .58 and that between 2 and 3 was .70. In another instance test-retest reliability for 47 male college students, seen individually, with three days intervening was .57. These values are low, but still permit meaningful appraisal of the Body Prominence variable. Incidentally, a tendency was observed for mean retest values to be consistently slightly higher than mean initial values.

As for norm values, it should be noted that the Body Prominence scores in numerous samples of college men, who were asked on an individual basis to give 20 awareness statements, have averaged about 3.3 [5] (range 0–17). Body Prominence scores obtained in a group setting tend to be lower. All score distributions were largely of a normal character.

In two samples of college males (N = 50, N = 48) no correlations of significance have been observed between Body Prominence and the following measures of response set: MMPI L and K scales and the Bass (1956) Social Acquiescence scale. No relationships have been detected in several studies between Body Prominence and measures of intelligence.

---

[2] Scores derived from each of these content subcategories do not differ appreciably in their correlations with total Body Prominence scores.

[3] Personal communication from Dr. Jerome Kutner.

[4] All correlation coefficients are product-moment unless otherwise specified.

[5] Body Prominence means will be presented for work to be described in this chapter only where major studies are involved or when the values are quite unusual or deviant.

Table 30.1
Means and Standard Deviations of Body Prominence Scores

M	σ	N
2.9	1.9	52
3.6	2.8	29
2.7	2.6	43
3.3	2.7	46
3.4	2.4	50
3.6	2.2	36
3.0	2.0	46
2.9	2.6	49
3.2	2.8	51
4.1	3.0	19

VALIDITY

The question whether Body Prominence validly measures what it purports to measure has been considered from a number of perspectives. One of the first approaches to the validity issue dealt with the relationship between Body Prominence and selective recall for body versus non-body words. As suggested and demonstrated in earlier chapters, body feelings and attitudes may be expected to exert significant influence upon cognitive processes. Therefore, if the Body Prominence score does, indeed, tap amount of body awareness, one might expect it to predict selective cognitive response to stimuli with body implications. It was conjectured that the greater an individual's awareness of his body (Body Prominence) the more likely he would be to manifest selectively high retention for terms with body reference learned from a list comprising both body and non-body words. That is, it was assumed that the sensory representation of one's body would serve as a persistent signal or anchor which would enhance the significance of any stimulus or symbol with body connotations. To evaluate this proposition the following design was employed. Body Prominence reports were obtained from subjects in a group setting. Memory for body versus non-body references was evaluated in terms of degree of recall for ten words pertaining to the body and ten involving non-body objects. Subjects were asked in a classroom situation to observe for one minute the following list of words which was projected on a screen.

Leg *	Hammer	Wrist *	Nose *
House	Scooter	Street	Glass
Car	Liver *	Head *	Neck *
Thumb *	Book	Tent	Hip *
Toy	Hair *	Skin *	Lamp

[Body words are starred]

The body and non-body words were chosen so as to be about the same average length. The non-body terms designated common and frequently experienced objects. After the subject had studied the list for one minute, it was removed from view. He was then told that he would have five minutes to recall and write down on a sheet of paper as many of the words as possible. His written recall was scored by summing the number of body words and subtracting the number of non-body words.

There were 92 subjects (25 men and 67 women) who were college students. Their median age was 20.

The median Body Prominence score was 0 (range 0 to 11). The median difference between the number of body and non-body words recalled was +1.0 (range +4 to —6).

The distributions of scores were skewed. Their relationship was therefore appraised with chi-square. A clearly significant positive relationship was discerned between the Body Prominence score and the inclination to recall more body than non-body words ($\chi^2 = 12.8$, df $= 1, p < .001$). The greater a subject's awareness of his body the more he displayed selective superior recall for words with body meaning. The results directly supported the hypothesis tested and therefore provided indirect evidence that the Body Prominence score taps a body awareness dimension.

A second approach to the validity issue was based on a comparison of Body Prominence scores with measures of the density of body sensations or experiences during a defined time period. It was assumed that the experiential prominence of one's body should be reflected in its sensory vividness, as defined by the total amount of sensation apparently emanating from it. It is important to specify that the assumption was not that degree of body awareness was positively correlated with *actual* amount of body sensation, but rather with the amount perceived by, or registering upon, the individual in question. Three studies were devised to appraise the matter. One involved male college students (N $= 52$) who were seen individually and asked to give 20 Body Prominence reports. They were then asked to concentrate upon their bodies and to indicate (by placing checks under appropriately headed columns on a sheet of paper) each time that they experienced a distinct sensation either in the upper (waist to head) or lower (below waist) regions of the body. Such reports were obtained for a five minute period. Upon completion of this task they were asked to indicate for a five minute period each time that they experienced a sensation in two interior sites (stomach, heart) and two exterior sites (skin, muscle). When the total numbers of sensation reports for the first task were related to Body Prominence scores, a correlation of .32 ($p < .025$) was found. For the second task, the correlation was .24 ($p < .10$). In both instances, the greater the body awareness as defined by Body Prominence scores the greater was the density of body sensations reported—although it is true that the correlation for the second sensation task was of borderline significance.

In a second study involving 46 male college students, Body Prominence protocols and the same two sets of sensation reports as those just described above were once again individually secured. Body Prominence was correlated .41 ($p < .01$) with the sum of upper and lower sensations and .43 ($p < .01$) with the sum of outer and inner sensations.

Finally, in a third project in which 60 male college students participated, Body Prominence scores and sensation reports for back plus front body sites and also sensation reports for outer plus inner sites were individually obtained. Body Prominence was correlated .29 (p .025) with the front plus back sensation scores and .27 ($p < .05$) with outer plus inner sensation scores.

Looking at the three sets of studies, one may conclude that an individual's Body Prominence score is meaningfully related to the density of his body sensory experiences. The more aware he is of his body, as defined by the Body Prominence score, the more frequently he perceives sensations as occurring in his body. This finding represents further support for the validity of the Body Prominence technique.

Another opportunity to look at the validity of the Body Prominence score was provided by an investigation of persons hospitalized for surgery. Certainly, one would expect that coming to a hospital and awaiting surgery and subsequently recuperating from it would make an individual unusually aware of his body. If so, Body Prominence scores should be higher in a group of surgical patients than in non-hospitalized persons. The Body Prominence procedure was administered to 20 men within a day or two prior to surgery and again a day or two after it. Patients with rather minor surgical problems were used so that they would not be too incapacitated at any point to respond to the test procedures. Average age of the patients was 40.8 (range 20-61); and average educational level 11.2 years (range 5–16). A score was computed equal to the average of the pre- and post-surgery Body Prominence scores. The mean for the group was 5.7 ($\sigma = 2.4$). This value was compared with that from 47 male college students to whom the Body Prominence was administered individually on one occasion and again three days later. Average age was 20.4 (range 19–23); and educational level 14.2 years. The mean of the two Body Prominence scores was 3.6 ($\sigma = 2.9$). A t test indicated, as predicted, that the value for the surgical patients was higher than that for the controls ($t = 3.1$, $p < .01$). One might ask whether this difference could be a function of the difference in age and education between the groups. However, an analysis of the surgical patients indicated, if anything, a trend ($p < .10$) for Body Prominence and age to be negatively correlated. That is, those with higher ages tended to obtain lower Body Prominence scores; and so the age difference between the groups would have worked against, rather than facilitated, the body awareness difference observed. The influence of the education difference can likewise be ruled out because no correlations between Body Prominence and education were found in these samples or in any previous ones studied. The results demonstrate that the Body Prominence score was elevated in a group of persons who, because of their exposure to surgery, would be expected to be unusually preoccupied with, and concerned about, their bodies.

A question that naturally arises is whether body awareness as defined by the Body Prominence score is related to body awareness as measured by the Secord Homonym test. To investigate this matter, both techniques were administered on an individual basis, with Body Prominence first in the sequence, to 50 male college students. A positive correlation of .28 ($p < .05$) was found. That is, the two procedures were positively correlated, as might be expected; but their degree of common variance is obviously low.

Other approaches to evaluating the validity of the Body Prominence measures have been attempted, but they involve female samples; and will therefore be described in a subsequent chapter which deals with general body awareness in women.

PERSONALITY AND ATTITUDINAL CORRELATES

In trying to comprehend the significance of one's habitual degree of body awareness, a study was undertaken in which Body Prominence was related to BFQ variables. The question was whether general body awareness was linked with awareness of focal body areas. Might awareness of one body area contribute more than other areas to general body awareness? A second question considered was whether body awareness was related to degree of boundary articulation. There are good theoretical and empirical reasons derived from what is known about perceptual phenomena in general for arguing that the more clearly an individual's body is differentiated from its environs the more vividly will it be experienced as a perceptual object. Fifty male college students were evaluated. These students, who were seen in small groups on three separate occasions (week intervals), were administered the Body Prominence, Rorschach ink blots (with response total controlled), and Body Focus Questionnaire procedures during the first session and the Body Prominence, among other tests, during the two subsequent sessions. For the Body Prominence measure, only ten responses were requested on each occasion. The sum of the Body Prominence scores proved to have only a chance correlation with the Barrier score.[6] General body awareness seemed not to be related to the degree of articulation of the body boundary. When the sums of the Prominence scores were related to the BFQ scores, the only relationship of significance to emerge was that involving BFQ Stomach

---

[6] In several other male samples Body Prominence and Barrier have consistently been observed to be unrelated.

($r = .34$, $p < .02$). The larger the Prominence score the greater was the stomach awareness.[7] This finding occurred at a time when the significance of stomach awareness had not yet been investigated and it was thought, for obvious reasons, to relate to oral attitudes. Consequently, it was interpreted as indicating that the best approach to understanding general body awareness in men was via oral concepts. Thus, for the wrong reason Body Prominence was viewed as a function of oral variables.[8] However, as will be seen, this was a fortunate mistake because oral attitudes did, in fact, turn out to be tied to general body awareness in men.

Taking as a model earlier observations that when awareness of an area is linked with a dynamic theme, it is usually anxiety about that theme which is involved, it was expected that the greater a man's body awareness the more anxiety he would display when confronted with oral themes and symbols.

It was with this view that the following was hypothesized:

1. The greater an individual's awareness of his body the higher will be his underlying anxiety about incorporation and therefore the more limited his ability to enjoy the incorporative process exemplified in eating.

2. If an individual's degree of body awareness derives from anxiety about incorporation one might expect that it would be negatively related to how altruistic he recalls his parents to have been. If there is anxiety about oral gratification, it could be a function of experiences with parents who were apparently unwilling to give.

Body awareness was measured in small groups by means of the Body Prominence technique.

The Byrne (Byrne, et al., 1963) Food Attitude Scale, described above, was once again used to determine the subject's enjoyment and interest in eating. Also, a measure of his preferences for a list of 103 foods (20 of which are part of the Byrne scale) was obtained. He was asked to indicate for each food item whether he liked or disliked it. His score was the total number of foods liked. It could range from 0 through 103.[9]

---

[7] However, in five other male samples in which Body Prominence was correlated with BFQ Stomach only one significant positive correlation was found. Obviously, the relationship is limited and inconsistent. Similar inconsistency characterized relationships with all of the other standard BFQ dimensions.

It should parenthetically be added that frequent negative correlations between Body Prominence and degree of awareness of one's arms have also been found. The significance of such data has remained obscure because it has not been possible to find consistent trait and attitudinal concomitants of arm awareness.

[8] Another reason why body awareness was early viewed as possibly involving orality was the finding that Body Prominence was positively and significantly correlated with selective superior recall for words referring to oral aspects of the body (e.g., mouth, tongue, throat, saliva) as compared to words not having oral implications (e.g., spine, kidney, heart, joint). This finding emerged in two different male samples (Fisher, 1965A).

[9] While responses to the Blacky Oral Eroticism and Oral Sadism pictures were also originally studied with a ranking procedure, these data will not be considered because the Blacky ranking procedure proved to be highly unreliable.

The amount of altruism attributed to each of the parents was appraised with the same series of nine items used to measure parental altruism in a study earlier described in the chapter dealing with eye awareness.

The subjects were 58 male college students (median age 20). The mean Body Prominence score was 3.7 ($\sigma = 2.5$). The mean Byrne Food Attitude Scale score was 34.8 ($\sigma = 5.4$).

Table 30.2
Correlations of Body Awareness with Indexes Relating
to Incorporation

Body awareness versus	r	Significance Level
Byrne Food Attitude scale	−.30 (N = 58)	<.05
Total number of foods liked	−.25 (N = 58)	.05
Father altruism	.03 (N = 54)	n.s.
Mother altruism	−.11 (N = 57)	n.s.

Table 30.2 indicates that the Body Prominence score was, as predicted, negatively and significantly correlated with the Byrne Food Attitude Scale ($r = -.30$, p $<$ .05). Included in the Byrne scale is a list of 103 foods, and the subject indicates which he likes and dislikes. The mean number of foods liked was 80.6 ($\sigma = 11.8$). Body Prominence proved to be negatively correlated with the number of foods liked ($r = -.25$, p .05). These data indicated that the less pleasurable eating appeared to an individual the greater was his body awareness. The Father Altruism mean was 10.1 ($\sigma = 3.3$) and the Mother Altruism mean 11.8 ($\sigma = 3.5$). Table 30.2 shows that Body Prominence was, contrary to prediction, not significantly related to these variables.

There was limited congruence between the data and the hypotheses. The best results were obtained for the prediction that Body Prominence would be inverse to satisfaction derived from eating. The Byrne scale and the index of number of foods liked were both related to Body Prominence in the fashion anticipated. With increased Body Prominence there was a corresponding negative attitude toward food intake which was interpreted as relating to anxiety about incorporation. The formulation relating Body Prominence, with its presumed concern about incorporation, to the subject's recall of the degree of selfishness of each of his parents was not affirmed by the findings.

The significant findings pertaining to the Byrne scale cited above were put to the test in cross-validation efforts. The negative correlation of Body Prominence with the Byrne score was evaluated in three samples. In sample 1, comprising 49 male college students, Body Prominence proved to be correlated .36 (p < .01) with the Byrne score. This was, indeed, a surprising finding. Instead of a duplication of the original negative correlation, there was a significant positive correlation in the opposite direction. This immediately suggested the possibility that if there are oral anxieties associated with body awareness they may find expression not only in unusually negative but also positive (perhaps compensatory) attitudes toward food and eating. In sample 2 (48 college males) Body Prominence and the Byrne scale manifested a chance correlation ($r = -.02$). Finally, in a third sample of male college students (N = 21) a correlation of $-.30$ (p > .10) was found.

The findings regarding the relationships of Body Prominence to the Byrne scale were so shifting as to be a bit discouraging. However, a variety of other approaches to the orality matter were available and they will be described below.

FURTHER STUDIES

While the view still seemed reasonable that amount of body awareness would be positively correlated with concern about oral matters, it was considered, on the basis of the shifting direction of correlations between Body Prominence and the Byrne scale described above, that the concern might possibly manifest itself in both diminished or augmented response to oral stimuli.

Average Week

Data obtained by means of the Average Week technique was used to determine whether body awareness is related to the amount of time the individual devotes to oral activities. As earlier mentioned, this technique involves the subject writing for a 15-minute period and detailing his routine during an average week in his life. A number of different scoring categories have been applied to analyzing such protocols (e.g., Work, Cleaning, Entertainment). The category particularly pertinent to the present issue was that concerned with references to food. It embraces all statements concerned with eating and preparing or buying food. The total number of food references divided by the total of all scored activities included in other categories was taken as an index of interest in food. Adequate interscorer reliabilities for the various categories have been demonstrated. In a sample of 54 college men, the mean percent of Food References was 1.9 ($\sigma = 1.0$). The mean Body Prominence score was 3.3 ($\sigma = 2.9$). A correlation of .39 (p < .01) was found between Body Prominence and percent of food references. That is, the higher the individual's body awareness the more he described himself as engaged in activities revolving about food.

Chain Associations

Chain association response patterns offered a way of inquiring whether persons differing in body awareness also differed in associative reactions to oral words. As previously described, the chain association technique required subjects to give ten associations to each of 13 words. Three of the words (taste, suck, swallow) had oral meaning; and the others diversely conveyed anal, aggressive, and masochistic themes. All associations were written down verbatim by the experimenter; and the time taken to complete ten associations to each was recorded. The associations given to each stimulus word were also scored in terms of how directly they adhered to its actual meaning. This was done to appraise the extent to which subjects sought to evade dealing with the themes conveyed by the stimulus words. It was expected, of course, that variations in Body Prominence would be paralleled by selectivity in response to the oral words.

Data were analyzed from a sample of 43 male college students. The mean response time rank for the oral words was 3.3 ($\sigma = 1.3$). It was found that Body Prominence was negatively correlated ($r = -.40$, $p < .01$) with the rank of the time required to complete associations to the oral words. The greater the subject's body awareness the more quickly did he complete the oral responses as compared to those for the other word clusters. Selective response to the oral themes was definitely associated with the body awareness dimension. It would be sheer guesswork if one tried to explain the direction of the selectivity. None of the correlations of Body Prominence with the ranks of the other four themes were significant.

No correlations of significance emerged between Body Prominence and the index indicating how directly the associations to the oral words adhered to their original meaning. However, Body Prominence was positively correlated with the directness of associations to the anal ($r = .33$, $p < .05$) and masochistic words ($r = .39$, $p < .01$). It was also positively, but not significantly, correlated with directness of associations to hostile words ($r = .23$). These findings suggest that persons with higher body awareness generally had less need to respond circuitously to emotionally charged material in a variety of areas.

While the index concerned with directness of oral associations was not related to Body Prominence, the time required to complete responses to oral words was so related. Further evidence was therefore provided that body awareness was involved with oral attitudes.

Proverbs

Attention will now be directed to results derived from responses to oral versus "neutral" proverbs. As stated earlier, Story (1963) developed a technique for evaluating oral attitudes which is based on responses to proverbs. Subjects are asked to explain the meaning of each of a series of 14 proverbs read to them. Seven deal with oral themes (e.g., Never show your teeth unless you can bite, The gentle sheep is sucked by every lamb) and seven deal with diverse matters that do not have oral significance (e.g., Too many chiefs, not enough Indians, The work praises the workman). Beginning with an oral proverb, the oral and neutral ones were presented alternately. The time from presentation of the proverbs to the beginning of definition (initial response time) was recorded, as well as the total time (total response time) to arrive at a definition. Two scores were computed:

1. Average of initial times for neutral minus average of initial times for oral.
2. Average of total times for neutral minus average of total times for oral.

These differences scores were originally devised to correct for gross tendencies to be either slow or fast in dealing with cognitive tasks such as represented by proverb definition. Although Story also evaluated the degree of abstraction of the proverb interpretations, this was not done in the present study.

Data from 45 male college students were analyzed. The mean neutral minus oral initial time score was —.18 seconds ($\sigma = .5$). The mean neutral minus oral total time score was 8.2 seconds ($\sigma = 2.0$). The score based on initial time was correlated .25 ($p < .10$) with Body Prominence. That is, body awareness was positively correlated at a borderline level with the tendency to respond initially faster to the oral than non-oral proverbs. The neutral minus oral total time score was negatively correlated at a borderline level ($r = —.27$, $p < .10$) with Body Prominence. The greater the individual's body awareness the longer he tended to require to complete his definitions of the oral as compared to the neutral proverbs. Apparently, those with relatively high body awareness were stimulated to respond more quickly to the oral than non-oral proverbs and subsequently spent more time explaining the oral proverbs. These observations indicated at a borderline level another connection between body awareness and attitudes pertinent to orality.

Humor

Reactions to jokes with various thematic contents provided the methodology for the work to be presented in this section. As depicted in other chapters, Weiss (1955) collected a series of jokes which clustered about specific themes. These themes were as follows:

> Oral Eroticism
> Oral Sadism
> Oedipal
> Anal Expulsive
> Castration Anxiety

The Oral Erotic jokes emphasized eating and incorporative wishes; whereas the Oral Sadistic jokes focused on biting, vomiting, and spitting themes. An example of an Oral Erotic joke is as follows:

Then there was the young nurse whose uniforms were cut so low at the neck that whenever she walked through the nursery the babies began to cry.

The Oral Sadistic category may be illustrated by the following:

Kind neighbor (to little boy eating an apple): "Look out for the worms, Sonny."
Little boy: "When I eat an apple, the worms have to look out for themselves."

Subjects were asked to rate each joke on a 6-point scale, indicating how much they liked it. The mean rating of all jokes in a given cluster was determined; and these means were then ranked (rank 1 = least enjoyable).

It was anticipated that significant relationships would be found to exist between body awareness and reactions to the Oral Eroticism and Oral Sadism jokes.

Body Prominence and humor scores had been secured from a sample of 45 male college students. The mean Oral Eroticism rank was 2.9 ($\sigma = 1.3$) and the mean Oral Sadism rank was 3.8 ($\sigma = 1.2$). Body Prominence scores were correlated .36 ($p < .025$) with Oral Eroticism ranks and $-.22$ ($p > .20$) with Oral Sadism ranks. The greater an individual's body awareness the more he enjoyed the Oral Eroticism jokes. But his response to the Oral Sadism jokes could not be predicted. There was also a significant negative correlation ($r = -.29$, p .05) between Body Prominence and Oedipal Intensity ranks. With greater body awareness, there was less enjoyment of the Oedipal Intensity jokes.

The finding of a significant positive correlation between Body Prominence and enjoyment of the Oral Erotic jokes was congruent with expectation.

Early Memory

Holleman's (1965) Early Memory procedure had, as previously reported, been used to obtain ten early memories from a sample of 54 college men. Among various categories of analysis applied to these memories was one concerned with oral themes. It embraced all references to eating, drinking, buying or preparing food, and illnesses caused by food. Adequate interscorer reliability for judging such themes has been shown. When the relationship of Body Prominence to number of oral themes was examined, it was found to be of a chance order.

Presentation of Blacky Themes Tachistoscopically

The relationships of Body Prominence to the two Blacky Oral themes presented tachistoscopically were perused. In a study described in detail earlier male college students ($N = 41$) were asked individually to identify six Blacky pictures (Oral Eroticism, Oral Sadism, Anal Sadism, Masturbation Guilt, Castration Anxiety, Sibling Rivalry) viewed tachistoscopically. Each picture was shown at six increasingly slower speeds. Body Prominence was found not to be significantly correlated with ability to identify the Oral Eroticism theme. However, it was correlated .25 (p .10) with the rank of the first speed at which the Oral Sadism picture was correctly perceived; but only at a chance level with the rank of the total number of correct identifications. There was, in terms of ability to make the initial correct identification, a borderline trend for degree of body awareness to be positively related to difficulty in perceiving Oral Sadism. Incidentally, two other significant results emerged which are not directly pertinent to the present inquiry and whose meaning remains obscure. Body Prominence was negatively correlated with the rank of the total number of times Anal Sadism was correctly perceived ($r = -.43$, $p < .01$) and positively so with the rank of the total number of times Masturbation Guilt [10] was accurately seen ($r = .32$, $p < .05$).

Tachistoscopic Perception

Data were reviewed which permitted relating body awareness to response to oral words presented tachistoscopically. In a previous study subjects ($N = 45$

[10] Of course, the obvious parallel was noted between a measure of body awareness like Body Prominence and Masturbation Guilt, which presumably taps anxiety about self stimulation of one's body. However, there are no other data to give this parallel further significance.

college males) tried to identify 14 words randomly presented tachisto-scopically. Each word was shown at five consecutively increasing time exposures (3.3, 3.4, 3.6, 4.0, 4.5 milliseconds); and the earliest speed at which it could be identified was established. Three of the words referred to homosexual themes; three had heterosexual implications; two dealt with narcissism; and three with orality (food, candy, suck). The rank order (relative to other word categories) of the average of the three oral word threshold values was determined. The mean rank was 2.2 (σ = 1.2). The rank index proved to be negatively correlated (r = —.26, p < .10) with Body Prominence. Correlations of Body Prominence with the rank values for the various other word themes were all of chance magnitude. There was a trend for increasing body awareness to be paralleled by increasing sensitivity to the oral words.

A week after the completion of the tachistoscopic task subjects had been asked to recall as many as possible of the words they had perceived. The number of oral words recalled divided by the total of all words recalled was found to be positively related to body awareness (χ^2 = 4.1, df = 1, p < .05). The findings did indicate a selective memory effect, such that body aware-ness was positively correlated with the tendency to recall a relatively high proportion of oral words.

Perceptual Selectivity in Terms of Ames Thereness-Thatness (T-T) Apparatus

The Ames Thereness-Thatness procedure involves the subject viewing pictures in an ambiguous setting and apparently adjusting their spatial positions to line up with a series of rods; but actually the judgments made relate to changing their size rather than their spatial positions. Such size judgments provide meaningful information about the evaluative responses evoked by a picture's content. In a study earlier outlined, T-T responses were obtained to six line drawings, one of which depicted an oral theme (ice cream parfait). Other pictures presented various heterosexual and homo-sexual themes. It will be recalled that a distinction was made between those who dealt with the pictures in a Repressive versus non-Repressive manner. This was done by testing at subsequent times the subject's memory of the content of the T-T pictures. Those making two or more recall errors were classified as Repressors (N = 25) and those making no errors as non-Repressors (N = 29).

The T-T index employed to represent the response to the oral picture was the average of the ranks of the settings for two nude figures minus the rank of the ice cream parfait setting. It was intended in this way to determine if the response to the oral stimulus was different from the response to the other two most ego-involving picture stimuli in the series.

Mean Prominence scores in the Repression and non-Repression categories were respectively 2.5 and 2.8. A chance relationship was observed in the Repression group between Prominence and the relative setting of the parfait picture. But the results in the non-Repression sample indicated that the chi-square (df = 2) depicting the relation between Prominence and the parfait index was 5.8 (in the predicted direction), which is just short of the 6.0 needed for significance at the .05 level. The greater the subject's body awareness the smaller (further away) did he set the parfait as compared to the nude pictures and presumably the greater was his defensive response to the oral theme depicted.

COMMENT

If one retraces the maze of results pertaining to body awareness and response to oral stimuli, the evidence suggests a trend for the two variables to be associated. While Body Prominence turned out to be inconsistently or not at all related to such variables as the Byrne scale, the number of food references in one's early memories, and amount of altruism recalled as characterizing one's parents, it did show fair consistency in its relationships to all of the other oral variables. It was clearly related to amount of energy apparently devoted to food relevant activities in an average week; speed of associative response to oral words; and degree of enjoyment of jokes with oral incorporative themes. It was linked at a borderline level with selective response to the Blacky Oral Sadism picture, speed and duration of response when interpreting oral proverbs, and selectivity in perceiving oral words or pictures during tachistoscopic and Thereness-Thatness presentation.

It is difficult to spell out the nature of the specificity of reactions shown by those differing in body awareness with respect to the various oral stimuli. The relationships of Body Prominence to the following variables would suggest that with increasing body awareness there is greater anxiety about oral themes: Blacky Oral Sadism picture (as defined by tachistoscopic response) and Thereness-Thatness parfait picture (non-Repressive group) But the relationships of Body Prominence with the following oral variables are less easily comprehended: food pertinent activities in an average week, chain associations to oral words, speed of perception of tachistoscopically presented oral words, time required to interpret oral proverbs, response to Oral Erotic jokes. Therefore, it would be sensible at this point to withhold judgment concerning the significance of the oral correlates of body awareness and simply emphasize the fact of interconnection. One can only say that body awareness is linked with feelings and attitudes concerning the whole process of incorporation and "taking in" from the environment.

FURTHER SEARCH FOR TRAIT CORRELATES

The data pertaining to Body Awareness and orality, while pointing up a general relationship between body awareness and a particular need or drive, did not spell out the nature of the relationship. They were not satisfying for this reason and also because they leave one without a picture of the traits or defense modes which possibly accompany varying amounts of body awareness. Therefore, additional exploratory work was undertaken in which Body Prominence was correlated with the scales of the Edwards (1954) Preference Schedule over a series of three successive studies. In two of the studies the Kuder (1956) Preference Record was also administered and in one the Allport-Vernon-Lindzey (1960) Study of Values was included. The question was whether Body Prominence would display consistent correlations with any of these measures. Three samples of male college students ($N = 53$, $N = 44$, $N = 46$) were evaluated with the Edwards scales. Body Prominence scores were obtained in small groups, as were the answers to the Edwards questionnaire. In the first and third of these samples ($N = 53$, $N = 46$) the Kuder Preference Record was administered and in the first ($N = 53$) the Study of Values was included.

For the Edwards, it was found that in sample 1 Body Prominence was positively correlated with Nurturance ($r = .27$, $p < .05$), Affiliation ($r = .22$, $p > .10$), and Aggression ($r = .23$, $p < .10$) and negatively so with Order ($r = -.30$, p .025). In sample 2 Body Prominence was not significantly correlated with any of the Edwards scores. In sample 3 it was positively correlated with Nurturance ($r = .31$, $p < .05$) and negatively with Deference ($r = -.32$, $p < .05$). It should be incidentally mentioned, apropos of other findings soon to be cited, that there was a slight trend for Body Prominence to be negatively correlated with Order ($-.19$, $p > .20$). In any case, the major observation worth mentioning with respect to the overall data was the positive correlation between Body Prominence and Nurturance in two out of the three samples. Nurturance is defined by Edwards in terms of perceiving self as motivated to do such things as help friends when they are in trouble, be generous with others, and treat others with kindness and sympathy. Since a nurturant attitude is the opposite of a taking one, it also represents the reverse of what is usually considered to be a passive oral orientation. One cannot but be impressed with the coincidence that Body Prominence was correlated with a variety of indicators of oral concern or interest and at the same time linked with an attitude which can be viewed as opposite in character to that of oral receptivity. Is it possible that with increasing body awareness in men there is a parallel inhibition of oral wishes and the adoption of a compensatory "giving" stance? Perhaps the inhibition of oral wishes plays a role in enhancing body awareness. Unsatisfied oral needs might result in activation of organ systems (e.g., stomach, mouth) or create physiological tensions which lead to a generalized increase in body sensations and experiences. However, one difficulty with this hypothesis is the fact that eye awareness (BFQ Eyes) which has been shown to be correlated with anxiety about oral wishes (and therefore presumably inhibition of such wishes) is not related to Body Prominence. If inhibition of oral wishes plays a role in increasing body awareness, why is this not evident in terms of the oral inhibition probably associated with increasing degrees of eye awareness? An adequate resolution of this discrepancy is not immediately evident.

To return to the studies mentioned above in which the Study of Values and Kuder Preference Record were considered in relation to body awareness, it was found in the first study (N = 53) that Body Prominence was correlated .23 ($p < .10$) with the Aesthetic, .23 ($p < .10$) with the Religious, and $-.24$ ($p < .10$) with the Economic scores of the Study of Values. In the same study, Body Prominence was correlated .24 ($p < .10$) with the Artistic, $-.28$ ($p < .05$) with the Computational, and $-.35$ with the Clerical scores of the Kuder test. The results in the other study (N = 46) indicated that Body Prominence was correlated .30 ($p < .05$) with the Artistic and $-.29$ ($p < .05$) with the Clerical scores of the Kuder.

Looking broadly at these data, one can see a definite trend for body awareness to be positively related to an aesthetic or artistic orientation and negatively so with clerical interests. Apropos of the negative correlation with the Clerical variable, it should be recalled that a slight trend was noted above for Body Prominence to be negatively correlated with the Edwards Order score. Body awareness seems to be low in those who have orderly-clerical interests and high in those with artistic interests.

To check further on the finding concerning the positive correlation between Body Prominence and artistic interests, a study was done with 50 male college students who were asked, in small groups, to give Body Prominence responses and also to list on a sheet of paper "ten occupations you consider most attractive or interesting." The number of artistic or literary occupations (e.g., artist, novelist, writer, poet) in each list was determined; and related to the Body Prominence scores. A correlation of .35 ($p < .025$) was found. The greater the individual's body awareness the greater was his expressed interest in artistic and literary occupations. It is interesting that this crude, but freely expressive, technique for ascertaining artistic-literary interests gave more significant results than the formal, more psychometrically sophisticated interest measures employed.

The specific implications of the value and interest findings remain to be seen. However, one is reminded of speculations by some psychoanalytic observers (e.g., Rose, 1966; Kris, 1952) that an important element in artistic creativity is the ability to translate body feelings and experiences into symbolic or pictorial representations. Rose states (pp. 778–779), "The artist's inborn heightened sensitivity to bodily sensations and rhythms as well as to the outer world causes a continual searching for harmony of balance between the two. The force of his own body feelings responds to and causes a kind of amalgamation of body imagery with outer forms in the world and leads to a state of mutual permeability or sense of fusion with the outer world. This is favored by a greater capacity for organizing sensory impressions. . . . The matrix of his experience is enriched throughout the whole spectrum of sensory modalities and responses—visceral, tactile, kinesthetic."

Perhaps a certain minimal level of body awareness is basic to an artistic orientation. This is an intriguing possibility which deserves further study.

COMMENT

To conclude succinctly, one may say that the greater a man's habitual body awareness the more likely he is to be concerned with oral themes; to adopt nurturant attitudes; and to have artistic rather than clerical (orderly) interests. Speculations have been offered that the high body aware individual may compensate for oral wishes via nurturant behavior toward others. It was also suggested that inhibited oral wishes may play a role in generating body awareness in men. Finally, it was pointed out that the association of artistic interests with intensified body awareness is congruent with psychoanalytic speculations about the role of body experiences in artistic creativity.

In using the Body Prominence technique, it would be well to keep in mind what factors influence it. The assumption has been made that there is an habitual level of body awareness characterizing persons. But obviously many different kinds of body experiences can contribute to a Body Prominence score. Being physically ill or hungry or cold could probably elevate the score. Therefore, so far as possible, such variables should be controlled when working with Body Prominence. Ideally, conditions should be arranged so that subjects produce their protocols in similar hunger, temperature and health states. Of course, these controls are difficult to arrange; and, in fact, were not observed in the studies carried out by the present author. But one can urge their potential value in permitting sharper tests of hypotheses.

31
General Body Awareness in Women

INTRODUCTION

The investigation of general body awareness in women was pursued with the same technique as that used with men. The identical procedure was adhered to which requested subjects to write on a sheet of paper "20 things that you are aware of or conscious of right now." A total score was derived from protocols which was based on the number of direct or indirect body references

Table 31.1
Means and Standard Deviations of Body Prominence

| | Scores | |
M	σ	N
3.2	2.4	50
4.2	2.6	52
2.6	2.2	41
3.9	2.8	34
4.0	3.2	42
3.5	2.1	40
3.3	2.0	50
3.9	4.0	20
3.9	2.1	31
3.2	2.5	59
4.2	2.9	16
4.2	3.1	15

made. Scoring criteria are presented in Chapter 30. Body Prominence values in 12 different female samples of college students have averaged 3.7 (range 0–18).[1] They have usually been normal in character.

[1] In general, Body Prominence values will be presented only when major studies are involved or when they are quite deviant.

Comparison of the 12 samples of Body Prominence scores in Table 31.1 with the ten samples of male Body Prominence scores represented in Table 30.1 in Chapter 30 indicated a real sex difference. The mean value for the women (N = 450) was 3.57 (σ = 2.63) and that for the men (N = 421) was 3.19 (σ = 2.18). This difference was statistically significant (t = 2.4, $p < .02$).

In two samples of college women, the K and L scales of the MMPI and the Bass (1956) Social Acquiescence scale were not significantly correlated with Body Prominence. Apparently, response sets do not play a role in the production of scorable responses during the Body Prominence procedure. Measures of intelligence have likewise proved not to be significantly correlated with Body Prominence.

With a week intervening, the following test-retest values have been obtained for Body Prominence in female college student samples:[2] .49 (N = 81), .60 (N = 59), .42 (N = 37). In one study in which Body Prominence protocols were obtained on three occasions (five days intervening between each) from 42 college women the correlation between sessions 1 and 2 was .45. The correlation between sessions 1 and 3 was .41 and that between 2 and 3 was .50. These values are low and indicate limited stability in the Body Prominence measure. It is interesting that, as was true for the BFQ variables, they are of lesser magnitude than those observed for men. Once again the women show less consistency in their responses than men do.

VALIDITY

Several approaches were taken to evaluating the validity of the Body Prominence score. The first, which is similar to one described with reference to studies of males, involves relating Body Prominence to the density of body sensations or experiences reported during a period of time. This approach assumes that the experiential prominence of one's body will be manifested in its sensory vividness, as measured by the total amount of sensation apparently emanating from it. Operationally the density of body sensations is determined by asking subjects to report for five minutes (by placing checks on a sheet of paper with suitable headings) each time they experience definite sensations at certain body sites. A study was done in which 67 female college students (who were seen in small groups) were asked to produce Body Prominence protocols and subsequently called upon to give two five-minute periods of body sensation reports. The first of the requested five-minute reports concerned four sites: right side of head, left side of head, right side of body, left side of body. The second of the reports concerned four other sites: front of head, back of

---

[2] All correlations are product-moment unless otherwise indicated.

head, front of body, back of body. Body Prominence was found to be correlated .33 ($p < .01$) with the sum of the right-left reports and .29 ($p < .025$)
with the sum of front-back reports. Both correlations significantly supported
the expectation that Body Prominence would be positively related to density
of experienced body sensations.

A second approach to the validity issue was afforded by an experimental
design [3] in which Body Prominence reports were secured from women in the
standard situation and then again (five days later) after they had removed
their clothing and participated in a procedure in which they were gyneco-
logically examined. In the standard situation the subject was wearing her
usual clothing and in the second situation had just completed being examined
and was wearing only a hospital gown and a sheet loosely draped over her. It
would be logical to expect that submitting to a gynecological examination
and being in a semi-nude state would intensify body awareness. Therefore, if
the Body Prominence score taps body awareness, it should increase from the
first to second sessions. The sample studied consisted of 42 women (average
age, 26.5, average educational level, 13 years).

When the Body Prominence protocols were scored (blindly), it was noted
that the mean for session 1 was 3.3 ($\sigma = 2.1$) and that for session 2 was 6.7
($\sigma = 3.3$). A t-test indicated that the difference was significant ($t = 5.6$,
$p < .001$) in the predicted direction. To determine whether this increase
might simply be a function of the test-retest condition itself, two samples of
college women ($N = 59$, $N = 81$) who were seen on two occasions (seven
days intervening), each time under the usual standard conditions, were
appraised. Slight increases in Body Prominence from first to second sessions
were found, but they were not significant.

One of the most direct efforts to validate the Body Prominence index
involved a study of the effects of an experimental procedure for intensifying
body awareness. The question was whether directing an individual's attention
to her body would increase her Body Prominence score. Prominence protocols
were first obtained individually from 16 female college students. Each subject
then listened to a 15-minute tape recording in which a woman's voice
instructed her to focus on various parts of her body, to move and experience
certain body regions, and in general to attain heightened awareness of her
body sensations. Subsequently, a second Body Prominence protocol was
obtained. For a control group of 15 female college students, the identical
design was pursued except that the subjects listened to a tape recording of the

---

[3] This design was part of a larger study (Fisher and Osofsky, 1967) concerned with sexual
responsivity in women. In this study it was found that body awareness was not correlated
with sexual responsiveness. However, the degree of increase in body awareness from the
standard to the semi-nude state was positively and significantly correlated with sexual
responsiveness. This finding was interpreted as indicating that sexual responsiveness was
partially a function of being able to experience the sexual attributes of one's body (as exemplified in a nude state) without defensive denial or "shutting out."

same female voice which asked for thought and attention to a variety of issues (e.g., observing a landscape painting, describing vocational preferences, thinking about certain aspects of college life) that had nothing to do with the body.

The mean shift in Body Prominence for the experimental group was $+3.9$ ($\sigma = 3.9$); whereas that for the control group was $+.7$ ($\sigma = 2.7$). A t-test indicated that the relatively greater increment in body awareness of the subjects exposed to the body awareness tape was significant ($t = 2.7$, $p < .02$). The Body Prominence score showed itself to be directly sensitive to the effects of the technique devised to magnify body awareness.

Several other experiments were done which provided information as to whether the Body Prominence score was differentially sensitive to a series of conditions with varying degrees of potential influence upon body awareness. The series included, at one extreme, conditions with no body reference at all and at the other extreme those in which the subject's body was an explicit object of attention. Between these extremes were two conditions, one of which highlighted the bodies of others and another which called attention to the individual's body only in an indirect fashion.

Conditions with no body significance were built into two studies. One involved the following sequence: obtaining a Body Prominence protocol and then ink blot responses from the subject; exposing her to a 15-minute film consisting of two technical and rather boring film excerpts; [4] securing ink blot responses and another Body Prominence protocol from her.

The second study took exactly the same sequence, except that the subject watched an exciting film about racing. [5]

For the first study, which involved 15 college women, the mean of the initial Body Prominence score was 4.2 ($\sigma = 1.8$) and the mean following the boring film was 5.2 ($\sigma = 3.2$). The difference between means was not significant. In the case of the second study, in which 20 college women participated, the initial Body Prominence mean was 2.5 ($\sigma = 2.5$) and the second 3.9 ($\sigma = 4.0$). The difference between the means was once again not significant. Neither the boring chemistry film nor the exciting racing film, which had minimal references to the body, produced a significant effect upon the Body Prominence score.

At the other extreme was an experiment designed to produce high body awareness. The subjects (25 college women) went through a sequence similar to that in the two experiments just outlined above. However, intervening between the first and second ink blot tests was a condition in which each subject was told that she was being watched by several observers (who were shown to her) who would photograph and record every aspect of her behavior while she was asked to perform a number of self-revealing tasks

---

[4] "Use and Care of the Analytic Balance" and "Techniques of Organic Chemistry."
[5] "The Indianapolis 500."

(e.g., free association, describing the most embarrassing incident ever experienced). Electrodes were also attached to her arm and she was told that her physiological responses were being monitored (although actually they were not). It was intended to create a stress situation in which there was an acute sense that one's body reactions were being watched, analyzed, and evaluated. The duration of this intervening experimental condition was 18 minutes. The mean initial Body Prominence score was 2.6 ($\sigma = 1.9$) and the mean of the Body Prominence score taken after the experimental condition was 5.9 ($\sigma = 3.3$). The difference between means was significant ($t = 5.0$, $p < .001$). Clearly, an increase in body awareness was effected. The subject's exposure to information which made her body an unusually outstanding part of the total perceptual field did increase her Body Prominence score. One could, of course, argue that it was merely the fact of having been exposed to a stress situation which resulted in the Body Prominence increase and that the focus upon the subject's body did not play an important role.

Some light was cast on the soundness of this argument by another experiment which was concerned with the impact upon body awareness of watching a stressful movie [6] containing much body mutilation. It should be underscored that this film, produced to encourage safe driving, consists of repeated gory incidents in which cars are shown smashed up and people bleeding, dying, and moaning. There is unanimity that it is highly stressful and distasteful to view. Subjects report wanting to look away and leave the room. Body mutilation is the primary theme. But it is mutilation of *others* that is portrayed. The design of this experiment was the same as those just described above, except that the condition intervening between the pre- and post-Body Prominence protocols involved the film with the mutilation theme. Twenty-three college women were studied. The mean of the initial Body Prominence scores was 3.7 ($\sigma = 2.6$) and the mean of the post-mutilation film Body Prominence scores was 4.7 ($\sigma = 3.4$). This difference was not significant. Despite the clearly stressful nature of the film, it did not result in increased body awareness. Also, and perhaps more surprisingly, exposure to vivid themes of body mutilation did not produce higher Body Prominence scores. This could be interpreted as indicating a lack of sensitivity on the part of the Body Prominence measure. Another possibility is that exposure to body mutilation themes, which are in pictorial form and not *directly* threatening to the viewer's *own* body, is not sufficient to elicit a perceptible augmentation of body awareness in most people.[7] Perhaps this is so because indirect mutilation threats cause many persons to adopt repressive and denying strategies that defensively dampen body awareness.

Additional pertinent information concerning the dynamics of shifts in

---

[6] "Signal 30." An edited 15-minute version was used.

[7] However, it should be indicated that Boyar (1964) demonstrated that exposure to a longer version of this film increased anxiety about death.

body awareness was offered by the results of an experiment with the same design as the others described—except that the intervening condition involved listening to vigorous march music [8] and also beating time and marching to it. It was intended by this procedure to direct the individual's attention to his body—especially his muscles. The marching, the beating time, the vigor, and the increase in breathing were considered likely to intensify the prominence of the body in the perceptual field. It should be noted that most subjects experienced the condition as enjoyable and exhilarating—and definitely not stressful. Sixteen college women were studied. The mean of the initial Body Prominence scores was 4.2 ($\sigma = 2.9$) and the post-marching music Body Prominence mean was 6.1 ($\sigma = 3.2$). This difference attained a borderline level of significance ($t = 1.8$, $p < .10$). Exposure to a condition involving *direct* arousal of one's body (especially muscularly) resulted in a discernible (although borderline) trend for body awareness to increase. It is interesting that this non-stressful, rather enjoyable direct experience led toward greater body awareness, whereas the indirect threat posed by frightening mutilation themes involving *others* did not give rise to such a trend.

The experiments just described represent a first exploratory effort to understand some of the factors that influence the Body Prominence score. A crude sampling of conditions has been perused. Those which had no obvious body significance (e.g., watching boring chemistry film or racing film) did not influence Body Prominence. Those which explicitly called the individual's attention to her body (e.g., apparently being photographed and physiologically recorded) or involved direct body arousal (e.g., marching) tended to increase Body Prominence scores. But an indirect threat to one's body (viz., mutilation film) did not appreciably add to body awareness. It was, as previously stated, surprising that the mutilation threat had so little effect; and obviously a good deal needs to be done to ascertain [9] which persons do and which do not become more bodily aware when indirect body threats are made.

[8] For example, Seventy-Six Trombones (M. Wilson), El Capitan (Sousa), and Stars and Stripes Forever (Sousa).

[9] In actual fact, as already reported in the chapter dealing with boundary phenomena, something is known about one variable involved in whether body awareness increases under the impact of indirect body threat. Barrier scores were available for the subjects in the mutilation film study. Such scores were found to be correlated .36 ($p < .10$) with the degree to which the post-film Body Prominence score was greater than the pre-film score. One way of interpreting this finding is that the more definite a woman's boundaries the more directly she translated the mutilation film into self referred body experiences—instead of denying them. Of course, one could also argue that the greater the boundary definiteness the greater was the body anxiety aroused. Which of these or other alternatives best fits the facts remains to be seen.

TRAIT AND DEFENSE CORRELATES

Two prime kinds of variables first were considered in the sweep [10] to collect information about the possible trait and defense correlates of general body awareness in women. One concerned the contribution of awareness of specific body areas to general body awareness. That is, it dealt with the relation of Body Prominence to the various Body Focus Questionnaire scores. The other concerned the role of boundary articulation in making one's body stand out as a perceptual object. Good theoretical reasons can be mustered for conjecturing that if an individual's body is clearly differentiated from its environs it should be experienced as a more vivid perceptual object than if it is not clearly differentiated. This idea, as mentioned earlier, did not show much promise when applied to men. But its applicability to women was also explored. Forty-two college women were studied. They were asked to respond to the Body Focus Questionnaire and to the Rorschach blots [11] which measured boundary articulation in terms of the Barrier score. Body Prominence scores were secured on three occasions (five days intervening each time) and it was the sum of these scores which was used as an index of general body awareness. The BFQ variables were all unrelated to Body Prominence.[12] No specified body sector seemed to be contributing particularly to the overall level of body awareness.

More encouraging results appeared when the relationship between Body Prominence and the Barrier score was determined. The median Body Prominence sum was 7 (range 1–14) and the median Barrier score was 7 (range 2–18). The two variables were positively and significantly related ($\chi^2 = 9.5$, df = 1, $p < .01$). There was evidence that a woman's amount of body awareness was positively related to her boundary definiteness. It was this lead which was followed up in a series of cross-validation efforts.[13]

A total of 11 more samples were studied in which the Body Prominence measure and the Barrier score were obtained. The results are summarized

[10] This study was actually a parallel of that which was initially carried out to pinpoint the behavioral correlates of general body awareness in men. Only ten Body Prominence reports, instead of 20, were secured from subjects each time.

[11] The blots were administered in the usual fashion which elicits a fixed number of responses per blot.

[12] It should be added that in subsequent samples Body Prominence was not found to be consistently related to any of the BFQ variables. However, there was a trend (in three of six samples) for it to be correlated positively (approximately .30) with BFQ Back.

[13] Because oral variables and Body Prominence were related in male subjects, a similar possibility was investigated with reference to women. Oral variables (e.g., Byrne Food Attitude Scale, memory for oral body areas) have, however, turned out not to be consistently correlated with Body Prominence in women.

in Table 31.2. In eight samples the observed relationships were in the predicted direction; and in seven they were significantly so. There was one

Table 31.2
Summary of Results Pertaining to Relationships of Body Prominence with Barrier Score in Multiple Samples of Women [a]

N	Result
112	$\chi^2 = 4.0, p \ .02$ [b]
74	$\chi^2 = 5.6, p < .01$
25	Not significant
21[c]	Rho $= .46, p < .05$
15	Not significant
61	Pearson $r = .26, p < .05$
35	Pearson $r = -.32, p \ .05$
42	$\chi^2 = 9.6, p < .001$
23	Pearson $r = .38, p < .05$
16	Pearson $r = .37$, not significant
20	Pearson $r = .40, p \ .05$

[a] All samples consist of college women, unless otherwise noted.
[b] All significance values stated in terms of one-tail tests.
[c] Female relatives of hospitalized psychiatric patients.

instance in which a significant negative rather than positive correlation was found. Seven of the 11 results were significantly in the expected direction. If one considers the original finding prompting these cross-validation efforts, one may say that a total of eight of 12 results support the proposition that body awareness and boundary articulation are positively linked.

OVERVIEW

The results for women may be contrasted with those for men. Women turned out to be slightly, but significantly, more aware of their bodies than men. This is not surprising in view of previous reports. Secord (1953), Van Lennep (1957), Weinberg (1960), Korchin and Heath (1961), and Mordkoff (1966) have all indicated on the basis of different methodologies that women are more aware of their body sensations and experiences than are men. In male samples body awareness and boundary articulation were quite unrelated. The only consistent correlate of degree of body awareness was selectivity in responding to oral themes and the extent to which Nurturant attitudes (as defined by the Edwards Preference Schedule) were apparently taken toward others. Body awareness seemed to be linked in some as yet unexplained way with the intensity of oral wishes and conflicts. But in female samples oral measures fail to relate to body awareness. One finds instead that Body Prominence is positively related to boundary definiteness. The fact that body awareness in women varies with respect to boundary definiteness may be most meaningfully interpreted within the context of previous findings concerning the Barrier score. Considerable data portray the person with well articulated boundaries as self steering, goal oriented, and possessed of a clearly stated sense of identity. Clear-cut boundaries seem to be accompanied by the ability to behave as a well-individuated person. From this perspective, it would appear that degree of body awareness in women is an expression of individuation. The woman who is relatively highly aware of her body may be viewed as one who expresses herself with a clear sense of identity. Her body awareness is perhaps one manifestation of her explicit differentiation from her environs. Contrastingly, the woman with relatively little body awareness might be characterized as lacking individuation.

It is perhaps not going too far beyond the facts to say that the data indicate that in women degree of body awareness is correlated with a kind of personal strength (viz., individuality and self steering). However, in men body awareness does not seem to be tied to a strength factor—but rather a focalized concern about oral stimuli.

The existence of the above sex differences probably reflects the contrasting attitudes one finds in Western culture toward body awareness in men and women. The socialization of the female child emphasizes a conscious concern with how her body impresses others. She is expected to devote considerable attention to adorning and shaping her body to make it attractive and to communicate her sexual interests. This is a normal and an important aspect of learning the role of a woman. However, the boy, while expected to develop muscular strength and agility, is not encouraged to attend to his body in this self-conscious manner, particularly as a potential object of display and attractiveness. It will be recalled that Van Lennep (1957) has found that typically girls show an increasing interest in body themes in stories elicited by pictures as they mature beyond adolescence, whereas boys manifest a decreasing degree of such interest. Relatedly, Harlow (1951) reported that men who devoted special attention to building up their bodies by means of weight lifting were likely to be insecure and in considerable conflict about being heterosexually expressive.

Korchin and Heath (1961) found not only that women report more sensations of autonomic arousal in various situations than do men but that men with high autonomic awareness scores are described as passive-dependent and ineffectual whereas women with high scores are depicted as active and aggressive. In view of this observation that women with high autonomic awareness scores were active and aggressive, Korchin and Heath suggested that persons with high autonomic feedback might be those "least successful in their sex roles." Mordkoff (1966) confirmed the fact of a sex difference in degree of awareness of autonomic sensations; and noted that high awareness of such sensations was associated with maladjustment in men but not in women. The contrast between men and women in attitudes and traits linked with body awareness which the present studies have uncovered bears a similarity to the Korchin and Heath and also the Mordkoff findings. One point of difference would relate to the fact that Korchin and Heath interpreted the patterns of sex differences in correlates of autonomic awareness to indicate that high awareness was paralleled by inadequate structuring of sex role in both men and women; while the data derived from the Body Prominence work suggests that high body awareness may betoken conflictual oral attitudes in men and clear self individuation in women.

There may be unlike interpretations of the various kinds of data which have accumulated pertaining to sex differences in awareness of body sensations, but the fact of some kind of basic difference now seems highly probable.

ARTISTIC VS. ORDERLY ORIENTATION

The fact that Body Prominence was found to be positively related in men to artistic interests and negatively so to clerical interests encouraged inquiry concerning similar possibilities for women. An initial sample consisting of 50 college women who were seen in small groups was studied. Body Prominence protocols were obtained and also responses to the Kuder (1956) Preference Record, the Allport-Vernon-Lindzey (1960) Study of Values, and the Edwards (1954) Preference Schedule. Body Prominence was found to be positively related to the Kuder Literary scale ($\chi^2 = 5.1$, df $= 1$, $p < .05$) and negatively at a borderline level with the Clerical scale ($\chi^2 = 2.8$, df $= 1$, $p < .10$). The relationship with Kuder Artistic was positive, but not significant.

No relationships of significance appeared between Body Prominence and any of the Study of Values scores (although that involving the Aesthetic score was positive in direction).

Body Prominence was not significantly related to any of the Edwards Preference Schedule scores. While it was linked negatively to the Orderly score, the χ^2 value was only 2.1.

In a second study of 55 college women who were seen in small groups Body Prominence was considered again with reference to the Kuder and the Edwards scores. It proved to be positively related to Kuder Artistic ($\chi^2 = 6.5$ df $= 2$, $p < .05$), but not to any of the other Kuder variables. There were negative relationships with both Kuder Clerical and Computational, but they fell merely at the $p < .20$ level.

The only relationship Body Prominence achieved with the Edwards scales was a negative one with the Order score ($\chi^2 = 3.9$, df $= 1$, $p < .05$).

These findings only hinted at a trend for body awareness to be positively linked with the artistic-literary attitude and negatively so with a clerical-orderly orientation.

The problem was explored in still another way in a third study involving 58 college women who were seen in small groups. Body Prominence protocols were obtained and subjects were asked to list on a sheet of paper "ten occupations you consider most attractive or interesting." A score based on the number of artistic and literary occupations mentioned was correlated .30 ($p < .025$) with Body Prominence. As was true for the male samples, a better demonstration of the link between body awareness and artistic interests was obtained by use of the rather crude spontaneous listing of occupations one likes than by means of psychometrically sophisticated interest measures.

The fact that in both male and female samples trends have been detected for amount of body awareness to be greater in those with elevated artistic and literary interests suggests this is a solid lead. Studies are now obviously needed which will compare Body Prominence in different occupational groups (e.g., artists and writers versus accountants and economists). One can even fantasy about the potentialities of experiments in which it would be possible to appraise the impact of increasing an individual's body awareness upon his artistic productions.

32
Sex Differences in Body Perception[1]

INTRODUCTION

Considering the gross contrasts in anatomy and style of clothing typifying the two sexes, it is surprising how few direct and simple distinctions in body perception have been detected between them. Looking back over the work presented in previous chapters, one finds that men and women did not differ significantly for any of the Body Focus Questionnaire scores except BFQ Eyes. They were quite similar in the amount of attention they focused upon specific body sectors.

But, on the other hand, certain sex differences in body concept have emerged. It has been shown both in adults and children that females obtain higher Barrier and lower Penetration scores than males. The female seems to have a more clearly demarcated body boundary than the male. In addition, while gross sex differences in BFQ scores have not appeared, the correlates of such scores have been patently unlike for the two sexes. For example, difficulties in heterosexual adjustment are associated with high right awareness in men; but women who are unusually right aware are distinguished by their intraceptive attitudes. Differences of a related order could be described for any of the BFQ dimensions. Another level at which BFQ sex differences occurred concerned the test-retest reliabilities of the BFQ dimensions. With minor exceptions, men displayed greater BFQ stability over time than did women. Sex differences were observed too for Body Prominence. Women tended to obtain slightly higher Body Prominence scores than men. Also, women with high Body Prominence scores turned out to have clear boundaries; whereas men with high scores seemed to be particularly sensitive to, and concerned about, oral themes.

The material cited above illustrated not only that sex differences in body

---

[1] Portions of this chapter appeared in a monograph by Fisher (1964E).

528

perception are complex in nature but also that when such differences are found they do not necessarily favor the widely held view that men have a "superior," more stable body concept than women. It is hardly supportive of the idea that the male body concept is superior to learn that women obtain higher Barrier scores than men, and to have evidence that heightened body awareness in women is associated with clearly delineated boundaries, whereas in men it is linked with sensitivity to oral themes.

The notion of the inferior female body concept was most forcefully promulgated by Freud (1938, 1959). He felt that the female becomes aware, by comparing herself to the male, that she lacks an externally projecting genital; and this engenders feelings of inferiority. Indeed, because the vagina is literally a "break" in the body wall she is stimulated to fantasy that she once possessed a projecting genital, but that it was removed. She is therefore presumably left with a permanent feeling of body inferiority. Freud theorized that the sense of body (penis) loss could result in compensatory "penis envy" and phallic attitudes. The phallic versus non-phallic approach to distinguishing the body concept of males and females has been considered in a few empirical studies. Erikson (1951) found that when male and female adolescents were asked to construct scenes with play materials, the males were inclined to produce upright, phallic structures and the females to fashion configurations which are open and easy of access. He suggested that these differences were symbolic statements of the genital distinction between the sexes and their contrasting phallic versus non-phallic modes of experiencing their bodies. Franck and Rosen (1949) discovered, quite relatedly, that when males and females were asked to complete vague line drawings, the males, in contrast to the females, were characterized by more completions with projecting phallic qualities. This was regarded, at one level, as an expression of a sex difference in body feeling.

The aura of male superiority conveyed by the relatively greater occurrence of phallic attitudes in the male is not reinforced when one looks at other studies which have examined sex differences in body perception. Katcher and Levin (1955) observed that when boys and girls were requested to construct human forms representing self, mother, and father by means of schematic body parts varying in size, the girls apparently had an earlier realistic appreciation than boys of the smallness of their own bodies relative to those of adults. It was conjectured that since body smallness is typically associated with femininity in our culture, this difference might indicate that girls learn more quickly than boys to assign sexual significance to their bodies. Pertinent to this matter is the fact that Jourard and Secord (1955) and others have demonstrated that women differ from men in preferring their body proportions to be small rather than large. Studies should also be mentioned which, congruent with the Body Prominence results obtained by the present writer, suggest that women may have greater awareness of their bodies than do men. Secord (1953) and also Weinberg (1960) noted that when associations to homonyms with body and non-body meanings were elicited, women gave more body oriented responses than did men. Van Lennep (1957) similarly reported that in story constructions females exceed males in the frequency of their references to body sensations.

Returning again to the distinction between the phallic and the non-phallic, one may recall that in the literature review in Chapter 3 studies were mentioned which indicated that boys tend to be more preoccupied than girls with castration fantasies when they enter the hospital for surgery. In general, boys seem to be a bit more upset than girls by a surgery experience. This no more fits with the idea that girls have an inferior body concept than do most of the other studies just cited.

Aside from the Barrier and Body Prominence studies which the present author conducted and which have already been described, there were several others he completed which were specifically pertinent to the question whether women feel less satisfied [2] and more insecure about their bodies than do men.

RESPONSE TO BODY DISTORTION

The first that will be described grew out of the Barrier and Body Prominence studies which implied that women have less difficulty than men in dealing with the whole problem of body awareness and arriving at a view of their bodies as distinct articulated entities. These studies implied that women more readily "come to terms" with their bodies and more easily make psychological sense out of them. As earlier suggested the socialization of the female child emphasizes a conscious concern with how her body impresses others. She is expected to adorn and "do things" to her body in order to render it attractive and to signify her sexual interests. This is an expected and paramount aspect of encompassing the role of a woman. Contrastingly, the boy, although encouraged to build up his body muscularly, is discouraged from attending to his body in a self-conscious, personalized fashion—particularly as a potential object of display and attractiveness. It is pertinent to note again that Harlow (1951) found that men who were unusually invested in building up their bodies by means of weight lifting were insecure and conflicted about their sexual identity. Only in the narrowest sense is it manly for a man to be sensitized to, or preoccupied with, his body.

With this general perspective, it was hypothesized that women are characterized by a clearer concept than men of the sexual identity of their bodies. It was assumed that they are better able to integrate their body experiences meaningfully with their societally defined sex role. Their body

---

[2] As measured at a conscious level by the Secord and Jourard Body Cathexis test (1953), men and women do not differ in their amount of dissatisfaction with their bodies.

attributes seem to make more sense to them in the context of the feminine role than do the male's body attributes in the context of the male role. If so, it should follow that women would be less confused or disturbed than men when perceiving themselves in a situation designed to introduce ambiguity concerning the sexual aspects of their appearance. If women have been better able than men to give meaning to their body experiences in a sex role sense, it should be more difficult to disturb or confuse them about such experiences. Translated closer to operational terms, this means that the more insecure one is about one's sexual identity the greater will be one's anxiety and disturbance when confronted with images of one's appearance that are ambiguous with regard to sexual categorization. Therefore, if men are more insecure than women about how to integrate their body experiences to their sex roles, they should be characterized by signs of relatively greater anxiety when confronted by a situation which introduces contradictions regarding the sex of their appearance.

In order to test this formulation a study was undertaken which involved the following procedure. Each subject was asked to describe his own mirror image while wearing a series of male and female masks. He was brought into a totally dark room; placed four feet from a full-length mirror; and told to keep his eyes closed until a signal was given. He was further told that a series of masks would be placed upon his face and that each time he was asked to open his eyes he would have a brief glimpse of his masked appearance in a mirror. His task was to examine his image until it was no longer visible; then he was to close his eyes and describe in as much detail as possible the appearance of his masked face. He was given a verbal preparatory signal ("Get ready") one second before he was to open his eyes; and then two lights (75 watt) were turned on for one second by a timer. Simultaneously with the turning on of the illumination, he was given a signal to open his eyes. Eight different rubber masks were placed upon his face in random order. Four represented males and four females. They were chosen so that their sex characteristics were clearly evident. When the subject described the appearance of his masked face, his words were written down as verbatim as possible. Scoring of his descriptions was entirely concerned with the correctness of his identification of the sex of each mask. The total number of misidentifications was tabulated. This total could range theoretically from o to 8. It was presumed that confrontation with a situation in which the sex of one's appearance could unpredictably vary would create a threat to the subject in proportion to his own insecurity about his sex attributes. Further, it was expected that the more intense the threat to the subject the greater the likelihood that he would experience anxiety of sufficient magnitude to interfere with the accurate perception of the sex characteristics of the masks. In terms of the hypothesis, this meant that men should make more errors than women in identifying the sex attributes of the masks.

Two separate samples of subjects were studied. Sample 1 consisted of 63 subjects (30 male, 33 female), and sample 2 comprised 78 subjects (29 male, 49 female). All were college students. The median age in both samples was 20.

Table 32.1
Chi-Square Analysis of Sex Differences in Misidentifications
of Masks in Samples 1 and 2

| | | Sample 1 | | | Sample 2 | | |
		Male	Female	χ^2	Male	Female	χ^2
Sex misidentifications	H	27	9	25.2 *	18	15	7.4 *
	L	3	24		11	34	

Note. H = above median; L = at median or below.
* $p < .001$

Sample 1. The median number of sex misidentifications in the male group was 3 (range 0–4) and in the female group 1 (range 0–2). As shown in Table 32.1, a chi-square analysis confirmed the prediction that the male subjects would report a larger number of sex misidentifications than the female subjects ($\chi^2 = 25.2$, df = 1, $p < .001$).

Sample 2. The median for sex misidentifications in the male group was 2 (range 1–3) and in the female group 1 (range 0–4). When the data in this cross-validation sample were examined by means of the chi square, sex misidentifications proved to be significantly more frequent in the male than female groups ($\chi^2 = 7.4$, df = 1, $p < .001$). It should be noted that an analysis of the specific types of misidentification errors in samples 1 and 2 did not reveal any significant trends for these errors to cluster on masks of the same sex or opposite sex as the subjects.

The differentiation between the men and women in number of sex misidentification errors was surprisingly sharp in two different samples. Men seemed less able than women to make valid discriminations between male and female sex attributes under the conditions set up in the experiment. It must, of course, be acknowledged that the fact that the subjects responded to masks on their own faces does not ensure that they identified them with their own appearance. The same results could perhaps have been obtained from reactions to the masks had they not been on the subject's own face. However, the fact must be considered that although many studies have been done of sex differences in responding to pictures and blots, none have ever indicated that men are less successful than women in making valid distinctions between that which is male and female. In any case, whether the results of the present study could be duplicated with masks not worn by the subject, the basic fact would remain that men evidence more disturbance than women in making the male-female discriminations required. One should also note that the relatively greater number of errors made by the men in this unstructured situation is opposite to the usual finding that women make more errors than men in vaguely defined judgmental situations (e.g., Witkin, et al., 1954).

INTERPRETATION OF CHANGES IN APPEARANCE

Another hypothesis pertinent to sex differences which was evaluated antici-pated that women would have less need than men to regard gross distorting changes in their appearance as having positive or enhancing value. Stated in another way, it was assumed that men would exceed women in assigning desirable implications to visual transformations of their bodies. This hypo-thesis was derived, first of all, from the view, already partially explored, that a woman feels more secure about, and basically accepting of, her body than a man because she can relate its attributes to her primary social (sex) role with greater clarity. Secondly, it was reasoned that women devote a good deal of energy to experimenting with cosmetics and various forms of body decoration in their striving to attain a "best appearance"; while men are limited by custom to a minimum of this kind of experimentation. Women therefore have more opportunity than men to "act out," or achieve reality for, their fantasies about how they would prefer to look to others. The freedom to experiment with her appearance would provide the average woman with a more realistic experiential background than is available to the man for judging what enhances one's appearance. In addition, it would mean that she would have fewer unexpressed wishes relating to the alteration of her appear-ance, and consequently have less motivation to capitalize wishfully on a random series of changes in her appearance by experiencing them as "improvements." Integrating these points, it may be said that women would be expected to appraise alterations in their bodily appearance more realis-tically than men because they have greater opportunities, by virtue of their sex role, to experience their bodies as related to real life goals and also to experiment with the actual effects of altering them.

In order to provide subjects with an opportunity to react to gross alterations in their appearance they were asked to stand four feet from a full-length mirror and to view themselves while wearing lenses that changed their apparent proportions. One set of lenses was designed to produce obvious lengthening of the vertical axis of the body. They consisted of a pair of equivalent meridional afocal iseikonic lenses of 14 percent magnification (right eye and left eye—14 percent [M = 1.20] meridional afocal lenses at axis 180°). Their effect was to make the subject look taller and thinner. A second set of lenses was used which produced obvious widening in the horizontal axis. They comprised a pair of equivalent meridional afocal iseikonic lenses of 14 percent magnification (right eye and left eye—14 percent [M = 1.20] meridional afocal lenses at axis 90°). They confronted the subject with an image of himself which was shorter and wider than usual. He was instructed to observe his mirror image and to describe the ways in which it appeared to be altered. Upon completion of his description, which was written down as verbatim as possible, he was asked to imagine the kind of person his altered appearance made him resemble. Responses were obtained first for the vertically and then for the horizontally distorting lenses.

The protocols were scored by rating the subject's description of his altered appearance as favorable or not favorable. Two judges who had no knowledge of the hypothesis under consideration attained 86 percent agreement in their classification of the responses for the total sample. Disagreements were later resolved by joint discussion. Examples of responses judged as favorable are as follows: Abraham Lincoln, movie star, agile, athletic, like a model, tall and slim. The following are illustrative of responses judged as unfavorable: lazy, fat, clown, weak, old maid.

There were 81 subjects (31 men, 50 women). They were college students whose median age was 20 years.

Table 32.2
Chi-Square Analysis of Sex Differences in Response to Vertical and Horizontal Lens-Induced Changes in Mirror Image

| | Vertical | | | Horizontal | | |
	Male	Female	χ^2	Male	Female	χ^2
Favorable	19	6	20.8 *	17[b]	11	11.7 *
Other	12	42		11	39	

[a] Only 48 female subjects are reported because two did not participate in the vertical distortion task.

[b] Only 28 male subjects are reported because three did not participate in the horizontal distortion task.

* $p < .001$

Without exception, all subjects detected the lengthening impact of the vertical lenses and the widening effect of the horizontal lenses. However, there were many individual differences in the interpretations that were placed upon these changes. Some subjects greeted them as highly desirable ("I wish I looked like that"), whereas others rejected them as "ugly" and alien. As can be seen in Table 32.2, the men were significantly more often approving than the women of the changes they observed in their mirror images. The differences were highly significant for both the vertical ($p < .001$) and horizontal ($p < .001$) conditions. It was the men who seemed to be intrigued with the potential improvement in body form suggested by the novel mirror image. Typically, this potential improvement was defined in terms of greater strength or forcefulness.

Although the data supported the original hypothesis and can therefore be explained in terms of the rationale underlying it, one could debate alternative explanations. Is it possible that the women, in rejecting the lens changes, were actually evidencing anxiety about perceiving gross alterations in their appearances rather than giving evidence that they could make discriminating realistic judgments? Perhaps the more favorable attitude of the men toward such alterations was indicative of their ease in accommodating to them. These possibilities cannot be dismissed, but they are contradicted by the fact that women are generally more daring and less embarrassed than men in exhibiting themselves publicly in novel clothing styles. It should also be pointed out that the favorable reactions of the men to their altered images occurred whether these alterations involved becoming taller and thinner or shorter and wider. That is, even though the two classes of alteration were directly opposite in character they both evoked favorable reactions from the men. This appears to be an expression of a diffuse set rather than of a discriminating openness to new body experiences.

Incidentally, it needs to be pointed out that the disapproving responses of the women to the lens distortions involved admitting publicly to defects which had been produced in their appearance. This raises the additional possibility that their level of body security made it easier for them to acknowledge the body defects they perceived in themselves than is the case for men.

Comment

As one considers the fact of sex differences with respect to Barrier, Penetration, Body Prominence, responses to wearing masks with confusing sex identity, and evaluative reactions to gross lens induced changes in one's mirror image, it is apparent that there is little support for the idea that women have an "inferior" or less stable body image than men. If anything, the opposite seems to be true. This does not correspond with Freud's views that women, because of their "castrated" state, are doomed to feel eternally that their bodies are defective. The idea of a defective female body concept has perhaps been encouraged by misinterpretations of the Witkin, et al. (1954) work which indicated that men were better able than women to make use of body cues in rendering spatial judgments and therefore presumably characterized by a better integrated and articulated body concept. The truth is that Witkin's data indicated only that women were not as effective as men in utilizing kinesthetic cues to make spatial judgments when they also had the choice of using visual cues for the same purpose. Actually, when women were allowed to make spatial judgments on the basis of kinesthetic information alone they did just as well as men. They were equally as capable as men of using their bodies as an orienting frame of reference.

Digressing for a moment, a word of puzzlement should be expressed about the earlier reported sex difference which was found in the test-retest reliabilities of the Body Focus Questionnaire. Women's BFQ scores turned out to be rather consistently less stable over time than men's. This suggests that a woman is less fixed than a man in the way she distributes her attention to her body over a period of time. Does this represent greater flexibility in the woman's organization of body experience or less integration and stability? Or is it a reflection of more periodicities (e.g., the menstrual cycle) in female physiology, which are capable of producing variations in body experiences? It is difficult to know at this point. However, one cannot help but note an analogy between the greater variation in women's BFQ scores and the fact that they do experiment considerably more than men with changing their body appearance. Over time, they are more likely than men to try new hair-dos, to change clothing styles radically, and to gird themselves with new modes of camouflage (e.g., wigs, false eyelashes, special girdles) which not only alter their appearance but also the patterning of their body sensations. This may reflect a greater freedom to change body experience in real life situations. Men may need to stabilize the existence of major body landmarks in a more rigid fashion. Of course, it could also be true that new modes of body adornment associated with a sense of being freer to experiment with one's body could themselves contribute to variation in responses to the BFQ. A woman might be wearing one type of costume when first responding to the BFQ and then have a radically new "get up" when respondng on a second occasion a week later. The two sets of costumes could conceivably emphasize, by decoration and pressure, quite different body sectors. Such radical costume changes would probably be less likely to occur in the case of the average man.

ANISEIKONIC PERCEPTION OF LOWER VERSUS UPPER BODY SECTORS

Before completing this chapter, several studies will be presented which deal with a special sex difference in body perception, originally reported by others, that is not directly involved in issues of male versus female superiority in body concept. These studies were first stimulated by the findings of Wittreich and Grace (1955) who compared male and female subjects with respect to the changes such subjects noted in their own appearance while observing their mirror images through aniseikonic lenses.[3] They discovered a trend for girls to report, among other things, fewer changes in their legs and feet than was true for boys. Several studies have demonstrated that perceptual targets

[3] Aniseikonic lenses result in the image of an object which is formed in one eye differing in size and shape from the image of the same object formed in the other eye.

which arouse anxiety in an individual are those which he is least likely to see as changed when viewing them through aniseikonic lenses. Perception of change in the appearance of an aniseikonically viewed stimulus seems to be facilitated if that stimulus is experienced as non-threatening (Wittreich and Radcliffe, 1955). With this viewpoint, Wittreich and Grace (1955) explained the sex differences they observed in frequency of aniseikonic change in one's own body parts as a function of differential anxiety about such parts. They focused especially upon the relative infrequency with which girls perceived alterations in their legs as compared to boys and theorized that this was due to the difference in meaning attached to their legs. They conjectured that the boy experiences his legs primarily as a means of locomotion and is frequently able to test out their effectiveness in this respect. Consequently, he has limited anxiety or uncertainty about them. However, they point out that for the girl her legs are not only a means of locomotion but also important objects of display that elicit responses from others which influence her judgment of whether she is attractive. As a result, she would perhaps be somewhat dependent upon the opinions of others for forming an evaluation of her legs. Her perception of her legs would be marked by relative uncertainty and anxiety. This explanation was tentatively proposed by Wittreich and Grace to exemplify the kind of variable that might cause a body area to be resistive to perceptual change.

Following this work, other findings [4] appeared which further suggested that males and females differ in their attitudes toward their legs. Bennett (1960) found that when subjects were asked to list any ten body parts, men more often mentioned the leg region (in terms of reference to the knee) than did women. Calden, Lundy, and Schlafer (1959) observed that when men and women rated their satisfaction with various parts of their bodies, the women were more critical of their legs and the lower sectors of their bodies than were the men. If one considers the Wittreich and Grace and Calden, et al. studies together, they imply that men are less dissatisfied with their legs than women and also better able to tolerate their perceptual alteration.

It therefore seemed reasonable to theorize that males and females do differ in the way they experience their legs. However, the Wittreich and Grace concept that this difference in attitude is due to the girl's dependence upon the reactions of others for arriving at an evaluation of her own legs did not seem to be an adequate explanation. One could argue that the boy too is dependent upon the responses of others in developing attitudes towards his legs. This dependence would not be so much in terms of reactions to the appearance of his legs as with reference to the amount of agility he displays in games or other athletic activities. The boy does not abstractly know that he is skillful in movement. He needs the positive response of others to establish that

[4] One should keep in mind, though, that no differences in leg or head awareness have been recorded in terms of BFQ measures.

such is true. It was conjectured that the basic difference between the sexes in attitudes toward one's legs is an expression of contrasting attitudes toward mobility and movement in space. The role of the female is usually defined as less mobile and more "stay put" than is the role of the male. The male is encouraged to learn to move his body aggressively and to venture forth boldly. But it is the custom to be more protective of the female as she moves out from the family circle. She is given the message that it is less proper and more dangerous for a woman to move about freely "out there" than it is for a man. Parsons and Bales (1955) and others have elaborated upon the division of labor between the sexes, such that the female's principal functions are inside the family group and the male's require contacting agents and institutions outside the family. Presumably, socialization experiences and standards render the female insecure about the type of mobility equated with leg activity. However, the male is made to feel that such mobility is a normal aspect of his life. This formulation will be tentatively favored to account for sex differences in leg attitudes which have been reported.

The main objective of the present study was to replicate with adult subjects the sex differences in aniseikonic perception of the legs which Wittreich and Grace found for children. Such a replication would establish that a sex difference in leg perception exists not only in children but also in adults.

There was a second objective which depended upon the results obtained with the aniseikonic procedure. It was intended, if it could be demonstrated that women do have a special degree of difficulty in perceiving aniseikonic changes in their legs, to show that their legs are less physiologically activated than are those of men. This proposition is derived from earlier work which demonstrated that specific attitudes toward given body areas may be accompanied by particular levels of physiological activation of those areas. Similar correlates have been described for exterior versus interior, right versus left, and front versus back body sectors (Davis, 1960; Fisher, 1958, 1961B; Fisher and Cleveland, 1959; Shipman, et al., 1964). More will be said about the theory underlying such work in a later chapter.

Aniseikonic judgments were obtained by asking each subject to stand 48 inches from a full-length mirror and to examine his image while wearing a set of aniseikonic lenses (right eye 4 percent meridional afocal, $\times 135°$; left eye 4 percent meridional afocal, $\times 45°$). He was simply told to note any changes in his appearance that might be produced by the lenses. After he had had five minutes to observe himself he was told:

I will read you a list of body areas. As I mention each one, tell me if it was changed in any way by the glasses.

The following list of body areas was then read to the subject: face, shoulders, chest, arms, hips, legs.

Two separate samples were evaluated. One consisted of 80 subjects (30 men, 50 women); and the other of 63 subjects (30 men, 33 women). They were all college students.

Table 32.3
Aniseikonic Changes in Body Appearance Reported by Men and Women in Two Samples

Body Part	Change [a]	Sample 1			Sample 2		
		Male	Female	χ^2	Male	Female	χ^2
Face	Yes	14	34	3.5	14	25	5.4 [b]*
	No	16	16		16	8	
Shoulders	Yes	14	18	NS [c]	18	14	1.7
	No	16	32		12	19	
Chest	Yes	12	30	3.1	14	15	NS
	No	18	20		16	18	
Arms	Yes	13	23	NS	20	21	NS
	No	17	27		10	12	
Hips	Yes	14	20	NS	18	16	NS
	No	16	30		12	17	
Legs	Yes	23	26	4.8 [d]*	25	17	7.2 [d]**
	No	7	24		5	16	

Yes = change seen; No = change not seen.
Two-tailed test.
Not significant.
One-tailed test.
* $p < .02$
** $p < .01$

Sample 1. As shown in Table 32.3, the male and female subjects in Sample 1 were differentiated in the same fashion as the boys and girls in the Wittreich and Grace sample. Men significantly exceeded the women in perceiving aniseikonically induced changes in their legs ($\chi^2 = 4.8$, df = 1, $p < .02$, one-tailed test). None of the sex differences for the other body parts were significant, although there was a weak trend for women to perceive more changes in the face ($\chi^2 = 3.5$, df = 1, $p < .10$, two-tailed test) and in the chest ($\chi^2 = 3.1$, df = 1, $p < .10$, two-tailed test) than the men. No real differences were present for shoulders, arms, or hips.

Sample 2. The results for Sample 2 reiterated that men perceive aniseikonic changes in the leg area with greater frequency than do women. Table 32.3 indicates that the difference is significant at the .01 level. The trend found in Sample 1 for women to exceed men in frequency of perceived change in the face was clearly supported ($\chi^2 = 5.4$, df = 1, $p = .02$, two-tailed test). Only chance differences between the sexes appeared for the other body sectors.

Comment

The data declare that men are more receptive than women to the perception of aniseikonic induced perceptual changes in the leg sector. The men did not exceed the women in aniseikonic change for any other body region. Since a sex difference in leg perception was also found by Wittreich and Grace to characterize children, the generality of this phenomenon is affirmed. There appears to be a difference between the male and female in our culture in their ability to experience perceptual change in the legs; and it begins in the early years. If one keeps in mind the available research regarding the factors influencing aniseikonic change, this suggests that the female finds her legs as perceptual targets to be a source of anxiety. She is not sufficiently secure about them to chance their visual transformation. It was previously proposed that her anxiety relates to having learned that mobility and movement in space, which are closely associated with the legs, are unsafe for a female. Her anxiety would mirror the limitations conventionally placed upon the female role.

The only other consistent aniseikonic difference which could be detected in both samples related to women perceiving alterations in the face region more frequently than did the men. One cannot but be impressed with the fact that this difference, which depicts the women as receptive to the perceptual alteration, involves a sector at the opposite end of the body from the legs. Since the face is the area most often used to register expressive emotion, this finding fits with Parsons' (Parsons and Bales, 1955) view that women are more specialized as expressive rather than instrumental agents in intimate situations (e.g., within the family) than are men. Perhaps the woman is more skilled in the use of her face for expressive communication and therefore less anxious about its functioning.

The work just reviewed demonstrates sex differences in body concept which are not related to obvious matters of anatomy but rather to particular cultural definitions of masculinity and femininity. Each culture's arbitrary concepts of masculinity-femininity may result in specific sex differences in body image. In a culture which favored female mobility and male passivity there might be a reversal of the present findings which suggested that anxiety about the leg region is greater in women than in men.

The data concerning the legs were sufficiently promising to stimulate an investigation of whether there are sex differences in amount of activation of the leg region. This work will be described next.

SKIN RESISTANCE REACTIVITY RATIOS

As previously noted, evidence exists in the literature which suggests that an attitude toward a body area may have its physiological correlate. It has been shown that the more clearly articulated an individual's body image boundaries the more he shows high reactivity in the boundary regions of the body (viz., skin and muscle) and low reactivity in interior sectors, e.g., heart (Davis, 1960; Fisher, 1963B; Fisher and Cleveland, 1968). Also, ratios of skin resistance between certain body areas have proven to be related to differential values assigned to these areas. Typically, it has been found that a body sector relatively less prominent than another in the body scheme is also relatively lower in skin activation. In one study the perception of one's head as small in relation to one's body was correlated with a high skin resistance level on the head (i.e., low activation) as compared to the body. Differences in size ascribed to the back versus front and upper versus lower areas of one's body have been analogously related to skin resistance differentials (Fisher, 1958, 1961B, 1961C).

One could, within the context of this work, expect that if men and women differ in the apparent role they assign to their legs in the body scheme, there should also be a corresponding physiological activation difference. Presumably, the female is anxious about her legs and conflicted about how to integrate them into her body scheme. As symbols of a potentially dangerous way of behaving, she minimizes their significance in relating to other body areas. If so, it would follow that activation of a woman's legs should be less in relation to other of her body regions than is true for men. It was therefore predicted that the ratio of leg skin resistance to that of an upper non-leg area should demonstrate lower leg activation for the female than the male.[5] Further, since Wittreich and Grace observed aniseikonic leg perception differences in children, it was expected that the same activation sex difference would occur in children.

Skin resistance was used as the index of relative physiological reactivity of upper body site in relation to lower body site. It was measured by means of a Brush direct-writing oscillograph. There was a constant current supply of 20 milliamperes and a direct current amplifier for measuring the voltage across subject. Calibration of the record was made directly in ohms. Separate balanced systems were utilized for the upper and the lower site measures. The area of recording from the sites was equalized by means of pieces of tape punched with two holes, each of 1/4-inch diameter.

[5] Other theoretical reasons for expecting such a relationship will be discussed in the final, integrative chapter.

The period of recording was based on the time required for both sites to stabilize to a point of no change for a 15-second period. A minimum of 30 seconds of recording was taken in any case. The median length of recording was 204 seconds. The upper site recording was taken from the dorsal surface of the middle joint of the middle finger of the left hand. A lower site recording was taken from a point 1/2 inch anterior to the ankle. The choice of the site was quite arbitrary and was based mainly on the ease with which electrodes could be applied. A final reactivity value was tabulated for each subject that was equal to the ratio of the hand resistance level to the lower site resistance level (hand resistance: ankle resistance) at the time of stabilization. The test-retest reliability of this procedure has been shown elsewhere to be adequate (Fisher, 1961B).

The subjects consisted of 275 college students (120 male, 155 female). Their median age was 20.

Included in the study were 230 children (117 boys, 113 girls). Their age range was seven–17, and they were recruited by payment of a fee.

Table 32.4
Chi-Square Analysis of Adult Sex Differences in Ratio
of Hand to Ankle Skin Resistance

Sex	Hand-leg ratio		
	High	Medium	Low
	$\frac{1}{(8.1 \text{ or higher})}$	$\frac{1}{(3.4-8.0)}$	$\frac{1}{(3.3 \text{ or less})}$
Men	25	49	47
Women	54	58	43

Note. $\chi^2 = 7.7$, df $= 2$, $p < .05$

The median skin resistance ratio in the adult male group was 1/4.4 (range 2/1–1/20) and in the female group it was 1/5.5 (range 2/1–1/60). When the scores were trichotomized into as nearly equal thirds as possible, a chi-square analysis indicated that the females had a significantly higher hand to ankle ratio than the males ($\chi^2 = 7.7$, df $= 2$, $p < .05$). That is, the women manifested, as predicted, a relatively lower degree of skin activation in the leg area (in relation to the hand) than did the men.

The medians and ranges for the children are depicted in Table 32.5. Because of the limited number of subjects at each level, the data have been analyzed by combined adjoining age groups (viz., seven–eight, nine–ten, 11–12, 13–14, 15–17). Table 32.6 indicates that in the seven–eight range significant sex differences do not appear. However, beginning in the nine–ten group the girls have, as predicted, a relatively lower level of leg skin activation than the boys ($\chi^2 = 4.6$, df $= 1$, $p < .02$, one-tailed test). This

Table 32.5
Medians and Ranges of Hand to Ankle Skin Resistance Ratios
in Boys and Girls in Age Range 7–17

	Age									
	7–8		9–10		11–12		13–14		15–17	
	M (N = 26)	F (N = 19)	M (N = 24)	F (N = 25)	M (N = 22)	F (N = 21)	M (N = 21)	F (N = 22)	M (N = 24)	F (N = 26)
Median	$\frac{1}{10}$	$\frac{1}{8.1}$	$\frac{1}{5.1}$	$\frac{1}{7.1}$	$\frac{1}{5.1}$	$\frac{1}{4.1}$	$\frac{1}{4.1}$	$\frac{1}{4.1}$	$\frac{1}{3.1}$	$\frac{1}{5.1}$
Range	$\frac{2\ 1}{1-25}$	$\frac{1\ 1}{1-21}$	$\frac{1\ 1}{1-20}$	$\frac{1\ 1}{1-22}$	$\frac{2\ 1}{1-19}$	$\frac{3\ 1}{1-18}$	$\frac{2\ 1}{1-15}$	$\frac{1\ 1}{1-19}$	$\frac{3\ 1}{1-13}$	$\frac{2\ 1}{1-20}$

Table 32.6
Chi-Square Analysis of Sex Differences in Ratio
of Hand to Ankle Skin Resistance in Age Range 7–17

Ages	Boys	Girls	χ^2
7–8			
H [a]	13	8	NS
L	13	11	
9–10			
H	9	17	4.6 [b]**
L	15	8	
11–12			
H	11	10	NS [c]
L	11	11	
13–14			
H	9	10	NS
L	12	12	
15–17			
H	7	14	3.2 [b]*
L	17	12	

[a] H = above median; L = at median or
below.
[b] One-tailed tests used.
[c] Not significant.
* $p < .05$
** $p < .02$

difference was not evident in the 11–12 or 13–14 groups, but reappeared at a
borderline level in the 15–17 category ($\chi^2 = 3.2$, df $= 1$, $p <. 50$, one-tailed
test). It is worth noting that children in the seven–eight age group have
significantly less leg activation than do children nine -17 or adults.

Comment

The skin resistance data were congruent with the hypothesis in the adult group, but merely in a borderline fashion for the children. Only at ages nine–ten and 15–17 could sex differences in ratio of hand-ankle skin resistance be shown. Why significant differences should appear at these points, but not in the seven–eight, 11–12, and 13–14 groups is not evident.

The findings of the aniseikonic lens procedure and the skin resistance measures point to a fundamental sex difference in the manner in which the legs are integrated into the body scheme. In turn, this difference has been speculatively linked with attitudes toward mobility and movement in space. A sex difference in leg skin resistance levels was predicted from the aniseikonic data, and the prediction was largely confirmed. This adds weight to the view, to be expanded at a later point, that body attitudes may contribute to (and also be affected by) the physiological activation of a body sector.

The mapping of sex differences in body concept has just begun. We possess minimal facts about what distinguishes the masculine and the feminine modes of body experience. What is the body "feeling" equivalent of a sense of being manly? What pattern of body sensations depicts femininity? One would guess that a number of the following variables will turn out to contribute to masculine versus feminine modes of body perception: mobility of body attention landmarks, awareness of areas (e.g., breasts, penis) with conspicuous sexual and reproductive significance, differentiation of attitudes toward upper and lower body sectors, feelings of smallness versus largeness, and the special role served by body awareness in the psychological economy.

One of the byproducts of an increasing knowledge of what is basic to the masculine and feminine body image would be a new approach to appraising variations in masculinity-femininity within each sex. Existing methods for measuring masculinity-femininity, which are largely based on analyzing interest patterns and activity preferences, have been disappointing. But perhaps a new perspective stated in terms of body experiences would achieve greater success. An evaluation of how closely an individual's experience of his body conforms to the masculine or feminine model may tell a good deal about his sex role identification.

VI

BODY STATES IN
DISTURBED PERSONS

33
Body Perception in Neurotic
and Schizophrenic Persons

INTRODUCTION

Deeply embedded in clinical lore is the idea that psychiatric patients are characterized by multifarious strange and distorted body experiences. Writers like Bleuler (1950), Schilder (1935), and Bychowski (1943) have described peculiarities of body perception in neurotic and schizophrenic patients. Reviews of some of this work may be found in Chapter 4. Many of the published accounts of distorted body experiences observed in schizophrenics depict phenomena so dramatically bizarre that one is left with the impression that radical body schema alterations are an inevitable accompaniment of serious ego regression.

However, as will be seen, the author encountered considerable difficulty in his attempts to delineate empirically the nature of the body scheme distortions which occur in those who are seriously maladjusted. This is perhaps not surprising if one considers how few positive results were netted by the review in Chapter 4 of past research dealing with body image parameters in schizophrenia. It is true that schizophrenics judge body position (and the relationship of non-self objects to body) differently than do normal controls (Wapner and Werner, 1965). Also, there are hints (e.g., Epstein, 1955) that schizophrenics are unusually positive in their evaluations of self representations when they are unknowingly confronted with them. But, on the other hand, the literature does not clearly indicate whether schizophrenics ascribe unusual size qualities to the body; whether they experience unique types of body distortions; or whether they have special difficulty in creating representations (e.g., drawings) of the human body. Also, schizophrenics are not consistently differentiated from normals in body awareness (as defined by Secord Homonym test scores), degree of positive or negative feeling about one's body, and response to distortions in one's mirror image. It should be added that the present author (Fisher, 1966B) and other investigators (Witkin, et al., 1962) have not been able to establish that schizophrenics differ from normals in the definiteness of their body image boundaries. Despite the fact that the Barrier score is positively correlated with ability to deal effectively with stress in the normal range, it is not significantly lower in schizophrenics than in normal persons.

The problem of disentangling what is typical of the body scheme of the individual who has serious reality testing problems was approached on several fronts. A review of this work follows.

BODY DISTORTION QUESTIONNAIRE (BDQ)

It seemed especially important to find out whether there are unique kinds of distorted body experiences associated with disturbances in reality testing. Toward this end the Body Distortion Questionnaire (BDQ) [1] was devised. It poses for the subject the task of answering Yes, No, or Undecided to 82 statements referring to a number of different kinds of distorted body experience. The exact instructions are as follows:

"Read each of the statements below. If your answer to a statement is Yes, put an X under Yes. If you answer is No, put an X under No. If you are not sure whether to say Yes or No, put an X under Undecided."

Statements included in the questionnaire involved seven [2] categories which are enumerated below:

 1. Large
  Perception of body as large (14 items)
  Examples: Parts of my body feel swollen.
      My hands feel big.
 2. Small
  Perception of body as small (14 items)
  Examples: My body feels small.
      My arms feel short.

---

[1] Referred to in earlier publications (e.g., Fisher, 1964C) as the Body Experience Questionnaire.

[2] There were originally nine categories. However, two (Miscellaneous, Size Change) comprised so few items that they proved to be extremely unreliable and are no longer used as separate scores. The entire BDQ form is presented in the Appendix D.

Only 76 of the 82 BFQ statements are formally scored in terms of the subcategories. But all 82 are used in deriving the total Distortion score.

3. Boundary Loss
   Loss of body boundaries (ten items)
   Examples: I feel like my body is unprotected.
   　　　　　I feel like the inside of my body has no protection from things that
   　　　　　　happen near me.

4. Dirty
   Body dirty or contaminated (six items)
   Examples: I feel like I should wash my hands.
   　　　　　The odor of my breath does not seem pleasant.

5. Blocked Openings
   Blocking of body openings (ten items)
   Examples: My ears feel stopped up.
   　　　　　My throat feels blocked up.

6. Skin
   Unusual skin sensations (ten items)
   Examples: My skin feels tighter than usual.
   　　　　　My skin feels more ticklish than usual.

7. Depersonalization
   Perception of one's body as alien or foreign (ten items)
   Examples: My hands feel like they are not mine.
   　　　　　My body feels like a non-living object.

These categories were developed on the basis of an analysis of the frequency with which diverse sources mentioned specific kinds of body image distortions as occurring in psychiatric populations. They represent those most often cited.

A total Distortion score is derived based on the number of items in the questionnaire checked either Yes or Undecided. The Yes and Undecided answers were combined because preliminary studies indicated high positive correlations between them. In addition to the overall Distortion score, indices are computed which indicate the percentage representation of each of the seven subcategories of distortion in the total Distortion score. The number of items in each category checked Yes or Undecided is divided by the total number of items checked Yes or Undecided in all categories. Percentage scores were utilized to minimize the effects upon the specific categories of general tendencies to check either large or small numbers of items.

The test-retest reliability of the total Distortion score has been consistently moderate to high in normal subjects. In one sample of 37 women (average age 26.5) who were administered the questionnaire individually on two occasions, seven days intervening, the test-retest coefficient [3] was .87. In a second sample of 49 women (average age 23.0), seen individually on two occasions 14 days apart, the test-retest coefficient was .81. For a group of 19 men (average age 40.8) who were evaluated individually the day before and

---

[3] All correlation coefficients cited are product-moment unless otherwise specified.

the day after minor surgery the two sets of scores correlated .96. Cardone (1967) reported that in a group consisting of 42 chronic schizophrenics and ten normal controls the test-retest coefficient for total Distortion score was .80. It is incidentally of interest that he found no correlation between the Distortion score and intelligence test scores.

The test-retest reliabilities of the subcategory scores, which were available for two of the samples just cited, were considerably lower. For the male pre-post operative group, only the Small and Blocked Body Openings test-retest scores were significantly positively correlated (.49, $p < .05$; .63, $p < .01$, respectively). The Large and Depersonalization test-retest correlations were just short of significance ($r = .41$, $r = .42$, respectively).

In the sample of 37 women, the test-retest correlations were as follows: Large ($r = .15$), Small ($r = .50$, p .001), Blocked Openings ($r = .27$, $p < .10$), Skin ($r = .30, p < .10$), Dirty ($r = .42, p < .01$), Depersonalization ($r = .47$, $p < .01$). A coefficient could not be computed for Boundary Loss because the distributions were too highly skewed. One can see that the highest test-retest values were found for the Small, Dirty, and Depersonalization categories. Those for Large, Blocked Openings, and Skin were not even statistically significant.[4] Across both samples, Small scores were most stable, with Depersonalization and Blocked Openings scores running a poor second.

The Marlowe-Crowne (1964) Social Desirability scale was found to have negligible relationships with the various BDQ scores in male (N = 34) and female (N = 31) schizophrenic groups. However, the MMPI K scale was correlated negatively with the total Distortion score in a sample (N = 60) of male college students ($r = -.38, p < .01$) and also in a sample (N = 47) of female college students ($r = -.52$, $p < .001$). The MMPI L scale was correlated with the total Distortion score in these samples respectively $-.04$ and $-.27$ ($p < .05$). However, none of the subcategory scores of the BDQ were correlated significantly with K and L. It is interesting that social desirability effects contributed more to the total BDQ Distortion score in the normal than schizophrenic samples.

The Bass (1956) Social Acquiescence scale was completely unrelated to any of the BDQ scores in a sample of 41 normal women.

In normal subjects, the total Distortion score has shown variable correlations with the seven subcategory scores.

One finds that in a normal male group (N = 20) it was significantly correlated with Small ($r = .70, p < .001$), Boundary Loss ($r = .44, p < .05$), and Depersonalization ($r = .44, p < .05$).

But in a normal female sample (N = 41) it was significantly correlated only with Depersonalization ($r = .48, p < .01$).

---

[4] Test-retest values for specific BDQ subcategories were not available for the Cardone (1967) sample or one of the female samples mentioned for which test-retest Distortion scores were cited.

Further, in a sample of college women (N = 47), it was not significantly related to any of the BDQ subscores.

Whereas in a sample of college men (N = 61) it was correlated significantly with Large (r = .48, p < .001), Small (r = .27, p < .05), and Boundary Loss (r = .28, p < .05).

The only consistency one can see is that in the two male groups the total Distortion score correlated positively with Small and Boundary Loss. However, these correlations were quite low (viz., .27 and .28) in one of the samples.

It should be added that in a number of samples no consistent correlations among the BDQ subcategory scores themselves could be observed.

Differentiation of Schizophrenic, Neurotic, and Normal Persons

Several studies were undertaken to permit comparisons of the BDQ scores in various groups differing in severity of psychiatric symptomatology.

The first exploratory venture [5] in this direction utilized an early, short version of the BDQ which consisted of 34 items organized into four categories (change in body size, depersonalization, boundary loss, body dirty). It was administered individually to 30 schizophrenic, 28 neurotic, and 25 normal women.[6] The groups did not differ significantly in age or education (median 12 years). The schizophrenics were all hospitalized and formally diagnosed as schizophrenic because of the presence of either delusions or hallucinations. None had received shock treatment within six months of being evaluated. About 30 percent were receiving tranquilizing medication. As for the neurotics, they were all in in-patient treatment; and about 20 percent were receiving medication. Special care was taken in recruiting the normal control group to choose persons who were without psychiatric symptomatology, but who were exposed to stressful conditions in some way comparable to that confronting a psychiatric patient by virtue of the fact that he is in trouble and coping with a crisis. Half of the group was composed of close relatives of hospitalized psychiatric patients; and the remainder were college students and housewives who were confronted with serious physical illness in some member of their immediate family. To some degree, then, all of the normal controls were exposed to a rather stressful life problem.

Analysis of the BDQ data indicated that the *combined* psychiatric patients obtained significantly higher (p .001) total Distortion scores than the

---

[5] This study has been described in detail in a paper by Fisher and Seidner (1963).

[6] Other tests were administered which are not pertinent to the problem under consideration.

Table 33.1
Medians for Body Distortion Questionnaire Scores and Chi-Square Tests of Group Differences

Variables	Medians			Group Differences								
	Schizo-phrenics (N = 30)	Neurotics (N = 28)	Normals (N = 25)	Schiz. vs. Neurotic χ^2	Signif. Level	Schiz. vs. Normal χ^2	Signif. Level	Neurotic vs. Normal χ^2	Signif. Level	Schiz. + Neurotic vs. Normal χ^2	Signif. Level
Total Distortion	8	8	5	ND [a]	NS [b]	.9	NS	1.5	NS	7.6	.001
% Size Change	14.3	16.7	14.3	.6	NS	.03	NS	1.0	NS	0	NS
% Depersonalization	11.1	12.5	12.5	.3	NS	.01	NS	ND		0	NS
% Boundary Loss	25.0	27.8	25.0	2.4	NS	ND		.2	NS	.1	NS
% Dirty	21.4	26.7	33.0	.4	NS	.9	NS	.5	NS	.3	NS

[a] ND = No difference
[b] NS = Not significant

normals.[7] Neither the schizophrenic nor neurotic groups taken alone differed significantly from the normals. Also, they did not differ from each other. None of the subcategory scores differentiated the groups. However, it was found that when six items specifically referring to sensations of decrease in body size were pooled, the schizophrenics, neurotics, and normals obtained scores which were in descending order. A chi-square comparison of the three groups was significant ($\chi^2 = 7.7$, df $= 2$, $p < .05$). The difference between the schizophrenics and neurotics was not significant. While sensations of body smallness were higher in the psychiatric than normal samples, no such differences could be found when six items pertaining to sensations of increase in body size were pooled.

These results led to the construction of a revised and longer version of the BDQ which has already been described. It was first administered [8] to the following males: 21 schizophrenics, 21 neurotics, 20 normal controls; females: 25 schizophrenics, 40 neurotics, 21 normal controls.[9] All schizophrenics were hospitalized. Forty-eight of the neurotics were hospitalized and 13 were being treated as out-patients. Sixty-six of the 106 psychiatric patients were not on medication at the time they were studied. The remainder were seen only after they had been taken off medication for at least three days. None of the patients had received shock treatment for at least six months prior to being evaluated.

Table 33.2
Median Scores for the Body Distortion Questionnaire in Normal, Neurotic, and Schizophrenic Groups

Variables	Male			Female		
	Normal (N = 20)	Neurotic (N = 20)	Schizo-phrenic (N = 21)	Normal (N = 21)	Neurotic (N = 40)	Schizo-phrenic (N = 25)
Total Distortion	3	11	10	3	13	11
% Larger	8	8	11	0	9	12
% Smaller	0	0	4	0	6	13
% Boundary Loss	0	0	8	0	6	11
% Blocked Body Openings	0	11	6	0	11	12
% Skin	0	14	12	5	13	12
% Dirty	0	20	16	0	9	6
% Depersonaliza-tion	7	6	12	0	12	14

[7] The patients receiving medication did not differ from those not receiving medication. Cardone (1967) likewise found that tranquilizing medication did not alter BDQ Distortion scores in male schizophrenics.

[8] Other tests were administered which are not pertinent to the immediate issue.

[9] A detailed description of this study may be found in a paper by Fisher (1964C).

Table 33.3
Comparisons of Normal, Neurotic, and Schizophrenic Male Subjects
for Body Distortion Questionnaire Scores

Variables	Normal (N = 20) vs. Neurotic (N = 20)			Normal (N = 20) vs. Schizophrenic [b] (N = 21)		
	Higher Score	χ^2	Signif. Level	Higher Score	χ^2	Signif. Level
Total Distortion	Neur.	7.0	0.001[c]	Schiz.	4.2	<0.02 [c]
% Smaller	Neur.	3.4 [a]	<0.05 [c]	Schiz.	3.9	<0.02 [c]
% Larger	ND [d]			ND		
% Boundary Loss	Neur.	2.4	>0.10	Schiz.	5.9	<0.02
% Blocked Body Openings	Neur.	8.8	<0.001	Schiz.	4.3	<0.05
% Skin	ND			ND		
% Dirty	Neur.	5.5	<0.02	Schiz.	5.5	<0.02
% Depersonalization	ND			ND		

[a] With Yates' correction.

[b] None of the differences between the neurotics and schizophrenics were significant.

[c] One-tail test.

[d] ND = No difference.

Table 33.4
Comparisons of Normal, Neurotic, and Schizophrenic
Female Subjects for Body Distortion Questionnaire Scores

Variables	Normal (N = 21) vs. Neurotic (N = 40)			Normal (N = 21) vs. Schizophrenic [b] (N = 25)		
	Higher Score	χ^2	Signif. Level	Higher Score	χ^2	Signif. Level
Total Distortion	Neur.	5.6	<0.01[c]	Schiz.	6.4	<0.01[c]
% Smaller	Neur.	6.1 [a]	<0.01[c]	Schiz.	12.0	<0.001[c]
% Larger	ND [d]			ND		
% Boundary Loss	Neur.	5.4	0.02	Schiz.	8.7	<0.01
% Blocked Body Openings	Neur.	4.0	<0.05	Schiz.	6.4	<0.02
% Skin	ND			ND		
% Dirty	Neur.	3.3	>0.05	Schiz.	3.7	>0.05
% Depersonalization	ND			ND		

[a] With Yates' correction.

[b] None of the differences between the neurotics and schizophrenics were significant.

[c] One-tail test.

[d] ND = No difference.

Once again the normal controls were chosen on the basis of the view that they should be facing some life crisis or difficult problem—with the intent of at least partially controlling for the fact that psychiatric patients are not only disorganized but caught up in a severe life crisis situation. The life crisis faced by the subjects in this group was a derivative of the fact that they were all relatives of patients who had been hospitalized for psychiatric treatment. Age and education differences between the groups were not significant.

The data disclosed in terms of chi-square tests that the male schizophrenics ($p < .02$) [10] and neurotics (p .001) experienced higher total Distortion scores than the normals. However, the schizophrenics and neurotics did not differ. As for the BDQ subcategory scores, certain differences between the psychiatric patients and the normals emerged. The schizophrenics ($p < .02$) and neurotics ($p < .05$) reported significantly more Small body experiences (i.e., body shrinking or becoming smaller) than the normals. But no differences occurred with respect to the Large category (body feels larger). The schizophrenics, but not the neurotics, exceeded the normals in Boundary Loss ($p < .02$); and the schizophrenics and neurotics both had higher Blocked Body Opening scores ($p < .05$, $p < .001$, respectively) and higher Dirty sensation scores ($p < .02$ in both instances) than the Normals. No differences were found for Skin or Depersonalization scores.

The pattern of results for the female subjects was similar. Both the schizophrenics ($p < .01$) and neurotics ($p < .01$) exceeded the normals in total Distortion scores. But the two psychiatric groups did not differ from each other. Also, neither of these two groups differed from the normals for Large scores. The schizophrenics and neurotics exceeded the normals in Boundary Loss ($p < .01$, p .02, respectively), Blocked Body Openings ($p < .20$, $p < .05$, respectively) and Dirty scores (borderline $p > .05$ level for both). No differences could be detected for the Skin or Depersonalization categories. The neurotics and schizophrenics did not differ significantly for any of the BDQ variables. Incidentally, no sex differences of significance were observed for the BDQ scores.

A third study was instituted to consider the solidity of these findings. The BDQ was administered individually to the following: male: 20 neurotics, 45 schizophrenics; female: 20 neurotics, 46 schizophrenics. The groups did not differ significantly in age or education. All the neurotics were hospitalized; and this was also true of the schizophrenics. None of the schizophrenics had received shock treatment within six months of the testing. About 50 percent of the patients were on tranquilizing medication. [11]

---

[10] One-tail tests were used for the Distortion and Small scores in this and all subsequent analyses to be cited because of the cross-validational nature of the studies. Two-tail tests are used for all other BDQ scores.

[11] Indices based on whether the subject was taking a drug and also the quantity did not correlate with any of the BDQ scores.

In order to have normal BDQ values for comparison, the controls available from the study last described above were utilized again. These normals did not differ significantly in age or education from either of the present patient samples.

Among the males, the schizophrenics and neurotics significantly

Table 33.5
Chi-Square Comparisons of Normal, Neurotic, and Schizophrenic Male Subjects for BDQ Scores

Variables	Normal vs. Neurotic				Normal vs. Schiz.		
	Normal Median (N = 20)	Neurotic Median (N = 20)	χ^2	p	Schiz. Median (N = 45)	χ^2	p
Total Distortion	3.0	8.0	4.9	<.02 [a]	21.0	14.1	<.001
Smaller	0	11.0	8.3	<.001	13.0	9.3	<.001
Larger	8.0	13.0	NS [b]		17.0	NS	
Boundary Loss	0	4.0	3.9	<.05	11.0	11.4	<.001
Blocked Body Openings	0	20.0	14.4	<.001	11.0	9.3	<.01
Skin	0	13.0	NS		9.0	NS	
Dirty	0	0	NS		7.0	NS	
Depersonalization	7.0	0	NS		10.0	NS	

[a] One-tail test used for Distortion and Small categories.
[b] NS = Not significant.

Table 33.6
Chi-Square Comparisons of Normal, Neurotic, and Schizophrenic Female Subjects for BDQ Scores

Variables	Normal vs. Neurotic				Normal vs. Schiz.		
	Normal Median (N = 21)	Neurotic Median (N = 20)	χ^2	p	Schiz. Median (N = 46)	χ^2	p
Total Distortion	3.0	8.0	4.9	<.02 [a]	7.0	3.6	<.05 [a]
Smaller	0	5.0	6.7	.001	8.0	9.8	<.001
Larger	0	10.0	NS [b]		9.0	NS	
Boundary Loss	0	7.0	5.2	<.05	7.0	7.1	<.01
Blocked Body Openings	0	6.0	NS		10.0	NS	
Skin	5.0	11.0	NS		6.0	NS	
Dirty	0	13.0	3.6	>.05	7.0	NS	
Depersonalization	0	7.0	NS		6.0	NS	

[a] One-tail tests used for Distortion and Small categories.
[b] NS = Not significant.

exceeded the normals for total Distortion scores ($p < .001$, $p < .02$, respectively), Small scores ($p < .001$, $p < .001$, respectively), Boundary Loss scores ($p < .001$, $p < .05$, respectively) and Blocked Body Openings scores ($p < .01$, $p < .001$, respectively). No differences were observed between the psychiatric groups and the normals for Large, Skin, Dirt, or Depersonalization scores. The neurotics and schizophrenics did not differ from each other significantly for any of the BDQ variables except total Distortions. The schizophrenics had, for the first time in three samples, higher Distortion scores than the neurotics ($p < .01$).

In the female samples, the schizophrenics and neurotics obtained higher total Distortion ($p < .05$, $p < .02$, respectively), Small ($p < .001$, p .001, respectively), and Boundary Loss scores ($p < .01$, $p < .05$, respectively) than the normals. No differences were found in this respect for the Large, Blocked Body Openings, Skin, Dirty, and Depersonalization categories. The schizophrenics and neurotics did not differ for any of the BDQ variables.

Significant sex differences in BDQ scores were not detected.

A fourth study was done which involved 31 male and 50 female schizophrenics. They were compared with the same normal group employed in the last two studies described. About 55 percent of the schizophrenics were taking tranquilizing medication.[12] The usual criteria relative to diagnosis, recency of shock treatment, and equating for age and education with the normal controls were applied in the selection of the sample.

A chi-square test indicated that the male schizophrenics had significantly higher Distortion scores (median = 18) than the normal controls ($p < .05$). They also had significantly higher ($p < .001$) Small (median = 13.0) and Blocked Body Openings scores ($p < .001$). Differences for the other BDQ categories were not significant.

The female schizophrenics had, as defined by a chi-square test, significantly higher Distortion scores (median = 13.0) than the female normals ($p < .02$). They also had significantly higher ($p < .02$) Small (median = 12.0) scores. Differences for the other BDQ categories were not significant.

Looking back over the four studies cited, what conclusions can one draw? First of all, the evidence is solid that neurotics and schizophrenics of both sexes grossly have a greater number of distorted body experiences than corresponding normal controls. This is also true with respect to the Small category. For males only, there has been a consistent trend for Blocked Body Openings scores to be higher in the psychiatric than normal groups. Consistent differences were not found in the males for the Large, Dirty, Boundary Loss, Skin, or Depersonalization scores. As for the females, consistent differences failed to appear with reference to the Large, Boundary Loss, Blocked Body Openings, Dirty, Skin, and Depersonalization scores.

---

[12] BDQ scores of medicated and non-medicated subjects were found not to differ significantly.

Neurotics and schizophrenics were found not to differ consistently for any of the BDQ categories.

A complication developed when the BDQ was administered to samples of college students. It was surprisingly discovered that they obtained considerably higher total Distortion, Small, and Blocked Body Openings scores than the normal controls who had originally been selected not only because they were equated with the psychiatric patients for age and education but also the fact of experiencing a life crisis. While both of the special male and female normal control groups had obtained median scores of 3.0, 0, and 0 respectively for the Distortion, Small, and Blocked Body Openings variables, one sample of normal male college students correspondingly obtained scores of 6.0, 6.0, and 13.0; and another male college sample obtained corresponding scores of 10, 10, and 13. In two female college samples, the scores were 10, 9, 3 and 9, 10, 7 respectively. When the pooled Distortion scores of all of the college students were compared by means of chi-square with the pooled Distortion scores of all of the psychiatric subjects, a significant difference was found ($p < .05$). This was similarly true for the Small score ($p < .05$). However, the difference for Blocked Body Openings was not.

The reason for the elevated scores in the college samples is not clear. Correlations between education and BDQ scores in the original normal and psychiatric samples had been non-significant; and one would therefore not expect the higher educational level of the college students to be the basis for their elevated BDQ scores. It is true that the college samples (median age 20) were considerably younger than the previous groups (median age in middle 30's) studied. One could look to this fact as a source of response difference. However, it is likely that the real explanation relates to a test taking attitude. The college student samples all comprised volunteers. They seemed to approach the BDQ items with an attitude which suggested not that they were concerned about pathology in themselves, but rather examining their body experiences with interest and intellectual curiosity. The studies with the non-college samples had all occurred in the context of a psychiatric hospital and perhaps for that reason may have elicited a different response set. There is no way of knowing whether this explanation is a valid one. In any case, even when the elevated scores of the college samples were considered, the psychiatric patients continued to have significantly elevated Distortion and Small scores, although this was not true for Blocked Body Openings.

In general, one may say that psychiatric patients are aware of more distorted body experiences than normals. They are especially likely to feel as if their bodies are shrinking and becoming smaller. This stands by way of contrast to the fact that they do not have a high number of sensations indicative of apparent increase in body size. The quality of the size change experienced is uniquely in the direction of smallness. There seems to be some factor basic to the development of psychiatric disturbance, or associated with the fact of occupying the role of a psychiatric patient, which results in experiences of body smallness. The sense of body smallness may be a translation into body terms of feelings of inferiority. It may be a very basic statement of a feeling of lacking worth, which perhaps arose so early as to be expressed primarily in the language of the body.[13] One is reminded, in this respect, of theories of schizophrenia which emphasize the etiological importance of inability to develop a sufficient sense of worth upon which to build ego or identity.

It should be noted that the predominance of Small rather than Large body sensations in the schizophrenics apparently contradicts those studies which report a tendency for schizophrenics to overestimate their body size (e.g., Cleveland, et al., 1962). However, as suggested in Chapter 4 and partially supported by work reported by Fisher (1966B), it is possible that the body size overestimation of schizophrenics represents a means of compensating for feelings of smallness.[14]

A word is in order concerning the lack of difference between the normals and psychiatric patients for Depersonalization experiences. As noted in Chapter 4, it has been a tradition among clinical observers that depersonalization is particularly pathognomic of serious regression. The present findings are not in agreement with this viewpoint. Relatedly, several other investigators (Sedman, 1966; Dixon, 1963) have now reported that depersonalization experiences are not at all unusual in normal persons.

It may be a particularly important finding that neurotic and schizophrenic patients do not differ from each other in total BDQ distortions or with respect to specific BDQ categories. Psychotic breakdown does not seem to be accompanied by body experience distortions which are uniquely unlike those discernible in troubled neurotic patients who still retain reality contact. If so, this raises questions about many previous clinical reports which depict schizophrenia as typically leading to gross distortions in the body scheme. One is reminded that although clinical reports would lead one to believe that the body boundary is severely impaired in schizophrenia, objective measurement of boundary definiteness by means of the Barrier score has not successfully differentiated neurotic or normal subjects from schizophrenics. It is possible that clinical reports have generalized unrealistically from outstanding dramatic instances where body image disturbance happened to occur.

It could be argued that the existence of differences between psychiatric patients and normals, but the absence of such differences between neurotics and schizophrenics, reflected the effects of unlike response sets. Perhaps normal subjects in general (even college students) are more reluctant than

[13] The BDQ Small and Large scores are not correlated with actual measures of height, shoulder width, and hip width.

[14] This view gains further plausibility when one considers that in one sample of male and two samples of female schizophrenics the Small score was positively and significantly correlated with ratings of the patient's degree of grandiosity. That is, the larger the number of Small sensations experienced the more likely the patient was to display grandiose attitudes and behavior. (indicative of feelings of psychological bigness).

psychiatric patients to admit to distorted body experiences and therefore come out with lower BDQ total Distortion scores. Whereas neurotics and schizophrenics, because of their patient status, are equally unguarded in their responses and therefore do not differ in their BDQ scores. This argument gains some force from the fact that the K score has been shown to be negatively related to total Distortion scores in normal samples. However, it is simultaneously true that the K score was not found to be related to the BDQ Small subcategory score. Therefore, the difference which occurred for this specific score could not be accounted for on this basis.

Another point which argues against response set as a major explanation for observed differences is the fact that some BDQ categories which one might expect to be most subject to social desirability censoring did not distinguish the normals and psychiatric patients. A good example of this is provided by the Depersonalization category. It deals with phenomena relating to the experiencing of one's body as strange and foreign. To indicate that one has had Depersonalization experiences would actually represent a blatantly open statement that one has had weird (socially undesirable) experiences. But it is this very category which has not differentiated psychiatric patients and normals in any instance. Another pertinent point is the fact that the BDQ Small score has consistently been higher in psychiatric than normal subjects, while the Large score has not. There is no apparent difference in the amount of social desirability implied in admitting to strange sensations of body smallness as against body largeness; and yet the two categories of items did evoke different patterns of response.

Further light is thrown on the BDQ results by studies which have been completed by other investigators. Keen (1966) administered the BDQ to 30 female chronic schizophrenics, 25 female acute schizophrenics, and 30 normal controls (attendants working in a psychiatric hospital). It was modified so that the term "Sometimes" was substituted for "Undecided" as one of the response choices. In addition to the BDQ, the following procedures were utilized:

1. Each subject was asked to look at a photograph of herself; to identify who it was; to indicate its degree of resemblance to herself; and to rate the degree to which her pictured body seemed to be "out of shape, irregular, distorted, or unusual."

2. Subjects were requested to draw a whole person on a blackboard and the drawing was photographed so that it could be submitted to judges for evaluation.

The results indicated that BDQ total Distortion scores were significantly higher in both of the schizophrenic groups than in the normal sample. Also, as predicted, the Distortion scores for the chronic schizophrenics were higher than those for the acute schizophrenics, although only at a borderline level ($p < .10$). An analysis of the BDQ subcategory scores was not undertaken.

A significant positive correlation was found too for the combined groups between the BDQ Distortion scores and the degree to which subjects judged their own bodies, as depicted in a photograph, to be distorted or out of shape. Judges' ratings of the degree of distortion of the figure drawings produced by the subjects were not consistently related to the BDQ Distortion scores. Only the distortion ratings of one of three judges correlated positively and significantly with total BDQ Distortion.

The results obtained by Keen were encouraging insofar as they supported the fact that the Distortion score could distinguish schizophrenics and normals. In addition, they showed that it was possible to discriminate (at a borderline level) between acute and chronic schizophrenics. It is of interest too, relative to matters of validity, that a measure of body image distortion based on ratings of one's own photograph correlated positively with the Distortion score.

As part of a study of the changes occurring in a group of schizophrenic patients being treated with tranquilizing medication, Cardone (1967) compared the BDQ Distortion scores of 42 male chronic schizophrenics and ten male psychiatric aides who represented normal controls. He did not find a significant difference between them. No attempt was made to analyze the subcategory BDQ scores.

The subjects responded not only to the BDQ, but also to the following:

Secord Body Cathexis–Self Cathexis Scale
Holtzman Ink Blots (Barrier and Penetration)
Adjustable Body-distorting Mirror (presenting subject with task of correcting distortions in his mirror image)

The Distortion score did not relate meaningfully to any of these variables. Actually, one wonders how much importance to assign to the lack of significant difference in Distortion between the normals and schizophrenics in view of the extremely small size of the normal sample ($N = 10$).

Cleveland and Sikes (1966) investigated BDQ scores in a group of male alcoholics ($N = 70$) who were compared with a group of male hospitalized neurotics ($N = 50$). The alcoholics were tested and then retested after a 90 day group therapy treatment program. No differences were initially found between the alcoholics and neurotics in total Distortion scores. However, the alcoholics were significantly higher in Blocked Body Openings and Dirt scores. Following treatment, the alcoholics displayed a significant decrease in both of these scores.

Relationship to Boundary Definiteness

Considerable space was devoted in Chapter 13 to an analysis of studies concerned with boundary attributes in psychiatric samples. It was concluded on the basis of Barrier score data that schizophrenics and seriously maladjusted neurotics do not differ from each other or normal controls in boundary definiteness. It was suggested that a psychotic person may maintain clearly delineated body boundaries as long as he continues to feel that he is a significant person with a meaningful role in the world. The paranoid schizophrenic, who delusionally portrays himself as the universal center of attention, exemplifies this possibility particularly well. Indeed, trends were found for the Barrier score to be positively correlated with the presence of paranoid and grandiose symptomatology in schizophrenic samples.

However, the possibility of a new perspective on the problem of how the boundaries of schizophrenic and normal individuals differ was provided by some interesting BDQ findings derived from the six samples of schizophrenics in which the Barrier score had been related to BDQ scores. Three samples were male and three female. No predictions had been made concerning the nature of the correlations that would occur. When the data were analyzed, it was found that Barrier was rather consistently unrelated to all of the BDQ variables except Blocked Body Openings. Its correlations with Blocked Body Openings in the male samples were as follows: .44 ($N = 21, p > .05$); .21 ($N = 42$); and .39 ($N = 27, p < .05$). In the female samples the correlations were as follows: .40 ($N = 25, p < .05$), .29 ($N = 46, p < .05$), .05 ($N = 46$). All of the correlations were positive and four were significantly so at the .05 level or better.[15]

There were available five samples of normal subjects in which the Barrier score could be correlated with BDQ scores. In no instance could one discern a significant positive correlation between Barrier and Blocked Body Openings. Only one borderline relationship ($r = .37, N = 20, p < .10$) occurred. It is also noteworthy that in two of the three normal male samples there was a trend for a negative relationship to exist between Barrier and Boundary Loss ($r = -.37, N = 37, p < .05; r = -.31, N = 20, p > .20$). Such a trend was not observed in the two female samples.

Data concerning the relationship of Barrier to Blocked Body Openings were examined in four neurotic groups. All correlations were of a chance order except one of borderline significance in a male sample ($r = .37, N = 27, p < .10$). Barrier likewise failed to have consistent meaningful relationships with the other BDQ scores.

The logical question to ask at this point is why the Barrier score was positively correlated with Blocked Body Openings in schizophrenic groups but not in normal or neurotic samples. Perhaps an answer can be derived from a review of what the Blocked Body Openings score means. This score indicates how much the subject endorses statements which describe body openings (including sense organs) and other organs usually thought of as

---

[15] Consistent correlations between Penetration and the various BDQ variables could not be established.

having interchange functions with the environment (e.g., stomach, lungs, kidneys) as feeling blocked. The following are examples of such statements:

My eyes feel like they are covered by a film.
My nose feels blocked up.
My throat feels blocked up.
My body feels like it is "stuffed" or too full.
My ears feel stopped up.

As a matter of fact, these particular items are those, from the entire series, endorsed with greatest frequency (by a ratio of 2 or 3 to 1) in most samples. Four of these items refer to blocked "openings" in the head region; and two (eyes and ears) involve the most important sense organs. It is of interest that items referring to the blocking of regions in other body areas (e.g., kidneys, stomach, intestines) are relatively rarely endorsed. It would appear, then, that the higher the Barrier score of the schizophrenic patient the more he feels that the principal sense organs and openings in his head are blocked— with lesser but similar feelings about other areas of his body. In other words, the more delineated the schizophrenic individual's boundaries the more he feels that his usual channels of input-output (particularly input) are blocked or somewhat closed off (e.g., My eyes feel like they are covered by a film; My ears feel stopped up). Since such feelings do not correlate with the existence of well delineated boundaries in the normal or neurotic individual, it seems reasonable to view them as representing a compensatory process which occurs in schizophrenia to help maintain the boundary. The "blocking off" process in the well bounded schizophrenic may be thought of as contrasting with the special alertness to the environment which was earlier described as typifying the normal person with a high Barrier score. One must seriously entertain the possibility that the maintenance of the boundary in the schizophrenic involves an active inhibitory process which dampens certain kinds of input. Does the boundary in the schizophrenic become delineating by virtue of its ability to "shut out" rather than by fostering alerted scanning functions? Perhaps the schizophrenic's boundary is "constituted" to an unusual degree by the sense of having a locus, a place of refuge that is shielded from input. This view is remarkably congruent with Federn's (1952) speculation that the schizophrenic may maintain just as firm boundaries as a normal individual, but that such boundaries are qualitatively different in their emphasis upon "sealing off" and excluding chunks of reality. The important point to be derived from the above presentation is that the Barrier score probably denotes quite different boundary structuring processes in the schizophrenic than in the normal or neurotic.[16]

[16] One is reminded that Reitman and Cleveland (1964) found that sensory isolation increased the Barrier score in schizophrenics and lowered it in non-psychotic individuals. Perhaps this was due to the fact that diminished sensory input reinforced the "shutting out",

How do the data pertaining to the relationship between Barrier and Blocked Body Openings mesh with those in Chapter 13 which depicted boundary definiteness in schizophrenics as depending upon the degree to which they are able to manufacture a good delusional "cover story" in which they retain importance and centrality? It is difficult to say. There is little about feeling that one's body openings are blocked which seems pertinent to the idea of assigning oneself delusional self-importance. Indeed, Blocked Body Openings scores of schizophrenics do not correlate with measures of grandiosity or paranoia. One can only speculate that the intensification of blocked body opening sensations and the unrealistic dramatization of self as important are both different aspects of a boundary preserving process.

One other point needs to be discussed with reference to the correlates of the Barrier score in schizophrenic patients. This concerns the relationship between boundary definiteness and self touching. Fifteen minutes of observation of self touching behavior had been secured in samples of schizophrenic patients while they were responding to questionnaires. The observer was always in the same room as the patient. The self touch data were obtained in three samples of male and four samples of female schizophrenics. It is interesting that in only one instance were the means of the self touch scores greater than the values prevailing for normal subjects. Self touching rates in schizophrenics [17] were not basically different from those typifying normal persons. Also, as is true in normals, the largest proportion of self touching was directed to the head. Barrier scores proved to be unrelated to self touching in male schizophrenics. However, in three of four female schizophrenic samples Barrier was positively correlated with total self touch scores (.46, N = 26, $p < .02$; .68, N = 25, $p < .001$; .50, N = 38, $p < .001$). At this point it should be recalled that in both *normal* male and female samples the Barrier score was not consistently related to total self touching. This means that the correlations found for the female schizophrenics were unique. What is to be made of this uniqueness? Does it mean that self touching plays a role in helping the schizophrenic woman to articulate her boundaries? By touching herself does she create skin and muscle sensations which in turn increase the prominence of the boundary layers of her body? This would exemplify self manipulation of body experience designed to produce effects analogous to those created in experiments earlier described, in which the Barrier score was increased by giving subjects tasks requiring them to concentrate their attention upon their skin and musculature. Another possibility to consider is that the greater the definiteness of a female schizophrenic's boundaries the more she receives skin sensations which stimulate her to self touching. This view

---

function of the boundary in schizophrenia; whereas limitation in stimulus input interfered with the role of the normally functioning boundary (see Chapter 13) as a *sensitive* and *alerted* interface.

[17] No relationship between self touching and drug dosage measures was found.

seems less plausible because it does not explain why others (e.g., male schizophrenics) do not show the same phenomenon. Why would the high Barrier schizophrenic male, who presumably would also be characterized by a good deal of skin and muscle activation, not show the same increased self touching as that found in the high Barrier female schizophrenic? There seems to be more logic to the view that the female schizophrenic, in contrast to the male, evolves a unique mode of boundary maintenance based on self stimulation. If one considers that women learn as part of the feminine role to change and camouflage their bodies directly by means of dress, cosmetics, and various appliances to a much greater extent than men do, it is perhaps not surprising that they "take" a more direct approach to augmenting boundary sensations at a time when crisis calls for special defensive measures. Women are much wiser about, and more practiced in, "doing" self enhancing things to their bodies than are men. A good deal more will be said about this matter at a later point.

Clinical Correlates of BDQ Scores

Returning again to the BDQ results, it should be indicated that neither the BDQ total Distortion score nor the various subcategory scores were correlated consistently with a series of indicators of the clinical status of the schizophrenic patients. Data from two samples of male and two samples of female schizophrenics demonstrated that the BDQ scores were not consistently related to number or length of hospitalizations, grandiosity, paranoia, or other aspects of behavior as defined by Lorr Inpatient Multidimensional Psychiatric Scale (Lorr, Klett, and McNair, 1963). They were also not correlated with age or whether the patient was taking medication. Further, in several samples they were not correlated with the frequency with which patients touched themselves.[18] One may add that self touching scores were generally unrelated to such variables as age, education, drug status, number of hospitalizations, and various Lorr ratings.

BODY FOCUS QUESTIONNAIRE (BFQ)

BFQ data were available in two samples of male and two samples of female schizophrenics. None of the BFQ scores for the schizophrenics were consistently different from those obtained for two neurotic groups and a variety of normal groups. Apparently, the manner in which schizophrenics distribute their attention to the various sectors of their bodies is not unusual or atypical.

---

[18] This was equally true in several neurotic samples.

Also, BFQ scores were not consistently correlated with any of the measures of clinical status such as exemplified by Lorr ratings, drug status, number of previous hospitalizations, and so forth.[19] The only exception, previously described, is that BFQ Back in men was positively correlated with a paranoid diagnosis in one sample.

The fact that the BFQ scores do not generally separate the individual with severe ego disturbance from the normal is not really surprising. Each BFQ score refers to a specific body area and in turn is pertinent to a particular conflict or problem. Since there is no empirical evidence that neurotic or schizophrenic disturbance is linked more to the occurrence of one type of problem than another, it is reasonable to expect that high or low BFQ scores in disturbed groups will be randomly distributed among the various BFQ categories.

COMMENTS

It must be admitted that despite the examination of a considerable number of samples of schizophrenics and neurotics by means of multiple body image measures, few definitive conclusions can be drawn concerning the nature of the body image phenomena associated with severe personality disorganization. It has not been possible to demonstrate that schizophrenics are characterized by unusually vague boundaries, nor by tendencies to be particularly more or less aware of specific body regions, nor by noteworthy differences in the frequencies with which they touch their bodies. They cannot be differentiated from neurotics in the frequency with which they experience strange or peculiar changes in their bodies. It is true, however, that neurotics and schizophrenics experience more body distortions than normals; and furthermore they experience more in the category pertaining to sensations of shrinkage and smallness. No consistent differences could be shown for BDQ categories concerned with body largeness, feelings of being dirty, blocked body openings, unusual skin sensations, feelings of boundary loss, and depersonalization. In other words, if one simply looks at the magnitude of various body image parameters, only a few distinguish the schizophrenic from the normal, and even these will not differentiate him from the neurotic. The fact that neurotics (largely hospitalized in the present studies) and schizophrenics do not differ at all suggests the possibility that distorted body experience is an important principal manifestation of disturbed ego integration right up to a threshold point where more serious indicators of reality distortion arise. That is, the degree of body image distortion shown by the

---

[19] It should be specifically indicated that BFQ Head did not correlate positively with amount of head touching in any of the psychiatric samples. Why the relationship appeared in normal groups but failed to do so in schizophrenic samples remains to be seen.

severe neurotics in the present samples may represent the usual upper limit of breakdown in the body concept that occurs before the individual becomes schizophrenic and grossly misinterprets the reality of objects "outside of" his body. This would imply that the pre-psychotic phases of ego disorganization are typified by a build-up of distortions in the body scheme and that further serious ego breakdown is expressed not primarily in body image terms but rather distortion of what is "out there."

Some measure of clarification emerged concerning what is specific to the way in which the schizophrenic individual structures his boundaries. In a unique fashion, Barrier was found to be positively correlated with Blocked Body Openings sensations in both male and female schizophrenics (but not in neurotics or normals). Apparently, sensations of blockage of body openings ordinarily involved in interchange with the environment may play a role in the schizophrenic's ability to maintain his boundaries. It remains to be seen whether the sensations of being "blocked" are a manifestation of a set to retreat from reality; whether they actually contribute to the sense of having a protective boundary by providing reassurance that the principal means of access into one's body are closed off; or whether both are true.

The data which were reported indicating that the Barrier score is positively correlated with self touching in schizophrenic women has been interpreted to mean that boundary maintenance in this group may be partially a function of self initiated sensory arousal of boundary regions of the body. Perhaps a sense of loss of boundary may motivate increased self touching which highlights the boundary. This may occur especially in the instance of the previously well bounded individual who has been accustomed to a clearly defined boundary experience and who, when boundary sensations decrease, is therefore most quickly aroused to provide an equivalent sensory experience for herself. This response might be analogous to the child who sucks his thumb or the adult who smokes or chews gum when accustomed oral gratifications are lost. It was conjectured that the reason why compensatory self touching occurs in women and not in men is that women have had much more experience in "doing things" directly to their bodies in order to achieve some idealized image or state of identity.

With such "compensatory" behavior as a paradigm, it will be interesting to look at other body image parameters to determine whether they are subject to self manipulation. If, as suggested by the Body Focus Questionnaire research, some of the control over an impulse or conflict is provided by an individual focusing attention upon a specific area of his body, what happens when the attention focusing process is disrupted? Does the individual initiate new ways of highlighting the area, such as by touching it with increased frequency or looking at it in the mirror more often? Some of the bizarre grimacing, posturing, and self mutilation observed in schizophrenics may represent compensatory attempts to restore patterns of body experience which have been disrupted and which previously had significant reassurance value and regulatory functions.

VII
CONCLUSION

34
Review, Formulation, and Speculation

INTRODUCTION

What closure can be attained with respect to the wide range of findings presented? Is it possible to weave connections between these findings and the diverse observations concerning body experience which have been offered by others? Is there continuity in the array of facts uncovered?

Let us contemplate some of the questions, problems, and issues that have emerged. It is obvious that the act of beholding one's own body is exceedingly multi-faceted. The experienced body is a world within a world. It is a complexly shaped and yet bilaterally symmetrically simplified object which has spatial and geographical features second to none in their diversity. As an experienced object, it often presents itself in a "strange" fashion which violates longstanding assumptions about the perceptual world. For example, the body possesses an interior which, though hidden from others and therefore socially invisible, continues to be evident to oneself with vivid intensity. One knows one's body from the inside, although the insides of other opaque objects are almost never perceivable. This "transparency" exemplifies but one of its numerous special qualities. Consider some of the others that may be enumerated: the fact that it is equated with self more than any other object; the immense worth and value ascribed to it; the potentiality it possesses of changing as the result of feedback during the very act of being perceived; and its ever present persistence as a "frame" for all perceptual experiences. Because of these unique conditions, the individual is confronted with a demanding task as he sets about learning to make sense out of his body as a psychological object.

It is evident, from the present author's research, that the process of organizing body experiences proceeds in several dimensions. First of all, quite different attitudes may be adopted with regard to the prominence that one's body experiences will occupy in the total perceptual field. The Body Prominence findings which were earlier presented indicated that individuals differ grossly in their relative awareness of their bodies as compared to other objects in their environs. The existence of such variations in body awareness was suggested too by the findings of Secord (1953) and Van Lennep (1957). One may speculate that long term tendencies to magnify or minimize the presence of one's body represent fundamental strategies in the process of learning to master body experiences. For some individuals (and for some cultures), the messages from one's body are shunted aside, avoided, and treated as unintelligible noise. For others, body experiences are of paramount importance and the state of the world is probably measured off against body "feelings." Formulations concerning the significance of body awareness differences are, unfortunately, much complicated by the fact that multiple, and even polar opposite, variables may contribute to a particular level of awareness. It has already been shown that the factors stimulating body awareness in women are not the same as those underlying such awareness in men. Similarly, the heightened body awareness of the chronically hypo-chondriacal woman is likely to be different in kind from the intensified awareness found in women who are mature and possessed of well delineated body boundaries. Much remains to be learned in this area. But what is of importance for the present discussion is the fact that one avenue of adaptation to body experience seems to relate to dampening and magnification. Sets can be established which either intensify or inhibit one's sensitivity to the sensations emanating from one's body. They obviously bear an analogy to the repression-sensitization dimension which has emerged in analyses of how experiences with the world in general are assimilated.

Another fundamental operation in organizing body experience concerns the establishment of a boundary. The conglomerate of results earlier presented concerning the nature of the body boundary and its role as a mediator in numerous behaviors leaves little doubt concerning its import. In order to perceive his body as possessing integrity and personal identity an individual needs to be able to see it as girded by a stable delineating surface. One would guess that without this elementary delineation it would be difficult, if not impossible, to set up other modes of controlling and interpreting body experiences. Unless an individual "knows" the limits of his body domain and can distinguish it accurately from all that is non-body he lacks an essential element in structuring other systems he might try to fashion to evaluate body experiences. He needs to know where his body "goes up to" in order to define the spatial limits of any body monitoring process. Without sharp clarity on this matter, body and non-body get confused with each other. The fundamental nature of boundary formation has been recognized in almost every major developmental theory. Whether the orientation is to Freud or Piaget, there is consensus that a primary step in individuation is learning the limits of one's body and, even more specifically, learning how to differentiate it from mother's body. Ego formation is predicated upon the initial step of body segregation. Empirically, the work of Witkin, et al. (1962) and Wapner and Werner (1965) with children leaves little doubt that the state of the child's boundary influences certain aspects of his decision making and also his general adaptability.

A third dimension of body image organization revealed by the author's research concerns the manner in which an individual distributes his attention to the major sectors of his body. The findings derived from the Body Focus Questionnaire indicate that each person learns to highlight certain body regions and to minimize others. He is absorbed with some; whereas others are almost non-existent for him. Evidence has accrued that the process of allotting attention selectively to body locales represents a way of linking one's body to life experiences and guiding values and intents. Each of the primary body areas apparently takes on a meaning and becomes part of a control system which influences approach or avoidance to certain types of situations. The control of long term directive states may be envisioned as inextricably bound up with an hierarchy of body experience signals. A good deal more will be said about this control system shortly.

The work which has been presented has rendered explicit some of the strategies for making sense out of one's body. We can, with moderate assurance, assign importance to such processes as boundary delineation, minimizing versus maximizing of body sensations, and allocation of attention to body areas in terms of meanings which have been ascribed to them. From the literature reviewed in Chapters 1–5 it is likely that other strategies are also important. The average individual arrives at an evaluation of how attractive his body is. He develops a concept of how much space it occupies (i.e., whether he is big or little). He formulates conclusions about the strength of his body and whether it can be easily injured. He decides how far his body exemplifies standards of masculinity or femininity. In addition, he engages in untold activities designed to implement or compensate for his decisions. It is with respect to such decisions that he dresses, cleans, camouflages, touches, mutilates, exercises, tranquilizes, and excites his body in particular ways. All of the "strategies" which have been cited may be thought of as "methods" for understanding and giving meaning to body experiences. They are part of a program of acquiring mastery over the perceived body. Incidentally, one would guess there are probably a fair number of body organizing strategies yet to be discovered.

A puzzling aspect of the present author's findings and also those reported by others is the fact that most body image dimensions seem not to be correlated with each other. For example, body awareness (as defined by Body Prominence) and the Barrier score are generally not related to the manner in which attention is distributed to the major sectors of the body.

Also, most of the BFQ measures are not consistently correlated. Similarly, there have been few instances in which parameters like the Secord Homonym test, the Jourard and Secord Body Cathexis index, indicators of over- or underestimation of one's body size, and accuracy of definition of one's position in space have been interrelated. The amount of independence among such measures, all of which are presumed to tap body attitudes, is somewhat surprising. But why should it be? No one is surprised at the fact that most "personality" indices are relatively independent of each other. Measures like those pertaining to ego strength, hostility, values, acquiescence, and cognitive style are presumably concerned with a common realm and yet they are largely unrelated to each other—or at an inconsistent low level, at best. It has come to be recognized that this is so because there are many specialized functions and subsystems in the personality realm; and further they are susceptible to influences that are situation specific.[1] Analogously, the term "body image" directly or indirectly embraces conscious and unconscious attitudes; verbal and motor modes of response; feelings about self worth, appearance, sex, hostility, anality; perception of body parts of diverse shape, location, size; experiences with sensations from visible and invisible sites; awareness of body events ranging from those which are highly acceptable to those utterly "disgusting." These phenomena are all semantically part of the body realm, but their diversity and unlike modes of reference are obvious.

BODY EXPERIENCE LANDMARKS

Probably one of the essential steps in mastering one's body experientially is discriminating its prime landmarks and assigning them to a cognitive map. This is as necessary for one's body as it would be for learning to live in any *terra incognita*. However, while a child may relatively quickly learn verbal labels for the major features of his body, this does not mean that he can with equal rapidity "know" what meanings to ascribe to them. He may be told that a part of his body is labeled "mouth" or "back," but even at the moment he learns the label he has already amassed a profusion of preverbal experiences about that part which impart to it confusing connotations requiring clarification. For example, a person's "back" is simultaneously a spatial designation, a rarely seen part of the body, a sector associated with anal functions, that which "faces away" from people, an area difficult to defend, a source of unique kinesthetic sensations, a locale particularly activated by certain emotions, a favorite site for the administration of punishment by one's parents, and so forth. In other words, to decide on the "place" and "significance" of the back, or any body region, is not a simple matter.

---

[1] Even different measures of physiological response to the *same* stimulus usually show only low order correlations with each other.

However, the research utilizing the Body Focus Questionnaire indicated that most of the major body regions, aside from their obvious semantic labels and designations pertinent to function, do acquire consistent specialized meanings—perhaps best described as symbolic in nature. Each signifies, though rarely within conscious awareness, an interest in, or a desire to avoid, certain types of experiences. Each becomes equated with a theme or a conflict. The themes largely concern basic life behaviors: incorporation, elimination, self-control, sexual aims, disposition of hostility, religiosity, exercise of power, defining the distance between self and others.

Table 34.1
Themes Associated with Body Awareness Dimensions
in Men and Women

Body Awareness Dimensions	Themes	
	Men	Women
BFQ Back	Anality	Anality
BFQ Right	Heterosexual inhibition	Intraception
BFQ Eyes	Incorporation	— [a]
BFQ Heart	Religiosity	Sociability
BFQ Mouth	Hostility-Masochism	Power
BFQ Stomach	Hostility-Masochism	Power
BFQ Head	Anality	Heterosexual inhibition

[a] The test-retest reliability of this dimension was too low to permit systematic investigation of its significance.

One must acknowledge that the data descriptive of the significance of various body regions are uneven. For men, the clearest findings have been obtained for the back-front, right-left, eyes, and heart dimensions. The results for the mouth, stomach, and head dimensions were much less impressive. For women, almost all of the BFQ findings must be viewed as tentative. Perhaps the most definite trends emerged with reference to back awareness. It is not yet clear whether the uncertain results obtaining for women represent methodological weaknesses in the studies concerned or stem from the relatively unstable nature of body awareness landmarks in the female.

One should also note that the meanings associated with awareness of specific body areas by men as compared to women are quite different. In only one instance was there a similarity. Relative awareness of the back versus the front was linked with anal variables in both men and women. But for all other awareness dimensions sex differences were marked. As one scans the themes or conflicts associated with heightened awareness of various body sectors in women, one cannot help but be impressed with the frequency with which they refer to either accommodation to, or gaining control over, other people. The Intraception theme associated with BFQ Right, the Sociability theme linked with BFQ Heart, and the Power theme associated with BFQ Mouth and BFQ Stomach all fall into this category. But the findings for the males rarely reveal an instance in which the theme associated with a BFQ variable explicitly concerns influencing or being influenced by others. The focus is consistently upon self oriented (intrapsychic?) problems and conflicts (e.g., whether it is acceptable to be incorporative; the need for self-control). One could say that the body signals of men largely concern matters related to internalized standards or conflict; while those of women convey information about social roles. This difference between males and females implies two things: first, that women are perhaps more concerned than men with the matter of social adaptation to others; and, second, that women assign more social connotations and meanings to their bodies than do men. One may suggest that the body as a psychological object is more involved in structuring of social roles in the case of women than is true for men. There is, of course, a good deal of common sense observation to support such an idea.

HOW DOES A BODY AREA ACQUIRE MEANING?

It has not been possible, as yet, to trace how equations occur between a theme or conflict and a specific body area. But let us review various alternatives.

1. One possibility is that parents may express attitudes about a matter in terms of how they treat a particular portion of the child's body. For example, parental attitudes about the badness of sex might result in restrictive behavior on their part which would prevent the child from freely seeing and touching his genitals. Or in a more subtle but related way they might call attention to his genitals by the extreme manner in which they avoided looking at, or referring to, them. Therefore, the child would begin to assume that sexual badness and his genitals were equivalent.

2. Another possibility, already conveyed by many of the BFQ formulations, is that an elaborate analogical language operates to give meaning to a body part. It will be recalled that in attempting to account for the equation of eye awareness in men with conflicts about incorporative wishes, it was speculated that the eye, because it is so devoted to "taking in" the environment, acquires incorporative connotations. That is, the apparent incorporative significance given to the eyes was thought to be derived from the metaphorical "taking in" implicit in looking and seeing. A similar use of metaphor may be discerned in certain explanations about how right versus left body sites could have become linked with attitudes toward heterosexuality. One of the speculations offered was that the difference in strength typically characterizing the right and left hands lends itself to a polarized representation of the masculine versus feminine which is itself often stereotyped in terms of

strong versus weak. Here again, it was an apparent metaphor (comparing masculinity-femininity to strength-weakness) which was presumed to account for the fact that attitudes toward heterosexuality were tied to right-left body sites.

The idea that metaphor might play such a role in giving symbolic meaning to body areas was developed by Freud (1910) and other psychoanalysts (e.g., Deutsch, 1952). Freud suggested that a body part could acquire unconscious significance because of its structural analogy (e.g., possessed of an opening) to the genitals or because it participated in functions which reminded one of a conflict (e.g., the throat might be equated with incorporative conflicts because of its involvement with swallowing).

3. The model offered by important figures in one's life could also be the origin of the special significance attributed to a body part. If, for example, a parent were particularly focused upon a region of his own body and used it to express complaints about a problem or issue, this could convey to the child a unique definition of that region. If mother complains of a headache every time she feels angry, the child may quickly learn to identify head with the whole problem of expressing or not expressing anger.

4. A further possible paradigm for the acquisition of body meaning that should be considered would derive from the juxtaposition of certain affects or emotions and the physiological activation of specific body parts. Lacey's (in Rubenstein and Parloff, 1959) work on physiological channeling makes it tenable to assume that a particular channel of activation in response to a stimulus situation may happen to predominate more in one individual than in another. One individual might customarily respond to sexually arousing stimuli with an unusual amount of heart activation, whereas another might respond with vasoconstriction which would produce vivid sensations in skin areas. Over a period of time this could result in an equation of either the heart or skin with matters pertaining to sex. This model would fit too those instances in which an individual feels inhibited about overtly performing certain types of acts or expressing certain affects, but wishfully keeps specific body parts (which would be involved in such expression) ready for possible action. The emotional drive or intent which was inhibited could then become linked with the body part which was chronically prepared to respond (and perceptually prominent because of its activation). An illustration of this process might be provided by a person with repressed anger who keeps preparing to express this anger by clenching his fists and tensing his arm muscles (as if he were going to hit or strike out). The juxtaposition of the repressed anger and the aroused arm and fist muscles could impart hostile connotations to these body parts.

5. One of the more obvious sources from which a body region might draw meaning, viz., its actual use and function, has not yet been mentioned. It would be expected that if a body part specialized in an activity, it would acquire connotations related to that activity. From this perspective, the mouth or stomach could assume incorporative significance because they are

so involved in the eating process. Or the head might be associated with intellectuality and control because it seems to be so patently involved (via the brain) in thinking and logical deduction. Paradoxically, although the function of a body part would seem to be one of the more obvious sources of the meaning assigned to it, the Body Focus Questionnaire findings supplied only one example congruent with this alternative (viz., back awareness and anality). Organs like the stomach and mouth which have such obvious eating functions were not found to be linked with orality or incorporation. Also, the head, with its intellectual and control functions, did not seem to have an analogous control significance.

One wonders why the explicit function of a body part should apparently play such a limited role in the "meaning" assigned to it. But before dealing with this question, it should be noted that the term "meaning" is used in the special sense that it has emerged with reference to the various BFQ dimensions. That is, it refers to a largely unconscious significance which typically has as its central theme some conflict or alternative way of dealing with the world. One can speculate that this element of conflict or indecision usually generates sufficient anxiety so that the individual wants it coded in a fashion that is at least partially camouflaged. That is, if a body part is assigned a meaning that can stir anxiety, it may best serve defensive aims to code the meaning in a concealing fashion. The failure to assign "meaning" to parts in terms of their obvious day to day function would mirror the need for such defensive concealment. If the meaning associated with an area derives from metaphor or analogy, it is probably less likely to attain an explicit awareness that would be embarrassing or alarming.

An important point to consider is the fact that the BFQ findings indicated considerable uniformity as to which body sectors become identified with given meanings. Illustratively, the eyes tend, among men in general, to be equated with incorporative problems. Likewise, among men, the right-left sectors are usually identified with attitudes about heterosexual interaction. Modal types of meanings characterize almost all major body areas. This suggests that there is uniformity in the culture in the "messages" given about body meanings. While one cannot really say which of the methods of learning of body meaning (e.g., imitation of parents, adoption of analogically suggested concepts) are most common, one can say that there is a good deal of commonality in what is conveyed.

BODY SIGNALS

Theoretical Considerations

As reiterated in previous chapters, it is doubtful that the distribution of meanings to body sectors is a mere "epiphenomenon." It seems to become part of a system for guiding behavior and evaluating alternatives. While such an idea is a bit dissonant in terms of the current emphasis on "central" theories of cognition and emotion, the actual fact is that one cannot think of a more reasonable proposition than the assertion that body feelings provide a way of evaluating one's experiences. It is quite probable that most of the early "preferences" and "sets" of the young child are determined by body states. If food relieves the tension of hunger, it has positive valence and is sought after. If a particular person like mother relieves certain body tensions by rocking or holding tightly, she acquires positive value. If something causes the body pain, it becomes unacceptable. All of the child's early "judgments" about the environment are non-verbal and highly influenced by his body states. Schachtel (1959) noted, apropos of this point, that children initially regard as real "only that . . . which is in the immediate environment and of which the physical impact is felt on one's body" (p. 143). Piaget and Inhelder (1956) have documented the degree to which early spatial relationships are egocentrically perceived in terms of the child's own body. It takes years before the child learns to make judgments based on introjected verbal standards which are relatively independent of his body "feelings." For a long, long time his body states "tell him" what is "good" and "bad." Even after he learns non-body based standards, the force of certain types of body arousal continue to press for influence in his decision making. It will be contended by the writer that the early trust in body experience as a guide in decision making is never given up and, indeed, continues to play an important role throughout life via an elaborate system based on the assignment of meaning to body areas and the monitoring of sensations from these areas. There are data suggesting that when important matters are at stake the individual returns to his body for guiding cues. Although the socialization practices of most cultures strive mightily to teach the individual to make decisions on the basis of "objective reality" and to ignore his body, it would, indeed, be surprising if he could neatly jettison the primary body guidance system of his early years.

It has been proposed in several theoretical contexts that one of the first steps in developing identity and autonomy is to become aware of one's body as separate from mother's. This means attaining awareness of one's body sensations as a separate "field." Ego differentiation and the beginning of a sense of self initially involve a special way of perceiving one's body (viz., "My existence *is* this body space and what I feel going on within it"). In other words, to be aware of one's own body responses to events is perhaps one of the first prime ways of identifying self. If so, it could be speculated that "knowing" how one's body is reacting remains a fundamental act of identity maintenance. Even further, one may ask whether identity maintenance does not require that the body as an experienced object participate in basic decision making? Does the child, as it is becoming aware of its separate body, begin to equate being a person with the act of receiving "information" that clearly emanates from his own body feelings and states? Indeed, if he is taught standards by others can he incorporate them into his own self structure without integrating them in some way into his perceived body field? The present author hypothesizes that a systematic process of assigning meaning to various body areas is a necessary step in the child's ability and willingness to take over standards from others and to regard them as his own. He has to evolve a framework of meanings embedded in his own body space [2] which can be applied evaluatively to experiences. Because he has for so long during the early formative years been guided by body feelings, one would conjecture he is unable to learn the guiding rules of the culture unless he is able to translate them to some degree into body feelings. He has to evaluate them and give them meaning against a body context so that there will be continuity between the early learned "body feeling guidance system" and the newer societally imposed non-body oriented guidance standards. Also, the need to maintain self integrity in the face of the culture's standards requires the translations of such standards into body feelings. Perhaps the standards would be experienced as foreign and obtrusive upon self as a separate object unless they were given "self" quality by being experienced as part of the individual's segregated body perceptual field. [3] This view parallels some of the "motor" theories of learning, as applied to the child's early development. They have assumed that the child evolves stable concepts and standards only insofar as he is able to experience and test out things in terms of motor experiences. The motor response with its kinesthetic feedback and information is deemed an essential component for building fundamental concepts about the world.

As previously proposed, the individual may be able to apply body experience standards to phenomena (and thus to make them acceptable or non-acceptable for inclusion into the self) by reacting to them in terms of persistent signals derived from differential awareness of body landmarks which have acquired specified meanings. The most elementary stage in the child's development of such a system might be illustrated by his having learned that if an object creates uncomfortable tension in his body he should avoid it and treat it as potentially harmful. Even adults continue to have experiences in which the perception of an object produces diffuse body discomfort without any apparent realistic reason for doing so. And it is not uncommon under such circumstances to make a "gut" decision to put distance between oneself and the offending object. At a more complex stage, the child's development of a body judgment standard may be illustrated by his having learned that there are negative consequences if he does not control his anal sphincter. He learns to "monitor" and regulate this sphincter. But since learning sphincter control is part of a generalized learning of self-control over things that are

[2] It is intriguing in this respect that Desoto, London, and Handel (1965) have shown that thinking and deduction in adults is often guided by conversion of ordered terms into spatial representations (e.g., along a vertical axis). One wonders whether the conversion of the body space into differentiated areas with specific meanings or connotations is in any way analogous to this phenomenon?

[3] The importance of the body frame of reference in giving meaning to the world has been beautifully depicted by Merleau-Ponty (1962).

regarded as messy and dirty by the culture, the "watched" anal sphincter also becomes a reminder to be careful in the presence of any temptations to be "dirty." When the child encounters a situation or object which is "tempting" in this respect, his focused awareness of the sphincter keeps cueing him that he must control himself. Similarly, as his eyes, mouth, and other body areas take on meaning in terms of his socialization experiences, he learns differential awareness of each in the proportion that its meaning provides cues about classes of objects he has learned are bad and should be avoided or good and approachable.

The basic "landmark" model which emerged from the BFQ research depicted each individual as varying in his degree of awareness of major body sectors, and displaying selective attitudes or sets toward given values and conflictual issues which paralleled the patterning of his body landmark awareness. It was proposed that as each individual works out attitudes toward prime issues in the world they become coded in terms of differential awareness of specific body parts. Such differential awareness was then viewed as part of a system of "peripheral" cues which acted as signals to remind the individual about the necessity for certain selective ways of thinking and responding. This system of peripheral cues [4] was considered to be integrated via feedback circuits with central attitudes. Central attitudes were seen as playing a role in shaping the manner in which attention gets distributed to body areas with special meanings; and in turn they seemed to be susceptible to reinforcement or inhibition by the peripheral signals which were established. Important aspects of this model are based on empirical data. It has, indeed, been shown that persons (particularly men) do distribute their attention in fairly consistent and stable ways to the major areas of their bodies. Also, it has been demonstrated that the amount of attention focused upon a body area by an individual is correlated with selective values and attitudes, as measured by a variety of techniques. Even further, the fact that degree of awareness of a specific body site can act as a signal which influences central sets has been repeatedly affirmed by experiments in which artificial sensory accentuation of peripheral sites exerted measurable selective effects upon learning and recall. Among the successful experiments (in male samples) related to this last point, one may illustratively enumerate the effect of right versus left body stimulation upon the learning of sex and non-sex words, the influence of eye enhancement upon memory for food words, and the impact of intensified back versus front awareness upon memory for dirt words. There were similar analogous successful experiments in female samples.

It would be well in future work to extend the generality of these findings

---

[4] The idea that peripheral body cues affect central cognitive and perceptual processes is certainly explicit in sensori-tonic theory and research (e.g., Werner and Wapner, 1949). This group has amassed countless observations of instances in which patterns of body experience find representation in decision making and perceptual interpretations.

by showing that stimulation of peripheral body sites can produce selective responses in other contexts. For example, it should be possible to demonstrate that such stimulation selectively influences the perception of appropriate tachistoscopically presented themes, responses to word associations stimuli, and even interpretations of ink blots.

Pertinent Literature

The idea that peripheral body cues influence selectivity in central perceptual processes was rather boldly stated by Solley and Murphy (1960). They were influenced by the work of Solomon and Wynne (1954) which had demonstrated that visceral sensations are capable of becoming conditioned stimuli. They were also intrigued with the clinical observations of a psychoanalyst, Braatoy (1954), who had noted that some persons seem chronically to inhibit specific anxiety laden memories by maintaining continuous tightening of muscle groups.[5] Their interpretation of Braatoy's observations was that, "The painful memories are 'locked' in a state of unawareness by the incessant feedback from the tightened muscles" (p. 244). It was their conclusion that perceptual and interpretative processes can become linked with, and partially controlled by, autonomic and proprioceptive feedback mechanisms.

If one scans the literature, it is apparent that there are numerous converging studies which support this view. The Werner and Wapner sensoritonic group has assembled much data pertinent to this issue. It has been shown, for example, that memory (Rand and Wapner, 1967) and tactual perception (McFarland, Werner, and Wapner, 1962) may be affected by body posture; and that asymmetrical body sensations may introduce asymmetry into the perceptual field. Razran (1961) has nicely summarized a considerable Russian literature in which it has been demonstrated that interoceptive stimuli may acquire conditioned control over a range of response systems. A particularly striking study by Belleville (1964) should be mentioned in which it was found that conditioning and extinction in dogs could be significantly influenced by the body experience milieu associated with the effects of certain drugs. The effects observed were apparently not a direct function of the central action of the drugs but rather the patterns of body sensations they aroused.

The work of Reiser and Block (1965) is also noteworthy because it demonstrated that the accuracy of reports concerning weak visual stimuli can be increased by giving the individual an opportunity to register and assimilate the body sensations associated with autonomic responses to the stimuli. Their

---

[5] Hefferline, Keenan, and Harford (1959) have since shown empirically that small muscle twitches (below conscious awareness) may be conditioned to occur as a means of avoiding aversive stimuli.

results indicated that individuals utilized the scanning of their own body experiences subsequent to a visual stimulus to augment the accuracy of their perceptions of that stimulus. In other words, they evaluated body information to make a cognitive decision. This was done in a fashion bearing some analogy to that proposed for the body landmark model.

Another line of important and ingenious work pertinent to this issue has been instituted by Valins (1966). He asked male subjects to rate the attractiveness of a series of pictures of semi-nude girls. They were told that while making the ratings their heart rates would be recorded; but that because of a defect in the equipment they would actually be able to hear their own hearts beating. The "heard" heart beat was manipulated so that it changed markedly while the subject was rating certain of the pictures; whereas no changes occurred with reference to the other pictures. It was found that the highest attractiveness ratings were given to those pictures which had apparently produced the greatest heart rate change in oneself. In later studies Valins (1967, A, B) showed that the effect of such apparent heart rate shifts were likely to be greatest for persons who were "emotional" and accustomed to observing their own internal reactions. It would appear that body experience information, when available and observed, can be integrated into, and influence, complex cognitive judgments.

Nature of the Signal

Let us now carefully review one of the most important ingredients of the body landmark model, viz., the nature of the "body awareness" signal which presumably guides behavior. The original model stated that when a body area possesses a meaning which is pertinent to some significant conflictual decision, the individual is centrally motivated to focus consistent attention upon that area as a way of giving "body meaning" to the decision (bringing it within the body realm) and also chronically reminding himself of what he has "decided" to be the "best way" of coping with (e.g., approach vs. avoidance) that class of conflict. The "signal," in this sense, would simply be the consistent perceptual prominence of a particular body area resulting from a selective attitude toward it. However, at a more speculative level, it has also been conjectured by the writer that when an individual focuses his attention upon a local body area he can produce physiological changes in it which might then independently increase its sensory prominence. Obviously, if an individual directs his attention to his biceps he can produce activation of muscle groups which become increased sources of sensory stimulation themselves. Likewise, is it possible that when an individual directs his attention for long periods to an area of his body he will alter its previous activation level in such a way that it becomes a semi-autonomous source of new sensory input? Perhaps focusing chronically upon one's back changes the level of skin and muscle activation in the back; and even if centrally derived attention to that area were decreased, local physiological changes would (perhaps for a period) continue to be a source of highlighting sensations. Similarly, focusing upon one's heart chronically could perhaps alter its usual rate; and so forth.

The kind of circuit envisioned in this model involves focus upon a body area because of its coded meaning which is congruent with a learned attitude or set; feedback from the resulting perceptually highlighted locale which reinforces the original set; consequent intensified drive to continue focusing upon that body locale which in turn might increase its degree of physiological activation and even render it a semi-autonomous source of sensory feedback directed centrally; and so forth until an equilibrium is established between central and peripheral conditions.

The idea that semi-autonomous physiological changes might occur at body sites which are focused upon was necessarily introduced into the model by the fact that several studies have now shown correlations between degree of awareness of body areas and measures of the physiological activation levels of these areas. Details of some of the studies have been presented elsewhere (Fisher, 1966A; Fisher, 1967B). But the following may be briefly reported. BFQ Back was found in male subjects to be positively and significantly correlated with the degree to which the skin resistance of the back of the neck was lower (indicative of greater activation) than that of the front of the neck. BFQ Heart was positively and significantly correlated with heart rate in male and female samples; and BFQ Stomach was correlated in a male sample with a measure of stomach motility. One possible way of interpreting such findings is that focusing attention on the back or heart or stomach may influence their respective activation levels.

However, another possible interpretation is that the BFQ scores are merely reflections of the physiological variables. A BFQ score could be regarded simply as an indirect statement about a physiological event. One could entertain the possibility that the themes or conflicts found to be associated with specific BFQ variables were actually linked with physiological parameters indirectly measured by the BFQ. Thus, the correlations of anal variables with BFQ Back might be due to their correlations with the activation level of the back. Or the correlation of religiosity with BFQ Heart might be basically a function of its relationship with heart rate. The following facts cast serious doubt on this perspective. First and foremost, when the physiological measures corresponding to given BFQ variables have in several instances been related to parameters (e.g., anality, religiosity, masochism) which seem to be consistently linked with these BFQ variables, completely chance findings have emerged. The physiological indices show no evidence of being associated with specific conflicts, themes, or attitudes. The level of activation of an organ or body part is not sufficiently related to pertinent themes and conflicts to qualify alone as the sort of peripheral signal required by the feedback model proposed. Secondly, with just a few exceptions, the degree of correlation between BFQ and physiological variables accounts for only a small part of the BFQ variance. Third, the reported stability of measures like heart rate and stomach motility over time is considerably less than that shown by the BFQ measures (at least, in male samples). Finally, there is the fact that very brief experimental alteration (e.g., by means of special instructions) of the amount of attention an individual directs to a sector (e.g., eyes, heart) produces measurable selective changes in learning and recall. But it is extremely unlikely, in view of past findings, for example, concerning the difficulty of altering heart rate in specific directions via attitudinal or "voluntary" manipulation, that briefly induced changes in the amount of attention directed to one's heart could have had sufficient effect upon heart activation to have resulted in the central cognitive effects which were observed. Even in experiments where heart rate changes have been produced by focusing attention upon one's heart (e.g., Bower, 1963), this has required time durations far exceeding those in the various body landmark stimulation experiments described.

What has been said does not at all rule out the possibility that a part of the BFQ variance is a function of how activated a body area happens to be when an individual inspects it to make his BFQ judgments. The immediate influence of physiological activation upon BFQ scores may be quite considerable in some situations and perhaps as a result reduce the validity of such scores as measures of long term body awareness patterns. Obviously, if an individual is hungry and his stomach therefore active or if he has been hurrying and his heart is pounding, the corresponding BFQ judgments will be affected.

But let us shift now and pursue further the idea that the amount of attention focused on a sector may influence its degree of physiological arousal. To assert that directing attention to a body part can affect it physiologically is equivalent to stating that the activation of a circumscribed body region can be influenced by the adoption of a specific attitude or set toward it. With increasing frequency it is possible to find studies which indicate that this hypothesis is supportable. Just in the last few years, clear evidence has been obtained that autonomic responses (e.g., GSR and heart rate) may be operantly conditioned. The work of Johnson and Schwartz (1967), Van Twyver and Kimmel (1966), Engel and Hansen (1966), Birk, Crider, Shapiro, and Tursky (1966), Frazier (1966), and numerous others testify to this point. A carefully designed study by Bower (1963) is especially striking because he was able to show that when subjects were simply asked to *think* over a period of time of cyclically slowing or speeding up their hearts they were able to produce significant effects in the intended directions. Somehow, they were able to manipulate their own heart rates, but interestingly with no conscious awareness of the maneuvers they utilized.

One also finds reports concerning the ability to change, via special attitudes and psychological sets, other physiological parameters besides heart rate and GSR. A few illustrations may be cited. Sternbach (1964) recorded gastric peristalsis rate from subjects under three conditions: in one instance they believed they had swallowed a drug which slowed stomach movement; in another the belief was that the drug speeded up stomach movement; and in a third they were told they had swallowed a placebo. Significant trends for actual stomach motility to conform to expected motility were observed. Brehm, Back, and Bogdonoff (1964) demonstrated that hungry subjects, for whom the perception of their hunger would be dissonant to their commitment to abstain voluntarily from food, not only decreased their perceived degree of hunger but also manifested changes in concentrations of plasma free fatty acids consonant with lower levels of physiological hunger. The authors suggest, "that a person who has convinced himself that he is not so hungry tends to respond physiologically as if he were not hungry" (p. 1).

Schultz and Luthe (1959) cited a series of studies in which the temperatures of circumscribed body areas could be changed by focusing attention upon them.

A study by Culp and Edelberg (1966) is a bit tangential to the matter under discussion and yet pertinent because it indicates how a physiological process which can be voluntarily initiated may influence one which is usually regarded as non-voluntary. This study indicated that the electrodermal response amplitudes in specific parts of the body may be influenced by local muscular activity. Muscular activation of an area was found to potentiate its electrodermal activity. For example, flexing the left foot augmented electrodermal response amplitude in the left hand. Obviously, this raises the possibility that persistent wishes or intents, which could be mirrored in the activation of musculature in body areas required for acting them out, might produce changes in skin conductance in such areas. It will be recalled that BFQ Back was found to be positively correlated in a male sample with the degree to which skin conductance of a back site exceeded that for a front site. In terms of the Culp and Edelberg data, one wonders whether this finding may not be due to long continuing differences in activation of back versus front muscle sites which reflect a selective intent to maintain control of the back. That is, the chronic incipient tightening of back muscles to "keep control" could increase the activation of the skin on the back.

In any case, there is empirical evidence in the literature that psychological sets can affect the activation of local body areas. It is therefore conceivable that the persistent concentration of attention upon specific body areas that is postulated in the body landmark model could affect their physiological reactivity—thereby intensifying their sensory prominence and perhaps also rendering them semi-independent of centrally determined channeling of awareness to maintain their effectiveness as directive signals.

An Experimental Attempt to Alter Local Body Reactivity

It seemed important, in terms of what has just been said, to ascertain whether actual manipulation of an individual's degree of awareness of a body sector constituting a BFQ dimension could produce physiological changes in that sector. A study was therefore designed toward this objective, which will be briefly described. It was intended to alter awareness of front versus back body sites and to determine how this affected the difference between back and front temperature and also back and front skin resistance. The study involved two groups, each consisting of ten male college students. The subject, with his shirt removed, was brought into a shielded room and various electrodes and thermistors were applied to his body. These made possible simultaneous recording of temperature from the front and back of the neck and skin resistance values from the front and back of the neck and front and back of the trunk (at a point equivalent to two inches above the sternum [6]).

One group of subjects participated in a procedure with the following sequence: 15 minutes of rest, 15 minutes of tasks focusing attention upon the front of the body, 15 minutes of rest, and 15 minutes of tasks focusing attention upon the back of the body. A second group followed the same procedure except that the back focusing tasks preceded those which were front focusing. In order to produce concentration of attention upon a front or back site, the following series of tasks was utilized:

Obtaining reports of back or front sensations.
Determining light touch threshold (at back or front sites) with nylon filaments.
Writing words very lightly with one's finger upon the skin [7] (distant from the electrodes) and asking the subject to identify them.
Obtaining reports of back or front sensations.
Lightly applying several bits of textured material to skin sites (distant from the electrodes) and asking which are preferred.
Urging a period of fantasy in which subject recalls past threats that came from either "in front" or "behind."
Making loud noise, unexpectedly, either in front or back of the subject (while his eyes were closed).
Whispering threatening words from in front of, or behind, subject (while his eyes were closed).

[6] Temperature was measured with the Yellow Springs Telethermometer 46TUC. Skin resistance was recorded on a Brush Polygraph (Model RP562100). Grass silver EEG electrodes recorded through 1/4 inch holes in masking tape which controlled for area. An electrode paste which maintains stability for extended periods of time was used.
   [7] Analysis of the data indicated that actual touching of the skin produced no greater physiological shifts than did the purely verbal techniques.

Telling the subject (eyes closed) that his picture was being taken from "in front" or "behind."
Obtaining reports of back or front sensations.

The physiological data were expressed as differences between the back and front measures (back minus front). This was done for each set of temperature and skin resistance values. The crucial values, with respect to testing the hypothesis, were considered to be those occurring at the completion of each 15-minute sequence of body focusing. If the back and front attention directing procedures were having differential physiological effects, they should be evident following the cumulative time impact of each.

For each physiological measure (and for each subject) an index was computed which equaled the back minus front difference for the first body focusing procedure minus the back minus front difference for the second focusing procedure. In the case of the temperature values, the higher the simple difference score for a given condition the higher the temperature of the back site as compared to the front site—and therefore presumably the more vaso-dilated the back in relation to the front. If the shift of the difference score from the first to the second condition was such that the back temperature increased more than the front temperature, the difference between the two difference scores became larger. As for the skin resistance values, the higher the resistance of the back site (and therefore the lower the activation) as compared to the front site the larger was the difference score. If the shift of the difference score from the first to the second condition was such that the back resistance increased (i.e., became less activated), the difference between the two differences became larger.

Table 34.2
Mean Shifts in Back-Front Temperature and Skin Resistance Values under Back-Front Attention Focusing Procedures

Physiological Scores (Back minus Front)	Front Attention Focus followed by Back Attention Focus (N = 10)		Back Attention Focus followed by Front Attention Focus (N = 10)	
	M	σ	M	σ
Temperature (Neck)	−.02 [a]	.75	−.04	.42
Skin Resistance (Neck)	−.60	3.90	+.30	1.61
Skin Resistance (Chest)	−4.55	4.43	+.95 [b]	4.14

[a] The more negative the score the relatively lower is the back value.
[b] The difference between the two means for this chest site is significant at the .01 level.

Analysis of the data involved t tests of the differences between mean shift scores derived from the front to back attention condition and mean shift scores derived from the back to front attention condition. If the attention focusing procedures were effective, one would expect that the front to back focusing procedure would increase the relative reactivity of the back; and the back to front focusing procedure would have the opposite effect.

Only chance differences were found for the temperature data. However, the skin resistance findings were consistently in the expected direction; and those for the chest level sites were clearly significant ($t = 2.9$, p .01). They indicated that the shift from front to back attention focusing increased relative back activation, whereas the shift from back to front attention focusing decreased relative back activation. It is indeed striking that the directionality of shift was opposite in the two instances. Data for the neck site showed the same shift in directionality, but did not attain statistical significance.

The physiological changes induced by the attention focusing technique were apparently not reflected in temperature measures. However, they were detected by skin resistance measures. It is possible that the skin resistance trends are directly referrable to muscle activation differences, as suggested by the previously cited work of Culp and Edelberg (1966) concerning the effect of muscle activation on skin conductance. That is, the attention driving techniques may produce increased muscle activation at the sites to which they are directed and these could result in corresponding skin activation changes. If the relatively brief period (15 minutes) of attention focusing in the present experiment is capable of producing measurable back-front activation differences, one can only speculate about the magnitude of possible difference that long continued patterns of differential focusing, over months and years, might produce.

Further Speculations

The general picture that one builds up from the BFQ findings is that each individual is characterized by a series of body awareness patterns. He may simultaneously have high awareness of his left side and little of his right; high awareness of his back and little of his front; low awareness of his eyes as compared to other parts of his face; intensified awareness of his heart as compared with certain more peripherally located points on his body; and so forth. Extremely complex permutations of high and low awareness nodes become possible. This awareness network presumably acts to provide multiple signals quite continuously about multiple classes of psychological objects and issues. One wonders how such a network is integrated. Or does it function as a series of largely autonomous processes? This last possibility is one that might logically be deduced from the lack of significant correlations among most of the BFQ variables. But it is still too early to arrive at solid conclusions about this matter.

A brief speculative word is in order concerning the extent to which it may be necessary to alter peripheral signals from the body in order to change basic central attitudes radically. If, for example, a man's responses to sexual or oral stimuli are chronically modified by the sensory prominence of a given body sector, how far can one change his responses to such stimuli if one ignores the peripheral component? Central cognitive changes may accomplish only part of an expected alteration process. Perhaps it is the existence of persistent body signals with their selective influence, which makes it so difficult for an individual to stop smoking, to give up a hypochondriacal symptom, to refrain from overeating, and to change his style of approach to others (e.g., being passively receptive or avoiding heterosexual contacts) while in psychotherapy. We must begin to think of the possibility that whenever we want to change a basic attitude we need to work on its peripheral as well as its central components. Perhaps the recently reported successes of behavior therapies, which emphasize alterations in certain body experiences (primarily kinesthetic) at the same time that specific central attitudes are modified, derive from the fact that both central and peripheral variables are considered.

PERIPHERAL THEORIES OF EMOTION

There is an obvious similarity between the body landmark model, which asserts that certain peripheral body signals modify central concepts and attitudes, and peripherally oriented models of emotion (e.g., the James theory). Note James' statement of his theory:

> An object falls on a sense-organ and is apperceived by the appropriate cortical center. . . . Quick as a flash, the reflex currents pass down through their pre-ordained channels, alter the condition of muscle, skin, and viscus, and these alterations, apperceived like the original object, in as many specific portions of the cortex, combine with it in consciousness and transform it from an object-simply-apprehended into an object-emotionally-felt. . . . My thesis . . . is that *the bodily changes follow directly the Perception of the exciting fact, and that our feeling of same changes as they occur Is the emotion* (James, 1892, p. 190).

From his view, emotional experience of an object *is* the pattern of body response it evokes, as it is experienced by the individual. The perceived physiological changes in one's body produced by seeing an object combine with the original perception of the object to give it emotional meaning. The peripherally perceived body cues interact with a central perception and modify it.

Although the Jamesian concept of emotion has been in disrepute for an extended period because of Cannon's (1927) work and criticisms which favor a more central theory, there have been those who have continued to defend it or offer analogous versions (e.g., Wenger, 1950; Freeman, 1948A, B). Wenger (1950) considers that an adequate experimental test of peripheral theories of emotion has yet to be designed. Gellhorn (1964) has vigorously supported the importance of the body experience component of emotion by pointing out, on the basis of an analysis of the appropriate physiological literature, that proprioceptive feedback from body posture and facial expression may play a significant role in influencing hypothalamic balance. He has even suggested that deliberately assumed postures and body attitudes be utilized to change, via their proprioceptive effects, unpleasant emotional states.

Laird (1967) boldly attempted an empirical test of the Jamesian theory of emotion by measuring the effects upon mood judgments of subjects assuming artificial emotional expressions. The faces of subjects were manipulated by the experimenter until they seemed to be either "smiling" or "frowning." These manipulations were rationalized to the subject as part of a procedure for studying the activity of the facial muscles. Self report judgments were used to evaluate the impact of the artificially imposed "smile" or "frown" facial experiences upon the subject's mood. The results indicated that the artificial expressions did produce significant expected effects upon mood. There was no evidence that the subjects suspected the nature of the expressions which the experimenter had indirectly caused them to assume. This represents one of the first studies in which alteration of a peripheral aspect of emotional expression has been shown to have a predictable central impact upon mood.

In actual fact, it is turning out to be an inaccurate oversimplification to talk about emotion as if it were primarily central or peripheral. There is obviously an important contribution from both sources—with their relative weights varying as a function of situational factors. This has been most explicitly clarified by Schachter and his associates (Schachter and Singer, 1962; Schachter and Latane, 1964). They have typically designed experiments in which body arousal is produced (e.g., by injecting adrenalin) in individuals and then special cognitive sets are introduced which diversely shape the ways in which the arousal is interpreted. Cognitive sets are created variously by verbal instructions, moving pictures with special content (e.g., humor), and the use of "stooges" who act out particular emotional states. It has been observed that the same matrix of body arousal may with one cognitive set be experienced as amusement; but with another set register as fear; and with still another eventuate in rage. What we call an "emotion" may turn out in most instances to be a fusion of body arousal experiences and expectations concerning these experiences which are derived from the context in which they occur.

If interpretations of peripheral body events do enter importantly into emotional states, this would represent another way in which the experienced body significantly influences behavior.

PERIPHERAL THEORIES OF THINKING

Conceptions of thinking in terms of peripheral body events are perhaps even more pertinent to the body landmark theory than are peripheral theories of emotion. Peripheralist theories of thinking insist, to varying degrees, that changes in body activation (largely muscular) accompany thought and are basic to it. Typically, it is assumed ". . . that the essential work of the thinking process is muscular work, of very small amplitude indeed, but still essentially muscular. Our thinking consciousness would be ultimately derived from the sense organs in the muscles and possibly the joints and tendons. . . . The thinking-experience would be fundamentally a perceptual one; perceptual, that is, of the fundamental peripheral processes . . ." (p. 198, Humphrey, 1963). Body experiences are seen as contributing to, supporting, and even constituting the essence of the thinking process. The whole realm of judgment and decision making is regarded as anchored in body reactions and the sensory feedback from these reactions. It is interesting to note that Titchener (cited by Humphrey, 1963) was so extreme in his concept of thought and judgment as derived from body sensation patterns that he linked, for example, a judgmental process like identifying a particular shade of grey with awareness by the observer that his stomach had "quivered" in a particular way upon his first having perceived the grey stimulus. Such peripheralist views are actually considerably more extreme than the body landmark theory concerning the role of body experience in cognitive and decision making processes.

A good deal of research has been stimulated in the course of investigating the peripheralist position. It has largely taken the form of attempts to demonstrate that reduction of kinesthetic experiences decreases imagery and thought (e.g., Jacobsen, 1929); that covert speech movements are necessary for thought to occur (e.g., Curtis, 1900; Rounds and Poffenberger, 1931; McGuigan, Keller, and Stanton, 1964); that subvocal language can become a conditioned stimulus (e.g., Roessler and Brogden, 1943); that induced body tensions and feelings affect thought (e.g., Freeman, 1948A, B); and that various motor patterns typify the individual while he is thinking (e.g., Lorens and Darrow, 1962; Roffwarg, Dement, Muzio and Fisher, 1962). The results of such experiments have failed to indicate a direct dependence of thought upon specific motor responses or modes of body experience. An extreme motor theory of thought is clearly not supported by the total array of findings. However, considerable evidence has been uncovered that body activation and body sensory information may influence thought processes.

CURTAILMENT OF BODY EXPERIENCE

We do not, of course, know very much about what happens to the perceived world if you take away the individual's experienced body. To be able to eliminate all body experiences requires the use of methods which do themselves cloud consciousness and also the ability to report verbally. From the lack of representations of body experience variables in most current theories of perception (with the notable exception of the sensori-tonic group), one might not expect very much to happen if the body context of experience could be removed. On the other hand, if one takes the extreme position of Merleau-Ponty (1962) who sees body experience as primary to the organization of the world, the removal of the body context would leave the perceived environs almost unrecognizable.

As one scans the pertinent literature, it is possible to find many anecdotes and observations which suggest that body feelings do consistently color the state of one's world. There are psychoanalytic theorists (e.g., Rose, 1966; Schilder, 1935; Fenichel, 1945) who trace the influence of body feelings into many forms of physiognomic perception. Presumably, the "aliveness" of a landscape, or the "cheeriness" of a scenic vista, or the "warmth" of a color may derive from body feelings projected to the appropriate stimulus. Congruently, it has been Werner's (1954) view and also the position of Gestalt theory (Asch, 1946) that all physiognomic interpretations (i.e., assigning human qualities to the inanimate) derive analogically from body experiences. It is not inappropriate to digress for a moment and describe a study by Gaughran (1963) dealing with physiognomic perception. He empirically examined the proposition (deduced from Gestalt theory) that the amount of physiognomic interpretation made by an individual is positively related to how well integrated and differentiated his body concept is. Propensity for making physiognomic interpretations was measured in terms of responses to several tasks (e.g., assignment of meaning to lines with potentially expressive configurations). Body image integration was evaluated with a variety of indices (e.g., Secord Homonym test, degree of overestimation of head size). Equivocal results were obtained. Only the correlation between propensity for making physiognomic interpretations and soundness of the body image, as measured by a figure drawing scale developed by Machover (in Witkin, et al., 1954), was positive and significant. This represents one of the first and only existing empirical studies of the relation between body image parameters and physiognomic perception. Further investigation in this area should have high priority. The assignment of human qualities to the inanimate (physiognomic perception) would seem, from a common-sense view, to have a high probability of somehow involving the projection of body derived feelings. If so, it should be extremely enlightening to find out how various states of the body image influence the amount and specific content of physiognomic elaboration. The analysis of physiognomic interpretation may provide a miniature system within which to determine with special clarity the principles governing the transformation of body experiences into qualities of objects "out there." The fact that transformations of this type are possible is explicit in those studies (e.g., Meltzoff, et al., 1953) which have shown that a build-up of kinesthetic tension (e.g., as a result of sitting immobile) can increase the amount of movement attributed to human figures perceived in ink blot stimuli. Similarly, Fisher (1965C) reported that the greater an individual's awareness of his stomach prior to interpreting ink blots the larger the number of percepts he produced which referred to eating and other oral activities.

In any discussion of how the experienced body "reaches into" perception one must mention its potential effects upon the way in which the space "out there" is structured. Obviously, body sensations are a necessary basis for maintaining equilibrium in space. But further, the sensori-tonic group (Wapner and Werner, 1965) has been able to show how the right-left, up-down, and sagittal dimensions of space may be altered by applying asymmetrical stimuli to the body or causing the body to assume special postures. Roland (1966) has observed that merely engaging in physical exercise may affect some aspects of perception of the vertical. Teitelbaum (1965) noted too that exercises which increased an individual's awareness of directionality on his own body improved his perception of directionality "out there." The question arises whether body experiences may not also affect many of the subtle subjective aspects of the appearance of space: how open or closed, how safe or dangerous, how expanding or contracting. Some of the descriptions in the psychoanalytic literature (e.g., Weiss, 1964; Schilder, 1935) of patients with claustrophobic or agoraphobic symptoms imply that unusual body sensations play a role in the distorted spatial impressions they experience.

Few empirical findings are available to clarify what happens to the perceptual field following a drastic curtailment of sensations from one's own body. However, there have been relevant experiments with curare, which creates a physiological state in which much of the usual muscle feedback from the body is blocked as the result of action upon peripheral sites. These experiments have involved animals primarily. Some effects have also been studied in man (Smith, et al., 1947). No evidence has emerged from such work that the elimination of proprioceptive feedback grossly alters central processes like thinking, learning, or clarity of awareness. However, there is serious question as to whether curare eliminates a sufficient proportion of body experience to represent a decisive approach to the issue.

Another opportunity to appraise the effects of curtailing body experience has been potentially available in instances in which severe spinal cord injuries interrupt afferent tracts conveying body sensation information centrally. Unfortunately, only a few studies relevant to this point have been done; and none have employed objective measurement techniques. Probably the best to date was carried out by Hohmann (1966). He was himself a paraplegic and therefore in a particularly favored role to gain the confidence of 25 male adult patients with cord lesions whom he interviewed. From his view this is of considerable importance because he doubts that the severely spine injured individual will divulge how he really feels to a person with an intact body. The reports he obtained suggested that gross loss of body sensations does affect one's emotions. Significant decreases in experienced feelings of anger, sexual excitement, and fear were described as having occurred. This report, by the way, does not agree with a much older study by Dana (1921) which found no loss in emotional experience as the result of spinal lesions. The Hohmann observations concerning loss of emotional experience need to be evaluated cautiously. If they could be substantiated, they would add a bit of support for the peripheralist view that body sensations can shape emotion. It should be added that they do not really give us any information as to the specific ways in which body experiences "frame" or provide a background for our perceptions of the world. In order to glean such information from the spinal injured it may be necessary to bypass defensive attitudes by use of perceptual methods which are subtle in their approach and also which are sensitive enough to detect small effects. For example, one wonders why the Ames Thereness-Thatness procedure (described in earlier chapters), which can evaluate the apparent perceptual vividness of objects, has not been used. Or why have content analysis procedures not been applied to projective productions to determine if certain affect categories or emotional references occur with unusually low frequency?

BODY CONSTANCY

While it has been suggested that the individual continues, even as an adult, to apply body experiences or body criteria to the evaluation of important matters, and to the definition of his own emotional responses, there is no doubt that the socialization practices of most cultures strive to introduce stringent controls which will minimize such body influences. Body feelings are typically equated with that which is emotional, impulsive, and irrational; and the individual is taught to control them as much as possible. To make decisions on the basis of body feelings is, in most contexts, regarded as a sign of immaturity or lack of self-control. One can find empirical evidence in the sensori-tonic research that with increasing "maturity" there is also an augmented set to eliminate one's body as a direct judgmental anchor. For example, the young child who is tilted and asked to judge when a rod is in a vertical position will shift the vertical in the direction of his own body tilt. But an adult will, under the same circumstances, shift the vertical in a direction *opposite to* his own tilt. The child's judgment indicates a "pull" to let his body position determine the vertical. But the adult's judgment may be interpreted as a compensatory effort to eliminate the "pull" of his own body. As quickly as possible the culture tries to conventionalize body experience: the body is covered with clothes congruent with sex and age role; rules are promulgated about the appropriate times to eat, urinate, and defecate; certain body zones are defined as publicly touchable and others are "off limits"; masturbation is forbidden. Also, there is regulation of how much the individual can publicly introduce his body experiences into his definitions and impressions of the world. If a person he meets arouses a particular pattern of excitation in his body, he would not (unless he were an artist or patient in psychotherapy) introduce such body feelings into his descriptions (even to himself) of the encounter. He would never say that the person had made his heart beat faster, his skin itch, his eyes feel tense, and his gut "tense." He might state that the person made him feel "excited" or "tense," but it would not be appropriate to introduce detailed informaton about the body experiences evoked. By and large, the culture enjoins one to keep one's body feelings out of descriptions, judgments, and communications. The socialization process attempts to render body experience a constant controlled variable. Perhaps some of the body image mechanisms which have been described (e.g., boundary delineation, regulated awareness of body sectors) contribute to such constancy. The importance of establishing a certain degree of "body constancy" in the experiential field becomes evident when controls break down or health crises occur and powerful body experiences intrude into everyday perceptions and interpretations. The pain of an illness, the hypochondriacal worry about an organ, anxieties about death and body fragility or a newly acquired body deformity can reach into every phase of experience and distort it in a way that is disadvantageous for realistic adaptation. Even transient conditions like lack of sleep, an upset stomach, a painful menstrual period, or an unsightly blemish have the potentiality, via their disturbance of body perception, for introducing sizable stresses and strains into interpretative processes.

It is actually surprising how well most persons are able to regulate the effects of their body experiences. This is true in spite of considerable fluctuations in one's body over the long run developmentally and in the short run situationally. Consider the enormous changes that occur in one's body from childhood, through adolescence, into adulthood, and finally into advanced aging. Consider the variations in weight, height, distribution of fat, size of facial features, sensitivity of sexual organs, and acuteness of receptors that occur. In any given day consider too the variations in clothes that are worn, the changes in degree of distention of organs, and the sharp muscle tonus shifts that are common. However, even in the presence of these body alteration phenomena the body "platform" from which one looks out on one's environs normally finds representation in the experienced world in a rather modulated and consistent fashion. This stability has nowhere been better shown than in experiments which have systematically deprived subjects of food, sleep, and kinesthetic feedback or placed them in strange spatial and temperature conditions and yet have been able to detect little or no effects upon batteries of measures of cognition and perception. The effects that do register require very sensitive sensors.

Body constancy probably results in part from the classificatory and defining mechanisms which the individual learns to use in the process of mastering and assigning meaning to his body experiences. For example, having arrived at a clear concept of his body boundaries, he does not experience the limits of his body as grossly altered when, in the process of filling and emptying it with food, liquid, or air, he produces sensations of body expansion and contraction. Similarly, having established an habitual level of body awareness in relation to the total perceptual field probably dampens the impact of sudden changes in the perceptual vividness of the body resulting from such factors as illness, drug effects, and sexual excitement. Even the assignment of meaning to body areas can introduce an element of stability by preventing irrational diffuse projection of anxieties and feelings upon one's body. Thus, an individual who feels extremely depreciated might be inhibited in ascribing inferior qualities like smallness and ugliness to a range of body areas because their prior assigned values would resist change. Relatedly, a woman's basic level of satisfaction with her body, in the sense that it is measured by the Jourard and Secord (1954, 1955) Body Cathexis technique, could provide a stable framework within which to assimilate the impact of a temporary facial blemish or even a more permanent kind of disfigurement capable of arousing feelings of body ugliness. It is the fact that one has defined one's body in certain ways and ascribed to it definite qualities which renders it a stable influence in perceptual situations.

PRIOR ENTRY INTO THE PERCEPTUAL FIELD OF THE EXPERIENCED BODY

The relative constancy of the experienced body may also (as suggested by Merleau-Ponty, 1962) provide a means for stabilizing adjustment to new or novel situations. By having available in such situations a psychological object which is familiar, the individual has an anchor or source of reassurance. His body functions, in a sense, like the familiar personal possession that a child carries about with him as a security prop. Greenacre (1953, 1955) has already commented, with great insight, that persons who have had difficulty in integrating and accepting their own body experiences may need to develop secondary objects which they can use for substitute support. As she sees it, there are elements of this substitutive process represented in the use of a fetish and also the need of the transvestite to wear his exotic garb. This seems like a reasonable view; and there is much room for study of how the average normal person uses clothing and other forms of body decoration to increase the reassurance value of his body experiences. The work of Compton (1964) and Kernaleguen (1968) has already shown that the woman with indefinite boundaries is especially motivated to wear clothes with compensatory body enhancing value. One would also like to know a good deal more about what compensatory strategies are adopted when, for various reasons (e.g., illness, feelings of loss of body vigor due to age), the individual finds that his body impressions lack the supporting security connotations to which he has been accustomed. One would guess that not only does he call upon "outside" objects for additional support, but also he may attempt to initiate and exaggerate those body sensations which have in the past been most comforting to him. If a relaxed and flaccid position on a bed has been especially comforting, he might seek that out. If intensified sensations from the mouth and stomach have been particularly pleasant, he might eat a lot. If mild pain, which provides license to put his body into a "sick" status calling for outside nursing has been especially reassuring, he might "tune in" for the slightest "twinge" and magnify its amplitude. One wonders if this last alternative, which involves focusing upon slight discomforting sensations as a way of magnifying them, may not be the source of some classes of hypochondriacal symptomatology.

The above comments are intended to underscore the security provided by one's body simply as a function of its familiarity. But quite speculatively, it will be proposed that another source of security provided by body experiences resides in the fact that they provide an active organized "screen" or "wedge" for moving into a complex, impinging world. The organized perceptual context of the body may be thought of as creating a field, *via its central representation*, into which all new stimuli must enter and thereby be modified. The articulation of the body sensory field, as it is represented centrally, provides a setting into which all new stimuli will be accommodated. There is certainly nothing novel about the idea that persons approach the world with sets or expectancies which serve as filters which allow certain inputs to gain prominence and others to be muted. Allport (1955) and others (Solley and Murphy, 1960) have nicely summarized past theory and research concerning this matter. It has even been pointed out that many sets have a significant peripheral component (e.g., kinesthetic) which contributes to the "filtering" process.

What is new in the present writer's formulation is only a matter of emphasis and detail. It is proposed that when an individual scans his environs he is doing so not only with the selectivity derived from certain special expectations, sets, and intentions—but also with the selectivity derived from the configured impact of the general experience of his body. Not only does this configuration provide a "familiar" pattern of arousal into which to assimilate new arousal, but also a guiding vector based on the feeling *that internal stimulation is prior to external stimulation.* The experienced body makes it possible to feel that there is a source of arousal which is prior to, and independent of, what is "outside" and therefore that one is "alive" and capable of initiating events—rather than simply registering stimuli. Although the matter awaits empirical investigation, one would speculate that a sense of purpose and self identity depends upon a feeling that the experienced body is present prior to what is "out there" and can therefore modify what will gain entry. The experienced body has to be perceived as "first" in a perceptual sequence and the outside stimulus as "second." If the sequence is reversed, feelings of purpose and intent probably cannot be maintained. Without the counterpoise of the field created by the massed and organized body sensations the individual would presumably equate himself more and more with any ordinary perceptual object.

The persisting body field which exists prior to the outside stimulus derives from multiple aspects of the organized body image: the boundary, the differentiation of areas in terms of their symbolic significance, the definition of body that goes along with sexual identity, the configured effect resulting from the sheer differences in central representations of body areas (homunculus), and many other factors. One would conjecture that a prime prerequisite for maintaining individuality is to ensure the continuance of the experience of one's body as that which *precedes* other experiences. In this respect, it is significant that with the onset of serious neurotic or schizophrenic disturbance it has been observed that the individual begins to experience his body as the site of a variety of unusual sensations and events. It feels "different." But especially, as shown by Fisher (1966B), it begins to "shrink" psychologically—to seem relatively less in its spatial extent than previously. The feeling that one's body has become smaller may be a reflection of its diminished importance or reduced contribution in providing an organized experiential context which can be equated with being "in control."

One wonders whether the "shield" of prior body experiences may not contribute considerably to what Freud called the *Reizschutz* and others have referred to apropos of the apparent need for mechanisms to cope with the incessant impact of outside stimuli. If so, it will be an interesting and demanding task to ascertain the relative contributory roles of various aspects of the body image organization to the "shielding" process. Is the maintenance of the boundary the primary aspect of the process? That is, does awareness of the prior existence of muscle and skin sensations (rather than internal regions) provide the greatest security? Or is there even a larger contribution from the organized hierarchy of awareness of different body parts and areas (as measured by the BFQ)? In the last instance, one might consider that not only might this patterned awareness give the body differentiated meaning but also provide sources for signals which define in "body terms" which stimuli in the outer world are "good" and which are "bad." The body signal presumed to be linked with the relative experiential prominence of a body sector might not only be *prior to* the perceived object but also provide a basis for "weighting" how much significance it should be given in the "inner" perceptual field.

Difficulty in maintaining an organized body field is probably particularly presented by stimuli which trigger diffuse body reactions. Diffuseness would tend to disrupt familiar articulated and hierarchical patterns. The mass visceral response (occurring in an "inside" region which is relatively unknown and lacking consistent perceptual organization) might exemplify the type of body event most disruptive of the need for a well-defined experienced body. On the other hand, one can conceive of the possibility that when the usual forms of body image organization begin to break down and become inadequate for marking one's body as a prior and important object in the field, experiences might be sought out which would produce gross, intense (emotional) body sensations capable of giving it great perceptual prominence. The task at this stage might be one of simply making one's body more prominent than that which is "out there." Apropos of this last point, one is reminded of the Kaufman and Heims (1958) observation that seriously disturbed delinquents may find the affects accompanying rage and aggression to have reassurance value—especially insofar as they are boundary defining.

The idea that the experienced body provides a "wedge" for relating to one's environs in an active selective fashion bears some relationship to Scheerer's (1931, 1954) concept of the "mine sphere." This concept refers to the fact that the individual learns to regard certain objects in his world as belonging to him and possessed of some of his "I" quality. ["An 'object' is related to the 'I' . . . if it can be signified or experienced as 'mine'."] A sphere of "I" influence is mapped out; and within this sphere the individual feels a special sense of intimacy, belongingness, and possessing control. Gupta (1962) has presented a particularly cogent description of the "mine-sphere." He states that it (p. 7) ". . . encompasses various shades of the experience of belonging-to-me which can be differentiated, depending on the referent of this experience. For example, it includes the experience of belonging-to-me as referred to the internal characteristics of a person—pain, hunger, anxiety, nausea, comfort, well-being, ideas—and the experience of belonging-to-me as referred to his external characteristics . . . bodily function, appearance, action, etc. It further includes the experience of belonging-to-me when the referent is another person—my child, my friend—and also when objects . . . personal property, possessions, etc. . . . are referents."

Via the feeling or attitude expressed in the concept of "mine" the individual may perhaps establish bounded areas in the "outer" space. This bounding process could be thought of as bearing some similarities to the way in which he establishes the basic boundaries of his own body.

It is important to emphasize that Scheerer regarded the foundation of the "mine" attitude to be derived from the body as a reference point. At some level, "mine" referred back to the fact that an object or a person had a special relationship to his experienced body. Gupta (1962) remarks with reference to Scheerer's views on this matter (p. 4): "The earliest and basic experience of *my body* and the *mine* relationship, which links it with bodily, psychological and situational events, is the fundamental nucleus from which the other attributes of the *mine-sphere* experience . . . take their roots. Included in this basic *body* experience are the first smiles of recognition in an infant, crying, squalling, gestures, grimaces, communication by movement and all other forms of bodily events that express and elicit a reaction. In common usage all such basic body expressions are verbalized in the phrase the *body speaks*. It is from this nucleus of experience that 'higher level' psychological references to the contents of mine-sphere develop, such as the contents, *my name, my honor, my friend, my uniform,* etc."

For Scheerer, the mine-sphere embraced both the phenomenal body experience and its multiple extensions into other aspects of the individual's psychological world.

It is an interesting affirmation of Scheerer's views that in sensori-tonic experiments (e.g., Glick, 1964) it has actually been shown that when objects are seen as related to an individual's body they are assigned different qualities than when they are not seen as having such a relationship. The perceptual qualities (e.g., apparent spatial position) of objects appear to alter as soon as an individual shifts from merely seeing them as "out there" to seeing them as related to his own body.

It should be possible to undertake a variety of empirical studies of the relationship of body image parameters to the special way in which each individual constructs his mine-sphere. Prelinger (1959) has already experimented with methods for measuring the extent of the mine-sphere. He has had subjects sort verbal references to a wide variety of objects (including one's own body parts) in terms of how intimately such objects are experienced as having mine quality. An immediate promising area of application of this methodology would be to determine the relationships of the "extent" of one's mine sphere to the definiteness of one's own boundaries. Does the individual with well delineated boundaries tend, because of his sense of security about his "base of operations," to extend his feeling of "mine" to a wide area of surrounding space and objects? Or does the individual with poorly defined boundaries do this because he cannot easily differentiate himself from his environs? It is unlikely that any simple linear models will apply adequately. One would conjecture, for example, that wide extension of the "mine" domain could occur both on the basis of a clear sense of boundedness and also as a derivative of inadequate boundedness.

BODY IMAGE COMMUNICATION

Our bodies influence, and are influenced by, the bodies of others. Such influences are apparent in the involuntary tensing of an individual's muscles in imitation of the movements of an athlete or dancer he is watching. They are apparent in reports that the sight of deformity in another individual usually arouses anxiety in self about body damage. They are further illustrated by the body experiences that one has in the presence of others who are unusually small or large, beautiful or ugly, awkward or graceful. Schilder (1935) has provided numerous examples pertinent to this matter; and he includes them under the general rubric of the "sociology of the body image." He postulates that information about body feelings and attitudes is constantly being interchanged in social relationships. He points out that by the use of clothing style, gesture, and posture the individual conveys basic body feelings.

In most situations there are constraints with regard to how we observe the bodies of others. We are not usually aware of these constraints; but we receive quick feedback if we violate them. If you focus too obviously upon the lower areas of another individual's body or upon his mouth or eyes, this will arouse anxiety and perhaps hostility which will be reflected back in appropriate signals to you conveying concern. It will be suggested that such anxiety and hostility are not merely a response to behavior that is a bit unusual or a violation of conventional standards of modesty. It may be a way of defending oneself against threatening outside intrusion and influence. Is it possible that by focusing attention upon a specific area of another individual's body we change its usual experiential prominence and thereby alter its signal functions in the body image? If a man has low awareness of his eyes and we grossly increase their sensory prominence by staring at them, do we institute a body landmark signal change which in turn affects the equilibrium of attitudes and conflicts related to incorporation? If we stare at his back, and he is aware of this fact, can we arouse anxiety associated with anal conflicts? That is, to make an individual aware of a body area might be equivalent, in some ways, to lowering the threshold for arousal of a specific drive on motivational state. This possibility may not be far-fetched in view of the fact that artificially imposed changes in the sensory prominence of body landmarks (e.g., via vibration, deliberately channeling attention) have been shown to affect central attitudes. Indeed, there is no reason why it cannot be empirically evaluated. It should be feasible to design experiments in which measures of central attitudes are taken before and after a person is made particularly aware of a body sector by "social interaction" procedures. These procedures might involve staring intermittently at some part of an individual's body or conspicuously calling attention to a part of one's own body with the intent that it will arouse in the other individual an analogous interest in his body.

One wonders whether the original development of body landmarks may not in part be a function of the fact that parents learn to influence their children in social interactions by directly or indirectly intensifying their awareness of particular body landmarks. Does a mother focus an unusual amount of attention (as indicated by the direction of her gaze) upon the lower rear of the child when she wants it to learn anal sphincter control? Does she learn to fixate the eyes of her child disapprovingly when she thinks it is "taking too much" or being greedy (i.e., too incorporative)? She may learn that she can, with such maneuvers, achieve a certain amount of control which does not require a word of explanation. In turn, she may reciprocate by responding to attention the child focuses upon certain areas of her body. The child who feels mother is being too possessive or incorporative may accusingly direct his gaze to her eyes and produce changes in her behavior. In other words, a repertoire of non-verbal strategies, based on calling the other person's attention to some part of his body, might develop in a family as a means of influencing each other. Obviously, a shared concept of the "meaning" of certain body areas would be implicit in such influencing procedures.

THE TASK OF PREDICTING BODY EXPERIENCE ITSELF

In the literature concerned with the body image one of the primary intents has been to find out whether measures of body perception will predict non-body categories of behavior. There is frequently interest in examining the relationships of body image variables to measures of self concept, stress tolerance, sociometric status, and so forth. While studies of this type are important, one may ask whether body image information does not provide us with a unique opportunity to make predictions about the experiential world of the body? Should we not be able to use body image information to foresee such phenomena as the need for special stimulation of certain body areas (e.g., via eating or smoking or drinking); the probability of developing hypochondriacal complaints (and also the body sites to which they are likely to be attached); ability to tolerate pain; differential tendencies to accentuate or minimize pain at specific body sites; and the body areas most likely to be highlighted by "unusual" sensory experiences consequent upon ingestion of placebos or diffusely acting drugs? There is, too, the whole question waiting to be explored regarding the unique patterning of body experience typifying various emotional states in an individual. Can we predict whether a person will experience anger primarily in one body sector, whereas a second will feel it largely in another? Some encouragement concerning the possibility of making such predictions may be derived if one recalls that in the chapter dealing with boundary phenomena a study was described which demonstrated that the individual with definite boundaries experiences certain emotions vividly in the body exterior (viz., skin and muscle), while the individual with indefinite boundaries frequently localizes these same emotions in the body interior (viz., heart and stomach). If there are differences in localization of emotions linked to the state of the boundary, there may also be differences shaped by BFQ patterns and also total body awareness. With reference to this last variable, it is conceivable that one whose strategy is to minimize the impact of his body in the total perceptual field might either experience emotions in a particularly muted fashion or try to limit them to sites of "low visibility" which would have fewer possibilities of generating widespread body awareness. To experience an emotion in an area like one's head or stomach might make it more vivid ("visible") than if it were perceived in the muscles of the back. Whether it is actually possible for the same emotion to be localized in different persons in highly unlike body areas remains to be seen. Mason's work (1961) dealing with reports concerning the localization of emotions in one's body indicated that there were modal loci for given emotions, but there also seemed to be some fairly wide individual variations. As an adjunct to clarifying some of these issues, it will be necessary to find out how consistently emotions and other repetitive body experiences (e.g., hypochondriacal concern, accentuating versus minimizing of pain) occur at specific body sites. Is there enough consistency to make the study of individual differences feasible?

It is a related matter to ponder whether body image variables can eventually be looked to for much assistance in predicting which body sites will develop psychosomatic symptoms. The term psychosomatic is used in the gross sense of referring to disturbances in body function which seem to be linked with the occurrence of stress and conflict of psychological origin. There has been little past success in defining the conditions which determine the site at which a psychosomatic symptom will flourish. The work of Fisher and Cleveland (1968) has demonstrated some consistency between a body image variable (boundary) and the site of symptomatology. This work, which indicated significant correlations between the Barrier score and the exterior versus interior sites of symptoms, was thoroughly reviewed in the chapter dealing with boundary phenomena.

There are possibilities, worth considering, of using the BFQ to predict aspects of psychosomatic symptomatology. It would seem logical to assume that areas of unusually high or low experiential prominence, as defined by the BFQ, might have a special potential for becoming symptom sites. There are two lines of thought which could lead to such an assumption. One, derived from the Alexander (1948) perspective, would be that a psychosomatic symptom reflects an acute psychological conflict which finds expression in the pathological activation of a body sector possessing a meaning appropriate to the conflict. Obviously, any elevated BFQ score would fit this view perfectly.

Each BFQ dimension has been shown to represent simultaneously a specific conflict and also the body area with which that conflict has become associated. The second line of thought would derive from the fact that the levels of physiological activation of several body sectors have been observed to be significantly correlated with the BFQ scores designating such areas. This would be pertinent to the view held by some that the psychosomatic symptom is likely to occur in a body area which has become a chronic target for channelized emotional activation or inhibition. Clearly, an area defined by a high BFQ score could be conceptualized as just such a persistently involved physiological target.

One wonders whether other body image variables may not prove to be predictive of psychosomatic phenomena. For example, are there long-term differences in the probabilities of symptoms occurring in those sectors of the body which the individual finds attractive versus those he finds unattractive? Is it possible that there are gross differences in amount of psychosomatic symptomatology as a function of how typically the individual is high or low in his awareness of his body in relation to the total perceptual field?

BODY IMAGE AND CURRENT PERSONALITY THEORY

There were several promising routes that body image concepts might have taken in gaining admittance to current personality theories. The psychoanalytic route was one possibility. Many of Freud's formulations stressed the importance of the body as a psychological object in the development of an ego structure and also in the etiology of psychopathology. Body image concepts were prominent in his theory of the developmental process, which was depicted as leaning heavily on "libido localization." They were explicit in his statements concerning the part played by fixation of interest upon a limited body zone in the derivation of character types (e.g., "anal character"); and were also apparent as he spelled out the role of body symbolism in conversion hysteria. Since psychoanalytic concepts did attain influence in American personality theories, one might have expected their body image content to have been absorbed and assigned significance. However, what actually happened was that psychoanalytic theory became increasingly "social" in its orientation; and concepts concerned with libido localization, castration anxiety, and body symbolism were attenuated and appraised as having little importance. The neo-Freudian theories almost entirely ignored the "gut" aspects of Freudian theory. Consequently, the psychoanalytic concepts which did gain prominence on the American psychological scene were largely devoid of references to the role of body feelings in organized and disorganized behavior.

Body image formulations might have acquired influence if peripheral theories of emotion and thought had been able to defend themselves adequately against the arguments of the centralists. If it had become acceptable to regard emotion and thought as possessing substantial peripheral components, much research energy would probably have been channeled into developing methods for controlling and measuring such components. The success of attacks on kinesthetic theories of learning; the effectiveness of Cannon's criticisms of James' concept of emotion; and the devaluation of introspection, which is an important method for becoming aware of the role of the experienced body, combined, along with other events, to obscure the contribution of the body experiential framework.

It is striking, however, that with time an enormous interest evolved in the "self concept." The essence of the self concept approach is that each individual has a unique area of perception which encompasses how he experiences himself. This experience has been largely defined in terms of value assigned to self, satisfaction with self, ideal goals set for self, and the tensions associated with the whole process of existing as an independent being. Presumably, an understanding of the individual's self perceptions would permit predictions of various aspects of his behavior. Body experience was only rarely and incidentally mentioned as contributing to the self concept. Self was largely portrayed in the language of central cognitive attitudes. But one wonders whether the appeal of the "self concept" was the fact that it represented an attempt to fill the void in theories which ignore the "base of operations" from which all experiencing occurs. Many motivational and personality theories present man as a central nervous system capable of learning, with attached endocrinological and autonomic subsystems; and there is little or nothing said about what it "feels like" to be alive, to have emotions, and to be a site for interacting sensory events. Self concept theory recognized that the way an individual experiences himself constitutes a potent element in his behavior. It indirectly recognized that there is a unique area of space belonging to self. However, it said little about the fact that this space is man's body and that "self experience" is often expressed in the domain of body sensation. It would be fair to add, as described in Chapter 2, that scattered attempts have been made to correlate self concept and body image measures. Also, a few self concept inventories which have been developed include ratings of body parts and processes (Wylie, 1961). In any case, one would guess that the absence of the "body" from most self concept formulations represented an overzealous reaction against biologically oriented theories of behavior. The "self concept" arose partially to humanize the image of man which biologically based theories had mechanistically oversimplified. Since such biological theories were identified with body functions, it was probably in the spirit of things to want to forget about the body entirely—even as an experienced object and even at a level where its biological attributes were not the prime consideration.

However, it is likely that self concept theory will, in the long run, have helped to lay a foundation for integrating body image concepts into the mainstream of psychological theory. It is not a large step from a recognition of the importance of the experienced self to a consideration of how the perception of one's body contributes to this "self." This is well illustrated in the following statement by Lundholm (1946, pp. 129–130):

> The self intuits itself as having a "whereness" within the body. The "whereness" is not strictly localized. The self, however, never identifies itself with the body. The body is one of its percepts, like all percepts projected into three-dimensional space. . . . The body is a coherent object having a definite contour extending all around the self— the latter always being with the contour. . . . The self intuits the relation of belonging-ness of the body to itself. The body is its body, it is termed "mine"; the self seems aware of itself embodied. . . . Though lacking extension, it (self) has "whereness." It is never *there* as the perceived thing; it is always *here*; and here means in a vague manner within the body-contour.

What are the principal forces on the current scene which are giving impetus to research related to the body image? It is difficult to answer this question because the number of investigators engaged in body image research has proliferated. However, as previously mentioned, the sensori-tonic work of Wapner and Werner (1965) and the studies by Witkin and his associates (1954, 1962) have certainly been in the forefront in calling attention to body perception phenomena. The findings of Schachter and his associates (e.g., Schachter and Singer, 1962; Schachter and Wheeler, 1962) concerned with the interaction of cognitive set and body experience have supplied an entirely new methodology for studying the experienced body. The rapidly growing literature on operant conditioning of autonomic responses and the poten-tialities of interoceptive conditioning has added intriguing alternatives for possible formulations about how body signals enter into behavior. The work of Jourard and Secord concerned with body attractiveness and body awareness continues to attract considerable attention. Shontz's (1963A, C, 1967) and also Cleveland's (Cleveland, 1960B; Cleveland, et al., 1962) systematic explorations of the variables affecting perception of body size have delineated the problems that need to be mastered in this area. One needs to single out also the work of Holzman and his associates (1966) which has highlighted the feasibility of studying self confrontation phenomena (e.g., hearing one's own voice without conscious awareness of its identity) in depth and yet experimentally. These are just a few of the active, productive lines of effort on the current scene that show special promise.

There are also many issues under investigation which seem tangential to body image matters, but whose pertinence is becoming increasingly clear. The growing field of psychopharmacology, with its interest in drug experi-ences, has begun to uncover a good deal of data indicating an interaction between the central effects of drugs and their impact upon the experienced body. Some of the new work concerned with adaptation to lens induced visual distortions (e.g., Rock, 1966) has defined the role of body experience and the body context in stimulating or inhibiting the adaptation process. Interesting possibilities for clarifying the contribution of environmental input toward sustaining the organization of the body scheme have come from sensory isolation data (e.g., Reitman and Cleveland, 1964). Many studies concerned with kinesthesia, e.g., how it participates in memory and the construction of fantasy (Feder, 1967), are of prime pertinence. One should also call attention to the potentialities for application to body image problems of research concerned with spatial orientation (Howard and Templeton, 1966); the use of muscle relaxation procedures in reducing anxiety; the entire range of issues related to the perceptual and motor differentiation of the right and left sides of the body (Palmer, 1963, 1964); the influence of postural sets on behavior (Jones, 1965); and so forth. If this recitation of interesting "leads" sounds amorphous, one can only plead that there are too many new lines of pertinent work opening up to permit their neat categorization.

Speaking boldly, one may predict that future work will eventually indicate that most aspects of an individual's behavior are appreciably influenced by the ways in which he has learned to deal with his body as a psychological object.

APPENDICES

A
Barrier and Penetration Scoring

This Appendix contains detailed definitions of the Barrier and Penetration scoring systems. It also includes sample ink blot protocols in which the scoring criteria have been applied and explained.

CRITERIA FOR BARRIER SCORING [1]

Score the following as Barrier:

1. All references to clothing, whether mentioned as separate articles (e.g., dress, girdle, sweater); whether described as worn by a person (e.g., He has a tie on); or whether indirectly referred to (e.g., There are pleats; It has a pocket).

This category embraces all forms of jewelry and body adornment (e.g., earrings, bracelet, comb in her hair, ring, wig, false eyelashes). It does not include special hairdos, beards, or long hair.

It pertains to all forms of body protection and camouflage, e.g., gas mask, armor, helmet, umbrella, shield, mask, halo, catcher's mask, disguise, false nose, cast, arm sling, bandage, sheet (wrapped around), veil.

It includes all mechanical attachments to the body (e.g., glasses, hearing aid, wax wings, scuba tank, flippers, skates, skis, badge).

2. All references to buildings and similar enclosing structures. Examples:

arch	closet	merry-go-round	store
barracks	cottage	mine	subway
basement	fence (also hedges)	mineshaft	tent

---

[1] This scoring scheme differs from that first published in 1958 (Fisher and Cleveland) insofar as it includes *all* references to clothing, buildings, and vehicles instead of selected instances of such classes. It also includes popular responses previously omitted. In addition, it includes all masks. These changes have been made to simplify scoring by reducing the number of exceptions. Correlations between scores based on the old and the new, more simplified, criteria are of the order of .98.

bomb shelter	hall	monument	tower
bridge	house	porch	tunnel
catwalk	hut	shelter	warehouse
church	kitchen	skyscraper	

It embraces images which indirectly connote the existence of such structures (e.g., city, metropolis, village, town, colony, airport).

Also, it includes parts of buildings and structures (e.g., chimney, roof, stairway, walls, ceiling) and adornments within or upon them (e.g., gargoyles, door knockers, wallpaper).

Further, it involves structures which delimit or organize an area (e.g., road, sidewalk, street, curb, alley, playground, backyard, football field).

3. All references to vehicles with some containing or "holding" qualities. Examples:

airplane	boat	motorcycle	ski lift	wagon
automobile	elevator	rocket ship	sled	
bicycle	magic carpet	scooter	train	

4. All references to that which contains, covers, or conceals. This may be subdivided into the following categories:

A. Container (or container-like shapes)

Examples:	ant hill	box	freezer	pouch
	bag	bubble	glass	radio
	bagpipes	cage	globe	sheath
	ball	candleholder	hammock	spoon
	balloon	chair	lamp	stove
	bed	couch	nest	tank
	bee hive	cup	net	throne
	bell	dish	oil well	toaster
	billfold	drawer	pillow	trap
	book	envelope	pipe	TV set
	book ends	flask	pocketbook	vat
	bottle	folder	pot	well

Includes living things with special container qualities (e.g., pregnant woman, kangaroo, camel).

B. Coverings

Examples:	bear rug	mountain with snow on it
	blanket	moss on a log
	rug	bowl overgrown by a plant
	table cloth	donkey with load covering his back

C. Concealment

(Includes references to hiding or being in a concealed position. Also includes references to objects with concealing functions)

Examples:	behind a rock	peeking out	shutters
	behind a tree	screen	smoke screen
	curtains	shades	

5. All living things (except human) described as having special surface qualities (e.g., fuzzy, rough, hard, smooth, striped, spotted, bristly, feathered, long-haired). Does not include references to the surface being light, dark, or possessed of specific hues (e.g., red, yellow).

This category also embraces a series of animals, listed below, considered to possess distinctive or unusual skins.

alligator	goat	mountain goat	Siamese cat
badger	hippo	peacock	skunk
beaver	hyena	penguin	tiger
bobcat	leopard	porcupine	walrus
buffalo	lion	prairie dog	weasel
chameleon	lizard	rhinoceros	wildcat
coyote	lynx	sea lion	wolverine
crocodile	mink	seal	zebra
fox	mole	sheep or lamb	

[These animals are scored Barrier only if more than the head is seen.]

6. All creatures possessed of shells or similar protective structures, e.g., snail, lobster, shrimp, clam, oyster, mussel, bug with shell, crab, cactus, scorpion, turtle.

7. All references to geographic or natural formations with delimiting or container-like qualities. Examples:

abyss	harbor	river
banks of river	island	spring
canal	lake	valley
cave	pathway in woods	volcano
	ravine	

When scoring a record, give a credit of 1 to each response which contains any of the above images. But no more than 1 credit can be assigned to any given response, no matter how many Barrier images it contains.

CRITERIA FOR PENETRATION SCORING [2]

Score the following for Penetration:

1. All references to the fact of disruption, penetration, damage, or destruction of any object or living thing. Examples:

amputated arm	man being shot
autopsy	man sick

[2] This scoring scheme is a revised version of that published in 1958 (Fisher and Cleveland). The intent was to simplify scoring by eliminating a few instances in which special exceptions were made to general categories. Scores derived from the old criteria correlate on the order of .98 with scores based on the new simplified criteria.

body cut open
bombed building
bullet entering flesh
cancer
deteriorated old house
diseased flesh
diseased flower
dog run over
hurt
house burning
killed
killing woman

man wasted away
operating on patient
saw cutting wood
scar
squashed bug
stabbing a person
tooth pulled
torn muscle
ulcer
wilted flower
worn out shirt
wound bleeding
wounded

[Includes instances of body distortion exemplified by responses like cripple, hunchback, paralyzed, cross-eyed, midget, blind, deaf.]

2. All references to body openings or to acts involving body openings. Examples:

anus
being born
bite
chew
chicken pecking

defecating
drink
eat
looking down someone's throat
mouth (separately)
nostril (separately)

spitting
stick tongue out
vagina
vomiting
yawn

[Do not score references to singing or talking or making sounds.]

3. All references to perceptions which involve a perspective of bypassing or evading the usual boundaries of the body or other objects. Examples:

can see through it
cross section of an organ
fluoroscope of chest

inside of body *
transparent gown
X-ray

[* Does not include references to the inside of objects which can ordinarily be entered without disrupting the boundaries, e.g., inside of house, inside of flower.]

4. All references to the process of entering or leaving structures and also the means for doing so. Examples:

came out the window
climbed out the chimney
door
doorway
entrance

exit
jet exhaust
rocket exhaust
smoke coming out of a pipe
walked through the door
window

5. All references to natural contexts that involve intake or expulsion. Examples:

> geyser
> oil spurting out of ground
> volcano erupting

6. All images that are insubstantial or vague in their delimitation. Examples:

ghost shadow spirit

Each response that contains one or more Penetration images [3] is given a value of 1. No more than a credit of 1 can be assigned by any response, no matter how many Penetration images it contains.

INK BLOT PROTOCOLS [4] TO ILLUSTRATE APPLICATION OF BARRIER AND PENETRATION SCORING CRITERIA

Ink Blot Protocol 1

Responses	Scoring
1. A man's tie and part of his jacket.	1. B * because of "tie" and "jacket."
2. Two widows in long black dresses holding on to tail of lizards.	2. B because of "dresses" and also "lizards."
3. Sting ray coming out from behind coral in ocean.	3. B because of reference to having been "behind" something.
4. Two people flying on back of turkeys over twin mountains.	4.
5. A horse with wings and bird flying overhead.	5.
6. Two grandmothers sitting back to back in plush chairs reading.	6. B because of "chairs."
7. Heads of two fish. Mainly see their mouths.	7. Not scored P,* even though mouth emphasized. Reference to actual use of mouth in some way would be required to score P. Or if only the mouth itself were seen it would be scored P.
8. Serpent sitting with tail dangling beneath him. Sort of monster. In	8.

* B = Barrier
P = Penetration

---

[3] Note that a response may simultaneously be scored Penetration and Barrier (e.g. "volcano erupting," "broken vase").

[4] All protocols in the Appendix A are based on responses to the Holtzman blots.

forepaw and back paw holding serpent.

9. Two horses rolling on their backs.

9.

10. Fight. Ready to punch each other.

10. Not scored P, even though "fight" mentioned. P would require that actual body damage be described.

11. Jet in distance flying between two storm clouds.

11. B because of "jet" which is a vehicle.

12. River in foreground. Huge bonfire and people running around it.

12. B because of "river."

13. Alligator.

13. B because of "alligator."

14. Two figures sitting on rock, tails like mermaids. Top not woman, but furry animals and furry arms. On rock.

14. B because of "furry animals."

15. Face—eyes and nose, mouth. Person. Black hair.

15. Not scored B despite mention of "black hair."

16. Aerial view of a turtle shell, who has purple spot disease.

16. B because of "turtle." P because of "disease"

17. Chalice with a wide brim, slim neck, rectangular base.

17. B because of "chalice."

18. Two birds very plush plumage looking opposite ways. Standing on top of knoll viewing area in distance.

18. B because of "plush plumage."

19. Two people waiting. Two running away and two cats.

19.

20. Ocean spray against the rocks and against cliffs. Sunset reflection in water.

20. Not scored B because the covering implications of the "spray" are not sufficiently explicit.

21. Birds and landscape.

21.

22. Mouth of an alligator at zoo. Going to catch meat someone's throwing.

22. P because of implication will "catch meat" with "mouth."

23. Queen of the night. Long black gown. Standing with hands over head. Very misty atmosphere.

23. B because of "gown." The reference to "misty" would not be scored B.

24. Castle—half-destroyed in ruins.

24. B because of "castle." P because "half-destroyed."

25. Two centaurs, dancing in a Bacchic rite.

25.

Ink Blot Protocol 2

Responses

1. Two people facing each other stand-

* B = Barrier

Scoring

1. B * because "wearing masks,"

ing between two Japanese trees. Very tall people wearing masks. Standing in shade of tree.

2. Two girls with backs to each other. Harvesting grain. Very gentle with plant, like a baby.

3. Two horses, both have riders. Gun shot caused horses to rise up on hind legs. They're throwing the riders off.

4. Scene from El Cid. Two fighters on horses. Sun is going down. Been a lot of fighting on battlefield; lot of death. Clouds from battle in sky. Two horsemen with swords going toward one another.

5. Stiff figure. Blind. Has a cane. Very foggy.

6. Two pigs' heads, happy and smiling. Background has about four people.

7. Picture from fairy tale. Two fairies in long flowing dresses dancing on tiptoes with hands joined.

8. Buildings beside the water. Boats with fisherman holding fishing poles.

9. Horse jumping over a bush. Rider thrust forward very close to horse, holding on for dear life.

10. Two people facing each other doing minuette. Lady with long hair in long dress ready to curtsy. Man with epaulettes on shoulder, fighter of Revolutionary War.

11. Baby swan still black. Ugly duckling.

12. People on desert or prairie. Sunset near. People around camp fires.

13. Swimmer doing crawl. Feet make splashes. Waves in water.

14. People standing up in foreground waving to someone. Men are waving to women going away. Men skinny. Women waving back wearing long dresses.

15. Building—Alamo or capital build-

* P = Penetration

"standing between trees," and "in shade of tree."

2. Not scored P * despite use of term "harvest." The cutting and destructive effects upon the plants are not sufficiently explicit.

3. Not scored P despite mention of "shots" and "throwing the riders off." Explicit body damage is not mentioned.

4. Scored P because of reference to "death."

5. Scored P because of reference to body damage implied by term "blind." "Foggy" not scored B.

6.

7. B because of "dresses."

8. B because of "buildings" and "boats."

9.

10. B because of "dress" and "epaulettes."

11. Not scored P, even though described as "ugly."

12.

13.

14. B because of "dresses."

15. B because of "building" and also

ing. Very beautiful sunset in background. Silhouette of bushes and
trees around building.

16. Science fiction. Head of person
exposing brain, with two people running around in it.

17. Man and woman in a boat in Venice
canal. Sail fish in water. People
around.

18. Two men ready to hit each other.
Wearing large kimonos and beards.

19. Two men on horses. Horses not
visible. Riding into home town after
battle. People cheering them. They're
waving their helmets.

20. Two birds flying over water. Boat in
water. Going toward boat.

21. Two people sitting with backs to
each other, facing ducks with very
long beaks. People are slouched over,
have long feet.

22. Two alligators in water. Heads and
part of bodies visible. Facing each
other. Talking because mouths are
open.

23. Night time, very bright moon. Castle
with three towers and moat with
towers, reflection.

24. Wash line with clothes blowing long
underwear and pants.

25. Two dancers both on one foot, other
raised, holding hands. Gypsies dancing in front of fire and smoke.

"bushes and trees *around* building."

16. P because of "exposing brain."

17. B because of "boat" and also
"canal."

18. B because of "kimonos," but *not*
because of "beards."

19. B because of "helmets" and "home
town."

20. B because of "boat."

21.

22. B because of "alligators."
P because "mouths open."

23. B because of "castle" and "moat."

24. B because of "clothes" mentioned.

25. Not scored B despite mention of
"gypsies" who might be thought of
as having distinctive costumes. The
reference to clothing must be more
explicit to justify scoring B.

Ink Blot Protocol 3

Responses	Scoring
1. Two people in middle facing each other. People fighting.	1.
2. Two women, back to each other. Heads are bent over.	2.
3. Rabbits.	3.
4. Knights on horses dueling.	4. B * because "knights" so strongly

* B = Barrier

suggests the wearing of armor. This is one of the few cases in which B is scored on the basis of an individual belonging to a general class of persons.

5. Cubist charcoal painting of a man holding a stick.

5.

6. Two pigs holding something between their hands.

6. "Between their hands" is not scored B.

7. Michelangelo's painting of hand of God almost touching.

7.

8. House on the edge of water and its reflection. Flat roof.

8. B because of "house" and also reference to the "edge of water" with its implications of a body of water with a boundary.

9. Forest—the roots of trees.

9.

10. Two people with legs disconnected from their bodies. They have tails.

10. P * because of "disconnected from their bodies."

11. Big dark cloud and a star.

11.

12. Two women on a desert. Big fire in middle, people around fire. Black clouds and sunset. Two women dancing.

12.

13. Landscape, hills and trees, very far away.

13.

14. Two skeletons on either side of a wall. They are trying to get over.

14. B because of "wall."

15. Pagoda with pond in middle.

15. B because of "pagoda" and "pond."

16. Ice skaters or ballet dancers with one leg up.

16. Scored B because of reference to idea of wearing ice skates.

17. Few people with long noses, talking to one another.

17.

18. Two men facing each other. One arm on other's shoulder. Other arm behind him.

18. Not scored B despite fact that man has his arm "behind" him. This refers to a posture and not to an act of concealment.

19. Group of people. Two women in center, one hand holding piece of cloth. Kneeling.

19.

20. Left side—bird. Purple elephant in back of him.

20. Not scored B despite reference to "purple."

21. Two women taking a bath.

21. Would be scored only if reference made to being in a bathtub or shower stall.

22. Crab with claws.

22. B because is creature with a shell.

* B = Barrier
  P = Penetration

23. Black bat.

23. Not scored B despite reference to "black."

24. Furry caterpillars.

24. Scored B because of use of term "furry."

25. Two matadors on horses, wearing berets.

25. Scored B because wearing "berets."

Ink Blot Protocol 4

Responses	Scoring

1. Little white furry animal. In middle, pile of stuffed animals.

1. B* because "furry." Not because "white."

2. Frog.

2.

3. Nuclear explosion.

3. Not P.* Explosions not scored P unless reference made to destruction of a specific object.

4. Sunset.

4.

5. Dirty window.

5. P because of "window" (an outlet to a structure).
"Dirty" not scored B because the covering implications are not sufficiently explicit.

6. A woman's head.

6.

7. Head and legs, body of animal.

7.

8. Mad scientist leaning over a test tube. Spitting out a big black cloud.

8. B because of "test tube."
P because of "spitting out."

9. Four dancers. Two people hanging in the middle or six dancers. That's nice.

9.

10. Ghost with two big black eyes.

10. P because of "ghost" (insubstantial).

11. Two buffalo.

11. B because of "buffalo" (one of animals considered to have distinctive hide).

12. Forest fire.

12. P because of "forest fire."

13. Pond water under a microscope.

13.

14. Two people fighting. Blood in between.

14. P because of association of terms "fight" and "blood."

15. Silhouette of forest or jungle with rocks sticking up.

15.

16. Two big and two little fish.

16.

17. Two big monsters about to tear each other apart.

17. P because "about to tear each other apart." The futurity of the action is not important. The reference to "tear apart" is primary.

* B = Barrier
  P = Penetration

18. Two Indians (India) and big moth above.

18.

19. War. People shooting each other, clouds and lot of dirt.

19. P because of "shooting each other."

20. Shirt worn in Shakespearean plays.

20. B because of "shirt."

21. Two mountain sides. Two vultures at bottom.

21.

22. Tree at night. Two owls, one on either side on different branch.

22.

23. Landscapes.

23.

24. Dropped and squashed orange popsicle.

24. P because of "squashed." Not because of "dropped."

25. Two ice skaters waltzing. Russian ice skaters.

25. Scored B because of "ice skaters"

Ink Blot Protocol 5

Responses	Scoring

1. Face with two eyes in center.

1.

2. Art nouveau design. Heart in center.

2. Not scored P * despite mention of "heart." Mere mention of an internal organ does not signify P.

3. Science fiction. Two big monsters confronting each other. Explosion in background. Comical, about to dance.

3.

4. Dragons. Japanese. Sunset in background. Dragons face to face.

4.

5. Painting of the seasons. Spring with budding tree. Black and white winter. Summer and fall too.

5.

6. Underside of a turtle or something in biology.

6. B * because of "turtle." Scored B even though "underside" rather than shell emphasized.

7. Person waving a big cloak. Wearing vest and bow tie. Very proud of himself.

7. B because of "cloak" and other articles of clothing mentioned.

8. Ballet. Costumed figure with elaborate headdress on.

8. B because of "costumed" and "headdress."

9. Stage. Black solid figures with tongues stuck out at each other, blowing smoke.

9. B because of "stage" (a delimited and containing structure).
P because "tongues stuck out" and "blowing smoke."
Note that the same response can be scored both B and P.

* P = Penetration
  B = Barrier

10. *Life* Magazine picture of Arabs fleeing homeland. Smeared photograph.

10. Not scored B despite reference to "Arabs" who could possibly be visualized as wearing a distinctive costume. A more explicit statement concerning costume is required for B.

11. Just rained, lot of trees.

11.

12. Very careful study of something. Veins and muscles.

12. Not scored P despite mention of "veins and muscles." P would be scored only if the "veins and muscles" were described as being inside the body or revealed by such means as X-ray or dissection.

13. Painting. Child's comical drawing of person, probably child himself—big head, long neck. Figure lying down. Cave painting.

13. Scored B because of reference to being a "*cave* painting."

14. Music. Dancers with backs hunched.

14.

15. Dogs' faces looking away from each other. Each has one wing with feathers.

15. Scored B because of "feathers."

16. Springtime. Pretty water color of castle and beautiful kingdom.

16. B because of "castle."

17. Fall. Bears coming out of hibernation. Looking up at two orange suns.

17. B because of fairly explicit reference to having been in "hibernation" *somewhere* (a contained area).
P because of reference to "coming out" of the place of hibernation.

18. Butterfly with one antenna hooked on leaf that looks like embryo.

18. Not P because reference to "hooked on" in this case is not clearly indicative of doing damage.

19. Devil with big horns, squatting on short legs like an insect. Large muscular arms. Huge monster in front of horse's head. A rider on horseback shooting guns or blowing bugles, saluting the Devil.

19. P because of "blowing bugle." But not P because of "shooting guns." Shooting is scored P only when reference to someone having been shot is made.

20. Love purple color. Abstract. Twilite. Birds in sky. Calm. Pink sunset.

20.

21. Two ladies very vain, looking at each other. Large hats.

21. B because of "hats."

22. Anatomical drawing, pelvis and rib cage.

22. Not P despite reference to "anatomical drawing." To be scored P some explicit reference to damaging or by-passing the usual boundaries is required.

23. Tree trunk with no top to it.

23. P because of reference to "no top to it." Any statement indicating that

some usual part of a living being is missing is scored P.

24. Something falling down. Close-up of a branch with a bird in it. Ashes coming thru the air. Orange because of forest fire.

24. P because of "forest fire."

25. Two dancers hopping on one foot. Polish or Italian. One on right has book.

25. B because of "book."

B
Body Focus Questionnaire

This section contains a copy of the Body Focus Questionnaire and also lists of the items comprising each BFQ scale. Scoring procedures are detailed.

Turn your attention upon yourself. Concentrate on your body. Below is a list in which different areas of your body are listed in pairs. In each case pick the area or part which is at the moment most clear in your awareness. If your answer is in the left column blacken in the two lines in the column marked A on the answer sheet. If your answer involves a word in the right column, fill in the two lines in the column marked B on the answer sheet.

1.	Chest	Back of head
2.	Mouth	Neck
3.	Eyes	Nose
4.	Head	Shoulder
5.	Left shoulder	Right shoulder
6.	Arms	Toes
7.	Back of head	Front of head
8.	Stomach	Elbows
9.	Right eye	Left eye
10.	Heart	Skin
11.	Chin	Mouth
12.	Mouth	Eyes
13.	Thighs	Head
14.	Chest	Back of body (at chest level)
15.	Legs	Arms
16.	Front of neck	Back of neck
17.	Head	Stomach
18.	Left arm	Right arm
19.	Muscles	Heart
20.	Mouth	Cheeks
21.	Back of knees	Front of knees
22.	Eyes	Chin
23.	Head	Chest

24.	Arms	Knees
25.	Back of shoulders	Front of shoulders
26.	Stomach	Thighs
27.	Right foot	Left foot
28.	Heart	Feet
29.	Eyebrows	Mouth
30.	Back of hips	Chest
31.	Scalp	Eyes
32.	Knees	Head
33.	Left wrist	Right wrist
34.	Soles of feet	Arms
35.	Front of hips	Back of hips
36.	Feet	Stomach
37.	Left knee	Right knee
38.	Hands	Heart
39.	Face	Back of shoulders
40.	Mouth	Eyes
41.	Eyes	Hair
42.	Head	Elbows
43.	Fingers	Toes
44.	Right side of mouth	Left side of mouth
45.	Back of thighs	Front of thighs
46.	Stomach	Muscles
47.	Right ear	Left ear
48.	Heart	Shoulder
49.	Ears	Mouth
50.	Back of neck	Chest
51.	Ears	Eyes
52.	Ankles	Head
53.	Legs	Fingers
54.	Front of legs	Back of legs
55.	Back of hips	Face
56.	Hands	Stomach
57.	Left elbow	Right elbow
58.	Neck	Heart
59.	Mouth	Nose
60.	Chest	Back of legs
61.	Eyes	Cheeks
62.	Head	Hands
63.	Fingers	Knees
64.	Right thigh	Left thigh
65.	Heart	Head
66.	Hair	Mouth
67.	Back of ankle area	Front of ankle area
68.	Eyebrows	Eyes
69.	Feet	Head
70.	Soles of feet	Fingers
71.	Front of neck	Back of head

72.	Ankles	Stomach
73.	Left ankle	Right ankle
74.	Elbows	Heart
75.	Mouth	Scalp
76.	Chest	Back of shoulders
77.	Right big toe	Left big toe
78.	Eyes	Forehead
79.	Head	Waist
80.	Elbows	Toes
81.	Stomach	Neck
82.	Right thumb	Left thumb
83.	Heart	Thighs
84.	Front of legs	Back of head
85.	Forehead	Mouth
86.	Neck	Eyes
87.	Toes	Head
88.	Legs	Elbows
89.	Knees	Stomach
90.	Left little finger	Right little finger
91.	Elbows	Knees
92.	Stomach	Skin
93.	Heart	Ankles
94.	Soles of feet	Elbows
95.	Heart	Stomach
96.	Knees	Heart
97.	Neck	Toes
98.	Stomach	Inside of throat
99.	Back of head	Front of thighs
100.	Legs	Neck
101.	Stomach	Lungs
102.	Heart	Lungs
103.	Knees	Neck
104.	Right hand	Left hand
105.	Inside of head	Stomach
106.	Inside of throat	Heart
107.	Neck	Soles of feet
108.	Inside of head	Heart

INDIVIDUAL BODY FOCUS QUESTIONNAIRE SCALES

BFQ Back

1.	Chest	Back of head
7.	Back of head	Front of head
14.	Chest	Back of body (at chest level)
16.	Front of neck	Back of neck

21.	Back of knees	Front of knees
25.	Back of shoulders	Front of shoulders
30.	Back of hips	Chest
35.	Front of hips	Back of hips
39.	Face	Back of shoulders
45.	Back of thighs	Front of thighs
50.	Back of neck	Chest
54.	Front of legs	Back of legs
55.	Back of hips	Face
60.	Chest	Back of legs
67.	Back of ankle area	Front of ankle area
71.	Front of neck	Back of head
76.	Chest	Back of shoulders
84.	Front of legs	Back of head
99.	Back of head	Front of thighs

BFQ Right

5.	Left shoulder	Right shoulder
9.	Right eye	Left eye
18.	Left arm	Right arm
27.	Right foot	Left foot
33.	Left wrist	Right wrist
37.	Left knee	Right knee
44.	Right side of mouth	Left side of mouth
47.	Right ear	Left ear
57.	Left elbow	Right elbow
64.	Right thigh	Left thigh
73.	Left ankle	Right ankle
77.	Right big toe	Left big toe
82.	Right thumb	Left thumb
90.	Left little finger	Right little finger
104.	Right hand	Left hand

BFQ Eyes

3.	Eyes	Nose
12.	Mouth	Eyes
22.	Eyes	Chin
31.	Scalp	Eyes
40.	Mouth	Eyes
41.	Eyes	Hair
51.	Ears	Eyes
61.	Eyes	Cheeks
68.	Eyebrows	Eyes
78.	Eyes	Forehead
86.	Neck	Eyes

BFQ Heart

10.	Heart	Skin

19.	Muscles	Heart
28.	Heart	Feet
38.	Hands	Heart
48.	Heart	Shoulder
58.	Neck	Heart
65.	Heart	Head
74.	Elbows	Heart
83.	Heart	Thighs
93.	Heart	Ankles
95.	Heart	Stomach
96.	Knees	Heart
102.	Heart	Lungs
106.	Inside of throat	Heart
108.	Inside of head	Heart

BFQ Mouth

2.	Mouth	Neck
11.	Chin	Mouth
12.	Mouth	Eyes
20.	Mouth	Cheeks
29.	Eyebrows	Mouth
40.	Mouth	Eyes
49.	Ears	Mouth
59.	Mouth	Nose
66.	Hair	Mouth
75.	Mouth	Scalp
85.	Forehead	Mouth

BFQ Stomach

8.	Stomach	Elbows
17.	Head	Stomach
26.	Stomach	Thighs
36.	Feet	Stomach
46.	Stomach	Muscles
56.	Hands	Stomach
72.	Ankles	Stomach
81.	Stomach	Neck
89.	Knees	Stomach
92.	Stomach	Skin
95.	Heart	Stomach
98.	Stomach	Inside of throat
101.	Stomach	Lungs
105.	Inside of head	Stomach

BFQ Head

4.	Head	Shoulder
13.	Thighs	Head
17.	Head	Stomach

23.	Head	Chest
32.	Knees	Head
42.	Head	Elbows
52.	Ankles	Head
62.	Head	Hands
65.	Heart	Head
69.	Feet	Head
79.	Head	Waist
87.	Toes	Head

BFQ Arms

6.	Arms	Toes
8.	Stomach	Elbows
15.	Legs	Arms
24.	Arms	Knees
34.	Soles of feet	Arms
38.	Hands	Heart
42.	Head	Elbows
43.	Fingers	Toes
53.	Legs	Fingers
56.	Hands	Stomach
62.	Head	Hands
63.	Fingers	Knees
70.	Soles of feet	Fingers
74.	Elbows	Heart
80.	Elbows	Toes
88.	Legs	Elbows
91.	Elbows	Knees
94.	Soles of feet	Elbows

DIRECTIONS FOR MAKING OVERLAY SCORING SHEETS FOR THE BODY FOCUS QUESTIONNAIRE

The questionnaire consists of a list of different areas of the body arranged in pairs. In each of the 108 pairs, the S is asked to mark on an IBM answer sheet (No. I.T.S. 1100 A444) the area or part which is at the moment most clear in his awareness. If his choice is in the left-hand column he makes a mark "A" on the answer sheet; if his choice is in the right-hand column he marks a "B" on the answer sheet. The answer sheet can be scored by using a series of overlay sheets made from blank answer sheets.

There are eight overlay sheets needed to completely score the answer sheet. Mark each according to the following patterns:

The eight areas: Arms
Back
Eyes
Head
Heart
Mouth
Right
Stomach

I. *ARMS:*   (9) A's   (9) B's
6, 24, 38, 43, 56,   8, 15, 34, 42, 53,
63, 74, 80, 91   62, 70, 88, 94

II. *BACK:*   (9) A's   (10) B's
7, 21, 25, 30, 45,   1, 14, 16, 35, 39, 54,
50, 55, 67, 99   60, 71, 76, 84

III. *EYES:*   (5) A's   (6) B's
3, 22, 41, 61, 78   12, 31, 40, 51, 68, 86

IV. *HEAD:*   (6) A's   (6) B's
4, 17, 23, 42,   13, 32, 52, 65,
62, 79   69, 87

V. *HEART:*   (8) A's   (7) B's
10, 28, 48, 65,   19, 38, 58, 74,
83, 93, 95, 102   96, 106, 108

VI. *MOUTH:*   (6) A's   (5) B's
2, 12, 20, 40,   11, 29, 49, 66, 85
59, 75

VII. *RIGHT:*   (8) A's   (7) B's
9, 27, 44, 47,   5, 18, 33, 37,
64, 77, 82, 104   57, 73, 90

VIII. *STOMACH:*   (7) A's   (7) B's
8, 26, 46, 81,   17, 36, 56, 72,
92, 98, 101   89, 95, 105

After you have filled in the eight overlay sheets and have checked your marks to make sure they correspond with the numbers in this booklet, take an IBM punch (or similar punch with a *long* arm) and punch out the items you have marked on each score sheet. Then take a magic marker and outline the punched holes.

Finally, label each sheet and then cut a rectangular notch at the right hand margin to provide an opening for the score or scores to be recorded directly on the answer sheet. There will be eight scores in all.

C
Body Prominence Protocols

This section contains five protocols in which illustrations of the application of the Body Prominence scoring criteria are provided.

Body Prominence Protocol 1

Responses	Scoring
1. My own existence—the fact that I am alive.	1. Scored because of reference to being "alive."
2. The fact that my feet are cold and wet.	2. Scored because mentions temperature sensation and tactile sensation ("wet").
3. The movie screen in front of me.	3. Not scored despite reference to "me." Incidental references to self or to spatial coordinates involving self (e.g., "on my left") are not scored.
4. That I will be here (in this room) for some time.	4.
5. That I don't know what's coming next.	5.
6. The flow of thoughts in my mind now.	6. Not scored despite mention of "my mind." If had said "my brain," would be scored.
7. That they are not greatly spontaneous.	7.
8. My ears are cold.	8. Scored because of "ears" and temperature reference.
9. A self-conscious gesture.	9. Not scored. Descriptions of body movement are scored only if a specific part of one's body is mentioned (e.g., "I moved my hand").

10. My quick passing thoughts about how someone else will perceive or interpret what I write.

11. The reassuring glitter of my ring.

12. My seeing it first as a thing to which I am accustomed.

13. It is beautiful.

14. Wondering if the kind of responses I am giving are what is wanted.

15. Realizing that it is probably exactly this that is to be studied, so worrying is irrelevant.

16. Still wondering.

17. A decision to look around the room.

18. A blackboard with pegs of some sort.

19. A sink with a lot of strange-looking faucets.

20. Wondering what they are for.

10.

11. Scored because of reference to ornament on one's body.

12. Scored because there is a repeated reference to the body ornament. It would not be scored simply on the basis of the use of the word "seeing." Reference to various kinds of visual or auditory experiences not scored unless eyes or ears are specifically mentioned. This is analogously true for olfactory experiences. However, any tactile experience is scored (e.g., "This feels rough").

13. Scored because there is still another repetition of the reference to the body ornament.

14.

15.

16.

17.

18.

19.

20.

Body Prominence Protocol 2

Responses

1. My head aches—it's pounding, thumping, and preventing me from thinking clearly.

2. It's not a very pleasant day—it's cold, damp, and penetrating, late winter weather.

3. Love is a wonderful state of mind— it sets your heart soaring and your mind at ease.

Scoring

1. Scored because "head" mentioned and also variety of head sensations.

2. Scored because of temperature ("cold") and tactile ("damp") references.

3. Scored because of "heart." References to love not scored. But mention of sexual feelings are scored (e.g., I would like to kiss a girl).

4. The room is bright and quiet, except for the scratching of pencils.	4.
5. Three other people in the room with whom I am not in contact, except through our similar situation here.	5.
6. That one has to work very hard to find employment that he likes and which suits him adequately.	6.
7. The switch box in the corner—open and almost forbidding because you don't know what the switches are for.	7.
8. That I'm not sure what I'm doing this for—it's puzzling and somewhat frustrating.	8.
9. My reflection in the glass case near me—it makes me wonder if that's really me or if that is the way others see me.	9. Scored because of reference to own "reflection."
10. That I have many things to do! I sometimes wonder if it will all get accomplished but, of course, it will.	10.
11. The sound of the fan—it's a sound you hear only if you start thinking about it, or are aware of only when it stops.	11. Not scored, despite use of word "aware."
12. That life moves along very rapidly— and seems to gain even more momentum as you grow older.	12. Not scored despite use of phrase "grow older." This is not sufficiently explicit in its body implications. If the subject had said, "I feel older," this would be scored.
13. My fingernail which is splitting— which is annoying and aggravating.	13. Scored because of "fingernail."
14. The movie screen in front of me—it's off white, austere, somewhat unaesthetic.	14.
15. That the walk back to campus is long and that I may be too tired to do it with enthusiasm.	15. Scored because of "tired."
16. The pencil is wearing down from use so that it doesn't form images as sharply as it did in the beginning.	16.
17. The gray cabinets on the wall—they cause me to wonder what they contain.	17.
18. That there is a great deal of trouble in the world which could be at least somewhat alleviated.	18.

19. That there is multitudinous knowledge that I do not know, am not even aware of, and will never be able to know, but which I continue attempting to discover.

20. That I've reached the last number and don't believe I've been aware of or conscious of much with much significance.

Body Prominence Protocol 3

Responses	Scoring
1. Sound of fan.	1.
2. Pressure of my hand on my cheek.	2. Scored because of "hand" and "cheek."
3. Sound of other pencils hitting on desk.	3.
4. Presence of other people.	4.
5. Black cloth at my left.	5. Not scored despite "at my left."
6. Whiteness of chair arm and black cloth.	6.
7. Ball of cotton stuck on bottom black cloth.	7.
8. Pressure of pencil on thumb, index, and third fingers.	8. Scored because of "thumb" and "third fingers" and also "pressure."
9. Foot going to sleep.	9. Scored because of "foot" and "going to sleep."
10. Pattern of gray and white tiles.	10.
11. Sound of someone erasing.	11.
12. Sound of squeaky steps in hall.	12.
13. Feel of wool on my legs.	13. Scored because of "feel" and "my legs."
14. Sharpness of pencil.	14.
15. Dull sound coming from somewhere overhead.	15.
16. Surrounding of gray metal cabinets.	16.
17. Predominance of grey-black-white colors.	17.
18. Smell of cigarette smoke.	18. Olfactory experiences not scored.
19. Coldness of chair arm, smooth and cool.	19. Scored because of temperature and tactile reference.
20. Coldness of my feet.	20. Scored because of "coldness" and "feet."

Body Prominence Protocol 4

Responses	Scoring
1. Pants—green, corduroy, worn at places.	1. Scored because of "pants." Some ambiguity exists as to whether subject is referring to own pants. But whenever clothes are mentioned and there is no explicit statement that they are someone else's, the policy has been to assume they are self-referring.
2. Shoes—maroon, dirty, wet, uncomfortable because of blister.	2. Scored because of "shoes," "wet," "uncomfortable," and "blister."
3. Coat—checked, warm, blues and maroons.	3. Scored because of "coat" and "warm."
4. Hands—holding paper, shape, color, texture.	4. Scored because of "hands." Once again there is ambiguity about whether the subject is referring to her own hands. But in the absence of an explicit mention that they are someone else's, it is assumed that she has her own in mind.
5. Pencil—in relation to way held in hand.	5. Scored because of "hand."
6. Paper—lined (blue) and yellow. Contrast yellow against white table.	6.
7. Hair—hanging in face, bothersome.	7. Scored because of "hair" and "face."
8. Nails—short, a mess at this point, dirty.	8. Scored because of "nails."
9. Freckles on hands—brown against white skin.	9. Scored because of "freckles on hands."
10. Table—white, clean, smooth.	10. Scored because of tactile experience implied in word "smooth."
11. Contact lenses—bothering my eyes this morning. Pressure against eyes.	11. Scored because of "eyes" and also reference to a body appliance one uses (i.e., "contact lenses").
12. Pipes.	12.
13. Words—already written down on this page.	13.
14. Mouth—dry, thirsty.	14. Scored because of "mouth," "dry," and "thirsty."
15. Head—thinking of things to write down.	15. Scored because of "head."
16. Wood—light in contrast to black it is against.	16.

17. Shoulders—tired, poor posture.

17. Scored because of "shoulders," "tired," "posture."

18. Blister on right big toe—it hurts.

18. Scored because of "blister," "toe," and "hurts."

19. Chair against body—color-wise and pressure-wise.

19. Scored because of "body" and "pressure-wise."

20. Handwriting—how poor it is, corrections made.

20. Not scored despite reference to own handwriting. This is based on a general decision not to score references to various kinds of self performance (e.g., "I run slow," "I draw poorly").

Body Prominence Protocol 5

Responses

1. Hum in the room.
2. Creaky shoes.

3. Dirty smudge on my hand from a railing.
4. Run in my nylon.

5. Scratch of pencils writing.
6. Hair tickling the back of my neck.

7. Itchy neck.
8. No smell here.
9. A full feeling in my stomach.

10. Dry lips.
11. Dirty fingernails.
12. Hair in my eyes.
13. Fluorescent lighting; I hate it.
14. The pimple on my nose.

15. Wondering what everybody else is writing.
16. Curiosity about what those slides are.
17. My leg itches.
18. The sound of rushing air in the room.
19. She lit a cigarette; now I smell smoke. It's a True cigarette and they smell icky!

Scoring

1.
2. Scored because of "shoes." In absence of statement to the contrary, it is assumed that the subject's own shoes have been mentioned.
3. Scored because of "hand."

4. Scored because of reference to own clothing ("nylon").

5.
6. Scored because of "hair," "tickle," and "neck."
7. Scored because of "itchy neck."
8. Olfactory experiences are not scored.
9. Scored because of "full feeling" in "stomach."
10. Scored because of "lips" and "dry."
11. Scored because of "fingernails."
12. Scored because of "hair" and "eyes."
13.
14. Scored because of "pimple" and "nose."

15.

16.
17. Scored because of "leg" and "itches."
18.
19. Olfactory experiences are not scored.

20. My overall feeling of expecting something—this should be fun, it's been a happy day.

20. Not scored despite reference to "my overall feeling." It is assumed that the term "feeling" is used not primarily with reference to a body experience but rather a cognitive expectation.

D
Body Distortion Questionnaire

This section includes the Body Distortion Questionnaire form and instructions for scoring it.

Questionnaire

Read each of the statements below. If your answer to a statement is Yes, put an X under Yes. If your answer is No, put an X under No. If you are not sure whether to say Yes or No, put an X under Undecided.

	Yes	No	Undecided
1. My body feels unusually heavy.			
2. My body feels small.			
3. I feel like I should wash my hands.			
4. My mouth feels like it is changing in size.			
5. My body feels numb.			
6. I feel as if my skin is sore.			
7. My eyes feel like they are covered by a film.			
8. Things seem unusually close to my body.			
9. I feel as if parts of my body have disappeared.			
10. My nose feels blocked up.			
11. My hands feel small.			
12. Parts of my body feel swollen.			

	Yes	No	Undecided
13. My armpits feel unclean.			
14. My hands feel like they are changing in size.			
15. My rectum feels unusual.			
16. My skin itches less than usual.			
17. I feel like hiding my body.			
18. My hands feel like they are not mine.			
19. My throat feels blocked up.			
20. My head feels small.			
21. My neck feels unusually large.			
22. My skin feels unclean.			
23. My head feels like it is changing in size.			
24. My genital organs feel unusual.			
25. The right side of my body seems different from the left.			
26. My skin itches more than usual.			
27. I feel like my body is unprotected.			
28. My stomach feels blocked up.			
29. My chin feels small.			
30. My hips feel big.			
31. I feel like I have a dirty taste in my mouth.			
32. My body feels like it is changing in size.			
33. The sex of my body seems different.			
34. My skin feels less ticklish than usual.			
35. I feel that germs can somehow more easily get into my body.			

	Yes	No	Undecided
36. My body is less sensitive than it usually is.			
37. My ears feel stopped up.			
38. My nose feels small.			
39. My legs feel long.			
40. My hands don't feel as alive as usual.			
41. My skin is more ticklish than usual.			
42. I feel like my skin is too thin.			
43. My body feels "dead."			
44. My intestines feel blocked up.			
45. My hips feel small.			
46. My arms feel long.			
47. My toes feel dirty.			
48. My skin is warmer than it should be.			
49. My arms feel short.			
50. feel like the inside of my body has no protection from things that happen near me.			
51. My body feels strange.			
52. My lungs feel stopped up.			
53. My eyes feel unusually large.			
54. The odor of my breath does not seem pleasant.			
55. My skin is colder than it should be.			
56. My eyes feel unusually small.			
57. Parts of my body feel as if they might become detached from me.			
58. My body feels like it is not mine.			

	Yes	No	Undecided
59. My kidneys feel blocked up.			
60. My mouth feels unusually small.			
61. My feet feel unusually large.			
62. I feel like I want to cover my body with something that will protect me.			
63. My skin feels looser than usual.			
64. My body feels like a non-living object.			
65. My nose feels big.			
66. My body feels like it is "stuffed" or too full.			
67. My feet feel unusually small.			
68. My ears feel unusually large.			
69. My skin feels tighter than usual.			
70. My body feels big.			
71. I feel less able to tell where my body ends and the outer world begins.			
72. I feel distant from my own body.			
73. My body feels blocked up.			
74. My ears feel unusually small.			
75. My mouth feels unusually large.			
76. My body feels too "open."			
77. I seem less aware of my body.			
78. My hands feel big.			
79. My body feels unusually light.			
80. My chin feels large.			
81. My neck feels unusually small.			
82. My legs feel short.			

SCORING INSTRUCTIONS FOR BODY DISTORTION QUESTIONNAIRE

Procedure:
  (1) Draw a line under numbers when answer is "yes."
  (2) Encircle the numbers when answer is "undecided."

Total Yes
Total Undecided
Total Yes plus
  Undecided Responses
  (Total Distortion Score)

		Yes + Undecided	%
	Items:		
Larger	1, 12, 21, 30, 39, 46, 53, 61, 65, 68, 70, 75, 78, 80		
Smaller	2, 11, 20, 29, 38, 45, 49, 56, 60, 67, 74, 79, 81, 82		
Boundary	8, 9, 17, 27, 35, 50, 57, 62, 71, 76		
Blocked Openings	7, 10, 19, 28, 37, 44, 52, 59, 66, 73		
Skin	6, 16, 26, 34, 41, 42, 48, 55, 63, 69		
Dirt	3, 13, 22, 31, 47, 54		
Deperson- alization	5, 18, 36, 40, 43, 51, 58, 64, 72, 77		

(To compute % for each category, divide total "yes" plus "undecided" for each category by the overall total "yes" plus "undecided" for all categories.)

References

Abraham, K. The influence of oral eroticism on character formation (1927). In *Selected papers of Karl Abraham*. London: Hogarth, 1927.

Ackner, B. Depersonalization. *Journal of Mental Science*, 1954, *100*, 835–872.

Adams, Nancy M., and Caldwell, W. E. The children's Somatic Apperception Test. A technique for quantifying body image. *Journal of General Psychology*, 1963, *68*, 43–57.

Adelson, J., and Redmond, Joan. Personality differences in the capacity for verbal recall. *Journal of Abnormal and Social Psychology*, 1958, *57*, 244–248.

Alexander, F. *Fundamentals of psychoanalysis*. New York: W. Norton, 1948.

Alexander, T. The effect of psychopathology in children's drawings of the human figure. *Journal of Psychology*, 1963, *56*, 273–282.

Allardice, Barbara and Dale, A. A. Body image in Hansen's disease patients. *Journal of Projective Techniques and Personality Assessment*, 1966, *30*, 356-358

Allen, M. K. Personality and cultural factors related to religious authoritarianism. Unpublished doctoral dissertation, Stanford University, 1955.

Allison, J. Cognitive structure and receptivity to low intensity stimulation. *Journal of Abnormal and Social Psychology*, 1963, *67*, 132–138.

Allport, F. H. *Theories of perception and the concept of structure*. New York: John Wiley & Sons, 1955.

Allport, G. W., Vernon, P. E., and Lindzey, G. *Manual. Study of Values.* Boston: Houghton Mifflin Co., 1960.

Alpert, Augusta. Notes on the effect of a birth defect on the pregenital psychosexual development of a boy. *American Journal of Orthopsychiatry*, 1959, *24*, 186–191.

Ames, Louise B. Children's stories. *Genetic Psychology Monographs*, 1966, *73*, 337–396.

Andrews, J. The relationship of body image to verbal learning and perceptual motor performance in young children. Unpublished doctoral dissertation, Syracuse University, 1968.

Apfeldorf, M. The projection of the body self in a task calling for creative activity. Unpublished doctoral dissertation, University of North Carolina, 1953.

Apfeldorf, M., and Smith, J. The representation of the body self in human figure drawings. Presented at annual meeting of Eastern Psychological Association, Atlantic City, N.J., 1965.

Appleby, L. The relationship of a Rorschach barrier typology to other behavioral measures. Unpublished doctoral dissertation, University of Houston, 1956.

Arieti, S. (Ed.) *American handbook of psychiatry*. New York: Basic Books, 1959.

Arkoff, A., and Weaver, H. B. Body image and body dissatisfaction in Japanese-Americans. *Journal of Social Psychology*, 1966, *68*, 323–330.

Armstrong, H. The relationship between a dimension of body-image and two dimensions of conditioning. *Journal of Consulting Psychology*, 1968, *32*, 696-700.

Arnaud, Sara H. Some psychological characteristics of children of multiple sclerotics. *Psychosomatic Medicine*, 1959, *21*, 8–22.

Arnheim, R. The gestalt theory of expression. *Psychological Review*, 1949, *56*, 156–171.

Arnhoff, F., and Damianopoulos, E. Self-body recognition: An empirical approach to the body image. *Merrill-Palmer Quarterly of Behavior and Development*, 1962, *8*, 143–148.

Arnhoff, F., and Damianopoulos, E. Self-body recognition and schizophrenia. *Journal of General Psychology*, 1964, *70*, 353–361.

Arnoult, M. D., and Duke, J. A. Japanese and American judgments of self-height. *Perceptual and Motor Skills*, 1961, *13*, 226.

Aronson, M. L. A study of the Freudian theory of paranoia by means of the Rorschach test. *Journal of Projective Techniques*, 1952, *16*, 397–412.

Arseni, C., Botez, M. I., and Maretsis, M. Paroxysmal disorders of the body image. *Psychiatry and Neurology*, Basel, 1966, *151*, 1–14.

As, A. *Mutilation fantasies and autonomic response*. Oslo, Norway: Oslo University Press, 1958.

Asch, S. Forming impressions of personality. *Journal of Abnormal and Social Psychology*, 1946, *41*, 258–290.

Azima, H., and Cramer-Azima, F. J. Effects of the decrease in sensory variability on body scheme. *Canadian Psychiatric Association Journal*, 1956, *1*, 59–72.

Bachelis, L. A. Body-field perceptual differentiation as a variable in creative thinking. Unpublished doctoral dissertation, Yeshiva University, 1965.

Baldwin, I. T. The head-body ratio in human figure drawings of schizophrenic and normal adults. *Journal of Projective Techniques and Personality Assessment*, 1964, *28*, 393–396.

Barendregt, J. T. *Research in psychodiagnostics*. The Hague: Mouton & Company, 1961.

Barglow, P. Pseudocyesis and psychiatric sequelae of sterilization. *Archives of General Psychiatry*, 1964, *11*, 571–580.

Barnes, C. A. A statistical study of the Freudian theory of levels of psychosexual development. *Genetic Psychology Monographs*, 1952, *45*, 105–175.

Barnes, C. M. Prediction of brain damage using the Holtzman Inkblot Technique and other selected variables. Unpublished doctoral dissertation, State University of Iowa, 1963.

Barron, F. An ego strength scale which predicts response to psychotherapy. *Journal of Consulting Psychology*, 1953, *17*, 327–333.

Barron, J. Physical handicap and personality: A study of the seen versus unseen disabilities. *Archives of Physical Medicine*, 1955, *36*, 639–643.

Barton, M. I. Aspects of object and body perception in hemiplegics: An organismic-developmental approach. Unpublished doctoral dissertation, Clark University, 1964.

Barton, M. I., and Wapner, S. Apparent length of body parts attended to separately and in combination. *Perceptual and Motor Skills*, 1965, *20*, 904.

Barts, G. J. The perception of body boundaries. Unpublished master's thesis, Ohio State University, 1959.

Bass, B. Development and evaluation of a scale for measuring social acquiescence. *Journal of Abnormal and Social Psychology*, 1956, *53*, 296–299.

Bass, B. M. Famous Sayings Test: General manual. *Psychological Reports. Monograph Supplement*, 1958, Supplement 6, 1958, 479–497.

Beigel, H. G. The influence of body position on mental processes. *Journal of Clinical Psychology*, 1952, *8*, 193–199.

Bell, Anita I. Some observations on the role of the scrotal sac and testicles. *Journal of American Psychoanalytic Association*, 1961, *9*, 261–286.

Bell, Anita I. The significance of scrotal sac and testicles for the prepuberty male. *Psychoanalytic Quarterly*, 1965, *34*, 182–206.

Beller, E. K. Dependency and autonomous achievement striving related to orality and anality in early childhood. *Child Development*, 1957, *28*, 287–315.

Beller, E. K., and Turner, J. Personality correlates of children's perceptions of human size. *Child Development*, 1964, *35*, 441–449.

Belleville, R. E. Control of behavior by drug-produced internal stimuli. *Psychopharmacologia*, 1964, *5*, 95–105.

Beloff, Halla. The structure and origin of the anal character. *Genetic Psychology Monographs*, 1957, *55*, 141–172.

Beloff, J., and Beloff, Halla. The influence of valence on distance judgments of human faces. *Journal of Abnormal and Social Psychology*, 1961, *62*, 720–722.

Bender, M. B., and Nathanson, M. Patterns in allesthesia and their relation to disorder of body scheme and other sensory phenomena. *Archives of Neurology and Psychiatry*, 1950, *64*, 501–515.

Bender, M. B., Shapiro, M. F., and Teuber, H. Allesthesia and disturbance of the body scheme. *Archives of Neurology and Psychiatry*, 1949, *62*, 222–235.

Benedek, Theresa. The organization of the reproductive drive. *International Journal of Psychoanalysis*, 1960, *41*, 1–15.

Benjamin, H. Transvestism and transsexualism. *American Journal of Psychotherapy*, 1954, *8*, 219–225.

Bennett, D. H. The body concept. *Journal of Mental Science*, 1960, *106*, 56–75.

Bennett, Virginia. Notes and comments. Does size of figure drawing reflect self-concept? *Journal of Consulting Psychology*, 1964, *28*, 285–286.

Benton, A. L. *Right-left discrimination and finger localization*. New York: Hoeber (Harper), 1959.

Berger, L. A comparison of the physiological functioning of normals and psychiatric patients. *Psychological Reports*, 1964, *15*, 183–187.

Bergler, E. *Fashions and the unconscious*. New York: Brunner, 1953.

Berman, S., and Laffal, J. Body type and figure drawing. *Journal of Clinical Psychology*, 1953, *9*, 368–370.

Bernstein, A. Some relations between techniques of feeding and training during infancy and certain behavior in childhood. *Genetic Psychology Monographs*, 1955, *51*, 3–44.

Bierman, J. S., Silverstein, A. B., and Finesinger, J. E. A depression in a six-year-old boy with acute poliomyelitis. In *Psychoanalytic Study of the Child*, Vol. 13. New York: International Universities Press, 1958, 430–450.

Birch, H. G., Proctor, F., and Bortner, M. Perception in hemiplegia. III. The judgment of relative distance in the visual field. *Archives of Physical Medicine and Rehabilitation*, 1961A, *42*, 639–643.

Birch, H. G., Proctor, F., and Bortner, M. Perception in hemiplegia. IV. Body surface localization in hemiplegic patients. *Journal of Nervous and Mental Disease*, 1961B, *133*, 192–202.

Birch, H. G., Proctor, F., Bortner, M., and Lowenthal, M. Perception in hemiplegia. I. Judgment of vertical and horizontal by hemiplegic patients. *Archives of Physical Medicine*, 1960A, *41*, 19–27.

Birch, H. G., Proctor, F., Bortner, M., and Lowenthal, M. Perception in hemiplegia. II. Judgment of the median plane. *Archives of Physical Medicine*, 1960B, *41*, 71–75.

Bird, B. Depersonalization. *Archives of Neurology and Psychiatry*, 1958, *80*, 467–476.

Birk, L., Crider, A., Shapiro, D., and Tursky, B. Operant electrodermal conditioning under partial curarization. *Journal of Comparative and Physiological Psychology*, 1966, *62*, 165–166.

Bishop, F. V. The anal character: A rebel in the dissonance family. *Journal of Personality and Social Psychology*, 1967, *6*, 23–36.

Black, A. H., and Carlson, N. J. The conditioning of autonomic responses under curare-like drugs. *American Psychologist*, 1957, *12*, 429.

Black, A. H., and Lang, W. M. Cardiac conditioning and skeletal responding in curarized dogs. *Psychological Review*, 1964, *71*, 80–85.

Blake, R. R., and Ramsey, G. V. (Eds.) *Perception: an approach to personality*. New York: Ronald Press, 1951.

Blank, H. R. Depression, hypomania, and depersonalization. *Psychoanalytic Quarterly*, 1956, *23*, 20–37.

Blatt, S. J., Allison, J., and Baker, B. L. The Wechsler Object Assembly Subtest and bodily concerns. *Journal of Consulting Psychology*, 1965, *29*, 223–230.

Blau, A. The master hand. *American Journal of Orthopsychiatry, Association Monographs*, 1946, *5*.

Bleuler, E. *Dementia Praecox*, or, *The group of schizophrenias*. New York: International Universities Press, 1950.

Blum, G. S. A study of the psychoanalytic theory of psychosexual development. *Genetic Psychology Monographs*, 1949, *39*, 3–99.

Blum, G. S., and Miller, D. R. Exploring the psychoanalytic theory of the "oral character." *Journal of Personality*, 1952, *20*, 287–304.

Blumberg, S., and Gonik, U. Psychophysiological reactions to some properties of specific auditory stimuli. *Texas Reports on Biology and Medicine*, 1962, *20*, 555–561.

Blumstein, A. Masochism and fantasies of preparing to be incorporated. *Journal of The American Psychoanalytic Association*, 1959, 7, 292–298.

Bonnard, Augusta. Pre-body-ego types of (pathological) mental functioning. *Journal of The American Psychoanalytic Association*, 1958, *6*, 581–611.

Boraks, F. C. Sex differences in body cognition. Unpublished doctoral dissertation, University of Kansas, 1962.

Boulanger-Balleyguier, G. First reactions before the mirror. *Enfance*, 1964, *1*, 51–67.

Bower, S. M. Self instructed heart rate change: A methodological evaluation. Unpublished doctoral dissertation, Vanderbilt University, 1963.

Boyar, J. I. The construction and partial validation of a scale for the measurement of the fear of death. Unpublished doctoral dissertation, University of Rochester, 1964.

Boyd, H. S., and Sisney, V. V. Immediate self-image confrontation and changes in self concept. *Journal of Consulting Psychology*, 1967, *31*, 291–294.

Braatoy, T. *Fundamentals of psychoanalytic technique*. New York: John Wiley & Sons, 1954.

Brehm, Mary L., Back, K. W., and Bogdonoff, M. D. A physiological effect of cognitive dissonance under stress and deprivation. *Journal of Abnormal and Social Psychology*, 1964, *69*, 303–310.

Breuer, J., and Freud, S. *Studies in hysteria*. New York: Nervous and Mental Diseases Publications Company, 1936.

Brodie, C. V. The prediction of qualitative characteristics of behavior in stress situations, using test-assessed personality constructs. Unpublished doctoral dissertation, University of Illinois, 1959.

Brodsky, B. The self-representation, anality, and the fear of dying. *Journal of The American Psychoanalytic Association*, 1959, 7, 1–4.

Brown, A. R. Differentiated handedness as related to perceptual style, stimulus seeking and associative learning. Unpublished doctoral dissertation, University of Texas, 1967.

Brown, D. G. Psychosomatic correlates in contact dermatitis: A pilot study. *Journal of Psychosomatic Research*, 1959, *4*, 132–139.

Brown, D. G., and Young, A. J. Body image and susceptibility to contact dermatitis. *British Journal of Medical Psychology*, 1965, *38*, 261–267.

Brown, Janet L. Prognosis from presenting symptoms of preschool children with atypical development. *American Journal of Orthopsychiatry*, 1960, *30*, 382–390.

Brown, N. O. *Life against death.* New York: Vintage Books, 1959.

Bruch, Hilde. Falsification of bodily needs and body concept in schizophrenia. *Archives of General Psychiatry*, 1962, *6*, 18–24.

Burton, A., and Adkins, J. Perceived size of self-image body parts in schizophrenia. *Archives of General Psychiatry*, 1961, *5*, 131–140.

Burton, A. C., and Edholm, O. G. *Man in a cold environment.* London: Edward Arnold & Company, 1955.

Buss, A. H. *The psychology of aggression.* New York: Wiley, 1961.

Buss, A. H., and Durkee, Ann. An inventory for assessing different kinds of hostility. *Journal of Consulting Psychology*, 1957, *21*, 343–349.

Buss, A. H., and Lang, P. J. Psychological deficit in schizophrenia: I. Affect, reinforcement, and concept attainment. *Journal of Abnormal Psychology*, 1965, *70*, 2–24.

Buxbaum, Edith. Hair pulling and fetishism. In *Psychoanalytic Study of the Child*, New York: International Universities Press, 1960, Vol. 15, 243–260.

Bychowski, G. Disorders in the body-image in the clinical pictures of psychoses. *Journal of Nervous and Mental Disease*, 1943, *97*, 310–334.

Bykov, Konstantin M. *The cerebral cortex and the internal organs.* New York: Chemical Publishing Company, 1957.

Byrne, D., Golightly, C., and Capaldi, E. J. Construction and validation of the Food Attitude Scale. *Journal of Consulting Psychology*, 1963, *27*, 215–222.

Calden, G., Lundy, R. M., and Schlafer, R. J. Sex differences in body concepts. *Journal of Consulting Psychology*, 1959, *23*, 378.

Caldwell, Willard E., and Matoon, C. U. The Somato-Chroma Apperception Test: A quantitative projective technique. *Journal of General Psychology*, 1966, *74*, 253–272.

Calloway, E., and Dembo, D. Narrowed attention. A psychological phenomenon that accompanies a certain physiological change. *Archives of Neurology and Psychiatry*, 1958, *79*, 74–90.

Cameron, N. *The psychology of behavior disorders.* New York: Houghton Mifflin, 1947.

Campos, J. J., and Johnson, H. J. The effects of verbalization instructions and visual attention on heart rate and skin conductance. *Psychophysiology*, 1966, *2*, 305–310.

Campos, L. P. The relationship between "anal" personality traits and temporal experience. Presented at annual meeting of California State Psychological Association, San Francisco, 1963.

Campos, L. P. Relationship between time estimation and retentive personality traits. *Perceptual and Motor Skills*, 1966, *23*, 59–62.

Cannon, W. B. The James-Lange theory of emotion: A critical examination and an alternative theory. *American Journal of Psychology*, 1927, *39*, 106–124.

Cannon, W. B. Again the James-Lange and the thalamic theories of emotion. *Psychological Review*, 1931, *38*, 281–295.

Cannon, W. B. *Bodily changes in pain, hunger, fear and rage.* New York: D. Appleton-Century, 1939.

Cantril, H., and Allport, C. Recent applications of the Study of Values. *Journal of Abnormal and Social Psychology*, 1933, *28*, 259–273.

Cappon, D. Morphology and other parameters of phantasy in the schizophrenias. *Archives of General Psychiatry*, 1959, *1*, 17–34.

Cappon, D., and Banks, R. Orientational perception. *Archives of General Psychiatry*, 1965, *13*, 375–379.

Cardone, S. S. The effect of chlorpromazine on the body image of chronic schizophrenics. Unpublished doctoral dissertation, Illinois Institute of Technology, 1967.

Carp, F. M. Psychosexual development of stutterers. *Journal of Projective Techniques*, 1962, *26*, 388–391.

Carpenter, Susanne. Psychosexual conflict, defense, and abstraction. Unpublished doctoral dissertation, University of Michigan, 1965.

Cassell, W. A. A projective index of body-interior awareness. *Psychosomatic Medicine*, 1964, *26*, 172–177.

Cassell, W. A. A tachistoscopic index of body perception. *Journal of Projective Techniques*, 1966, *30*, 31–36.

Cassell, W. A., and Duboczy, J. B. Cardiac symptoms and tachistoscopic recognition of the heart image. *Canadian Psychiatric Association Journal*, 1967, *12*, 73–76.

Cassell, W. A., and Fisher, S. Body-image boundaries and histamine flare reaction. *Psychosomatic Medicine*, 1963, *25*, 344–350.

Castaldo, V., and Holzman, P. S. The effects of hearing one's own voice on sleep mentation. *Journal of Nervous and Mental Disease*, 1967, *144*, 2–13.

Cath, S. H., Glud, E., and Blane, H. T. The role of the body-image in psychotherapy with the physically handicapped. *Psychoanalytic Review*, 1957, *44*, 34–40.

Centers, Louise, and Centers, R. A comparison of the body images of amputee and non-amputee children as revealed in figure drawing. *Journal of Projective Techniques and Personality Assessment*, 1963A, *27*, 158–165.

Centers, Louise, and Centers, R. Body cathexis of parents of normal and malformed children for progeny and self. *Journal of Consulting Psychology*, 1963B, *27*, 319–323.

Chorost, S. B. Parental child-rearing attitudes and their correlates in adolescent hostility. *Genetic Psychology Monographs*, 1962, *66*, 49–90.

Christrup, Helen J. An exploratory study of the effect of dance therapy on the concept of body image, as measured by projective drawings, in a group of chronic schizophrenics. Unpublished master's thesis, George Washington University, 1958.

Claparide, E. Note sur la localization du moi. *Archives de Psychologie*, 1924, *19*, 172.

Clark, C. M., Veldman, D. J., and Thorpe, J. S. Convergent and divergent thinking of talented adolescents. *Journal of Educational Psychology*, 1965, *56*, 157–163.

Cleveland, S. E. Body image changes associated with personality reorganization. *Journal of Consulting Psychology*, 1960A, *24*, 256–261.

Cleveland, S. E. Judgments of body size in a schizophrenic and a control group. *Psychological Reports*, 1960B, *7*, 304.

Cleveland, S. E., and Fisher, S. Body image and small group behavior. *Human Relations*, 1957, *10*, 223–233.

Cleveland, S. E., and Fisher, S. A comparison of psychological characteristics and physiological reactivity in ulcer and rheumatoid arthritis groups. I. Psychological measures. *Psychosomatic Medicine*, 1960, *22*, 283–289.

Cleveland, S. E., Fisher, S., Reitman, E. E., and Rothaus, P. Perception of body size in schizophrenia. *Archives of General Psychiatry*, 1962, *7*, 277–285.

Cleveland, S. E., and Morton, R. B. Group behavior and body image: A follow-up study. *Human Relations*, 1962, *15*, 77–85.

Cleveland, S. E., Reitman, E. E., and Brewer, E. J., Jr. Psychological factors in juvenile rheumatoid arthritis. *Arthritis and Rheumatism*, 1965, *8*, 1152–1158.

Cleveland, S. E., and Sikes, M. P. Body image in chronic alcoholics and non-alcoholic psychiatric patients. *Journal of Projective Techniques and Personality Assessment*, 1966, *30*, 265–269.

Cleveland, S. E., Snyder, Rebecca, and Williams, R. L. Body image and site of psychosomatic symptoms. *Psychological Reports*, 1965, *16*, 851–852.

Coats, J. W. The use of symbols as related to areas of the human body. Unpublished master's thesis, University of Utah, 1957.

Cohen, C. P. Reactions to perceived somatic vulnerability. Unpublished doctoral dissertation, University of Kansas, 1963.

Cohn, R. *The person symbol in clinical medicine.* Springfield, Ill.: Charles C. Thomas, 1960.

Comalli, P. E., Jr. Effect of unilateral above-the-knee amputation on perception of verticality. *Perceptual and Motor Skills*, 1966, *23*, 91–96.

Compton, N. Body image boundaries in relation to clothing fabric and design preferences of a group of hospitalized psychotic women. *Journal of Home Economics*, 1964, *56*, 40–45.

Conquest, R. A. An investigation of body image variables in patients with the diagnosis of schizophrenic reaction. Unpublished doctoral dissertation, Western Reserve University, 1963.

Corah, N. L., and Corah, Patricia L. A study of body image in children with cleft palate and cleft lip. *Journal of Genetic Psychology*, 1963, *103*, 133–137.

Cormack, P. H. A study of the relationship between body image and perception of physical disability. Unpublished doctoral dissertation, State University of New York at Buffalo, 1966.

Cornelison, F. S., Jr., and Arsenian, Jean. A study of the response of psychotic patients to photographic self-image experience. *Psychiatric Quarterly*, 1960, *34*, 1–8.

Cornelison, F. S., Jr., and Bahnson, C. Conference on Self Image. Department of Psychiatry, Jefferson Medical College, Philadelphia, Pa., December 1966.

Couch, A., and Keniston, K. Yeasayers and naysayers: Agreeing response set as a personality variable. *Journal of Abnormal and Social Psychology*, 1960, *60*, 151–174.

Cowden, R. C., and Brown, J. E. The use of a physical symptom as a defense against psychosis. *Journal of Abnormal and Social Psychology*, 1956, *53*, 133–135.

Craddick, R. A. The self-image in the Draw-A-Person test and self-portrait drawings. *Journal of Projective Techniques and Personality Assessment*, 1963, *27*, 288–291.

Craddick, R. A., and Stearn, M. R. Effect of pre- and post-stress upon height of drawings in a perceptual motor task. *Journal of Perceptual and Motor Skills*, 1963, *17*, 283–285.

Critchley, M. *The parietal lobes.* London: Edward Arnold and Co., 1953.

Crowne, D. P., and Marlowe, D. *The approval motive.* New York: Wiley, 1964.

Cruickshank, W. M. The relation of physical disability to fear and guilt feelings. *Child Development*, 1951, *22*, 291–298.

Culp, W. C., and Edelberg, R. Regional response specificity in the electrodermal reflex. *Perceptual and Motor Skills*, 1966, *23*, 623–627.

Curtis, H. S. Automatic movements of the larynx. *American Journal of Psychology*, 1900, *11*, 237–239.

Damaser, Esther C., Shor, R. E., and Orne, M. T. Physiological effects during hypnotically requested emotions. *Psychosomatic Medicine*, 1963, *25*, 334–343.

Dana, C. S. The autonomic seat of the emotions: A discussion of the James-Lange theory. *Archives of Neurology and Psychiatry*, 1921, *6*, 634–639.

Dannenmaier, W. D., and Thumin, F. J. Authority status as a factor in perceptual distortion of size. *Journal of Social Psychology*, 1964, *63*, 361–365.

Davidon, R. S. Body space: Tactile-kinesthetic schema, Technical Note No. 1, 1960. Report for Contract AF 46(638)–726 with Air Force Office of Scientific Research, Washington, D.C.

Davis, A. D. Some physiological correlates of Rorschach body-image productions. *Journal of Abnormal and Social Psychology*, 1960, *60*, 432–436.

Davis, R. C., Buchwald, A. M., and Frankmann, R. W. Autonomic and muscular responses, and their relation to simple stimuli. *Psychological Monographs*, 1955, *69*, No. 20.

Davis, R. C., and Williams, J. G. A study of somatic responses under psychotherapeutic drugs. Technical Report No. 2, 1960. Contract No. 908–15 with Indiana University.

Davison, G. C. Anxiety under total curarization: Implications for the role of muscular relaxation in the desensitization of neurotic fears. *Journal of Nervous and Mental Disease*, 1966, *143*, 443–448.

Deno, Evelyn. Self-identification among adolescent boys. *Child Development*, 1953, *24*, 269–273.

Des Lauriers, A. M. *The experience of reality in childhood schizophrenia.* New York: International Universities Press, 1962.

DeSoto, C. B., London, M., and Handel, S. Social reasoning and spatial paralogic. *Journal of Personality and Social Psychology*, 1965, *2*, 513–521.

Deutsch, F. Analytic posturology. *Psychoanalytic Quarterly*, 1952, *21*, 196–214.

Deutsch, F. Basic psychoanalytic principles in psychosomatic disorders. *Acta Psychotherapeutica*, 1953, *1*, 102.

Deutsch, F., and Murphy, W. F. *The clinical interview*, Vol. 2. New York: International Universities Press, 1955.

Devereux, G. The significance of the external female genitalia and of female orgasm for the male. *Journal of The American Psychoanalytic Association*, 1958, *6*, 278–286.

Dillon, D. J. Measurement of perceived body size. *Perceptual and Motor Skills*, 1962A, *14*, 191–196.

Dillon, D. J. Estimation of bodily dimensions. *Perceptual and Motor Skills*, 1962B, *14*, 219–221.

Dixon, J. C. Development of self recognition. *Journal of Genetic Psychology*, 1957, *91*, 251–256.

Dixon, J. C. Depersonalization phenomena in a sample population of college students. *British Journal of Psychology*, 1963, *109*, 371–375.

Doidge, W. T., and Holtzman, W. H. Implications of homosexuality among Air Force trainees. *Journal of Consulting Psychology*, 1960, *24*, 9–13.

Donelson, Frances E. Discrimination and control of human heart rate. Unpublished doctoral dissertation, Cornell University, 1966.

Dorsey, D. S. A study of the relationship between independence of group pressure and selected measures of body image. Unpublished doctoral dissertation, University of California, Los Angeles, 1965.

Douty, Helen I. The influence of clothing on perceptions of persons in single contact situations. Unpublished doctoral dissertation, Florida State University, 1962.

Dow, T. E., Jr. Social class and reaction to physical disability. *Psychological Reports*, 1965, *17*, 39–62.

Drellich, M. G., and Bieber, I. The psychologic importance of the uterus and its functions. *Journal of Nervous and Mental Disease*, 1958, *126*, 322–336.

Eagle, M. The effects of subliminal stimuli of aggressive content upon conscious cognition. *Journal of Personality*, 1959, *27*, 578–600.

Easson, W. M. Body image and self-image in children. *Archives of General Psychiatry*, 1961, *4*, 619–621.

Edgerton, R. B., and Dingman, H. F. Tattooing and identity. *International Journal of Social Psychiatry*, 1963, *9*, 143–153.

Edwards, A. L. *Edwards Personal Preference Schedule* (Manual). New York: Psychological Corporation, 1954 (Revised, 1959).

Eigenbrode, C. R., and Shipman, W. G. The body image barrier concept. *Journal of Abnormal and Social Psychology*, 1960, *60*, 450–452.

Elkisch, Paula. The psychological significance of the mirror. *Journal of the American Psychoanalytic Association*, 1957, *5*, 235–244.

Elkisch, Paula, and Mahler, M. On infantile precursors of the "influencing machine." *Psychoanalytic Study of the Child*, Vol. 14, New York: International Universities Press, 1959, 219–235.

Endicott, N. A., and Endicott, Jean. Objective measures of somatic preoccupation. *Journal of Nervous and Mental Disease*, 1963, *137*, 427–437.

Engel, B. T., and Hansen, S. P. Operant conditioning of heart rate slowing. *Psychophysiology*, 1966, *3*, 176–187.

Epstein, L. The relationship of certain aspects of the body-image to the perception of the upright. Unpublished doctoral dissertation, New York University, 1957.

Epstein, S. Unconscious self-evaluation in a normal and a schizophrenic group. *Journal of Abnormal and Social Psychology*, 1955, *50*, 65–70.

Epstein, S. J. A critique of the body-boundary hypothesis as related to apparent body-part size perception. Unpublished doctoral dissertation, University of Kansas, 1965.

Epstein, S., and Shontz, F. C. Attitudes toward persons with physical disabilities as a function of attitudes toward one's own body. Presented at annual meeting of American Psychological Association, St. Louis, 1962.

Epstein, S., and Smith, R. Thematic apperception, Rorschach content, and ratings of sexual attractiveness of women as measures of the sex drive. *Journal of Consulting Psychology*, 1957, *21*, 473–478.

Erikson, E. H. *Childhood and society*. New York: Norton, 1950.

Erikson, E. H. Sex differences in the play configurations of pre-adolescents. *American Journal of Orthopsychiatry*, 1951, *21*, 667–692.

Falstein, E. I., Judas, Ilse, and Mendelsohn, R. S. Fantasies in children prior to herniorrhaphy. *American Journal of Orthopsychiatry*, 1957, *27*, 800–807.

Farber, M. L. The anal character and political aggression. *Journal of Abnormal and Social Psychology*, 1955, *51*, 486–489.

Feder, J. An investigation into the relationship between vividness of recall of early childhood experiences, proximal sensory modalities, and proprioceptive awareness. Unpublished doctoral dissertation, New York University, 1967.

Federn, P. *Ego psychology and the psychoses*. New York: Basic Books, Inc., 1952.

Felix, R., and Arieli, S. The pattern of the human hand. *Israel Annals of Psychiatry and Related Disciplines*, 1966, *4*, 30–42.

Fenichel, O. *The psychoanalytic theory of neurosis*. New York: Norton, 1945.

Ferenczi, S. Stimulation of the anal erotogenic zone as a precipitating factor in paranoia (1911). *Selected papers of Ferenczi*. New York: Basic Books, 1955.

Fillenbaum, S. How fat is fat? Some consequences of similarity between judge and judged object. *Journal of Psychology*, 1961, *52*, 133–136.

Fineman, D. Preliminary observations on ego development in children with congenital defects of the genito-urinary system. *American Journal of Orthopsychiatry*, 1959, *29*, 110–120.

Fink, L., and Shontz, C. Body-image disturbances in chronically ill individuals. *Journal of Nervous and Mental Disease*, 1960, *131*, 234–240.

Finney, J. C. The MMPI as a measure of character structure as revealed by a factor analysis. *Journal of Consulting Psychology*, 1961, *25*, 327–336.

Fish, J. E. An exploration of developmental aspects of body scheme and of ideas about adulthood in grade school children. Unpublished doctoral dissertation, University of Kansas, 1960.

Fisher, Rhoda. The effect of a disturbing situation upon the stability of various projective tests. *Psychological Monographs*, 1958, *72*, No. 14.

Fisher, Rhoda. Body boundary and achievement behavior. *Journal of Projective Techniques and Personality Assessment*, 1966A, *30*, 435–438.

Fisher, Rhoda. Failure of the Conceptual Styles Test to discriminate normal and highly impulsive children. *Journal of Abnormal Psychology*, 1966B, *71*, 429–431.

Fisher, Rhoda. Mother's hostility and changes in child's classroom behavior. *Perceptual and Motor Skills*, 1966C, *23*, 153–154.

Fisher, S. Patterns of personality rigidity and some of their determinants. *Psychological Monographs*, 1950, *64*, No. 1.

Fisher, S. Body image and asymmetry of body reactivity. *Journal of Abnormal and Social Psychology*, 1958, *57*, 292–298.

Fisher, S. Body image boundaries in the aged. *Journal of Psychology*, 1959A, *48*, 315–318.

Fisher, S. Extensions of theory concerning body image and body reactivity. *Psychosomatic Medicine*, 1959B, *21*, 142–149.

Fisher, S. Prediction of body interior versus body exterior reactivity. *Journal of Personality*, 1959C, *27*, 56–62.

Fisher, S. Head-body differentiations in body image and skin resistance level. *Journal of Abnormal and Social Psychology*, 1960A, *60*, 283–285.

Fisher, S. Right-left gradients in body image, body reactivity, and perception. *Genetic Psychology Monographs*, 1960B, *61*, 197–228.

Fisher, S. Achievement fantasy and directionality of autokinetic movement. *Journal of Abnormal and Social Psychology*, 1961A, *63*, 64–68.

Fisher, S. Body image and upper in relation to lower body sector reactivity. *Psychosomatic Medicine*, 1961B, *23*, 400–402.

Fisher, S. Front-back differentiations in body image and body reactivity. *Journal of General Psychology*, 1961C, *64*, 373–379.

Fisher, S. Body image boundaries and hallucinations. In J. West (Ed.), *Hallucinations*. New York: Grune & Stratton, 1962A, Pp. 249–260.

Fisher, S. Developmental sex differences in right-left perceptual directionality. *Child Development*, 1962B, *33*, 463–468.

Fisher, S. Body image and hypnotic response. *International Journal of Clinical and Experimental Hypnosis*, 1963A, *11*, 152–157.

Fisher, S. A further appraisal of the body boundary concept. *Journal of Consulting Psychology*, 1963B, *27*, 62–74.

Fisher, S. Body awareness and selective memory for body versus non-body references. *Journal of Personality*, 1964A, *32*, 138–144.

Fisher, S. The body boundary and judged behavioral patterns in an interview situation. *Journal of Projective Techniques and Personality Assessment*, 1964B, *28*, 181–184.

Fisher, S. Body image and psychopathology. *Archives of General Psychiatry*, 1964C, *10*, 519–529.

Fisher, S. Power orientation and concept of self height in men: Preliminary note. *Perceptual and Motor Skills*, 1964D, *18*, 732.

Fisher, S. Sex differences in body perception. *Psychological Monographs*, 1964E, *78*, 1–22.

Fisher, S. Body-boundary sensations and acquiescence. *Journal of Personality and Social Psychology*, 1965A, *1*, 381–383.

Fisher, S. The body image as a source of selective cognitive sets. *Journal of Personality*, 1965B, *33*, 536–552.

Fisher, S. Body sensation and perception of projective stimuli. *Journal of Consulting Psychology*, 1965C, *29*, 135–138.

Fisher, S. Sex designations of right and left body sides and assumptions about male-female superiority. *Journal of Personality and Social Psychology*, 1965D, *2*, 576–580.

Fisher, S. Body attention patterns and personality defenses. *Psychological Monographs*, 1966A, *80*, No. 1.

Fisher, S. Body image in neurotic and schizophrenic patients. *Archives of General Psychiatry*, 1966B, *15*, 90–101.

Fisher, S. Motivation for patient delay. *Archives of General Psychiatry*, 1967A, *16*, 676–678.

Fisher, S. Organ awareness and organ activation. *Psychosomatic Medicine*, 1967B, *29*, 643–647.

Fisher, S. Selective memory effects produced by stimulation of body landmarks. *Journal of Personality*, 1968, *36*, 92–107.

Fisher, S. The body boundary and perceptual vividness. *Journal of Abnormal Psychology*, 1968, *73*, 392–396

Fisher, S., and Abercrombie, J. The relationship of body image distortions to body reactivity gradients. *Journal of Personality*, 1958, *26*, 320–330.

Fisher, S., and Cleveland, S. E. The role of body image in psychosomatic symptom choice. *Psychological Monographs*, 1955, *68*, No. 17.

Fisher, S., and Cleveland, S. E. Body image and style of life. *Journal of Abnormal and Social Psychology*, 1956, *52*, 373–379.

Fisher, S., and Cleveland, S. E. Relationship of body image boundaries to memory for completed and incompleted tasks. *Journal of Psychology*, 1956, *42*, 35–41.

Fisher, S., and Cleveland, S. E. *Body image and personality*. Princeton, New Jersey: D. Van Nostrand Co., 1958.

Fisher, S., and Cleveland, S. E. Body image boundaries and sexual behavior. *Journal of Psychology*, 1958, *45*, 207–211.

Fisher, S., and Cleveland, S. E. A comparison of psychological characteristics and physiological reactivity in ulcer and rheumatoid arthritis groups. II. Difference in physiological reactivity. *Psychosomatic Medicine*, 1960, *22*, 290–293.

Fisher, S., and Cleveland, S. E. Personality, body perception, and body boundary. In S. Wapner and S. H. Werner (Eds.), *The body percept*. New York: Random House, 1965, Pp. 48–67.

Fisher, S., and Cleveland, S. E. *Body image and personality*. (New revised edition.) New York: Dover Press, 1968.

Fisher, S., and Fisher, Rhoda. A developmental analysis of body image and body reactivity. *Child Development*, 1959, *30*, 389–402.

Fisher, S., and Fisher, Rhoda. Body image boundaries and patterns of body perception. *Journal of Abnormal and Social Psychology*, 1964, *68*, 255–262.

Fisher, S., and Fisher, Rhoda. The complexity of spouse similarity and difference. In G. H. Zuk and I. Boszormenyi-Nagy (Eds.) *Family therapy and disturbed families*. Palo Alto, California: Science and Behavior Books, 1967, Pp. 118–132.

Fisher, S., and Mirin, S. Further validation of the special favorable response occurring during unconscious self-evaluation. *Perceptual and Motor Skills*, 1966, *23*, 1097–1098.

Fisher, S., and Osofsky, H. Sexual responsiveness in women: Psychological correlates. *Archives of General Psychiatry*, 1967, *17*, 214–226.

Fisher, S., and Renik, O. Induction of body image boundary changes. *Journal of Projective Techniques and Personality Assessment*, 1966, *30*, 429–434.

Fisher, S., and Seidner, R. Body experiences of schizophrenic, neurotic, and normal women. *Journal of Nervous and Mental Disease*, 1963, *137*, 252–257.

Fisher, S. H. Mechanisms of denial in physical disabilities. *Archives of Neurology and Psychiatry*, 1958, *80*, 782–784.

Fitzgerald, W. E. A psychological factor in Legg-Calve-Perthes disease. Unpublished doctoral dissertation, Harvard University, 1961.

Flaccus, L. W. Remarks on the psychology of clothes. *Pedagogical Seminary*, 1906, *13*, 61–83.

Flescher, J. On neurotic disorders of sensibility and body scheme. *International Journal of Psychoanalysis*, 1948–49, *29–30*, 156–162.

Fliess, R. *Ego and body ego*. New York: Schulte Publishing Co., 1961.

Flugel, J. C. *The psychology of clothes*. London: Hogarth Press, 1930.

Forrest, D. W., and Lee, S. G. Mechanisms of defense and readiness in perception and recall. *Psychological Monographs*, 1962, *76*, No. 4.

Fox, H. M. Body image of a photographer. *Journal of The American Psychoanalytic Association*, 1957, *5*, 93–107.

Francis, R. W. A study of the relationships among acceptance of psychological disability, self concept and body image. Unpublished doctoral dissertation, State University of New York at Buffalo, 1968.

Franck, Kate, and Rosen, E. A projective test of masculinity-femininity. *Journal of Consulting Psychology*, 1949, *13*, 247–256.

Frazier, T. W. Avoidance conditioning of heart rate in humans. *Psychophysiology*, 1966, *3*, 188–202.

Frede, Martha C., Gautney, D. B. and Baxter J. C. Relationships between body image boundary and interaction patterns on the MAPS test. *Journal of Consulting Psychology*, 1968, 32, 575–598.

Freeman, G. L. *The energetics of human behavior*. Ithaca: Cornell University Press, 1948A.

Freeman, G. L. *Physiological psychology*. New York: Van Nostrand, 1948B.

Frenkel, R. E. Psychotherapeutic reconstruction of the traumatic amnesic period by the mirror image projective technique. *Journal of Existentialism*, 1964, *5*, 77–96.

Freud, Anna. The role of bodily illness in the mental life of children. *Psychoanalytic Study of the Child*, Vol. 7. New York: International Universities Press, 1952, 69–81.

Freud, S. The origin and development of psychoanalysis. In J. van Teslaar (Ed.), *An outline of psychoanalysis*. New York: Modern Library, 1924.

Freud, S. Character and anal eroticism (1908). *Collected papers*, Vol. 2. London: Hogarth Press, 1924.

Freud, S. On narcissism: An introduction. *Collected papers*, 1914, Vol. 4. London: Hogarth Press, 1925.

Freud, S. *The ego and the id*. London: Hogarth Press, 1927.

Freud, S. *Collected papers*, 4 vols. London: Hogarth Press, 1938.

Freud, S. Three contributions to the theory of sex (1910). In A. A. Brill (Ed.) *The basic writings of Sigmund Freud*. New York: Modern Library, Pp. 553–629.

Freud, S. Psychoanalytic notes upon an autobiographical account of a case of paranoia (1911). *Collected papers*, Vol. 3. London: Hogarth Press, 1950.

Freud, S. *The interpretation of dreams* (1900). Standard edition. Vol. IV. London: Hogarth Press, 1953.

Freud, S. The infantile genital organization of the libido (1923). In *Collected papers*, Vol. 2. London: Hogarth Press, 1956, Pp. 244–249.

Freud, S. Some psychological consequences of the anatomical distinction between the sexes. In *Collected papers*, New York: Basic Books, 1959.

Freytag, Fredericka. *Hypnosis and the body image*. New York: Julian Press Publishers, 1961.

Friedemann, M. W. Reflection on two cases of male transvestism. *American Journal of Psychotherapy*, 1966, *20*, 270–283.

Fromm, E. *Escape from freedom*. New York: Rinehart, 1941.

Fuhrer, M. J., and Cowan, C. O. Influence of active movements, illumination, and sex on estimates of body-part size. *Perceptual and Motor Skills*, 1967, *24*, 979–985.

Funkenstein, D. H., King, S. H., and Drolette, M. A. The direction of anger during a laboratory stress-inducing situation. *Psychosomatic Medicine*, 1954, *16*, 404–413.

Gaughran, E. P. Physiognomic perception: A study of a cognitive style in relation to qualities of body experience. Unpublished doctoral dissertation, New York University Press, 1963.

Gellert, Elizabeth. Children's beliefs about bodily illness. Presented at annual meeting of American Psychological Association, New York City, 1961.

Gellert, Elizabeth. Children's conceptions of the content and functions of the human body. *Genetic Psychology Monographs*, 1962, *65*, 293–405.

Gellert, Elizabeth. Comparison of children's self drawings with their drawings of other persons. *Perceptual and Motor Skills*, 1968, *26*, 123–138.

Gellert, Elizabeth, and Stern, Joan B. Age and sex differences in children's judgments of their height and body proportions. Presented at annual meeting of American Psychological Association, Los Angeles, 1964.

Gellhorn, E. Motion and emotion: The role of proprioception in the physiology and pathology of the emotions. *Psychological Review*, 1964, *71*, 457–472.

Gemelli, A. Orienting concepts in the study of affective states. *Journal of Nervous and Mental Diseases*, 1949, *110*, 198-214; 249–314.

Gendlin, E., and Berlin, J. Galvanic skin response correlates of different modes of experience. *Journal of Clinical Psychology*, 1961, *17*, 73–77.

Gerstmann, J. Problem of imperception of disease and of impaired body territories with organic lesions. *Archives of Neurology and Psychiatry*, 1942, *48*, 890–913.

Gibson, R. M. An exploratory study of the effects of surgery and hospitalization in early infancy on personality development. Unpublished doctoral dissertation, University of Michigan, 1959.

Gill, M. M., and Brenman, Margaret. *Hypnosis and related states*. New York: International Universities Press, 1959.

Giller, D. W. Some psychological correlates of recovery from surgery. Unpublished doctoral dissertation, University of Texas, 1960.

Gittleson, N. L. Psychogenic headache and the localization of the ego. *Journal of Mental Science*, 1962, *108*, 47–52.

Gittleson, N. L. A phenomenological test of a theory of depersonalization. *British Journal of Psychiatry*, 1967, *113*, 677–678.

Glass, D. C. (Ed.) *Neurophysiology and emotion*. New York: Rockefeller University Press, 1967.

Gleser, Goldine C., Gottschalk, L. A., and Springer, K. J. An anxiety scale applicable to verbal samples. *Archives of General Psychiatry*, 1961, *5*, 593–605.

Glick, J. A. An experimental analysis of subject-object relationships in perception. Unpublished doctoral dissertation, Clark University, 1964.

Glud, E., and Blane, H. T. Body-image changes in patients with respiratory poliomyelitis. *The Nervous Child*, 1956, *11*, 25–39.

Goertzel, V., May, P. R. A., Salkin, J., and Schoop, Trudi. Body-ego technique: An approach to the schizophrenic patient. *Journal of Nervous and Mental Disease*, 1965, *141*, 53–60.

Goldfarb, J. H. The concept of sexual identity in normals and transvestites: Its relationship to the body-image, self concept, and parental identification. Unpublished doctoral dissertation, University of Southern California, 1963.

Goldfarb, W. Self-awareness in schizophrenic children. *Archives of General Psychiatry*, 1963, *8*, 47–60.

Goldman, Freida. Breast feeding and character formation. Part I. *Journal of Personality*, 1948, *17*, 83–103.

Goldman, Freida. Breast feeding and character formation. Part II. The etiology of the oral character in psychoanalytic theory. *Journal of Personality*, 1950, *19*, 189–196.

Goldstein, M. Physiological theories of emotion: A critical historical review from the standpoint of behavior theory. *Psychological Bulletin*, 1968, *69*, 23–40.

Gordon, Carol M. Some effects of information, situation, and personality on decision-making in a clinical setting. *Journal of Clinical Psychology*, 1966, *30*, 219–224.

Gordon, Carol M. Some effects of clinician and patient personality on decision-making in a clinical setting. *Journal of Consulting Psychology*, 1967, *31*, 477–480.

Gordon, Gail. Developmental changes in responses on the Holtzman Ink Blot Technique. Unpublished master's thesis, University of Texas, 1964.

Gottesman, Eleanor G., and Caldwell, W. E. The body-image identification test: A quantitative projective technique to study an aspect of body image. *Journal of Genetic Psychology*, 1966, *108*, 19–33.

Gottheil, E. Conceptions of orality and anality. *Journal of Nervous and Mental Disease*, 1965, *141*, 155–160.

Gottschalk, L. A., Gleser, Goldine C., D'Zmura, T., and Hanenson, I. B. Some psychophysiologic relations in hypertensive women. *Psychosomatic Medicine*, 1964, *26*, 610–617.

Grace, W. J., and Graham, D. T. Relationship of specific attitudes and emotions to certain bodily diseases. *Psychosomatic Medicine*, 1952, *14*, 242–251.

Granit, R. *Centrifugal control of sensory measures. Receptors and sensory perception.* New Haven: Yale University Press, 1955.

Grayden, C. The relationship between neurotic hypochondriasis and three personality variables: Feeling of being unloved, narcissism, and guilt feelings. Unpublished doctoral dissertation, New York University, 1958.

Green, A. H. Self-mutilation in schizophrenic children. *Archives of General Psychiatry*, 1967, *17*, 234–244.

Green, S. L., Schur, Helen, and Lipkowitz, M. H. Study of a dwarf. *Psychoanalytic Study of the Child*, Vol. 14, New York: International Universities Press, 1959, 236–249.

Greenacre, Phyllis. Certain relationships between fetishism and faulty development of the body image. *Psychoanalytic Study of the Child*, Vol. 8, New York: International Universities Press, 1953, 79–96.

Greenacre, Phyllis. Further considerations regarding fetishism. *Psychoanalytic Study of the Child*, Vol. 10, New York: International Universities Press, 1955, 187–194.

Greenacre, Phyllis. Toward an understanding of the physical nucleus of some defense reactions. *International Journal of Psychoanalysis*, 1958A, *39*, 1–9.

Greenacre, Phyllis. Early physical determinants in the development of the sense of identity. *Journal of The American Psychoanalytic Association*, 1958B, *6*, 612–627.

Greenfield, N. S., and Roessler, R. Hypochondriasis: A re-evaluation. *Journal of Nervous and Mental Disease*, 1958, *126*, 482–484.

Greenson, R. R. A transvestite boy and a hypothesis. *International Journal of Psychoanalysis*, 1966, *47*, 396–403.

Grygier, T. G. *Dynamic Personality Inventory.* London: National Foundation for Educational Research in England and Wales, 1956.

Guillaume, P. *L'Imitation chez L'enfant.* Paris: Alcan, 1925.

Gunderson, E. K. Body size, self evaluation, and military effectiveness. *Journal of Personality and Social Psychology*, 1956, *2*, 902–906.

Gunderson, E. K., and Johnson, Laverne C. Past experience, self evaluation, and present adjustment. *Journal of Social Psychology*, 1965, *66*, 311–321.

Gunvald, G. The nature and changes of the body schema of girls nine, ten, and eleven years old with special reference to age, body type, and height. *International Record of Medicine and General Practice Clinics*, 1951, *5*, 558–564.

Gupta, V. On the meaning of "Mine": A psychological study. Unpublished doctoral dissertation, University of Kansas, 1962.

Guthrie, E. R. *The psychology of learning.* (Revised edition.) New York: Harper, 1952.

Guthrie, T. C., and Grossman, E. M. A study of the syndromes of denial. *Archives of Neurology and Psychiatry*, 1952, *68*, 362–371.

Haber, R. N. Nature of the effects of set on perception. *Psychological Review*, 1966, *73*, 335–351.

Haber, W. B. Effects of loss of limb on sensory functions. *Journal of Psychology*, 1955, *40*, 115–123.

Haber, W. B. Observations of phantom limb phenomena. *Archives of Neurology and Psychiatry*, 1956, *75*, 624–636.

Hall, G. S. Some aspects of the early sense of self. *American Journal of Psychology*, 1898, *9*, 351–395.

Hamilton, R. G., and Robertson, M. H. Examiner influence on the Holtzman Inkblot Technique. *Journal of Projective Techniques and Personality Assessment*, 1966, *30*, 553–558.

Hammerschlag, C. A., Fisher, S., DeCosse, J., and Kaplan, E. Breast symptoms and patient delay: Psychological variables involved. *Cancer*, 1964, *17*, 1480–1485.

Harlow, R. G. Masculine inadequacy and compensatory development of physique. *Journal of Personality*, 1951, *19*, 312–323.

Harris, J. E. Elucidation of body imagery in chronic schizophrenia. *Archives of General Psychiatry*, 1967, *16*, 679–684.

Hart, H. H. The eye in symbol and symptom. *The Yearbook of Psychoanalysis*, 1950, *6*, 256–275.

Hartley, R. B. A homonym word association measure of the barrier variable and its comparison with the inkblot barrier measure. Unpublished doctoral dissertation, University of Washington, 1964.

Hastings, P. K. A relationship between visual perception and level of personal insecurity. *Journal of Abnormal and Social Psychology*, 1952, *47*, 552–560.

Hastorf, A. H. The influence of suggestion on the relationship between stimulus size and perceived distance. *Journal of Psychology*, 1950, *29*, 195–217.

Head, H. *Studies in neurology*, Vol. 2. London: Oxford University Press, 1920.

Head, H. *Aphasia and kindred disorders of speech.* London: Cambridge, 1926.

Heath, Helen A., Oken, D., and Shipman, W. G. Muscle tension and personality. *Archives of General Psychiatry*, 1967, *16*, 720–726.

Hefferline, R. F., Keenan, B., and Harford, R. A. Escape and avoidance conditioning in human subjects without their observation of the response. *Science*, 1959, *130*, 1338–1339.

Hefferline, R. F., and Perera, T. B. Proprioceptive discrimination of a covert operant without its observation by the subject. *Science*, 1963, *139*, 834–835.

Helmreich, R. L. Prolonged stress in Sealab II: A field study of individual and group reactions. Unpublished doctoral dissertation, Yale University, 1966.

Herner, T. Significance of the body image in schizophrenic thinking. *American Journal of Psychotherapy*, 1965, *19*, 455–466.

Herring, F. H. Response during anesthesia and surgery. *Psychosomatic Medicine*, 1956, *18*, 243–251.

Herion, E. W. Changes in inkblot perception with presentation of the Holtzman Inkblot Technique as an "intelligence test." *Journal of Projective Techniques and Personality Assessment*, 1964, *28*, 442–447.

Hertz, R. *Death and the right hand.* Glencoe, Illinois: Free Press, 1960.

Hetherington, E. M., and Brackbill, Yvonne. Etiology and covariation of obstinacy, orderliness, and parsimony in young children. *Child Development*, 1963, *34*, 919–943.

Himelstein, P. Sex differences in spatial localization of the self. *Perceptual and Motor Skills*, 1964, *19*, 317.

Hinckley, E. D., and Rethlingshafer, D. Value judgments of heights of men by college students. *Journal of Psychology*, 1951, *31*, 257–262.

Hirschenfang, S., and Benton, J. G. Assessment of phantom limb sensation among patients with lower extremity amputation. *Journal of Psychology*, 1966, *63*, 197–199.

Hirt, M., Ross, W. D., and Kurtz, R. Construct validity of body-boundary perception. Proceedings, 75th Annual Convention, American Psychological Association, 1967.

Hoch, R., Kubis, J. F., and Rouke, F. L. Psychogalvanometric investigations in psychoses and other abnormal mental states. *Psychosomatic Medicine*, 1944, *6*, 237–243.

Hohmann, G. W. Some effects of spinal cord lesions on experienced emotional feelings. *Psychophysiology*, 1966, *3*, 143–156.

Holden, R. H. Changes in body image of physically handicapped children due to summer camp experiences. *Merrill-Palmer Quarterly of Behavior and Development*, 1962, *8*, 19–26.

Holleman, J. L. Explorations in human development with an early memories inventory. Unpublished doctoral dissertation, University of Oklahoma, 1965.

Hollender, M. H. Observations on nasal symptoms: Relationship of the anatomical structure of the nose to psychological symptoms. *Psychiatric Quarterly*, 1956, *30*, 375–386.

Hollender, M. H., and Boszormenyi-Nagy, I. Hallucinations as an ego experience. *Archives of Neurology and Psychiatry*, 1958, *80*, 93–97.

Holt, R. R. Gauging primary and secondary process. *Journal of Projective Techniques*, 1956, *20*, 14–25.

Holtzman, W. H. Intelligence, cognitive style, and personality: A developmental approach. In *Intelligence: Perspective*. New York: Harcourt, Brace, and World, 1965.

Holtzman, W. H., Gorham, D. R., and Moran, L. J. A factor-analytic study of schizophrenic thought processes. *Journal of Abnormal and Social Psychology*, 1964, *69*, 355–364.

Holtzman, W. H., Moseley, E. C., Reinehr, R. C., and Abbott, E. Comparison of the group method and the standard individual version of the Holtzman Inkblot Technique. *Journal of Clinical Psychology*, 1963, *19*, 441–449.

Holtzman, W. H., Santos, J. F., Bouquet, Susana, and Barth, P. *The Peace Corps in Brazil*. Austin, Texas: University of Texas Press, 1966.

Holtzman, W. H., Thorpe, J. S., Swartz, J. D., and Herron, E. W. *Inkblot perception and personality*. Austin, Texas: University of Texas Press, 1961.

Holzman, P. S. On perceiving oneself. Presented to the Interdepartmental Institute for Training in Research in the Behavioral and Neurologic Sciences at Albert Einstein College of Medicine, May 7, 1964.

Holzman, P. S., Berger, A., and Rousey, C. Voice confrontation: A bilingual study. *Journal of Personality and Social Psychology*, 1967, 7, 423–428.

Holzman, P. S., and Rousey, C. The voice as a percept. *Journal of Personality and Social Psychology*, 1966, *4*, 79–86.

Holzman, P. S., Rousey, C., and Snyder, C. On listening to one's own voice: Effects on psychophysiological responses and free associations. *Journal of Personality and Social Psychology*, 1966, *4*, 432–441.

Horney, Karen. *Our inner conflicts*. New York: W. W. Norton, 1945.

Horowitz, E. L. Spatial localization of the self. *Journal of Social Psychology*, 1935, *6*, 379–387.

Horowitz, M. J. Human spatial behavior. *American Journal of Psychotherapy*, 1965, *19*, 20–28.

Horowitz, M. J. Body image. *Archives of General Psychiatry*, 1966, *14*, 456–460.

Horowitz, M. J., Duff, D. F., and Stratton, Lois O. Body-buffer zone. *Archives of General Psychiatry*, 1964, *11*, 651–656.

Howard, I. P., and Templeton, W. B. *Human spatial orientation*. New York: John Wiley & Sons, 1966.

Howell, Mary C. Some effects of chronic illness on children and their mothers. Unpublished doctoral dissertation, University of Minnesota, 1962.

Hozier, Ann. On the breakdown of the sense of reality: A study of spatial perception in schizophrenia. *Journal of Consulting Psychology*, 1959, *23*, 185–194.

Humphrey, G. *Thinking*. New York, Wiley, 1963.

Humphries, Ogretta A. Effect of articulation of finger-tip through touch on apparent length of outstretched arm. Unpublished master's thesis, Clark University, 1959.

Hunt, R. G., and Feldman, M. J. Body image and ratings of adjustment on human figure drawings. *Journal of Clinical Psychology*, 1960, *16*, 35–38.

Hunt, Valerie, V., and Weber, Mary E. Body image projective test. *Journal of Projective Techniques*, 1960, *24*, 3–10.

Hunt, W. A. Localization of bright and dull pressure. *American Journal of Psychology*, 1932, *44*, 308–313.

Huntley, C. W. Judgments of self based upon records of expressive behavior. *Journal of Abnormal and Social Psychology*, 1940, *35*, 398–427.

Ingram, C. G. Some findings in the autonomic nervous system in schizophrenia. *Annals of the New York Academy of Sciences*, 1962, *96*, Article #1.

Ittelson, W. H., and Kutash, S. B. (Eds.). *Perceptual changes in psychopathology*. New Brunswick, N. J.: Rutgers University Press, 1961.

Jabin, Norma. Attitudes toward the physically disabled as related to selected personality variables. Unpublished doctoral dissertation, New York University, 1965.

Jacobsen, E. *Progressive relaxation*. Chicago: University of Chicago Press, 1929.

Jacobson, Edith. Depersonalization. *Journal of The American Psychoanalytic Association*, 1959, *7*, 581–610.

Jacobson, G. R. Reduction of sensory environment: Effects on measures of body image and perceptual orientation. Unpublished master's thesis, College of William and Mary, 1965.

Jacobson, G. R. Effect of brief sensory deprivation on field dependence. *Journal of Abnormal Psychology*, 1966, *71*, 115–118.

Jacobson, W. E., Edgerton, M. T., Meyer, E., Canter, A., and Slaughter, Regina. Psychiatric evaluation of male patients seeking cosmetic surgery. *Plastic and Reconstructive Surgery and the Transplantation Bulletin*, 1960, *26*, 356–372.

Jaffe, J., and Slote, W. H. Interpersonal factors in denial of illness. *Archives of Neurology and Psychiatry*, 1958, *80*, 653–656.

James, W. *Psychology*. New York: Henry Holt, 1892.

James, W., and Lange, G. C. *The emotions*. Baltimore: Williams and Wilkins, 1922.

Janis, I. L. *Psychological stress*. New York: Wiley, 1958.

Jarvis, J. H. Post-mastectomy breast phantoms. *Journal of Nervous and Mental Disease*, 1967, *144*, 266–272.

Jaskar, R. O., and Reed, M. R. Assessment of body image organization of hospitalized and non-hospitalized subjects. *Journal of Projective Techniques and Personality Assessment*, 1963, *27*, 185–190.

Jasper, H. H., and Raney, E. T. The physiology of lateral cerebral dominance. *Psychological Bulletin*, 1937, *34*, 151–165.

Jessner, L., Blom, G. E., and Waldfogel, S. Emotional implications of tonsillectomy and adenoidectomy on children. *Psychoanalytic Study of the Child*, Vol. 7, New York: International Universities Press, 1952, 126–169.

Johnson, H. J., and Schwartz, G. E. Suppression of GSR activity through operant reinforcement. *Journal of Experimental Psychology*, 1967, *75*, 307–312.

Johnson, L. C. Body cathexis as a factor in somatic complaints. *Journal of Consulting Psychology*, 1956, *20*, 145–149.

Johnson, O. G., and Wawrzaszek, F. Psychologists' judgment of physical handicap from H-T-P drawings. *Journal of Consulting Psychology*, 1961, *25*, 284–287.

Jones, F. P. Method for changing stereotyped response patterns by the inhibition of certain postural sets. *Psychological Review*, 1965, *72*, 196–214.

Jortner, S. An investigation of certain cognitive aspects of schizophrenia. *Journal of Projective Techniques and Personality Assessment*, 1966, *30*, 559–568.

Jourard, S. M. An exploratory study of body accessibility. *British Journal of Social and Clinical Psychology*, 1966, *5*, 221–231.

Jourard, S. M., and Remy, R. M. Individual variance score: An index of the degree of differentiation of the self and the body image. *Journal of Clinical Psychology*, 1957, *13*, 62–63.

Jourard, S. M., and Secord, P. F. Body size and body cathexis. *Journal of Consulting Psychology*, 1954, *18*, 184.

Jourard, S. M., and Secord, P. F. Body cathexis and the ideal female figure. *Journal of Abnormal and Social Psychology*, 1955, *50*, 243–246.

Jung, C. J. *Psychology of the unconscious*. New York: Dodd, Mead, and Company, 1931.

Jung, C. J. *Psychology and alchemy*. New York: Pantheon Books, 1944.

Jurko, M., Jost, H., and Hill, T. S. Pathology of the energy system: An experimental clinical study of physiological adaptive capacities in a non-patient, a psycho-neurotic, and an early paranoid schizophrenic group. *Journal of Psychology*, 1952, *33–34*, 183–198.

Kagan, J., and Moss, H. A. *Birth to maturity*. New York: Wiley, 1962.

Kagan, J., Rosman, B., Day, D., Albert, J., and Phillips, W. Information processing in the child: Significance of Analytic and Reflective attitudes. *Psychological Monographs*, 1964, *78*, No. 1.

Kamano, D. K. An investigation of the meaning of human figure drawing. *Journal of Clinical Psychology*, 1960, *16*, 429–430.

Kaplan, S. M. Psychological aspects of cardiac disease. *Psychosomatic Medicine*, 1956, *18*, 221–233.

Karush, A., Hiatt, R. B., and Daniels, G. E. Psychophysiological correlations in ulcerative colitis. *Psychosomatic Medicine*, 1955, *17*, 36–56.

Katcher, A., and Levin, M. Children's conceptions of body size. *Child Development*, 1955, *26*, 103–110.

Kaufman, I., and Heims, Lora. The body image of the juvenile delinquent. *American Journal of Orthopsychiatry*, 1958, *28*, 146–159.

Keen, R. Body image disturbance in chronic and acute schizophrenia, Unpublished master's thesis, University of Oklahoma, 1966.

Keiser, S. Disturbances in abstract thinking and body-image formation. *Journal of The American Psychoanalytic Association*, 1958, *6*, 628–652.

Keisman, I. Stuttering and anal fixation. Unpublished doctoral dissertation, New York University, 1958.

Kenyon, F. E. Hypochondriasis: A clinical study. *British Journal of Psychiatry*, 1964, *110*, 478–488.

Kenyon, F. E. Hypochondriasis: A survey of some historical, clinical, and social aspects. *British Journal of Medical Psychology*, 1965, *38*, 117.

Kernaleguen, Anne P. Creativity level, perceptual style and peer perception of attitudes towards clothing. Unpublished doctoral dissertation, Utah State University, 1968.

Kestenberg, Judith S. The role of movement patterns in development. III. The control of shape. *Psychoanalytic Quarterly*, 1967, *36*, 356–409.

Kilpatrick, F. P. (Ed.) *Human behavior from the transactional point of view*. Hanover, New Hampshire: Institute for Associated Research, 1952.

Kimmel, J. A comparison of children with congenital and acquired orthopedic handicaps on certain personality characteristics. Unpublished doctoral dissertation, New York University, 1958.

Kinsey, A. C., Pomeroy, W. B., and Martin, C. E. *Sexual behavior in the human male.* Philadelphia: W. B. Saunders Company, 1948.

Kitamura, S. Studies on sensory deprivation. II. On the estimation of the body image. *Tohoku Psychological Folia*, 1964, *22*, 69–71.

Klein, D. F., and Fink, M. Behavioral reaction patterns with phenothiazines. *Archives of General Psychiatry*, 1962, *7*, 449–459.

Klein, G. S. The personal world through perception. In R. Blake and G. Ramsey (Eds.). *Perception: An approach to personality.* New York: Ronald Press, 1951, Pp. 328–355.

Klein, G. S., Spence, D. P., Holt, R. R., and Gourevitch, Suzannah. Cognition without awareness: Subliminal influences upon conscious thought. *Journal of Abnormal and Social Psychology*, 1958, *57*, 255–266.

Klein, Melanie. *The psycho-analysis of children.* London: Hogarth Press, 1932.

Kleitman, N. *Sleep and wakefulness as alternating phases in the cycle of existence.* Chicago: University of Chicago Press, 1939.

Klepper, I. L. The effect of body attention procedures on field dependence. Unpublished master's thesis, Syracuse University, 1968.

Klerman, G. L., DiMascio, A., Greenblatt, M., and Rinkel, M. The influence of specific personality patterns on the reactions to phrenotropic agents. *Biological Psychiatry*, 1959, *1*, 7–15.

Koechel, J. W. Perceptual defense and perceptual vigilance in individuals with obvious and hidden disabilities. Unpublished doctoral dissertation, University of Houston, 1964.

Kolb, L. C. Disturbance of the body-image. In S. Arieti (Ed.). *American handbook of psychiatry,* New York: Basic Books, 1959, Pp. 749–769.

Korchin, S. J., and Heath, Helen A. Somatic experience in the anxiety state: Some sex and personality correlates of "autonomic feedback". *Journal of Consulting Psychology*, 1961, *25*, 398–404.

Korin, H., Weiss, S., and Fishman, S. Pain sensitivity of amputation extremities. *Journal of Psychology*, 1963, *55*, 345–355.

Korner, I. N., Allison, R. B., Jr., Donoviel, S. J., and Boswell, J. D. Some measures of self-acceptance. *Journal of Clinical Psychology*, 1963, *19*, 131–132.

Koschene, R. L. Body image and boundary constancy in kidney transplant patients: A test of the Fisher-Cleveland hypotheses. Unpublished master's thesis, University of Colorado, 1965.

Kotkov, B., and Goodman, M. Prediction of trait ranks from Draw-A-Person measurements of obese and non-obese women. *Journal of Clinical Psychology*, 1953, *9*, 365–367.

Kris, E. *Psychoanalytic explorations in art.* New York: International Universities Press, 1952.

Krout, M. H. An experimental attempt to determine the significance of unconscious manual symbolic movements. *Journal of General Psychology*, 1954, *51*, 121–152.

Krout, M. H., and Tabin, Johanna K. Measuring personality in developmental terms: The Personal Preference Scale. *Genetic Psychology Monographs*, 1954, *50*, 289–335.

Kuder, G. F. *Kuder Preference Record (Examiner Manual).* Chicago: Science Research Associates, 1956.

Kuethe, J. L. Social schemas. *Journal of Abnormal and Social Psychology*, 1962, *64*, 31–38.

Kuramochi, H., and Takahashi, R. Psychopathology of LSD intoxication. *Archives of General Psychiatry*, 1964, *11*, 151–161.

Kurtz, R. M. The relationship of body attitude to sex, body size, and body build in a college population. Unpublished doctoral dissertation, University of Cincinnati, 1966.

Lacey, J. I. Individual differences in somatic response patterns. *Journal of Comparative and Physiological Psychology*, 1950, *43*, 338–350.

Lacey, J. I. Psychophysiological approaches to the evaluation of psychotherapeutic process and outcome. In E. A. Rubenstein and M. B. Parloff (Eds.). *Research in psychotherapy*. Washington, D. C.: National Publishing Company, 1959, Pp. 160–208.

Lacey, J. I., Bateman, Dorothy E., and Van Lehn, Ruth. Autonomic response specificity: An experimental study. *Psychosomatic Medicine*, 1953, *15*, 8–21.

Lacey, J. I., and Lacey, B. E. Verification and extension of the principle of autonomic response-stereotypy. *American Journal of Psychology*, 1958, *71*, 50–73.

Lacey, J. I., and Van Lehn, R. Differential emphasis in somatic response to stress: An experimental study. *Psychosomatic Medicine*, 1952, *14*, 71–81.

Ladee, G. A. *Hypochondriacal syndromes*. New York: Elsevier Publishing Company, 1966.

Laird, J. D. The effect of facial expression on emotional experience. Presented at the annual meeting of the Eastern Psychological Association, Boston, Massachusetts, 1967.

Landau, Miriam F. Body image in paraplegia as a variable in adjustment to physical handicap. Unpublished doctoral dissertation, Columbia University, 1960.

Landis, B. A study of ego boundaries. Unpublished doctoral dissertation, New School for Social Research, 1963.

Lane, R. W. The effect of preoperative stress on dreams. Unpublished doctoral dissertation, University of Oregon, 1966.

Lasagna, L., Mosteller, F., von Felsinger, J. M., and Beecher, H. K. A study of the placebo response. *American Journal of Medicine*, 1954, *16*, 770–779.

Lasky, J. J., and Berger, L. Blacky test scores before and after genito-urinary surgery. *Journal of Projective Techniques*, 1959, *23*, 57–58.

Lazare, A., Klerman, G. L., and Armor, D. J. Oral, obsessive, and hysterical personality patterns. *Archives of General Psychiatry*, 1966, *14*, 624–630.

Lebovitis, B. Z., and Lakin, M. Body image and paralytic poliomyelitis. *Journal of Nervous and Mental Disease*, 1957, *125*, 518–523.

Leeds, D. P. Personality patterns and modes of behavior of male adolescent narcotic addicts and their mothers. Unpublished doctoral dissertation, Yeshiva University, 1965.

Lehner, G. G., and Silver, H. Age relationships on the Draw-A-Person Test. *Journal of Personality*, 1948, *17*, 199–209.

Leigh, D., Marley, E., and Braithwaite, Dorothy. *Bronchial asthma*. London: Pergamon Press, 1967.

Lerner, B. Auditory and visual thresholds for the perception of words of anal connotation: An evaluation of the "sublimation hypothesis" on philatelists. Unpublished doctoral dissertation, Yeshiva University, 1961.

Lerner, Barbara. Rorschach movement and dreams: A validation study using drug-induced dream deprivation. *Journal of Abnormal Psychology*, 1966, *71*, 75–86.

Lerner, Barbara. Dream function reconsidered. *Journal of Abnormal Psychology*, 1967, *72*, 85–100.

Lerner, Mildred S. The relationship of certain aspects of the body image of female schizophrenic patients to therapeutic success or failure. Unpublished doctoral dissertation, New York University, 1960.

Lester, D. Attempted suicide and body image. *Journal of Psychology*, 1967, *66*, 287–290.

Levi, Aurelia. Orthopedic disability as a factor in human-figure perception. *Journal of Consulting Psychology*, 1961, *25*, 253–256.

Lewinsohn, P. M. Some individual differences in physiological reactivity to stress. Unpublished doctoral dissertation, Johns Hopkins University, 1954.

Lewinsohn, P. M. Relationship between height of figure drawings and depression in psychiatric patients. *Journal of Consulting Psychology*, 1964, *28*, 380–381.

Lewis, M. D. A case of transvestism with multiple body-phallus identification. *International Journal of Psychoanalysis*, 1963, *44*, 345–351.

Liebert, R. S., Werner, H., and Wapner, S. Studies in the effect of Lysergic Acid Diethylamide. *Archives of Neurology and Psychiatry*, 1958, *79*, 580–584.

Linn, L. Some developmental aspects of the body image. *International Journal of Psychoanalysis*, 1955, *36*, 36–42.

Linn, L. Some comments on the origin of the influencing machine. *Journal of The American Psychoanalytic Association*, 1958, *6*, 305–308.

Linton, Harriet B., and Langs, R. J. Empirical dimensions of LSD-25 reaction. *Archives of General Psychiatry*, 1964, *10*, 469–485.

Lippman, C. W. Certain hallucinations peculiar to migraine. *Journal of Nervous and Mental Disease*, 1952, *116*, 346–351.

Little, K. B. An investigation of autonomic balance in peptic ulcer patients. Unpublished doctoral dissertation, University of California, 1950.

Lorens, S. A., Jr., and Darrow, C. W. Eye movements, EEG, GSR, and EKG during mental multiplication. *Electroencephalography and Clinical Neurophysiology*, 1962, *14*, 739–746.

Lorr, M., Klett, J. C., and McNair, D. M. *Syndromes of psychosis*. New York: Macmillan Company, 1963.

Lorr, M., Rubenstein, E., and Jenkins, R. L. A factor analysis of personality ratings of out-patients in psychotherapy. *Journal of Abnormal and Social Psychology*, 1953, *48*, 507–514.

Lukianowicz, N. Autoscopic phenomena. *Neurology and Psychiatry*, 1958, *80*, 199–220.

Lukianowicz, N. "Body image" disturbances in psychiatric disorders. *British Journal of Psychiatry*, 1967, *113*, 31–47.

Lundholm, H. The psychological self in the philosophies of Kohler and Sherrington. *Psychological Review*, 1946, *53*, 119-131,

Lundin, W. H. Projective movement sequences: Motion patterns as a projective technique. *Journal of Consulting Psychology*, 1949, *13*, 407–411.

Luria, A. *The role of speech in regulation of normal and abnormal behavior*. London: Liveright, 1961.

Lussier, A. The analysis of a boy with a congenital deformity. *Psychoanalytic Study of the Child*, Vol. 15, New York: International Universities Press, 1960, 430–453.

Macgregor, F. C. Social and cultural components in the motivations of persons seeking plastic surgery of the nose. *Journal of Health and Social Behavior*, 1967, *8*, 125–135.

Macgregor, F. C., Abel, Theodora M., Bryt, A., Louer, Edith, and Weissmann, Serena. *Facial deformities and plastic surgery*. Springfield, Illinois: Charles E. Thomas, 1953.

Machover, Karen. Human figure drawings of children. *Journal of Projective Techniques*, 1953, *17*, 85–91.

Machover, Karen. *Personality projection in the drawing of the human figure*. Springfield, Illinois: C. C. Thomas, 1949.

Machover, Karen. Drawing of the human figure: A method of personality investigation. In H. H. Anderson and E. L. Anderson (Eds.). *An introduction to projective techniques*. New York: Prentice-Hall, 1951, Pp. 341–369.

Magnussen, M. G. Body size and body-cathexis replicated. *Psychological Newsletter* (NYU), 1958, *10*, 33–34.

Maher, J. J. Barrier score—body image, or behavior tendency? Unpublished doctoral dissertation, University of Georgia, 1968.

Malerstein, A. J. Post-hysterectomy pseudocyesis of phantom visceral organ. *American Journal of Psychiatry*, 1963, *119*, 1102.

Malev, J. S. Body image, body symptoms and body reactivity in children. *Journal of Psychosomatic Research*, 1966, *10*, 281–289.

Mandel, H. A Q-methodology investigation of the oral and anal characters as described in psychoanalytic theory. Unpublished doctoral dissertation, New York University, 1957.

Mandler, G., and Mandler, Jean M. Associative behavior and somatic response. *Canadian Journal of Psychology*, 1962, *16*, 331–343.

Mandler, G., and Kremen, I. Autonomic feedback: A correlational study. *Journal of Personality*, 1960, *26*, 388–399.

Mandler, G., Mandler, Jean M., and Uviller, Ellen T. Autonomic feedback: The perception of autonomic activity. *Journal of Abnormal and Social Psychology*, 1958, *56*, 367–373.

Marais, H. C., and Strumpfer, D. J. W. DAP body-image disturbance scale and quality of drawing. *Perceptual and Motor Skills*, 1965, *21*, 196.

Martin, Irene, and Grosz, H. J. Hypnotically induced emotions. *Archives of General Psychiatry*, 1964, *11*, 203–213.

Mason, R. E. *Internal perception and bodily functioning*. New York: International Universities Press, 1961.

Masserman, J. H. *Principles of dynamic psychiatry*. Philadelphia: Saunders, 1946.

Masson, R. L. An investigation of the relationship between body-image and attitudes expressed toward visibly disabled persons. Unpublished doctoral dissertation, University of Buffalo, 1963.

May, P. R. A., Wexler, M., Salkin, J., and Schoop, Trudi. Non-verbal techniques in the re-establishment of body image self identity—a preliminary report. *Psychiatric Research Reports*, 1963, No. 16, 68–82.

Mayer-Gross, W. On depersonalization. *British Journal of Medical Psychology*, 1935, *15*, 103–126.

McClelland, D. *The achieving society*. Princeton, New Jersey: Van Nostrand, 1961.

McClelland, D., Atkinson, J. W., Clark, R. A., and Lowell, E. L. *The achievement motive*. New York: Appleton-Century-Crofts, 1953.

McClelland, D. C., and Watt, N. F. Sex-role alienation in schizophrenia. *Journal of Abnormal Psychology*, 1968, *73*, 226–239.

McConnell, O. L., and Daston, P. G. Body image changes in pregnancy. *Journal of Projective Techniques*, 1961, *25*, 451–456.

McFarland, J. H. The effect of asymmetrical muscular involvement on visual clarity. Presented at the annual meeting of Eastern Psychological Association, New York, 1958.

McFarland, J. H., Wapner, S., and Werner, H. Factors affecting body image as measured by perceived arm length. Presented at annual meeting of Eastern Psychological Association, New York, 1960.

McFarland, J. H., Werner, H., and Wapner, S. The effect of postural factors on the distribution of tactual sensitivity and the organization of tactual-kinesthetic space. *Journal of Experimental Psychology*, 1962, *63*, 148–154.

McGlothlin, W. H., Cohen, S., and McGlothlin, Marcella S. Long-lasting effects of LSD on normals. Presented at annual meeting of American College of Neuropharmacology, San Juan, Puerto Rico, 1966.

McGuigan, F. J. *Thinking: Studies of covert language processes*. New York: Appleton-Century-Crofts, 1966.

McGuigan, F. J., Keller, Barbara, and Stanton, Eleanor. Covert language responses during silent reading. *Journal of Educational Psychology*, 1964, *55*, 339–343.

McHugh, Ann. Children's figure drawings and school achievement. *Psychology in the Schools*, 1964, *1*, 51–52.

McNeil, E. B., and Blum, G. S. Handwriting and psychosexual dimensions of personality. *Journal of Projective Techniques*, 1952, *16*, 476–484.

McPherson, Marion W., Popplestone, J. A., and Evans, Katherine A. Perceptual carelessness, drawing precision, and oral activity among normal six-year-olds. *Perceptual and Motor Skills*, 1966, *22*, 327–330.

Meerloo, J. A. The fate of one's face. *Psychiatric Quarterly*, 1956, *30*, 31–43.

Megargee, E. I. Relation between barrier scores and aggressive behavior. *Journal of Abnormal Psychology*, 1965, *70*, 307–311.

Megargee, E. I., Lockwood, Vicki, Cato, Jeraldine L., and Jones, Joanna K. Effects of differences in examiner, tone of administration, and sex of subject on scores of the Holtzman Inkblot Technique. Presented at annual meeting of American Psychological Association, Boston, 1966.

Meissner, Ann L., Thoreson, R. W. and Butler, A. J. Relation of self-concept to impact and obviousness of disability among male and female adolescents. *Perceptual and Motor Skills*, 1967, *24*, 1099–1105.

Meketon, Betty W., Griffith, R. M., Taylor, Vivian H., and Wiedeman, Jane S. Rorschach homosexual signs in paranoid schizophrenics. *Journal of Abnormal and Social Psychology*, 1962, *65*, 280–284.

Meltzoff, J., Singer, J. L., and Korchin, S. J. Motor inhibition and Rorschach movement responses: A test of the sensory-tonic theory. *Journal of Personality*, 1953, *21*, 400–410.

Merleau-Ponty, M. *Phenomenology of perception*. London: Routledge and Kegan Paul, 1962.

Mcycr, B. C. Psychoanalytic studies on Joseph Conrad: II. Fetishism. *Journal of The American Psychoanalytic Association*, 1964, *12*, 357–391.

Meyer, B. C., Blacher, R. S., and Brown, F. A clinical study of psychiatric and psychological aspects of mitral surgery. *Psychosomatic Medicine*, 1961, *23*, 194–218.

Meyer, B. C., Brown, F., and Levine, A. Observations on the House-Tree-Person Drawing Test before and after surgery. *Psychosomatic Medicine*, 1955, *17*, 428–454.

Meyer, E., Jacobson, W. E., Edgerton, M. T., and Canter, A. Motivational patterns in patients seeking elective plastic surgery. *Psychosomatic Medicine*, 1960, *22*, 194–203.

Michel-Hutmacher, Rosalie. The inside of the body in the imagination of children. (German trans.) *Schweizer Zeitschrift fur Psychologische Anwendung*, 1955, *14*, 1–26.

Miller, A. A., McCauley, J. M., Fraser, Constance, and Culbert, Catherine. Psychological factors in adaptation to hearing aids. *American Journal of Orthopsychiatry*, 1959, *29*, 121–129.

Miller, D. R., and Stine, Margaret, W. The prediction of social acceptance by means of psychoanalytic concepts. *Journal of Personality*, 1951, *20*, 162–174.

Miner, H. M., and DeVos, G. *Oasis and Casbah: Algerian culture and personality in change.* Ann Arbor: University of Michigan Press, 1960.

Money, J. Phantom orgasm in the dreams of paraplegic men and women. *Archives of General Psychiatry*, 1960, *3*, 373–382.

Moore, F. J., Chernell, E., and West, M. J. Television as a therapeutic tool. *Archives of General Psychiatry*, 1965, *12*, 217–220.

Moore, R. A., and Selzer, M. L. Male homosexuality, paranoia, and the schizophrenias. *American Journal of Psychiatry*, 1963, *119*, 743–747.

Moos, R. H. Behavioral effects of being observed: Reactions to a wireless radio transmitter. *Journal of Consulting Psychology*, in press.

Moos, R. H., and Engel, B. T. Psychophysiological reactions in hypertensive and arthritic patients. *Journal of Psychosomatic Research*, 1962, *6*, 227–241.

Moos, R. H., and Solomon, G. F. Psychologic comparisons between women with rheumatoid arthritis and their nonarthritic sisters. I. Personality test and interview rating data. *Psychosomatic Medicine*, 1965A, *27*, 135–149.

Moos, R. H., and Solomon, G. F. Psychologic comparisons between women with rheumatoid arthritis and their nonarthritic sisters. II. Content analysis of interviews. *Psychosomatic Medicine*, 1965B, *27*, 150–164.

Mordkoff, A. M. Some sex differences in personality correlates of "autonomic feedback". *Psychological Reports*, 1966, *18*, 511–518.

Morris, Freda, and Young, H. H. A test of a body image hypothesis of hand extinction in double simultaneous stimulation. *Journal of Consulting Psychology*, 1967, *31*, 103.

Morton, Joyce C. The relationship between inkblot barrier scores and sociometric status in adolescents. Unpublished master's thesis, University of British Columbia, 1965.

Moseley, E. C., Gorham, D. R., and Hill, Evelyn F. Computer scoring of inkblot perceptions. *Perceptual and Motor Skills*, 1963, *17*, 498.

Mosher, D. L., Oliver, W. A., and Dolgan, J. Body image in tattooed prisoners. *Journal of Clinical Psychology*, 1967, *23*, 31–32.

Murphy, W. F. Some clinical aspects of the body ego. *Psychoanalytic Review*, 1957, *44*, 462–477.

Murray, H. A. *Explorations in personality*. New York: Oxford University Press, 1938.

Nafe, J. P. The psychology of felt experiences. *American Journal of Psychology*, 1927, *39*, 367–389.

Nagy, Maria H. Children's conceptions of some bodily functions. *Journal of Genetic Psychology*, 1953, *83*, 199–216.

Nakoshima, T. Contributions to the study of the affective processes. *American Journal of Psychology*, 1909, *20*, 157–193.

Nash, H. The estimation of body size in relation to actual body size, personal ethos and developmental status. Unpublished doctoral dissertation, University of California, 1951.

Nash, H. Assignment of gender to body regions. *Journal of Genetic Psychology*, 1958, *92*, 113–115.

Nathanson, M., Bergman, P. S., and Gordon, G. G. Denial of illness. *Archives of Neurology and Psychiatry*, 1952, *68*, 380–387.

Nichols, D. C., and Tursky, B. Body image, anxiety, and tolerance for experimental pain. *Psychosomatic Medicine*, 1967, *29*, 103–110.

Nichols, R. C. and Strumpfer, D. J. W. A factor analysis of Draw-A-Person test scores, *Journal of Consulting Psychology*, 1962, *26*, 156-161.

Nickols, J. Size judgment and the Draw-A-Person test. *Journal Psychological Studies*, 1962 *13*, 117-119.

Niederland, W. G. The "miracled-up" world of Schreber's childhood. *Psychoanalytic Study of the Child*, Vol. 14, New York: International Universities Press, 1959, 315–382.

Nisbett, R. E. Birth order and participation in dangerous sports. *Journal of Personality and Social Psychology*, 1968, *8*, 351–353.

Nisbett, R. E., and Schachter, S. Cognitive manipulation of pain. *Journal of Experimental Social Psychology*, 1966, *2*, 227–236.

Noble, D., Price, D. B., and Gilder, R. Psychiatric disturbance following amputation. *American Journal of Psychiatry*, 1954, *110*, 609–613.

Noblin, C. D. Experimental analysis of psychoanalytic character types through the operant conditioning of verbal responses. Unpublished doctoral dissertation, Louisiana State University, 1962.

Noblin, C. D., Timmons, E. O., and Kael, H. C. Differential effects of positive and negative verbal reinforcement on psychoanalytic character types. *Journal of Personality and Social Psychology*, 1966, *4*, 224–228.

Noonan, J. R. Personality determinants in attitudes toward disability. Unpublished doctoral dissertation, University of Florida, 1966.

Numberg, H. *Principles of psychoanalysis*. New York: International Universities Press, 1955.

Oberndorf, C. P. The genesis of the feeling of unreality. *International Journal of Psychoanalysis*, 1935, *16*, 296–306.

Obrist, P. A. Cardiovascular differentiation of sensory stimuli. Presented at annual meeting of American Psychosomatic Society, Rochester, New York, 1962.

Obrist, P. A., Hallman, S. I., and Wood, D. M. Autonomic levels and lability, and performance time on a perceptual task and a sensory-motor task. Presented at annual meeting of Society for Psychophysiological Research, Detroit, Michigan, 1963.

Offord, D. R., and Aponte, J. F. A comparison of drawings and sentence completion responses of congenital heart children with normal children. *Journal of Projective Techniques and Personality Assessment*, 1967, *31*, 57–62.

Ohzama, M. The changes of body image boundary scores under conditions of alcoholic intoxication. *Tohoku Psychologica Folia*, 1964, *22*, 100–107.

Orbach, J., Traub, A., and Olson, R. Psychophysical studies of body image. II. Normative data on the Adjustable Body Distorting Mirror. *Archives of General Psychiatry*, 1966, *14*, 41–47.

Orlansky, H. Infant care and personality. *Psychological Bulletin*, 1949, *46*, 1–41.

Osgood, C. E., Suci, G. J., and Tannenbaum, P. H. *The measurement of meaning*. Urbana, Illinois: University of Illinois Press, 1957.

Osofsky, H. J., and Fisher, S. Psychological correlates of the development of amenorrhea in a stress situation. *Psychosomatic Medicine*, 1967, *29*, 15–23.

Ostow, M. The illusory reduplication of body parts in cerebral disease. *Psychoanalytic Quarterly*, 1958, *27*, 98–100.

Paige, A. B., McNamara, H. J., and Fisch, R. I. A preliminary report on sensory stimulative therapy with chronic schizophrenic patients. *Psychotherapy*, 1964, *1*, 133–136.

Palmer, R. D. Hand differentiation and psychological functioning. *Journal of Personality*, 1963, *31*, 445–461.

Palmer, R. D. Development of a differentiated handedness. *Psychological Bulletin*, 1964, *62*, 257–272.

Pantleo, P. M. An investigation of body image in adolescents. Unpublished master's thesis, New Mexico Highlands University, 1966.

Parkin, A. On fetishism. *International Journal of Psychoanalysis*, 1963, *44*, 352–361.

Parsons, T., and Bales, R. F. *Family socialization and interaction process*. Glencoe, Illinois: Free Press, 1955.

Peabody, G. A., Rowe, A. T., and Wall, J. H. Fetishism and transvestitism. *Journal of Nervous and Mental Disease*, 1953, *118*, 339–350.

Pedersen, F., and Marlowe, D. Capacity and motivational differences in verbal recall. *Journal of Clinical Psychology*, 1960, *16*, 219–222.

Peto, A. On so-called "depersonalization." *International Journal of Psychoanalysis*, 1956, *36*, 379–386.

Peto, A. Body image and archaic thinking. *International Journal of Psychoanalysis*, 1959, *40*, 1–9.

Petrovich, D. V. The Pain Apperception Test: A preliminary report. *Journal of Psychology*, 1957, *44*, 339–346.

Petrovich, D. V. The Pain Apperception Test: Psychological correlates of pain perception. *Journal of Clinical Psychology*, 1958, *14*, 367–374.

Petrovich, D. V. The Pain Apperception Test: An application to sex differences. *Journal of Clinical Psychology*, 1959, *15*, 412–414.

Petrovich, D. V. Pain apperception in chronic schizophrenics. *Journal of Projective Techniques*, 1960, *24*, 21–27.

Pezzella, Mariann A. Verbal and non-verbal self-references of children. Unpublished doctoral dissertation, New York University, 1964.

Piaget, J., and Inhelder, B. *The child's conception of space.* New York: Humanities Press, 1956.

Pishkin, V., and Blanchard, R. J. Auditory concept identification as a function of subject sex and stimulus dimensions. *Psychonomic Science*, 1964, *1*, 177–178.

Pishkin, V., and Shurley, J. T. Auditory dimensions and irrelevant information in concept identification of males and females. *Perceptual and Motor Skills*, 1965, *26*, 673–678.

Pitcher, Evelyn G., and Prelinger, E. *Children tell stories—an analysis of fantasy.* New York: International Universities Press, 1963.

Poeck, K., and Orgass, B. Die entwicklung des Korperschemas bei Kindern im Alter von 4–10 Jahren. *Neuropsychologia*, 1964, *2*, 109–130.

Pollack, M., and Goldfarb, W. The face-hand test in schizophrenic children. *Archives of Neurology and Psychiatry*, 1957, *77*, 635–642.

Pomp, H. C. A study of self-concept distortion in physically disabled and non-disabled seventh and eighth grade students. Unpublished doctoral dissertation, New York University, 1962.

Popper, Juliet M. Motivational and social factors in children's perceptions of height. Unpublished doctoral dissertation, Stanford University, 1957.

Popplestone, J. A. A scale to assess hyperchondriasis: The converse of hypochondriasis. *Psychological Record*, 1963, *13*, 32–38.

Popplestone, J. A., and Van Every, P. Contrasting forms of somatic over-concern. *Psychological Record*, 1963, *13*, 26–31.

Porzemsky, J., and Wapner, S. Effect of self-object cognitive set on body perception, object perception and their relationship. Presented at annual meeting of Eastern Psychological Association, Atlantic City, N.J., 1965.

Posner, M. I., and Konick, A. F. Short-term retention of visual and kinesthetic information. *Organizational Behavior and Human Performance*, 1966, *1*, 71–86.

Postman, L., and Schneider, B. H. Personal values, visual recognition and recall. *Psychological Review*, 1951, *58*, 271–284.

Potter, Eileen G., and Fiedler, F. E. Physical disability and interpersonal perception. *Perceptual and Motor Skills*, 1958, *8*, 241–242.

Prater, G. F. A comparison of the head and body size in the drawing of the human figure by hemiplegic and non-hemiplegic persons. Unpublished master's thesis, University of Kentucky, 1950.

Prelinger, E. Extension and structure of the self. *Journal of Psychology*, 1959, *47*, 13–23.

Price, D. B., Thaler, Margaret, and Mason, J. W. Preoperative emotional states and adrenal cortical activity. *Archives of Neurology and Psychiatry*, 1957, *77*, 646–656.

Quartermain, D., and Miller, N. E. Sensory feedback in time-response of drinking elicited by carbachol in preoptic area of rat. *Journal of Comparative and Physiological Psychology*, 1966, *62*, 350–353.

Ramer, J. The Rorschach barrier score and social behavior. *Journal of Consulting Psychology*, 1963, *27*, 525–531.

Rand, G., and Wapner, S. Postural status as a factor in memory. *Journal of Verbal Learning and Verbal Behavior*, 1967, *6*, 268–271.

Rapaport, C. Character, anxiety, and social affiliation. Unpublished doctoral dissertation, New York University, 1963.

Rapaport, D. *Emotions and memory.* Baltimore: Williams and Wilkins, 1942.

Ray, T. S., Dickinson, W. H., and Morehead, S. D. Immediate effects of self-image confrontation with chronic schizophrenic women. Presented at annual meeting of Southwestern Psychological Association, Six Flags, Texas, 1966.

Razran, G. The observable unconscious and the inferable conscious in current Soviet psychophysiology: Interoceptive conditioning, semantic conditioning, and the orienting reflex. *Psychological Review*, 1961, *68*, 81–147.

Reed, G. F., and Sedman, G. Personality and depersonalization under sensory deprivation conditions. *Perceptual and Motor Skills*, 1964, *18*, 659–660.

Reese, W. G., Dykman, R. A., and Galbrecht, C. R. Psychophysiological reactions of "normals" and psychiatric patients. *Psychiatric Research Report*, 1961, No. 14.

Reich, Annie. The structure of the grotesque-comic sublimation. *The Yearbook of Psychoanalysis*, 1950, *6*, 200–207.

Reich, W. *Character analysis.* New York: Orgone Institute Press, 1949.

Reiff, Carolyn G. An investigation of relationships among body image and some ego functions involved in formal thought processes. Unpublished doctoral dissertation, New York University, 1962.

Reiser, M. F., and Block, J. D. Discrimination and recognition of weak stimuli. III.: Further experiments on interaction of cognitive and autonomic-feedback mechanisms. *Psychosomatic Medicine*, 1965, *27*, 274–285.

Reitman, E. E. Changes in body image following sensory deprivation in schizophrenic and control groups. Unpublished doctoral dissertation, University of Houston, 1962.

Reitman, E. E., and Cleveland, S. E. Changes in body image following sensory deprivation in schizophrenic and control groups. *Journal of Abnormal and Social Psychology*, 1964, *68*, 168–176.

Renik, O. D., and Fisher, S. Induction of body image boundary changes in male subjects. *Journal of Projective Techniques and Personality Assessment*, 1968, *32*, 45–48.

Richardson, S. A., Goodman, N., Hastorf, A. H., and Dornbusch, S. M. Cultural uniformity in reaction to physical disabilities. *American Sociological Review*, 1961, *26*, 241–247.

Richardson, S. A., Hastorf, A. H., and Dornbusch, S. M. Effects of physical disability on a child's description of himself. *Child Development*, 1964, *35*, 893–907.

Richman, J. L. Need structure and environmental perception in groups with external and interior symptomatology. Unpublished master's thesis, Syracuse University, 1966.

Richter, Helen G. Emotional disturbances of constant pattern following non-specific respiratory infections. *Journal of Pediatrics*, 1943, *23*, 315–325.

Richter, R. H., and Winter, W. D. Holtzman Ink Blot correlates of creative potential. *Journl of Projective Techniques and Personality Assessment*, 1966, *30*, 62–67.

Riese, W., and Bruck, G. Les membres fantomes chez l'enfant. *Revue Neurologie*, 1950, *83*, 221–222.

Riklan, M., Zahn, T. P., and Diller, L. Human figure drawings before and after chemosurgery of the basal ganglia in Parkinsonism. *Journal of Nervous and Mental Disease*, 1962, *135*, 500–506.

Roach, Mary E., and Eicher, Joanne B. (Eds.). *Dress, adornment, and the social order.* New York: John Wiley & Sons, 1965.

Roberts, W. W. Normal and abnormal depersonalization. *Journal of Mental Science*, 1960, *106*, 478–493.

Rock, I. *The nature of perceptual adaptation.* New York: Basic Books, 1966.

Rockwell, G. J., Jr., WISC object assembly and bodily concern. *Journal of Consulting Psychology*, 1967, *31*, 221.

Rodrigue, E. M. Notes on menstruation. *International Journal of Psychoanalysis*, 1955, *36*, 328–334.

Roessler, R. L., and Brogden, W. J. Conditioned differentiation of vasoconstriction to subvocal stimuli. *American Journal of Psychology*, 1943, *56*, 79–86.

Roessler, R. L., Burch, N. R., and Childers, H. E. Personality and arousal correlates of specific galvanic skin responses. *Psychophysiology*, 1966, *3*, 115–130.

Roffwarg, H. P., Dement, W. C., Muzio, J. N., and Fisher, C. Dream imagery: Relationship to rapid eye movements of sleep. *Archives of General Psychiatry*, 1962, *7*, 235–258.

Rogers, A. H., and Coleman, P. Impunitiveness and unwitting self-evaluation. *Journal of Projective Techniques*, 1959, *23*, 459–461.

Rogers, A. H., and Walsh, T. M. Defensiveness and unwitting self-evaluation. *Journal of Clinical Psychology*, 1959, *15*, 302–304.

Roland, B. C. The influence of body exercise on the perception of kinesthetic and visual stimulus objects. Unpublished doctoral dissertation, University of Houston, 1966.

Rorschach, H. *Psychodiagnostics*. New York: Grune and Stratton, 1921.

Rose, G. J. Body ego and reality. *International Journal of Psychoanalysis*, 1966, *47*, 502–509.

Rosen, G. M., and Ross, A. O. Relationship of body image to self-concept. *Journal of Consulting and Clinical Psychology*, 1968, *32*, 100.

Rosenblatt, B. Influence of affective states on body image. Unpublished master's thesis, Clark University, 1956.

Rosenbluh, E. S. Verbal concept identification and the body percept. Unpublished doctoral dissertation, University of Oklahoma, 1967.

Rosencranz, Mary L. The application of a projective technique for analyzing clothing awareness, clothing symbols, and the range of themes associated with clothing behavior. Unpublished doctoral dissertation, Michigan State University, 1960.

Rosenwald, G. C., Mendelsohn, G. A., Fontana, A., and Portz, A. T. An action test of hypotheses concerning the anal personality. *Journal of Abnormal Psychology*, 1966, *71*, 304–309.

Rosenzweig, N., and Gardner, L. The role of input relevance in sensory isolation. *American Journal of Psychiatry*, 1966, *122*, 920–928.

Rosenzweig, S., and Shakow, D. Mirror behavior in schizophrenic and normal individuals. *Journal of Nervous and Mental Disease*, 1937, *86*, 166–174.

Ross, W. B. The Rorschach performance with neurocirculatory asthenia. *Psychosomatic Medicine*, 1945, *7*, 80–84.

Rothstein, R., and Epstein, S. Unconscious self-evaluation as a function of availability of cues. *Journal of Consulting Psychology*, 1963, *27*, 480–485.

Rotter, J. B. Generalized expectancies for internal versus external control of reinforcement. *Psychological Monographs*, 1966, *80*, No. 1.

Rounds, G. H., and Poffenberger, A. T. The measurement of implicit speech reactions. *American Journal of Psychology*, 1931, *43*, 606–612.

Rowe, A. S., and Caldwell, W. E. The Somatic Apperception Test. *Journal of General Psychology*, 1963, *68*, 59–69.

Rubenstein, E. A., and Parloff, M. B. (Eds.). *Research in psychotherapy*. Washington, D.C.: National Publishing Co., 1959.

Ruddick, B. Agoraphobia. *International Journal of Psychoanalysis*, 1961, *42*, 537–543.

Rudofsky, B. *Are clothes modern?* Chicago: Paul Theobald, 1947.

Sabbath, J. C., Morris, T. A., Menzer-Benaron, D., and Sturges, S. H. Psychiatric observations of adolescent girls lacking ovarian function. *Psychosomatic Medicine*, 1961, *23*, 224–231.

Sachs, Lisbeth J. On changes in identification from machine to cripple. *Psychoanalytic Study of the Child*, Vol. 12, New York: International Universities Press, 1957, 356–378.

Salfield, D. J. Depersonalization and allied disturbances in childhood. *Journal of Mental Science*, 1958, *104*, 472–476.

Sanford, R. N., Adkins, M. M., Muller, R. B., and Cobb, E. Physique, personality, and scholarship. *Monograph of the Society for Research in Child Development*, 1943, 7, No. 34.

Saperstein, J. L. On the phenomena of depersonalization. *Journal of Nervous and Mental Disease*, 1949, *110*, 236–251.

Sarlin, C. N. Depersonalization and derealization. *Journal of The American Psychoanalytic Association*, 1962, *10*, 784–804.

Sarvis, Mary A. Psychiatric implications of temporal lobe damage. *Psychoanalytic Study of the Child*, Vol. 15, New York: International Universities Press, 1960, 454–482.

Savage, C. Variations in ego feeling induced by d-lysergic acid diethylamide (LSD–25). *Psychoanalytic Review*, 1955, *42*, 1–16.

Schachtel, E. G. *Metamorphosis*. New York: Basic Books, 1959.

Schachter, S. The interaction of cognitive and physiological determinants of emotional state. In L. Berkowitz (Ed.), *Advances in experimental social psychology*, Vol. 1, New York: Academic Press, 1964, Pp. 49–80.

Schachter, S. Cognitive effects on bodily functioning: Studies of obesity and eating. In D. C. Glass (Ed.), *Neurophysiology and emotion*. New York: Rockefeller University Press, 1967, Pp. 117–144.

Schachter, S., and Latane, B. Crime, cognition, and the autonomic nervous system. In D. Levine, *Nebraska symposium on motivation*. Lincoln, Nebraska: University of Nebraska Press, 1964, Pp. 221–273.

Schachter, S., and Singer, J. Cognitive, social, and physiological determinants of emotional state. *Psychological Review*, 1962, *69*, 379–399.

Schachter, S., and Wheeler, L. Epinephrine, chlorpromazine, and amusement. *Journal of Abnormal and Social Psychology*, 1962, *65*, 121–128.

Schaefer, E. S. A circumplex model for maternal behavior. *Journal of Abnormal and Social Psychology*, 1959, *95*, 83–104.

Schaefer, E. S., and Bell, R. Q. Structure of attitudes toward child rearing and the family. *Journal of Abnormal and Social Psychology*, 1957, *54*, 391–395.

Schaefer, E. S., and Bell, R. Q. Development of a Parental Attitude Research Instrument. *Child Development*, 1958, *29*, 339–361.

Schafer, R. Bodies in schizophrenic Rorschach responses, *Journal of Projective Techniques* 1960, *24*, 267–281.

Schechter, M. D. The orthopedically handicapped child. *Archives of General Psychiatry*, 1961, *4*, 247–253.

Scheerer, M. *Die Lehre Von der Gestalt*. Berlin: Walter de Gruyter, 1931.

Scheerer, M. Cognitive theory. In G. Lindzey (Ed.), *Handbook of social psychology*, Vol. 1. Cambridge, Massachusetts: Addison-Wesley, 1954, Pp. 91–140.

Schiebel, D. R. Tactile behavior in psychopathology. Unpublished doctoral dissertation, University of Michigan, 1965.

Schilder, P. *The image and appearance of the human body*. London: Kegan, Paul, Trench, Trubner and Co., 1935.

Schilder, P., and Wechsler, D. Short communication, What do children know about the interior of the body? *International Journal of Psychoanalysis*, 1935, *16*, 355–360.

Schlesinger, Vera J. Anal personality traits and occupational choice: A study of accountants, chemical engineers and educational psychologists. Unpublished doctoral dissertation, University of Michigan, 1963.

Schmidt, L. D., and McGowan, J. F. The differentiation of human figure drawings. *Journal of Consulting Psychology*, 1959, *23*, 129–133.

Schneider, D. E. The image of the heart and the synergic principle in psychoanalysis (psychosynergy). *Psychoanalytic Review*, 1954, *41*, 197–215.

Schneider, S. C. Analysis of presurgical anxiety in boys and girls. Unpublished doctoral dissertation, University of Michigan, 1960.

Schneiderman, L. The estimation of one's own bodily traits. *Journal of Social Psychology*, 1956, *44*, 89–99.

Schoen, Z. J., and Scofield, C. F. A study of the relative neuromuscular efficiency of the dominant and non-dominant eye in binocular vision. *Journal of General Psychology*, 1935, *12*, 56–181.

Schonfeld, W. A. Gynecomastia in adolescence: Effect on body image and personality adaptation. *Psychosomatic Medicine*, 1962, *24*, 379–389.

Schonfeld, W. A. Body-image disturbances in adolescents with inappropriate sexual development. *American Journal of Orthopsychiatry*, 1964, *34*, 493–502.

Schultz, J. H., and Luthe, W. *A psychophysiologic approach in psychotherapy*. New York: Grune & Stratton, 1959.

Schumacher, A. S., Wright, J. M., and Wiesen, A. E. The self as a source of anxiety. *Journal of Consulting and Clinical Psychology*, 1968, *32*, 30–34.

Schwartz, M. *Heredity in bronchial asthma*. Copenhagen: Munksgaard, 1952.

Scodel, A. Heterosexual somatic preference and fantasy dependency. *Journal of Consulting Psychology*, 1957, *21*, 371–374.

Searl, M. N. A note on depersonalization. *International Journal of Psychoanalysis*, 1932, *13*, 329–347.

Sears, R. Studies of projection: I, Attribution of traits, *Journal of Social Psychology*, 1936, *7*, 151–163.

Sears, R. R. Experimental analysis of psychoanalytic phenomena. In J. McV. Hunt (Ed.), *Personality and the behavior disorders*, Vol. 1, New York: Ronald Press, 1944.

Secord, P. F. Objectification of word-association procedures by the use of homonyms: A measure of body cathexis. *Journal of Personality*, 1953, *21*, 479–495.

Secord, P. F., and Jourard, S. L. The appraisal of body cathexis: Body cathexis and the self. *Journal of Consulting Psychology*, 1953, *17*, 343–347.

Sedman, G. Depersonalization in a group of normal subjects. *British Journal of Psychiatry*, 1966, *112*, 907–912.

Shaffer, Juliet P. Social and personality correlates of children's estimates of height. *Genetic Psychology Monographs*, 1964, *70*, 97–134.

Shakow, D. Psychological deficit in schizophrenia. *Behavioral Science*, 1963, *8*, 275–305.

Shapiro, G. E. Sensory function in amputation stumps. Unpublished doctoral dissertation, Yeshiva University, 1965.

Shellow, R. S. Perceptual distortion in the spatial localization of emotionally meaningful stimuli. Unpublished doctoral dissertation, University of Michigan, 1956.

Sherick, I. G. Body image, level of ego development and adequacy of ego functioning. Unpublished doctoral dissertation, Washington University, 1964.

Sherman, M., and Jost, H. Frustration reaction of normal and neurotic persons. *Journal of Psychology*, 1942, *13*, 3–19.

Shipman, W. G. Personality traits associated with body-image boundary concern. Presented at annual meeting of American Psychological Association, New York City, 1965.

Shipman, W. G., Oken, D., Grinker, R. R., Goldstein, Iris B., and Heath, Helen A. A study in the psychophysiology of muscle tension: II. Emotional factors. *Archives of General Psychiatry*, 1964, *11*, 330–345.

Shontz, F. C. Body-concept disturbances of patients with hemiplegia. *Journal of Clinical Psychology*, 1956, *12*, 193–195.

Shontz, F. C. Body-part size judgment in contrasting intellectual groups. *Journal of Nervous and Mental Disease*, 1963A, *136*, 368–373.

Shontz, F. C. Reanalysis of data from "Some characteristics of body size estimation". *Perceptual and Motor Skills*, 1963B, *17*, 438.

Shontz, F. C. Some characteristics of body size estimation. *Perceptual and Motor Skills*, 1963C, *16*, 665–671.

Shontz, F. C. Estimation of distances on the body. *Perceptual and Motor Skills*, 1967, *24*, 1131–1142.

Shultz, T. D. A comparison of the reactions and attitudes toward stress of two psychosomatic groups. Unpublished doctoral dissertation, Washington University, 1966.

Sieracki, E. R. Body-image as a variable in the acceptance of disability and vocational interests of the physically disabled. Unpublished doctoral dissertation, State University of New York at Buffalo, 1963.

Siller, J. Psychological concomitants of amputation in children. *Child Development*, 1960, *31*, 109–120.

Siller, J., and Chipman, A. Attitudes of the nondisabled toward the physically handicapped. Final report on Vocational Rehabilitation Administration Project RD–707. May, 1967. New York University School of Education.

Silverman, Sylvia S. *Clothing and appearance: Their psychological implications for teen-age girls*. New York: Columbia University Press, 1945.

Silverstein, A. B., and Klee, G. D. A psychopharmacological test of the "body image" hypothesis. *Journal of Nervous and Mental Disease*, 1958, *127*, 323–329.

Silverstein, A. B., and Robinson, H. A. The representation of orthopedic disability in children's figure drawings. *Journal of Consulting Psychology*, 1956, *20*, 333–341.

Silverstein, A. B., and Robinson, H. A. The representation of physique in children's figure drawings. *Journal of Consulting Psychology*, 1961, *25*, 146–148.

Simmel, Marianne L. Phantoms in patients with leprosy and in elderly digital amputees. *American Journal of Psychology*, 1956, *69*, 529–545.

Simmel, Marianne L. Phantoms, phantom pain and "denial". *American Journal of Psychotherapy*, 1959, *13*, 603–613.

Simmel, Marianne. Developmental aspects of the body scheme. *Child Development Monographs*, 1966, *37*, 83–95.

Simmons, A. D. A test of the body image hypothesis in human figure drawings. Unpublished doctoral dissertation, University of Texas, 1966.

Sims, N. Analysis of the human figure drawings of orthopedic and nonorthopedic children. Unpublished master's thesis, University of Nebraska, 1951.

Singer, J. E., and Lamb, Patricia F. Social concern, body size, and birth order. *Journal of Social Psychology*, 1966, *68*, 143–151.

Singer, J. L., Meltzoff, J., and Goldman, G. D. Rorschach movement responses following motor inhibition and hyperactivity. *Journal of Consulting Psychology*, 1952, *16*, 359–364.

Smith, S. M., Brown, H. O., Toman, J. E., and Goodman, L. S. The lack of cerebral effects of D-Tubocurarine. *Anesthesiology*, 1947, *8*, 1–14.

Smits, S. J. Reactions of self and others to the obviousness and severity of physical disability. Unpublished doctoral dissertation, University of Missouri, 1964.

Solley, C. M., and Murphy, G. *Development of the perceptual world*. New York: Basic Books, 1960.

Solomon, P., Kubzansky, P. E., Leiderman, P. H., Mendelson, J. H., Trumbull, R., and Wexler, D. *Sensory deprivation*. Cambridge, Massachusetts: Harvard University Press, 1961.

Solomon, R. L., and Howes, D. H. Word frequency, personal values, and visual duration thresholds. *Psychological Review*, 1951, *58*, 256–270.

Solomon, R. L., and Wynne, L. C. Traumatic avoidance learning: Anxiety conservation and partial irreversibility. *Psychological Review*, 1954, *61*, 353–385.

Speisman, J. C., Lazarus, R. S., Davison, L. A., and Mordkoff, A. M. Experimental analysis of a film used as a threatening stimulus. *Journal of Consulting Psychology*, 1964, *28*, 23–33.

Sperling, Melitta. Fetishism in children. *Psychoanalytic Quarterly*, 1963, *32*, 374–392.

Spiegel, L. A. The self and perception. *Psychoanalytic Study of the Child*, Vol. 14. New York: International Universities Press, 1959, 81–109.

Staffieri, J. R. A study of social stereotype of body image in children. *Journal of Personality and Social Psychology*, 1967, 7, 101–104.

Stagner, R., Lawson, E. D., and Moffitt, J. W. The Krout Personal Preference Scale: A factor-analytic study. *Journal of Clinical Psychology*, 1955, *11*, 103–133.

Stamm, J. L. Altered ego states allied to depersonalization. *Journal of The American Psychoanalytic Association*, 1962, *10*, 762–783.

Starcke, A. The reversal of the libido-sign in delusions of persecution. *International Journal of Psychoanalysis*, 1920, *1*, 231–234.

Stern, G. G. Scoring instructions and college norms for Activities Index and College Characteristics Index. Syracuse, New York: Syracuse University Psychological Research Center, 1963.

Sternbach, R. A. The effects of instructional sets on autonomic responsivity. *Psychophysiology*, 1964, *1*, 67–70.

Sternbach, R. A. Autonomic responsivity and the concept of sets. In N. S. Greenfield and W. C. Lewis (Eds.), *Psychoanalysis and current thought*. Madison: University of Wisconsin Press, 1965, Pp. 215–226.

Story, R. I. The relationship between the effects of conflict arousal and oral fixation on thinking. Unpublished doctoral dissertation, University of Michigan, 1963.

Stuntz, E. C. The beard as an expression of bodily feelings in a schizophrenic. *Psychosomatic Medicine*, 1959, *21*, 28–33.

Swartz, J. D. Performance of high- and low-anxious children on the Holtzman Inkblot Technique. *Child Development*, 1965, *36*, 569–575.

Sweetland, A. Hypnotic neuroses: Hypochondriasis and depression. *Journal of Genetic Psychology*, 1948, *39*, 91–105.

Swenson, C. H. Sexual differentiation on the Draw-A-Person Test. *Journal of Clinical Psychology*, 1955, *11*, 27–41.

Swenson, C. H., and Newton, K. R. The development of sexual differentiation on the Draw-A-Person Test. *Journal of Clinical Psychology*, 1955, *11*, 417–419.

Syz, H. C. Psychogalvanic studies in schizophrenia. *Archives of Neurology and Psychiatry*, 1926, *16*, 747–760.

Szasz, T. S. Physiologic and psychodynamic mechanisms in constipation and diarrhea. *Psychosomatic Medicine*, 1951, *13*, 112–116.

Szasz, T. S. The psychology of bodily feelings in schizophrenia. *Psychosomatic Medicine*, 1957, *19*, 11–16.

Szasz, T. S. *The myth of mental illness*. New York: Hoeber (Harper), 1961.

Tait, C. D., Jr., and Archer, R. C. Inside-of-the-body Test: A preliminary report. *Psychosomatic Medicine*, 1955, *17*, 139-148.

Takala, M. Asymmetries of the visual space. Helsinki: Suomalaisen Kirjallisuuden Seuran Kirjapainon Oy, 1951.

Tausk, V. On the origin of the influencing machine in schizophrenia. *Psychoanalytic Quarterly*, 1933, *2*, 519–556.

Teitelbaum, M. The role of internal body orientation in perception of spatial direction. Unpublished doctoral dissertation, Yeshiva University, 1965.

Thomas, E. L., and Stasiak, E. Eye movements and body images. *Canadian Psychiatric Association Journal*, 1964, *9*, 336–344.

Thorndike, E. L. Valuations of certain pains, deprivations, and frustrations. *Journal of Genetic Psychology*, 1937, *51*, 227–239.

Thurstone, L. L. Thurstone Interest Schedule. Psychological Corporation, 1947.

Thurstone, L. L. *Examiner manual for the Thurstone Temperament Schedule*. Chicago: Science Research Associates, 1953.

Timmons, E. O., and Noblin, C. D. The differential performance of orals and anals in a verbal conditioning paradigm. *Journal of Consulting Psychology*, 1963, *27*, 383–386.

Titchener, E. B. *The psychology of feeling and attention.* New York: Macmillan, 1924.

Titchener, J. L., and Levine, M. *Surgery as a human experience.* New York: Oxford University Press, 1960.

Tolor, A., and Jalowiec, J. E. Body boundary, parental attitudes, and internal-external expectancy. *Journal of Consulting Psychology*, 1968, *32*, 206–209.

Tomkins, S. S., and Miner, J. B. *The Tomkins-Horn Picture Arrangement Test.* New York: Springer Publishing Company, 1957.

Traub, A. C., Olson, R., Orbach, J., and Cardone, S. C. Psychophysical studies of body-image. III: Initial studies of disturbance in a chronic schizophrenic group. Proceedings, 75th Annual Convention, American Psychological Association, 1967.

Traub, A. C., and Orbach, J. Psychophysical studies of body-image. I: The adjustable body-distorting mirror. *Archives of General Psychiatry*, 1964, *11*, 53–66.

Travis, L. E., and Herren, R. Y. Studies in stuttering. V. A study of simultaneous antitropic movements of the hands of stutterers. *Archives of Neurology and Psychiatry*, 1929, *22*, 487–494.

Twente, E. W. Patterns of awakening. *The Clinical Counselor*, 1964, *1*, 7–17.

Ullman, M., Ashenhurst, E. M., Hurwitz, L. J., and Gruen, A. Motivational and structural factors in the denial of hemiplegia. *Archives of Neurology*, 1960, *3*, 98–110.

Ueno, H. Particular way of perceiving body in persons who have disease image: From the point of view of body boundary theory. *Tohoku Psychologica Folia*, 1967, *25*, 3–4.

Valins, S. Cognitive effects of false heart-rate feedback. *Journal of Personality and Social Psychology*, 1966, *4*, 400–408.

Valins, S. Emotionality and autonomic reactivity. *Journal of Experimental Research in Personality*, 1967A, *2*, 41–48.

Valins, S. Emotionality and information concerning internal reactions. *Journal of Personality and Social Psychology*, 1967B, *6*, 458–463.

Van De Mark, S. N., and Neuringer, C. The effect of physical and cognitive somatic arousal on Rorschach responses: An experimental test of the assumption that body image influences the perceptual organization of unstructured stimuli. *Journal of Consulting Psychology*, 1969, *33*, 458–465.

Van der Valk, J. M., and Groen, J. Electrical resistance of the skin during induced emotional stress. *Psychosomatic Medicine*, 1950, *12*, 303–314.

Van der Werff, J. J. Onbewuste zelfbeoordeling. *Psychologie*, 1967, *22*, 150–161.

Van Kaam, A. (Ed.) *The human body.* Duquesne University Press, 1966.

Van Lennep, D. J. Projection and personality. In H. P. David and E. Von Bracken (Eds.), *Perspectives in personality theory.* New York: Basic Books, 1957, Pp. 259–277.

Van Twyver, H. B., and Kimmel, H. D. Operant conditioning of the GSR with concomitant measurement of two somatic variables. *Journal of Experimental Psychology*, 1966, *72*, 841–846.

Vaughn, Ogretta H. Organization of body space: An exploratory study. Unpublished doctoral dissertation, Clark University, 1967.

Vernon, D. T., Foley, Jeanne M., and Schulman, J. L. Effect of mother-child separation and birth order on young children's responses to two potentially stressful experiences. *Journal of Personality and Social Psychology*, 1967, *5*, 162–174.

Vernon, D. T., Foley, Jeanne M., Sipowicz, R. R., and Schulman, J. L. *The psychological response of children to hospitalization and illness.* Springfield, Illinois: Charles C. Thomas, 1965.

Victor, G. Fluidity and regression of body image in relation to errors in distinguishing between external events and inner experiences: A test of Federn's theory of ego boundary changes. Unpublished doctoral dissertation, New York University, 1964.

Vinck, J. Body-image and the diagnosis of schizophrenia. *Gawein*, 1967, *15*, 306–323.

Von Ophuijsen, J. H. On the origin of the feeling of persecution. *International Journal of Psychoanalysis*, 1920, *1*, 235–239.

Wachs, H., and Zaks, M. S. Studies of body image in men with spinal cord injury. *Journal of Nervous and Mental Disease*, 1960, *130*, 121–127.

Wadeson, R. Anxiety in the dreams of a neurosurgical patient. *Archives of General Psychiatry*, 1966, *14*, 249–252.

Walker, Helen, and Lev, J. *Statistical inference.* New York: Holt, Rinehart, and Winston, 1953.

Wapner, S. An experimental and theoretical approach to body image. Presented at XVI International Congress of Psychology, Bonn, Germany, 1960.

Wapner, S. Body image and pathological states. Part 1: Perceptual properties of the body qua object. Transcript of symposium at the Veteran's Administration Hospital, Houston, Texas, June, 1961A.

Wapner, S. Body image and pathological states. Part 2: Effect of spatial context on perceptual properties of one's own body. Transcript of symposium at the Veteran's Administration Hospital, Houston, Texas, June, 1961B.

Wapner, S., and Krus, D. M. Behavioral effects of Lysergic Acid Diethylamide (LSD–25). *Archives of General Psychiatry*, 1959, *1*, 417–419.

Wapner, S., McFarland, J. H., and Werner, H. Effects of visual spatial context on perception of one's own body. *British Journal of Psychology*, 1963, *54*, 41–49.

Wapner, S., and Werner, H. An experimental approach to body perception from the organismic-developmental point of view. In S. Wapner and H. Werner (Eds.), *The body percept*. New York: Random House, 1965, Pp. 9–25.

Wapner, S., Werner, H., and Comalli, P. E., Jr. Effect of enhancement of head boundary on head size and shape. *Perceptual and Motor Skills*, 1958, *8*, 319–325.

Ware, K. E., Fisher, S., and Cleveland, S. E. Body-image boundaries and adjustment to poliomyelitis. *Journal of Abnormal and Social Psychology*, 1957, *55*, 88–93.

Warren, H. C. *Elements of human psychology*. Boston: Houghton-Mifflin, 1922.

Washburn, M. F. *Movement and mental imagery*. Boston: Houghton-Mifflin, 1916.

Watson, E. J., and Johnson, Adelaide M. The emotional significance of acquired physical disfigurement in children. *American Journal of Orthopsychiatry*, 1958, *28*, 85–97.

Webb, Ruth C. Perceptual modes and familiarity in social acceptance of physically disabled college students. Unpublished doctoral dissertation, University of Illinois, 1963.

Webb, W. L., Jr., Slaughter, Regina, Meyer, E., and Edgerton, M. Mechanisms of psychosocial adjustment in patients seeking "face lift" operation. *Psychosomatic Medicine*, 1965, *27*, 183–192.

Weckowicz, T. E., and Sommer, R. Body image and self-concept in schizophrenia. *Journal of Mental Science*, 1960, *106*, 17–39.

Weinberg, J. R. A further investigation of body-cathexis and the self. *Journal of Consulting Psychology*, 1960, *24*, 277.

Weinstein, E. A., and Kahn, R. L. *Denial of illness.* Springfield, Illinois: Charles C. Thomas, 1955.

Weinstein, E. A., and Kahn, R. L. Symbolic reorganization in brain injuries. In S. Arieti (Ed.), *American handbook of psychiatry*. New York: Basic Books, 1959, Pp. 964–981.

Weinstein, S. Deficits concomitant with aphasia or lesions of either cerebral hemisphere. *Cortex*, 1964, *1*, 154–169.

Weinstein, S., Johnson, Linda, and Guerra, J. R. Differentiation of human figure drawings made before and after temporal lobectomy and by schizophrenics. *Perceptual and Motor Skills*, 1963, *17*, 687–693.

Weinstein, S., Sersen, E. A., Fisher, L., and Vetter, R. J. Preferences for bodily parts as a function of sex, age, and socio-economic status. *American Journal of Psychology*, 1964, *77*, 291–294.

Weiss, E. *Agoraphobia in the light of ego psychology*. New York: Grune & Stratton, 1964.

Weiss, J. L. An experimental study of the psychodynamics of humor. Unpublished doctoral dissertation, University of Michigan, 1955.

Weiss, S. A. The body image as related to phantom sensation: A hypothetical conceptualization of seemingly isolated findings. *Annals of the New York Academy of Medicine*, 1958, *74*, 25–29.

Weiss, S. A., and Fishman, S. Extended and telescoped phantom limbs in unilateral amputees. *Journal of Abnormal and Social Psychology*, 1963, *66*, 489–497.

Weiss, S. M. Psychological adjustment following open heart surgery. Unpublished doctoral dissertation, University of Arizona, 1965.

Wells, H. P. Relationships between physical fitness and psychological variables. Unpublished doctoral dissertation, University of Illinois, 1958.

Wenger, M. A. Measurement of individual differences in autonomic balance. *Psychosomatic Medicine*, 1941, *3*, 427–434.

Wenger, M. A. Studies of autonomic balance in Army Air Force personnel. *Comparative Psychology Monographs*, 1948, *4*, No. 101.

Wenger, M. A. Emotion as visceral action: An extension of Lange's theory. In M. L. Reymert (Ed.), *Feelings and emotions*: The Mooseheart symposium. New York: McGraw-Hill, 1950, Pp. 3–10.

Wenger, M. A. Pattern analyses of autonomic variables during rest. *Psychosomatic Medicine*, 1957, *19*, 240–244.

Werner, H. *The comparative psychology of mental development*. New York: Harpers, 1940.

Werner, H. *On expressive language*. Worcester, Massachusetts: Clark University Press, 1954.

Werner, H., and Wapner, S. Sensory-tonic field theory of perception. *Journal of Personality*, 1949, *18*, 88–107.

Werner, H., and Wapner, S. Toward a general theory of perception. *Psychological Review*, 1952, *59*, 324–338.

Werner, H., Wapner, S., and Comalli, P. E., Jr. Effect of boundary on perception of head size. *Perceptual and Motor Skills*, 1957, 7, 69–71.

Wertheimer, Rita, and Bachelis, L. A. Individual differences in hue discriminations as a cognitive variable. Presented at annual meeting of American Psychological Association, New York City, 1966.

White, W. F., and Gaier, E. L. Assessment of body image and self-concept among alcoholics with different intervals of sobriety. *Journal of Clinical Psychology*, 1965, *21*, 374–377.

Whiting, J. W. M., and Child, I. L. *Child training and personality: A cross-cultural study*. New Haven: Yale University Press, 1953.

Wieder, A., and Noller, P. A. Objective studies of children's drawings of human figures. Part I: Sex awareness and socio-economic level. *Journal of Clinical Psychology*, 1950, *6*, 319–325.

Wieder, A., and Noller, P. A. Objective studies of children's drawings of human figures. Part II: Sex, age, and IQ. *Journal of Clinical Psychology*, 1953, *9*, 20–23.

Williams, R. L. The relationship of body image to some physiological reactivity patterns in psychosomatic patients. Unpublished doctoral dissertation, Washington University, 1962.

Williams, R. L., and Krasnoff, A. G. Body image and physiological patterns in patients with peptic ulcer and rheumatoid arthritis. *Psychosomatic Medicine,* 1964, *26,* 701–709.

Winnicott, D. W. Transitional objects and transitional phenomena. *International Journal of Psychoanalysis,* 1953, *34,* 89–97.

Witkin, H. A. Psychological differentiation and forms of pathology. *Journal of Abnormal Psychology,* 1965, *70,* 317–336.

Witkin, H. A., Dyk, R. B., Faterson, H. F., Goodenough, D. R., and Karp, S. A. *Psychological differentiation.* New York: John Wiley & Sons, 1962.

Witkin, H. A., and Lewis, Helen A. Presleep experiences and dreams. In H. A. Witkin and Helen A. Lewis (Eds.), *Experimental studies of dreaming.* New York: Random House, 1967, Pp. 148–225.

Witkin, H. A., Lewis, H. B., Hertzman, M., Meissner, P., Machover, K., and Wapner, S. *Personality through perception.* New York: Harper and Brothers, 1954.

Wittkower, E., Rodger, T. F., and Wilson, A. T. M. Effort syndrome. *Lancet,* 1941, *1,* 531–535.

Wittreich, W. J., and Grace, Marea. Body image and development. Technical Report, March, 1955, Princeton University, Contract N6oNR–270 (14), Office of Naval Research.

Wittreich, W. J., and Radcliffe, K. B., Jr. The influence of simulated mutilation upon the perception of the human figure. *Journal of Abnormal and Social Psychology,* 1955, *51,* 493–495.

Wolfenstein, Martha. *Children's humor.* Glencoe, Illinois: The Free Press, 1954.

Wolff, H. G. *Life stress and bodily disease.* Baltimore: The Williams and Wilkins Co., 1950.

Wolff, W. *The expression of personality.* New York: Harper, 1943.

Woodbury, M. A. Altered body-ego experiences: A contribution to the study of regression, perception, and early development. *Journal of The American Psychoanalytic Association,* *14,* 273–304.

Woods, Marcella D. An exploration of developmental relationships between children's body image boundaries, estimates of body space, and performance of selected gross motor tasks. Unpublished doctoral dissertation, Ohio State University, 1966.

Wulff, M. Fetishism and object choice in early childhood. *Psychoanalytic Quarterly,* 1946, *15,* 450–471.

Wylie, Ruth C. *The self concept.* Lincoln: University of Nebraska Press, 1961.

Wysocki, B. A., and Whitney, Eleanor. Body image of crippled children as seen in Draw-A-Person test behavior. *Perceptual and Motor Skills,* 1965, *21,* 499–504.

Yazmajian, R. V. The testes and body-image formation in transvestitism. *Journal of The American Psychoanalytic Association,* 1966, *14,* 304–312.

Yokoyama, M. The nature of the affective judgments in the method of paired comparisons. *American Journal of Psychology,* 1921, *32,* 357–369.

Young, P. T. Studies in affective psychology. *American Journal of Psychology,* 1927, *38,* 157–193.

Yuen, C. W. Attitudes of individuals with visible and invisible physical impairment toward their disability. Unpublished doctoral dissertation, New York University, 1963.

Zane, M. D. The hypnotic situation and changes in ulcer pain. *International Journal of Clinical and Experimental Hypnosis,* 1966, *14,* 292–304.

Zazzo, R. Images du corps et conscience de soi: Materiaux pour l'etude experimentale de la conscience. *Enfance,* 1948, *1,* 29–43.

Zierer, E. Dynamics and diagnostic value of creative therapy. *Acta Medica Orientalia,* 1950, *9,* 35–43.

Zimny, G. H. Body image and physiological responses. *Journal of Psychosomatic Research*, 1965, *9*, 185–188.

Zion, Leela C. Body concept as it relates to self-concept. *Research Quarterly*, 1965, *36*, 490–495.

Zucker, Luise J. Evaluating psychopathology of the self. *Annals of the New York Academy of Sciences*, 1962, *96*, 844–852.

Zuckerman, M., Barrett-Ribback, B., and Monashkin, I. Normative data and factor analysis on the PARI. *Journal of Consulting Psychology*, 1958, *22*, 165–171.

Zuk, G. H. Psychodynamic implications of self-injury in defective children and adults. *Journal of Clinical Psychology*, 1960, *16*, 58–60.

Zuk, G. H. Relation of mental age to size of figure on the Draw-A-Person Test. *Perceptual and Motor Skills*, 1962, *14*, 410.

Name Index

Subject Index